D1015733

BOOKS BY RONNIE DUGGER

Dark Star: *Hiroshima Reconsidered in the Life of Claude Eatherly* (1967)

Three Men in Texas: *Bedichek, Webb, and Dobie, Essays by Their Friends in the* Texas Observer (editor, 1967)

Our Invaded Universities: *Form, Reform, and New Starts* (1974)

The Politician: *The Life and Times of Lyndon Johnson—The Drive for Power, from the Frontier to Master of the Senate* (1982)

THE POLITICIAN

The Life and Times of Lyndon Johnson

The Drive for Power, from the Frontier to Master of the Senate

by RONNIE DUGGER

W · W · Norton & Company · New York · London

 Published simultaneously in Canada by George J. McLeod Limited, Toronto. Printed in the United States of America.

THE TEXT *of this book is composed in photocomposition Gael. Display typeface is Garamond. Composition and manufacturing are by the Haddon Craftsmen. Book design is by Marjorie J. Flock.*

Library of Congress Cataloging in Publication Data
Dugger, Ronnie.
The politician.
Bibliography: p.
Includes index.
1. Johnson, Lyndon B. (Lyndon Baines). 1908–1973. 2. Texas—Politics and government—1865–1950. 3. United States—Politics and government—1933–1945. 4. United States—Politics and government—1945– 5. Presidents—United States—Biography. I. Title.
E847.D78 1982 973.923'092'4 [B] 81-22507
AACR2

ISBN 0-393-01598-X

W. W. Norton & Company, Inc. 500 Fifth Avenue, New York, N.Y. 10110
W. W. Norton & Company Ltd. 37 Great Russell Street, London WC1B 3NU

1 2 3 4 5 6 7 8 9 0

For my mother and father

Contents

Illustrations follow pages 40, 88, 122, 178, 214, 236, 260, 288, 340 and *380.*

Introduction: From Roosevelt to Reagan, the Johnson Period

Because of electric speed, we can no longer wait and see. George Washington once remarked, "We haven't heard from Benj. Franklin in Paris this year. We should write him a letter."

— Marshall McLuhan and Quentin Fiore in *The Medium Is the Message,* 1967

The burdens and terrors of the twentieth century are embodied in the politician as in no other professional. Wilson, La Follette, and Taft, Churchill, De Gaulle, and Sadat, Lenin, Stalin, and Hitler (somehow once we call a man a dictator we forget that he is also a politician). Of the great American politicians of the century—Huey Long, Franklin Roosevelt, Lyndon Johnson, George Wallace—Johnson was the master; he was the archetype. Through the refractions of his life we can see the causes for our collective progress and our common peril.

We may scorn politicians, but politics dominates us, and the politician who is the president dominates our politics. "We kid ourselves all the time about our personal lives," wrote the critic Alfred Kazin. "It's politics that rules the roost, that makes much of our 'personal feeling' these days."

Yet the politicians seem to be as helpless as everyone else. Something rather subtle has overtaken American politics. It was the tradition that society and citizens should be left alone as much as possible; things would work themselves out. Since 1931, however, we have had to evolve an entirely new idea. We expect politics to correct reality. The politicians, therefore, have taken up the habit of claiming that they do just that. But reality is not sufficiently corrected; politics is not sufficient to the new expectation for it. The Reagan-led reaction against this general failure of reform politics would carry us, if it could, clear back to the nineteenth century.

What has gone wrong? What should we learn?

As C. Wright Mills said, "During most of human history, historical change has not been visible to the people who were involved in it, or even to those enacting it." We are so close in among these present events, they come so thick and fast, and they recede into the past at such an accelerating rate, we are not sure what anything means, and even what we know has happened seems like a series of dreams. Yet we also, in this same period, feel that we here and now are participating in the re-formation or destruction of civilization for a long time, perhaps forever. We are living with weapons of entirely new kinds and dimensions, monsters that we mass-produce ourselves. Things go awry so quickly and so dangerously, we know we will fail if we and our leaders go on as before—as A. Powell Davies said, "The world is now too dangerous for anything but the truth." We must understand the present in the present or self-destruct. By the iron laws of evolution, to survive as a species or as a nation we have to change in response to the governing realities no matter how phantasmagorical they have become. As quickly as we can, we must agree on what these realities are and think together about them so we can do what can be done.

This work is my attempt to understand, in the life and times of Johnson, what Mills called "the history of the present." More narrowly stated, the subject before us is Lyndon Johnson and his heritage as it was delivered through his career and presidency into the life of the world. The present volume relates Johnson's life to the moment when he attains the Senate Democratic leadership, with some sections broken free of the chronology to let us consider some subjects by themselves, move forward or backward in time as the implications of the subject may indicate, and think in the present.

We begin by looking back to his origins in the culture of the northern Europeans who had settled in the American Southwest. His people were salt of the earth southern farmers and western frontiersmen. What formed him both expressed and falsified us as a people and helped cause the difficulties that have descended upon us. Christian-American patriotism in Texas, Johnson's own southwestern raunchiness, his cynical idealism, and the unmanageable mysteries of the times converged into the early-American, frontier-style presidency that finally forced us to begin to redefine our nationhood.

Lyndon Johnson was rude, intelligent, shrewd, charming, compassionate, vindictive, maudlin, selfish, passionate, volcanic and cold, vicious and generous. He played every part, he left out no emotion; in him one saw one's self and all the others. I think he was everything that is human. The pulsings within him, his energy, will, daring, guile, and greed for power and money, were altogether phenomenal, a continuous astonishment.

He was not an idealist, but he served ideals when it suited and pleased him. He was not a reactionary, but he fanned reaction when it helped him advance himself. He was tireless and diligent, but he was also narrowly political, and he was suspicious of new ideas. He berated intellectuals because he envied them. He knew that he was the product of a rural culture and that he had neglected to take the time out from his headlong ambition to broaden himself.

His career was one person's experience of nearly everything important that has happened in American public life since 1931, and he was as personally responsible for American history since 1950 as any other man of his time. Throughout his career he was consolidating his private wealth by a calculating use of public power, and there is an affinity between this squalid side of his success and the corruptive commercialism in the national ethos.

He used the American political system with such skill, audacity, and originality, his career is a tour through that system and a study in what is wrong with it. But business power is now the musculature inside the skin of our politics. In recent decades we have learned that the federal government is neither as moral nor as benign as many of us for a long time thought and that the big business-military economy that overtook the political system during World War II has become the foundry where we will have to forge a new national conscience. In Johnson's career and period we can plainly see that conventional politics is just the puppet show of economic power.

While the present work can be regarded as biography, history, politics, and economics, it is meant to be a study of the United States in its president. There used to be a clear demarcation between biography and history. Now, however, when the president comes into control of the national nuclear arsenal, his merest bent of personality or slant of attitude is so consequential, he himself is history. His biography is history because what has happened to him becomes, through his power, history. Whatever made him is magnified through him into our common life. The chance influences and events of his days and nights, tugging at his decisions one way or another, can save or kill millions of us. Myths in his mind change the history of the world.

Seeing a period through a representative life, there is danger of distortion. One may not imply, nor should anyone infer, that a representative person is an accurate microcosm—that because he or she was thus and so to such and such an extent, so was the era. Stimulated by the suggestive indications of Johnson's life, we must nevertheless turn to the record and pattern of the period.

Precisely what period are we considering? We have a natural tendency to think of the presidencies or the slogans of the administrations as the spans of recent history. Actually, though, the New Deal, the Fair Deal, the Eisenhower years, the New Frontier, the Great Society, the New Majority, Jimmy Carter's fumblings, and Ronald Reagan's retrenchments have been one long and exhausting era, a period of palliatives, a half-century of collapse, improvisation, reaction—war, prosperity, injustice—rhetoric, privateering, and degeneration.

Between 1929 and 1931 the illusions of the preceding period had dissolved. By the time Johnson arrived in Washington as a congressional secretary in 1931, the United States had already become the world's leading Corporation Society. Desperately, the New Dealers fiddled with this condition as if handouts could humanize it, as if antitrust suits could control it, as if pilot programs could redeem it. Eased for a little while, the depression returned savagely, only to be erased and replaced by the larger calamity of the war. After that war, we lived through a twenty-year scramble of incorporated commercialism, maldistributed prosperity, anticommunism as a shield for rapacious corporate power at home and abroad, and an increasingly bristling and independent militarism. In 1965, during the brief but dazzling burst of progressive legislation under President Johnson, all this sank into the pit of the Vietnam War, dragging us down into its strangeness and immorality. After a few years there was Watergate, criminality in the White House, corrupt presidential connivance with major corporations, impeachment hearings—the resignation. Brushing aside the afterthought presidents Ford and Carter, Reagan came then to do vengeance.

Gus Tyler has described what he calls "the Roosevelt Era that ran from 1932–68." In the two spells, 1933–38 and 1965–66, when progressives had a majority or near majority in Congress, their accomplishments were real, but have certainly been exaggerated by partisans of Roosevelt and Johnson. The Supreme Court had important effects, but not on the continuously centralizing economic structure. The Congress was in the hands of a conservative coalition more than two-thirds of the time, as it still is to this day. To think of the half-century since the New Deal as the Roosevelt Era, climaxing in the social legislation of the mid-sixties, gives our time too cheery, too gallant a glow. Neither has this been the era of the transitional Truman or the decent, muddled Eisenhower, nor of the amiable, moderate Kennedy, nor of the presidential perverter of the Constitution nor of his pardoner, nor of the Georgian breaking his most important promises, nor of the Radical Avenger, blowing up the social works of the period one after another.

These last five clustering decades from Roosevelt to Reagan are best understood as the Johnson Period because Johnson, more than any of the other presidents of the time, helped generate the values and participated in and then presided over the trends that ultimately prevailed. Arriving in Washington at the beginning of his era, he was himself—in his origins, the plastic aggression of his passion and ambition, his real but expendable compassion, his subordination to his corporate sponsors, his jingoism, McCarthyism, and militarism, and his renascent idealism about the blacks and the other poor—the embodiment of the events and the shapes of power that have become our present situation. He adapted himself idealistically, pragmatically, radically, cynically, above all opportunistically, to the New Deal, the War, and the Reaction, he led the Congress into militarizing the government, he finally seized and worked, all by himself, the levers of the national power. Then the onrushing darkness of the period overcame him, and his war and his programs were ridden out to their demoralized consequences by his eventually disgraced or defeated successors.

He was a victim, a victim of his heritage, his energy, his gifts, his ambition, his cynicism, and the forces of his times, but there was what one writer has called "the tragedy of Lyndon Johnson" only in a sentimentalizing personal sense. What really matters is the social degeneration over which Johnson was his period's chosen impresario. He served as president during the turbulent confluence of the failure of the western American heritage in our militarized foreign policy, the failure of the New Deal even as it was accomplishing the last of its goals, and the disappearance of the confidence that the democracy is based on an economic system of small-unit competitive free enterprise. His presidency enshrined into law new standards of civil rights for all and social compassion for the poor, but it was also responsible for the general calamity. Nine years buried in his forebears' country cemetery, Johnson's knowing but saturnine presence haunts our continuing disarray.

As I write this afternoon in 1981, we are still mired in the third great depression of the period. The first was the economic one, "The Depression." The second was the cultural and political demoralization from 1963 to 1968, from assassination to assassination. This third one now, from Watergate to Ford to Carter to Reagan, is perhaps our first national psychological depression.

All this wasn't anyone's fault—who had control? In 1974 J. Paul Getty, probably the richest man in the world, said, "Things burst and the devil drives. . . . I kind of take industrial growth and its complications in my stride. I didn't have any control over things." Neither, obviously, did American presidents or international corporations.

Yet we can see that if we had had, at this place of power, at that particular time, a different person, or if the man there had chosen, rather than the course he did, another one that lay latent in him but he let go for some reason, why, then!—the whole period, the very world, would be different. Our leaders have more choices than they admit or even realize and higher liability for history than they will accept when things go wrong. Expecting to be forgiven their political self-interest, they do not keep enough in mind how paltry that motive is when we can all die together in a thirty-minute war.

My method is a combination of reporting and research. As Quincy Howe wrote, "The accelerated pace of the twentieth century has merged the functions of the journalist and the historian." I have lived in libraries and roamed the field, stomped off the cold in west Texas, wandered about Washington, driven winding roads into the mountains of northern California, reading, asking, investigating.

You will find here not just what I have learned, but my thoughts about our time, what I have been thinking. As I told Johnson, in response to his suddenly telling me he wanted "a friendly book," it will be fair and accurate, but my opinions are in it; "No deal," I asked George Christian to tell him—and that ended our interviews. I ask my readers to enter this work with me as an effort to make the governing realities and a more rigorously humanist ethic into a foundation, a base, for the future. While watching the sky for portents, for what the Texas naturalist Roy Bedichek called "authentic tidings of invisible things," we must do as Henry Adams said the historian should, we must triangulate from the widest possible base to the farthest point we think we can see, "which is always far beyond the curvature of the horizon." To see toward the future we have to sense and imagine what we cannot either measure or prove, the connections among events, the accepted ideals and values, and the controlling purposes of our time. Sensing these connections (in a powerful man's mind, in the awakenings of millions of people, in the failure of a war or the success of a new idea) we must proceed with utmost care and utmost seriousness of purpose.

"Political history is far too criminal a subject to be a fit thing to teach children," [W. H. Auden, the poet,] said. "Teachers all know this, so they bowdlerize it, but the trouble with that is, to bowdlerize history is to falsify it."

Mr. Auden said he thought children could safely, and truthfully, be taught art history or literary history, but not political history.

—*New York Times,* December 16, 1970

THE POLITICIAN

The Drive for Power

A NOTE TO THE READER

Italicized reference numbers designate notes that add information other than the sources. Numbers set in ordinary Roman type designate notes that contain only sources. A reader who might want more information on a point, other than the sources, can save time by turning to the reference note only if its number in the text is printed in italics.

Prologue: The Man in the Special House

. . . At Hiroshima when the first atomic bomb exploded . . . a new era was born—the Atomic Age. The power that ended the world's greatest war within 48 hours became ours to use, either to Christianize the world or pulverize it.

— Lyndon Johnson on the day in 1948 when he announced for the U.S. Senate

Lyndon Johnson was the president, but he was personal. He took you on directly with his thrust, charm, wit, charge and parry, power, and menace. He was a force of nature; as Hopkins said of Churchill, "God, what a force that man has."[1] Leading you through the White House as if he owned it, which for his time he did, he cuffed you with his rough anger. He occupied his rocking chair with an indifferent authority, as if, should it squeak, he would maul it. There was threat, ferocity, real danger in him.

"We killed Diem," he said during interviews in 1967 and 1968.[2] But, he told me, we didn't have anybody in Vietnam to take his place, and we'd be a lot better off with him than we are now! Listen, he said, "If Ronnie Dugger's my lawyer, and we've got to kill him, we want to be damn sure we've got another lawyer before we kill him."

From the Oval Office he went into the bathroom adjacent, leaving the door open behind him. Around the corner from me loud expulsive sounds mixed in with his continuous talking. One of his young men squatted down just outside the open door and made notes. Another was hovering around him somewhere inside the bathroom.

Returning, he sat down in front of his telephone console so that he was facing, above the fireplace, the Shoumatoff portrait of one of his teachers, Franklin Roosevelt. Explaining, explaining, explaining the war he was conducting, he compared the Vietnamese people with his grandson, Patrick Lyndon. Extending his right forefinger stiffly in front of him as though a toddler was holding onto it for balance, he notched the air back toward his belly as if he was drawing the child closer to him, saying, ". . . he takes one step, then another, and then another, but it's slow; it just takes time." Master of a national power greater than any in history, he thought the Vietnamese were children he was teaching.

Upstairs in his bedroom, he sprawled down on a rubbing table and a blank-faced boy, about eighteen, massaged his gargantuan body with a white oil. Aides brought him reports to read and a new book of his speeches to look at, and from the rubbing table he watched any of the three television screens when something caught his interest. He said again, "We killed Diem," and he said, "We killed Trujillo," and he said, "We were going after Castro." He looked at me sideways with a smile and added, "Us liberals," meaning, of course, the Kennedy liberals. Hoisting himself to a seated position on the massage table, facing me, he continued to challenge me as if daring me with his nakedness, his pot belly, his dangling legs, his power-glowing self. Though I knew he was a country boy, he looked and seemed to be, in these strange moments, a Chinese war lord.

Later on that night I walked the streets of Washington, which are well known to me. Huddled in my overcoat against the cold, looking through the bars of the iron fence at the power-glowing White House, I thought about Johnson in there that night. Half a million Americans were fighting in Vietnam at his command. He personally, at that exact moment which I was also living, could destroy hundreds of millions of people, he personally could destroy human civilization from this venerable old house. With a start I fully believed what before I had only realized: this man I had been watching carefully for a dozen years, increasingly convinced of his desire to do good and his affinity for evil, was the most powerful and the most dangerous ruler until then in history. It seemed to me then, and still does, that the problem for the American people is to realize and believe that this immaculate White House is what it actually is, a house wired for universal death, instant after instant, president after president after president. My shoulders stiffening from the cold there in the Washington night, I decided to ask Johnson, at our meeting the next evening, a forbidden question.

In the family dining room in the early evening of December 14, 1967, he was seated at the head of the table, pushed back in his chair, right knee off at an angle, as if we were on a picnic. Two men sat across the table from me, Frank Reynolds of ABC and Tom Johnson, an assistant press secretary, who is now the publisher of the *Los Angeles Times.*

When there was a pause in the talk, I told the president I had been walking around outside there beyond the windows the night before and got to thinking about all those nuclear weapons he, and he alone, had to decide whether to use, thinking about the hundreds of millions of people who would die, how it would be worse for those left living than for those who were killed . . . civilization gone. . . .

"I guess you just always believe and hope," he said, "that whoever's here—you know it of yourself, and whoever you're dealing with—can be as candid and prudent and concerned as you. . . . Today we think the Soviets know the awesomeness of it all." The greatest danger was the Middle East, and in a few years from then it would be China, he said, but "We see that the Soviets have come a long way since the bomb, and we think intelligent men are leading 'em maybe," and this might be true of China, too. "Otherwise you're just helpless and throw up your hands."

"But," I asked him, "how do you feel about it?" I was trying to ask him, Would he really drop the bombs? I did ask him, "What are we who are supposed to try to explain such things to the people out there"—I gestured toward the dining room windows and the evening beyond them—"what are we supposed to tell them?" I knew I wasn't putting the question well, I said—

"I know exactly what you're asking," he said. As he thought, his eyes were down. We waited. I think a minute passed. The silence was like a presence.

At last, rearing back in his chair, he said it put him in mind of a story he would tell us. One stormy night he was being flown from Mineral Wells, Texas, to Galveston in a small single-motor plane which belonged to a company that was supporting him. He was the only passenger, alone in the plane with the pilot. The wind and the rain were just hell, knocking the frail little craft first one way and then the other, dropping them suddenly in mid-air, butting them head-on. Suddenly, out the left window, a ball of lightning exploded on the wing!

Well, after they flew on a while, Lyndon asked the pilot, "Is this the company's regular plane?"

"No sir," the pilot told him, "this is just a little plane we use to run errands in."

They bumped on through the violent storm, and then, God *damn!* —*another* bolt of lightning banged out, dancing lightning balls of fire down the other wing all white-hot sputterin' and snappin' . . . and he decided he would ask the pilot another question.

"Are you the company's regular pilot?"

"No sir," the fellow said, "I'm not. I'm an accountant during the day."

Johnson said he thought then, "Well, Dear Lord, there's not anything I can do about it," and laid his head back on the seat and after a while dozed off.

"When I woke up," he said, "we were on the ground."

That was the president's answer. Maybe when we wake up we'll be on the ground. But he must have felt the horror of the trap he was in, because his gorge rose now against me and my question, against the dissenters, the criticizers, the kibitzers who have none of the burden, none of the inside knowledge, and none of the responsibility. Pushed completely back from the table now, glowering at me with his inescapable power for mass nuclear killing fresh in his being and his feelings, he exclaimed that *he* is the one who has to decide whether to bomb, *he* is the one who has to decide whether to send in troops—he shouted at me with a terrible intensity, jamming his thumb down on an imaginary spot in the air beside him, *"I'm* the one who has to *mash* the *button!"*

This is the meaning of the White House.

PART I
Origins of American Bellicosity in Johnson's Southwest

Let no one mistake the American purpose. Our nation is dedicated to Christ's quest for peace—not the false peace of evasion and retreat, but the divine peace which comes as the fulfillment of striving and the climax of commitment.

We will never falter in that dedication.

—Johnson at the Christmas Pageant for Peace, White House Ellipse, Dec. 20, 1961

1. The Preacher and the Cowboy

"About my background," he said, "you might say that Lyndon Johnson is a cross between a Baptist preacher and a cowboy." On another occasion he said, "If I hadn't gone into politics, I think I would have been a teacher or a preacher."[1]

In his name, Lyndon Baines Johnson, he carried forward the two families that converged in his birth. The Baineses were southern slave-owners, the Johnsons western cattle-drivers. Baines men made their ways in religion, journalism, and law, Johnson men in ranching, farming, and politics. From the Baineses through his mother Lyndon had laid on him the piety and cant of Puritan gentlemen in high collars and their women fretting about how things will look. From the Johnsons through his father he got the gaminess and radicalism of the West and the craftiness that helped make a hard life livable.

On the frontier, women tended the children and kept up the home, they warmed and took care of their men, but being captives, they often became tough and resentful; they fought the men's freedom. The men were roaming at large, having adventures, and earning distinctions while the women were staying home, doing the dirty work and praying with the children. Vassals and galley-slaves, in good time the women became mothers-in-law and grandmothers and turned on the men with a righteousness that could sanctify hate. They inherited and conserved a realm of their own—religion, morality, honor in defense of womanhood—wherein they, too could have a little splendor.

The primness of the women and the preachers drove men to drink and wenching and to cussing so dedicated it was the finest of the local arts and crafts. When, in mid-life, Johnson said he was both a liberal and a conservative, he was converting into political labels the influences of his youth that sent him ranging out to California in a roofless Model T, but then drew him back to home, college, and career. He was a wild Christian, a woman-ridden outlaw, complexly mixed from the day of his birth in the slave-owning whites' honor-ridden South, the Indian-fighting range riders' West, and the state that gloried in itself as if it was still a nation.

"Grandpa came in '53; then grandmother came," he said. His forebears were southern. Talking southerners into wanting him for president, he said, "Both my grandfathers served in the Confederacy." One of his remote southern ancestors left to a wife who survived him "my Negro whench Luce," and Lyndon's great-great-grandfather willed to each of two daughters "one Negro girl." As historian Frederick Jackson Turner wrote, "Fundamentally, the colonization of Texas resulted from . . . the advance of the southern stock," who brought with them some of the slaves of the cotton culture. When Johnson's great-grandmother, the widowed Phoebe Bunton, loaded up a wagon train of goods and struck forth to join her son John in Texas, she brought her slaves with her. The 1860 census showed that about a third of the people of Texas were enslaved. Gillespie County in the hill country where Lyndon was born had "white population, 2,700; slaves, 102; blind, one person; orphans, 25. . . ." In the area from which Mother Johnson's Blanco County was later carved, there were fewer than 200 slaves among the 4,000 whites, but the *Texas Almanac* said, "The disposition of the people is to own slaves as soon as able," and there were "No free persons of color." In Lyndon's own memory, "There was a colony of Negroes out of Blanco," he said.

Venturing west across the state, the settlers fought with the Indians and Mexicans who had been there long before them. Texas became the battlefield of the southern American, the Indian, and the Mexican; what we now call the Southwest formed in this tri-cultural struggle for the range. Southerners had settled Texas, all right—Stonewall, the town nearest Lyndon's birthplace, was named, not for stone walls, but for Stonewall Jackson. But scrambling to survive in the dry, scrubby hills and the drier plains beyond, they had to become westerners. As Turner also said, "The experience of the Carolina cowpens guided the ranchers of Texas."[2] Sixty miles east of Lyndon's birthplace the country people today still farm the fertile blackland, but in the hill country mostly they have to ranch. And just here, in the rocky fracture of the one great American state that is both South and West, Lyndon Johnson received his being.

The firmest values in him were those that were lodged in his family's stories about the heroes among their Texas ancestors. From family, school, and church he received and internalized, too, the southern and western American heritages. He grew into an old-fashioned man and a very American president, patriotic, sentimental, and ruthless. Those who turned away from his escalation of the war in Vietnam were turning away from a heritage that had failed the present.

Geneology was the avocation of Johnson's mother, Rebekah Baines Johnson. Paging through books in libraries, making notes at tombstones in graveyards, turning dusty pages in county courthouses, she learned that one of her antecedents had been on the staff of Colonel Frances Marion, 'the Swamp Fox' in the Revolutionary War. She was convinced, as she wrote in a sketch of son Lyndon published in the thirties, that she was "a direct descendant of Thomas Jameson, who served on Washington's staff," and she wrote that Jameson was "well acquainted with General Washington and was within twenty steps of him when Cornwallis surrendered." Johnson had the impression, when he was in the White House, that Jameson might have been a member of the first president's cabinet. Reading her German Grandfather Huffman's letters from the battlefields of the Civil War, Rebekah wrote about "the great strain and suffering he felt as a surgeon ministering to the wounded soldiers, and his sorrow over the losing cause."

Had we dropped in on a tea-party of an afternoon at the charming old Driskill Hotel in Austin and heard, perchance, Mrs. Johnson saying her family line could be traced back to a signer of the American Declaration of Independence, we might have thought it odd, in modern times, to cling to such a circumstance, but it was more than odd, it was serious.

Three years before she died, in the period when Lyndon was consolidating his domination of the United States Senate, Rebekah gave him the book she had written on their family. During the month he was laid out on his back by a heart attack, she went to him often and told him about the ones who had gone before them in their family. He had heard of Uncle John Bunton at the battle of San Jacinto, of Grandfather Johnson driving cattle, and his own father had told him how he had saved the Alamo, but now, here, at his bedside, in the shadow of his death, his Mother. No eyelash-batting belle, she was a Christian matriarch, a strong-willed woman marshaling within her graciousness a certain anger, driving her son, her Christian soldier, onward. Proud of the family escutcheon he was restoring to its rightful place, determined that he would get well and become president, she gave him her special gift to him, the authenticated venerability of their ancestors.[3]

Johnson was a cynic, all right, but vain. His ancestors? He didn't know then, their times were over—they were dead. Yet he saw that they could be useful to him, and he felt a special wonder. His people, after all, were daguerreotype American, religious and political, English, Irish, Scotch, French, German, farmers, preachers, cattlemen, soldiers, a governor of Kentucky, a secretary of state for Texas, and makers of the Texas laws. He was of them, these real people of his own body's feeling who had given life to the same land, worked the same fields, seized their measures, and died and lay in the graveyard by the river where he would lie dead, too. Determined to shoulder himself into immortal company, he found in his own family some men and women who were worthy contemporaries of Thomas Jefferson and Sam Houston, he saw ahead of himself the sacred ground that he in turn would tread. His ancestors were in him. He really knew about them, and he often invoked them in speeches when he was where they had been or when they somehow might validate him.[4]

A man may be an opportunist and strongly selfed, yet never let go of ideals as his last resort from the burdens of being. Even a man who sees everyone and everything first for the uses of his own interest may all the while be harboring the noblest ideals. A man may gain, but he must dream. He may crush a rival, betray an ideal, deceive his colleagues, yet it costs him nothing to wish that everything were love, and when he wins all that he wants, then, *then,* he can make his bid for greatness, and much will depend on the values that are stored away inside him.

Not given to philosophical reflection, reading almost no books after college, Johnson more than most leaders was a man of his region and his friends. He was not an original breaking unexpectedly toward possibilities in the future, he was a weathercock politician who uses and is used by the winds of circumstance and time and who, in a crisis, reenacts the past and thus transmits it into the present. When at the end of his life he held in his hands the powers of the president, he thrust his heritage, just as he had received it, into the life of the world.

---

2. From the Alamo to Khe Sanh

Texas broke free from Mexico in the battle of San Jacinto, on the coastal plains near the Gulf. There is a famous painting of General Sam Houston after the battle. Lying on a pallet surrounded by his men under a big oak tree, his bandaged right leg extended, he receives the surrender of Santa Anna, the captured Mexican commander, who stands before him. Lyndon Johnson said he was told as he grew up that his great-great-uncle, John Bunton, is in this picture, standing off beside a tree. Once Lyndon kidded his mother that he would get the picture out of sight because it looked as if their kinsman was hiding behind the tree to stay out of the line of fire. She did not think that was funny—she flared up, "Well, if you're as courageous and fearless and amount to as much in life as your Uncle John Wheeler Bunton—!"[1]

One of the earliest of the Anglo-American settlers, Bunton arrived in Texas in 1833. His wife was widely admired as a musician and a crack shot. As talk of war with Mexico increased, Bunton became first sergeant in a company of volunteers. The Mexicans occupied San Antonio. Texans bent on revolution and war, Bunton among them, camped outside the town and trained for several months, but to their surprise their commander then ordered a withdrawal. One of their number asked the question beloved in Texas history books, "Who will go with old Ben Milam into San Antonio?" The odds against them were four-to-one, but Bunton and several hundred others went in. For five days they fought house to house. Milam was killed, but the Mexicans were driven out.

Three months later about 185 Texans, still holding San Antonio and barricaded inside the Alamo mission, were attacked by Santa Anna's entire army. Inside the Alamo, Travis, the Texans' commander, drew a line in the dust with his sword and asked those who would stay and fight to step across it. This time the odds were thirty-to-one, but except for one, all the men stayed, fought to the end, and were slaughtered (unless, as may have happened, seven of them surrendered and then were slaughtered, too). Their bodies were stacked and burned.

During that siege Bunton was serving as one of the fifty-nine delegates to the convention of 1836 in Washington, Texas, a town in the woods on the bank of the Brazos River. "About a dozen wretched cabins or shanties constitute the city," wrote a visitor at the time; "not one decent house in it, and only one well-defined street, which consists of an opening cut in the woods. The stumps still standing." The convention hall was a house with no doors; the cotton cloth stretched across its windows snapped in the March wind. Most of the delegates were from the southern states, and only about ten of them had been in Texas longer than a decade, but here in this woebegotten village they were all Texans, and here like the Americans before them they wrote their declaration, echoing Jefferson's: "When a government . . . becomes an instrument in the hands of evil rulers" oppressing the people, "a consolidated central military despotism, in which every interest is disregarded but that of the army and the priesthood," when agents bearing petitions and remonstrances are thrown into dungeons, and mercenary armies are sent forth, "in such a crisis, the first law of nature . . . enjoins [the people] . . . to abolish such government and create another in its stead. . . . We, therefore, . . . appealing to a candid world for the necessities of our condition, do hereby resolve and declare . . . that the people of Texas do now constitute a free, sovereign, and independent Republic. . . ." Thereunder, at Washington-on-the-Brazos even as sixty years earlier at Philadelphia, the Texans pledged their lives, their fortunes, and their sacred honor . . . Richard Ellis . . . Lorenzo de Zavala . . . Thomas Jefferson Rusk . . . Sam Houston . . . Saml. A. Maverick . . . and the great-great-uncle of President Lyndon Johnson, John Wheeler Bunton.

Bunton also served on the committee that wrote the new country's constitution, modeled on the American system. The convention adjourned, and Houston, having heard of the terrible fall of the Alamo, retreated his army eastward, Santa Anna in pursuit.[2] On the afternoon of April 21, 1836, at San Jacinto, the Texans attacked the Mexicans and broke them in eighteen minutes of hard fighting. Bunton, one of the forty-three privates in Captain Jesse Billingsly's Company C, First Regiment, the Texian Volunteers, charged the Mexican breastworks, and Billingsly is the authority that Bunton's "towering form could be seen amidst the thickest of the fight. He penetrated so far into the ranks of the defenders of the breastworks that it is miraculous that he was not killed. But he came out of the deadly conflict unscathed." He was given 320 acres of land for his part in the Storming of San Antonio and 640 for his heroism at San Jacinto.[3]

At San Jacinto, Texas became the only American state that won its independence by fighting a foreign power alone. The battle of San Jacinto was one of the decisive events in American history—a deed "so marvelously far-reaching and strikingly momentous," said a college editorial probably written by Johnson, "that the whole world paused in astonishment."[4] Having freed herself from Mexico, the Republic of Texas was annexed to the Union, and this implicated the United States even more than before in the passions and claims of the Texans against Mexico and ramified into the Mexican War by which we wrenched half the national territory of Mexico into our own.

In Washington on the Potomac, a dissenting congressman in his late thirties, Abraham Lincoln, suspected that President Polk had ordered American troops into a peaceful Mexican settlement "purposely to bring on a war . . . trusting to escape public scrutiny by fixing the public gaze upon the exceeding brightness of military glory. . . ." Warned of political devastation his dissent was causing him in his home district, Lincoln retorted that the Constitution gave Congress the war-making power because "kings had always been involving and impoverishing their people in wars, pretending generally, if not always, that the good of the people was the object," that this was "the most oppressive of all kingly oppressions," and that a defense of Polk "places our President where kings have always stood."[5]

When he was excoriating his Vietnam critics, President Johnson often called up Lincoln in his defense, but the Lincoln of the Civil—not the Mexican—War.[6] A country's heritage is drawn from, but is more potent than its history, because the heritage is what is left after the writers of anthems, schoolbooks, and orations, in their pride, idealism, romanticism, enthusiasm, and glossing in the services of patriotism, have emphasized what they want remembered and left out what they want forgotten. Lincoln's dissent did not become part of the heritage because the manifest destiny of westward expansion did. There was never a likelihood that Johnson would value or want to tolerate dissent from what he as the president said was the national destiny. The Texans' revolutionary war culminated ten years later in the Americans' stunning land grab, but that was only history—what had made it through the filters of the heritage to the future president was his mother's picture of his great-great-uncle as a courageous founding father of the Republic of Texas. Like the stone of a hill-country peach, the son was clenched into the myths of his forebears.

If only Bunton had died at the Alamo!—then the Johnsons could almost *be* the heritage of Texas. Eight decades after the Alamo fell, Lyndon's father filled in this gap in the Johnsons' heroic lineage by becoming a "savior of the Alamo." Being like his son after him a politician morning till morning, he probably knew, either exactly or generally, what he was doing.

The state had been protecting the mission church of the Alamo, but the rest of the convent had been occupied by a liquor business, and a hotel was planned for the site. Three years before Lyndon's birth his father, State Representative Sam Johnson, Jr., introduced a bill in the legislature to save the Alamo for posterity. A famous young lady of the period—pretty, wealthy, well-traveled—provided money to stop the debasement of the shrine. Lyndon said his Grandfather Joseph Baines helped with the drafting of the bill, and his father Sam "got Miss Clara Driscoll to lend them $25,000 till he got his bill passed." Sam and his six cosponsors succeeded: the legislature authorized the governor to buy the endangered part of the mission.

In 1917, when Lyndon was eight or nine, Sam Johnson was honored at the state capitol, along with Clara Driscoll, as a savior of the Alamo. He told his boy all about it and led him into the Alamo with pride. "He took me as a little boy down there and showed it to me many times," Johnson told me.[7] A visitor in this high-domed old mission church, hallowed and hollow, a holy tomb, hears his own footsteps echoing into the thick stone heights. Here almost two hundred men took the stand they knew would be their deaths, here they fought, parapet to parapet, room to room, as they were shot, rushed, hacked down, driven through. Bowie, Travis, Davy Crockett, right here. A little boy will remember these things.

When Lyndon was an ambitious young schoolteacher in south Texas, the Austin paper ran a feature that opened like a western song:

"Santa Anna took the Alamo.
"That was 1836.
"Sam Johnson saved the Alamo.
"That was 1905."

In a campaign handbill for Lyndon's first try for Congress the only thing mentioned about his father's complex legislative career was his signature on the Alamo bill. In Lyndon's first Senate race his major listed contributor was Clara Driscoll; during this campaign he and his mother stopped at the Alamo, where he spoke of his father's Alamo bill. As the Germans crushed Europe, he asked Texans to "step over the line" again for liberty,[8] and ever after, any embattled military situation turned his thoughts back to the time of the Alamo. When the French were about to lose Dien Bien Phu he opposed sending U.S. troops without allies, demanding, "Would you tell us who will go in with old Ben Milam?" Confronted, during the first days of his presidency, with the prospective fall of South Vietnam, he told the National Security Council, "Hell, Vietnam is just like the Alamo. Hell, it's just like if you were down at that gate and you were surrounded and you damn well needed somebody. Well by God, I'm going to go—and I thank the Lord that I've got men who want to go with me, from McNamara right on down to the littlest private who's carrying a gun."[9]

Wishing for a son, President Johnson was proud of his son-in-law Pat Nugent's four hundred combat missions. Jack Valenti, Johnson's aide, said, "He has a new lease on life with a son-in-law who is gung-ho for Vietnam . . . who wants to go, who has asked to go, who believes it is right to go. It is the greatest thing that has happened to the president." Looking at a picture of Nugent kissing his wife Luci with their child, Patrick Lyndon, hanging onto Nugent's arm, Johnson said, "This is the kind of men I want fighting for me." His sons-in-law became, emotionally, his sons. One night he and his friend, Texas rancher Jess McNeel, were talking in the White House about two-thirty in the morning when Charles Robb, the Marine officer who had married the president's other daughter Lynda, came in "raising hell," McNeel said, "because he wanted to go back to Vietnam and take command of his battalion, or whatever it was." Lynda was expecting, and Robb had been wounded and was not yet fully recovered. "Goddamn," Johnson told McNeel, "isn't that a son for you. Wounded, not even out of the hospital, and he wants to go back." McNeel said Johnson "was really proud." Presenting medals of honor to four Vietnam veterans, Johnson said with pleasure that one of them came from the unit "where I have a load-master son-in-law, and the other one is in the Marine Corps, that we have represented out there, too."

Like Travis, Johnson vowed for the men in Vietnam, "We shall not ever retreat," but unlike Travis he did not die with them, and this may have bothered him. He was especially moved in the presence of young men who had been wounded over there. Visiting some of them in Maryland when he was himself recovering from an operation, he told them, "I feel like one of the casualties. . . ." After addressing troops at Cam Ranh Bay, he taped a report for replay in the U.S. in which he said something like, "Do you know that some of those men had just climbed out of their foxholes to be with me, they had just come from battle carrying their guns on their backs?" (His staff cut this from the statement that was released.) Visiting more casualties, he said, "Some were on crutches; others were in wheelchairs. Some were still suffering from shock, others were missing a leg or an arm." Again he said, "Our fighting men have contributed themselves, their bodies, their arms and their legs. . . ."

During a tour of Asia, while he was addressing servicemen at Camp Stanley in Korea, suddenly he told the young men in uniform massed before him, "My great-great-grandfather died at the Alamo. There was the battle of San Jacinto or Texas wouldn't have its independence."

No kin of Johnson's died at the Alamo. What had happened that moment in the president's mind? He had identified the Vietnam War with the Alamo, his blood kin with the Alamo, and so himself with the boys dying in Vietnam. In one quick but irretrievable slip, his father's saving the Alamo from the merchants had somehow blurred over into his great-great-uncle's heroism at San Jacinto.

When I asked him about this, Johnson explained, with some pain: "A few boys had been killed the night before, or maybe it was the next night," and "it was a very emotional speech. I was thinking of those boys." The picture of Sam Houston, his leg extended, with Bunton at the tree, was also in his mind, he told me. He thought he had said Bunton had fought at San Jacinto—"That's what I thought I said. I don't believe I said it yet." His aides brought him the official record to prove to him what he'd said but he sent them away—he didn't want to see it, he said. "I was seeing this picture of Sam Houston with his leg up like this. . . ."

Explaining the slip to his aide Joe Califano, Johnson cracked about Hugh Sidey, the *Life* writer on the presidency, "If Hugh Sidey ever had a crowd like that, he'd claim he was a great-grandson of George Washington." But Johnson knew the slip was serious—he probably understood why it happened; the context shows what he meant by it.

Just before the slip in the speech, he complained against critics who were asking, "Why don't we let the old men go fight? . . . Why do we snuff out all these young lives?" After saying his ancestor had died at the Alamo, the president went on: "In all the years we have been represented in some way down through the years." The opacity of the thought does not block what was really worrying Johnson. He was suffering because he was not fighting and dying in the carnage for which, increasingly, he was being blamed, and he was arguing that he had been "represented in some way down through the years."[10]

Not only had Bunton neither fought nor died at the Alamo, he hadn't died at San Jacinto, either.[11] Apparently Johnson needed to believe that he, his ancestors, something about him personally, was suffering as finally as the young Americans the war was killing. Presenting Silver Stars to pilots for gallantry over North Vietnam, he surprised one of them by removing his own Silver Star cloth lapel pin and placing it in the pilot's hand.[12] One evening late in his term, remembering exactly, as one never forgets an anthem, a poem his mother coached him to recite in his childhood, he reared back in his rocking chair and bellowed out gustily:

> Santa Ana came storming, as a storm might come;
> There was rumble of cannon; there was rattle of blade;
> There was cavalry, infantry, bugle and drum—
> Full seven thousand in pomp and parade,
> The chivalry, flower of Mexico;
> And a gaunt two hundred in the Alamo!
>
> And thirty lay sick, and some were shot through;
> For the siege had been bitter, and bloody, and long.
> "Surrender, or die!"—"Men, what will *you* do?"
> And Travis, great Travis, drew sword, quick and strong,
> Drew a line at his feet. . . . "Will you come? Will you go?"
> *I* die with my wounded, in the Alamo.[13]

In Vietnam the siege of Khe Sanh, which came to its peak in March, 1968, brought the Alamo to mind, but was very different. Within the surrounded base 199 Marines died, but the siege was broken by aerial attack—one hundred thousand tons of bombs and seven hundred thousand rounds of machine-gun fire, killing about 10,000 of the besiegers. The men at the Alamo fought with the weapons of their time; Khe Sanh was defended with a greater bomb tonnage than had ever been dropped on a single target, including Hiroshima.[14]

Nevertheless, one night the correspondent of the London *Times* went to see Johnson and found him talking about the spirit of the Alamo. "It seemed," the Britisher thought, "an unfortunate parallel. Colonel William Travis and the 150 defenders were all annihilated, but one could hardly point that out to a Texan President. In any case, he remembered only the grim courage of his brother Texans, the ruthless fighting, and Mexican duplicity."

Johnson was also capable, although bitterly, of seeing the Viet Cong as the heroes of the Alamo. Failing to get a response from them to a peace offer, he said their answer was "just like the answer that Travis gave at the Alamo when they asked if he would surrender. A cannon shot."[15]

Through their son who was president, the Johnsons of the Southwest were manifesting that Texans stand equal with New Englanders and Virginians in the American pantheon, that Texas, too, is part of the American grandeur. The Texans of the 1830s, declaring themselves free of Mexico, were modeling themselves, in principle and in bloody action, on the Americans six decades earlier who declared themselves free of England. Each cause prevailed, and in Lyndon Johnson's mind they fused. San Antonio was the Texans' Boston, March the Second their Fourth of July, the Alamo their Bunker Hill, and San Jacinto, Yorktown. To understand how Johnson felt about John Bunton, an American who is not a Texan may wish to imagine having a great-great-uncle who was one of the American colonists who attacked Boston, signed the Declaration of Independence, and fought with Washington's army the day the redcoats were whipped. By blood kinship, sectional pride, and martial patriotism, Johnson was bonded into the most sacred memories of the American people.

"When we studied the Alamo," Lyndon's girl in high school, Kitty Clyde Leonard, has been quoted, "it was the heroes who were impressed upon our minds. Heroes who were willing to fight for liberty. They stayed rather than retreated. Hard, strong, sturdy, patriotic men, willing to die for what they believed."[16] In the scene that is central to the Alamo story, the commander drew a line in the dust with his sword and told all the men who would stay and fight to the death with him to step across the line. The one who did not, the arch-coward of Texas history, skulked away one night before the massacre and survived in immortal disgrace, an object lesson for generations of Texas schoolchildren, including Lyndon B. Johnson. The powerful story of the Alamo, structured into the president's character, was one cause of Vietnam. The Alamo became Khe Sanh, San Jacinto the Tet offensive, and victory, defeat. He had not expected it would come to that. But it was not, after all, his fault alone, for each of us is a child of our heritage, and how was he to know that the ghosts he saw and the poems he believed in would become the trap and the trauma, the bombs and the broken bodies, the moral calamity and the mortifying defeat of Vietnam.

---

3. Indians and Communists

A French botanist and zoologist, Jean Louis Berlandier, traveled in Texas for the Mexican government in the late 1820s. Finding the Indians tolerably friendly, he lived with two Kickapoos. When he went buffalo hunting with a large party of Comanches in 1828, they ranged into the valley of a river the Indians called the Pedernales, on a bank of which the Johnson homestead was built a generation later.

As the French scientist knew them, the Indians of Texas were hardy, intelligent, and loyal to their codes. Theft within a tribe was prohibited, but theft from a stranger or an enemy was admired as a feat. They had much generous community; some of their customs about sex were almost as modern as life in a commune. Their religious rites were little more bizarre than, viewed as objectively, some of ours. Even their hideous cruelties to captured enemies can be understood in comparison, say, with Germany's murders of the Jews, Britain's firebombings of Dresden, or the American atomic bombings. Wrote the Frenchman who knew the first natives of Texas, "Those beings upon whom we have pinned the badge of 'savages' because they fled from what they did not know are often more closely united with each other than those who live in our cities and villages."[1]

The way Americans were taught until the 1960s, the Indians were barbarous and treacherous thieves and murderers, pagans we conquered and Christianized. Only now do we more generally realize that the Europeans invaded their lands and imposed on them, and as the Indians reacted in often savage ways, we wiped them out with responsive savagery, aggressively, treacherously, genocidally.

Lyndon Johnson's forebears were implicated participants in the western pioneers' exterminations of the Indians, and Johnson received and internalized the Anglo-Americans' cover story about it. Perhaps partly because his idea of the frontier was misshapen in this way, he often justified the Vietnam War with the argument that we should fight the Communists on the frontier to save the good people and civilize, in time, the savages.

Some of the Indian fights on the frontier happened on the river along which Johnson spent his boyhood. In the 1830s on the Pedernales, Captain Jack Hayes and about fourteen of his Texas Rangers, trying out the Colt revolvers against about seventy Indians, proved they could chase the Indians on horseback and shoot them with the repeater pistols at the same time.[2] As John Speer reported, the Indians were "the Red Savage" to the Blanco County settlers, who included Baineses and Johnsons. Speer, a merchant in the county, wrote about a later company of Rangers who had headquartered on the Blanco River (alongside which Lyndon's mother spent some of her girlhood) that "It was claimed by some that they did no good, for they had no fights with Indians." Certain white outlaws were even more dreaded than Indians because "If we espied a red man we knew he was an enemy. . . ."[3]

Stephen F. Austin, "the father of Texas," saw the Karankawa Indians during his first venture into the state and observed that "there will be no way of subduing them but by extermination." He later led an expedition that killed half of them. An Indian fighter, Noah Smithwick, who lived as a friend among Comanches a few months and understood their grievances, discussed the subject with the great Sam Houston, who had lived among Indians with an Indian wife and had fathered, it was said, Indian children. Houston told Smithwick that the conflict had to go on until the Indian was exterminated or forced into exile, and he was powerless to stop it.[4] As president of Texas, Houston tried to get his countrymen to respect the Indians' lands and seek peace, but they would not, and he was succeeded by Mirabeau B. Lamar, "the father of Texas education," whose policy like Austin's was extermination.

The hill-country invaders' written records are full of accounts of the Indians' outrages, although not of the invaders' own. In Blanco County, of which Lyndon's home town Johnson City is the county seat, Indians were identified after the Civil War as the stealers of horses, mules, and pistols. On the Little Blanco River a man, his wife, and their baby were "shot with Balls & pierced Arrows." A man about twenty-two was shot with balls; a man and his son were shot with balls and arrows.

After dinner one summer evening in 1869 on Cypress Creek in Blanco County, Thomas Felps, twenty-seven, and his wife, a young woman of nineteen, "walked down to the creek to catch some fish; in a short time the Indians cut them off from the house and murdered them both near each other." Felps was shot and stabbed, his wife was speared in the heart, her arm and face were broken with a club, she was scalped, and both were stripped of their clothes. One account said the Indians "passed on to the residence of Mr. Johnson, where they murdered one of his sons, about twenty-one years of age, and took his twelve-year-old boy a prisoner, tied him on a horse and departed. The Indians, twenty-one in number, were overtaken by fifteen whites near Fort Mason, and being hotly pursued, they untied their little prisoner, set him down unhurt and then continued their flight. Having recaptured the boy, the Texans abandoned the chase and went home." What Johnson, which son was killed, which one was kidnapped, the tale doesn't tell.[5]

According to a story Johnson told in the White House as it had been passed on to him by his mother and his cousins when he was a boy, Lyndon's grandfather, Sam Johnson, Sr., left his wife Eliza Bunton to join the hunting party that went out to avenge the murders of Felps and his wife. Evidently the Indians had doubled back, and they came upon the Johnsons' cabin while Sam was away hunting them.

"In those days that's where the expression 'going to the well with you' originated," Johnson said. "The well was usually located a distance from the house, and you'd have to go to the well and take the rope or the chain and haul the water, the bucket that held two or three gallons of water, up fifty or sixty or seventy feet, and then empty the water out. . . . My grandmother had gone to the well . . . and just as she emptied the bucket of water, with her little baby in one arm, and the bucket in the other hand, she heard the Indian war-whoops coming over the hillside, and she threw down the bucket of water and ran to the house as quickly as she could, picked up a diaper for the baby and opened the trap door, and crouched down in the cellar of the log cabin, and remained there very quietly. For fear the baby'd cry she took the diaper and put it in the baby's mouth. She stayed there all day." The Indians stormed around overhead, ransacking the house and killing a horse outside.

"Late that night," Johnson said, "her husband and some of his companions came in. They saw that the horses had been stolen from the corrals, the house had been torn up and the silver was gone, and nowhere could he find his young wife and first child, so he was very disturbed. But going out someone said something and my grandmother heard what she thought was my grandfather's voice, and she listened again, and then he laughed, something—something was said that made him laugh, and she knew that was her husband, and she opened the trap door and came up and called to him, and told him where she'd been."[6]

Soon afterward, Lyndon's mother has written, the hill-country men routed the Indians in the battle of Deer Creek, and the three whites who were wounded in the battle were carried to the Johnson ranch to be cared for.[7]

A boyhood friend of Lyndon's, Tom Crider, said there is a spot over on Croft's Ranch near Johnson City where the Indians attacked another couple. "They scalped her and they wouldn't scalp him because he was red-headed. They tell me that a Indian won't scalp a red-headed person," Crider said. "They had a Indian fight in our pasture. That grass was real high and them Indians crept through it."[8]

A young man who was helping build a stock ranch in the early 1870s, probably for the Johnsons, on a creek that runs into the Pedernales, wrote home that he was cautioned not to get out of sight of the wagon because Indians had "come in here last Month & stole between 250 & 300 head of horses and killed & stole 2 or three persons, but soon several companies of Rangers were organized & they have been scouting the country ever since." The fellow decided to join the Rangers so he could be with them "going right out where the Comanchee dwells not to make a war treaty neither."[9]

Hunting Indians, like hunting the wild game, was sport. Even the thoughtful frontiersman Smithwick said when they raided settlements he "hunted them as mercilessly as anyone." Once when he helped kill an Indian, he was awarded the scalp because "according to all rules of the chase, the man who brought down the game was entitled to the pelt." A Presbyterian clergyman traveling through Texas said that among his hosts, "sporting and the killing of Indians were merely synonymous terms."[10]

As the Indians were killed out, this changed. A cowboy passing through Oklahoma around 1871 with a herd of cows belonging to the

Johnson family wrote that buffalo, antelope, and Indians were much in evidence, and chasing and shooting the buffalo "afforded great sport, but as for chasing Indians, that was out of the question, for at that time they were under the watchful care of government agents."[11] But the adventures of extermination quickly became the legends that would become the myths. As the century ended, Johnson's father, Sam Johnson, Jr., was teaching school near Hye and happened to be boarding in a house where an old Indian fighter, Captain Rufus Perry, was living out the end of his life. In the evenings around the fire, Sam, Jr., "listened with great interest" while Captain Perry spun his tales. Perry had fought Comanches and Mexicans since 1836. On Turkey Creek, attacked by Indians, abandoned by his sidekicks, he was pierced by arrows in his shoulder, temple, and hip, and the Indians left him for dead. One of the arrows had cut all the way through him—he pulled it out of his back. Somehow, walking for seven days, eating prickly pear apples and mesquite beans, he reached San Antonio. There, so the story goes, they counted twenty-one arrow holes in his clothes. "His handsome face all drawn and scarred, his eye distorted, and twitching while he walk[ed] with a cane," this was the man Lyndon's daddy listened to around the fire.[12]

Was there another way, hidden behind one of the screens of the heritage, perhaps even somewhere in the history of Johnson's own region? There was. Peace was made and kept between the Comanches, the most ferocious of the Texas tribes, and the Germans who settled Gillespie County a morning's ride upriver from the Anglo-Saxons of Blanco County. In the contrast between the war-making courage of Johnson's forebears and the peace-making courage of John O. Meusebach there is much to think about.

Germany was becoming a reactionary nationalist state, and young Baron Meusebach, immersed in the values of the American and French Revolutions, decided to go to Texas for the rest of his life to "Stand on free soil among a people free." The Germans had preceded the American southerners into the hill country by six or seven years and had the same Indian problems they did, but back in Germany Meusebach wondered whether the Indians could be approached with a fair proposition. Arriving in the hill country to take charge of the German colony, Meusebach must have known about the Anglo-Indian carnage involving Johnson's forebears, but he decided to take the chance that even the Comanches were human beings who could, with risk, be sought out and befriended.

Meusebach led about seven Germans north from the Pedernales across the stony hills into the Comanches' San Saba River country. The governor, hearing of this folly, sent a messenger warning them to turn back, but they went on.

The Comanches did not kill them on sight; instead, Indian emissaries approached them to talk. Meusebach tentatively convinced them he came seeking a peace treaty. When the moon came full, on March 1, 1847, he and his men rode to a peace council with the head chiefs of the western bands of Comanches on the lower San Saba River.

Approaching the place of the meeting, the small band of Germans saw ahead of them, arrayed on a hill in a military formation, several hundred Comanches. Meusebach in the lead, the Germans rode up into the midst of them. They took this mortally dangerous risk for peace. One of Meusebach's companions later recalled, "Several hundred warriors faced us and great numbers were behind us. Each one was well-armed—many with guns, a number with spears, and all with bows and arrows."

To give proof of trust Meusebach and his companions fired their rifles in the air. The Comanches responded—by doing the same thing. The Germans went into the Indians' camp and distributed gifts among the chiefs, and a peace treaty was drawn up and signed.

A German historian has written that by the treaty of 1847, "A vast territory of over three million acres was opened to civilization." Meusebach later related that Captain Hays (the celebrated Indian fighter who led the first raid with repeater pistols on the Pedernales) "returned from a trip to El Paso . . . in 1858 or '59, I believe, stopped at my house at Comanche Springs, and told me that he was astonished that the Indians kept their treaty so well. That he was never molested nor lost any animals during his travel within the limits of our colony, but as soon as he had passed the line he had losses."[13]

After the Civil War Meusebach founded Loyal Valley, named for the Union, forty-five miles northwest of Johnson City. In his weakening years there he cared for his "garden in the wilderness," sixty varieties of roses, sixty of pear and forty of peach, apples, oranges, grapes, plums, yucca and crepe myrtle, flowering willows, violets and trumpet vines. Under a trellis, the former German baron who had made peace with the Comanches built an open-air Roman bath of reddish native stone, with steps rising up over the side into it. Sometimes he would emerge from it wearing a long white shirt, reciting verses in Latin. In his last years, free, he wondered what he was free for.[14]

Although Johnson was raised in the very part of Texas where Meusebach's treaty with the Comanches kept the peace, he made nothing of it. Rather, he relished the danger and romance of the frontier in the lives of his own ancestors. He and his baby girl were photographed being shown the basement where Eliza Bunton hid with her baby during the Indian raid. An old man told Lyndon that at nine years of age he had gone up the trail with Lyndon's forebears and that coming home they brought back a sack of gold and, Johnson told a reporter, "the Indians sometimes would try for the gold."

"Mr. Johnson told about that," the reporter wrote, "while driving

Huddle's 1886 painting, "The Surrender of Santa Anna," Santa Anna (in white pants) standing before Sam Houston, reclining, in the Mexican surrender after the battle of San Jacinto in 1836. The arrow points to the man almost behind the live oak tree, identified as "Buntin" in a document six years after the painting was made and probably Lyndon Johnson's great-great-uncle John Wheeler Bunton. In a story Johnson told the author, Johnson's mother took offense at a jest that Bunton was hiding behind the tree.

COURTESY OF TEXAS HIGHWAYS

EXPRESS-NEWS CORP.

Left to right, Texas Governor Price Daniel, U.S. Senator John Kennedy of Massachusetts, and Johnson chat during a campaign visit to the Alamo in 1956. Johnson's father helped preserve the Alamo from commercial encroachment.

Johnson talks to old cowboy Berry Roebuck and an unidentified old-timer.

JOHNSON LIBRARY

Old cowboy Berry Roebuck shows Johnson and little Lynda Johnson the cellar where Johnson's grandmother Eliza hid from marauding Indians.

JOHNSON LIBRARY

PETER HALPERN

Killing the Indians is a commonplace in the history of the frontier, but there was another way of relating to them. John O. Meusebach made a treaty with the Comanches that kept the peace in Johnson's hill country. Retiring to Loyal Valley, about 45 miles from Johnson's birthplace, Meusebach planted gardens and built a Roman bath, which can still be seen, above, unattended by history, on Ralph Russell's farm. The "M" scratched on the adjacent structure, shown below, is assumed to be Meusebach's initial.

PETER HALPERN

back to his home in the darkness after a tour of his ranch and visits with neighbors. He directed the driver to pull into the yard of a little home . . . where his ancestors fought off the Indian raiders. He flashed the car lights on the old stone buildings, which served at times as forts. You could still see the slots in the stone—arranged for pointing rifles at the raiding Indians." Johnson when president told a network audience that his grandfather Sam would put his gun in the slot, and the neighbors would stand inside and watch for the Indians to come.

Johnson identified with the feared, but fearless lawmen of the frontier. Tom Crider has a snapshot of a skinny, grinning Lyndon at the age of about ten dressed up in a Sunday school suit and standing bolt upright on a saddled horse, holding both his arms out, crooked upward for balance, and in his right hand, pointed to the sky, a pistol; maybe a toy. There was a Texas Ranger in Lyndon's own family background, Eliza's brother Joe.[15] During his first year as president, Johnson said: "In my country, we were very proud of what we call the Texas Rangers. Sometimes when we have a little row or misunderstanding in our country, they call a Ranger. One of our old cow-puncher friends took some cattle up to Kansas City to sell, and one of the fellows out in the stockyards said to him, while they were waiting for the bidders to come in, 'Please tell me what is really the difference between a Sheriff and a Texas Ranger?'

"The old man, a Ranger for many years, ran his hand through his hair and deliberated, and he said, 'Well, the Ranger is one that when you plug him, when you hit him, he just keeps coming. And we must let the rest of the world know that . . . if they ever hit us it is not going to stop us—we are just going to keep coming."[16]

The Vietnam president especially admired Captain L. H. McNelly, who fought Indians and Mexicans on the frontier. McNelly and his men once saw a dozen Mexicans driving stolen cattle and in a running gunfight killed every one of the bandits. When McNelly's men captured a Mexican bandit spy (or someone they thought was one), they would fake hanging him until he talked, and then they'd hang him. In McNelly's most famous exploit, pursuing bandits in 1875 he took thirty of his Rangers into Mexico and ordered them to ride into the headquarters of Las Cuevas Ranch and kill everybody except women, old men, and children. They galloped in and killed all the men they saw, but it was the wrong ranch. A Mexican force gathered, but McNelly, ignoring orders to get back to American soil, fought back in Mexico as long as he could. Historian Walter Prescott Webb believed he was trying was to provoke another war with Mexico.

Webb, who was a Texan, wrote a book about the Rangers, and President Johnson signed (and must at least have approved personally) a foreword for an edition of it. Johnson's foreword closed: "Captain McNelly repeatedly told his men that 'courage is a man who keeps on coming on.' Dr. Webb would explain to me, 'you can slow a man like that, but you can't defeat him—the man who keeps on coming on is either going to get there himself or make it possible for a later man to reach the goal.' In the challenging and perilous times of this century, free men everywhere might profitably consider that motto. . . . We can . . . be the kind of people who 'keep on coming on.'—Lyndon B. Johnson, May, 1965." This was just about when Johnson was ordering the bombing of North Vietnam and sending American boys into war in the Indo-Chinese jungles.[17]

Any fine day one can drive into the Texas hill country, a little on past Johnson City, and getting directions from people in Loyal Valley to what they call "the bathtub," one can walk out by a farmhouse there, through a field of clinging weeds, to Citizen John O. Meusebach's Roman bath. His garden and orchard, the terrace and trellis, are gone without a trace, but the stone bath lies untended, somehow naked, on the open ground. It is comfortably wide, surprisingly long. Except for a few stones that have slid into the weeds, it has not crumbled. On the side of an open stone water tank that still stands nearby, an "M" is scratched in the mortar, as if with a stick, but there are no historical markers. Nobody comes here. Except for the few citizens of Loyal Valley, nobody even knows the place exists. The patriotic historians who left John Meusebach out of the American heritage held forth, instead, the myths that Lyndon Johnson acted out when he escalated, while refusing to compromise, the Vietnam War. He would fire no rifles in the air. He would sign no treaty with the savages. His principle, like his grandfather's before him, was retaliation.

---

4. From Deer Creek to Pleiku

The United States lurched into the Vietnam War in 1964 and 1965 like a feudist in the hills of Kentucky and West Virginia or the river valleys of Texas. The president from Texas, sensing that something in the American character would require that he be backed up, made his first two lunges in the name of retaliation. We "struck back," we "retaliated," and the ethic of revenge is so deep in the instincts and memories of the people that the immorality of the greatest power on earth bombing a tiny country with no air force of its own on the basis of retaliation has escaped most of us to this day.

During the 1964 presidential campaign the United States alleged that three North Vietnamese torpedo boats had fired torpedoes and machine guns at a U.S. destroyer in the Gulf of Tonkin about thirty miles from the Indo-Chinese mainland. Two days later the government alleged that two more of the Reds' boats had fired at two U.S. destroyers. Each time, we said, the other side took losses, but we, none. Whether President Johnson believed all this was true, or despite contrary evidence chose to say he believed it to justify what he wanted to do, he ordered retaliatory air attacks on the torpedo-boat bases and their oil storage depots—for the first time the United States bombed North Vietnam on grounds of retaliation. "... when they fired on our flag," Johnson said, "we retaliated in kind.... But we didn't drop a bunch of bombs on civilian women and children in an act of desperation or in a thoughtless moment." That was to come later, in many thoughtful moments.

In February, 1965, when Johnson again wanted public support for bombing Vietnam, again he fell back on the devil's brew of the feud. Viet Cong guerillas attacked an American installation at Pleiku north of Saigon, killing seven U.S. soldiers and wounding more than a hundred. When Johnson bombed North Vietnam then for the first time, he said it was retaliation for Pleiku; his secretary of defense, Robert McNamara, said "retaliatory" three times in his press conference about it. Congress and most of the people accepted it. The *New York Times*, while questioning what we were doing over there, said, "The average American will not question that if the Vietcong hits the Americans, our forces must hit back," and Texas papers were exultant. Johnson had decided "to retaliate," said the *Houston Chronicle*—he showed the Reds, said the *Houston Post*, that the U.S. "will not hesitate to retaliate directly"—"Retaliation in kind," said the *San Antonio Express*, "will be the order of the day."

For a short while thereafter the government maintained that all we were doing was retaliating some more for further wrongs done us, in kind and in proportion. But at the end of that month, having involved the people emotionally in his war-making, Johnson cast off the retaliator's righteousness and announced continuous bombings against North Vietnam. Then he sent troops, and the United States was at war without a declaration by Congress. The excuse, having done its psychological work, was forgotten. The American people, who normally would have been stunned and confused by their government suddenly bombing a small country ten thousand miles away, had been tricked through the instinct of revenge into accepting it.

Explaining about the war in 1967, Johnson said he had done everything a human being could, but the North Vietnamese had dropped a bomb "right on top of our people," and "Our people said they've got to be told this they cannot do." We could not, he said, "just sit there as a bunch of Quislings. . . . If you rape my daughter . . . tit for tat." This was the way Undersecretary of State George Ball remembered the justification, too, "giving tit for tat."[1]

Brutal revenge had been one of the common values among the Indians, and individuals had the right to administer it. In Texas Berlandier heard Indian parents commending revenge as a virtue, and the thirst for vengeance became, among them, "like the instinctive fury of wild beasts. . . . It is invariably the desire for vengeance that incites them to make the raids which occupy most of their days. Every friend of a man killed by the enemy tries to start one of these private wars."[2]

Enraged by the barbarities of the Indians, the settlers, availing themselves of their own cultural precedents, retaliated barbarously. Revenge, personally settling scores, feudal raiding—commonplaces in medieval Europe—had become, in the southerners' own places and times, the feud and the lynching bee. These ways, drifting along West with the wagontrains like succubi in men's dreams, matched the Indians' vengefulness to become the primitive justice of the frontier. When Captain McNelly, on the eve of his raid into Mexico, said to his men, "We will learn them a Texas lesson,"[3] his was the voice of the ancient tribal feud.

For every inhumanity there's a theory. Among Europeans and Americans the theory for revenge is honor. In his book *I'll Die Before I Run,* C. L. Sonnichsen speculated that the traditions of honor entered the South through memories of the English cavaliers and the Scots, the surviving codes of French and British army officers, the novels of Sir Walter Scott. With the force of law weakened by the rural nature of the South and by the slaveowners' power, the code of honor was stronger than law.[4] Whatever was literally true about the Knights of the Round Table, the myth about them became the southern heritage.

Lyndon's mother, Rebekah, dreamed, the first half of her life, of writing a great novel. She wrote, instead, a romanticized story of her family, but her novel probably would have conjured up again the gallantry and blush of Ivanhoe and Rowena, Quentin Durward and the Countess Isabelle, Francis and Diana, the exploits of Andrew Fairservice, Rob Roy, Robin Hood, cads of vile intent and maids betrayed, tournaments and knights, castles under siege. Of one of her earliest known ancestors, George Bains, who served in the American Revolution, she wrote that his life "embodied the glorious heritage of his ancestry of Scottish kings." In the book she did write she called Lyndon's grandmother Eliza, who hid with her baby from the Indians, one of "the heroines of the highlands of Southwest Texas."[5]

The battle of Deer Creek, shortly after the murder of the Felps couple in Blanco County, was a retaliatory raid. The Felpses were killed, Lyndon's mother wrote, and "The countryside was aroused and a few days later ten young men of this section met a band of Indians and engaged in the battle of Deer Creek, in which the Indians were routed."[6]

Rebekah well knew the traditions of those "ten young men of this section" she was conveying to her favorite son. In Johnson's hill country, neighbors killed each other over points of honor and stormed the law for revenge. "Those feuds up there," Johnson said when he was president, "can be pretty bitter ones."[7] Growing up in the little town of Blanco at the turn of the century, Rebekah probably heard early on about the Blassingame shoot-out on the Blanco River just before the Civil War. Texas Ranger James Callahan, believing he or his wife had been slandered by Woodson Blassingame, led a small party in an attack on the Blassingames in their home and was shot dead, along with a friend who was riding with him. Blassingame and his son, arrested and guarded by twenty-eight men, were released to a mob of fifty or one hundred others who dragged father and son, locked in each others' arms, into the open and shot them both dead, piercing them with many wounds.[8]

During the Civil War three companies loyal to the Union were raised in the German counties, but disbanded. Three score or so of the Germans lit out for the safety of Mexico, but were hunted down and many of them killed in a fight in the early dawn, the wounded prisoners shot or hanged. About fifty Unionists were hanged soon after in Gillespie County, upriver from Johnson country.[9] After the war Blanco was one of the Texas counties that had permanent committees of vigilantes enforcing the laws of the time.[10]

Jim Johnson, a nephew of Sam and Tom Johnson (who were Lyndon's great-grandfather and great-uncle), decided while he was laying out Johnson City that he wanted the county courthouse there, although it was already in Blanco. By the tales one still hears in the area, some Johnson City men went over and stole the records from the courthouse in Blanco, took them to Johnson City, and declared their town the county seat. The feud lasted twelve years. There were a few killings over it, Johnson told me, and when he ran for office, in northern Blanco County he was "old man Sam's boy," but in the southern part he was "Miss Rebekah's son." For little towns on the frontier, politics meant success or failure. There was the usual feverish athletic competition in Johnson City, but it was grim in the games against Blanco. Emmette Redford said that not rarely, the baseball games between these two towns would end about the fifth inning, in a fist fight—feuds die hard in the hill country! "They used to say that Percy Brigham, the banker in Blanco, said he'd teach his children to teach their children to hate Johnson City," Redford recalled. "I don't know if he *said* it, but people in Johnson City said he'd said it."[11]

Johnson's Populist grandfather Sam ran for the legislature in 1892 against his own son-in-law, Democrat Clarence Martin—"My grandfather ran against his son-in-law," as Johnson put it to me. According to what Lyndon said his Uncle Clarence told him, there was nothing feudlike about this; but the *Dallas Morning News* half a century later said Martin "suffered a serious stab wound in a public speaking" at a town in the area.

In the next generation, Lyndon's father and Albert Moursund were bitter political enemies (Moursund won out), and it was pitiful, Lyndon said—his mother and Mrs. Moursund had been college roommates and were good friends, but they dared not be seen together. They would phone each other while keeping an eye on the door to be sure their men didn't come in.

Clarence Martin's son Tom was opposed to Lyndon for Congress in 1937, and in 1941 Lyndon had to deal with a threat from Tom to run against him for reelection to Congress. Lyndon and his brother, Sam Houston Johnson, later blamed this on the envy an older man felt about his kinsman's success. The Second World War broke out and Tom Martin did not, after all, run against his first cousin.[12]

Whatever the events these facts are clues to, the Johnsons had toughed it out in a frontier environment full of feuding and vengeance, and Lyndon knew it. After World War II he exchanged reminiscences with a lady in central Texas who, a newspaper reported, recalled "an occasion when Johnson's grandfather had started out to fight a duel to settle a quarrel."[13] The feuding traditions of the South had found their forms in the region and in the family of the man who was to be the president of the country.

"In Texas," wrote Sonnichsen, "the folk law of the frontier was reinforced by the unwritten laws of the South and produced a habit of self-redress more deeply ingrained, perhaps, than anywhere else in the country. . . . What a few years of feuding does to . . . kindly Christian people is one of the darkest figures in the pattern. They grow used to the thought of killing and lose all compunction about how it is to be done. Shooting an unarmed man or killing from ambush does not seem dishonorable any more than 'commando' tactics seem dishonorable to a seasoned soldier. . . . The matter of broken treaties comes in here, too. Many times . . . feudists have signed an agreement to cease fighting. Usually these documents, like other treaties we have heard of, were just scraps of paper. Why? Because each side reasoned that the other was unworthy of trust or honorable treatment." The pattern "seldom stops or dies out of its own accord. . . . More and more people are drawn in, even the women being involved . . . and telegrams go out to the adjutant general, the governor, and sometimes to the president of the United States."[14] Sending President Johnson a telegram to stop the bombing of North Vietnam was asking a Hatfield to stop killing the McCoys.

PART II
Populism and Compromise in Johnson's Family

That is Mr. Olds as he is, as he was; the prologue to the future which he now seeks. Once more, let me repeat the words of Justice Black: "Here we have a man in an environment which we know, and no man can honestly deny that he knows, that environment creates the trend of thought and develops the bent of mind."

—Johnson opposing President Truman's nomination of Leland Olds for the FPC, Oct. 12, 1949

5. Johnsons on the Chisholm Trail

The dusty, river-swimming cattle drives of the western frontier never involved more than a few ten thousand Americans, but two of them were Tom and Sam Johnson, Lyndon's great-uncle and grandfather. The biggest cattle-drivers in the seven counties west of San Antonio, the Johnson brothers assembled large herds and drove them up the trails to Kansas, Montana, and Wyoming until plunging prices wiped them out.

In 1846 the Johnson clan—Jesse Johnson and his wife, eight of their children, and several slaves—had trundled into east Texas from Georgia. Three of the sons, Tom, Sam, and Jack, moved on further west to the hill-country valley of the Pedernales in the vicinity of Johnson City. Lyndon Johnson said his grandfather moved from the prairies to the hills for "more freedom. He wanted to get away from the trains that passed through every night and disturbed him. He went out into a new, uncharted wilderness."

In the Civil War, Sam enlisted as a private in DeBray's Regiment. According to his daughter, his horse was killed under him, he risked his life to carry a wounded companion from the battlefield on his back, and he steadied wounded soldiers while their limbs were being cut off.[1]

Meanwhile, in the hill country, Jack and Tom were accumulating cattle. Jack supplied beef to the Confederate forces and was the agent for sixty or seventy horses Sam and Tom owned early in the war.

A. W. Capt, a cowboy who worked for the Johnson brothers, has left us a good account of those days. He got his start as a youngster in the hill country in the early sixties when older hands were away to war. It was good, he wrote, "to ride the range alone, everybody's 'roustabout,' to gather their scattered cattle, brand their calves, and hunt their lost horses."

There were disputes in Blanco County over who owned the cattle that had been multiplying during the war.[2] According to the historian Lawrence Goodwyn, immediately after the war rustling was commonplace, "about the only workable method of capital accumulation for men who had no other resources. Less easily explained . . . are the loose values and primitive cynicism that wholesale stealing inculcated into the way of life; few objective Texans would claim their land has yet fully escaped this darker aspect of its heritage."[3] There is no evidence that Johnson's cattlemen forebears did or did not do any rustling, but obviously those who stayed home during the war gained advantage over those who joined the fight.

After the war Jack evidently moved out of the area, but Tom and Sam carried on. Their headquarters at Johnson City was a log cabin and the rock barn that had the slit holes in it for firing out at marauding Indians. Their pens extended, Lyndon was told later, from the barn all the way down to the river a mile or more away. They were big operators, capitalists of the range. Cattle were driven to their pens from an area bounded by Fredericksburg on the west, Llano on the north, Austin on the east, and San Antonio on the south. Expanding mostly on credit, by 1869 they were able to drive north a herd large enough to bring home ten or twelve two-horse wagons and pay off their debts. In 1870 they drove seven thousand head to Kansas, and coming back with one hundred thousand dollars, they paid off their debts in the "cold, sleety year" of 1871 and began to buy up for that year's drives.

Johnson said of his grandfather's cattle drives from the Pedernales Valley to Abilene between 1869 and 1872, "He had a hundred cowboys on the drives. Some of them were not cowmen, they were literally cowboys, some ten, eleven, twelve years of age, and they'd drive as many as three thousand longhorn cattle up the trail to Kansas in different groups. They'd have to swim the Red River. They would have their stampedes and lose some of their cattle—many of them would die goin' up. They had many drives through the years. They had as high as thirty thousand in one year, and they would assemble these longhorns from a hundred miles around, and the central focal point of assembly was in Johnson City. They called it 'the Johnson Brothers ranch.' "[4]

Those, those were the days!—the days, Capt wrote, when "cowboys were sure-to-goodness cowboys" and the job was "to round 'em up and hold them up before they struck the breaks." Of one of his buddies Capt said, "No better cowboy every graced or disgraced the hurricane deck of a Spanish pony . . . if he did usually hang his long carcass on the left side of his mount with his hind leg in his flank and roped with his left paw. . . ."

And Capt remembered: "Beginning in the spring of 1870, when large herds were being driven to Texas up the Chisholm Trail to Kansas and beyond, I got my best experience, joining the 'roundup' for Sam and Thomas Johnson, the then largest individual trail-drivers operating in Blanco, Gillespie, Llano, Burnet, Hays, Comal, and Kendall Counties, with headquarter pens and branding stall at the mouth of Williamson's Creek in Blanco County and headquarters at Johnson's ranch on the Perdenales River, Johnson City. . . .

"The roundup or range hands and range boss usually gathered, road branded and delivered a herd of from 2,500 to 3,000 head of cattle, which a trail boss and his outfit received at headquarters ranch, but sometimes we delivered them at the Seven Live Oaks on the prairie west of Austin. After a good night's rest the ranch hands, bidding their relief 'So long, we'll meet you later in Kansas,' with pack and ponies, hit the back trails for another herd for the next outfit."

That last year of the Johnson boys' lives as big cattlemen, Capt and fifteen other cowboys, riding for the Johnsons, headed north with an oxen-drawn chuck wagon, a horse wrangler, and "64 rode-down mounts," driving along a herd of three thousand. Water was scarce and the thirsty cattle stampeded again and again. Taking out his small interest in the herd, Capt established himself on a river above Abilene, Kansas, where, he said, he "wintered and suffered. Thawing out in the spring, I hit the grit for Sunny Texas, a poorer but wiser man."[5]

"Hod" Hall, a seventeen-year-old boy on the roam, had bribed a train conductor to let him ride from Illinois to Kansas that fall, and in Abilene, right off he got a job with "a big cattle dealer," Sam Johnson of Blanco County. Before Hod left Abilene with the Johnson group for Texas, he met Wild Bill Hickok. Lyndon Johnson's forefathers were living men in the adventures that really happened and then, filtering through the fantasies of millions of people through the decades, became the myth of the West.

"Dear Ma and Pa," Hod wrote on a Sunday in 1871, "I am in Johnsons camp now, out at the cattle pens and I am writing on the bread board in the smoke of the fire, a fellow cant get out of the fire to day for the wind blows in every direction, so I had to put on an extra shirt this morning for the winds cut a fellow through and through. The boys have sold all of their cattle and to morrow they will commence 'outfitting,' and then go to Texas; hands here get from $30 to $100 a month and board. . . . The Johnson boys have brought up 25 herds this season the smallest of which was 1500. Captain King is the biggest cattle man that comes here I guess. . . ." ("Captain King" was the founder of the horizon-to-horizon King Ranch, a later proprietor of which gave young Lyndon the break that took him to Washington for the opening of the New Deal.)

With fourteen spring wagons, the Johnson party set out down the East Shawnee Trail for Texas. By then Sam had married Eliza Bunton, the daughter of a Kentucky planter. Hod, riding along eight miles ahead of the outfit in the Indian territory with a Mrs. Johnson who might have been Eliza, chased and killed a deer with a revolver.

Five months later, writing from "Johnsons Ranche Blanco Tex," Hod told his folks, "This is a beautiful country through here: mountains, clear rocky streams, live oaks, mesquite, with rich valleys and bottom lands for farming and mountains for stock, abondance of game and Indians once a year. Blanco city is the county seat, a store, and black smith shop. . . . I have never been with out money, friends and credit, the last wages I have received is 30.00 gold as they use nothing else."

The boy worked hard, running cattle, cutting corn, chopping wood —once driving the axe through his cowhide boots and corduroy britches deep into his shin. He had fun, too, breaking stallions, swimming in the river, hunting and fishing. In one morning he caught a trout that weighed six or seven pounds and three catfish about the same size. A rough sketch he sent home showed that Tom Johnson had a horse ranch of 720 acres and possibly Sam had another 960 acres, all on the Pedernales.[6]

Elias Roebuck, who was raised by Lyndon's father's parents, first rode the Chisholm Trail in 1873. When he was eighty-nine, chatting with Lyndon in the fall of 1946, he said, "For three hundred miles we saw only wild Indians, wild buffaloes, cactus, snakes, and sand. . . . I roped and rode the blue mustang seventy-three years ago. I've roped a buffalo cow so wild it took four men to turn her loose."[7]

They were a long way from Harvard Yard and the Back Bay, Wall Street and Washington. "The men as a general thing," wrote John Speer, "did not put on much style: hickory shirts with woolen over shirt, jeans-breeches with buck or goat skin leggings, a six-shooter and butcher knife, hung by a broad belt around the waist, and large jingling spurs. The Sunday dress was about the same with the exception of a calico shirt instead of the hickory. Very few had overcoats, but used their camp blankets instead. All carried six-shooters, from the cowboy to the minister; and, strange to say, there were very few personal difficulties and no quarrels, for a quarrel between well-armed men meant blood."[8]

Insecurity was the common condition. Outlaws and Indians lurked everywhere. Help was too far to come in time, and since courage was required, cowardice was inevitable. Even today the people in the Texas hill country are "full of fears," a journalist raised among them, Winston Bode, has written. If you hurt yourself, how long before the doctor comes? What if you get sunstroke on the back forty? Nor was it wise to travel after dark. One evening, dusk caught Bode's grandfather traveling the road by wagon. A swarthy, tough-looking fellow appeared from nowhere and climbed into the bed of the wagon, leaving only when Bode's grandfather held a pistol on him.[9]

Even the most successful settler could be wiped out in one bad season. By 1871 Tom Johnson had become the second-largest taxpayer and property owner in Blanco County. For 775 gold dollars he bought the land grant on which Johnson City was later established and sold it to Sam for 3 dollars fewer than that, in specie. Sam, too, owned both land and cattle in Blanco County in 1870 and 1871, but Speer, writing from memory in the decade afterward, told about the market collapse that brought the Johnson boys down:

"They took receipts [for cattle bought for the trail drive, evidently] and very soon had a large carpetbag full, and in such a shape that there is no doubt in my mind that a good many beeves were paid for twice and some of them three times, and some of the cattle were never paid for. . . . But, when called on the third time to pay for the same steer, I never heard of him [Tom Johnson, evidently] demanding a receipt. . . . But so it was that in a few months the Johnsons had paid out all their money. . . . Johnson had no trouble in getting cattle and drove out this year about 10,000 head, and many trades were made and some notes taken, payable when Tom Johnson comes back from Kansas, but this was a hard year for the cattle drivers. The financial pressure was so great that the large drive of Texas cattle could not be sold and many, among them Johnson, were obliged to winter a large part of their cattle, and a great many died, Johnson lost heavily, and was forced to sacrifice some valuable property in Fredericksburg and a fine farm in Gillespie County. So with all his mishaps he failed to pay his debts, which was a great loss to the people, and destroyed confidence. Some were disposed to say, and no doubt believe, hard things about Johnson, but in justice to a dead man I will say that while he prospered no one condemned him."

Was it "the market," Wall Street, freight rates, the bankers—who knew for sure? In what came to be known as "The Crime of '73," Congress dropped the silver dollar and placed the country on the gold standard. Wartime bondholders prospered in the ensuing depression while farm prices dropped along with the value of silver. In the hill country of Texas in 1872 a judgment was rendered against Tom and Sam Johnson in a county south of Blanco, and Sam's land was sold to pay it. Tom's taxable worth dropped two-thirds that year. In two years he went from $17,000 to $180, and then he owned nothing. From time to time Lyndon Johnson claimed that his grandfather founded Johnson City, but the unprettified truth was part of Lyndon's inherited bitterness against the market-profiteering capitalists of the eastern seaboard. Johnson City was surveyed and established in 1879 by a nephew of the Johnson brothers who had worked for them and got Sam's land in the early 1870s.[10]

Tom Johnson died by drowning in the Brazos River in 1877.[11] Sam and Eliza just left the hill country, settling in Buda, a central Texas town, where they had a family. The fifth of their nine children was Sam, Jr., the father of a president. But then, in an incident that shadowily illuminates the character of Lyndon's grandfather, they moved again.

According to an old-timer in Buda, when a trouble-maker who had killed a number of people started a fight with an old, frail farmer, Sam, Sr., took the old man's side and broke it up. The rough-houser left the store threatening to settle the score with Johnson with guns, and rather than kill a man or be killed, Sam moved his family back home to a frame house on the bank of the Pedernales, near Johnson City.[12]

---

6. A Populist Johnson Runs for Office

For forty years, from the farmers' revolts of the last fifth of the nineteenth century to the death of the Progressive movement in the 1920s, social idealism in the United States wavered between populism and the Democratic party, between radicalism and regulationism, and the conflict can be seen in the political adventures of Lyndon Johnson's grandfather, father, and uncle, adventures that gave him his own sensings of the political limits as plain and real as the markets and the weather that limit farming.

Returning to the Pedernales country where he and his brother had been wiped out by the mysterious brutalities of the northern cattle market, grandfather Sam ran for the state legislature as a Populist, thereby publicly associating himself with the Populists' radical doctrines of 1892. Lyndon's Uncle Clarence Martin, who had married Sam, Sr.'s daughter, ran for the same seat as a Democrat, opposing his father-in-law.

By the time Sam had returned, the farmers' radical movement had swept the hill country. The Farmers' Alliance, a precursor of the Populists, was founded about fifty miles north of Johnson City in 1877 "to clean up thieves, 'cattle kings,' and loan sharks." As the robber barons of railroads and finance took over the government, the farmers, foreseeing the end of their independence, shifted their emphasis from self-administered justice to financial cooperation in their own interests. The alliance had 182 chapters in Texas by 1882 and was active in Blanco

County by the mid-1880s. To weaken the revolt, the Democrats moved leftward toward government regulation of railroads and trusts, but when Sam was settling himself and his family back down on the Pedernales the Texas Alliance had two hundred and fifty thousand members, many cooperative stores, more than two thousand clubs, and eighty-five or so journals.

The chief reform the farmers sought was freedom from the bankers and tight money. As Lawrence Goodwyn explains in *Democratic Promise,* the definitive history of Populism, Texan Charles Macune, an organizer of large-scale cooperation among the farmers, proposed a system whereby the government would create a farmers' subtreasury with its own county warehouses, credit system, and currency. By this one plan the farmers would cut themselves free of the bankers, the furnishing merchants, and the chattel mortgage companies. Storing their crops in the warehouses if they needed to wait for prices to rise, the farmers would borrow on the crops within the subtreasury system.

In 1891 the Texas Populists first formed the People's party, and it spread into the farmers' movement cross-country, adopting the subtreasury plan as its own. Lyndon's grandfather was a candidate of the new third party that also wanted government ownership of railroads, telephone, and telegraph, abolition of the national banks, and government control of the financial system.

The party's candidate for governor in Texas, a well-read judge named Tom Nugent, was dealt with respectfully by the *Dallas Morning News* as "a quiet, self-contained, intellectual and scholarly man, and an accomplished lawyer. . . . It would be supreme folly to despise and belittle a movement that is leavened with such moral stuff as this," the paper said.

Nugent declaimed that Wall Street had always asserted the right to dictate the candidates of the two regular parties: "Wall Street must, at any cost, be appeased. . . . The big bankers and money lenders, the stock jobbers, the men who bull and bear the market, must be kept in good humor. . . . A million tramps trudge along our highways and gaze despairingly over illimitable areas of unused land, monopolized and withheld from settlement by the speculator, the syndicate, and the corporations," while thousands of poor in the cities were paid pittances and driven to begging, women either whoring or starving. In 1892, Nugent said, one-twentieth of one percent of the people of the country owned three-fifths of the wealth. The banker was rich, the farmer poor; the banker had the money, but the farmer could not get credit.

The Populists' long-term worry was losing their land. In Texas the legislature had given the railway companies more than thirty-two million acres of the public domain, and the same thing was happening across the West. Through standard-bearer Nugent, old man Sam's party proposed "undying opposition to land monopoly": the government should see that every person could buy at a reasonable price the land needed to make a living, all the public lands should be reserved for people who built their homes on them, and corporations should be prohibited from owning more land than they had to have to conduct their business.

The Democrats' candidate for governor in Texas, reformer Jim Hogg, was concerned enough about the Populists in Blanco County the year Sam Johnson ran to take a train out to Johnson City for a barbecue and campaign rally. Hogg won the state, but Nugent carried Blanco County by a plurality, and the Populists' candidate for lieutenant governor did, too. District-wide, though "Uncle Clarence told me," Lyndon said, "that he ran against my grandfather and he beat him by thirty-seven votes." Sam and Clarence would ride together to a speaking, Sam would cuss his daughter's husband as "a reactionary so-and-so" and Clarence would cuss Sam as a wild radical, but then they would happily "get back on the double buggy on the front seat and ride to the next speaking," Lyndon said.

Sam had a ferocity of conviction that reappeared later as his grandson's ferocity of ambition. At one rally in 1892, fire-eating Sam predicted civil war if the Populists lost and said Grover Cleveland should be hanged. Cleveland, the mild reform Democrat who had served as president in the preceding decade, was seeking another term, running against the incumbent Republican, Benjamin Harrison, and Populist James Weaver.

According to a pro-Democratic writer in the *Blanco News,* "We had lots of speaking here last Thursday night." Clarence Martin, the Democrat, and Sam Johnson, the People's party nominee, held a discussion, with Tom Haines also speaking for the Populists' side. "Clarence Martin held his own . . . very well," the report said. "He gave them some arguments which could not be refuted. Mr. Johnson stated in his speech that if the People's Party did not win at the polls there would be war. This no doubt sounds nice from a speaker but how does it look on paper? Mr. Johnson and Mr. Haines both stated in their speeches that Cleveland ought to be hung."

Nationally, Weaver received less than a tenth of the vote as Cleveland won his second term. There was no civil war—the president was not hanged—but Cleveland's performance probably intensified old Sam's convictions in the matter. By achieving repeal of the Silver Purchase Act, Cleveland further enraged the farmers who were suffering from tight credit, and he broke the Pullman strike with federal troops. In 1896 the Democrats completed their absorption and defeat of the Populists' causes by the nomination of pro-silver William Jennings Bryan for president and Bryan's anticlimatic loss to Republican William McKinley.

In Texas the year Sam ran and lost to his Democratic son-in-law, the

People's party finished a strong third for governor. Blanco County went Populist again in 1894 and 1896 as the People's party candidates for governor moved up to second—then nearly won. Goodwyn concludes that the new party was counted out in 1894 by vote fraud in seven Texas congressional districts.

Governor Hogg had weakened the movement by establishing the Texas Railroad Commission. The railroads, the land speculators, and the lumber interests were taking over the social system, and the commission was supposed to correct this, but like nearly all regulatory agencies the commission either never had or else lost any real independence of the private business that it regulated. When oil became the major element in the state's industrial structure, the railroad commission (with no change in name) became in effect the production control division of the international oil cartel.

Defeated like Populism itself, old Sam lived out his life holding to his views, and he gave some of them, gifts shortly before his death, to his grandson. When Lyndon was passing through his earliest years, his Grandfather Johnson lived up the road about half a mile. "I remember," he said, "walking along the banks of the Pedernales when I was four, five years of age, walking from the little home where I was born down the river up to my grandfather's house, where he would always give me peppermint stick candy or a big red apple." He had a gray horse named Dan and would put Lyndon up on him. "He would laugh, he was a happy fella, gay," Lyndon said. After a while he would take the boy back home, and Rebekah would get after the old man for encouraging Lyndon to run off to him like that. "My earliest memories," Lyndon said, "were hearing my grandfather talk about the plight of the tenant farmer, the necessity for the worker to have protection for bargaining, the need for improvement of our transportation to get the farmer out of the mud with blacktop roads, particularly the red schoolhouse and the tenant purchase program where a worker could attain something of his own."[1]

---

7. Like Father, Unlike Son

When Sam, Jr., a boy of ten or eleven, returned with his family to the Pedernales about 1889, the largest farmer in the region had only three hundred acres. "We are not ashamed," said the *Blanco News,* "that we have no big plantations, nor sheep and cattle kings." Never recovering from the collapse of their cattle drives, the Johnsons were poor. One year all Big Sam could give his boy to help him in his schooling was a few cattle.

Growing up, Sam, Jr., taught school a while and then rented his father's farm and operated it with some hired hands. In 1902 "Little Sam" was elected justice of the peace and, as Otto Lindig said, "married more boys and girls than any pastor in Gillespie County because he just charged five dollars." In 1904 he ran for the legislature and served four years. An agrarian reformer, he was his Populist father's son, but like the times he was milder. He supported a franchise tax on corporations, a pure-food bill, city regulation of utility rates, an eight-hour day for railroad workers, and the regulation of lobbyists.

Financially it was scratch and patch for young Sam, too. After he was first elected he went into Rob Crider's grocery story in the town of Hye, near his farm. "Sam," Crider said, "you don't have much money, do you?" No, he didn't, Sam said, but he wasn't going to borrow any, either. Crider exclaimed that they couldn't have their man "not going to Austin in style" and forced a three-hundred dollar loan on him. At times, then, Sam owed Crider one thousand dollars for groceries; he would have to borrow money for gas to go to Austin to help a widow get a pension. His service in Austin paid him only three hundred dollars a year, the income from the farm was meager, and like his father in the 1870s, young Sam was cold-cocked by the distant forces of the market; his dreams of a seat on the cotton exchange burst when the depression of 1906 wiped out his cotton holdings and saddled him with debt.[1]

He was still the cotton buyer at the gin at Stonewall three miles down the river from his dad's farm. His neighbors across the river, a young man and his wife, depended for their only cash income on the three or four bales they carried down to him at the gin over the course of a season. Those days women were not allowed in the saloons, and after the ginning of the couple's bale Sam would take a bottle of beer out to the wagon for them.

One day the young man told Sam he had an extra mule he would like to sell. Sam asked how much, his neighbor said five dollars, and Sam opened "his old clickin' purse," as Lyndon later told it, and took out a five-dollar bill. "When you get back down there," Sam said, "turn the mule over to my side of the river."

The neighbor's father-in-law, though, told him he'd been robbed—the mule should have brought ten dollars—and the young fellow became depressed; this had been his first trade since he had married. The next time they went to the gin his wife needled him to speak up about it, but he was too embarrassed. Sam brought them out a beer as usual, but as they finished it and the young man picked up the reins and took off the brake to drive home, his wife punched him and said, "Tell Mr. Johnson what my father said." So the young man did. Later on she told Lyndon what happened then:

"Your father, you could hear him laugh all across the river. . . . He rared back and just laughed a good hearty full laugh, and reached in that same purse, and he got another five-dollar bill, just like that first five-dollar bill, and he said, 'Well, Edmunds, you asked me five dollars for the mule, and I gave you what you asked for it. But neighbors mustn't ever fall out over five dollars.' "[2]

The farm people's lives were going on as before, regulated by their amiable country values, but beyond these surfaces everything was changing. The new capitalists were swaying the farmers' politicians and turning the elections.

The U.S. senator from Texas, Joe Bailey, held himself forth as the people's champion against plutocratic power, but he had taken money from a front for Standard Oil in Texas, and in 1906 he was exposed. The direct election of senators was still in the future, and the legislature had to approve of Bailey's reelection. The issue that obsessed young Sam in 1906 and 1907, whether to condemn Bailey for selling out to Standard Oil, must have stirred, too, his most important neighbor, his Populist father, who was following his son's career from the banks of the Pedernales.

Either you were all-out for Bailey or he saw you as an enemy. With his eloquence and political power enforced by his splenetic and threatening execrations of his critics, he founded the personalist school of Texas politics in which Lyndon Johnson was a later master. "Every Socialist in Texas," said the vengeful Senator Bailey, "is standing on the streetcorner reviling me day and night," and he would drive his enemies into the Gulf of Mexico—they were anarchists, thieves, liars, hyenas, dogs, and hessians.

Bailey had gone to work for several corporations, one secretly. At the turn of the century, disbelieving the denials that it was part of Standard Oil, Texas authorities had ordered the Waters-Pierce Oil Company out of the state as a monopolist. Texas Democrats were choosing Bailey as their senator then, and he assured them that although the rich chieftain of the company, H. Clay Pierce, had asked him to be his lawyer, he had declined. What Bailey had not told his fellow citizens was that Pierce had loaned him money. Then, after he was confirmed as senator, Bailey helped Waters-Pierce get back into Texas. The public learned that Standard did own Waters-Pierce and Bailey admitted he had borrowed five thousand dollars from Pierce, who had charged it to the company as legal expenses. At one point Bailey even said he had done $20 million worth of business for the company. He had also diversified: a Texas lumber baron had paid him $149,000 for "legal services," and he had represented a group of St. Louis capitalists.

On January 8, 1907, despite the fact that his brother-in-law Clarence Martin was close to Bailey, Sam Johnson was one of a dozen legislators who met and demanded an investigation. Called up to the vicious senator's hotel room in Austin, Sam told Bailey that most of the hill-country people favored the inquiry. Sam later testified that Bailey told him "he would see that these men who opposed him . . . would never hold another office. . . . He was telling about how . . . he wanted the chance of a free nigger. . . ."

Bailey's threats were bludgeons, for several reasons. He was the senator. He had a reputation for violence—he was accused of going at one opponent with a knife, and once on a train he had drawn a gun from his satchel to silence some critics. Finally, he had big money behind him now. Nevertheless, Sam told him he'd always been his friend and doubted the charges, but wanted them cleared up.

Asked later if Bailey had scared him any, Sam replied, "No, I did not become very badly frightened." Bailey, admitting he had made a few threats, denied threatening Sam. "Mr. Johnson," he said, "is a brother-in-law of one of the best friends I have in this state. . . . I treated him courteously. . . . Mr. Johnson still thought I ought to be mild; in other words, he thought, or seemed to think, that although these men stand upon street corners and denounce me as a traitor to my country, insinuate that I have not been an honest man, that I ought to draw my cloak around me, and with meekness and humility say, 'Pray, sirs, don't do that' . . . I think I deserve great praise for not taking a shotgun and killing them, and if I could have gotten around, that is what I would have done."

Only seven members of the legislature refused to approve of Bailey's reelection, and one of them, in the year before Lyndon was born, was his father Sam. The legislature then, rejecting a minority opinion that said Bailey had been "indiscreet," approved a report clearing him. Later President Johnson remembered his father voting on the anti-Bailey side.

The triumphant senator was carried on the shoulders of his supporters into the House chamber, where he scourged his enemies with a wild-eyed menace that Lyndon was to read about, admire, and himself emulate. Bailey swore his enemies "have made their own graves. . . . We are going to bury them face down, so that the harder they scratch to get out, the deeper they will go towards their eternal resting place. . . . I will not forgive them this side of the grave. . . . The man who tries to fight between the lines is certain to be killed." A reporter wrote of Bailey's performance that his slogan was "relentless retaliation." But as he throttled his enemies, conversely he would embrace and reward his friends: "I owe no grudges that I have not tried to pay my enemies, and I owe no obligations that I have not tried to pay my friends."

The ensuing scene stayed alive in Lyndon Johnson's imagination all his life. "His followers were all applauding," Johnson told me in the White House, "and his detractors were kind of holding their heads down. He said he was going to take two pictures of this legislature, this group of men. And over the picture of his detractors and those who had fought him, he was going to put the sign 'The Rogues' Gallery.' And over those who had supported him in his hours of difficulties, he was going to put 'The Roll of Honor.' And he said he was going to teach his children to love the one and to hate the other." When Bailey said " 'The Rogues' Gallery,' " Lyndon added, "he 'looked right at my father."

A committee of lawmakers acting for the anti-Bailey element charged that the senator had betrayed the people for money, officially helping companies that helped him financially. The committee called him a boodler, a pirate, and a hypocrite whose doctrine was "Put money in thy purse."

But Sam Johnson did not run for reelection in 1908. His son said this was not from fear of Bailey, but because his wife Rebekah "wouldn't let him"; she wanted him home. Only after a full decade passed did Sam return to the legislature.

Despite his father's role, Lyndon admired Joe Bailey without reserve. In an editorial Lyndon wrote as a college freshman, he singled out Bailey as an exemplary politician. As his own little brother entered college, Lyndon gave him a biography of Bailey with passages underlined in ink. Later Lyndon gave his wife Sam Acheson's biography of Bailey, which presented the boodler as a hero.

But hold on—hadn't Bailey sold out? Not as Johnson saw it. He told me his father "thought it was improper" for Bailey to take the loan from the oil company and race horses with it, but for his own part the president thought Bailey had probably been "indiscreet," but not improper. Well, I said, the trouble was, the man who made the loan ran it through the company account as a company expense. "They always do that," the president of the United States said. "Those fellas, they say, 'I'm gonna help you,' but their companies do it. And they do." Confronted with his father's principled resistance to Joe Bailey's unprincipled success, Lyndon Johnson chose Joe Bailey.[3]

---

8. A Frontier Baptist Mother

His mother was the dominant woman in Lyndon's life. He knew it; he said so. There was between them, he said, not only love, but also "a special feeling, something we felt when we looked at one another." Her values molded him; her ambitions for him, which she told him defined her life as they should his, propelled him; her love held him to her even after she was dead. She sent him forth in the world to make up to her all her disappointments in her father, her husband, her life of hardships, and herself. He set her on a pedestal, plunged into politics to make good for himself and for her, and bore to her, before she died, the proofs of their realization together. This made him a mama's boy.

In the early fifties when he was a senator, he would break off a conference, reach for the phone, and say, "Let's see what Mama thinks." In rebellion against that he was mean and strong—pragmatic and raunchy —in the world of men, but when he attained the presidency, deep in him, perhaps well beyond his control, her values in him tied him to old-world obsessions and dreams. Although in matters of style it did not so appear, from the first to the last she was his mother, and he was her son.

As a boy he would put his arm around her and kiss her on the cheek, and this feeling in him about her carried over to treatment of other women. "He was attentive to elderly ladies," Emmette Redford said, he played up to this grandma or that great-aunt, "he'd go down and call on them and put his arm around 'em, and hug 'em and kiss 'em."[1] He wrote his mother when he was a young man, "There is no force that exerts the power over me that your letters do." They always gave him, he told her, "more strength, renewed courage, and that bulldog tenacity so essential to the success of any man." As he saw other mothers shopping at Christmastime, he wished he was with her, he thought about her hardships that he meant someday to relieve—he enclosed a small sum of money. At twenty-two he sent the newspaper in San Marcos, where he was going to college, an unsolicited editorial, "To our mothers." Whatever else happens, he wrote, "mother's love abides to the end. . . . There is no love on earth comparable to that of mother. . . . Of all types of earthly love, it most nearly approaches the divine." Indeed, he wrote, "the mothers of men" were the most potent and vital force for good in the world.

"A man who has been the indisputable favorite of his mother," wrote Sigmund Freud, "keeps for life the feeling of a conqueror, that confidence of success that often induces real success." While Sam, Jr., tried cotton speculation, tried farming, tried politics, tried real estate —tried politics again—Rebekah poured into her open son Lyndon a sense of station intensified by the very absence of station in her own life —she planted ambition in him as sure-handedly as she laid seed in the furrows. She was loving up in Lyndon that driven energy nature can give a boy and a mother can make glow like power.

Rebekah realized she had laid all her own ambitions on her elder son. His election to Congress, she wrote him, compensated her for her disappointment when her father had failed to achieve the same office. "How dear to me you are you cannot know my darling boy," she wrote him, "my devoted son, my strength and comfort." His little brother, Sam Houston Johnson, said, "She was very proud of Lyndon. He felt Mother was his closest friend. I do think I came second." When Lyndon was rising in the Senate she said, "Naturally, I love all my children, but Lyndon was the first, and to me he was the greatest marvel in the world. I had always dreamed of a career for myself, but Lyndon was career enough for me." In 1954, while denying, as had become his custom, the slightest ambition to be president, Lyndon said, ". . . nobody but my mama ever thought I'd get as far as I am." She was quoted, as to the talk of his becoming president, that "from the first time I looked into his eyes, none of his accomplishments have surprised me."[2]

Conservative in her goals, Rebekah was shrewd in her pursuit of them. Two Johnson staffers who knew her regarded her as formidable. For an outsider, said Charles Boatner, she inspired, not love, but respect and admiration. "I wouldn't want her as an enemy," he said. Johnson's longtime press aide, George Reedy, believed that because of the influence of Lyndon's mother he was "terribly vulnerable to women." Lyndon thought his mother soft and feminine, but, said Reedy, "His mother was actually hard, she was awfully hard. But he couldn't see it." She knew people better than her husband or Lyndon "ever thought about knowing. She could read you like a book," her niece said.

Lyndon thought of his father as "adventure, political adventure," but his mother as stable and conservative. "My father was a liberal, progressive fella that dealt in helping the poor. Mother, her people were more preacher and educator types," he said. He attributed his impulses and his love of people to his father, but his moderation to his mother.

Though he liked his father's daring, he came down firmly on his mother's side. Showing a writer the family album she compiled, he choked up and said, "I can't read this. I'm sorry for letting my emotions carry me away, but I can't help it. My mother was a saintly woman. I owe everything to her." Hubert Humphrey said, "One of the things I used to like about him was that he would get tears in his eyes when he talked about his mother." Johnson said to me in the White House, "My mother was everything—religion, character, and right and wrong," she was "faith, pure gold, the greatest female I have ever known, without any exceptions."[3]

Genteel and severe, a southern woman in the western hill country, she personified to him the two cultures within which he came to know history. She was patriotic and very religious. Born into a Baptist family on the Texas frontier, she was enclosed all her life within the rigid idealisms of Biblical fundamentalism. When she spoke of high ideals, she meant gallantry, chivalry, courage, piety, sobriety. Some men might feel fear, but not her men. Into the driven, egocentric young Lyndon she poured all this past of piety and glory, gentility and exploitation, pride and gunfire. God, Mother, Country—these were the three figures in his temple of honor.

Rebekah's grandfather, George Washington Baines, Sr., was a paragon, a theologian, a leader of the church—almost like a figure among the prophets. The son of a minister who was the son of a minister from Scotland, he served a term in the Arkansas legislature, organized churches, preached around Louisiana, and bounced himself and his family along the trails for seventeen days to take up the work of God in east Texas. There he met Sam Houston. As editor of the first Baptist paper in Texas his orthodoxy was "never questioned, among Baptists." During the Civil War he was the president of a Baptist school in Texas, Baylor University.[4]

His status as the enduring patriarch of her family was much enhanced for her by a famous conversion he had made. She said to Lyndon when he was reading *The Raven,* Marquis James's biography of Sam Houston, "Why Lyndon, didn't you know it was Brother Baines who brought Sam Houston into the Baptist Church?"

The swashbuckling Houston was afraid his soul was so stained by his sins that if he dared to be baptized God would take vengeance on him. When he had been a boy a Presbyterian minister taught him that anyone who was not converted but took the Lord's Supper anyway would roast forever in hell. Reaching the decrepit stage at which he had little to lose from religious piety and a sharpening interest in what he might gain from it, Houston had become a Baptist, but he told his friend Baines of his fear that a passage in Corinthians meant that if he joined the church he might never be forgiven. Baines convinced him to the contrary, and the Father of Texas was captured by the Baptist Church.[5]

Houston loaned Brother Baines three hundred dollars and renewed the note, knocking off the interest. Of this, in a letter to Baines, the old general made much, as if arguing for his saddle in paradise. However, as Lyndon Johnson noticed later, Houston was actually asking Baines to renew the note because nothing had been paid on it.[6]

George's son Joseph, Rebekah's father, was a politician, but modeled himself on the patriarch. "A Baptist and a Democrat," he started out as a newspaper editor in McKinney, Texas, where Rebekah was born. He trained her that "a lie is an abomination to the Lord." His brother wrote of him, "To hear a preacher indulge in unclean jokes or suggestions gave him a real disgust, and he never wanted to hear him preach or pray. . . . His was a Christian home, in which piety was practiced, the old doctrines of the Bible believed and taught, God loved and honored. His wife and children walked with him in the way of the Lord."[7]

The fundamentalist churchgoers in McKinney were terrified of hellfire. In one of the early churches there, a low wall ran down the middle of the church to separate the women and the girls from the men and the boys. During open-air camp meetings in and around the town, "The congregation, which sometimes numbered into the thousands, usually indulged in complete emotional freedom. . . . They cried, shouted, groaned, or repeated the spoken phrases over and over again in unison in ever-increasing tempo. During the services some would rush to unsaved friends with tears of compassion, urging them to turn to the Lord;

some, struck with terror, would try to escape from anxious relatives; some fainted, remaining in a state of semi-consciousness for long periods of time. . . . Men, women, and children exhorted each other, prayed, wept, and even preached, often continuing until dawn."[8]

After a turn as secretary of state in Texas, Rebekah's father moved his family to a house high up on the bank of the Blanco River in the town of the river's name, and she grew up amidst sermons and prayer meetings. For almost twenty years, her father's brother wrote of him, "he was the chief pillar of the Blanco Church," and camp meetings were a regular part of the religious life in the hill country, too. About that time the young cowhand "Hod" Hall wrote that one summer day "I was at 'preaching' at an arbor on Rocky Creek, some of the feminines 'got happy,' put 'old Satan aside' and 'was bound to see Jesus' at least I took their word for it 'for they just knew they were going up there.' "

Rebekah grew up as a sheltered southern lass. She wrote later, "I love to think of our home, a two-story rock house with a fruitful orchard of perfectly spaced trees, terraced flower beds, broad walks, purple plumed wisteria climbing to the roof, fragrant honeysuckle at the dining room windows whose broad sills were seats for us children." She took a few courses, including oratory, at the state university, but then she studied at a Baptist college where her Uncle George, a fourth-generation preacher, held the Bible chair.[9]

Her life darkened, though, when a four-year drought, striking as her father's health was failing, ruined her family financially. There were two or three bad crops, and they lost everything but the house, Lyndon said. In 1903 they moved to Fredericksburg, their circumstances much reduced. Her father turned to writing political dispatches for a Galveston newspaper.

One day he sent Rebekah to interview State Representative Sam Johnson, Jr., for him. Sam refused to say anything on the record, but he told her he was delighted to be interviewed by her, and this was the beginning of their life together. As a correspondent herself for a San Antonio paper, she wrote him thanking him for a news tip and asking for others. He took her to a Confederate Reunion where they heard speeches by Senator Bailey and the governor of the moment, and they were together again listening when William Jennings Bryan addressed the legislature.

On August 20, 1907, they were married. Otto Lindig said without elaborating that "their honeymoon was in a topless one-horse buggy, riding from Fredericksburg to a place about 500 yards from the old Johnson place where he was raised." Settling down on Sam's father's place on the Pedernales, farming between legislative sessions, they lived in a little cabin upriver from Sam, Sr.'s homestead. Of their five hundred acres, they had about a hundred in cultivation, and they had forty or fifty head of cattle. Cooking for the farmhands and running the house, Rebekah took her place in the last American generation of pioneer women.

Her brother Huffman, who was temporarily out of work, helped her and Sam for a few months in 1907. "They were busy on the farm and needed help," Huffman wrote. "I helped them by doing all kinds of work—milking, feeding, hoeing, plowing, cutting wood, etc. We, like all farmers, were up early but late in getting the farm work done." Often he rode a horse to Hi Brown's store hoping there would be a letter there calling him to a job in town. "One mid-afternoon," he wrote, "while I was plowing a good distance from the house, my sister came and told me that Dr. Brown was calling me by telephone." It was a job, and Huffman never went back to the plow.

Rebekah was with child, and the summer of 1908 her sister Josefa and their mother visited, helping make the baby clothes and otherwise get ready. Rebekah set a full table every meal, always using a cloth, never an oilcloth. "They would go and pick grapes and they had so many peaches there, canned peaches, peach preserves, and all," Josefa said. "I remember the vegetables that they would bring in—fresh corn and tomatoes. . . ." Sam and Rebekah kept chickens. They had fresh honey.

A lady, Rebekah never raised her voice; in every way she was refined. She liked to do charcoal sketches, and she was a serious reader. "She was a cultured, delicate-looking woman," said one old-timer. Her first son was certain she could have been a great novelist, but she told him that her father's failure and death had so destroyed her own confidence and ambition, by the time she married she had given up, and her first year with her husband was the worst of her life. In vulgar contrast to the elevated concerns of her Baptist elders, her Sam would sit up half the night with his friends at dominoes, drinking beer and telling stories. "Then," said her first son later, "I came along and suddenly everything was all right again. I could do all the things she never did."[10]

---

9. "A Sharp, Compelling Cry"

The lamps burned all night in the tiny three-room cabin among the lashing pecan and sycamore trees, casting shadows into the rain down the slope toward the river aflood in the storm. The nearest doctor was twenty miles away, so Big Sam mounted a horse and forded the river half a mile above the crossing to fetch the midwife, Mrs. Christian Lindig, who lived two miles west.

At daybreak, in the west bedroom with the fireplace, a boy was born —his mother heard "a sharp, compelling cry." The child was handed first to Rebekah's mother, who pronounced him wonderful. You could see the Bunton favor in the brown eyes and the large ears, but Rebekah saw her father in him. He weighed about ten pounds.

In *A Family Album,* Rebekah implied a doctor delivered the infant. Sam, Jr.'s sister, Jessie Hatcher, explained that Rebekah would not have wanted it said that a midwife had done it, "She just wanted everything just so." But Otto Lindig, who was the midwife's husband, explained that everyone used a midwife; it took the doctor too long to come.

The new child breathed his first breaths as the Pedernales raged downstream on a Thursday morning in August, 1908, on the twenty-eighth. Sam saddled his gray horse Fritz and rode up the river to his parents in the next farmhouse and told them, "It's a boy!" He rode on to tell some other kinfolks nearby and went back to his house. When the baby was four hours old, Otto turned up, coming onto the porch, its roof supported by five thin posts. You could see through the breezeway to a tree behind the house. Otto told Sam he wanted to sell him a span of horses. "I'm not interested in horses.—Come in the house," Sam said. "I want to show you something." Otto stepped inside and looked at the baby. "That boy is going to be governor of Texas some day," Sam said. But Otto made Sam mad for a minute by saying, "He's certainly got his mother's head."

Rebekah tried a lot of names on Sam, but he wouldn't agree to any of them. For three months the boy was called Baby. One morning that November, lying in bed, watching the infant in the crib close by, thinking, "Such a beautiful, such a wonderful baby," she realized with a snap of anger, "No name yet."

Sam, lacing his boots at the fire, said, "Time to get breakfast, Rebekah. The room is warm."

"Sam," she replied, "I'm not getting up to cook breakfast until this baby is named." Sam usually laid down the law, but when she did, she did. "Now you suggest and I'll pass judgment."

Thinking of the boy's uncle, Clarence Martin, Sam said, "How do you like Clarence?" She disliked her heavy-drinking brother-in-law. "Not one bit, try again."

"Then what about Dayton?" Dayton Moses was a lawyer friend of Sam's. "Much better; but still not quite right for this boy."

W. C. Linden, a San Antonio lawyer and a friend of Sam's, liked to stay the night with the Johnsons when he had a case in the area. "What do you think about Linden for him?" Sam asked.

She considered that. It crossed her mind that Linden was a drinking man.

"That's fine," she said, "if I may spell it as I like. Linden isn't so euphonious as Lyn*don* would be."

"Spell it as you please, he will still be named for my friend Linden."

They realized the thing was settled.

"So now the boy is named Lyndon Baines Johnson," Sam said. "Come cook breakfast; the naming is over." Rebekah kissed the babe's cheek and was soon in the kitchen making the biscuits.[1]

A few months later a neighbor took a snapshot of the child, and when Sam came home with the picture, Rebekah said, "he raised his hand holding the package as he saw me waiting on the porch and began to run. I ran to meet him and we met in the middle of the Benner pasture to exclaim rapturously over the photograph of our boy. We had never seen a picture more beautiful—nor did we ever!" She wrote a letter to the child's aunt as if he had written it, she signing his name, and she had him say, "I can sit alone now and perform many amusing capers. My father says that I am quite an orator and translates my speech into political axioms."[2]

"The first memory I have of my mother, I was three or four years old," Johnson told me. "She was crying, it was nine or ten o'clock. My father was a cotton buyer. He had to stay at the gin till twelve or one at night till the cotton was ginned. She was frightened, afraid. I told her I'd protect her. I remember standing there by the well."

His second memory of his mother, he was dipping his toes in the river down from the house when, frightened and angry, she pulled him away and told him not to go near the river again. In his third memory about her, on a hot day she pulled her sewing machine into the breezeway and worked the foot pedal wondrously fast.[3]

There was nothing near them except farm houses like their own; the nearest post office was four miles away. At night they burned kerosene lamps for light. Their bathroom was an outhouse, a "two-holer." Rebekah did her washing in the back yard with homemade soap in a zinc tub, pushing the clothes up and down with a black plunger and scrubbing them on a corrugated washboard. They pumped their water by hand, and Rebekah did her pressing with a flat iron she heated on the wood stove in the kitchen. Once little Lyndon said to her, "Mama, when I get big I'm gonna see you don't have to wash clothes any more." Years afterward she was embarrassed by her large red knuckles, and once during a luncheon, attended also by her son the congressman, suddenly she wrapped her hands in a napkin to conceal them.[4]

Before Lyndon was two she taught him the alphabet from blocks, and all the Mother Goose rhymes, and when he was three she had him reciting poems from Longfellow and Tennyson. He learned to say grace at her knee, and she told him stories from the Bible, history, and myths, "especially" she said "the ones that really happened." Sam would pick up Noah Webster's spelling book and give the boy words to spell—at four he could spell and read some.[5]

Like all farm people they were up early and worked till dark, plowing with the horses, hoeing, feeding the cows and chickens, chopping the wood. When he was three or four Lyndon would toddle out to meet his father coming in from the field, and all his life Lyndon felt "tied in" to farm life.[6]

About this age, too, the boy had his first dog, a collie named Rover. They would take walks together down the road along the river and through the oat fields. Once they were gone for about three hours, and Rebekah, fearing that the boy might have drowned, frantically searched for him at the river, the school, the back pasture. She ran up to Sam at the plow and cried out, "He's gone! And the dog's gone." But as Sam tied up the reins he noticed the oats, which were higher than Lyndon, moving, and he thought the boy might have come to find him. "Lyndon, Lyndon!" he called. No answer. Then he called "Rover!"—the dog barked. When Lyndon and the collie came out Rebekah almost collapsed with relief. Sam asked the boy where he'd been. He answered, "Rover wanted to see the country, and I wanted him to see it."[7]

When Lyndon was three or four he started going to the dilapidated one-room Junction School with his six-year-old friends, hanging around and playing with them at recess, so Rebekah persuaded the teacher to take him on as a pupil. Accompanied by two cousins, he rode to and from the school where the teacher was handling eight grades in the one room. When she asked Lyndon to read aloud, he insisted on sitting on her lap because this was the way he read for his mother at home. His attitude was, "If I can sit in your lap I will do my best to learn," his teacher, Kate Deadrich, said. "He would wear his father's cowboy hat and then he would have his father's boots—a little bit difficult for him to have them. . . . He had them over his little shoes and he looked just like a little cowboy."[8]

Lyndon recalled, "My mother used to lead me from that house to this little schoolhouse when I was four. . . . With a baby in her arms. . . . She would lead me down and turn me over to the teacher at the side door." His mother was the figure in his life who was powering him. "She never wanted me to be alone," he told Doris Kearns. "She kept me constantly amused. I remember playing games with her that only the two of us could play. And she always let me win even if to do so we had to change the rules. I knew how much she needed me, that she needed me to take care of her. I liked that. It made me feel big and important. It made me believe I could do anything in the whole world."[9]

His mother and father struggled for his essence—his basic style—even when he was three or four. Rebekah curried his hair into long yellow curls and dressed him up like a girl. Although, those days, there was nothing from Freud in the folk wisdom about mothers inclining sons toward the homosexual by dominating them, among men there was a strong contempt for sissies. Men knew the roles they played and wanted their sons to play, and Sam hated those long curls. "He's a boy, and you're making a sissy of him," he would tell his wife. "You've got to cut those curls." She would not, so one Sunday when she was at church he took the scissors into his own hands and cut off his little son's hair until he looked the way a boy was supposed to look.[10]

During Lyndon's earliest years, he remembered, when his father was away he slept beside his mother. After she scrubbed his face and hands at the washbowl and tucked him into bed, he would watch her unpin her hair and shake it from side to side, and he would count, every time, her fifty strokes on each side. After she washed her face, arms, and throat and said her prayers at the bed, she would get in beside him and read to him from Browning, Milton, Dickens—or tell him about her girlhood, which he liked better.[11]

Sam's sister, Lyndon's Aunt Frank, had married the prosperous legislator and district judge Clarence Martin (he who had defeated Sam, Sr., in 1892), and during Lyndon's first year of life the Martins had bought a stone house and 350 acres on the Pedernales upriver a mile from Sam and Rebekah. As Judge Martin prospered, several rooms, more stonework, and an elevated fireplace were added. No plain frontier cabin, this spread placed the Sam Johnsons in the position of poor relations. "This was the *big* house on the river," Lyndon said of the place after it had become his own home. His uncle and aunt "would always ask all the in-laws to come here to spend their Christmas, and here in front of this house and around this yard we would shoot off our firecrackers and play with our dogs. . . . Christmas Eve night, we took the presents from the chimney." Lyndon also went to the Martins' for summer family reunions, Thanksgiving dinners, "or the family would gather come a Sunday or something like that." Barely able to walk, he would stand on the apron of the elevated fireplace and recite poems his mother had taught him.

"I came here at Christmastime when Judge Martin gave a big Christmas party, and he had a box of apples, and a big eight-by-ten box of peppermint 'n banana 'n lemon stick candy, and we had the Christmas tree in by the big fireplace.

"After we'd eaten all the candy and all the apples that we wanted, we came out here [in the yard] and Judge Martin had some bird dogs. And he would enjoy 'em and he'd have these bird dogs precede him, and [they'd] sniff out the quail and the Judge would hunt them. And my little cousin and I conceived the idea that we would get a tin can and fill it full of rocks, close the top of the can, and tie it onto the dog's tail. So he got one hound dog and I got the other and we wrapped the baling wire around his tail and we got the tin can securely fastened to his tail and we turned 'em loose, and they started runnin' the length of the lawn, and the Judge walked out just as the last dog cleared with his tin can that fence over there. And he looked at us very disapprovingly. And he gave us a little talk. I'll never forget what he said.

"He said, 'A dog is loyal, and a dog is grateful, and a dog appreciates what you do for him, and I would think that you boys could at least be as good as my dogs.' Said 'Here I've gone to Fredericksburg, bought a whole case of apples, brought 'em down here and saved 'em for Christmas for you. I bought you candy, Aunt Frank's baked ya cake, we've gone out and killed a turkey, we invite you to come here an' enjoy the Christmas season, and then you go an' show your appreciation by tin-canning every damn dog you can find on the place.'

"My little cousin went around one side of the house, and I went around the other," Lyndon said, "and I remember I stayed there quite a while crying, just thinking about what I had done to Judge Martin's dogs, after he'd done so much for us."[12]

Lyndon's grandfather Sam and his grandmother Eliza lived up the road from his own family about a fourth of a mile, and according to Rebekah, Grandpa Johnson wrote his daughter Lucia out West, "I have a mighty fine grandson, smart as you find them. I expect him to be a United States Senator before he is 40." This became the basis for a myth that the day Lyndon was born his grandfather had ridden about the countryside declaring that a United States senator, his grandson, had just been born. "That about my grandfather saying I'd be a senator by the time I was 40—they always taught me that," Johnson said. He allowed as how he wasn't sure it had happened because of his age at the time, but "I guess as soon as I could hear, they told me I'd be a senator." He was the eldest son, and his family had set his course for him. "That was my ambition."[13]

His grandpa meant a lot to little Lyndon. He heard his father talking about grandpa getting his horse shot out from under him in the Civil War. "We would always go up to his house at Christmas," Lyndon said. "Up at Grandpa Johnson's on Sunday," Rebekah labeled an old picture of all of them gathered there, the women decked out in the high-necked, long-flowing dresses of the frontier.[14] When his grandfather died and was buried, Lyndon, standing in a corner of the family cemetery by the riverside, watched the coffin lowered into the ground, saw his father crying, and was frightened.

In their own house by the river, Rebekah had given birth to a daughter, Rebekah; then another, Josefa, came. In Lyndon's memory, in front of the house he and his sister Rebekah were throwing a baseball around, their mother watching and, behind mother, baby Josefa crying in her crib. As Lyndon threw the ball their mother, big with her fourth child, stepped in the way and the pitch hit her in the middle of her stomach, knocking her off balance. She fell. Terrified, the five-year-old Lyndon was "certain that her belly would pop just like a balloon," but she got up and comforted him. Later that day, he skipped down to the river for a drink, but tripping on a tree root, he fell and banged his head, and when he couldn't get up he thought it was his punishment to be left forever. But his parents came and carried him to bed, and that night their loving voices talking at the foot of the bed made him so happy, he felt that the day's mishaps were worth it.[15]

His first close playmate was a Mexican-American boy, Huisso, who lived in a cabin across a big field from the Johnsons. "We raced our horses together, when we were both just learning to ride," Lyndon said. Huisso's horse, having been poorly fed, was thinner and weaker than Lyndon's, so, Lyndon said, "I will solve that problem. We will make him as fat." They fed him from the Johnsons' oat bin until his stomach stuck out. "Then," Lyndon said, "we filled him full of water, and then we took him out and ran the race." Lyndon's horse won easily, so they ran it over, but with the same result. In the third race Huisso's horse collapsed and died. The boys cried inconsolably.[16]

Following his Aunt Jessie around in her garden, Lyndon figured out that to get a watermelon to eat you cut a plug out of it (you "plug it") to find out if it's ripe, so he would plug them on the sly. "I used to stake him," she said. "I had to hide-tie him to keep him from getting into the watermelon patch, till I could go do what I was doing."

But Lyndon's mother was never far. According to Aunt Jessie, when Lyndon was four the governor of the state came to Johnson City and, rehearsed by Rebecca, said, "Well, suppose they let Lyndon make us a speech." The little four-year-old crawled up on an apple box and recited the Preamble to the Constitution.

Early in the winter of 1913–14 the Johnsons moved from the river to a pleasant white house in the town of Johnson City. Baby brother Sam Houston was born in town the first month of 1914, and two years later a new sister, Lucia, completed the family of Sam Johnson and Rebekah Baines.

"She put us all in her lap," Sam Houston said later, "and taught us the first, second, third and fourth grades before we even went to school."[17]

---

10. The School and the Churches

Johnson City was several hundred people, their houses, the school, the three churches, and a couple of cafés. No trains came, and there were only a few cars and a few phones. Everybody knew everybody, and people sat around together a lot, talking. If anyone was sick or hurt everyone cared. When a man of the village collapsed in a seizure, a woman near him immediately began massaging his arms. Sam Johnson hurried over and rubbed one of his legs and Emmette Redford rubbed the other one. When a person died, everyone brought food to the closest survivor, and the whole town went to the funeral.

Lyndon absorbed the southern heritage from his parents, but there was little in the daily life of the town to make him a racist. No blacks lived there, and the only Mexican had been stoned out of town by some of the older boys. When the farmer needed his cotton chopped, said one of Lyndon's boyhood friends, "there wasn't any Mexicans or niggers to do it," so everybody, the kids included, went out to do it.

"In those days," Otto Lindig said, "when a house was built all the neighbors helped. Maybe they had one carpenter, but all the neighbors helped. . . . In those days everybody helped everybody. There was no money or anything. If one man worked two days and another man worked only half a day, they forgot about it. There was no settling up or anything like that. There was no money to pay anyhow." A dollar was as hard to get as five hundred dollars now, and "The good land was a dollar an acre and the hills sold for 25 cents an acre."

"It was just a town," said Tom Crider, "where everybody come to town on Saturday." Nobody on the ranches ever worked past noon that day. "That's when you quit work, took a bath, and went to town." But everybody who was any good worked. Work was the dominant ethic, education was the way to get ahead, and together they were respectability, the Lord's answer to the Devil's drifting and gunplay.

You were knit into the values and attitudes of your peers. "In a small community," said one of Lyndon's pals, "everybody knew what was right and wrong. Everybody had a feeling of wanting to have the approval particularly of those who were older than you. . . . Patriotism, it was taken so much for granted, it was something—you never would even think about it." If you grew up there, that was the way you were.

When there was to be a party for the young people, the word just got around and all the kids of the right age would gather in the back yard at so-and-so's. Except for these parties there was, as kids would say, "nothing to do." When the Johnsons first arrived in town there wasn't even a moviehouse, and anyway a student was suspended if he went to any entertainment on school nights without school permission. About three times a year a circus would come through and the school board would decide whether the kids could go, usually letting them if there were animals for them to see.

There was a dance hall at nearby Hye, Gene Waugh, who grew up around there, said, and "Everybody went to the dance, mothers, daddies, kids, and the babies would be put in the back on a pallet, and they danced till 4 o'clock in the morning!" They had accordions and banjo and fiddle music, but mostly brass bands, as this was German country. What else did people do? "They *visited* a lot. They *talked* a lot," said Waugh. They had dances for the youngsters in their homes.

The two-story, six-room, five-teacher school was the center of the town. The people backed the school with a unity that transcended all their differences. The three rooms of the first floor were given over to the elementary grades, and high-school classes were conducted in two rooms upstairs. In the middle room upstairs there was a stage, and the walls of the rooms on each side of it could be slid back to turn the whole upper floor into the auditorium, which the people always filled up for the plays, declamations, readings, medleys, and commencements. To finance special school projects the parents of girls would fix box suppers, the boys would bid on them, and a boy got to eat with the girl whose supper he won, the proceeds going to the school.

Tom Crider's brother, Otto, said, "There's nobody realizes what kind of poverty we went through. We had damn little." To keep the other kids from seeing his lunch of fat meat and cornbread with homemade molasses, Otto would hide it when he got to school and eat alone.

Although there was sharp rivalry among the three churches, the Baptist, the Christian, and the Methodist, there was also the tolerance that was necessary in such a small town. Even the practice of baptism by total immersion in the river, which the Methodists did not believe in, could not separate the people. In those days a single circuit-riding preacher would serve three or four churches in the hill country. The Methodists in Johnson City were a little better off financially than the other two congregations, but no one could afford a full-time preacher. Each church held its own Sunday school, and then people would go to services at the Baptist church once a month, the Christian once, and the Methodist twice. The young people went to whichever church was running a youth meeting at the moment.

At the festive picnics after church, the ladies would spread their tablecloths and put out their plates and silver for their family groups. The kids clustered close because, as Redford said, "it was about the best spread you ever got. Everybody always had lots of fried chicken, lots of potato salad, two or three vegetables, and then cake 'n' pie! . . . The kids would go up and down the line, getting what they liked the most," pecan pies, pumpkin pies, apple pies. . . .

"If any one of 'em had a camp meeting," Tom Crider said, "everybody went to 'em. If the Baptists were havin' a camp meetin' we was there every night, the whole town was." Sometimes there were so many people they'd set up a tent in the churchyard. The services were held daily throughout a meeting—at 11 in the morning, 2:30, and 7:30. After the afternoon service the kids would go swimming in the river. Each of the churches sponsored one of these praying marathons every summer, and altogether they seemed to string out from the end of spring to the start of fall. Actually any one of them usually lasted about ten days, Friday through Sunday week. Sometimes they would go on a full two weeks, but during the summer and harvest-time it was hard to hold people in town that long.[1]

11. Poems, Curls, Hymns, and a Rabbit

"Mother, all of us could run over her," Lyndon said. "My father, he'd take a razor strap and just whip hell out of us. We looked upon him as a king. Everybody looked up and respected him." In Johnson City, Sam traded in real estate and cattle and made a good living, acquiring a small interest in the local bank and coming to be, Lyndon said, "among the top three" in town in respect, influence, and money. "I would say I was not deprived in my youth of anything," within reason, Lyndon said. The Johnson children were generally thought to be the best-dressed kids in town—in the school pictures Lyndon was the boy with the tie on. His little brother thought they lived in probably the nicest house in town. They had one of the few automobiles, one of the first Model T's in their part of the country, and it was a great occasion for them to get all dressed up and go out for a spin.[1]

The Johnson house had two bedrooms, a living-dining room with a big fireplace, a kitchen with a wood-burning stove, and a screened-in back porch. The girls slept on the porch, Lyndon and Sam in the bedroom next to their parents' room. Sometimes the father would call little Sam, about three, to "come in here and get me warm," which the little tyke would do (getting warm himself, too) until his daddy went off to sleep. Then Lyndon would call him to come on back—*he* was getting cold.

Rebekah kept a pot of pinto beans suspended over the coals from a metal arm in the fireplace and baked sweet potatoes in a large iron skillet in the coals, with more coals piled on the lid (the "Dutch oven" of the frontier). At the dinner table she would say, "The one who eats the most cornbread gets the most cake." The family had a well, a watertank, and some outbuildings on their block-sized lot, and when a small house came into Sam's possession as part of a swap, he moved it onto the lot for guests. This extra house quickly replaced the barns as the kids' favorite playing place. Early in the fall, though, when the barns were full of fresh peanut hay, they would romp in the hay and eat the peanuts they picked out of it. Once when he was playfully carrying Josefa from the barn, Lyndon broke his leg.[2]

When he was five or so Lyndon would drift over to the neighbors' place. "He'd come over many, many evenings when I was milking and watch me milk," said C. S. Kinney. "He got a big kick out of it, standing there trying to torment the cows." Once when the Pedernales was flooding Rebekah missed Lyndon again, and C. S.'s brother saddled up and went and found him down at the river, bringing him home perched on the back of the horse.[3] The boy was five or six the first time his daddy took him to Austin to see the state capitol. Sam would put the children in the wagon with him and give the first one who saw the capitol dome a nickle.[4]

To help with expenses Rebekah taught public speaking—then called "expression"—in the Johnsons' comfortably furnished front room, its walls lined with books. "She prepared my declamation contest—she wrote my speech for me," a neighbor kid remembered. For Otto Crider, too, "She used to write my debates for me." With never more than six teachers in the school, all the students in public speaking were trained by her or Mrs. C. C. Redford. Mrs. Redford didn't charge, but Mrs. Johnson did. Rebekah also helped with the school plays.

Lyndon's mother believed in shaping children from infancy. Long before one of her students had learned to read or write, Rebekah was teaching her to recite rather long poems for the banquets in Miss Tiny Spaulding's hotel.[5] The teachers of "expression" taught, not just how, but what to speak. Into the boys they inculcated national pride, patriotism, and the concept of the male hero, and into the girls, the correlative admirations and contempts. Rebekah Johnson was a teacher on the frontier transmitting just such values. Lyndon remembered the rhyme he learned at her knees—"In back of every noble enterprise / The shadow of a noble woman lies." In her five-page biography of him she wrote that when he was five, in the first grade, he delivered at the closing of school "a poem of his own selection, 'I'd Rather Be Mama's Boy.' "

"I'll never forget," Johnson said, "how much my mother loved me when I recited those poems. The minute I finished she'd take me in her arms and hug me so hard I sometimes thought I'd be strangled to death."

When he was six she taught him the poem about the Alamo for him to recite at a Confederate Reunion. He again had "long hair with golden curls," he said, but before the reunion he wandered into the barbershop and there was told they would give him a free haircut. "Well, it's free," he said, and he had his head shaved "slick as an onion." Back home his mother broke into tears. "My darling child, who did that to you?" she exclaimed. "I did it myself—I got it free." She canceled his performance and refused to go to the reunion.[6]

At seven, Lyndon was already a third-grader. His report card for the fourth grade showed A's in everything except deportment (C-plus). One of his teachers remembered a warm-hearted kid who "would crawl up in my lap and pet and pat me" and who "almost seized learning." He was aggressive with his fellow students, but never cruel or unkind, she said. He took to his mother two paragraphs he had written on the *Courtship of Miles Standish,* but she thought that he could do better. "What do you expect of me," he asked her, "to write one better than the author?"[7]

After supper Rebekah would position a coal-oil lamp in the middle of the kitchen table and three or four of the children would sit in the light while she went over their school assignments and saw that they did the work. "I never forget those days of the kerosene lamp," Lyndon said. "It never was a very good light. A little wind would make it smoke and you'd have to stop and clean the chimney. After a while, seemed almost every night, you would have to change the oil and go out . . . to get the old gallon coal-oil can and pull the potata off its snout 'n' pull the wick out 'n' fill the lamp with kerosene."

Never was Rebekah happier than when she was helping her children with their themes and studies. If Lyndon didn't do his homework, Rebekah and Sam stayed up with him until he did it, but "Many times," Rebekah said, "I would not catch up with the fact that [he] was not prepared on a lesson until breakfast time of a schoolday. Then I would get the book and put it on the table in front of his father and devote the whole breakfast period to a discussion with my husband of what my son should have learned the night before. . . . That way, and by following him to the front gate nearly every morning and telling him tales of history and geography and algebra, I could see that he was ready for the work of the day."[8]

Still in grammar school, Lyndon and his fellow students were listening one day to the state commissioner of agriculture, Cone Johnson, in the auditorium. He told them about a boy who was standing beside a girl telling her, "I wish I was a centipede." "Why?" she asked him. "So I'd have a thousand arms to hold you," he said. "Why don't you use the arms you have?" she asked. After the laughter the speaker made his point. "Young men," he said, "if you make use of the opportunities you have, some day one of you may be President of the United States."

When a new courthouse was built Sam got title to the old one and set up his real estate office there, and Rebekah helped produce plays there. In the same building Harold Withers showed movies, and Lyndon, earning his way in by passing out advertising handbills, rarely missed the cowboy thrillers.[9]

The Crider and Redford boys were Lyndon's pals, and one or more of them often spent the night with him. "I was the closest friend Lyndon ever had," Ben Crider said. "We were inseparable," Otto said. "We were together every damn day and nighttime. . . . We were so poor that Lyndon would give me half of anything he had." Ben and Lyndon would idle in the cedar brakes whittling the sumac (if it was wet, they would whittle it down to the dry inside), and the boys swam naked at the "Baptizin' Hole," the spot on the river under the bridge where true believers were dunked.

Weekends, Lyndon and his sisters visited the Crider boys on their family's place a mile or so out of town; sometimes Lyndon stayed a week. "We didn't ever get up till sun-up," Tom Crider said. "We had about a thousand head of sheep. We had to be sure to get 'em all into the house and put 'em in a pen with a high net wire because the wolves [coyotes] were bad." The boys fooled around by the river, for the hell of it Lyndon would ride a pig or a steer, they hiked around the eleven-hundred-acre ranch. And Lyndon learned the origin of Texas hospitality—necessity. "Back in those days," Tom said, "a man come through out there on the ranch, you take 'em in just like it was a hotel, feed 'em, put 'em up, feed the horses." A generation earlier, if you turned away a stranger overnight, you were exposing him to the Indians.[10]

"My own heritage," Lyndon said later, "is heavily weighed with Baptist influence." Not "weighted"—he said "weighed." "My mother was a highly religious person," he said. "She never missed church. She took all the children to Sunday School," where she taught a Bible class. Every summer she, all the kids, and aunts, uncles, and grandparents would go to the camp meetings. The preachers, Lyndon said, were "the Billy Graham type" who would get people to thinking they were "goin' to hell in a hack." These fears lasted; they stayed. "I got to believin' it pretty deep," Lyndon said. Fifty years later, presenting an award to Billy Graham, President Johnson could still recite a few lines from a hymn he sang as a boy—

> Throw out the life-line across the dark wave,
> There is a brother whom someone should save. . . .

Rebekah also joined a temperance society—a sign of future trouble. Lyndon's father, raised a Baptist, joined the more liberal Christian Church as a young man, and in later years he affiliated with the Christadelphians, who, having no churchhouse in Johnson City, held a camp meeting on the river nearer Fredericksburg. The Johnsons attended the Christadelphians' camp meetings, but Sam "didn't practice much of anything," his younger son said. "Though not exactly an atheist or agnostic, he never seemed to give much thought to a formal religion."

One Sunday everybody was at the Baptist church in town for a camp meeting, "and at 12 o'clock," Tom Crider said, "Sam Johnson figured he'd come in and pick up his wife and children. About that time they were taking up donations and the preacher had asked people to stand up and say what they'd give, and he said, 'Well, there's Mr. Johnson standing up. What's your donation?' There was nothin' he could say but 'Ten dollars.' "[11]

When Lyndon was seven or eight he crossed his mother, with singular results. Knowing, probably, that "real boys" bucked wild away from the influences of their mothers, she had enrolled him in violin and dancing lessons and had even bought him a violin. But he balked. For days then, he said, "she walked around the house pretending I was dead. And then to make it worse, I had to watch her being especially warm and nice to my father and sisters."[12]

He was running with boys older than he was, hanging around the barbershop because they did, too. George Corley, fifteen years older than he was, said he was "the most mischievous little dickens you ever did see. He was always up to something, picking at you." He loved to play pranks, and Luzia Casparis remembered, "sometime' we'd go on these family fishings, he would flip the hats in the water with a fishing pole." Once with his sisters at the home of the Gliddons, where his mother was hoping he would learn how to dance, he teased the girls so much, Mrs. Gliddon spanked him.

He liked ice cream—once he made a deal with the two women at the Crider Café to use their freezer to make some. He brought in all the makings, including a box of Grapenuts he dumped into the mix to make it chewy. After sharing a lot of it with the women at the café, he took the rest home to his mother. But things didn't always work out this well.

When he was eight or so he passed by the ice cream parlor downtown and spat at the woman running it. She grabbed him and shut him into a big icebox. Terrified, he screamed and kicked at the door, and when she opened it he fell out and bloodied his nose. Thinking he would tell his mother, the woman went by and said to her, "I suppose you noticed he had on a bloody shirt," but he had taken it off before he'd gone home. Rebekah once asked a friend for advice how to control him, and her friend told her to tie him to a bedpost. "Oh, I don't believe I could do that," said Rebekah, aghast.[13]

His grandmothers frightened him more than his mother ever did. The rigid and disapproving Eliza Johnson, whose uncle had fought at San Jacinto and who had saved herself and her baby in the Indian raid, suffered a stroke when Lyndon was three or four, and at times during the next five years until she died he helped tend her. Her twisted body had to be carried to a wheelchair when visitors came—at the end she was unable to move even her hands or to speak understandably. She was a terrifying figure to him, and all his life he dreaded being paralyzed. Perhaps the return of his horror of winding up paralyzed like her, which he expressed to me in the White House in the midst of the Vietnam War, was connected with his fear that he was failing her frontier values. He did not like, either, his grandmother on his mother's side, Ruth Baines, whom he remembered as "very conservative, very Baptist, anti-boys." His little brother said Lyndon always resisted her authority, while she regarded him as a disobedient delinquent and predicted, "That boy is going to end up in a penitentiary—just mark my words!"[14]

Hazing young boys was part of the frontier life, carried over from the Deep South, and when Lyndon was eight or nine some of the older boys, including Payne Roundtree, took him "snipe hunting." Snipes? "We didn't tell him what they was. He didn't ask," Roundtree said. On a drizzly night they took him and an old dog he had named Gip into a dark pasture, gave him a sack, and told him to stand there, they'd round up the snipes and drive them toward him, and they'd just jump into the sack. Lyndon was frightened as the older boys scattered and ducked behind bushes to watch him, but, Roundtree said, "He caught on pretty fast—about two minutes." (Later, thinking how he felt when the United States learned that Russia was installing missiles in Cuba, Johnson said, "I have been scared most of my life, ever since they took me snipe hunting when I was a kid and they left me out in the dark.")[15]

As he got a little older he learned how to use guns and went hunting squirrels and rabbits with the other boys. In the winter the boys would run trap lines, skin the animals they caught, and sell the pelts to Austin Casparis, who ran the café on the square. Lyndon tagged along once to get Luzia Casparis to bake a possum some of the older boys had killed.

But Lyndon didn't want to kill an animal himself. He told Doris Kearns he would point his gun, but just wanted to know he could kill if he had to. One day his father asked how come he hadn't killed anything—"Was I a coward?" The next day he went into the hills, a rabbit jumped out at him from behind a bush, and "I shot it in between the eyes." Then he threw up.

Throughout his boyhood he usually had a dog of some kind, and when "Evelyn," a dog of his the boys were using for hunting, had a litter of pups, he put up a sign in the barbershop window, "See me first for hound pups, Lyndon B. Johnson," and sold them all.[16]

He worked on farms and ranches around the town, building fences, hauling adobe, herding goats for twenty-five cents a day. Said Otto Lindig, "I can remember Lyndon following a double-shovel plow when he was eight." He picked cotton with the Redford boys, but one of them said he didn't work as hard as they did because he had a father and they didn't.

Even in the cotton patch he was beginning to think about politics, as a story he told later showed. One of his friends left the field a little after lunch to hear Senator Bailey speak at a Confederate Reunion. The boy didn't get back until about dark, and the boss asked him if the senator had talked all evening. "Mighty near, mighty near," the boy said. What, the boss asked suspiciously, did he talk about? "Well," the boy replied, "I don't recall precisely all the senator talked about, but the general impression I got all afternoon was that he was recommending himself most highly."

On Saturdays the father of Lyndon's cousin Ava rounded up all the town kids he could to help pick his cotton. If they worked hard enough they were treated to homemade ice cream. One Saturday the old man promoted a competition to see whether the boys or the girls could pick the most. Lyndon and four of the boys cut their noon nap short to return to work ahead of the girls, but began bragging who could ride the steers over in the feeding trap the best, got to riding them, and made it back to the cotton patch, pretty skinned up, late in the afternoon. The girls had the ice cream to themselves.[17]

Sam would shake Lyndon's leg in the morning to wake him up, telling him every boy in town had a head start on him. Late in the afternoon, Lyndon would take a ride with his dad in the hills and listen to him talk. Politics was Sam's overwhelming ambition for the boy. He told him that if he could not go into a room full of people and tell right away who was for him and who against, he had no business in politics. "When you're talking," he would say, "you ain't learnin' nothin'." Nearly everybody came and sat on Sam's porch for advice and talk, often about politics, and "I'd just sit there and eat it up," Lyndon said. Sometimes he would lurk in the bedroom listening through the window to the porch.

His friends sensed he was becoming different from them. "Ol' Lyndon had more guts than the rest of us," Tom Crider said. Even when Lyndon was ten, the governor was on a platform in Johnson City and "Ol' Lyndon went right up on the platform and shook his hand." Tom remembered Lyndon saying he wanted to be a congressman, and John Fritz Koeniger said that one day when he and Lyndon were playing hooky they told each other they would meet someday in Congress.

One morning on the porch, with Lyndon listening, a friend brought Sam the news that seventy clannish German voters in a nearby area were going with the other side in the next election. Sam told his caller to visit the leader of the Germans and tell him that people were thinking that he would be the logical man to become the next county judge. The next day the friend came back and told Sam he had found the German "sitting on a zinc bucket, milking his cow into another bucket. His wife was up in the loft throwing hay down for the cattle. I told him what you said, Sam, and he came up off that bucket like it was hot. And she nearly fell out of the loft." The German votes went Sam's way.[18]

So Lyndon was already learning political guile while he was still a boy doing the things boys do, shooting marbles, swimming, sitting on the bank afterward eating pork and beans. "Hey, Crider," Helmer Fox of Cypress Hill would say to Otto, "how about you gettin' Linten Johnson and we play baseball?" Over at Hye Lyndon played first baseman and outfielder in the back yard of a family whose nine boys could make up a whole team.

There was a town donkey the boys would take to baseball games and picnics, or to a vacant lot in town, to try to ride. The critter belonged to Louis Roundtree, who charged a boy ten cents or a quarter if he was thrown. "If you could ride 'im, you got a free ride," Louis' brother explained—"they had to ride 'em slick, see, and they wasn't any of 'em ever rode 'im, see, he'd throw 'em every time." But cousin Ava said, "Lyndon had pretty good long legs and he would ride that donkey all evening long for ten cents a fall."

"D'ja ever run for the knife?" Otto Crider asked me. You get a pearl-handled knife and tell three or four boys, one of them in it with you, that you're going to bury it and the first one to find it can keep it. You dig out a hole and fill it with water and mud and then cover it over with a layer of dry dirt. The confederate leads the other boys toward the spot, "they run for that knife and—!"[19]

Still in knee britches, Lyndon shined shoes at the barbershop to pick up a little extra change. A rancher came in with some dirty boots and asked how much for a shine. "A dime," Lyndon said—but then he looked down at the boots and added, "a quarter for yours." If a customer didn't have a dime Lyndon would shine him up for cigarettes, or *a* cigarette. He took some ribbing for his big ears—"I'll give you a quarter," a customer said, "if you'll flip your ears."

One day his father came home with two gifts for his mother, a Victrola and a deed to the *Johnson City Record-Courier,* the town weekly. For several years Rebekah sold the ads and did the writing and make-up for the paper, penciling out the copy on yellow tablet paper, all the while corresponding for dailies in Dallas, Austin, and San Antonio. Around the paper for a time Lyndon was the printer's devil and tried to set type. Hearing a lecturer in town on the theme that it pays to advertise, he went to his mother and bought space on the front page to advertise his shoe-shine stand. His father came back from a trip to Austin in time to get one of the first copies of the issue. "What are you doing? You've made a bootblack out of yourself!" he told Lyndon. Sam told people how he had bought a newspaper so his wife could advertise that his son was a bootblack.

Once in the barbershop Ben Crider put a little mustard in a chair, and when Lyndon sat down it burned him. Lyndon ran to his daddy, who was about to sell a piece of real estate at his office in the basement of the opera house, so, Ben said, "he beat hell outa Lyndon without waitin' for him to say anything and sent him home."[20]

A boy of ten awhirl in his already special life, Lyndon followed the news of the drive by American doughboys across France toward the Germans' railroad supply line, part of the Meuse-Argonne offensive in the fall of 1918.[21]

---

12. Siding with Another Grafter

Lyndon was growing closer to his Uncle Clarence Martin, the conservative Democrat who had defeated grandfather Sam in 1892 and lived in the big house on the river. Martin and the boy made trips together in a wagon, sleeping out on a blanket, and summers Lyndon worked on Martin's land, baling hay, looking after cattle. "Sometimes," Lyndon said, "we wouldn't come back to the house at night. We'd take our coffee with us, make a fire, cook our own coffee, sometimes a little bucket we had some food in, and we'd sleep on our saddle blankets, out in the open skies."[1]

The son of a frontier judge, Uncle Clarence was himself a legislator, then a judge. In the mornings he walked to his law office in Johnson City in a high top hat and a black string tie. He and his wife, who was named Frank, were the Johnsons' rich and powerful kinfolks in the big house upriver. "Clarence Martin was the power," Ben Crider said. "He was the one we looked to when we wanted anything from the state."

After defeating Lyndon's Populist grandfather for the legislature, Martin took Lyndon's father under his tutelage, interesting him in the study of law in the 1890s and in running for the legislature in 1904, when Sam Junior was first elected. But Rebekah did not like Clarence or his wife. Aunt Frank was jealous of Rebekah's education and talent, and Rebekah had to deal with her sister-in-law's superior social position. As for Judge Martin himself, "Mother hated him," said her younger son. Martin was a tippler, and Rebekah blamed him for Sam's own attraction to the swinging doors.[2]

Sam had opposed Joe Bailey despite Martin's support of the senator, but when scandals enveloped Governor Jim Ferguson in 1917, Sam stood alongside Martin in the governor's defense.[3] Martin was Ferguson's chief defense lawyer at his impeachment trial. In 1917, Lyndon's eighth year, his daddy was egging his uncle on as the judge conducted the governor's defense.

"Farmer Jim," a small-town banker, had been elected as the tenant farmers' friend. He fostered the creation of rural high schools and inaugurated free school textbooks. For the tenant farmers, who paid the owners of the farms they worked with fixed portions of crops, he fought for lower rents. Under Ferguson in Texas, the new regulationism began to blend with welfare-state liberalism. He persuaded the legislature to pass a workmen's compensation law; the state's spending for its wards increased. Sam and Clarence stumped four counties around Stonewall for Ferguson. When a fellow named Ball ran against their man, Clarence composed a square-dance call that ended, "Vote for Jim Ferguson and scratch Old Ball."[4]

No respecter of intellectuals, Ferguson vetoed the whole appropriation for the University of Texas because some professors there had opposed him politically, and this started his downfall. Like Joe Bailey, this champion of the common man was reached by the corruptions of his times. Early in his second term it became known that he had "borrowed" $156,000 in currency from sources he refused to reveal. Common talk said this fat wad of green bills had come from the beer lobby. Ferguson was also accused of depositing state money in banks in which he held stock, profiting himself. He was impeached on twenty-one charges of misconduct, and the Texas Senate sat in judgment on him.

Lyndon's Uncle Clarence pleaded to the senators that Ferguson had every right under the First and Fifth Amendments to deny them the right to look at his books and to refuse to say who had advanced him the $156,000, whether the loan was secured, and what the rate of interest was. Martin proclaimed that the governor stood before the senators "in the God-given majesty of a Texan and demands his rights"; but the senators voted that even such a majestic Texan as Jim Ferguson should tell them the facts. Undaunted, Martin took flight again to the oratorical lofts of Texas gothic. Ferguson "had the courage and the manhood to stand up in the majestic splendor of his manhood and stand for . . . the great toiling masses." Surely he would not be ruined for just a suspicion of wrongdoing, surely the senators would "have the God-given courage and the manhood to stand up in the sight of that manhood" and clear him. Unmoved—in fact delighted to kill off a friend of the poor—the senators threw Ferguson out of office. On the $156,000 they voted against him twenty-seven to four.[5]

But serious scandals had not finished off Bailey, and they didn't finish off Ferguson, either. In 1920 Lyndon's father and uncle teamed up to campaign for Bailey again in fifty-five south Texas counties. A few years later Sam pitched in for the Fergusons as Jim's wife "Ma" was elected governor, with everyone in chauvinist Texas knowing that "Farmer Jim" would be the governor in fact. Watching his father and uncle fend for their tarnished heroes in the politics of their times, Lyndon would draw his own conclusions.

---

13. A Resolve at Recess

When Lyndon was ten his family went back to the country. The cabin on the river, where they had lived until 1913, had reverted to Sam's father. With Sam, Sr., and Eliza dead, the question in the family was who would take over the farm. After a conference of the eight surviving sons and daughters, Lyndon's father sold the opera house and his other property in Johnson City and bought out his siblings' interests. Probably about January, 1919, Sam, Rebekah, and their five children moved back to the riverbank and the farm.

Lyndon would get up early, milk the cows, feed the horses, and walk or ride to school, his lunch bucket in hand. He walked three miles to the school at Stonewall, then to the school in Albert three miles south from home. Rebekah sent him to the Lutheran church on the river to learn German. But she could never get him to read fiction. He would ask, "Did it really happen?" and if she said it was made up he wouldn't look at it.

As he reached his teens, his father gave him a horse and a donkey, and on very special occasions, Lyndon said, "I could ride the horse to school, but most of the time I rode the donkey. The other boys, a good many of 'em had horses, most of the others walked. Three or four miles was a rather long walk for a boy in junior high school.

"I remember one day, one of my best friends was a very tall boy, much taller than I was, I guess at that time he was over six feet, and I said to him 'I ride this donkey every day and you ride the horse. Now why don't you let me ride the horse for a while. I'm tired of the donkey. You ride the donkey, you'll see that after all he has a nice gait, and you might enjoy that too. . . .' So I got on Alton's horse and he got on my donkey, and after we'd ridden about a mile Alton called to me and said 'Let's trade,' and I said 'No I like this horse better,' and every time he'd whip the donkey and spur the donkey and get him in a trot and get up real close to me, I'd run the horse a little faster, and I stayed ahead of him all the way home. And he said 'If I ever catch you, you little devil, I'm gonna whip you!'—but he never did catch me, until we got home."

There was a nice swimming hole on the river close to the Albert Lutheran Church—sometimes there were twenty boys in there swimming. One rainy morning Otto Lindig went down on the river, which "had on a little rise," and saw that Lyndon and a black boy were fishing. (This was during the cotton harvest, and the boys got to fish only on rainy days.)

"All at once," Otto said, "the boy slipped in the water and Lyndon jumped after him," grabbing him and pulling him back onto the bank. "Say, Lyndon," Otto told him, "you ought to have a medal for this." "Oh," Lyndon replied, "he had my chewing tobacco in his pocket."

Otto, who was twenty-six years older than Lyndon, said of him and his crowd, "It was nothing unusual if they went to the neighbor's watermelon patch and got them a watermelon to eat. Or if they passed a peach orchard, where there were ripe peaches, they also went in there and got some. . . . They ate all the peaches they could hold, like everybody else in those days."[1]

Lyndon saw his father as "Six-foot-two, with coal-black hair, quick in his movements, and an excellent rider. He was a warm man, loved people, while my mother was sort of aloof." Wright Patman, Sam's desk-mate in the legislature, remembered him as "just a nice good cowboy type fella with a fair education and the intent to do right by everyone." Where Patman came from men were either pot-bellied or pan-bellied, and "Sam was a pan-bellied man." He took shortcuts, he shouted slogans when he talked, and, Patman said, "Sam was a very persuasive man; he would get right up to you, nose to nose, and take a firm hold. . . ." But he had a strain of violence in him. "He was high-tempered," said Ben Crider. "He knocked one or two heads, one with a gun barrel." Otto Crider remembered, "He laid a guy out with a goddamn rail fence there one day." Lyndon told Ben, " 'I got my temper from my Daddy and my brains from my Mommy.' " Rebekah, loath to record anything that reflected on her family, admitted Sam "was impatient of inefficiency and ineptitude and quick to voice displeasure. . . ."

Lyndon spoke of his father and his grandfather Johnson as prophets on the frontier. Of his father he said, "He was a liberal, almost a radical Democrat. . . . He believed in the peepul—he spelled it that way—p,e,e,p,u,l—that was the way he separated a guy for the folks and the phony. . . . He told me, 'Your job is to look after these folks.' "

Emmette Redford believed Lyndon's interest in the poor came from his father. "I never saw Sam Johnson too busy to sit down and talk to people," Redford said. "To Sam Johnson, government was something that could do things personally for people." He had the reputation of a hard-working man who sometimes neglected his own affairs to help others. "If he had a dollar," postmistress Stella Gliddon said, "He'd give you ninety cents of it." Lyndon remembered his father spending two or three days at a time in the library digging in the records to help old people get Indian War pensions, and he helped hundreds of them. Seeing people coming around urging his father to run for office, Lyndon "thought his Daddy was a great man," Otto Crider said. Lyndon told Otto, "I want to wind up just like my Daddy, gettin' pensions for old people."[2]

After a decade out of office, Sam decided to run for the legislature again. Although, Lyndon said, his father ran as an independent because the Republicans in his district wouldn't vote for a Democrat, Sam himself was so much a Democrat he named his good horses for Democrats and his nags for Republicans.

Sam took office in time for the "Burn the Germans" session of the spring of 1918. R. E. Thomason, a legislator from El Paso, first saw Lyndon around the House chamber at this time, running errands for his father and other members, "a very bright and alert boy, with plenty of energy and personality."

Representing heavily German Gillespie County, Sam opposed without success a bill that made it a felony, punishable by twenty-five years in prison, to use disloyal or abusive language about American participation in the war, the military services, or the flag. He did prevent the law from authorizing any citizen to make an arrest for disloyalty. In a speech in the House that his son later bragged about, Sam pleaded that patriotism should be tempered with common sense and justice. Just as his grandfather Johnson had sympathized with the Texas Germans who had opposed the Civil War, Lyndon said, so his father thought that "burning their books" in 1918 was a terrible thing. In 1967, Lyndon said his father "was a great civil libertarian. He would almost be a protester now." The newspaper in Fredericksburg, understanding the risks Sam had taken for the native Germans, said he knew from the start "that the small bunch of liberals would lose out," but stood by the Germans despite vicious attacks on his loyalty.

Campaigning for his father's reelection that year, Lyndon licked stamps, delivered mail, and handed out literature. Sam, moving about the towns and the countryside, the county fairs and the ice cream suppers in his Stetson hat, his stiff high collar and his four-in-hand tie, was a handsome figure stepping right out of the nineteenth century, his tall young son tagging along with him. Lyndon said, "We drove in the Model T Ford from farm to farm, up and down the valley, stopping at every door. My father . . . would bring the neighbors up to date on local gossip, talk about the crops and the bills he'd introduced." They'd be given homemade ice cream, or hot tea if the weather was cold, and between farms on the road they'd stop and Sam would smear homemade jam on homemade bread and split the slices with his boy. "I'd never seen him happier," Lyndon said. "Christ, sometimes I wished it would go on forever."

During this first campaign, he heard his dad opposing prohibition; heard him explaining why, although he favored letting women vote, he had equivocated when his male constituents voted against it. Renominated, Sam won out over a neighbor who filed an election contest alleging that his name had been left off the ballot in one county and that intimidation had been practiced for Sam in another one. The legislature backed Sam.

Little Lyndon's visits to the capitol with his legislator-father, he said, were "the thrill of my boyhood days." Sitting in the gallery, he would watch his father and the others milling around the floor, or he would wander through the halls, watching and listening. "I heard my father pleading for seven-months school and for building little red schoolhouses," he said. "I heard him pleading for a way to get the farmers out of the mud. I heard him pleading for a rural route that would bring us our mail during the week."[3]

The thrills of school weren't much competition. "Mama wrote all our themes in school," Sam Houston said. Lyndon had his mind on other things. Ernest Hodges, who lived near the Johnsons, said Lyndon once asked him, "Do you think a fellow from Stonewall could get to be president of the United States?" One day at the Albert School, just before a ball game during recess, a resolve took form in Lyndon's mind. He and a fellow student, Anna Itz, were resting under a tree. Sitting with his legs folded, he looked up and said to Anna, "Someday I'm going to be President of the United States."[4]

Often when Sam went to Austin he would leave Lyndon, as the oldest boy, in charge of seeing that the children's chores were done, and Lyndon would assign them to the other four kids—chopping wood and filling the wood box, feeding the chickens and bringing in the eggs, tending the pigs, horses, and cows.[5]

Playing man of the place, he learned early that water is basic to life. "In the summertime," he said, "the Pedernales used to run dry as a bone, not a trickle," and "they used to have to bring water in with wagons. . . . We got our drinking water out of cisterns," pulling it up in a bucket tied to a rope. When the ponds and rivers were full the crops grew and the animals flourished, but droughts meant the opposite—and floods left them helpless. Several times in his life Lyndon was up all night moving things to higher ground.[6]

"I milked cows, dipped cattle, picked cotton, weighed it up, and occasionally got to take the cotton to the gin," he said. At eleven he was hauling cotton bales by horse and wagon. He told how his dad once agreed to give a green hand a chance to chop cotton. Sam took the boy out to the cotton patch, handed him a hoe, and pointed out the cotton and the cockleburrs, but in about an hour the fellow had "the prettiest stand of cockleburrs you ever saw, and there wasn't a stalk of cotton in sight."[7]

---

14. Lyndon's Father Fails

All the while there was politics. Sam, working for a candidate for Congress in 1920, kept a big placard for his man at the side of his desk. And at the dinner table Lyndon learned an unforgettable lesson in the meticulous vote-counting that he would himself perfect in the United States Senate.

Pat Neff, a Baptist who had been a friend of Rebekah's family, was running for governor in 1920 against whiskey and Joe Bailey. "The saloon," Neff would say, "is the home's worst enemy. It wraps its tightening coils around the head of the home and drags him to his death." Sam liked a libation or several, and by this time he liked Bailey, too, and handled south Texas for him. In the Johnsons' home precinct, Neff received only eleven votes, but Sam, who prided himself as a nose-counter, could account for only ten of them.

Rebekah set a good table—her specialties were spoon bread, fried chicken, dewberry cobbler—but even his wife's food couldn't calm Sam down one day at Sunday lunch. That one renegade who had evaded him! He muttered, "Someone double-crossed me. Some sneaky, two-faced louse lied to me."

Suddenly he looked directly at his wife. "My God," he said, "it wasn't *you,* was it Mama?"

"Yes, sir, I voted for Pat Neff!" Rebekah said. "He's a good decent Baptist. . . . You won't catch me voting against my own people."[1]

During the dances in the Johnsons' house, the young people would roll up the rugs and, to records on the Victrola, dance. Lyndon liked to sing, too—"In the Shade of the Old Apple Tree" was one of his favorites, and "Carolina Moon." Every Saturday night the kids played "Snap," a game of puppylove like kissing under the mistletoe. The kids would dart around chasing each other until a boy and a girl were tapped on the back—"caught." The caught couple had to hold hands and stand in the middle while the others ran around trying to "snap" each other, the new caught boy and girl would replace the couple in the middle, and the game resumed. They played this by the light of a smoky lantern. "We didn't much care about a lot of light," as Ben Crider said. Winters, inside, it was "Spin the Platter" or "Musical Chairs."

In another game they played, "Swords," they would choose up sides (the Johnson kids tried to get all on one side), the leader on one side would choose a passage from Scripture, and then the kids on the other side had to quote it correctly. Lyndon became the fastest and best Scripture-quoter. In the little playhouse outside, said Lyndon's sister Rebekah, "Sometimes we'd play church and Lyndon would be the preacher." She added, "I think he thought he was papa. He was always bossy."

Ben Crider, seven years older than Lyndon, said, "He wouldn't run with anyone his own age. . . . He wanted to be with the older boys, and he always went with older girls than he was." At the Criders' ranch, "he'd ride yearlings—calves, you know. He couldn't ride very well but he'd try, and we'd chase the sheep around and pen them. And we went deer hunting, squirrel hunting, even went fishing. . . . we'd go down there and catch fish and camp out."

All his life Lyndon would remember the hill-country land. He spoke later about riding in the pasture from daylight to dark, seeing the deer run through the oak trees and jump the fences, watching the grazing white-face cattle and the sheep with their lambs, seeing the goats scrambling to eat the leaves off the small shrubs and trees. It always fascinated him to see a goat climb to the top of a tree to get the last leaf.

Withal, he was still clasped in his mother's religiosity—"We used to get up in the morning and go down the road to church, and then when the services were over," he said, "we would have dinner-on-the-ground on the river bank and have a real reunion with our neighbors." The minister was a part of the Johnsons' homelife; once Sam Houston told a visiting preacher he wished he would come to dinner every Sunday so they could eat so well more often.

"As a boy of twelve," Lyndon said, "I attended a revival meeting and felt an urge to be saved." Showing his independence of his mother, he said, he joined his father's Christian Chruch and was baptized along with quite a number of children. Later he told Reverend Billy Graham that he had gone to a revival, but had not gone forward to be saved, and back home he felt terrible that he had not, so the next night he returned to the revival and was converted.

His mother didn't like it, but there was nothing she could do about it. The preacher who baptized him was a retired evangelist named Morgan Morgans. He had preached at revivals all over the country; once he said that in twenty-five years of preaching he had given four more sermons than there were days in the years. Emmette Redford remembered, "He was an elderly man, long beard—looked like Moses."

To a Johnson staffer, Lyndon's mother later explained his conversion as more a matter of puppy-love than of faith. He was smitten, Rebekah told Charles Boatner, with a girl who was a member of the church, and he escorted her to its brush arbor revival every night. The last night of the revival, when the preacher was really working for converts, he joined. A couple of weeks later Mother Johnson took the other children except Lucia and joined them into the Baptist Church.

One of Lyndon's older friends, who would not be quoted, said Lyndon didn't join the church until late 1923, when he was fourteen—"He didn't even go to Sunday School much—sometimes his Mama would get him to go." As his Aunt Jessie summed up Lyndon's boyhood in this realm, "Well, she [Rebekah] always wanted him to be a child that went to church and lived right, in that way. Of course, he wasn't too much that way, but, then anyhow, her influence was that way."[2]

So he could start in at the Johnson City High School, Lyndon went to live with his Uncle Tom and Aunt Kitty Johnson on their ranch near town. Woodrow Wilson was still the Democrats' hero, and Lyndon and Cecil Redford, studying the presidential campaign, argued in school for the League of Nations and "knew it backasswards."

In the legislature Sam went to work for rural education and transportation and for stabilizing cotton prices to guarantee cotton producers, of whom he was one, a reasonable profit. One of the farm liberals who early on wanted a welfare state for farmers, he supported using state money to buy seed for "those who are too poor and unable to obtain seed" and feed "for the workstock of such people."

Land dealer, legislator, friend of the persecuted and the poor, Sam was somebody, and his adoring, tag-along son knew it: the comings and goings of "Hon. S. E. Johnson and little son Lyndon" were news in the Blanco County paper. Taken to Austin once or twice a week, Lyndon

EXPRESS-NEWS CORP.

AUSTIN STATESMAN

A rare old photograph of the Johnson clan perhaps at the turn of the century. Johnson's mother, Rebekah, wrote under this picture, "Their first home at Stonewall. . . . The house above is the one in which Sam Ealy and Rebekah Johnson lived during the first six years of their marriage and is the birthplace of Lyndon." Lyndon was born in the left bedroom, above. Note the breezeway. At left, a more recent view of the birthplace.

JOHNSON LIBRARY

BARKER HISTORY CENTER

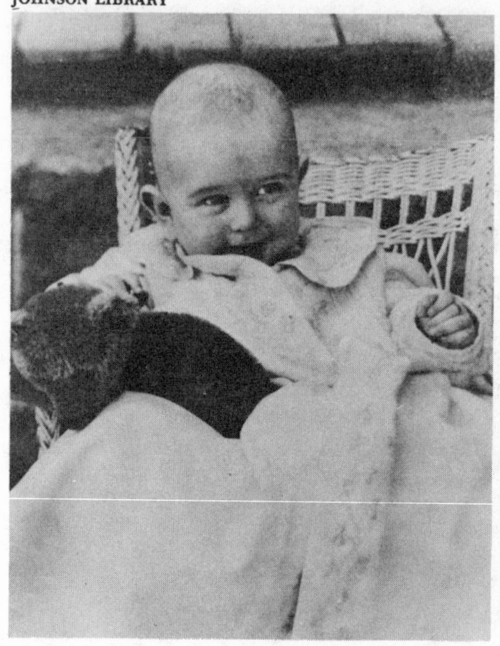

Lyndon at six months, and three of the Texas politicians whose influences in his family forced him to choose between Populist idealism and compromise with new industrial forces: above right, Thomas Nugent, Populist candidate for governor of Texas in 1892 when Lyndon's grandfather ran for the legislature as a Populist, too; below left, U.S. Senator Joe Bailey, charged with corruption and at first opposed by Lyndon's father, but later idolized by Lyndon; below right, Governor Jim Ferguson, impeached and removed on charges of corruption, but defended in the impeachment trial by Lyndon's Uncle Clarence.

BARKER HISTORY CENTER

BARKER HISTORY CENTER

JOHNSON LIBRARY

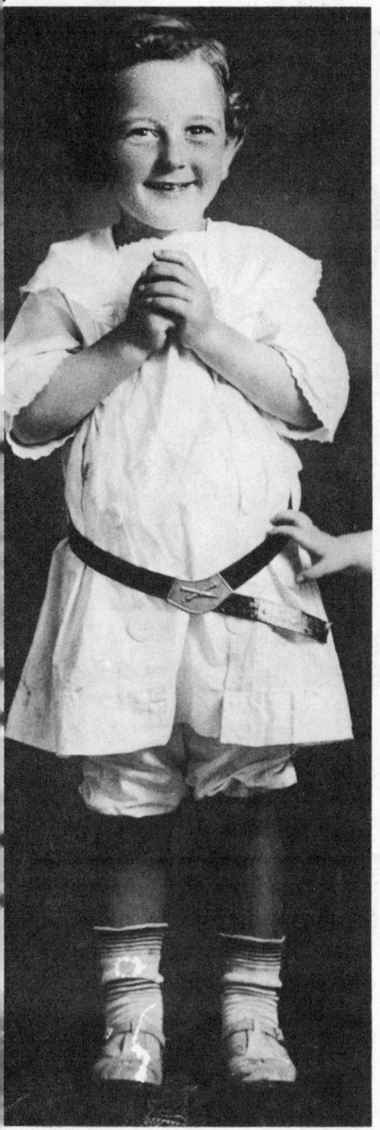

JOHNSON LIBRARY

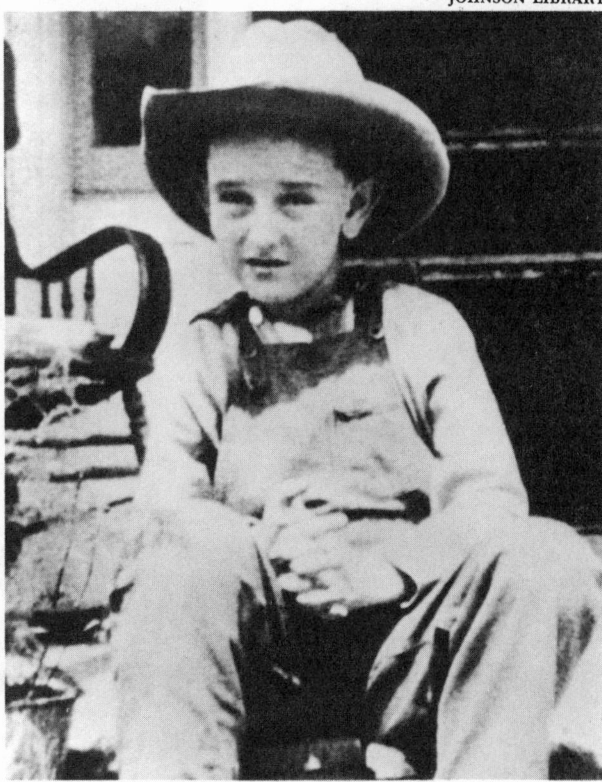

Left, Lyndon dressed up in girl's clothes as his mother wished. (The hand at his belt is that of a little sister.) Right, little cowboy Lyndon after his father began having his way on the boy's appearance.

The Johnsons' home in Johnson City about 1915. The boy by the car may be Lyndon.

JOHNSON LIBRARY

JOHNSON LIBRARY

Lyndon's mother, Rebekah Johnson, about 1917.

JOHNSON LIBRARY

Lyndon at the time of his high-school graduation, about May, 1924.

listened to the debates standing or sitting with his daddy. Wright Patman first saw the boy in the chamber in 1920 or 1921. "He was nearly six feet tall and nearly twelve years old."—To Patman he seemed to be twice as tall as another boy his age, and "so much like his father that it was humorous to watch. They sort of looked alike, they walked the same, had the same nervous mannerisms, and Lyndon clutched you just like his daddy did when he talked to you. He was a little on the rough side, too."[3]

The *Blanco County Record* said Sam Johnson had "one of the largest and best farms in this section of Texas." When not in school, a barefooted Lyndon followed a double shovel from morning till night (as Otto Lindig said), and on Sundays Lyndon saddled his horse and rode around like all the other boys. In 1919, when the cotton crop in Gillespie County was better than anyone could remember, Otto saw Lyndon coming to the cotton gin barefooted with a bale of raw cotton, to have it ginned. "I don't think he wore shoes before he was about 15," Otto said.

In 1921, though, a sharp drop in cotton prices broke Sam Johnson and dashed the pride of his watching son. Sam held cotton that was selling at forty-four cents a pound expecting it to go to fifty only to see it skid to six. He owed money on some tractors and the larger acreage he had taken over, and he had to pay a couple of families that were helping him work the land. He was standing good for other people's bills at the stores, and as the depression spread they couldn't pay, so he had to. Two or three bad crops and the collapsing prices just wiped him out, and the Johnsons lost their homestead. "We had dropped to the bottom of the heap," Lyndon said. "As a boy thirteen years old, I saw the 'boom and bust' . . . saw my own home place sold because cotton dropped from 40 cents to six." In three or four years in the early twenties, Lyndon said, his father lost one hundred thousand dollars, and "he never recovered."

"The experts on children tell us," he said later, "that one of the necessities for children is the feeling of security in their formative years. I know that as a farm boy I did not feel secure, and when I was fourteen years old I decided I was not going to be the victim of a system which would allow the price of a commodity like cotton to drop from 40 cents to six cents and destroy the homes of people like my own family. Because it was the same cotton. We had fought the same boll weevils to grow it. We sweat the same amount of sweat to hoe and pick it. It cost the same amount to gin it; the freight rates on it were unchanged."[4]

Crushed in the market like his own father and uncle fifty years earlier, Sam gave up on the farm, and he and Rebekah brought their family back into town, into Johnson City. "It wasn't as bad as the Hoover depression," Lyndon said, but "it was bad enough; we were advised to eat rabbits in summertime."[5]

15. The Boy Turns Away

Sam's drinking became a problem. He was "fond of liquor, a drinker," Stella Gliddon said. Ben Crider said more directly, "He would drink too much." If he was going to take out the car when he was squiffy, he would call on some boy to open the gate for him. The drunker he was the slower he drove. But setting out for Austin he would pull up a little way out of town and say, "Wait, boys, let's take a drink before we cross the county line," and he wouldn't lift his elbow again until he was back in his home county.

Rebekah had hoped he would run for the same congressional seat her father had tried for, but now she saw her dream, indeed her man himself, disappearing into his emptied bottles. "There was nothing Mother hated more than seeing my daddy drink," Lyndon said. She blamed their financial ups and downs on it, "and then she cried a lot. Especially when he stayed out all night," the oldest child said. Passing by the Johnsons' house you might see a happy scene, the children and their friends playing "Snap" under the shade trees in the yard, perhaps Rebekah and Sam on the porch watching them. But Lyndon was old enough to see what was happening to his father, and he didn't like it. "He'd lose control of himself," Lyndon said to me. "He used bad language. He squandered the little money we had on the cotton and real estate markets."

Frequently Sam disappeared into the Johnson City saloon with his political cronies for a few hours. One such afternoon in 1921 or 1922, Lyndon rounded up a few of his pals, and together they gathered outside the saloon and yelled for their daddies. "Come on home! Come on home!" they chanted, holding open the swinging doors so their fallen fathers could see them. Sam, seeing his very own son, thought it was a joke and offered him a quarter to leave, but Lyndon refused it. After a while, mortified and annoyed, Sam went home.

Here was the older son publicly siding with his mother against his father. Naturally little Sam Houston, who would get up every morning at six o'clock to build the fire and have breakfast with his father, became the favorite. "I'd kiss his ass," Sam Houston said. But, "between Lyndon and Daddy, there were two dominating personalities. . . . Daddy didn't want him tellin' him how to run a campaign. Lyndon wanted to show he could make it without Daddy." The little brother saw Lyndon learning the brashness he needed to resist his father from the father he was resisting.[1]

In Sam's last three terms in the legislature, he persisted as a progressive. He supported bills regulating the employment of women and minors and fixing a minimum wage for them, taxing corporations, and placing taxes on sulphur and oil production. He proposed free railroad passes for persons on state pensions. There was a law regulating the sale of securities, and he sponsored and passed a bill to create a regulatory office to try to stop "wholesale swindling . . . by oil promoters and other stock-fraud specialists." In addition to farm welfare legislation, he proposed a state system of public highways and the appointment of a state forester. Most of his votes "were liberal," Lyndon said, and "He was very proud of his tenant farm law and his blue sky law."[2]

Sam also backed a bill by Wright Patman, the leader of the anti-Klan forces in the House, to make it a prison offense to wear masks. "We just fought 'em all the time," Patman said. Once Patman's group prevented a known Klan leader from using the House chamber for a meeting. Lyndon said his daddy "would just fight the hell out of 'em. . . . All over the hill country he denounced 'em and dared 'em." In east Texas rocks were thrown through Patman's windows, and Rebekah quailed for Sam's safety. Lyndon, too, was fearful "that my Daddy would be taken out and tarred and feathered." As a result, Johnson said, "I never had any bigotry in me. My daddy wouldn't let me. He was a strong anti-Klansman. He wouldn't join the Methodists. The Klan . . . threatened to kill him several times." Baby Sam, who thought "KuKlux-SonofaBitch" was one word because he heard it from his father so often, said that one night when the Klan threatened to kill his father Sam replied, "Just come on ahead, you yellow bastards!" and stationed himself and two of his brothers on the porch with shotguns and waited—but no one showed up.[3]

In fact, though, nobody cared much about Sam Johnson any more. "There wasn't anything wrong with him," said an editor of the Austin daily then, "he just wasn't a very prominent man." Another old-timer (his view perhaps jaundiced by his later dislike of Lyndon) said Sam was "a cadaverish-looking fellow with an Adam's apple. . . . He was never as much as a vice-chairman of a committee. A deadbeat. He loved to pose as a fixer—behind the scenes."

After he left the legislature he continued to hang around Austin. "Sam was a drunkard," said one friend of the family. "He'd spend all his time in the Driskill bar." There was a wagonyard then at Second and Congress, and Sam would "lay off his drunks there in a wagon." He was called "Judge" because he sat around the courthouse a lot.

Even on the skids, mostly he kept to a kindly way. Lyndon remembered one Christmas Eve, when they were all sitting down to dinner, a road hand and his seven children came up to the house with a cake for Sam, to express affection for him. "It was a green cake, and terrible tasting—nobody could eat it." Rebekah was upset, but Sam was pleased and told them all to come on in.

"I think alcoholism's got a tendency to run in families," Lyndon said later. "Some men take to women, others to food; still others to drink.

Well, for my father and for his friends it was always drink." In the eyes of the boy, his father had lost their homestead, he was a lush, and he was nothing politically, living it out boozing and job-hunting. By Lyndon's fifteenth year his idealistic father had become a failure.

His mother, he said, "always had some pin money hid under the pillow to take care of our needs in time of distress." Much later, when he was vice-president, standing in a mud hut in Senegal, "I saw," he said, "an African mother with a baby on her breast, one in her stomach, one on her back, and eight on the floor, that she was trying to feed off of $8 per month. As I looked into her determined eyes, I saw the same expression that I saw in my mother's eyes when she, the wife of a tenant farmer, looked down upon me and my little sisters and brothers, determined that I should have my chance and my opportunity, believing that where there was a will, there was a way."[4]

The main political influences in Lyndon's youth were populism felt through his grandfather Johnson, farm-liberal romanticism felt through his father, and conservatism felt through his mother and his Uncle Clarence. Ambitious, looking for models, he found in his own family the leading alternatives.

The most wealth people had ever had in one country, flowing into private hands and corporate forms, was determining that the political struggle during the middle half of the twentieth century in the United States would be, not populism against liberalism, but liberalism against conservatism. Lyndon's grandfather, the Populist, had lost to his uncle, the conservative Democrat who lived in the big house. ("All of the Johnsons have been Democrats from time immemorial," Lyndon wrote in 1965,[5] dropping from time immemorial the one Johnson who had breasted the tide.) Lyndon's idealistic father fought the corrupt senator, but cheered Uncle Clarence's defense of the corrupt governor. Finally the liberal, his father, failed, intensifying the boy's loyalty to his conservative mother. "He was too adventurous, although not as much as a lot of them," Lyndon said of his father. "He was trying to better humanity. He didn't have too much to show you for it."[6] So in his own family the boy associated political idealism with defeat, poverty, and failure, and in these other lives and events too—Joe Bailey the oilman's friend, Jim Ferguson the farmer's friend, scandal and vindication, impeachment and restoration, crusading and disaster—the men of principles lost, the men of the opportunities won. It did not do to draw too clear a line.

From time to time as he made his way toward the presidency Lyndon tested himself by the values of his progressive elders. In 1955, for instance, as the editor of a liberal paper in Texas, I was upbraiding him and some others for what I took to be a sell-out to Texas conservatives, and he summoned me to supper at his ranch to give me what-for. I asked him why he, the Senate majority leader, would bother himself about what a weekly paper said about him. Shifting his weight in the chaise lounge beside his swimming pool, he bawled out, "I don't want people to think I've gone back on my raisin'." But to himself, he justified his increasingly serious departures from the humanist principles of his father and his grandfather by the fact that both men had failed. Stand too hard by your principles and you don't *succeed.* Well, if that was the game, that was the way he would play it, nobody would be able to do *him* in as the liberal, even though, yearning as he drove for power to be worthy of his father and the old man who gave him apple candy, he wanted to see himself as just as radical as they were.

PART III
Hell-Raising and Wandering

For we know in part, and we prophesy in part. . . . For now we see through a glass, darkly; but then face to face: now I know in part; but then shall I know even as also I am known.

— 1 Corinthians 13:9, 12

16. Bootleg Wine and Berry Vines

His pride wounded by his father's failure just as his own body was rippling with a boy's new sexual energy, for six years, from 1921 to 1927, Lyndon wavered between aspiration and abandon. Sometimes after supper he would walk out under the broad sky and wonder what those stars had seen, what they would see, what they would bring to him —but he was also one hell of a hell-raiser.

A beanpole, all angles and height, he was full of bravado, he talked a lot, and he was a great kidder. Although intelligent, he was not brilliant. In high school, he said, he was about a B student. Otto Crider, who knew Lyndon best, said there wasn't much studying going on.

Lyndon still ran with the Crider boys and the Redford boys. The Redfords, two blocks away from the Johnsons, had vacant lots on either side of them, and they used one for sandlot baseball and made a tennis court on the other one. Mrs. Redford kept her boys around the house to help her, and besides, she just wanted them around home, but Lyndon, down the street with his younger sisters and little Sam, had the run of the town in the summers. "Sometimes he didn't get home for dinner and they'd have to look for him," Emmette Redford remembered. "Many a time his mother would call our house wanting to know if Lyndon was there." The future president didn't miss a thing in town —"Whenever there was a fight or whatever, he was there first. . . . If there was a drummer in town, he'd be up front watching," Redford said.

Rebekah became in effect a servant to her elder son. "Lyndon never waited on his mother, he had her in the palm of his hand," Otto said. "When he spoke, Mrs. Johnson jumped. Lyndon would come in and say, 'Where's my shirt, where's my britches?' and Mrs. Johnson would *run* to get his clothes." He also got the upper hand over his diminished father. He "could turn on the tears," he could "talk him out of anything." Sam Houston said that he himself had to wheedle and be diplomatic to get the car, but "not Lyndon. He took it with authority. Wouldn't anybody've said anything to him about it." Otto remembered Lyndon coming out of the house twirling the car keys around his finger, whistling.

Otto said Lyndon had no religion as a boy, and as for himself, "I was never inside a church except to sleep off a hangover." Running in a pack of kids, they would stay out until three or four in the morning. "We'd do damn near anything," Otto said, but he added, "We stayed within the law," which in fact they did not.

The school superintendent was dating a pretty teacher. Lyndon and his friends piled boxes under the window of her parlor and took turns climbing up and watching them court.

Despite prohibition they could get booze in the nearby German town of Fredericksburg, which they called "the Hindenburg line." Said Otto, "We'd ride a jackass across the river, get the liquor, take a rope and hook it around its belly and tie the booze in the loop and bring it across." Occasionally they bought wine made from mustang grapes by an old German with a flowing beard. One night they jumped the old German's fence, sneaked up to his barn, tore off boards battening the door, and rolled a fifty-five-gallon barrel of the wine to a patch of berry vines on the edge of his field. Later the German matched up some tire tracks at the fence to the boys' car and threatened to file a complaint, but Lyndon, who knew the man was seeing a married woman, sent him word that everybody in town, including his own wife, would know, too, if he didn't drop the matter. Naturally, he did.

According to a story about his boyhood that Johnson told in the White House, he and some of his friends burned down a barn. They rushed into Johnson City and went to playing dominoes to look innocent, but the sheriff came up and said to them, "I know you did it—you never have been worth a damn."

There was, among them, a cynicism about the self-important officers of the law. To goad a horse-riding deputy sheriff named Hogan who was "always after us," Otto said, "somebody would set off a charge of dynamite on the north side of town, and he would flog his horse with both hands to get there."

In Fredericksburg Otto and Lyndon saw an old country sheriff standing beside a car that had Pennsylvania license plates. "Sheriff," they asked him, "what are you doing?" He said he'd learned on the wireless that this was a stolen car. They waited with him until at length a salesman, dressed in a seersucker suit and well-shined shoes, came up to the car. "Ah-ha!" the sheriff exclaimed. "Where you from?" "Pittsburgh," the salesman answered. "Well then what the hell are you doin' with that Pennsylvania license plate?" the sheriff demanded. The boys doubled up.

In the eyes of the churchified leaders of Johnson City, Lyndon and his rowdy friends were bad kids. For instance, Otto said, "Mrs. Redford was very strict—if you took a drink of whiskey they thought you should go to the penitentiary." But very early Lyndon had seen through the hypocrisies of the rules that bar access to the privileges of power. Once he and Cecil Redford were guilty of some infraction in school. The principal kept them after school to give them a switching, but he was plumb out of switches, so the three of them crawled through a fence into a pasture and the boys went to work cutting some. They whittled and diddled along, taking their time, for they wanted to make the very finest of switches. Finally they couldn't stall any longer, and Lyndon said to the principal, "You ought to think this over. You can switch me, but you won't want to switch Cecil, because his uncle's on the school board." They didn't get switched.[1]

In school Lyndon was fairly careful. "He pretty well stayed out of fights," for instance. "He didn't want to fight, and this was a place where you had a lot of 'em," Emmette Redford said. "Lyndon didn't like to fight, and he'd *persuade* you, to get out of 'em. . . . He'd lean over into your face, talking all the time, and lean right into your face until you were leaning *backward.*" Once, though, when he was making fun of bashful, left-handed John Dollahite because he was shy of girls, "John got him between two cars," and they came to blows.[2]

Lyndon did not like a certain bully in the school who picked on one quiet boy, especially, following him home, slapping and kicking him sometimes right up to his own front porch. One day, Lyndon related with relish, the kid turned on the bully, "got him down and began to hit his head on the concrete till his brains almost spilled out."[3]

Johnson led a pack of boys in what was meant to be a gang attack on a teacher they didn't like. "He was a kind of bully and not a very good teacher either," Johnson said. "A bunch of us talked about giving the teacher a good lesson by punching him around a bit. Sure enough, about seven of us boys ran into the teacher as he was crossing a small footbridge. Somebody said let's get him and I took the lead, trotting toward the teacher. When I got right on him I realized he was a pretty big fellow, and he was ready to take us on. So when I turned around to get support from my friends, to my surprise and to my horror, they had turned tail and run. I was with the teacher alone. I got out of there fast."[4]

Neither was Lyndon above taking advantage of his nine-year-old brother. Sam Houston, by working behind the counter at a restaurant and running errands for the general store and shining some shoes, had saved up eleven dollars and twenty cents, a lot of money for a little boy. "How about you and me goin' partners, Sam Houston?" Lyndon asked him one day. "Get together and buy us a secondhand bicycle." Delighted that his tall, handsome big brother, six years his elder, was offering to be partners with him, Sam dashed into the house and got his money, which he'd hidden in an old tobacco pouch under a loose floorboard in the pantry, and followed Lyndon to the bicycle shop. Sam's savings covered the whole price of the shining machine, a fine bike with curved racing handlebars and a practically new red-and-white paint job.

However, Sam's toes barely reached one of the pedals when it was at the top of its arc. The bike waas at least eight inches too high for him. Seeing his little brother's sudden doubts, Lyndon told him, "I'll let you have the first ride. You can be the senior partner." With the bike held up against his body, Lyndon helped Sam on and gave him a shove down a dirt road. The pedals spun around fast, but Sam couldn't reach them —he panicked, cut the handlebars, and sprawled into a ditch, scratching his elbow. He busted out crying as Lyndon ran up. "Don't cry, Sam," he said, putting his arm around Sam's shoulders, "I'll teach you how to do it right." But that night their father made Lyndon give the money back and told him never to do anything like that again. At least that's how Sam Houston told the story.[5]

Their father got Lyndon a job in Rob Crider's grocery store "to teach him how to work and keep him out of mischief," and Lyndon was a good worker and resourceful, honest, and nice to old ladies. A teen-age girl who was wearing her first silk stockings came into the store, and some Karo syrup spilled all over her when the handle came off the container. As she left the store in a state, Crider turned to his helper and said, "We're about to lose a customer." Lyndon dashed out to the water pump, pumped water into a bucket, ran down the street, caught the girl, and talked her into letting him clean up her new stockings. She kept on trading at the store, and Rob Crider put Lyndon down as a good young politician.

Lyndon took his first girlfriend, Kittie Clyde Ross, to silent pictures at the old opera house and to the women's temperance parades in town. The mores in the town were so strict, probably he and Kittie Clyde didn't even kiss. Once he said that one of his classmates, Louise Casparis, had copied out his themes for him, and Kittie Clyde had to help him on other things.[6] As he also said he "did a reasonable amount of helling around on Saturday night." In that time and place the boys did most of their girl-chasing as far away from their own elders' eyes as possible—you "went out among 'em" by traveling fifteen or twenty miles to nearby towns. There were dances on the second floor of the old courthouse, but the boys also went to the dances Saturday nights at Stonewall, Hye, Twin Sisters, Mountain View, singing along as they flivvered up and down the hills, "Just Keep on Doing What You're Doing, 'Cause I Love What You're Doing to Me." At the dance the music might be German or country-and-western with square dancing, provided by a string band with a fiddle, guitars, and perhaps a banjo.[7]

In the summer of 1923 Tom and Otto Crider went to Robstown in south Texas, and three days later Lyndon turned up, too. He was related to a family there and got a job in a cotton gin. John Koeniger heard that Lyndon didn't take to the hard work much and wrote to Ben Crider to get him home somehow. When Ben's brother Walter let it drop to Lyndon's father how every year there was an explosion at that gin and the people who lived near it wouldn't work there, Sam told Walter to take the car and go get Lyndon. Another summer Lyndon worked in Robstown in a café.[8]

Back in Johnson City the kids of the town played baseball after supper, sometimes even in the moonlight, with Lyndon at first base. A boy's image of himself can have a lot to do with his fantasies of himself at bat. Explaining his indifference to trouble he was having with President De Gaulle of France, President Johnson said that when he was a boy he was feared as a power hitter, and when the pitcher for the other team would try to dust him off, he "would just lean back and let the ball go into the catcher's mitt." Once the merchants in Johnson City told the boys on the team that if they beat Blanco High the merchants would buy them uniforms. "So," Tom Crider remembered, "we went out and beat the socks off Blanco. Lyndon played a mighty good game that day." Each place of business contributed a gray uniform with its name on the back.[9]

In the school there wasn't much interest in science—they didn't have any laboratories. There was math, there was English, and there was politics. "I doubt whether there ever has been a group of kids with more intense interest in politics than the group that went through school with Lyndon," said Emmette Redford. Lyndon and Cecil Redford pored through the *Congressional Record,* which somebody was bringing to school.

Lyndon was "real clever," said Joe Crofts, a fellow student. "When he was unprepared, he had a favorite trick. He'd start an argument with the teacher. I remember when Mr. Scott Klett was teaching us. One day Lyndon didn't know the lesson, so he started an argument about a wagon. 'Which travels furthest,' he'd ask Klett, 'the front or rear wheels of a wagon?' Whichever side the teacher took, Lyndon would take the opposite. He'd march up to the blackboard and draw diagrams and make up formulas and by the time he got through, class was out."

At Klaerner's opera house in Fredericksburg in 1921, Lyndon won his first debate on the subject of whether to divide Texas into a number of states. His last year in the high school he and his partner won first in

Blanco County debate and third in the district tournament in San Marcos, and he took some honors in declamation.[10]

For Lyndon and a couple of his friends, the courthouse was one of the main centers of entertainment. Otto remembered a lawyer discrediting a witness in a bootlegging trial by comparing him with "a bottle-scarred veteran of a thousand drunks." Another lawyer, sneering about the saddened demeanor of an adverse witness, said "His cheeks are streaked with dollar marks." When a notorious drunk, explaining what kind of a car he was in, said, "Well, I guess it was a towering car—it was a one-seater," Lyndon and Otto broke up laughing in the courtroom (the fellow had meant "a touring car").

They watched Lyndon's Uncle Clarence perform, too. "He would come in with the emotional stuff and have 'em wiping their eyes," Otto said. Defending a county commissioner for committing the felony of carrying a jug of booze, Martin declaimed, "If you send my dear old gray-haired friend to the penitentiary, you're going to inscribe over the doors of the courthouse in scarlet letters, 'Abandon hope, all ye who enter here!' "[11]

In Lyndon's senior year there were only ninety students in the Johnson City school, six of them graduating. That spring, in a baseball game on a big flat opposite the old Johnson farm on the Pedernales, he pitched and played first base as the Johnson City team defeated the boys from Albert and Hye. At the graduation exercises in May, 1924, president of his class of six, standing six feet tall and "too thin to throw a shadow at high noon," he read the class poem. The motto of the class was "Give to the world the best that you have and the best will come back to you."[12]

Sam and Rebekah had given their best, but the best had not come back to them. Lyndon later compared his family's struggles with those of black people. "My family was poor and I was poor," he said.

His parents wanted him to go to college, but "his mild interest in books," Rebekah said, "was discouraging." Armed with what Lyndon called "a terrible knife-like voice," she pressed him to go, but getting no agreement from him, she shut him out, at supper talking only to her husband and the other children. "We'd been such close companions, and boom, she'd abandoned me," Lyndon said later.

But he was appalled by the idea of spending four more years in schoolrooms, and he felt that going "would make me a sissy again." Their sudden plunge back into poverty was a factor, too. "When time came for us kids to go to college," he said, "the money wasn't there. We couldn't go to the university."[13]

17. "I Felt on My Own"

One day in the summer of '24, Walter Crider and Payne Roundtree, both about twenty-five, had the idea of getting together some boys to go to California in Walter's Model T. There were already three young fellows from Johnson City out there, Ben Crider, who was working at a cement plant in Tehachapi, John Koeniger, working in the same town, and Tom Martin, practicing law in San Bernardino. Tom was the son of Judge Martin, Lyndon's Uncle Clarence.

Payne went around and asked who wanted to go, and Lyndon was counted in. So were two of the Crider boys, Otto, then about sixteen, and Tom, about nineteen, Otho Summy, and Payne. "None of us had been off the farm for a trip longer than the road to town," Lyndon said. They were aiming for Ben Crider in Tehachapi.

Why did Lyndon want to go? He told Kearns he decided against college because he felt so pressured to go by his mother, who literally refused to talk to him for months, so finally he ran for California. He went west in search of—what kind of adventure, he could not say. "I know what he . . . told me about it," said his later associate George Reedy, "and most of it came out in terms of talking about something else." Lyndon said, "I ran off to California because that's where I thought my fortune was," they started out to follow "the old philosopher's advice, Horace Greeley, and 'go west, young man.'" His Aunt Jessie thought it was more for the trip than anything else, but his cousin Tom Martin was out there, and he knew, she said, that Tom was "a dipnailing good lawyer."

"Going West," the five young men chipped in five dollars apiece and bought the Model T from Walter, who had decided to stay home. Their seat up front was salvaged from an old buggy; on the back seat they improvised a bed. The car had a windshield, but no roof, so they fixed some wagon bows in place from the windshield to the rear and stretched a wagon sheet over the bows.

According to Lyndon's little brother, their father said all over town that if Lyndon dared to start out he was going to grab him and carry him home. Rebekah was not objecting, though. Lyndon packed his suitcase and stashed it under the bed, and one day, as soon as his dad left town to see about a farm for sale, Lyndon grabbed his bag, kissed his mother and Sam Houston goodbye, and bolted from the house to gather the other boys and get on the road.

Lyndon had twenty-six dollars in his pocket, and each of the others had about as much. (Those days, filling up at forty cents a gallon, you could ride all day.) Clambering into their flivver loaded with fatback, several cases of pork and beans, homemade pickles and molasses, cornbread, onions, jarred tomatoes, five-gallon jugs of water, and a single-shot .22 rifle, they waved goodbye to their friends and townspeople who had gathered to see them off and "hauled loose for California," roaring out of town at nearly thirty miles an hour.

Lyndon's mother phoned his Aunt Josefa in Fredericksburg to tell her he had forgotten to take a pillow, would she try to stop the boys as they passed her place and give him one?—Rebekah would replace it. But Aunt Josefa did not stop them, and Lyndon was spared running away from home with a pillow from his mother. Sam, finding the boy gone, cranked up the phone and called sheriffs from Johnson City to El Paso demanding they arrest him and send him home, but none did. There was just too much of Huck and Jim, the Model T raft drifting along the road-river through the desert, for anyone to want to stop them.

Many times before, hunkered down by the river or lying around in a barn, Lyndon and Otto had looked out to the east, then over to the west. Nothing was more magical to them than the idea of California or New York. Crusty old Otto, selling real estate in California half a century later, cast his mind back and reveled in the memories. "It was the most beautiful trip I ever made . . . five of us boys . . . because I was young, and everything was new to me. What can I see now? What the hell is the difference between New York and Los Angeles? We were young, we were fresh, and every corner we turned was new—every adventure was new."

The first day, near Kerrville, they shot a snake that was sunning on some rocks. Driving into Van Horn in west Texas that night, Otto said, they must have looked like something out of *The Grapes of Wrath.* They stopped to get some supplies when, as Lyndon said, "two or three fellas, look just like cowboys, wearing leggings and toting guns on their hips, said, 'Boys, how about a poker game?' " The Johnson City boys said no, and "We took offa there," Otto said, "like a spotted-ass ape," driving into the night for two hours to get as far away as they could. "There was a car on the road behind us," Payne said. "Hardly ever you'd see a car on the road those days. Lyndon would start hoo-rawin' Otho about those guys following us. Otho really got scared."

When they stopped to camp, Otho, refusing to sleep on top of his money like the others, took it out behind a hill and started digging.

"Otho, what're you diggin'?" they asked him.

"I'm burying my money, but I'm savin' a little change," he said. I've heard they'll kill you if you don't have a little change."

Every night thereafter when they stopped by the road to camp, their first chore was digging a money hole. "Always the heaviest member of the party was assigned to sleep over the cache," Lyndon said—"We didn't propose to be robbed."

Their Model T was a lot like a chuck wagon, with the mattress fixed for them to lie out on while one of them drove. "Oh," Payne remembered, "we'd sing old songs like 'Carry Me Back to Old Virginny,' we'd build a fire, cook bacon and eggs, some old sowbelly, for breakfast, pork 'n beans, corn." As Otto said, "We done our cookin' on the ground." There were no motels, but they couldn't have afforded them, anyway; they slept on the ground in World War I army blankets. One night Otho spread his blanket down onto a rattlesnake and they were all so spooked they drove through the night and the next day.

"Well," Tom Crider said, "we didn't see nothin' to speak of, just country." Everybody took turns at the wheel. The roads were dirt tracks, gravel, sand—they were "ridgety, washboard roads," Otto said. Sometimes they had to stop to open livestock gates. For a long way in Arizona they had to keep to the old board roads. "That road would just shake under you," Payne said. The drifting sand covered the boards in spots and they had to detour around these, carefully. "If you ever got off in that sand," Payne said, "why you were there, that was it, you never got out." When they stopped to eat, the sand got in their food.

In Arizona they were rained on, they had a flat tire, and making a wrong turn, they went forty-two miles the wrong way. Lost, they clomped into a little store in Tombstone and asked, "Which way is Arizona?" Getting directions, they told the people in the store they had seen only two cars the whole forty-two miles. One of the locals remarked to another, "These boys have been in a traffic jam."

At Blythe, for fifty cents, they were ferried across the river, just about sundown. When they walked up and down the streets of the California towns the natives called them hillbillies, but that didn't bother them. After a week on the road—Lyndon remembered it was about ten days—the boys reached Tehachapi.

Some of them went to work in the town and some in the citrus and grape orchards of the San Joaquin Valley. None of them wanted the car, so Payne drove it down by the side of the railroad tracks, got out, and walked off. For the first several months Lyndon sent his brother short notes—the boys had picked grapes a while, but gave it up because the work was too hard for too little pay, and warm grapes were tiresome for breakfast, lunch, and supper.[1]

Lyndon hitchhiked to Los Angeles to see his cousin Tom Martin, who hired him and John Koeniger to run errands and keep the law office open and let the boys live with him. "He was going to make lawyers out of both of us," Koeniger said. They helped him deal with clients in divorce cases, and Lyndon carried his briefcase to the courthouse. Often the lawyer rescued a bootlegger from the law and received, as his fee, "a case of alleged Gordon's gin," delivered to the office. ("Lyndon was no prude by any means," Koeniger said, "but I never saw him really intoxicated.")

On Labor Day, 1925, the three of them had to drive from Los Angeles to San Bernardino in time for Martin, who was already soused, to make a speech. Every time the boys said, "Let's go," Tom would say, "Let's have another one!" Lyndon had to speed through heavy traffic. The horn didn't work, and if anybody slowed them down he just banged on the outside of the car door. "Everybody would look—people would glare at him—but they would move over!" Koeniger said.

For some reason the work with Martin did not last, and Lyndon took a series of odd jobs, hashing in a beanery, washing cars, running an elevator. He slept in rooming houses and at times outdoors, and, he said, he almost starved to death. Probably it was during this time that he sat around in an employment office waiting for a job. He began to think his father was a lot more intelligent than he had given him credit for. Running an elevator for ninety dollars a month, "I found at the end of the month, after I paid for three meals and paid for my room and my laundry, that I was probably better off back there eating mama's food than I was in California."

Once Lyndon changed work shifts on the elevator so he could see the vice-president of the United States, Charles G. Dawes, who was in the area, but only got a glimpse of him—Dawes just waved and left. We get as little a glimpse of Lyndon out there, really. Broken free, for the first and the last time, from the values and the political ambitions that were to animate and control the rest of his life, half a continent from the gossipy, censorious matrons of Johnson City, he may have begun to turn away from the hill country culture. In an interview in the White House, all he would say about it was, "I felt on my own those two years."

Back in Johnson City his mother, learning that Clarence Martin was going to California, made the old man promise to bring her son home. Lyndon said later there was a plot to get him back, but they didn't let on to him or he wouldn't have gone. He helped his uncle with the driving. For twenty months he had lived out a boy's dream, roaming and job-hopping in the American West, but "The prettiest sight I ever saw," he said, "was my grandmother's patchwork quilt on the foot of my bed when I got home." He said to his Aunt Jessie about the lawyer he had worked for, cousin Tom, "Well, I'll just tell you right now, he charged them actresses from two to five thousand dollars to get them a divorce. Aunt Jessie, you know that wasn't right. I knew that wasn't right, quickly I got enough money to come home and I come home. I just went off and left him." His dad said to him, "Son, you've come up against the grindstone of life, and it'll get you."[2]

18. Working and Helling Around

Returning to Texas "with empty hands and empty pockets," Lyndon found that times were still hard for his family, too. Once they had to wait for groceries until his mother borrowed twenty-five dollars from a cousin. At the table one day, thinking the meat tasted like venison but knowing deer were out of season, he asked what it was. "Mountain goat," he was told.[1]

The upkeep of the roads was a county affair run on a patronage basis, and Governor Ma Ferguson had appointed Lyndon's father maintenance engineer over the roads in Blanco County. As Stella Gliddon said, this was "a piddling little political job," but Sam could not even claim credit for getting it. "Ma Ferguson got him the job through Clarence Martin," Ben Crider said. "Sam didn't do nothin'. The gasoline and trucks stayed at his house in Johnson City."

But at least Sam could give his prodigal son a job on the road gang. For about a year, Lyndon and Ben (who had also come back from California) worked six nine-hour days a week for $92.50 a month. "We didn't have to get to work until sunup, and we got to quit every night at sundown," Lyndon said. "We did have to go to work on our own time . . . and that was usually twenty or thirty miles down the road." (Lyndon said he started out for a dollar a day, but Ben was definite about the pay, too.) They loaded sand and gravel onto dump trucks, drove the trucks, shoveled the sand and gravel back off, pushed wheelbarrows, and swung picks and shovels. Lyndon drove a tractor, and he guided a dirt-scraper (a "fresno") pulled along by a team of mules, with his hands on the tool's handles and the reins either wrapped over a shoulder and under an arm or tied together and held stretched around his back. When he shoved down on the handles the scraper blade would lift up from the ground; when he let them back up the blade would cut into the dirt and get a load.

One of the boys working with him remembered Lyndon was full of fun, but he "always talked big . . . he had big ideas . . . and he wanted to do something big with his life." Perhaps this was what caused the trouble when he went to Austin to get some supplies for his tractor. While there he talked with the district highway engineer, and whatever it was that was said the engineer appeared on the road the next day and nearly fired everybody. Sam told his son, "Lyndon, I don't know what will happen to you, but I will tell you right now I don't believe that you are smart enough to talk to a highway engineer."

Racism was not a strong presence in Johnson City as Lyndon grew up mainly because blacks were seldom seen. There was a residual prejudice that ran back to the years just before the Civil War when the hill country was slave territory, despite the abolitionist sentiment among liberal Germans. But right after the Civil War the *Texas Almanac* remarked, "There were about forty negroes in the county, and some of them have left," and by Lyndon's time young people could choose prejudice or friendliness. Lyndon indicated by a story he told in the White House that he was instinctively unprejudiced. When a young road foreman, Melvin Winters, brought a gang of black construction workers to Johnson City, a heavy-drinking redneck told him to get them out of town before sundown—Winters refused—and the two men fought a marathon fight in the street. People gathered to watch, Lyndon cheering for Winters. As Lyndon told it, Winters got the bully down, beat his head against the concrete curb, and screamed, "Do my niggers stay? Do my niggers stay?" "Yes," the redneck answered. "Yes."

Big at sixteen and seething with energy, Lyndon got into some fights. George Corley, who was then about thirty-one, said, "He always wanted to rassle me. I'd have to let him throw me once in a while, just to keep him in good humor." Otto Crider said, "Lyndon wasn't afraid of nothin'. He'd stand up toe to toe with them. He had a lot of fist fights around Johnson City, over any damn thing. . . . If somebody jumped him he'd fight. He wasn't any damn coward." Ben remembered pulling Lyndon out of some rough ones. On the way to a dance Lyndon and Otto, fighting on a flatbed truck, pitched off together into an agarita bush. "He fought my brother all the time," Ben said, "but they'd sleep together that night."

Lyndon's boss used to pick up him and other workers in town early in the morning, but one morning Lyndon said that riding in the boss's car wasn't much better than walking and the boss immediately fired him. Their father had gotten him the job, as his sister Rebekah said, "to keep him out of mischief," but here he was again, nothing in his hands but himself and time. His wild doings in his late teens made his parents unhappy, as he later admitted.[2] Once he was trying to get a pretty girl to go to a dance with him and then let him take her home, but Tom Crider claimed her for the evening, so to hell with it—Lyndon and some of the boys climbed into a touring sedan and drove to Fredericksburg to get some bootleg wine. On the way back they let Payne drive because they thought he was the soberest. The car turned over twice and Lyndon was thrown about fifty feet into the pasture. His coat was torn about where a mackinaw would be cut, so he ripped it on around and had himself a mackinaw.

Well, the middle of prohibition, wine all over the car turned upside down in a pasture—he couldn't go back and face his dad and get the hell beaten out of him. With some money one of the boys loaned him he got on a bus to go to his uncle in San Antonio.

Walking into his uncle's office, he heard him through the open transom over the door, saying, on the phone, "Hello, Sam! How are you?

. . . Lyndon? No, he hasn't been here. . . . What happened? . . . Oh, a wreck . . . good." Lyndon sat down in the anteroom to wait and listen as his uncle continued. "Well, he's not here. . . . Wait a minute, I heard somebody come in."

The door opened, and his uncle saw Lyndon sitting there. The boy couldn't move.

"Come on, Lyndon, your dad wants to talk to you." He got up and went to the phone.

"Lyndon," his father said, "I know about that touring car thing, but there's something more important than that I want to talk to you about now. I've bought a sedan, cost a little money, but it would have anyway and I've wanted one, mighty good-lookin' car. Now you go over there and pick it up for me, catch the ten o'clock bus over there, you can do that, and bring it on to Johnson City. But don't come home first. First go to the square and drive that car around the square two or three times. I've been raised around here and I don't want people to think my son is a coward. So you go on and do that."

"Yes, daddy, where did you say it is. . . ."[3]

Throughout these drop-out years, Lyndon's mother kept after him to go to college. Physical work was honorable, she would tell him, but education gave "opportunity in every way." One Saturday night, after a dance, he came home with his nose bleeding from a fight, and late the next morning she went to him lying in bed and said, "My boy, my boy, I never thought he'd be a truck driver all his life. I never thought that's all he'd ever amount to." Crying, she sat on his bed, and she said to him, "To think that my eldest son would be satisfied with a life like this. . . ." He turned his head to the wall, ashamed.

His father frequently told him he was going to wind up being a black sheep. "It's fine to be satisfied with the simple things," Sam would say, too. "A simple man who is satisfied to be a laborer will never have much on his mind. Of course there won't be much in it, but those willing to devote all their lives to a road job really don't need much." Or he would say, "You don't have enough sense to take a college education."

All this got to him, too. He told his mother about it, and she smiled. He made his decision. "I'll go if I can get a job," he told her. She went for the phone and called the teachers' college in San Marcos to make the arrangements.

"Are you going?" his father asked him.

"Why?" he asked back.

"You haven't got sense enough," Sam said. "It won't penetrate: your head's too thick."

Yes, he was going. As Stella Gliddon said, "Lyndon finally decided that he'd rather go to school and learn enough not to have to work so hard." For a little while he had been a common laborer, a worker. He had picked cotton, clerked in a grocery store, sweated in the grapes, carried a lawyer's briefcase, run an elevator, washed dishes, and worked on the highways in the Texas heat. Now he was ready for college. "For me," he said, "it was a passport out of poverty."

Later he said the conversation with his father had decided him, but he knew at a deeper level that he was driven by his mother. "My mother finally convinced me that I would enjoy life more if I would use my head instead of my foot," he said. "I missed being an elevator boy just about that much, when my mother just reached up and made me go back to school. . . ." Determined to recapture his mother's love, but not at the price of his father's respect, he had decided, he said, that he would please his father by becoming a political figure, but "I would finish college; I would build great power and gain high office. Mother would like that. I would succeed where her own father had failed; I would go to the capitol and talk about big ideas. She would not be disappointed in me again."

Sam and Rebekah could give him only a few dollars, and he was turned down for a loan at the Johnson City bank. In Blanco he received a small loan, probably seventy-five dollars, from Percy T. Brigham, a banker who had once studied law under his maternal grandfather. Hitchhiking to San Marcos, Lyndon had about one hundred dollars, hardly enough to cover the cost of enrolling. There would be no more money from his parents.[4]

PART IV
The Politician Emerges

It had been astonishing to me, throughout the Affair, how far stubbornness could take him. He was a supreme political manager. Nevertheless, his instincts had ridden him. . . .

— C. P. Snow in *The Affair,* 1960

19. Start at the President's Office

Rebekah's decision that Lyndon would go to San Marcos was a protective one. Although the state university in Austin was closer, it was larger and more formidable. Nearly everyone around Johnson City went to Southwest Texas State Teachers College.

Founded early in the century, the college was dominated by "Old Main," a castlelike building with peaks and spires decorating the steeply-pitched red roof. The library had only twenty-one thousand books, but most of the professors had masters' degrees. There were eight other school buildings, along with shops, labs, gyms, sports fields, and a small demonstration farm. The seven hundred students came from the farms and towns of the area, Anglo-Saxons, Germans, Czechs, Poles, Bohemians, all of them whites except for a few Mexican-Americans. Tuition was nominal, but even so more than half the boys had jobs. Learning to be teachers, the students practice-taught in three local schools.

They lived in boardinghouses, and the rules were strictly antisexual: curfews, the girls prohibited from riding in cars with boys, skirts required to cover the knees. Attendance at the weekly chapel service was required. Because there were three times as many girls as boys, the boys were expected to date more than one girl. But, there were dances and parties, the students walked to the drugstore or the theater downtown, they swam and picnicked on the river near the campus. Each summer on the river there was "The Bathing Regatta and Red Cross Life Saving Annual Review," the floats bestrewn with girls in swimming suits drifting past thousands of oglers on the banks. Hazing was customary—the freshmen had to make speeches between classes and run errands for the seniors.

The dominant religion was Protestant, the dominant occupation, farming. About the only industry in town was the cotton mill and compress. There was a local gentry, but their children attended a finishing academy for ladies and gentlemen in the town. Thus for his entire education Lyndon was to be immersed in the ways and values of the farm people in the hill country and south-central Texas.

Right after he settled in, he wrote his grandmother thanking her for two suits she had sent him (they fit) and saying, "I am not going to be the black-sheep of the family after all." At first he lived in a boardinghouse. Mrs. Gates, who provided the boys their meals, had a rule that they could eat all they wanted, but they had to keep one foot on the floor when they reached for the meat, and she cooked only one pork chop for each boarder. When somebody was slow getting to the table Lyndon would spear his chop.

"When Lyndon brought boys and girls home from college," his sister Lucia once recalled, "daddy would sing at the parties."—His favorite song was "Let Me Call You Sweetheart." The first time Sam and Rebekah went over to San Marcos to eat supper with Lyndon and the forty or so other boys at his boardinghouse, Sam rallied the boys in the front yard and asked them to introduce themselves. A boy said he was from a certain town, and Sam lit up and said, "Yes, that's where the redheaded woodpeckers eat up the courthouse." As each boy said where he was from, Sam had something special to say about the place.

"I'm Dee Russell, and I'm from Victoria, Texas," Dee told him.

"Yes, but how far from Victoria?" Sam asked.

"Well," Dee said, "you can get on top of our windmill and see the water tower."

"Not as bad as I thought," Sam said.[1]

Since the Johnson City high school was not fully accredited, Lyndon had to enroll for six weeks in "the sub-college" at San Marcos to prove he was qualified. He turned in an English paper on current politics that was so good that the teacher asked several of her colleagues if she was being taken in. He qualified easily, except in one subject—his mother worked with him all night before the geometry exam, which he barely passed.[2]

He was his parents' son from the day he hit San Marcos. Having learned from his father the simple secrets of politics and power, he used what he knew shrewdly. His mother said he wrote her almost every day. Often he mailed her his themes and editorials, which she returned with corrections and comments.[3]

His first job was cleaning up buildings, tending shrubs, helping lay sidewalks, picking up trash, and (as he once said) "raking rocks" on the campus. But striding into the office of President Cecil Evans, he asked for a better job, and he was made assistant to the janitor of the science building.

One day Dee Russell, going into "Old Main" to get his job assignment, met Lyndon coming out. "I got a job working over two fellows," Lyndon told him.

"What in the world—how did you manage to do that?" Dee asked.

"I'm sweeping on the third floor and they're sweeping on the first and second," Lyndon said. Laughing, they went their ways.

Later, Lyndon said he recited his lessons aloud as he worked alone after the other students had left the school—he practiced oratory in the halls he was sweeping, he made speeches to the walls he wiped down, he told tales of the ancients to the doormats he was shaking the dust out of. "I literally swept my way through teachers' college," he liked to say.

"It makes a good story," said Dean Alfred Nolle, "but nothing could be further from the truth. He quickly worked his way in as an aide to the college president." In a more candid mood Lyndon admitted, "I knew there was only one way to get to know Evans and that was to work for him directly." For most of Lyndon's time at the college he held the plum of a job, special assistant to the president's secretary, occupying a desk next to the secretary's. "It took Lyndon about thirty days, I would say, to work his way out of that janitor's job," his pal Willard Deason said. Since one of Lyndon's duties was taking messages from the president to various departments, he came to be regarded as a representative of the administration. People began hearing around campus that they had to get Lyndon's permission to see President Evans.

Lyndon made $15 a month picking up rocks, $30 as a janitor, then $37.50 in Evans' office. Nevertheless, money was tight for him. When he developed a toothache, he hitchhiked to San Antonio where his uncle put in the filling free. He wanted to be editor of the student paper because the position paid $30 a month.

His friend Ben Crider visited him in San Marcos, and they double-dated some. "He was lonesome, you know," Ben said. Lyndon showed him the student paper and said he was going to edit it someday.

But at one point, deeply discouraged, Lyndon almost dropped out to rejoin Ben in California. In a letter, Ben recalled, "Lyndon said it was embarrassing to go to class with the seat of his pants worn. He said he didn't have any money to operate on. He didn't ask me for any money —he wanted to come out there and go to work." But Lyndon's mother wrote Ben asking him to keep Lyndon from going. " 'Don't tell him I asked you,' " she added. Ben wrote Lyndon back—*I never had a chance, but you do. I'm sending you every dollar I've got. Now you stay in school.* Lyndon hung on.

When his sister Rebekah enrolled in the college he took a second job downtown after midnight, stuffing envelopes for twenty-five cents an hour, to help her. He sold hosiery door-to-door, "real silk socks" he called them, and lots of people bought them. "He was such a salesman, you couldn't resist him," a professor said.[4]

His first roommate remembered him standing in front of a mirror smoothing down his hair, "drawing his neck down into his collar so that it would not look so long," bantering about how irresistible they were to girls. Though pinched for money, he dated different girls two or three nights a week. He had few clothes, but he was neat, and the bow tie was his trademark. When he and some other boys wanted to spend the weekend in Nuevo Laredo on the Mexican side of the border, where there were women available for money, Lyndon sold enough silk socks to make twenty dollars they needed for the trip.[5]

He was sweet, seriously, on twenty-year-old Carol Davis, the daughter of the right-wing mayor of the town. To Doris Kearns, Johnson spoke lovingly of this memory. Carol, he said, was "very beautiful, tall—and blond with dark blue eyes. Her skin was pale and very soft. She was very clever and everyone admired her. I fell in love with her the first moment we met. She seemed so much more alive than all the other girls I knew, interested in everything; she played the violin and wrote poetry but also liked politics and loved out-of-doors. I still remember the summer evenings we spent together, lying next to the river in a waist-high mass of weeds, talking about our future. I had never been happier. After a while we began to talk about marriage."[6]

He promoted a small group including Carol and her father to drive over to Houston with him for the Democratic national convention of 1928. Wangling his way into the press section as a student journalist, he got Carol and her father into the gallery. Here Lyndon probably saw for the first time the crippled Franklin Delano Roosevelt, managing Al Smith's campaign for the nomination from the floor and making the nominating speech. Returning to San Marcos to explain his absences to Dean Nolle, Lyndon charged in waving the program of the convention over his head, bubbling with excitement.[7]

His first item in the student paper, the *College Star,* was printed his second month in school, and by the summer, when an editorial appeared saying hero worship was "rather wholesome," he was an assistant editor. His first signed editorial showed that before he turned nineteen, he already had a bold will to suck up to power and a penchant for the uses of contempt. Students had been using the college bulletin board for lost and found messages and other personal matters. Freshman Johnson wrote that "certain college celebrities" were misusing the board, which "must be kept free for school matters." He hoped the school's officials would not have to take steps to stop "this ridiculous practice. It is appallingly undignified and grossly ignorant of seniors and sophomores to indulge in such . . . silly practices." Here is the shrewd freshman depreciating certain popular older students to gain favor with the college president.

Another editorial Lyndon probably wrote pled for courtesy, which was described as kindness and unselfishness growing out of the "desire to please." The picture of him in the 1927 student annual showed a canny face, intelligent eyes, his hair slicked down. "Lyndon was always respectful and all," said the dean of the college.[8]

"He had a peculiar effect on both the faculty and the students," English teacher Mattie Allison said. "You either liked him or you didn't. But Dr. Evans had the highest regard and respect for Lyndon. . . . Lyndon as a student knew how to ingratiate himself. . . ."

One day he was walking along on campus with his cousin Ava, who was just "a little country girl" who worked hard at her books. She was carrying her copy of the student annual, and as they walked along she showed Lyndon that a professor had written in the annual for her, "Keep your mind open. There is lots to be learned that is not written in books."

"Ava," Lyndon said, "this is the best thing that was ever written for you. The first thing you want to do is to know people—and don't play sandlot ball; play in the big leagues . . . get to know the first team."

"Why, Lyndon," she said, "I wouldn't dare to go up to President Evans's office!"

"That's where you want to *start,*" he told her.

Chosen editor of the *Star* by the student council in the summer of 1928, he at once began running sketches of people in the administration, and in the editorial about his boss he practiced shameless flattery, "Dr. Evans is greatest as a man. . . . With depth of human sympathy rarely surpassed, unfailing cheerfulness, geniality, kind firmness," and so on. Lyndon "was in and out of Dr. Evans's office all the time," as an assistant registrar remembered. Little wonder that Evans took a shine to him. "I was tremendously fond of him," Evans said. "We promoted him to increasingly responsible positions. . . . He could handle people extremely well."

Using the paper as a tool in his personal advancement, Lyndon was laying the basis (in his example to himself) for his lifelong attitude toward newspaper people, judging them according to whether they had the good sense to help him or the stupidity to hurt him. Glomming onto Evans, Johnson was also beginning his practice of the art of protégéship. Older men, seeing his energy, ability, and willingness to serve them without doubts, used him and, in return for his loyalty to them, advanced him.

Evans, a moderate with a keen sensitivity to shifts in the winds, a politician who had never run for office, enjoyed the young man's boldness and dash, later kidding him, "I could hardly tell who was president of the school, you or me." Having no son of his own, Evans taught Lyndon the ropes as if he was his own boy. He may have turned him away from teaching toward politics, for he told him, "A teacher is a law unto himself in the classroom. His views aren't challenged very much —you don't have to develop to your full potential."

Lyndon and a football star, Alfred "Boody" Johnson, moved into a tiny room above the president's garage. They slept on cots; since there was no shower they shaved and showered at the men's gym down the road. To help them pay the rent, Evans let them paint the garage, and one spring they painted it three times.

Some of the students began to resent this audacious young man, suddenly so close to the power, and students who put together the college annual let him have it. In the spoof section there was a drawing of a jackass made to resemble him, with this caption:

> Lyndon Johnson: *As he looks to us on the campus every day* from far away, and we sincerely trust he is going back. Sophistry Club. Master of the gentle art of spoofing the general public.[9]

That first year he had been practicing sophistry literally as a member of the debate team. Assigned to uphold or discredit a fixed proposition, a college debater has to use the arguments that come to mind. The topics Lyndon debated often concerned international organization and the League of Nations, but once he and his partner, Elmer Graham, won defending the proposition that the United States should continue "to protect, by armed force, capital invested in foreign countries except after formal declaration of war."

Another time they debated the topic, "Should the U.S. Use Marines in Nicaragua," and Graham said Lyndon "delighted in arguing the affirmative." Graham added, "I think he really believed that we ought to send the Marines in there." Arguing the case for it, Lyndon would tell a story about some boys who were stealing a farmer's fruit up in his tree. He tried to reason them not to, but they kept right on, so without saying anything he got a handful of rocks and started throwing them at the boys, and in just a few minutes, they came down.

The debate coach, H. M. Greene, a professor of government who influenced Lyndon more than any other teacher, put him in the second speaker's position because he was best at tearing up the opposing team's arguments. Greene said Lyndon was "ready with the arguments at any time" and "just went down the line, no eloquence at all . . . and he just pulled the string!" That is, Greene said, ". . . when he knew he had [his opponent] logically and had the advantage of him, why he could become ruthless."[10]

The football players were not only, as usual, favored by most of the girls, they also went to the head of the line at the cafeteria, registered first during enrollment, cut chapel without punishment, and got the best housing. Through a fraternitylike organization, Beta Sigma, which chose its members on the blackball system, they dominated campus politics, too. Lyndon said they elected the editor, controlled the beauty contest, and so on. Outsiders, knowing the organization only by its initials B.S., speculated that its name was "Black Stars," which thus became the public name.

Nolle said Lyndon wanted to get in Black Stars and tried out as a baseball pitcher so he could be considered an athlete. By a Black Star's account, he was considered for membership because of his influence in the president's office, but there was a blackball. Lyndon believed it was cast by a student about whom he had put a snide item in the paper.

Rejected, he "became somewhat incensed," Nolle said. The Black Stars would rue their mistake. According to his brother, Lyndon figured that only a tenth of the students were jocks and that it stood to reason other students secretly hated and resented them. "Since every practical politician knows that hate and fear offer more forceful tools for organizing than love and respect," Sam Houston said, "Lyndon had a rather fertile field. . . ."

The head of the Black Stars was "Boody" Johnson, Lyndon's roommate, and one night in 1928, while Boody was taking a shower, Lyndon said, the constitution of the outfit "fell out" of something and he read it, naturally. In this way he learned that only football players could belong to it. Boody told him he had no business reading it, but it was too late—"I organized the White Stars."

Six or seven boys, including Lyndon, laid the counterplot, selecting the secret name Alpha and Omega. They decided to choose promising boys, the comers with brains and savvy, but they, too, used the blackball. One of the founders, Horace Richards, said he swore in the first members, including Lyndon, with a candle and a Bible in the dead of night on the banks of the San Marcos River. The ten members that night took vows of brotherhood and secrecy. They had a rule that no more than two of them could be seen together on campus—if three came together without thinking, they would signal with their eyes which one was to leave.

Turning at once to the campus elections, Lyndon's White Stars studied the voting blocs, counted the votes, figured out how they could split up the opposition. They gained a one-vote majority on the student council and, through it, control of the student paper and the annual.[11] But before he could enjoy the fruits of victory, strapped for money as usual, Lyndon dropped out of college to go teach for a year in Cotulla, a dusty little town in south Texas.

20. "He Was After Everybody"

Hair parted in the middle, skinny, twenty years old, Lyndon was a caring and creative school teacher in the authoritarian tradition. Qualified by a two-year elementary school teachers' certificate, he was principal and teacher at Welhausen Ward Elementary School on the poor side of Cotulla, a dreary town of about three thousand people, three-fourths of them Mexican-Americans. His $125-a-month salary, fairly good for the time, enabled him to finish college.

The school, still there, is just a little place, shaped like a block, with the auditorium, the baseball bats with colored handles, the secretary and the paddle in the principal's tiny office . . . the school bell ringing. Lyndon taught a combined fifth-, sixth-, and seventh-grade class of about thirty students. In the morning after he rang the bell he would stride into class and his girls and boys would greet him with a song he had taught them to sing to the tune of a vaudeville jingle:

How do you do, Mr. Johnson,
How do you do?
How do you do, Mr. Johnson,
How are you?
We'll do it if we can,
We'll stand by you to a man,
How do you do, Mr. Johnson,
How are you?

"I disciplined 'em, I gave 'em hell," he said—"I'd drive 'em, whip 'em." Once he left the room and one of his better students, thirteen-year-old Daniel Garcia, hopped up in front of the class and clowned around making funny faces. The giggling stopped when Johnson came tiptoeing back into the room. Without a word he took Danny by the hand, led him to the office, and turned him across his knee and whacked him hard on his rear-end, quite a few times.

It was at Cotulla, Johnson said, "that my dream began of an America . . . where race, religion, language, and color didn't count against you." The Mexican-Americans lived in hovels on the wrong side of the railroad tracks, and the Anglos treated them "just worse than you'd treat a dog," he said. His realization of their poverty and oppression was a sort of religious experience. "I could never forget," he said, "seeing the disappointment in their eyes and seeing the quizzical expression on their faces when they had to come to school that morning, most of them without any breakfast, most of them hungry, and all the time they seemed to be asking me, 'Why don't people like me? Why do they hate me because I am brown?' . . . I swore then and there that if I ever had a chance to help those underprivileged I was going to do it."

One day in the grocery store before school he saw a girl he expected in his class. She said her mother did not want her to go alone, and her brother couldn't go because he had failed. Lyndon persuaded the superintendent to let her brother back in. And the new man would stay after school with the young school janitor, Tomas Coronado, teaching him the ABC's with a Spanish-English dictionary.[1]

Working with a Mexican-American merchant, Lyndon persuaded some of his students' parents to join a parent-teacher association. He meant to propose job training for the kids after school, but the parents wanted games and hobbies for them, so he went to work on that with the ceaseless energy that was coming to characterize his life. "I took my first paycheck," he said, "and bought them a volleyball net, singing books for the choir, second-hand musical instruments." During recess the four other teachers usually went into the bathroom and smoked, but one day he said to them, "You take the north corner. And you take the south one. And you take the east one. And you take the west one. And let's have volleyball!" He organized volleyball and baseball teams and horseshoes, or something like that game. Around a big slab of concrete where the students had their dances, he said, "I planted all the flowers, put out shrubs." He asked his mother to send him two hundred packages of toothpaste for the students.

To stimulate competition he gave the students the chance to perform at school assemblies, and he invited teams from the surrounding area to a field day for contests in spelling, speaking, and sports. Over at the high school in town he took on the job of coaching basketball, and if the boys weren't ready for him when he got there he would coach the girls' softball team. He even started a debating team at the high school, although it was difficult to get information in Cotulla on topics like "the British parliamentary system." As he said, "I couldn't understand them, they couldn't talk English and I couldn't talk Spanish"—but his debaters swept all events in their county meet. He thought the high-school football coach, who was his roommate, wasn't worth a damn, so he got into that, too, going to the games with the team and getting back to town sometimes at midnight. Teachers and parents who had cars were soon carrying the school's teams to other towns. Sometimes on their return everybody would gather at a small store across the street from the school for refreshments Lyndon bought. And all this while he was taking an academic quarter's worth of college courses by mail.

Trying to assign each of the teachers one of the new activities, he ran into a revolt. "One of them was the sister of the mayor," he said, "another was the sister of the postmaster, and they kind of had it pretty good—very influential friends around town. One of them was the daughter of one of the important men, one of the bankers." They did not like all the supervised play, and one Friday when Lyndon was out of town with the football team they called on the superintendent and their spokeswoman said, "Our traces are down and we have balked." The next morning the superintendent told Lyndon he was in trouble, "Every one of your teachers struck on you."

They had underestimated the young man. "There was a lady in town who was on the schoolboard that had been to Randolph Macon," Lyndon said. Evidently he went to her and told her what had happened, for by his account she said to him, " 'Well, they don't like to go through these recesses and hot lunch hours supervising these children. They just let them fight all the time. They have had nothing to play with, and they just let them fight. But you just accept every one of their resignations and go back to that teachers college you came from and hire you five more that *will* come here and supervise." The school board sided with her, and the teachers backed down.[2]

Lyndon already knew, too, when not to fight. For instance, he and his roommate, the coach, left the school cafeteria smoking cigarettes, and the next day the superintendent called them in. "It looked like the building was on fire, the smoke was just flowing, the wind was blowing," he told them. Lyndon figured they must have looked like a locomotive. "I am not sure that is a good example to set for the children," their boss continued. "If you could just keep those cheroots in your pocket until you get home in the evening, or do your smoking before you come to school in the morning, it would please me."

Both the young men were ticked off. "It's none of his business what I do in my personal life," the coach said to Lyndon. "I don't think he has any right to tell me what I can do, do you?"

"Well," Lyndon said, "I don't know whether he has a right to or not but he has already done it, and as far as I am concerned I am going to keep my Camels in my inside pocket when I see him in the vicinity."

That was a Tuesday. On Friday they started out walking together again, and the coach lit one up. The superintendent spied them, smoke a-blowin', and Lyndon made sure their superior could see that he had nothing in his mouth. They were called back in.

The superintendent asked Lyndon, "Didn't I see you smoking today?"

"No, sir," Lyndon said.

"Well, I beg your pardon, I thought I did." Turning to the coach, he asked, "Didn't I see you smoking?"

"Yes, sir, I was smoking."

"Didn't I tell you you shouldn't do that? Why do you continue?"

"Well, I feel this way about it, Mr. Superintendent, this is my personal life, and I consider what I do on my lunch hour is my own damn business."

The superintendent smiled and looked reasonable.

"Well," he said, "you're right, it is your own business, but I've got to recommend the coach to the county school board, and that's my business. I'm giving you notice."[3]

Constantly on the move, sparking with ambition, Lyndon was an amazement to the ordinary Texas people he was among. "Everyone in town knew him," a student in the high school said, "he was tall and thin and completely full of energy." When some of the students from the college at San Marcos came down to watch a football game, Lyndon persuaded the superintendent to let him refund the fifty-cent admission fee to them, and one of them remembered, "He came around and slapped the fifty cents into my hand, and *hug* you. . . . Good grief, we thought something was the matter, he'd get his mouth about an inch from yours and look you right in the eye. He was after everybody." All he talked about, said a teacher in the school, was politics. "That was his chief topic of conversation. He always said he was going into politics—like his father."[4]

He kept company with a pretty young woman who taught school in a town about thirty-five miles away, and he fell in love with her, but they did not decide to stay together. One problem for him was that she earned twenty-five dollars a month more than he did, and he considered this "very humiliating."[5]

For the school picture of his class in the spring, he arranged his students in a single line across the front of the school and stood behind them, his arms folded, his back to the arched school door. The school board wanted him to stay on, but he was returning to college. By some accounts, when he left in the summer of 1929 he took along with him a slow student named Juan Gonzalez for tutoring by his mother, or his brother, or perhaps both of them, in Johnson City. Once he was gone most of the activities he had organized just melted away because nobody else had the energy, or cared enough, to keep them going.[6]

---

21. Taking Over in College

With his White Stars controlling student politics in San Marcos, Lyndon was made editor of the student paper for his first summer back, and his editorials reflected his reverence for politicians and his affection for hero-worship.

"Restless, energetic, purposeful, it is ambition that makes of the creature a real man," he wrote. Again, "It is direction behind force that makes power. . . . If one wishes to make something of his life he must have steadfast purpose, subordinate all other hopes to its accomplishment, and adhere to it through all trials and reverses."

He believed that journalists and writers should celebrate heroes—"It seems to be the tendency now," he wrote, "to discover in historic characters rather disappointing and unadmirable traits and to reveal these. . . . This practice deserves pronounced condemnation. The great have their weaknesses, but for these weaknesses to be magnified and exploited works no good to the reading public. Hero worship is a tremendous force in uplifting and strengthening humanity. Let us have our heroes. . . . Petty biographyers with inferior souls and jealous hearts would rob us. . . . Down with the debunking biographer."[1]

The students, experiencing his charging ambition and seeing his gravity about his own balderdash, nicknamed him Bull. He was becoming thoroughly political. He went over to Austin when he could to see the legislature in session or hear Jim Ferguson speak, and President Evans took him over there, too, and put him to work writing reports to state agencies and letters to politicians.

Flattery gushed out of him. After he and a friend consumed some ordinary chili at a roadside café, Lyndon went up to the woman in charge, shook her hand, and said that was the finest bowl of chili he'd ever had. Whenever he wanted a favor of someone he considered his quarry well and then really laid it on. He wanted to help a young woman friend get a teaching job, and he knew that George P. Barron, who had an office in the capitol, was going to become the superintendent of schools at Pearsall in south Texas. Barron's account of Lyndon's massage of him reads like a scene in a stilted novel, but something like it must have happened.

The lad who came into Barron's office was about six-three and looked as if he had missed a few meals, but his general demeanor gave one confidence in him at once. "Mr. Barron," he said, "I am Lyndon Johnson of Johnson City. You don't know me, but I know a lot about you Barron folks."

After returning the greeting, Barron hankered to know if the young man knew anything *good* about his family. "Yes, I do," he replied straight off. "I know that you Barrons stood up to be counted when the Ku Klux Klan started their unholy fight against Negroes, Catholics, and Jews. Good citizens of Texas, like your family and mine, rallied behind the banner of Ma Ferguson for governor and forever put a stop to the lawless acts of the tar and feather brigands."

The superintendent, concluding on the spot that this young man was a good judge of families, asked him about his own hill country. "Mr. Barron," Lyndon said, "we don't have much in the way of products of our soil about which we can boast. We produce a few peaches, potatoes, a lot of billy goats and too much bull nettle. But we have one thing of which we are proud—the finest people under God's green heaven."

By this time Barron was ready to give his caller anything he wanted short of eternal life. He also figured out shrewdly that the young fellow wanted *something,* so he asked him if there was anything he could do for him.

"Yes, there is," Lyndon said. "I hear you are going to Pearsall as superintendent of schools and that you are in need of a history teacher. If my information is correct, I should like to have you meet a young lady who is waiting out in the rotunda of the capitol." Barron went out to meet her, and he hired her.[2]

Wheeling and dealing on campus, Lyndon took over student politics completely. The White Stars put up Willard Deason for president of the senior class, but the night before the election they counted noses and figured they were twenty votes short. Deason said he told Lyndon "we were beat. I said we might as well go on to bed and forget it. . . . He spent all night going around to men's dormitories, moving behind the scenes, giving them that Johnson 1-2-3 pep talk." As Deason said, "When the average man gives up, he's just beginning." Concentrating on the third campus bloc, the independents, Lyndon worked until four in the morning, and Deason won by eight votes.

The White Stars directed the student activity fee away from athletics into debate, dramatics, and musical programs. Lyndon told me that as a member of the student council, "I didn't give one damn dime to athletics." Working through the president's office, he made the Black Stars pay for that blackball in other ways, too. Even though his roommate was a Black Star, Lyndon helped him get on as "inspector of buildings," but with that exception he worked systematically to place his fellow White Stars in good student jobs in offices and the library. One student concluded that the White Stars had control when he noticed they had all the inside jobs, while the Black Stars were working outside on construction and painting crews. As Ben Crider said, Lyndon "just beat hell out of those athletes."[3] More to the historical point, he had practiced himself and found that he enjoyed Joe Bailey's black-and-white antiphony of revenge and loyalty.

"Lyndon was brilliant," said Horace Richards, one of his friends, "he had a high IQ; but he always wanted to be the head man. He kept his eye on what he wanted. Every action was calculated to advance his career. He left no stone unturned." A journalism teacher said, "he was quick. He was no four-flusher. . . . Johnson made friends, he systematically destroyed his opposition, and he made them like it . . . almost. . . . He was a vain boy, determined, and when he accomplished something, he saw to it that everyone knew he was responsible." Deason said, "he wasn't popular with the other students. They felt he was arrogant, and there was a lot of jealousy of him because he was able to accomplish so much." He was always in a hurry, walking "always with long, loping strides, almost like a trot." A student who worked with him said, "it pained him to loaf." Deason said, "He was the only fellow I ever knew who could see around the corner. He was just smarter than the rest of us."[4]

Majoring in American history and minoring in government and the social sciences, he took courses in economics, sociology, psychology, the social teachings of Jesus, race relations, education. He petitioned the dean to start a course in journalism and came up with five others and himself to take it. But a course in novels was difficult for him because just as he had rejected the make-believe stories his mother had tried to read to him, still now in college he was interested only in books that were true.[5]

The Associated Press once quoted him, "I took forty courses and got thirty-five A's," but this was not true. He told me he was a B-average student, and he resented the fact that in his first year, although he had made the debating team, he was given a D in argumentation. Dean Nolle, after studying his records, said he had about a B average, a little better in his major, but not as well in his other courses—"he had too many irons in the fire." Ben Crider said Lyndon "didn't give a damn" for his studies, his mother continuing to write themes for him even in college. After he made an F in physical education he arranged, probably through the president, to take the rest of his PE in special written form.[6]

In classes on government, though, he was alert and sharp. His preceptor was the only government professor at the school, H. M. Greene, who was a welfare-state Populist and a war-minded patriot. Dressed usually in a faded khaki shirt and rumpled trousers, Greene met his classes of fifteen or so students in a room in Old Main. He fortified Lyndon's disposition to believe that politics should help people, but stressed with a dogmatic emphasis that democracy has to mean compromise. H. M. Greene taught Lyndon Johnson that the only time a young man should never compromise is when he hears the call to arms.

Shortly before he died, the old professor remembered class discussions, with Lyndon taking part, in which everyone agreed that unless government paid for the elections, politicians would be corrupted and "we'll go fascist. In other words, 'We hire you, by God we expect you to work for us, not any damn corporation.' " Greene taught his students that campaign contributions were just as bad as any other graft.

"I was a populist, I guess," Greene told me. "Government from out point of view was action of the people in the interests of the people. How much government? As much as was necessary, you savvy, to properly do it. We weren't afraid of the government. . . . You either legislate for the welfare of the rich or the welfare of the poor." Even forty years later, a merry old gentleman with quick eyes, he was holding hard to his view: "The government is working for the welfare, but the welfare of whom? Of the rich."

But in Greene as in the South and West, populist liberalism coexisted with martial nationalism. "Lyndon," Greene said—"he's no boy for allowing an enemy of the country to get by with anything. There's old Sam Houston and others like that, you know. . . . Let's put it this way: He loved a hero. . . . He appreciated a hero."

Greene encouraged his students to argue with each other in class, and two of the most ardent antagonists were Lyndon, taking the liberal side, and Henry Kyle, the conservative. "I don't know how many times I saw Henry Kyle almost get Lyndon down. He never did, though," Greene said. "I *never* saw Lyndon 'outdone' by a student, although Henry Kyle often pushed him to his best."

Greene regarded Lyndon as the best student he ever had and encouraged him to go into politics. "Son," he would say to him in class, "if I were headed for the political arena, I would bear in mind that the United States Senate is one spot where a man of integrity has a real opportunity to serve his country."[7]

As a student teacher, Lyndon taught freshman government and perhaps history. His students, he said, "were constantly raising questions about the constitutional government and the necessity for revolutions here and there and the requirement that we have social changes and so forth. I liked that."

Evans, the college president, told Lyndon, though, that he was too competitive for the classroom or the pulpit—that through politics he could plunge into the combats of the present.[8] If either Greene or Evans was afraid Lyndon would aim too low the fear was misplaced, for Lyndon told a fellow student, "Politics is a science, and if you work hard enough at it, you can be president. I'm going to be president."[9]

To get there, though, he had to work through Texas politics, and the issues those days were local. Until the New Deal, as he said, most of the Texas elections were decided by whether you were wet or dry, Klan or anti-Klan, for or against the local bridge, for or against the "ins."[10] While he was still a student Lyndon plunged into this grown-up, but down-home politics.

For years country people had been gathering for political rallies in a grove of live oak trees at Henly, a town east of Johnson City on the road to Austin. In the summer of 1930 several hundred people congregated there to hear pitches for the candidates in various races. The speakers clambered onto the back of a wagon, its tailgate dropped open, beneath a tree in the grove. State Senator Alvin Wirtz was retiring, and Welly Hopkins, who was running for the seat, turned up to make the case for himself. "I got up on the tailgate of the spring wagon," he said, "and I spoke my virtues."

JOHNSON LIBRARY

Lyndon with pal John Fritz Koeniger in California about 1925.

Returned to the Texas hill country, where he worked on road gangs and helled around, Lyndon with friend Sherman Birdwell, in or near Johnson City, Christmas, 1926.

JOHNSON LIBRARY (SHERMAN BIRDWELL PAPERS)

Lyndon with an unidentified girl about 1926.

JOHNSON LIBRARY

Right, the assessment of Lyndon in the 1928 student annual at his college.

Below left, Lyndon and his roommate Alfred "Boody" Johnson about 1927. Right, Lyndon, far right, as a college debater. The debater in the middle was Lyndon's partner Elmer Graham (young man at left unidentified).

LYNDON JOHNSON

As he looks to us on the campus every day.

From far away, and we sincerely trust he is going back.

Sophistry Club. Master of the gentle art of spoofing the general public.

PEDAGOG AND DEBATERS, EXPRESS-NEWS CORP.

OHNSON LIBRARY

OHNSON LIBRARY

Lyndon with students (he coached as well as taught) at Welhausen School in Cotulla, Texas, the year he took off from college to practice-teach.

JOHNSON LIBRARY

Sam Ealy Johnson, Jr., Lyndon's father, about 1930.

Then someone clambered onto the wagon to speak for an opponent of Pat Neff, the Johnsons' candidate for the state railroad commission. Why, Pat Neff had never fired a gun or wet a fishhook, the speaker said —he wouldn't know what to do outside a pulpit, unlike his sports-loving opponent. The emcee called out for someone to speak for Neff, but no one stepped forward. Lyndon had come with his mother and father. "You get up there and make a talk, Lyndon," Sam told him. "Out of the crowd," Hopkins remembered, "I heard a boy say, 'I'll make a speech for Pat Neff.' I saw a bushy-tailed, bright-eyed young fellow go up." Lyndon vaulted onto the back of the wagon.

"I'm a prairie dog lawyer from Johnson City, Texas. I want to tell you about Pat Neff," the young man began.

"You have heard a man say that Pat Neff doesn't hunt or fish. I want to remind you of the way these Austin sports come out into your hills and shoot your cattle when they're supposed to be hunting deer. I ask you if you want a city-slicking hunter who doesn't know a cow from a deer to be in charge of your railroad business and your bus line business and your oil business, or do you want a man whose character is unimpeachable, and whose experience is already tested and proved?"

"For the next five or ten minutes," Hopkins said, "he made the goddamn most typical speech you ever heard . . . a damn affecting, arm-swinging speech, all in the style typical of the customs of the region and the politics of the time," and he got some applause for it.

Hopkins sought him out in the crowd and asked him, "Why in the hell did you make a speech for Pat Neff?" "Well," Lyndon said, "I just couldn't let it go by default. He did a favor for my dad one time—got him a job." On the spot Hopkins recruited the young man as, in effect, his own manager. Lyndon had not graduated from college yet, but he agreed to help as soon as he did.[11]

Except for the nine months in Cotulla, he had attended Southwest Texas State Teachers College continuously, including summers, from his admission in March, 1927, until his graduation with a bachelor's of science degree in history and his teacher's certificate in August, 1930. Into this period he had packed eleven quarters of courses, a dozen odd jobs, the nine months teaching, and the quarter's work in extension courses while he was in Cotulla. "I went through the course in less than three years," he said. "I never let daylight catch me in bed." Some months he was able to save thirty dollars, and when he graduated he had two hundred in the bank.

In the 1930 school annual's one-line squibs there were glimmerings of his fellow students' attitudes toward him. Said one little item: "Lyndon Johnson was recently asked if he was a college man or had a horse kicked him!" And another: " 'What makes half of your face black and the other half white, Mr. Johnson,' asked the little Politicus bird." Two one-liners used his nickname. According to one, "Bull Johnson cannot out-talk Senator Heflin." The other one said, "Bull Johnson has never taken a course in suction," meaning, one guesses, that he didn't need it.

On the night of graduation, Welly Hopkins was in the audience, and after the ceremonies he and Lyndon slipped off to Nuevo Laredo and Monterey on one hundred dollars Hopkins had saved up for the celebration.[12]

His romance with Carol Davis blew up. As they had marriage in mind, one evening in June she arranged for him to be invited to dinner at her home. "Mr. Davis," Johnson told Kearns, "was a wealthy banker, an extreme conservative in politics, and a member of the Ku Klux Klan," and at dinner, as Lyndon, after some wine, talked freely of his experiences in California and college, the atmosphere turned very cold: "Carol's father hated everything about me." Not only did the host attack Lyndon's father's politics, he said everyone in Blanco County knew that Lyndon's grandfather Sam had been "nothing but an old cattle rustler."

After he left that night Lyndon said to himself, "To hell with the whole family." He vowed he would never see Carol again. Back in his room he sat frozen a long time, immobilized by anger. The next morning Carol went to his room, her face red from crying, exhausted, and said that although it would give her terrible pain the rest of her life, she had to go against her father and marry him. According to Lyndon's brother, Carol told Lyndon her father had forbidden her to marry into "that no-account Johnson family . . . one generation after another of shiftless dirt farmers and grubby politicians." But his brother said Lyndon cut her off: "To hell with your daddy. I wouldn't marry you or anyone in your whole damned family. . . . And you can tell your daddy that someday I'll be president of this country."[13]

---

22. Teacher on the Run

"Old Sam was in poor circumstances, no question," said Governor Jim Ferguson's secretary. "He hung around the governor's office for I don't know how long for Ferguson to get him a job. He was trying to get him a job, any job, for $150 a month." In 1930, the year his son was plunging into politics, Sam got on as inspector of buses for the Railroad Commission. "His duties were made duties. He'd get on a bus and ride to Waco," said Harry Crozier.

"I had to support my brother, sisters, aunts, uncles, Cousin Oriole," Lyndon said. "During those years, my daddy never made more than $150 a month himself, and yet all of us children got through college by helping each other. When I graduated and started teaching, I helped the younger ones. When my sister graduated and began teaching, she helped the younger ones. We all did whatever was needed."[1]

Lyndon had applied for a teaching job at Sam Houston High School in Houston, where his favorite uncle George Johnson was chairman of the history department. Lyndon was hired as soon as a vacancy occurred, but nothing opened up by the fall term. One day the principal at the high school in Pearsall, Roy LaBauve, was passing through, and Lyndon wrapped his long arm around his shoulders and said, "Roy, I have got to have a job." LaBauve, knowing nothing about the Houston situation, took him on, evidently as vice-principal working in the book room.

Lyndon told the teachers in Pearsall he came by politics naturally. "I was raised down there at the legislature, playing around my daddy's desk," he'd say. But the teachers thought it was bizarre, in fact they thought it was "kind of off," that he was talking about becoming president, and when he would go up to a bunch of them they would scatter.

He had been in Pearsall only a short time when one day while eating with LaBauve in the Sunshine Café he said suddenly, "Roy, I could just about cry my eyes out." He had been offered a job in Houston. The situation was delicate, even for as precocious a politician as Lyndon.

He went into Superintendent Barron's office and sat down on the corner of his desk. "George," he said, "I look upon you as an older brother. I feel somehow that you have a kindred feeling toward me. If I didn't feel that way toward you, I wouldn't make this request." He had used flattery before to soften Barron up to hire his woman friend; now Lyndon affected intimacy with him to soften him up to accept a breach of contract. "I don't want to leave you," he continued, "but what I am looking for in life will not be found in Pearsall, although I do love this little city and all its people."

A bit stunned, but his emotions confused, Barron consented to Lyndon's departure, provided a replacement could be found. Lyndon was ready with his sister Rebekah and a young woman friend of hers both of whom he said could be hired for what they were paying him. As Rebekah moved in, Lyndon took out for Houston.[2]

A stripling named Gene Latimer walked into his debating class at Sam Houston High one October day expecting to find his easygoing old coach as usual, but instead there was "a tall young man with black curly hair and a confident air," the twenty-two-year-old Johnson. Gene soon realized that to stay on the team he would have to spend time after school researching into the jury system, that year's topic. Johnson reminded another dazzled young debater, Luther Jones, Jr., of "a steam engine in pants" (a phrase from Macaulay that had lodged in Luther's mind). Lyndon organized interclass speaking contests and awarded prizes of money to the winners. Teachers in Houston, like the teachers in Cotulla, found themselves impressed into service to judge debates after school or chauffeur the speakers to other schools. That winter and spring Lyndon's best teams toured the lower half of the state with him. One group, spending the night at the home of his parents, listened to "a stream of political talk" between him and his father.

Lyndon's goal for his debaters was his goal for himself—to win. When a teacher complimented him for the good sportsmanship of one of his debaters who had lost, he replied, "I'm not interested in how they lose, I'm just interested in how they win." A teacher listening to his debaters tried to whisper her criticisms of them to Lyndon, but he would shout out to them what she'd said. He would cut Gene off in the middle of a sentence to correct him. "He'd roam all around the room," Luther said. "He was liable to be over in the corner or in the back. You couldn't sit still and not do anything."

"If they'd take one side of a question I'd take the other," Lyndon said. "I'd just try to run 'em under ground, just almost stomp 'em, but always would make it clear that I loved them, where they'd never run completely off. I would humiliate 'em and embarrass 'em and make fun of 'em and everything until they got to where they could take care of themselves, which they did."

Gene and Luther won the city debating championship, and the school's speakers swept the city forensic tournament. Lyndon and his debaters were honored at a banquet, and the next day he was rehired with a raise. In all his teams, he said, won sixty-five or sixty-six debates, losing only one. Gene and Luther made it on into the state finals, but there, the five judges' votes were announced one by one, and the outcome was not decided until the last vote. "There was a great deal of suspense for a moment," Lyndon said. "The next vote was negative and I got sick at my stomach"—he made a rush for the bathroom. "He really did," Gene said. "He got plumb sick at his stomach."[3]

As a teacher, too, he worked fiercely, staying up all night grading papers to hand back the next day. Again he was respected as a disciplinarian—a student told another teacher, "You better get things right or Lyndon's gonna *pound* you." But even as a teacher he was a politician. He went to Austin as a lobbyist for the Houston teachers and helped put a tax on cigarettes to help pay them more. "He was ambitious," said a math teacher, Jessie Roy. "He intended to go on up in politics. Everybody thought, his father had been in politics, that he wanted to go into it." At night to make extra money he taught public night school and a Dale Carnegie course for businessmen, part of a program of the American Institute of Bankers. "I used to stand along the side wall and heckle these successful businessmen to death while they gave their talks, so they'd gain some confidence." he said.[4]

As his reputation for political savvy spread he got his first experience working with George Parr and other south Texas political bosses, who were well known already to his father. Bill Kittrell, the campaign manager for a candidate for lieutenant governor in 1930, said, "In Austin everybody kept talking about this kid teaching school in Houston. They all said he knew more about politics than anyone else in the area." Kittrell sent Lyndon into the south Texas boss counties and Kittrell's candidate won every one of them.[5]

Lyndon roomed with his Uncle George at his Aunt Jessie Hatcher's home ten blocks from the school. Lyndon said his uncle, whom he called Senator, was "the best man I ever knew," hard-working, thorough, careful, and frugal, he kept up his sisters, "he cussed me out for spending a nickle"—they actually argued over whether Lyndon should spend five cents for an ice cream cone after school. Lyndon thought his uncle knew about every senator in American history and just about everything there was to know, while George, Miss Roy said, "thought Lyndon just hung the moon. . . . George Johnson was an old-time Democrat, his voice would go up and down," she remembered. "He woulda voted for a yellow dog if he was running on the Democratic ticket. . . . Mr. Johnson was just *shocked* that there would be more Republicans than Democrats."

George's special field was Andrew Jackson, but he also held up Henry Clay as a great compromiser. "I think that's where Lyndon got his admiration for Henry Clay," said Mrs. Roy Dealey, a teacher at Sam Houston. If Lyndon had any doubts about the corrupt Joe Bailey, they were dissolved as his favorite uncle recited from memory long passages from Bailey's speeches and even quoted a poem about him. George thought Bailey was a great orator and one of the greatest Texans.

Walking home one day with the band director, Lyndon said, "I don't know whether I want to stay in teaching or not. I think I'd like to get into politics." His uncle told him he would never amount to much as a schoolteacher and ought to run for something; to a fellow teacher George confided that Lyndon wanted to be a U.S. senator. Mrs. Dealey heard that a real estate agent told Lyndon the way to get into politics was to become a secretary to someone already in office.

Traveling with his debaters, Lyndon would spend the night sometimes with Welly Hopkins, who lived with his mother in Gonzales. Later Hopkins' mother told Welly that during long talks with her, Lyndon said to her, several times, "Mrs. Hopkins, I am going to be president some day."[6]

The chance he had been waiting for came early in November, 1931, upon the death of the Republican congressman from the district extending from south Texas northwestward into Lyndon's own hill country. With the House of Representatives in Washington almost evenly divided between the parties, the outcome of the quickie twelve-day election to replace the Republican was important for the candidacy of Texas Democrat John Nance Garner for Speaker. Richard Kleberg, a scion of the family that owned the King Ranch dominion in south Texas, became a leading Democratic candidate. Anyone associated with Kleberg also became associated with one of the world's fantastic private domains. (In 1977 the oil and gas royalties, alone, from the 860,000 acres of the ranch approximated $680 million a year.) Uncle George told Lyndon he should go help Kleberg, and evidently Lyndon did, handing out posters at a rally and the like in Corpus Christi. Kleberg, a conservative but, far more importantly, a Kleberg, won easily.[7]

Who would be the new congressman's Man Friday? The politician closest to Kleberg was his campaign manager, Roy Miller, the notorious lobbyist for Texas Gulf Sulphur whose wife was a member of the King family which, along with the Klebergs, owned the King Ranch. Miller, moving into the vote-laden Mexican-American west side of San Antonio with decisive amounts of money, had put Kleberg over. As a lobbyist Miller had become a close friend of Lyndon's father, and furthermore, "Roy Miller, a conservative, was Lyndon's hero even when he was teaching," according to Luther Jones. Senator Welly Hopkins, whom Lyndon had helped elect, also knew Miller. The ambitious young schoolteacher had special access to the congressman through the lobbyist.

According to Lyndon's brother, their father went first to Hopkins, then straight to Miller. Hopkins journeyed to Houston to talk things over with Lyndon and then called on Miller and proposed Lyndon as Kleberg's private secretary. Although Miller had not met the young man, he was persuaded and agreed to arrange for Lyndon to talk with Kleberg.[8]

A history teacher, Helen Weinberg, happened to be in the office at Sam Houston High one day late in November, 1931, when a phone call came for Lyndon from Corpus Christi. "He was so excited he didn't know what to say," she remembered. "He said that he would consult his uncle and call back in a few minutes. When he hung up he turned to me and said with great excitement, 'Mr. Kleberg wants me to be his private secretary. I'll have to go up and tell Uncle George.' "

Lyndon and his father, on their way to see Kleberg, called on Welly Hopkins at his home in Gonzales. The next evening Lyndon phoned and told Hopkins excitedly that he had the job and was going to resign in Houston—a friend would replace him there. Kleberg announced Lyndon Johnson's appointment on November 29, 1931, nine days before Congress was to convene.

A fire-eating liberal tax collector in San Antonio, Maury Maverick, Sr., had supported Kleberg with the understanding that if he won he would help carve out a new congressional district Maverick could run in. When Maverick's assistant, Malcolm Bardwell, first met Kleberg's new secretary in a San Antonio hotel that winter, Bardwell said, Lyndon drew him out about what was going on in San Antonio "and acted like he wanted to be of personal service to you, so it made every one of us feel good."

Lyndon seemed to know that whatever ordinary life he had in Texas was over. All day before the train left for Washington he felt "excited, nervous, and sad. . . . I felt grown-up, but my mind kept ranging backward in time. I saw myself as a boy skipping down the road to my granddaddy's house. I remembered the many nights I had stood in the doorways listening to my father's political talks . . . the evenings with my mother when my daddy was away." On the railroad platform, he wanted to say something important to his mother, but couldn't think what it might be. The train came. He kissed his mother and father and climbed aboard, joining Congressman Kleberg, with whom he shared a stateroom.

Lyndon never forgot the moment when, lugging his belongings in a cardboard suitcase, he stepped off the train into the national capital that would be his home for the next thirty-seven years.[9] As he looked for the first time across the blocks of green to the Senate office building he was also lugging, within himself, the bulging, tightly knotted bundle of his heritage.

PART V
The Heritage in Action

A President's hardest task is not to *do* what is right, but to *know* what is right. . . . The answer was waiting for me in the land where I was born. . . .

A President does not shape a new and personal vision of America.

He collects it from the scattered hopes of the American past.

—Johnson in his State of the Union address, 1965

I say the dead are come to slay the living.

—Attendantin *The Choephori,* Aeschylus, translated by E. D. A. Morshead

23. Pioneers, O Pioneers!

As Johnson necessarily carried forward into history the influences that formed him, he acted out in his personal way the contradiction of the frontier ethic: build homes, towns, and law and order, and draw and shoot at the twitch of a wrist. He contained both the aggressive and the pacific, the warlike and the peacelike, the rough and the gentle; one could see the tensions in his rhetoric and his conduct.

Philip Geyelin has written that upon becoming president, Johnson "had a profound, even exaggerated distaste for war, an aversion beyond that of the ordinary man. Yet even this was counterbalanced by a simplistic approach to the evils of appeasement."[1] The western people simply lived with the contradiction between the community's need for peace and the requirement that a man defend his honor, and so did Johnson. His foreign policy killed Communists while building schools and hospitals and civilizing the friendly natives. This was perfectly compatible with, and faithfully expressed, the western heritage of killing the Indians while Christianizing those among them who would go along. Intellectuals—easterners perhaps—may shrug off the myth-norm of Christian pioneering as a cliché. Yet in 1939 Johnson was closer to the high-minded missionary yearnings of the American people when he wrote to Catholics in one Texas city, "By the efforts of the ever-faithful missionary father, the cross has inevitably arisen above the sword of conquest. And by the courage and sacrifice of the men and women who have followed the pioneers, our civilization has been infused with the truths and precepts of the Redeemer of mankind."[2]

"We know how the West was won," he said in Reno while campaigning against Barry Goldwater. "It wasn't won by men on horses who tried to settle every argument with a quick draw and a shot from the hip. We here in the West aren't about to turn in our sterling silver American heritage for a plastic credit card that reads, 'Shoot now; pay later.'

"This land was settled and made to prosper by sober and responsible men and women who built the homes, tilled the soil, and looked after the stock and raised their families. . . ."[3]

Johnson made connections; he proceeded by intuition. To him, the people of Asia and the people of the Texas hill country were somehow basically the same, and that fact had effects on history that are still working themselves out. As he identified his own people's problems with those of people in distant lands, he also returned to his own people's methods back when they were as primitive as those Asians out yonder.

On his tour of Southeast Asia as vice-president he said often that the revolution in the living conditions of the people of his own rural Texas could happen for the people of Asia, too.[4] On returning to Austin he said, "From the Colorado in Texas to the delta of the Mekong in Southeast Asia is half a world away. . . . I have taken great satisfaction in going among those peoples and being able to tell them that the Vice President of the United States had lived a boyhood life not unlike their own. I have taken satisfaction in telling them of the work we have done here in Austin and along the Colorado, because this is the work the people of the world need and want to do for themselves. . . ."[5] Conversely, he had confidence that he also knew who the good people's enemies were, out there.

"So many of our pioneer ancestors," he said, accepting the 750-millionth Bible distributed by the American Bible Society, "often ventured into the wilderness with only three possessions—their rifle, their axe, and their Bible. And of the three, the Bible was by far their greatest personal treasure."[6]

Not, however, the most *necessary*. The rifle and the axe were that, as the historian Turner made clear. Whether Johnson had ever read Turner, he had another historian of the frontier, Walter Webb of Texas, on his staff for a time, and Johnson learned more from talk than reading. Webb had already written *The Great Plains,* applying the frontier thesis and analysis to the central plains including west Texas, and *The Great Frontier,* generalizing that same approach to the world, particularly the Western world.

Speaking informally in 1967, Johnson saw Asia as the "outer frontier of disorder" in these times, to be tamed, he said, by the methods of the pioneers who "had a rifle in one hand and an axe in the other." The question raised by the analogy—what moral right have Americans to kill en masse with super-weapons when the frontier isn't American—was for Johnson just another problem in rhetoric. "We are fighting for freedom for ourselves," he said. "The war is not in San Francisco, but the war wasn't in this country when the Battle of Britain started."[7] As though, if any nation bombed or invaded San Francisco, their home base would last long. As a word-juggler Johnson knew his argument was eyewash, although it might work with some people. With his Bible, his rifle, and his axe, he wanted to help those people over there, and knowing that this missionary motive alone would not carry the country along with him in the bloody course he had set, he contended we were in mortal danger in Asia.

What, historically, do the rifle and the axe of the pioneer mean? "They mean," wrote Turner, "a training in aggressive courage, in domination, in directness of action, in destructiveness. . . . [F]ired with the ideal of subduing the wilderness, the destroying pioneer fought his way across the continent, masterful and wasteful, preparing the way by seeking the immediate thing, rejoicing in rude strength and wilful achievement. But even this backwoodsman was more than a mere destroyer. He had visions. He was finder as well as fighter—the trail-maker for civilization, the inventor of new ways. . . . He appealed to lynch law with little hesitation. He was impatient of any governmental restriction upon his individual right to deal with the wilderness. . . . But quite as deeply fixed in the pioneer's mind as the ideal of individualism was the ideal of democracy."[8]

Carrying forward John Kennedy's own coupling of the Peace Corps and counterrevolutionary guerrilla warfare on the "New Frontier" abroad, at once visionary and destructive, Johnson's fundamental foreign policy was the promise and purpose of a worldwide war on poverty for the values of individualism and democracy, along with the use of our fearful force to attain the immediate thing—stopping the revolution in Santo Domingo without waiting for the Organization of American States, stopping the Viet Cong in Vietnam without as much as a by-your-leave to the United Nations.

People could not believe Johnson was *serious* when he said we were doing Vietnam many kindnesses. The press, condemned from official Washington to official Saigon for paying more attention to the mayhem than the "village-building," bore up as well as possible. Johnson of course knew that the little country was double-damned as the battleground for what he regarded as our war against aggressive communism for the whole of Asia, but nevertheless he said, even as the friars on the American frontier must have said about the Indians who were not butchered before they could be pacified and converted:

"Captain Carpenter giving an order to come in and bomb his position is much more dramatic than a Marine who is washing the kids, treating their wounds, and teaching them to read and write—a Marine who has fought all day, working all night to help in these things.

"What we are doing in education, in health, in conservation and in beautification, in housing, and in the slums in this country is contagious. It is moving to other countries.

"We are setting an example for other countries."[9]

Frontiers are exciting and romantic. The explorer scouts forward into the unknown and dangerous wilderness, acting for those he comes from. Anything can happen and something new is happening that history will look back to.

The one great trouble with a foreign policy for pioneers is that you need savages for it. For Communists the savages may be capitalists; for Americans, Communists.

America is a mainly Christian nation, a business nation, and we are free. The national purpose that came upon us as ours in the Vietnam War was a long time gathering. To name it is to oversimplify it, but it was Christian anticommunism. The national theology and the national economics converged into the one ideal most universally valued among Americans—personal liberty—and Americans became pioneers again, holy crusaders set forth in the world. Perhaps it will happen soon again.

---

24. Two Patriotic Cowboys

Patriotism with a vengeance, which characterizes the administration of actor-cowboy Ronald Reagan, has also been a hallmark of two other presidencies in this century.

Running in 1964, Lyndon Johnson observed, ". . . what Theodore Roosevelt said back there a half century or more ago is as true tonight as it was then: 'Speak softly and carry a big stick.' . . . We speak softly, we carry a big stick."

"I was sent a copy of the *New York Times,* the front page, for the day I was born in 1908," President Johnson told a press conference on his birthday in 1966. "You will see that the Presidents of that period and the President of today have a good many things in common—and we are getting more of them done now. . . . Here are some headlines . . . 'Roosevelt To Stop Big Man's Rascality—Instructs Farmers in Their Duties.' "[1]

Teddy Roosevelt, Johnson told me in the White House in 1967, was one of his heroes, "a great conservationist . . . a great cowboy." As a boy

Lyndon learned about the Rough Rider in civics class, and "Papa made me name all the presidents when we were little boys," he said. Sensitive to the obvious implications concerning Vietnam, Johnson specified that he admired the first Roosevelt not for his exploits at San Juan Hill, but for his work for conservation and his "courage to stand up to predatory interests." To Kearns he said that Teddy was the local hero, and "Whenever I pictured Teddy Roosevelt, I saw him running or riding, always moving, his fists clenched, his eyes glaring, speaking out against the interests on behalf of the people."[2]

Early in the first year of Johnson's elected term, however, he wrote a letter to Alice Roosevelt Longworth on the occasion of the forty-sixth anniversary of the death of her father, Theodore Roosevelt. A month after this letter, Johnson sent the first waves of American bombers over Vietnam. One can see that the intention of doing it was in his mind as he wrote to the daughter of the Rough Rider.

Theodore Roosevelt, Johnson wrote Mrs. Longworth, was "the first modern President," and "he pioneered in making the economic and social welfare of the whole population a fundamental concept of government. Perhaps above all—at a time when American eyes were turned doggedly inward—he recognized that the United States had to play a continuing role in the world and he outlined with far-seeing realism the nature of that role."

Johnson quoted T.R. saying in 1911, "The United States of America has not the option as to whether it will or will not play a great part in the world. It *must* play a great part. All that it can decide is whether it will play that part well or badly. And it can play it badly if it adopts the role either of the coward or the bully."[3]

Eight years before saying what Johnson had quoted, the first Roosevelt had declared the emotional basis of his nationalism. "I believe," he said in Wisconsin in 1903, "that we are now, at the onset of the twentieth century, face to face with great world problems; that we cannot help playing the part of a great world power. . . . The man who is a weakling, who is a coward, we all despise, and we ought to despise him. If a man cannot do his own work and take his own part, he does not count; and I have no patience with those who would have the United States unable to take its own part, to do its work in the world."

There was something about the way Johnson charged around the White House in 1967 and 1968 that suggested the way Teddy Roosevelt must have charged around in it in his day. Nor can one dismiss the parallel between Johnson sending thousands of American troops to the Dominican Republic in 1965 and Teddy Roosevelt's own intervention in Santo Domingo. Johnson ceaselessly insisted that Franklin Roosevelt was "like a daddy to me," and FDR was certainly his daddy in domestic policy, but the first Roosevelt was just as unmistakably his daddy in military adventurism abroad. The main difference was that Theodore used men and gunboats and Lyndon used men and aircraft carriers, high-flying bombers, bombs, napalm, and herbicides.

Theodore had been a sickly and nervous child, he wrote in his autobiography, yet from reading about the soldiers of Valley Forge and Morgan's riflemen, "from hearing of the feats performed by my Southern forefathers and kinsfolk, and from knowing my father," he said, "I felt a great admiration for men who were fearless and could hold their own in the world, and I had a great desire to be like them."

If the young T.R. had any of the scruples that tormented Babel's Jewish Cossack into "imploring fate to grant me the simplest of proficiencies—the ability to kill my fellow man," he overcame them. Boxing and wrestling, practicing with the rifle, he went West to "take hold" of two cattle ranches, and he has provided us with memorable descriptions of the same free cowboy life on the Little Missouri that was also lived by Johnson's forebears on the Pedernales.

"It was still the wild West in those days," wrote T.R. "It was a land of scattered ranches, of herds of long-horned cattle, and of reckless riders who unmoved looked in the eyes of life or death. In that land we led a free and hardy life, with horse and with rifle . . . and as the men usually carried revolvers, and as there were occasionally one or two noted gun-fighters among them, there was now and then a shooting affray. A man who was a coward or who shirked his work had a bad time, of course; a man could not afford to let himself be bullied or treated as a butt; and, on the other hand, if he was 'looking for a fight,' he was certain to find it."

Soon after he was made assistant navy secretary, the first Roosevelt wrote, he became convinced war would come: "When the Maine was blown up in Havana Harbor," he said, "war became inevitable. A number of peace-at-any-price men of course promptly assumed the position that she had blown herself up. . . . [I]n any event, it would have been impossible to prevent war. The enlisted men of the navy, who often grew bored to the point of desertion in peace, became keyed up to a high pitch of efficiency, and crowds of fine young fellows, from the interior as well as from the seacoast, thronged to enlist."

Roosevelt's Rough Riders in Cuba were just that; they included, perchance, half a dozen Texas Rangers. One historian reported that as an officer among them at San Juan, Roosevelt, waving his sword, called on them to follow him up the hill. "His horse was shot, but the rider fell upon his feet and, seizing a rifle, climbed up, firing as he went." Roosevelt told about it, too:

"I waved my hat, and we went up the hill with a rush. Having taken it . . . I ordered our men to open fire on the Spaniards in the trenches. . . . When Haskins' soldiers captured the blockhouse, I, very much elated, ordered a charge on my own hook to a line of hills still farther on. Hardly anybody heard this order, however; only four men started with me, three of whom were shot. I gave one of them, who was wounded, my canteen of water, and ran back. . . . This time away we went, and stormed the Spanish entrenchments."

After he had taken office, Theodore wrote in his autobiography: "a revolution in Cuba broke out. . . . We promptly sent thither a small army of pacification. . . . The situation had become intolerable by the time that I interfered. . . . It cannot in the long run prove possible for the United States to protect delinquent American nations from punishment for the non-performance of their duties unless she undertakes to make them perform their duties."

When Theodore's youngest son Quentin was killed in a plane over German lines in 1918, the former president wrote in a magazine: ". . . the man who is not willing to die, and the woman who is not willing to send her man to die, in a war for a great cause, are not worthy to live. . . . At this moment there are hundreds of thousands of gallant men eating out their hearts because the privilege of facing death in battle is denied them.

"If the only son who is killed at the front . . . is the only son because the Unseen Powers denied others to the love of his father and mother, then we mourn doubly with them because their darling went up to the sword of Azrael, because he drank the dark drink proffered by the Death Angel."[4]

Theodore and Franklin Roosevelt and Johnson were connected by one biographical similarity winding through three generations of American politics. Each of them had in his career an influential interest in naval affairs.

The first Roosevelt made his mark as an assistant navy secretary. He was Franklin Roosevelt's fifth cousin once removed. The young Franklin, admiring his presidential cousin and his works, told his fellow law clerks in 1907 that he intended to be elected to the New York assembly and then to become, in sequence, assistant secretary of the navy, governor of New York, and president of the United States. After a term as state senator, FDR served as assistant navy secretary for seven years, including all of World War I.[5]

A generation after Franklin had cocked his hat for the navy job, Lyndon arrived in Washington and watched raptly as the second Roosevelt renewed the first's conception of the presidency as the active use of federal power in the general interest. The war appeared in distant news, and when Lyndon was elected to Congress Franklin Roosevelt saw to it that he was appointed to the House naval affairs committee. Made a lieutenant commander, Johnson had a short tour of active duty and then resumed his congressional career, investigating the war effort through naval affairs subcommittees. One New Deal source said in 1944 that Johnson had often spoken of himself as secretary of the navy; from time to time rumors were denied in print that his appointment was imminent.

But more than by their common interest in the navy, T.R. and L.B.J. are connected in American history by their coercive uses of patriotism as a tool for the achievement of their presidential goals. In whipping up jingoistic feeling to back himself up as he wielded military power to control lesser nations, Theodore Roosevelt was a presidential model every bit as powerful for Johnson as the second Roosevelt.

When Johnson was a senator, despite frequent reliance on patriotic pizazz, he was first a politician, an operator with flexible principles getting himself ahead, so people paid little attention to his flag-waving. As president, however, he came through to the country as a hill-country Dixie Doodle, born on the Second of March. Responsible personally for the life or death of the nation and politically for the record of the Congress, he took strength from his belief that he was carrying on the heritage of Lincoln and both Roosevelts. In his oval study he had the dauntless Andrew Jackson by Thomas Sully on the wall to his left, Gilbert Stuart's Washington on the wall to his right, and facing him, over his fireplace, a large, new portrait of Franklin Roosevelt by Elize Shoumatoff.[6] He spoke gruffly or angrily, with the authority of his office, about the nation's security, honor, commitments, and power. As Uncle Sam he was pot-bellied and wore a Stetson, but his colors were red, white, and blue.

When Jim Bishop went on a cruise in Johnson's party on the yacht *Honey Fitz,* the engines were reduced in power as they passed Mount Vernon and everyone stood at attention while "Taps" was played. Someone told Bishop the president "insists that this be done for George Washington on every trip. Mrs. Johnson says, 'He thinks it's the least we can do for the father of our country.' "

Johnson's patriotism began in his childhood when his father was having him name off the presidents and he was pledging allegiance in class. When he had fourteen thousand American troops in the Dominican Republic and felt he was "the most denounced man in the world," his mind turned back to that schoolroom. "As a little boy," he said, "I learned a declamation that I had to say in grade school. . . . It went something like this: 'I have seen the glory of art and architecture. I have seen the sun rise on Mont Blanc. But the most beautiful vision that these eyes have ever beheld was the flag of my country in a foreign land!"

A congressman functioning within the magnetic field of Franklin Roosevelt, he served through thirteen years of an era that proved strong presidential rule was necessary to cope with economic and military crises. The second Roosevelt, too, set an example for the young congressman in the uses of patriotism to support his own purposes.

In 1944 Texas oil people and conservatives began a revolt within the

Texas Democratic party. Though it was wartime, the "Texas Regulars" refused to pledge to back FDR if he was renominated. Johnson said, "A man publicly acknowledges his allegiance to his country and to his church and to his party. . . . Republicans who posed as Democrats in the Texas Democratic convention have the comfort of knowing their consciences are clear. They did not take, and refused to take, the pledge of allegiance." In wartime, his meaning was clear. In a radio speech entitled, "What Shall I Write Joe?"—Joe being the boy at the front—Johnson said the convention's resolutions committee rejected an expression of confidence in the commander-in-chief of the American armies. The anti-Roosevelt Democrats, he said, were marching under a false banner "toward secret, hidden goals." In his victory statement on Roosevelt's reelection he accused the Regulars of trying to "sabotage democracy."[7]

After the war, patriotic antifascism was readily convertible into patriotic anticommunism. As Johnson argued the case, support of President Truman's aid to Greece and Turkey and the Marshall Plan was required by patriotism. "It is an American, not a political foreign policy that we have in the United States," he said in 1948. "This is a question of patriotism, not politics." Six years later, still putting down politics as a noisome thing, really beneath the contempt of serious patriots, he said that "the politics of partisanship must be subordinated to the politics of patriotism."

About this time the Central Intelligence Agency, with Eisenhower's approval, helped overthrow the government of Guatemala. Eisenhower charged that the government was Communist-dominated, but the evidence is stronger that the provocation was Guatemala's expropriation of more than two hundred thousand acres of the United Fruit Company's holdings on the Pacific slope. When the strafing and invasion of Guatemala was occurring, Johnson declaimed on the Senate floor, "We have got to be for America first," to "cut out this distrust and hatred of each other which certain ones have been fomenting."[8]

Few paid much attention to what he said as vice-president, but calls to the colors rippled through his oratory. "They came in the thousands and tens of thousands, just to touch the hands of an American," he said of his first Asian tour. After visiting Europe and Middle Eastern nations, he said—while breaking ground for a new dam at Somerville, Texas—that "Everywhere I have gone the people came running and cheering after the American flag." In short, "They love America." He seemed to want to mean that the Lebanese, Cypriots, Iranians, Turks, Greeks and Italians were American patriots—there was prevalent "almost a fanaticism for our way of life and a deep gratitude for what we have done for them."[9]

As president he left the superpatriots nothing to add. "My plane," he said in 1964, "has landed in many continents, touched down in more than thirty countries in the last three years. . . . [T]he door has never opened and I have never looked upon any faces that I didn't think would like to trade citizenship with me."[10]

Patriotism seemed to be the remedy he thought would cure the ailments of American society, too—the racism, alienation, dropping out, and turning on. Out in Pocatello, Idaho, during the 1966 election, he said that when you start feeling sorry for yourself and think, before you turn over and go to sleep, that no one loves you, just ask yourself who in another nation you would trade places with, "which flag you would rather exchange for ours."

Mounted around the wall of his Oval Office were not only the American and the presidential flags, but also, clockwise away from his desk, those of the navy, Marines, army, air force, and Coast Guard, all bedecked with the battle streamers of the major engagements of U.S. history. In Korea, Vietnam, Berlin, he said as Teddy Roosevelt might have in his place that men die together regardless of race or religion, "protecting our flag." Declaiming in South Carolina during the 1964 elections, he said, "There is not a boy in that crowd that wouldn't gallantly march down to that railroad station and put on that khaki uniform if he thought this flag was in danger tomorrow. The blood of the sons of South Carolina is strewn through many nations because they have carried that flag many places in the world and they have brought it back without a stain on it.

"When they lead your boy down to that railroad station to send him into boot camp and put a khaki uniform on him to send him some place where he may never return, they don't ask you whether you are a Republican or Democrat," he said in Pittsburgh. "They send you there to defend that flag, and you go."

In San Diego, during the period when he was considering the decisions which were to lead to his sending half a million American boys to Vietnam, he recited again, but as his own, his schoolboy peroration that "the most beautiful vision that these eyes ever beheld was that American flag in a foreign land." Visiting the Smithsonian in Washington, he spoke of the flag there displayed that flew through the bombardment of Baltimore in the War of 1812 and inspired Francis Scott Key to write "The Star-Spangled Banner." A month after ordering the bombing of North Vietnam, he said, "Of course an American's spine tingles when he looks at the Stars and Stripes. . . . I defy anyone to look at that flag above me and not feel in his bones and in his heart an inexpressible pride and excitement."[11] Patriotism and military adventures abroad blended together in his mind just as they had in Theodore Roosevelt's.

25. The Politician as Western Hero

There is a simplicity in the language of force. Musing on why he had sent his "army of pacification" into Cuba, Theodore Roosevelt said all we could do with delinquent American nations was "make them perform their duties." Ad-libbing to the press in June, 1965, as the people began to realize what he was doing in Vietnam, Johnson said, "If we can get those people some food and clothing and housing and some education and health, we would not be having all this bombing. It would not be necessary to make them." If a fellow is after you, he asked me, "are you just gonna kind of goose him, or sit there and let him kill you?"

On the western frontier, of course, the way to get somebody to do what you wanted him to was to make him. Throughout Johnson's career he had bit-played his favorite roles in the western myth, and that was just rhetoric, a handy metaphorical framework for a bored speechwriter, grist for an idle joke. "Sell the Johnson image," Lyndon told President Kennedy's press secretary, Pierre Salinger, in 1960, "as one of a big, tall, tough Texan." "He is the nation's first cowboy President," wrote journalist Douglas Kiker (forgetting about Teddy Roosevelt). "Possibly," Johnson's fellow Texan Wright Patman reflected, "he is the last Frontiersman."[1]

But just as President Reagan's gun-slinging anti-Communist rhetoric is no longer funny now that he is president, neither was Johnson's once he occupied the White House. The danger of myth as national policy is the myth's very similarity to the past it romanticizes. When myth becomes policy, men who are otherwise practical, mistaking the myth for the past, enact the lessons of the myth instead of the lessons of the past. A legendary compromiser like Johnson refused to compromise about Vietnam because he thought he was acting in the light of experience.

Possibly, too, Johnson himself became, in his own mind, the hero Frontiersman, the Texas Ranger riding down the Indians. Deciding that he had been forced by events to try to civilize the frontiers of the world, he could draw some strength to proceed from his already wildly improbable success with his dreams. After all, he was the president.

One assumes that the frontiersmen of the Old West were not simple bad guys and good guys, but the myth has made them so. The Zane Greys, the Owen Wisters, the thousands of dime-western novelists, the western magazines, the shoot-'em-ups from Tom Mix to John Wayne, are merely variations on a single theme. Wallace Stegner, the novelist and a modern westerner, noticed that the characters of the western tale never change. Apparently, he has written, their fantasies of self-reliance and aggression ("sexually symbolic or curiously a-sexual depending on which critic you read") will be serviceable for another century and maybe forever.

As Stegner sees it, the staples of stock western writing are the freedom, adventure, and aspirations of the men contrasted to the caution, fear, and nest-building of the women. These staples, the thrill of wildness—the security of civilization, the tonic of danger—the tameness of home, are as basic for the western writer as brutalities and subtleties of racism are in the literature of the South. Western dramas are threaded through again and again with the conflict between the sheriff and the vigilantes, between the law and personal anger "enforced by gun, fist, or rope," and often the story line is set by the testing of the hero, a High Noon "walkdown" or the personal administration of justice. Western writing is heroic, Stegner says, and "even the better Western writers do not ever question the validity of heroism."

Like the western myth, western writing suffers, according to Stegner, from "the amputated Present." Writers of the West despise our own times and do not write about them. Conversely, Stegner continues, to modern critics the literature of the western myth seems "anachronistic, belated. For heroism does not survive into modern literature, and writing which deals with the heroic and the rural seems to have little to say to people whose lives are fully urban and whose minds have grown skeptical or scornful of heroes."

"If one assumes that fantasy has no social consequences," Stegner concludes, "then one can take all Westerns and some western literature as harmless ways of discharging the aggressive ego. If one assumes otherwise, then some Western books are unconsciously immoral, and perhaps dangerous, in the terms of the civilization that has replaced the frontier."[2]

If that is right—if the western myth as fantasy is dangerous to civilization—then an important element in American foreign policy has been overlooked by sophisticated analysis, and it will be well to admit the fact in time to affect not only ourselves, but perhaps also other nations that are now going through their own approximations of the Wild West phase. Cuba, for instance; Israel; Libya; South Africa. Although the western myth in Johnson's career began as rhetoric—we sense we are seeing, at one level, mere mummery and froth—eventually the winds and currents of circumstance whipped this very froth into the devastating storm of the Vietnam War.

Some of Johnson's living-out of the myth came through as barnyard theater. As late as 1959 he was serving his guests ground steak molded into the shape of maps of Texas,[3] and his Texas campaigns could become literally theatrical. In 1946 he hired a western music string band that played "Sioux City Sue" and "Home on the Range," as well as requests from the voters. By the time the cowboy crooner and actor Gene Autry joined the Johnson troupe you couldn't tell a rally from a roundup.

Lorraine Barnes, a feature reporter on the Austin paper, reported one day:

"Lyndon Johnson, that old vote-wrangler from Johnson City, paced a fast election-eve campaign Friday through seven Central Texas towns to the lyrical refrain:

> 'I'm back in the saddle again,
> Out where a friend is a friend . . .'

"The voice was the clear tenor of another Texan of some renown—Gene Autry, top movie cowhand, who played through seven successive mob scenes at the hands of Central Texas youngsters. . . .

" '. . . . Just a ridin', rockin', ropin',' Autry sang. 'Poundin' leather all day long. . . .' "[4]

In 1948, hopping from place to place firing from the hip at Joe Stalin and villainous labor bosses, Johnson would spin his Stetson down into the crowds from his quivering, rearing-back helicopter. Sometimes his aim was off, and the hat got stained with mud and grass before the kids reached it. "I'd give a buck to kids who found it," he said. "They battled for it, picking it off the tops of buildings, out of swamps, and off the tops of cars driving down the street."[5]

A regional rhetoric is more than a way of talking, it has a content. Southern American experience is embedded in the southern literary rhetoric—nostalgia for gallantry and the splendor of returning cavalry officers; defeat; bitterness; revenge; personal racial guilt; a melancholy. The western rhetoric, though, is lit up by the new hope and adventure of the frontier, the spirit of conquest, a man's pride in taking a risk, in offhand daring. Did Johnson believe the ideas embedded in the western rhetoric even into nuclear times? Did he say this and that in the western way for effect so often that he finally came to regard himself as controlled by these values as a matter of identity? Or was it all just his habitual way of blustering as he sought to justify what he would have done anyway?

One can canter along to his speakings for years, listening to the western echoes in his language, as all the while the seriousness of what he is saying escalates into the seriousness of what he is doing.

Taking his seat in Congress for the first time, he said it was beautiful to remember that his predecessor had "passed away as he wished, 'in the saddle—riding hard.' " In 1940 he wrote Speaker Rayburn that but for him and others, some of the Democrats running for Congress "would have been out in the bitter winter wind without any firewood." When Lyndon's opponent for the Senate in 1948, a real west Texas rancher, Coke Stevenson, would not come clear on a controversial subject, Johnson tried to hoo-raw him into or all the way out of the corral: "I predicted that my opponent would finally get stuck on the top rail of the fence. . . . I challenge him to lift either his right leg or his left leg off the top rail and get off on one side or the other."

If filibusters were curbed, Johnson told his new Senate colleagues in 1949, "the bridle will be upon the tongues of all minorities, and no mount is free, once the bit is in its mouth." Of a tour he made to see central Texas voters he said, "I like to look 'em in the eye" and see that Texans "want no backing down from the communists." In the fall of Dien Bien Phu to the communists, we had been "caught bluffing by our enemies."

During hearings after the Russians' launch of Suptnik in 1957, he said sundowners ought to be put in charge of the U.S. space program, and a sundowner (in case anyone was wondering) was a man who runs a taut ship, gets his men back aboard at sundown, and is ready for any fight. Johnson was sure that the Russian leader Khrushchev, during a visit to the U.S., had not been able to brainwash "the people who ride the range in the Texas hill country"—Khrushchev was not going to convert "the lean, spare Texan who runs the cattle on my ranch . . . into a communist." The thing that worried him, he said, was that by letting the Russians get ahead of us in space, we had fallen down in "an American specialty from the beginning—pioneering."

In Texas after a tour abroad in 1962, the vice-president was proclaiming that ". . . we will never turn back from any danger. . . ." In his first state of the union speech, President Johnson said we must build bridges to the East, all the while "facing danger boldly wherever danger exists." As the year advanced, he took satisfaction in our military power "because it protects our scalps."

We could not pride ourselves on a time "when outlaws roam the range," he said, but in the Cuban missile crisis, "As Kennedy and the leader of the Soviet Union came eyeball to eyeball, and their thumbs started inching up . . . their thumbs started getting closer to that nuclear button, their knives were in each other's ribs almost, literally speaking, and neither of them was flinching or quivering"—until Khrushchev backed down.

In the midst of his invasion of the Dominican Republic, President Johnson said that country and Vietnam were "freedom's frontiers . . . under attack." Asserting that Hanoi would not negotiate, he added, "I have searched high and wide and I am a reasonably good cowboy and I can't even rope anybody and bring him in that is willing to talk and reason. . . ." Even so, of talking to Russian Premier Kosygin he allowed, "it does help a lot to sit down and look at a man—right in the eye—and try to reason with him. . . ."[6]

Raconteur Cactus Pryor, program director of the Johnsons' radio-TV station, introduced Johnson in 1964 at the Johnson ranch as "the boss of this range" and noted that his range had expanded quite a bit. Autry came back to the ranch for a visit, but there was no danger this time he would upstage the politician, either as a cowboy or an actor. As columnist Joseph Kraft pointed out, Johnson's western shirts were monogrammed, the barbecues were catered, and Muzak piped "The Yellow Rose of Texas" to the sound-system outlets. On the frontier, menaced by Indians, a person tried not to go to the water well alone, and President Johnson was still saying, "He's a good man to go to the well with." Or he'd say, as if nuclear-age Americans still lie behind logs to fight off the savages, "He's a good man to get behind the log with." "There are times," commented Edward P. Morgan, "when Lyndon Johnson gives the appearance of an old-fashioned western range sheriff —alert, narrow-eyed, suspicious of strange faces and sudden movement, cruel in his methods of protecting his home county."[7]

The way Johnson saw the Vietnam War was western, also. Addressing field commanders at Cam Ranh Bay, he asked the Lord to bless them "until you come home with the coonskin on the wall." Gene Autry played on Johnson's stage in the forties; two decades later the stage was the world and reality was the play.

Entertaining one day at the LBJ ranch, Johnson relentlessly reenacted the western myth, serving up western barbecue and six-shooter coffee, jogging along on his walking horse, "Lady B," through herds of panicky cameramen, giving away a western saddle, a bridle, a horse blanket, spurs—even a cowboy outfit for the twenty-two-month-old crown prince of Iran. Dressed in his Stetson, tan sports shirt, poplin jacket, boots, and spurs, he told foreign diplomats who were guests out there during his vice-presidency, "We think you've been in Texas long enough to think like Texans, and act like Texans, so now we want you to look like Texans," and gave them each a Stetson.

Harry Rolnick's Byer-Rolnick Hat Corporation of Garland, Texas, made a million and a half hats a year in the mid-sixties. His sales increased ten percent after he became President Johnson's hatmaker; the company was netting half a million a year. Johnson sometimes ordered batches of as many as three hundred of the "LBJ" silver beaver ranch hats to give away.

In the spring of 1967 he flew about thirty Latin-American ambassadors from Washington to the ranch, presented them with Texas hats, fed them barbecue on red-checkered tablecloths, and had them entertained with a "Texas Fandangle," a cowboy act with covered wagons and buckboards as the props. When Vice-President Humphrey turned up in Dallas to tout the escalation in Vietnam, he was given a Stetson, which he put on amiably. (This led the *Dallas News* to ask, not so amiably, in a caption under a photograph of him wearing it, if he was not the "fastest tongue in the West.") The man on the moon would have been a Stetsonized Texan, too, if Johnson had had his way. He gave Wernher von Braun, director of the Marshall Space Flight Center in

Alabama, a Stetson out at the ranch and told him "to put it on the moon by 1970."[8]

Here he was, running the country, he the one that would have to "mash the button," restaging and exploiting the western passion play. In the White House he cried out, "Why do they want me to put my pistol on the table and just sit here while the enemy is killing my boys?" But this was no longer just scripting or rhetoric, a politician's protective coloration. The myth of the American West had become the mission of the American people. Roughriding into Santo Domingo, pioneering into Vietnam with half a million men, Johnson had brought the West back to life in the world of nations.

---

26. Honor, and the World in Ruins

Regal, moral, tragic, uplifting, like a calm, coercive presence, the concept of honor underlies our trades and ennobles our love affairs, inhabits our dreams and our debates, and inspirits our wars and our make-believes. Adapted from the feudalisms of Europe to the feudalisms of the American South, it still controls southern life in the name of romanticized white womanhood, and borne along on the Westward Expansion, it casts into the wide open sky of the West the hues and majesty of a cathedral. Out there, the southern tradition of the duel became the western tradition of the draw. They were the same tradition, the requirement that a man be bravely quick to kill or die for honor, personally administering justice and revenge, which were often the same.

Lyndon Johnson took honor for granted the way church was taken for granted, or burying the dead. Honor, which the group had the power to say you had or did not have; honor, as much a question of the way a thing looked as the way a man was inside. "So, our hope and our purpose," the president said, is "to preserve our honor without a world in ruins."[1]

Well, then, a man must be willing to die for honor or he is nothing at all. Whether a nation, too, must be willing to die for honor, this has become the subject before us. Now that the great nations have weapons that can destroy civilization, the question penetrating everything is not whether men want to use these weapons (they of course do not unless they are insane), but whether they adhere to ideas that they think might require them to.

The one idea which, as an idea alone, does have the power to bind our minds absolutely is this very southern-western notion of honor. It has such a long, one must say, such an honorable, history, we habitually think about it in terms of itself. Johnson used it so often to justify and validate the war in Vietnam, his mind became so rigid about it, American foreign policy under him became a dependent function of it.

In this, he was carrying forward his own intense regional experience of an ideal norm that is little examined, but nationally accepted.

When the United States went into Korea, Speaker Sam Rayburn wrote a constituent of his, "everybody in Washington, members of both parties, said that we had to go in to keep our word." Before Vice-President Johnson pledged to the West Berliners "our lives, our fortunes, and our sacred honor," President Kennedy approved. During the Middle Eastern crisis of 1967, after Nasser of Egypt had closed the straits of Tiran to Israel, Theodore Draper was authoritatively told that former President Dwight Eisenhower was telephoned and asked what commitment he had made in 1957. "He answered forthrightly," Draper wrote, "that he considered it a 'commitment of honor' for the United States to live up to his assurance to former Prime Minister Ben Gurion that the Straits would be kept open," and thereupon Johnson affirmed that the blockade was "illegal and potentially disastrous. . . ."[2] A commitment of honor made in 1957? Ten years later we had no choice.

Surely the idea of honor is as old as the expectation that "a man will keep his word," but the business ethic about contracts reinforced the concept. Johnson was not one to take bankruptcy the first time he got in debt. What were we going to *do* about that contract—just tear it up? "If America's commitment is dishonored in South Vietnam, it is dishonored in forty other alliances or more," he said. The courts will enforce a contract, but honorable men do not need such compulsion, because *honor requires them.*[3]

It follows that we do not have flexibility of foreign policy contrary to these contracts, even though we now live in a world in which the inflexibility of a great nuclear power can close down civilization in half an hour. Honor, as we have received it from the pre-Hiroshima heritage, compels us, not because it proceeds from a situation that objectively compels us, but because it is regarded as mandatory in itself. We continue to accept, in nuclear times, the imperative element of its prenuclear content: "We gave our word: *we have to.*"

Raging around the White House under political siege on Vietnam, Johnson may have overstated the importance of honor in his own mind, and he certainly overstated the case that the U.S. was bound to Vietnam by an unconditional commitment of honor made before he became president. Again and again, justifying, justifying, justifying the war, he spoke of the Southeast Asia Treaty Organization, the pact that bound us in honor. In fact, the SEATO treaty did no such thing.

Johnson's national security adviser, Walt Rostow, misrepresented the facts about SEATO, too, claiming, in 1966, that the U.S. obligation under its terms "has from the outset guided our actions in South Vietnam." The Vietnam escalation was based on "our word," which we had given, that we could not be "disloyal" to "our treaty obligations," he said in 1967. In 1964, in secret testimony later released, the same Rostow had told senators that while the SEATO treaty had been "a substantiating basis for our presence" in Vietnam, "we are not acting specifically under the SEATO treaty."

Richard Goodwin said that, as a Johnson staffer, he sat in on the discussions where the decisions were made to send in U.S. troops and bomb the North, and "I never heard *any* person say to President Johnson that we had to do this because a treaty required it." Instead, "They came and said, 'Look, we're losing.' There was a lot to it, but that's what it came down to. . . . If anyone had brought [the treaty] up, we'd have laughed."[4]

Johnson also argued that Eisenhower had bound the U.S. to Vietnam by a letter he sent to the then president of South Vietnam offering assistance in "developing a strong viable state, capable of resisting attempted subversion or aggression through military means." Johnson said, "Ike has made a promise. I have to keep it." Eisenhower's offer, however, was conditioned on the Diem government "undertaking needed reforms," which obviously it did not do.[5]

But even as the sophistry in Johnson's arguments for honor must be disallowed, it must be conceded that he also believed he was speaking for the nation when he said honor required his policies in Vietnam—and he may have been. "We love peace. We hate war. But our course is charted always by the compass of honor," he said. "Our national honor required us to pursue the course of conduct that we have followed." He meant, and he said he meant, that we had no choice: "We are there because . . . we remain fixed on the pursuit of freedom as a deep and moral obligation *that will not let us go."*

Just as with personal honor, in the final extremity national honor means we will keep on with it, *no matter what.* "We must do whatever must be done to insure our success," he told congressmen in 1965. "This is the firm and irrevocable commitment of our people and our nation, whatever the risk and whatever the cost." True, "there is a world to be helped. *Yet we do what we must."* (Italics provided.)

Even, say, to the deaths of whole nations, including our own? Johnson as president seldom discussed that question in public. Once, though, he did say that men like the black hero Milton Olive "die for honor. Nations that are without honor die, too, but without purpose and without cause." Here still and here again was Mark Twain's Sir Walter Scott with his fair ladies and gallant knights, his adventures and enchantments, setting the world "in love with dreams and phantoms; with decayed and swinish forms of religion; with decayed and degraded systems of government; with the sillinesses and emptinesses, sham grandeurs, sham gauds, and sham chivalries of a brainless and worthless long-vanished society . . . and the jejune romanticism of an absurd past that is dead, and out of charity ought to be buried."[6]

A person's life is not so dear that any price should be paid to go on living it. A person's willingness to risk loss and death or to die for a belief or others is one of the meanings of personal honor.

Yet personal honor assumes the life continuum: Even if dying we commit our own mortality to the memory and reality of others. A president who, consciously or unknowingly, put his personal honor ahead of humanity's right to live would have put himself ahead of everyone. This would be, not honor, but ultimate vanity. A president who mistook his concern for his own honor as his concern for his nation's would be guilty of an unforgivable confusion. A president who paid with his people's whole life and being for his conception of their beliefs and interests would have committed the terminal "arrogance of power." And a president who killed another nation on behalf of his idea of the honor of his own would never be forgiven by the human race or history.

Yet here we still are. "The lessons of Vietnam" have faded. President Jimmy Carter proclaimed the doctrine that the U.S. will use force if necessary to protect U.S. oil supplies in the Middle East; President Reagan announced, quite casually, that the U.S. will not permit another revolution like Iran's in Saudi Arabia. Like Eisenhower in 1957 concerning the Straits of Tiran, American presidents again are giving their word —therefore, the nation's—and committing their honor—therefore, the nation's—concerning the use of force on the other side of the world. We continue to accept, in nuclear times, our governance by the element in the idea of honor that compels our conduct, not because a situation actually compels us, but because our word is given. We said we would —or he said we would—he gave our word—we *have* to. The idea of honor is still the southern and western idea in the service of which otherwise rational men gravely risk and in foreseeable circumstances will commit upon humanity the hideous crime of nuclear war.

---

27. The Nationalization of Courage

The military castes of the nation-states rely on a weapon that is more important than rifles and cannons, flamethrowers and bombs. This is the concept of coward, associated as closely as possible with treason.

Fear on behalf of one's body is natural; anyone without such fear is abnormal. Conscience about what you are doing personally is natural; anyone without such conscience is psychopathic. To get young men to march in formation into hails of bullets and cannonbursts, to get them to burn their fellow men alive and bomb cities full of civilians or jungles peopled by whom they know not, the military has developed and institutionalized the fear of being called a coward. The most powerful coercives for young men in battle are the association of battlefield cowardice with treason, everyone's contempt for a coward, and the government's menace to a coward or a traitor.

In tribal and earlier national times, these coercives worked, just as the weapons worked. Now, however, the mass killing power of the weapons invented in the last four decades has made absurd the idea of personal heroism in all-out war and likewise absurd the inverse concept of coward-and-traitor in such a war's battlefield situations. The need for personal courage, sacrifice for the welfare of others, and loyalty to one's country are as valid as before, but the new technologies of killing radically change every situation they reach.

Presiding over the Vietnam War, Lyndon Johnson ruthlessly and consistently wielded the military's most potent weapon, to call a man a coward. It was not, therefore, a quirk of history, but rather it was the emergence of a new pattern in history, that during his administration there occurred the large-scale citizens' revolt against the war in the midst of it.

Although, for what Walter Webb speculated were physiological reasons, there were a few western gunmen who were literally fearless, most men, especially on a frontier, know fear. They cannot admit it or act on it—that's the point. President Johnson made this western tradition of courage the test of national policy.

One may not take too seriously the talk of a politician who talks as much as Johnson did, but one of his obsessions in his conversation and speeches about Vietnam was courage. And he exuded a certain feeling that is the more important to specify because it was so elusive. He said again and again that we must be brave, but what he seemed to be meaning and thinking, and sometimes what he said, was that *he* must be brave.

Although he had been cool under fire, his brief service in the navy during World War II had hardly established his military heroism, at least not beyond the doubts of skeptics. No doubt he resented the published report—from a source close to President Kennedy—that after Kennedy asked him to go to Saigon in 1961, he "balked for almost two weeks" and then one day responded, "Mr. President, I don't want to embarrass you by getting my head blown off in Saigon." ("That's all right, Lyndon," Kennedy reportedly replied, "if anything happens to you out there, Sam Rayburn and I will give you the biggest funeral in the history of Austin, Texas.")[1]

The call to courage had long been one of the high notes of Johnson's rhetorical bugling. Supporting Truman's cold war aid to Greece and Turkey in 1947, he objected to Henry Wallace speaking against it in

Texas because "the forum for him and his appeasement doctrine is not before the clear-eyed, stout-hearted Texans."

After San Jacinto, Mexicans are supposed to have cowered all over Texas crying out, "Me no Alamo," meaning they were not with Santa Anna at the Alamo, and Anglos came to use the phrase as a comic way of saying (sometimes with a bigoted meaning) that they hadn't done something they were suspected of. In the 1948 Senate campaign in Texas, Governor Coke Stevenson, realizing that Johnson was seeming the more anti-Communist of the two, me-tooed Johnson's stress on military preparedness. Johnson jibed back that his opponent "says 'me no isolationist.' " Texans viscerally understood the implication, which unmistakably had to do with courage. "Texans of all people," Johnson said, "should go on record against isolationism and appeasement."

"The West prefers courage to cowardice," he said in 1964. "Your grandpa wasn't a cry baby and your daddy wasn't either, or they wouldn't be out here in the land of the West."

Charles Roberts related in his book on Johnson that during the Dominican crisis of 1965, the president telephoned A. W. Moursund, his friend in Johnson City, and asked him to go out and see if he could find one Texan who opposed what he was doing in Santo Domingo. Moursund had a meeting of the electricity co-op there in the little town, but he said he would try. A few hours later he called Johnson back to report that he had not found one critic. "This," Roberts said, "pleased the President."

By the evidence of what he was saying privately, Johnson was motivated in his critical Vietnam decisions by fear of being regarded as lacking in military will. One of his closest aides from that period told me that as soon as he became president in 1963, concern built up in his circle that he had to act on Vietnam or be damned by hawks in the press corps and the government. Courage, his courage, was in his mind. After he had ordered bombing raids in Vietnam, allegedly in retaliation for Viet Cong terrorist attacks, he said, "They thought they could frighten the president of the United States. They just didn't know this president."

"[W]e are not going to tuck our tails and run home," he said after his bombing of Vietnam started. "When we are attacked," he told congressmen, "we must not turn tail and run, we must stand and fight." Announcing he was sending more men, he said, "we are not going to duck tail and run." This is the way he talked about these things, on and off guard. "Some would pull out, run out," he answered at a press conference, as though the nation should be ruled by the personal concept of courage. We must not "send up the white flag." The least the soldiers are entitled to "is for you to be as brave as they are." "The American people will not run. . . ."

Johnson told Kearns that in 1965 he feared that if he did not escalate the war, his critic and rival, Senator Robert Kennedy, would say "that I was a coward. An unmanly man. A man without a spine.

"Oh," Johnson said, "I could see it coming all right. Every night when I fell asleep I would see myself tied to the ground in the middle of a long, open space. In the distance, I could hear the voices of thousands of people. They were all shouting at me and running toward me: 'Coward! Traitor! Weakling!' They kept coming closer. They began throwing stones. At exactly that moment I would generally wake up . . . terribly shaken."

"He was caught," his college politics teacher, H. M. Greene, told me, "by the actions of his predecessors, second by his traditions of studying Texas history: it wasn't in him to back out, you know. . . . How in the hell are you going to get out, except tuck tail and run?"—that, said the professor just as his pupil the president felt, makes you "a yellow-belly."[2]

The fates of nations and peoples in the nuclear era may depend on one leader's concern—perhaps even his merely political concern—not to be thought a coward. To some extent Johnson thought the Vietnam situation was a challenge to his own courage, and he projected his bravado about his own courage into a bravado about the nation's. For Johnson not being a coward was not only a personal requirement, it was a foreign policy. International questions of judgment and justice were to some extent reduced to questions of personal manhood. People trying to think, "What is wise?" were pummeled with the question, "What is brave?"

Once a president nationalizes courage, he can himself personify it. If national policy is courageous, the president is courageous, like the fighting men themselves. His need not to be a coward has gone into his shaping of policy, and his satisfaction in regarding himself as courageous goes into his perpetuation of it. By psychological processes going on in the president beyond anyone's close observation, the frontier requirement of personal courage became a requirement of national policy. The president will be as fierce as he has to, he can because he has the weapons, and he makes all this clear.

---

28. Myth-Norms and Maladaptations

Citizens who elect presidents have to try to decide what values they want in the White House. The difficulty for the citizen reflecting on the heritage in action through Johnson's presidency (and by extension through any presidency) is guessing, or divining, how a president thinks.

Johnson did not seem to know what to do to avoid having to "mash the button," as his chilling response to my question about that showed. Perhaps the best way to think about all this is by imagining one's self in the president's place. "What would you do?" Johnson sometimes liked to ask, and it was a fair question.

The most dangerous tendency in the American presidency now (perhaps because it has also been the most dangerous tendency in the prevailing national psychology) is the application of the personal ideas of patriotism, honor, and courage to foreign policy as if the present national and international situation is even remotely similar to personal situations.

The nation can be blown away in fifteen minutes. In thirty minutes or so, perhaps an hour, civilization can be razed. What would it gain the flag to blow away the continent over which it flies? What would it gain a president to save his honor and destroy his nation? What would it gain a nation to prove its courage and destroy life on earth?

The vague but governing ideals of a nation, its myth-norms, arise from evolution and the nation's own cultural and political history. The myth-norms are generally accepted without question among the citizenry. Their salient characteristic is their power, when invoked, to suspend thinking and carry themselves into public action. Each myth-norm has a powerful obverse, for instance, patriotism: treason; courage: cowardice; honor: dishonor. The power of a myth-norm to move people to action abides as much in its negative as in its positive content. There is the Do (the myth) and the Don't (the norm).

Myth-norms are the rhetorical crystallizations of profound collectively experienced, tested, and remembered needs and decisions. But these needs and decisions can become obsolete long before the myth-norms do, and this can cause evolutionary maladaptations. The ideas that control us are no longer matched up to objective reality. An evolutionary maladaptation that can cause the use of nuclear weapons is closely analogous to physical maladaptations that have caused lower animal species to become extinct.

In President Johnson's mind there were certain myth-norms that coerced his thinking: Patriotism, Honor, Courage—especially, not to be a coward. The creators and transmitters of the patriotic heritage—historians, teachers, preachers, and parents—had better think this thing over. If politicians and the prevailing psychology of the people require decisions to use the new weapons in some situations whatever the consequences, the life of the species has become hostage to ideas handed down to us from the recent, but radically different past.

These considerations come new upon us, and old values cling fast to our feelings. In my opinion, President Johnson had not thought this matter through and very well might have responded to a nuclear crisis as a westerner defending his country, his honor, and his manhood to the death of civilization. Increasing talk since the election of Ronald Reagan to the White House that nuclear war can be in some sense survived and won suggests that while much has happened since Johnson, nothing has changed. The leader of a nuclear nation now needs the courage to break all rules and codes if he must to save the life on earth. That is a hard thing, no doubt, for a president to bear personally, but he must, and that is what he should be expected to do. No heritage can be or should be cast off lightly. But the heritage of this and any other nuclear nation that compels mankind toward the nuclear holocaust is the enemy. Only the clearest thinking about this can get us through.

---

29. God Visits the President

A mighty American ruler believed that during his long nights in the White House when his boys were flying bombers over Vietnam, God visited him. We know that when President Johnson feared that an escalation he had ordered might start World War III, he prayed to "the little monks" of Saint Dominic's Church. According to certain evidence of spoken events, he also believed that he was visited by God, in the form of the Holy Ghost, in the wee hours of the morning in the White House.

In the Bible, Enoch, after he begat Methuselah, walked with God for three hundred years. God gave Noah detailed instructions for the fashioning of the three-story Ark in which he was to save his family and two of every other sort of living thing. God descended in the cloud and stood with Moses on Mount Sinai, giving him the Commandments. God answered Job out of the whirlwind, "Hast thou an arm like God? Or canst thou thunder with a voice like him?" A religious president, knowing the nuclear power he commands, well might believe or fear that God has chosen him to deliver the earth into fire.

The boy Lyndon was such a rake-heller, he cannot have been much controlled by the fundamentalist Christian faith he was given, and as he crouched down for the life-long race that was his career he seemed to use the faith as a sprinter uses a starting block. Who could tell if the politician's practiced Christian piety was the real thing? But by the time Johnson was the president, the starting block had become a foundation in him to which he returned again and again for the reassurance he needed. In him the heritage was the action, the Christian crusade of aggressive soul-saving became the Christian crusade of aggressive nation-saving. But in the middle of the night, close by, "unto the thick darkness where God was," he felt an unbounded terror.[1]

The president believing the Holy Ghost visited him is so astonishing, the story must be approached slowly, and in the round.

Regularly President Johnson addressed the annual presidential prayer breakfast, which had been started by Eisenhower. In Johnson's third month as president he told his first of these breakfasts:

"In my childhood, I . . . had the great blessings of a devout and faithful mother. In our home, as in yours, there was always prayer—aloud, proud, and unapologetic. Through the . . . years since, observance of some of that training became irregular, especially the practice of returning thanks before each meal. But in those first dark days of November, when the pressures were the heaviest and the need of strength from Above the greatest, Lady Bird and I sat down together to eat a meal alone. No word or glance passed between us, but in some way we found ourselves bowing together, and I found myself speaking the words of grace that I had learned at my mother's knee so many years ago."[2]

An ordinary man would not admit that even in fantasy he thinks he is God's chosen agent, but Johnson, when he was president, did suggest that God may have taken a hand in his own career to make him an instrument in the war against the Axis powers. After his defeat for the U.S. Senate in 1941, Johnson cast one of the votes in the House that resulted in the extension of the draft by a margin of 203 to 202. In 1966 he said, "I am not sure that some higher force didn't contribute to it . . . that I was there to cast one of those 203 votes that did not send the Army home."[3]

Johnson also seemed to believe during World War II that "God is on our side." Speaking in 1944 to a Baptist church service in Austin, he said the war was "the age-old struggle between God and the forces of evil," and American fighting men had "discovered that God can be in the jungle swamps, in their wet foxholes, in their bombers. . . . In the middle of battle they have known the amazing, loving presence of God." In passing he said that "God gives us the right to know what is right,"[4] and he introduced a theistic qualification to his tolerance for the social forms on the earth. President John Kennedy had proclaimed his commitment to a world safe for diversity, with reciprocal tolerance between democracy and communism, but when Johnson repeated this idea less than a month after Kennedy's assassination, he gave it a new twist. He told the United Nations, "Man's age-old hopes remain our goal, that this world, under God, can be safe for diversity. . . ."[5]

Within the boundaries of Christianity, President Johnson was an ecumenical movement all by himself. His family was Christian unity realized.

Born a Baptist, he had become an elder in the Christian Church (Disciples of Christ) in Johnson City, and he also attended the services of the Presbyterians, Methodists, Episcopalians, and Catholics. Bird was first a Methodist, but had become an Episcopalian. At the ranch the Johnsons might go to mass at eight o'clock and Episcopal services at eleven so they could worship with both their daughters, Luci, a Catholic, and Lynda, an Episcopalian. Or they would go first to Episcopal services in Fredericksburg, then to the president's church in Johnson City the same morning.[6]

Luci, raised an Episcopalian like her sister, was confirmed a Catholic in August, 1966. Both her parents were reported to believe the decision was hers to make, and beyond that, Johnson said, "She comes in and says to me, 'Don't you feel the need to come have a prayer with me?' "[7] and they would go off and pray together. By a story to be related, Johnson considered becoming a Catholic himself.

What part of Johnson's religiousness was political, what part spiritual? Did he feel the need to pray? How deep was his religious feeling, how influential was his faith in his action, how literally did he believe what? Only he could answer, and he did, by signs and more.

He gave generously into the church collection plates, sometimes a hundred-dollar bill. His minister in Johnson City indirectly confirmed that he helped finance air-conditioning for the church there; the priest at the Catholic Church in Stonewall said, "I only know that when the president is here we always have $150 more in the collection plate."

A journalist reported that a certain Sunday morning in the First Christian Church in Johnson City, Johnson was sitting directly in front of the choir of four men, four women, and a young boy and girl, and "The choir sang directly into Mr. Johnson's face and he sang directly back." At a service in the same church the next year he was saying "Amen" aloud and joined in singing "Onward Christian Soldiers."[8]

One night while he was standing on the concrete drive under the giant elm trees at the White House, asked about his faith, Johnson replied, "My faith?" He paused a few seconds, looked off toward the Washington Monument, and then said, stamping the driveway, "It's just as solid as this."

Hugh Sidey, *Life*'s reporter assigned to the presidency, reported this and continued: "Once while walking on the White House grounds he suddenly broke into a stanza of 'Where He Leads Me, I Will Follow.' He has told guests that his mother instructed him, 'There's a great difference between saying prayers and praying.' He grumbled one Sunday morning following an Episcopal service about the modernistic and discordant hymns they had sung. He wanted the old rousers." Sidey concluded quoting one of Johnson's closest friends and advisers saying, "The root of the President's religion goes so deep now as to be out of sight."[9]

In 1964 Johnson had told a group of southern Baptists that the faith of men like his Grandfather Baines might become the folly of their children "if individually we fail to see God face to face. No man knows that better than I do." A story in 1966 quoted him as once having said, "Now I pray several times a day, but I don't seem to get any answer. When I get real low, I call the preacher." He said as president, "I would estimate that I say a prayer about a dozen times a day. . . . I say it every time I am confronted with a difficult situation or if something good happens." In a book entitled *I Believe in Prayer,* Johnson was identified as the author of an article declaring that prayer is daily communion with God and that for Johnson a belief in prayer was "a matter of sure and certain knowledge."[10]

As the Vietnam War tore apart Vietnam, the body politic in the United States, and the Johnson administration, the war became connected in the president's mind with the idea of Christian fortitude. From the pulpit in a cathedral, a Catholic archbishop told Johnson that all he could do was ask for divine guidance and compared his position with Washington's at Valley Forge. A reporter noticed that Johnson "brushed his fingers across his eyes."

Archbishop Robert E. Lucey of San Antonio, one of Johnson's observers of the South Vietnam elections in the fall of 1967, flew back to Texas from Washington with Johnson; they came off the plane arm in arm, Lucey telling the press that he opposed negotiations with Vietnam. Two days later, at his chancery, the archbishop added that if Americans do not believe in force we will be subjugated, and the world, too; "You cannot have peace unless you use force on the evil men of the world," he avouched. As for the president, Lucey said "he's a deeply religious man. . . . He's a deeply religious man."[11]

Despite Johnson's ecumenicism, he was particularly close to Baptist evangelist Billy Graham, who prayed with every president from Truman to Nixon, but said he was probably closer to Johnson than to any of them. During Johnson's first two or three nights in the presidency Graham lived at the White House. "He got up at three in the morning," Johnson said, "and got down on his knees and prayed for me. At six, he'd have coffee with me, and we'd talk over the problems facing the country."

"When I need some good tall prayin', I get Billy," Johnson told me in 1967. "He prays over me at night at two or three before bed, and he gets up at six in the morning and prays over me again. When the family is gone I get him to come stay with me."[12]

The president associated Graham with his own Grandfather Baines. "I guess [Baines] got so much religion here in the land of Billy Graham," Johnson said in North Carolina, "that he became a Baptist preacher in a land of Baptist preachers. . . ." It was at Graham's suggestion that Johnson closed his 1965 inaugural address with a prayer from King Solomon,[13] and speaking at the prayer breakfast that same day, Graham said that symbolically, Sam Houston's letter to Baines about the old general's conversion meant that Johnson had respect for "the 'old faith' that has guided his family, his state, and his nation through generations."

Many times Graham spent weekends in the White House or at the ranch or Camp David. "I remember one morning," Graham related, "he called up to me and I was still in my pajamas. He said come down to his bedroom and have coffee.

"When I got there he was talking about prophecy and he asked me if it was in the Bible. 'Where is it?' he asked, and I called for the Bible. I read it to him and he started to get out of bed. I said 'Just stay there,' but he climbed right out and got down on his knees to pray."

Johnson talked over his serious problems with Graham. "If I happened to be in England, I'd come back and spent a couple of nights with him—things like that," Graham said. Sometimes Johnson had Graham brought to the ranch by jet to conduct services for him, and the evangelist would be caught up in Johnson's tours of the ranch, counting his eggs and chickens with him, drinking glass after glass of buttermilk upon the president's prescription, bouncing across the ranch in Johnson's convertible—"Sometimes," Graham told Marshall Frady, "I was just about scared to death." The two friends would stay up well past midnight discussing Vietnam and other things.[14]

Graham regards himself as "a New Testament evangelist rather than an Old Testament prophet." Be that as it may, the Baptist faith is Calvinistic, with elements of predetermination in it—fatalism in theological form, submission to the God-determined universe. As some theologians see it, Johnson's Christian Church broke away from the Baptists, for one reason, because of a need for a more thoroughgoing belief in free will. Taking Graham as his special mentor, Johnson was turning back toward fatalism—a fatalism he was also expressing in his answer to me that implied he well might not be able to do anything, in a nuclear crisis, to avoid nuclear war. Perhaps the most political part of Johnson's religion was his ecumenicism. Whether he had been affected by the modern scholarship that has mellowed Biblical literalism, even Johnson's friend and pastor in Austin, Dr. John Barclay, did not know.[15]

True, Johnson well knew the political value of his friendship with the famous evangelist. In the White House one of Johnson's belly-whacking stories concerned Baptists' opposition to his program to provide federal aid to parochial schoolchildren.

A powerful Dallas Baptist, reaching Johnson's Baptist press secretary Bill Moyers by telephone, told him, "I didn't know the Pope of Rome would ever take over the White House." Moyers asked what he meant. "Johnson has surrendered," the caller said. "I never thought anybody with Baines in his name would surrender to the Pope of Rome."

The caller wanted Johnson on the phone, but Moyers told him he couldn't come to the phone just then. "Oh, is he too big to talk to me now?" "No," Moyers replied, "he's swimming with Dr. Graham."

"Our Billy?" the Dallas Baptist asked.

"Yes," Moyers replied, "he's been here two days, talking with the

President." Should Johnson return the call? "No, never mind," said the caller. "Send 'em both my warm regards."

"We passed the bill that night," Johnson said with relish.

But Johnson also really relied on Graham. Bill Moyers, a Baptist preacher himself, who as Johnson's press aide often watched the president and Graham together, has said, "Billy Graham represented a basic kind of patriotism in this country—an unquestioning, obeying patriotism, a loyalty to the authority of the president. Billy was always uncritical, unchallenging, unquestioning. . . . [Johnson] found Billy filled a need."

Moyers also said, "Billy, I sometimes noticed while the two of them were talking, seemed to have a touch of secret wickedness," enjoying Johnson's tales about other famous people. "It was an obvious delight Billy received, that you could see in his eyes, from hearing Johnson tell him those little inside stories and things like, 'You know what Brezhnev told me the other day?' He would have Billy completely riveted. And most of all, when he would let him in on state secrets, especially about the war, he'd say, 'Here's how I chose those bombing targets, Billy,' and there'd come this light in Billy's eyes."

At the least, Johnson gave Graham the impression he might follow the evangelist's advice; at the most, Johnson did. For instance, Graham related to Frady that during dinner at the White House the evening before the 1964 Democratic convention, with Graham's wife Ruth also present, Johnson "went down fourteen names with me that he was considering for Vice-President. 'Who do you think?' he asked. Ruth kicked me under the table then, and Johnson noticed it. 'Now, why'd you kick him?' he asked her. She told him, 'I think Billy ought to limit his advice to religious and spiritual matters.' He said, 'Oh, I agree! I agree!' But then when dinner was over and the ladies had gone out ahead of us, he quietly closed the door for a second and turned and asked me, 'All right, what's your choice?' I said, 'Hubert Humphrey.' He just nodded."

Graham also revealed later that once while he and Johnson were swimming in the pool at Camp David, the president gravely proposed that the evangelist run for president. Johnson asked him if he had ever thought of being president, adding, "You may be the only person who could pull the country together. . . . If you ever decide to run, I'll be your campaign manager." Graham replied he thought his own calling was "the highest in the world."

Graham fully believed in the authenticity of Johnson's Christian faith. He said early in Johnson's presidency that the Texan was "a very religious person. He has attended many of our crusades, and he comes from a religious family." Graham also said Johnson had "a great reverence for religious things. . . . He could use some earthy language. He didn't claim to be perfect. But in his heart and mind he believed in Christ."

It must be said that Graham thought this about Richard Nixon, too; but he had some remarkable grounds for believing it about Johnson. At Camp David one Sunday morning he and his wife Ruth walked to the porch of the main lodge to find presidential aide Jack Valenti reading to Johnson, at the president's request, a sermon given by an evangelist in Texas a hundred years before. Johnson said to the Grahams, "What do you think of a Catholic like Valenti reading a Baptist sermon to the President of the United States?"[16]

It was Graham's historical part in the Vietnam War to provide important reassurance in the midst of it to the religious and patriotic president who was conducting it. This became very clear at the 1966 prayer breakfast in Washington. By then dissent against the war was determined and desperate. After grilled lamb chops, hash brown potatoes, fried apples, and fried tomatoes—a sumptuous meal before the fire-breathing camp meeting that was to come—Graham began to preach to the president and the assembled congressmen, businessmen, and professional and civic figures:

Jesus said, "I am come to send fire on the earth," and Jesus said, "Think not that I am come to send peace on earth: I came not to send peace, but a sword. For I am come to set a man at variance against his family. And a man's foes shall be they of his own household."

"Certainly," Graham continued, "this is the generation destined to live in the midst of crisis, danger, fear, war, and death. When we read of the scores of little wars in many parts of the world . . .—when we read the threatening statements of the Red Chinese and of their growing nuclear capabilities—we sense that something is about to happen. . . .

"There are those who have tried to reduce Christ to the level of a genial and innocuous appeaser; but Jesus said, 'You are wrong—I have come as a fire-setter and a sword-wielder.'

"There were thousands of people in Christ's day who could not understand what He meant when he said He would set fire to the earth. They were good-hearted, kind people who were anxious to have a better world. They were idealistic, but they were ignorant of the deep-seated disease of human nature."

In the present day, too, Graham told official Washington assembled before him, "Even today in America, if you are a patriot, salute the flag, sing 'The Star Spangled Banner,' and say you believe in America, you are immediately in conflict with those who are saying patriotism is passé.' " He closed with the Battle Hymn of the Republic. . . . "Our God is Marching On."

Johnson, his Biblical Christianity and his patriotism freshly stirred, rose then and recited from Isaiah, that ancient voice of God: "They that wait upon the Lord shall renew their strength; they shall mount up with wings as eagles; they shall run, and not be weary; and they shall walk and not faint."

The president said he had received a letter from "a dear little lady" whose son had been killed in Vietnam, and he read from it: "Mr. President, I wish I could tell you all I feel in my heart. There just aren't words, so we ask God to bless you and your little family, that He will guide you in all the terrible decisions that you must make. As long as we believe, our strength is in our faith in God and He will never fail us."

His voice blurring with emotion, Johnson concluded, "So, my countrymen, in those words from that dear mother are to be found the greatness of this nation and also the strength of its President."[17]

Graham, in his remarks at this breakfast, hinted that the end of the world was coming. In mid-1968 he openly advanced the view that the end was near. Preaching to twenty-eight thousand people in San Antonio, he quoted Bertrand Russell saying "the world is coming to an end in five years" and added for himself, "Everybody knows it; everybody feels it; it's in the air. . . . This world as we know it . . . will come to an end." As the seventies passed he was still predicting, but with less suggestion of imminence, the coming of an antichrist who will be a world dictator and then "the Battle of Armageddon with their nuclear weapons or whatever kind of weapons they'll have at that period of time."[18]

Whatever part of Johnson's piety was political, he was Old Testament in style, and he was a southern-western American patriot. As he unleashed the fury of American firepower on the Vietnamese, only a feeling as ferocious as Jehovah's against "the deep-seated disease in human nature" could sustain the presidential righteousness. As the Lord of old smote his enemies with sword and fire, Johnson smote his with bombs and napalm. But there arose in Johnson, too, the stricken fear that he might start World War III.

He told "the story of the little monks" to many people in Washington, and finally a fragment of it was slipped into the society page of a local newspaper. A White House spokesman said the item was out of context, so other reporters, including Erwin Knoll, who was then with the Newhouse News Service, gave the context.

The night of June 29, 1966, Johnson was working late in his office as U.S. pilots ("my boys," as he called them) flew their bombers toward the oil depots near Haiphong. This was a new escalation Johnson had authorized, and he was deeply troubled. Luci came in and told him he looked tired and worried, and he acknowledged he was, he had a lot to worry about.

"Your Daddy may go down in history as having started World War III," he quoted himself telling his daughter. He talked about the risk, the possibility that the mission might result in Soviet retaliation. "You may not wake up tomorrow," he told her.

Luci told her father that when she was feeling downhearted, she went to "my little monks" at Saint Dominic's Church, and it helped. So the president and his daughter, with a Secret Service escort, drove to the church, entered, knelt, and prayed. After some minutes the president rose and shook hands with one of the monks, and they returned to the White House.

That night only one American plane was lost, and the pilot was rescued. The Soviets did not retaliate. The next day, after a good sleep, Johnson told Luci he felt much better, and she replied, "I knew my little monks would come through."[19]

According to an episode at a small dinner party in 1967 in Middleburg, Virginia, related to me by one of the guests, Mrs. Clyda Edwards, the wife of the Democratic congressman from California, Don Edwards, Johnson believed that God visited him in the White House.

The hosts at the party were skiing friends of the Edwardses. Clyda was seated next to the Austrian ambassador, Dr. Ernst Lemberger. Austria is, of course, a Catholic country.

Mrs. Edwards said that the ambassador told her that he wanted to talk to her about a very, very serious matter, very privately. He had attended a diplomatic function at the White House, and the president had drawn him aside in a corner. At great length, Johnson talked about what an important influence Billy Graham had been having on him.

Ever since Luci had become a Catholic, the ambassador continued, Johnson had wanted to become a Catholic, too. Although the ambassador was a Catholic himself, he told the lady he was talking to that he did not want the president of the United States to become one.

Johnson had talked to him for a very long time, ambassador Lemberger continued. The president had asked him if he thought the Holy Ghost was making visitations to the earth. (In Catholic doctrine, God is the Holy Trinity, the Father, the Son, and the Holy Ghost, three in one and one in three.) Johnson wanted to know when the ambassador thought the last such visitation had occurred, and the ambassador told him he did not think the Holy Ghost had made any visitations for quite some time.

With this answer the president displayed some irritation and became agitated. Didn't the ambassador think, Johnson asked him, that the Holy Ghost might visit the leader of a very powerful country now that we had nuclear weapons? The ambassador still did not think so, and he told the president he did not. With that, the president told him that he knew the Holy Ghost was making such visitations, because the Holy Ghost was visiting him.

"Really!" the ambassador said, displaying amazement in a manner that conveyed acceptance.

Yes, President Johnson told the ambassador, the Holy Ghost was visiting him around two or three o'clock in the morning at about the time he received reports from Vietnam.

The diplomat, according to Mrs. Edwards, expressed a deeply concerned opinion about this conversation. Then he recounted to her the story of the little monks, which the president had told him. By this version, the president had prayed on his knees for an hour and a half, and he said how goddamn sore his knees got. When Johnson told the ambassador that there had not been a loss on that mission, the ambassador had taken him to mean (he told Mrs. Edwards) that this was because of the Holy Ghost.

Clyda Edwards said that at this point in this astonishing conversation, she tried to pass the whole thing off with a little joke. She had been raised a Catholic, she told her dinner companion, and she thought the president would "find out pretty soon how that old Holy Ghost will let you down."

But the ambassador insisted intensely that he was very, very concerned. He said this was the sort of thing he had to tell his government, since Johnson was probably saying this to others, and what if such news got around the world about the president of the United States?

Ambassador Lemberger, asked about the story at that time, seemed to deny it. "All I could have said," he told me curtly, would have been a banal observation—in connection with another occasion—that the president was a very religious man.

When Mrs. Edwards told me the story—in 1968—she specified that I not quote her or name her husband. In 1981, before closing this volume, I tried again to get the couple on the record about it. "I certainly do remember it—Holy Smoke!" Edwards told me. He authorized me to tell Clyda, from whom he was by then divorced, that it was "OK with me" to go on the record and that he regarded it as historically important to do so. The former Mrs. Edwards, who is now Mrs. Clyda Gugenberger of San Jose, California (where she is president of the Valley Title Company, an underwriting and title firm), had me read back to her my account of the 1968 interview with her, confirmed it as correct, and agreed that she could be identified as the source. She also added some sobering detail.

The ambassador had not, Mrs. Gugenberger recalled, merely expressed concern that such news might get around the world about Johnson. "He said, What if this got to the Russians, and they decided he was crazy, and they are afraid he's unstable and go into a pre-emptive strike," Mrs. Gugenberger said.

She continued, "I think that that was the concern: Suppose the Soviets heard about this and concluded that he was mentally unbalanced, you wouldn't know what they would do, if they thought he was under this kind of strain—especially considering what he was already doing in Vietnam."

Had the ambassador definitely mentioned "a pre-emptive strike"? She said she does not remember now for sure, she may have brought it up or he may have, but the possibility that the Russians might launch a nuclear attack on the United States out of fear that the American president was unstable arose between them during the dinner party in Virginia. Mrs. Gugenberger said the ambassador told her, "If the Soviets think he's completely crazy, they might be forced into doing something."

Perhaps there is some mistake, although Congressman Edwards and his former wife (who is now more conservative than she was in 1968 and looks with some favor upon President Reagan) now stand forward on the matter. Or perhaps Johnson, worried about Vatican disapproval of the war, wanted what he said to get back to the Pope. Or perhaps Johnson was just engaging in the hyperbole for which he was famous.[20]

But it stands to reason that the story is true. Just as the heritage unexamined had become history unbidden, Bible stories and a teenage boy's religious conversion had become a president's visitations from the Holy Ghost in the White House wired for universal death.

PART VI
Moving into Position

One has to be a lowbrow, a bit of a murderer, to be a politician, ready and willing to see people sacrificed, slaughtered, for the sake of an idea, whether a good one or a bad one. I mean, those are the ones who flourish.

— Henry Miller in a *Paris Review* interview in September, 1961

30. Signing Letters with Bleeding Hands

We return now to the moment when, suitcase in his hand and heritage in his heart, Lyndon first arrived at the national capital in 1931. As he looked out across from the railroad station to the Senate office building he was vowing that he would come here someday as a congressman, not as an aide to one.

Until they got settled Congressman Kleberg and Lyndon checked into a thirteen-dollar-a-day room at the Mayflower Hotel. When Lyndon arrived at the office his first morning, lobbyist Miller and Richard Fleming, a Texas liberal who worked in the New York headquarters of the sulphur company, were there waiting for him, but Fleming took an immediate dislike to him. "Most arrogant young kid I ever saw," he said. Lyndon went along that day when Kleberg called on Garner (who greeted the new congressman, "Hello Dick, you old cow puncher!"). Although it was hard for Johnson to keep still, he just listened. A few days later he called in a debt. A congressman from El Paso, R. E. Thomason, owed the Johnsons because Sam had once helped him get elected Speaker in the Texas House. Lyndon told Thomason his daddy had said to ask him to give his son the same help Sam once gave Thomason.

Carrying his boss's briefcase, Lyndon heard Congressman Carl Hayden of Arizona say to Kleberg, "there are two kinds of horses in the Congress—the showhorses and the workhorses. There will be a time when it comes for you to speak. . . . But wait for that time, and always remember that you don't have to explain something you didn't say."

In the mornings about seven in their hotel room Kleberg had a large pot of coffee sent up, which Lyndon took as a hint that he should soon be hopping a taxi to the House office building.

At the office he at once set a killing pace.

On Saturday, December 5, for instance, he dictated 320 letters to Kleberg's constituents. That evening he and his boss met Senator Morris Sheppard of Texas at the Occidental, which the youngster from the hill country excitedly described, in a handwritten letter to Luther Jones, as "an exclusive Washington eating place where they advertise 'Where Statesmen Dine.'" He had met "several political celebrities" and most of the Texas delegation, and "I will go on the floor of the House and see John Garner elected Speaker," he wrote Luther. "I'm crazy about my work—Have a Very efficient stenographer—Jew girl about 28 who was formerly Sec. to several prom. Congressmen. . . . All in all I'll have three assistants. . . . Give all the debate class my love and I mean love too. . . . Write long letter at once. LBJ." At the top of the letter he scrawled the afterthought, "Burn this—Others probably won't understand the personal references."

Shortly before noon on Monday, December 7, 1931, in the House chamber, the loud hum of talk died down: the Seventy-second Congress was about to begin its work. Young Robert Jackson of Corpus Christi, an aide to another Texas congressman, was seated in the Speaker's box at the front of the chamber when his attention was drawn to "this tall, countrified boy, talking loud, embarrassing me," squeezing into a seat about three rows behind him and bumptiously introducing himself to everyone near him. Jackson turned back toward the rostrum, but feeling a tap on his shoulder, he turned to hear this same yokel, his hand extended, saying, "My name is Lyndon Johnson. I'm secretary to Congressman Richard Kleberg of the 14th District of Texas." Not knowing what else to do, Jackson stood up and gave his name and connection, too.[1]

Johnson needed a place to stay, and after the ceremony Jackson told him about a good deal he had at the Dodge Hotel, a short walk from the Capitol buildings. The Dodge was filled mostly with aging widows, but the basement was home for low-paid congressional secretaries. On one side below the street level there was the long row of cell-like bachelors' quarters, each room rented to two men for twenty dollars a month each, four men sharing a connecting bath. On the other side of the basement, with no doors connecting to the men's side, single girls occupied another row of rooms.

Johnson settled in, sharing a bath with Jackson for the next three-and-a-half years. "We were about as close as two people could be,"

Jackson said. "We worked together. We lived there together. Ate our meals together—We were just thick." When Johnson later brought his two star debaters, Gene and Luther, to Washington to work for him, all three of them occupied one room, connected by a bath to another room Jackson occupied alone. Texans Malcolm Bardwell and Carroll Keach lived in the basement, too. When Houston Harte, later a major Texas newspaper publisher, went to Washington seeking a community loan, he spent a night on one of four cots in one room with Johnson, Jackson, and Arthur Perry, Texas Senator Tom Connally's secretary who would later work for Johnson. These were close quarters, and fast friendships formed. "When four men are on adjoining cots," Harte said, "they just naturally get to know each other."

Usually the boys took their meals at the All States Restaurant, where they could get what the Texans called "Fo' bitters," all you could eat for fifty cents. Just before payday they would go to the Childs cafeteria near the post office, where they could eat for a quarter. To be able to afford the sumptuous Sunday lunch at the Dodge, they saved up. Jackson said Johnson's eating habits were weird. "He ate such odd mixtures of food, and he ate so damn much of it. He'd eat chili and steak at odd hours."

But Jackson was struck most by Johnson's "absolutely incredible restless energy." When they went to the movies, "we'd no sooner get there than he'd get up and leave." In the cafeteria he would get at the head of the line, sprint for the table and wolf down his food, and then shoot political questions at his friends while they were still eating.

"Lyndon was the greatest argufier any of us had ever seen," Perry said. He seemed to argue just to hear the answers to what he was saying. He was well read in political history, and he spoke well, but, Jackson said, "He mispronounced many words. His English was poor. He was aware of it, though. He wouldn't use words he couldn't pronounce."

"Lyndon dropped in my office almost every day," said Sam's friend Wright Patman, by then a congressman. "He wanted to talk politics—who was doing what and what the probable outcome would be. He seemed especially interested in the fight I had started to impeach Hoover's Secretary of the Treasury, Andrew Mellon, on a serious conflict-of-interest charge. . . . Lyndon also liked to ask questions about the dirty political fighting that was part of Texas electioneering, and he enjoyed hearing whatever you told him about the earlier-day doings in local politics."

Sam Rayburn, who had also served with Lyndon's father in the Texas legislature, had become chairman of the powerful House commerce committee, and naturally Lyndon now cultivated him, too: the story was later told that when Lyndon developed pneumonia Rayburn went to his bedside and offered to help him with money or any other way. On Sunday afternoons, when Marvin Jones of Amarillo, the chairman of the agriculture committee, was in his office across the hall from Kleberg, Johnson would drift over to talk about how Congress operated. Consorting with all the other committee chairmen he could, too, he learned fast.

His interest was always the same. When he went to a ball game with the boys at the Dodge, Arthur Perry said, he would argue politics through every inning. "He had the most narrow vision of anyone you can imagine," Jackson said. "Sports, entertainment, movies—he couldn't have cared less. It was so narrow it was almost ludicrous." They said among themselves that even when he went to the bathroom he considered the political implications. But according to Gene Latimer, Johnson "had an eye for girls with pretty faces and figures and did not regard too much what was behind those faces," and once a young woman he met at Childs "succumbed almost instantly," and Johnson returned to his room in the wee hours.

In letters Johnson wrote Luther Jones in the winter and spring of 1932, he showed some of his feelings as he settled into Washington. He was homesick—"write me," he told Luther. "Have you forgotten me?" He signed, "All my love, Lyndon B. Johnson." Luther did write, and Johnson replied that the letter made him "long for Texas and dear old Houston and my boys and girls. I had almost begun to think you had quit me." He had heard President Hoover delivering a speech. "Its now after 12 and I've just finished work." His fifth month in Washington he wrote Luther:

"Haven't been out of the office all day. Didn't get up until late this morning so I was forced to rush to work and have been at it until only a few minutes [ago]. I never get time to do anything but try to push the mail out to the people back home. Received over 100 telegrams today. The public has gone wild over the tax bill, bonus, salary cuts, etc.

"You are a real boy. I love you and Gene as if you were my own. I know you are going places and I'm going to help you get there. . . ."[2]

All the while the depression was spreading. About one out of four workers was out of a job, people formed breadlines in the streets, banks were failing, factories were closing, farms were being seized.

Huey Long, the brilliant American leftist with a penchant for tyranny, had arrived in the Senate in January, 1932, and had at once begun a series of electrifying speeches condemning the concentration of the country's wealth in the hands of a few people, proposing a tax on profits, and predicting that the country faced revolution if social justice was not done. He exposed the Democrats' Senate leader as a corporation attorney, ridiculed the Senate's rules, denounced sales taxes, told "nigger" stories, quoted philosophers and the Bible, and recited poetry.

A radical running for president in the midst of the depression, he was a dangerous, exciting man, and Johnson, like the country, was fascinated. The wondrous Huey had proposed that all cotton production be stopped for 1932, and Johnson, on a visit to New Orleans before he had gone to Washington, "became," he said, "an admirer of his because I thought he had a heart for the people."

Robert Jackson did not take his friend Lyndon's political ideas seriously. "I don't know how deep his convictions were," Jackson said. "His political thinking, if you could call it that, was Populist." But Johnson had a standing agreement with the pages' office that every time Long took the floor, a page would phone Johnson, "and I would go over there and perch in the gallery and listen to every word he said." All his life he remembered people rushing avidly to the Senate to hear the Kingfish, and he realized Long was speaking for people who couldn't speak for themselves. "He hated poverty with all his soul and spoke against it until his voice was hoarse," Johnson said. "For leading the masses and illustrating your point humanly, Huey Long couldn't be beat."[3]

Long had been taken with Hattie Caraway, the first woman elected to the U.S. Senate, because she voted progressively and especially because she voted for his bill to limit incomes to one million dollars a year. Though she was supposed to be just warming the seat held by her late husband, she decided to run for reelection in 1932, and Huey stumped Arkansas for her. One afternoon Lyndon, watching from the Senate gallery, was mesmerized watching Long as he was being denounced by one senator after another for invading Arkansas for Hattie Caraway. "He had this chocolate silk suit on—I'll never forget it—and his bright-toned brown-and-white shoes, and he was just marching back and forth," Lyndon recalled.

"And it came his time to answer them, and he got up and said, 'Mr. President, I have been denounced all afternoon.' He looked over at Senator Robinson, who was the majority leader and the most powerful man in the Senate—a very robust man, a very rotund man, he had a great big stomach and had a cigar that he always smoked and kept in the corner of his mouth—he was the most powerful man in the Senate.

"He walked right over to Joe Robinson, put his hand on his shoulder in a very affectionate and friendly way, and said, 'I wasn't in Arkansas to dictate to any human being. All I went to Arkansas for was to pull these big, pot-bellied politicians off this poor little woman's neck.' "[4]

(Long used this line over and over during his seven-day blitz of Arkansas. Attracting huge crowds, he told the Arkansas farmers that 540 men on Wall Street made more money every year than all the farmers in the country combined. Although she had been given no chance, Mrs. Caraway swamped the field. Long's biographer concluded that he had aroused the farmers' vague resentments "into a full fury . . . into a genuine class protest."[5])

Lyndon saw the long bread lines, and he was moved, too, by "the Bonus Army," the twelve thousand World War I veterans who converged on Washington in the summer of '32, demanding that bonsuses payable to them later be paid at once to ease their hardships in the depression. The government said no. Half of them refused to leave the city, so General Douglas MacArthur and the army drove them out with tanks and tear gas. When Johnson remembered these scenes later his feelings for the wretched veterans sometimes gave his words a headlong power—"I went down in time to see the Bonus Army being driven down Pennsylvania Avenue by quirts like sheep by a man on a white horse to the flats."[6]

A bushy-haired young economist from Texas, Robert Montgomery, had gone to work in the Department of Agriculture in Washington, and one afternoon that summer he, his wife Gladys, Kleberg, Johnson, and some others had a long bull session. Johnson repeatedly returned them, whatever the subject, to the political probabilities. He gauged the futures of congressmen whose names came up. When the discussion turned to pending farm bills, he would say confidently, "Congressman X will be for us," or "Congressman Y will be against us." He knew that this congressman represented eleven agricultural counties in Kansas, while that one represented a southern part of the city of Chicago. That night, Gladys Montgomery said to her husband that they had never known anyone like Johnson before, he was a modern version of Plato's political animal, a political specialist who "just *knew.*"[7]

As the Democratic national convention approached, Kleberg was asked to speak for Garner for president, and he and Lyndon worked up a lengthy spiel for an occasion at Johns Hopkins University. Only a few people turned up, and about halfway through Kleberg's speech a few of those began slipping away, too, but Jackson (who was along) said Johnson didn't notice that—"he was thoroughly entranced with the whole affair, as if it had been a Democratic national convention." He had come, after all, from a cabin on a river bank, and here he was having something to do with the presidency.

Once Roosevelt was nominated, with Garner on the ticket for vice-president, Johnson and two other young men appeared at the law office of Harold Young in Houston to talk about doing something for Roosevelt in Texas. Johnson, although gifted and articulate as Young remembered him, "was a tall skinny smiling boy with no brains. He wasn't the leader of that group."

Johnson more or less managed Kleberg's reelection campaign that year. One night during the campaign he and Kleberg dropped by the home of Sam Fore, a newspaper editor in Floresville. The editor took off his shoes in front of the fire in his living room and they had what Fore used to call "a sock foot reunion." "Now Lyndon," he said, "there's just two ways to do a thing—you can coast along and do it halfway with the pilot light on you know, but if you want to get the job done, you got to turn on the giant burner." After the guests left Fore told his wife,

"Elma, you know I think that fella's gonna be in the White House some day."[8] Johnson was frequently underestimated by intellectuals, but more ordinary people, who often have a greater respect for sheer drive, were overwhelmed.

The young, thin-faced Dick Kleberg was a private, emotional man, a conservative rancher-gentleman, scholarly but dashing, athletic but delicate. He was a horseman, a naturalist, a good shot with rifle and pistol, a golfer, a musician, and an authority on farming, genetics, Latin America, and classical Spanish. He would sit out on the screened porch of the Klebergs' house on upper Broadway in Corpus Christi, taking in the bay. Sometimes, when he played the piano, tears would form in his steel-blue eyes.

But Kleberg, Jackson said, "was not very smart, and his interests were not in any drudgery. He and Mrs. Kleberg lived at the Shoreham. The last thing he wanted to do was answer letters from constituents crying during the depression." Gene Latimer, who joined the staff late in 1932, thought Kleberg had no interest in being a congressman except for the prestige and the chance to live it up in Washington. Montgomery said the rich, apolitical congressman from the King Ranch "was never there—he was up in New York playing polo."

In this situation Johnson was the congressman-in-fact. He ran the show. "Kleberg didn't do anything," said Luther Jones, who worked in Kleberg's Corpus office. "Johnson had carte blanche authority." Johnson did not clear letters with the congressman before sending them out —he would even write letters to Kleberg's mother and sign them with Kleberg's name. "He'd call up people and say, 'This is Dick Kleberg calling,' and they always thought it was," said Dan Quill, the San Antonio postmaster. "Lyndon *was* the congressman," Montgomery said. "It was the best training you could get," Johnson himself said. "I would write every letter and sign every letter." Kleberg spent a lot of his time on the golf course, "but he'd back you."

Johnson worked from seven to seven, seven days a week. Often at the end of a day he, Perry, and Jackson would walk to the Dodge and have dinner at Childs', but then Johnson might go back and work until midnight. "His idea of a good time," Latimer said, was "to pick out a holiday, and everybody go down to the office and work." In the car on the way to work in the morning he could "issue enough instructions in ten minutes to put a hundred people to work for a month."

His first rule was, answer every letter the day it arrives. Latimer once saw Johnson signing letters with his right hand wrapped up in a towel so that blood that was dripping from it because of a severe rash would not stain the letters. He got people jobs as elevator operators, postal workers, or doorkeepers—provided they would do extra typing for him after hours. After Luther Jones had joined the Washington staff, Johnson would play off Jones and Latimer against each other, telling one or the other he was doing the most that day. When there was a telegram to be sent he would have Luther phone one of the two telegraph companies and Gene the other, and the messenger who skinned over there first got the telegram.

To control who saw Kleberg, Johnson put his desk just inside the entrance to the congressman's office. Daily he gave Kleberg memoranda with new ideas, assigned tasks in the office, received visitors, read the *Congressional Record,* sought credit for Kleberg in his home district, maintained relationships for him with other congressmen, and worked with the bureaucracy on behalf of constituents. When the mail level fell off he decided that each boy and girl graduating from high school in the district should get a letter of congratulations from Kleberg, and with this he began his lifelong habit of collecting lists.[9]

He drove himself and others so hard, so fast, and so long, "We just couldn't understand what motivated Lyndon at times," Jackson said. Certainly he had already decided that sincerity was no virtue in the practice of politics. Dictating replies to letters from Kleberg's constituents, "he'd have a pile of letters," Luther said, "and he'd just sit there and make a few comments, 'Say yes, say no, put him off, butter him up.' " Nor did he have any compunction about making Luther work until midnight redoing letters he had corrected.

Yet Latimer once saw Lyndon crying as he read a letter from his mother. Jones remarked on "the warmth of his personality during this period. He was inclined to be emotional. He was fiercely loyal to those he loved."

Ben Crider, who had helped Lyndon through school, could not find work, so Lyndon got him a government job and took him to a clothier in San Antonio and bought him a suit. Then Lyndon signed a lot of blank checks and told Ben to use them, but to keep track of what he spent. "That kind of a friend, that kind of a man, is very few and far between," Crider said. Gene ran up bills he could not pay, whereupon every payday Lyndon had him sign his paycheck over to him and from it made small payments on the bills and allowed him ten dollars cash.

Lyndon certainly wasn't flush, himself. One evening about dusk, a pal and he stepped out of the House Office Building. It was snowing. Rummaging in his coat pocket, Lyndon drew out two papers. "Look, Dan, what I've got." They were two $25 savings bonds. "I'm going to save one of those every payday," he said.

Lyndon loved practical jokes, but Jackson thought some of them were almost childish. One of their friends, Glenn Stegall, was crowing-proud of a new car he had just bought. Johnson had someone call him and tell him his car had been stolen and then turned to Jackson and said with delight, "Glenn Stegall is going to run right by here!"

A young Texan named William S. White was covering Texans for the Associated Press and marveled at Lyndon's "furious, almost incredible energy" and his "endlessly varied" questions on the one subject that fascinated him, "Who has the power and how is it exercised?" Vice-President Garner was snubbing White as a young cub, and when White told Lyndon about this, Lyndon put him onto a story that Garner was trying to snatch the postal patronage from Texas congressmen. From then on Johnson and White were friends.[10]

As for girls, "He was quite a ladies' man when he would go on a spree," Jones said, "but his work was his love." He went along with his friends to the socials of the Texas State Society, but according to one contemporary, he usually danced, not with the single girls, but with the wives of the Texas congressmen. Meanwhile, he made peace among their husbands. In the dispute in the Texas delegation over post office patronage, Johnson drew up a "gentleman's contract" splitting up the jobs and with Kleberg's consent won agreement on it from all the other Texas congressman and both senators.[11]

The depression intensified. Boys and men were ranging the country in boxcars trying to find work, and as Johnson later said, "the banks were popping like firecrackers . . . the farmers were burning their produce because they had no market to sell it in . . . soup lines were stretched around the corners of city blocks." Roosevelt was the hope. The day of his inauguration, March 4, 1933, it was raining and fairly cold in Washington, and Johnson and Jackson went to Vice-President Garner's office to watch. Stretched out before their eyes, gathered before the Capitol rotunda, there was a great throng. "The crowds," Eleanor Roosevelt said, "were so tremendous, and you felt that they would do anything—if only someone would tell them what to do." They were in serious mood; guards manned machine guns. Lyndon saw Roosevelt, garbed in striped trousers and silk top hat, front and center upon the canopied stand, and heard him speak, to the thousands below him and the millions listening at their radios, the ringing challenge: "the only thing we have to fear is fear itself." And he heard the new president enunciate a broad new theory of presidential power. If the Congress failed to provide what was needed, Roosevelt said, "I shall ask the Congress for . . . broad executive power to wage a war against the emergency, as great as the power that would be given to me if we were in fact invaded by a foreign foe." On the eve of the Hundred Days Lyndon felt as his mentor Montgomery said: Here was a world to be made.[12]

Johnson's contribution to the early New Deal was persuading Kleberg, who did not believe in it, to vote for it. The patrician rancher regarded the new ideas, Johnson said, as "socialism, very dangerous," and the two would argue. "There were many, many earnest discussions, with Lyndon arguing for these new bills," Luther Jones said. "Lyndon would always re-emphasize the liberal position. It wasn't contrived—he was sincere. Generally speaking Kleberg always went with Lyndon—not without argument."

Kleberg was a power in the agriculture committee, but he would return from the hearings on Roosevelt's farm production control proposal, the Agricultural Adjustment Act, in doubt and confusion, and Johnson would take him on. Johnson was still twenty-four when he listened to the House debate on the farm bill (later he would remember a racist, sexist story Congressman Everett Dirksen told on the House floor then, and throw it up to him.[13]). According to an account that probably came from Johnson, when he learned his boss was going to vote against AAA, he studied the mail and perceived a thirty-to-one trend for the bill; he polled congressional secretaries and learned it was going to pass. "The bill is socialistic," Kleberg said. "Then I quit," Johnson replied. The people wanted the bill—besides it would pass anyway, "I've polled the House and I know it." Kleberg voted aye.

A little later, when Social Security was to be voted on in the House, Lyndon had an intense discussion with Kleberg in the Speaker's office. Kleberg, Johnson said, was talking "about the socialism of Social Security—how dangerous it was. He was close to me, he was such a good man—and so genuinely believed that it would destroy this country. And I pled with him: Please, please, please go and support that measure; and he finally did."[14]

Lyndon attended one meeting of the "Little Congress," the organization of House secretaries and clerks, and decided to take it over. The group elected their "Speaker" by seniority, but at his first meeting Johnson announced he would be a candidate in the election the next week. The old hands snickered, but "Hell," Jackson said, "he just went up and down the corridors talking to people. He got about six or eight of us to tout him."

At the meeting the next week a crowd of new people packed the room and spilled out into the corridor. There was much anger and shouting, and attempts were made to keep the newcomers from voting, but they voted and Johnson won two to one.

From then on the group's meetings were livelier, and members of Congress were often the speakers. Huey Long was acting like a candidate for president, and there had been some bomb scares. As he was speaking to the "Little Congress," poised with his arm lifted dramatically, a flash bulb exploded, frightening everyone and causing moments of bedlam.

Long arranged the publication of his autobiography, *Every Man a King,* only after some difficulty, and then he had trouble getting it distributed, but Johnson got a copy and read it eagerly. He insisted that Jones, Latimer, and Jackson listen while he read passages to them. But evidently it was not so much Long's passion for the redistribution of wealth as it was his charisma and the threat he was to Roosevelt that fascinated Johnson. "I think he thought Huey was destined to shake the country up," Jones said. "Lyndon dictated to me, and I wrote in shorthand in the book, a statement that 'Roosevelt's spending too much money, and if we're not careful he'll lead the country into disaster.' Maybe this was Roy Miller's influence." Miller was in Kleberg's office constantly (Jones did his letters for him).

Through the secretaries Lyndon hobnobbed with in the Little Congress he learned a good deal about the members of Congress—their enemies back home, drinking problems, fears of the next election. Then, he said, although he made $267 a month one session "I asked for the privilege" of being a page in the House for $165 a month to hear the debates and get to know more of the congressmen. "He wanted to get in on the excitement," his brother said. Kleberg consented, and the canny young man made it a point to know every congressman who went through the door. Jennings Randolph remembered "he was there a few months, bringing into the chamber cards from visitors who wanted us to go out to the lobby for a chat. He got to know dozens of us that way." Lyndon knew exactly what he was doing. "I had the list and I studied it," he said. "He knew more people of his age and generation in the bowels of the government than any other fellow on Capitol Hill," said Paul Porter, the Washington lawyer who was a contemporary.[15]

Even when he was a page Lyndon worked for Kleberg after hours without pay. He would wake up Gene and Luther at the Dodge around five in the morning, and seldom did they return before midnight. "Though he was not much older than us, and though he liked females to the usual degree," Jones said, "he worked so hard and such long hours that there was almost no dating at all by him during any of this period. There simply was not enough time left for romance."

Despite his youth, Johnson was considered for the presidency of the Texas College of Arts and Industries at Kingsville (the Klebergs dominated the college and the town). For hours he talked with Jones about how he was going to get scholarships for the students and reorganize the faculty. A lobbyist beseeched him to join the corps of special-interest pleaders in Washington.[16]

In 1934 he went to San Antonio to help elect Maury Maverick congressman. Congressman Kleberg's secretary presided at a table strewn with large sums of money in five-dollar bills and surrounded by older politicians, some of them fifty or sixty. Mexican-American leaders would come in, get their money, and leave. It was the cover story that the leaders were "paying workers," and no doubt there was some truth to it. Johnson was undisturbed by what he was doing, but another young man present was so surprised he felt like his tongue was hanging out.

Luther Jones, whom Kleberg had lent to the Maverick campaign along with Lyndon and Gene Latimer, said, "One of the problems was distributing money to these Latin families. If a particular family had five voters, then that family would be given five times X. I don't know how much a vote. Like if it was $5, you'd get $25. Lyndon and some other people, there were several workers like Lyndon, were mistaken, handing this money out. . . . I don't know where the money came from."

Inevitably Lyndon tied up with Alvin Wirtz, a former state senator, an ardent Democrat, and probably the author of the dream for a series of power-producing dams, "a little TVA," on the Colorado River that winds down out of the hill country past Austin to the Gulf. Wirtz had known Lyndon's father, he was the promoter and lawyer of the Colorado project, and he was the lawyer for the contractor, Herman Brown. Liberal New Dealers like Creekmore Fath, the Austin attorney, looked on Wirtz as cautious and pragmatic—"He was a liberal when it didn't cost him anything," Fath said.

One day in 1934, Mary Rather, working as a secretary in the law offices where Wirtz was practicing in Austin, was astounded when a young man came in and turned the place upside down in short order. "He was very fast and quick and busy and having some of us put in some phone calls for him in between talking to Senator Wirtz," she said. "And yet he wasn't anything but a secretary, too, just like we were." She had the feeling it was awfully important, so she had better help. She thought of Josephine saying, upon meeting Napoleon, "He's like a tornado, that young man." Of course it was Lyndon.[17]

---

31. Suddenly, Courtship and Marriage

Lyndon never forgave his college sweetheart, Carol Davis, for her father's contempt for his family. To be with their other children in the college at San Marcos, Rebekah and Sam had moved there, and according to Sam Houston, Carol, hearing that Lyndon was coming home on a visit from Washington, would turn up at the house, but Lyndon would walk in and see her, say "Come on!" to Sam Houston, and take off.[1] In her stead he met a woman he wanted to marry and proposed to her within twenty-four hours.

Claudia "Lady Bird" Taylor was a lovely woman in the southern sense, feminine, intelligent, well-educated, and she had an unfailing personal courtesy. She had been a student at the University of Texas over at Austin, earning her degree with honors in 1933. There was no need for her to go to work—she drove a new Buick, she had an open charge account at the exclusive Neiman-Marcus store in Dallas—and she enrolled to take a second degree in journalism. As a graduation present in June, 1934, her father gave her a trip to the East. Her best friend, Gene Boehringer, had been telling her for years about this fellow Lyndon Johnson, and learning of Bird's trip she started in about him again, "He's just the brightest young man. He knows everything about Washington. I'm going to write him that you're coming, and here's his name and address and telephone number, and you call him!" Bird put the note in her purse and carried it with her on her boat trip to New York and the train ride down to the capital, but she saw the sights in the capital without phoning him. "I was having a good time," she said, "and I just hesitated to call somebody I didn't know." A southern lady, she was not going to be forward.

Planning to live at home a year with her father, doing nice things for him and fixing up their old house, she went to Austin at the end of the summer to see an architect about the house. On the last day of August or the first of September, she called on her friend Gene at the Texas Railroad Commission (where Gene was a secretary) and during the visit Lyndon came in to see Gene. Cupid's coincidence, perhaps, arranged by Gene or Lyndon or both. No one said so, but Gene exclaimed, "Oh, Lady Bird, here he is at last. Now I'm going to make sure you all get together!"

Lady Bird was twenty-one, and he was twenty-six. He seemed, to her, "excessively thin but very, very good-looking with lots of hair, quite black and wavy." The three of them went somewhere to have a drink, and Bird found him "terribly, terribly interesting" and "the most outspoken, straightforward, determined young man I had ever met. I knew I had met something remarkable, but I didn't quite know what."

Lyndon already had a date that night, but asked her, "Can you have breakfast with me?" She pondered it. He was kind of tense, "like a tight spring," a whiplashing kind of person, "a little bit scary—so dynamic and so insistent." She was drawn to him, but afraid. "He came on very strong, and my instinct was to withdraw."

"Yes," she said.

"Well, meet me in the dining room of the Driskill" at a certain time, after her meeting with the architect, he said.

The next morning she left the architect already half an hour or so late for the breakfast, and she decided to stand Johnson up. But the architect's office was almost next door to the Driskill, and as she walked past the big windows of the hotel dining room, there Lyndon was, sitting at the front table watching for her. "He just flagged me down. So I went in," Bird said. "I dare say I was going all the time, but just telling myself I wasn't going."

During breakfast she was astonished as he broke, pell-mell, the rules of reticence. "He began to tell me all about his job, his family," she said. "And he just kept on asking the most probing questions: What did you take in school? What's your family like? What do you want to do? He also was telling me all sorts of things I would *never* have asked him, certainly on first acquaintance."

He told her what his job was like, his salary, how much insurance he had. He told her about all the members of his family, his father's being in the legislature and going broke, his own job with the road gang, the adventure in California, his mother keeping after him to go back to school—how he once gave up a visit home for Christmas to save money, how Ben Crider loaned him money to stay in school.

He told her his ambitions, too. He thought he would stay in politics, and Washington was where it was. She knew little about politics, but she heard him say "constituents" frequently.

They spent the day together, riding all over the countryside in a Ford roadster convertible with leather seats that had one of the King Ranch brands stamped into them. "He was rather gallant," Bird said, "but he was a salesman through and through. But he was also very fair." He broke into the stream of what he was saying to tell her, "Listen, you're seeing the best side of me. I'm trying to, but I think you ought to know that."

Before the day was over he asked her to marry him. They had not known each other a single rounding of the sun. "I was so surprised I couldn't believe it," she said. "I thought it was some kind of joke." She could not understand how he could be so daring with his future, so decisive, so sudden.

"He was tall and gangling, and he talked incessantly," she said later. "At first, I thought he was quite a repulsive young man. But then I realized he was handsome and charming and terribly bright." She really didn't know what to make of him. "I was terrifically interested and a little bit scared, not wanting to let him go and not at all sure I wanted to have any closer relationship."

Like any young lady in her situation, Bird must have been wondering with some alarm, why had this remarkable young fellow—almost a stranger—popped the question to her before he had known her twenty-four hours. Perhaps she wondered if there was something calculating in him. A politician, after all, would need a good wife. He had no money; she did. He had fallen in love with her the very day he met her? Yet, there is such a thing as love at first sight. And she must have admired with wonder the honesty in his directness.

The practical advantages of this match were not lost later on Lyndon's friends. His friend Otto Crider said about the boys emerging from the Johnson City area, "Hell, we had no chance out there!—neither would Lyndon if he hadn't married Claudia." Lyndon's friend William S. White wrote, "She was the daughter of an East Texas landowner, and there was comfortable money in her background. All this was useful, of course, to her husband. . . ." Later Lyndon read in advance of publication and said he liked a book written by one of his staff people in which it was said that after he married Bird he realized "he had won a double prize. He not only had the one possible wife for Lyndon Johnson but also had the ideal helpmate for a going-places politician."

Having chosen his profession, at twenty-six he had now chosen his wife and partner. He resolved, he said, "to keep her mind completely on me until the moment I had to leave for Washington four days later."

He wanted her to meet his parents in San Marcos and continue down to the King Ranch headquarters to meet Kleberg and Kleberg's mother, whom he extolled as kind of a duchess, a great figure in the family and the countryside. "I wasn't sure until the last minute," Lady Bird said, "whether I was going to get in that car and go with him. So. Anyhow, I did. . . ."

He told his mother that Bird was the most interesting woman he had ever met. Rebekah didn't much like the sound of that. Bird, meeting Sam and Rebekah, thought Lyndon's father was "pretty much used up," worn out and discouraged, and she sensed in his mother the feeling, "What are you going to do with my young son? Are you friend or enemy?" The young woman wanted to tell her not to worry, "I just sort of wanted to reassure her that really I had no interest in taking her son away from her and wasn't at all sure that I wanted any part of him, myself, and on the other hand if I did, it wouldn't do her any harm."

Johnson was welcome at the Klebergs' King Ranch and made free use of the place. Once when Wright Patman attended an American Legion convention in south Texas, he said Lyndon "told me to collect as many of the Legionnaires as I wanted, and he'd take us out on a wonderful outing on Dick Kleberg's big boat. He was the host when we came on board, and he impressed everyone." Lyndon had business with Kleberg at the ranch when he took Bird there, but also, he said, "I knew she'd be impressed by seeing me walk so comfortably around this famous ranch," and she was. Later she told a friend it was so big they had to use compasses instead of watches. The ranch house, she said, was "a great baronial sort of place" with huge halls, and palm trees out front. Kleberg was gracious to her, and she was glad the Duchess liked her.

From the ranch Johnson had to return to Washington by car. He and Bird decided that on their way they would visit her father, T. J. Taylor, in his brick house in Karnack in northeast Texas. In San Antonio they picked up some other Washington-bound politicians, and in two carloads the group set out for the capital. Lyndon met Bird's father in his high-ceilinged living room, dazzling with white furniture on a red carpet. It is part of the Johnson legend that after dinner Taylor said to Bird, "Well, daughter, you've brought home a lot of boys, but this time you brought home a man!"

Malcolm Bardwell, Maverick's secretary, who along with Lyndon stayed the night, said, "we were put on the second floor, a great big wide bedroom, both of us slept there, two tremendous beds in this big,

Young Lyndon in Washington in the opening years of the New Deal, the Washington Monument in the background.

JOHNSON LIBRARY PHOTOS

Lyndon with his two young debaters from Texas, Luther Jones, left, and Gene Latimer, whom he had recruited as staffers to work with him in the offices of Congressman Dick Kleberg in Washington.

ʟyndon and Lady Bird on
heir honeymoon in Mex-
co City, standing in a gar-
anded boat.

Returned to Washington, the couple were photographed in front of the Capitol, about 1934 or 1935.

JOHNSON LIBRARY PHOTOS

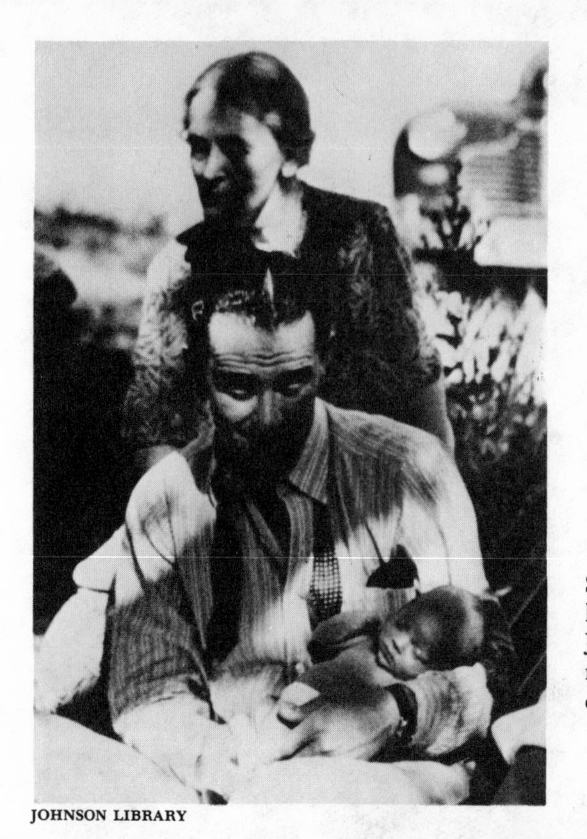

JOHNSON LIBRARY

Studies of Lyndon and his mother, Rebekah, during a picnic. The author quotes Johnson saying that his mother was the most important woman in his life, with no exceptions.

JOHNSON LIBRARY

Left to right, Lyndon and his sisters and brothers, Rebekah, Josefa, Sam Houston, and Lucia.

JOHNSON LIBRARY

Rebekah and Sam Ealy Johnson, Jr., the parents of the president, about 1936.

JOHNSON LIBRARY

tremendous room." The next morning, in his pajamas, Bardwell wandered downstairs to tell the cook what he wanted for breakfast, but when he got back upstairs Johnson jumped him, fuming, "I'm going to marry this girl! You're going to ruin my marriage if you run around that way!"

From Washington Johnson kept up his whirlwind courtship, writing or calling Bird every day. He sent her a picture of himself inscribed "For Bird, a lovely girl with ideals, principles, intelligence and refinement, from her sincere admirer." But she was talking now about their waiting a year to decide. Perhaps to impress and win her, less than three weeks after they'd met he enrolled in Georgetown Law School (he had turned over control of Kleberg's office to his brother). The next day he wrote her:

"This morning your letter indicated that you too had planned places for us to go together. Every interesting place I see I make a mental reservation and tell myself that I shall take you there when you are mine. I want to go through the Museum, the Congressional Library, the Smithsonian, the Civil War battlefields and all of those most interesting places. One week we must go over to New York together. Why must we wait twelve long months to begin to do the things we want to do forever and ever?"

Attending law school at night, he would get restless when the professor went over ground they had already covered in the homework—"He's not telling me anything I don't know," he'd mutter to the boy beside him. Luther Jones, who had also enrolled, said it quickly became obvious this was not for Johnson, "it was too slow, it was unemotional, he thought it was a lot of crap, briefing all those cases." After three weeks he quit (later he joked "I earned only a B.A. degree—for Brief Attendance"). As Jones saw it, "This was a fork in the road—the smartest thing he ever did."

"My Dear Bird," Lyndon wrote her October 24, "This morning I'm ambitious, proud, energetic, and very madly in love with you—I want to see people—want to drive thru the throngs—Want to do things with a drive—If I had a box I would almost make a speech this minute—Plans, ideas, hopes—I'm bubbling over with them. . . ."

"Lyndon," she wrote him from the brick house, "please tell me as soon as you can what the deal is . . . I am *afraid* it's politics. . . . Oh, I know I haven't any business . . . not any 'proprietary interest' . . . but I would hate for you to go into politics. Don't let me get things any more muddled for you than they are though, dearest."

This was a kind of eyes-down encouragement, but Lyndon wanted a commitment, and she wasn't giving it. "I see something I *know* I *want* —I *immediately exert efforts* to get it—I do or I don't but I try and do my best," he wrote her. "You see something you *might* want. . . . You tear it to pieces in an effort to determine if you should want it. . . . Then you wonder why you want it, and conclude that maybe the desire isn't an 'everlasting' one and that the 'sane' thing to do is to wait a year or so, and then if you still want it, to decide at that time whether or not you *should* make an effort to get it."

One Monday night she wrote him that she'd received a letter about him from a friend of hers in Cotulla saying that "Everybody down here likes him and says he is brilliant, so I think you're lucky." Bird went on to tell about her excursion with Dorris Powell, who was her surrogate mother:

"This morning after breakfast I went down to Dorris' and we hied forth in search of cape jasmine bushes and a little magnolia and jonquil bulbs, me thinking I could find them somewhere—and in the florists' sketch they are quite numerous and expensive. We walked through the woods to the old Haggerty place—site of an old colonial mansion, now quite dilapidated and doleful looking. It always gives me a very poignant feeling to go over there—It must have been a *lovely* place—there are the tallest magnolias I've ever seen, and great Liveoaks, and myriads of crepe myrtle, and a carpet of jonquils and flags in the Spring."

As the fall began her feelings moved closer to him: "Dearest . . . I've been reading *'Early Autumn'* and am enthralled. If we were together I'd read it to you. . . . There's nothing I'd like better than being comfortable in a nice cozy place and reading something amusing or well-written or interesting to someone I like. All good things are better shared, aren't they?"

Seven weeks after they'd met he returned to Karnack and she let him take her to an Austin jewelry store where they picked out a ring with a small diamond, but they didn't buy it—the thing was not settled. She bought a trousseau and left for Alabama to consult her Aunt Effie, who kept asking her what the hurry was. "If he loves you as much as he says he does, he'll wait for you," she'd say. He was waiting for her, all right—at her home when she returned. "What are you waiting for?" her father asked her. "Some of the best deals are made in a hurry. If you wait till your Aunt Effie's really ready you'll never marry anybody." Then Lyndon gave her an ultimatum. "We either get married now, or we never will," he said. If she didn't marry him right away she didn't love him. He couldn't go back to Washington wondering if it would ever happen.

In San Antonio about eight o'clock the morning of November 17, 1934, postmaster Dan Quill picked up his ringing telephone. It was Lyndon, 450 miles away in Texarkana. "Lady Bird and I want to be married at eight o'clock tonight at St. Mark's Episcopal Church. Fix everything up," he said, and hung up before Quill could object. They set out driving for San Antonio. But still she hadn't said yes.

Quill went to the rector of the church, Reverend Arthur R. McKinstry, and told him what was wanted. The minister thought that was ridiculous. He wasn't a justice of the peace, he said—"I don't marry people that fast. I want to get to know them, meet with them two or three days, talk with them and explain the seriousness of marriage." But Quill had just helped the church get a mailing permit for its weekly paper, and he was able to persuade the good reverend. All day Saturday Quill was busy, writing out the marriage license himself, getting the county clerk to sign it, inviting a few people, arranging a reception, making reservations for the couple at the Plaza Hotel. He proposed that Henry Hirschberg, a lawyer and friend of Lyndon's, be the best man, and Hirschberg, protesting that Quill should do it, agreed.

Lyndon and Bird came in about six-thirty. Although she still had her doubts, she had decided to go through with it. In the church she turned to Lyndon and asked, "You did bring a wedding ring, didn't you?" He snapped his fingers—"I forgot!" She turned to Quill, "Dan, did you get the ring?" "You've been passing jewelry stores all day long on your way from Texarkana!" Quill exclaimed—but he dashed across the street to Sears, which was open late Saturday, to buy one. They asked him what size, but he hadn't known wedding rings had sizes, so pointing to a batch of inexpensive ones he said, "Just give me a dozen of them." Holding aloft the dozen rings on a stick he dashed back to the church. Bird chose one that fit.

With one of Bird's classmates as maid of honor, the wedding went smoothly, but as they left the church the minister muttered, "I hope that marriage lasts." The newlyweds and their ten or so guests walked across the park from the church to a dinner reception at the ritzy St. Anthony Hotel. The wine list was too expensive for them, but, Quill said, "we told an old boy if he would bring a bottle of wine down, we'd let him come to the wedding," so they had some wine to toast the bride and groom. Quill took the extra rings back to Sears and paid three dollars for the one Bird had kept.

The next morning, after their wedding night at the Plaza, Lyndon phoned his parents and Bird called her father and the woman who had acted as her surrogate mother, Dorris Powell. There is a picture, pasted in Rebekah Johnson's scrapbook, of the honeymooners standing in a flower-filled boat at the floating gardens in Mexico City.

Rebekah wrote them two weeks after the wedding she and Sam had not attended. "My dear Bird," she wrote, "I earnestly hope that you will love me as I do you. Lyndon has always held a very special place in my heart. Will you not share that place with him dear child!" She hoped Lyndon would be as good a husband as he had been a son. She signed the letter "Mamma."[2]

32. Favors, and a Falling Out

Back in Washington after their honeymoon, Bird and Lyndon stayed first at the Dodge, then in a furnished one-bedroom apartment on Kalorama Road in a section that was regarded as inelegant. When Congressman Maverick and his wife Terrell arrived at the apartment for Bird's first dinner party, Terrell saw a Fanny Farmer cookbook lying open at a recipe for boiled rice. Accustomed to servants, Bird was on her own. The baked ham and lemon pie were good, but to Terrell the rice tasted like library paste.

From Lyndon's salary with Kleberg at this point, $267 a month, Bird gave him $100 to make their car payment and funded the household, including the rent of about $65, with the rest, he told me. Somehow she also managed to save enough to buy an $18.75 government bond every month. "I couldn't get five cents out of her I didn't deserve," he said. From the Federal Home Owners Loan Corporation he borrowed $3,500 on the house in Johnson City, and several years passed before he could pay it back.[1]

He continued wheedling Kleberg to vote for the New Deal. When Kleberg was disposed to oppose a veterans' bonus that was pending, the young man pounded on his boss's desk and cried out, "Mr. Kleberg, Mr. Kleberg, you can't do this!" One among the twenty-five million Americans who heard Huey Long's effective radio speech for his "Share Our Wealth" plan in the spring of 1935, Lyndon believed that the social security system probably resulted from the broadcast. Arguing with Kleberg about social security, Lyndon said, "I heard all the scare arguments and all the fright that they tried to put into men. They said it is socialistic; it is compulsory, it is evil, it will destroy our form of government."[2]

New Dealer though he was, Johnson was already using his public power in a private cause to obtain special treatment for a close kinsman. Accused by customs authorities of the criminal offense of importing merchandise into the country under false declarations of value, the kinsman telephoned Johnson, who wired him back that Kleberg had phoned the customs collector, "who assured just treatment." Kleberg also wired a border lawyer asking him to take the case. With the hostility of the customs people forestalled, a cash restitution was accepted from the man in trouble.

The lawyer billed Kleberg five hundred dollars for legal services, but then received a letter signed by the congressman saying that the offender was already handicapped by the cash settlement and adding, as if Lyndon might have to pay the fee, "All the matters pertaining to the arrival of this settlement were handled by my secretary, I having introduced him to Mr. Dow, Commissioner of Customs. . . . My secretary, Mr. Johnson has been subjected to unusual expenses due to the serious illness of his father and to the fact that his home folks are in desperate financial plight." If something could be done about that five-hundred-dollar fee, Kleberg wrote, "you will again place me greatly in your debt" and "likewise add to the obligation" Johnson and the offender "already owe you in this matter." The fee was reduced to one-hundred dollars, and Lyndon wrote the lawyer on Kleberg's stationery, "I am ready to serve you or your friends at any time, day or night."[3]

Lyndon would use his public position just as quickly to get an unfair advantage for a friend. Gene Latimer was in love, but his girl decided she would entrain for California to finish her studies. Almost bawling, Gene turned to Lyndon, who challenged him, "Why don't you marry her before her train leaves?" Gene proposed and she agreed. Lyndon got them a $100 wedding present from Kleberg, arranged a car for them to use, phoned to get them a marriage license even though it was a holiday, and had them swing by his house to borrow the Sears-Roebuck ring Quill had bought for Bird. As the couple left town the girl wired her father that due to a wedding, she would not be using her train ticket. When Latimer returned to work, Lyndon had Kleberg get him a cushy spot in the Federal Housing Administration. With Johnson on one extension of the phone and Latimer on another, Kleberg discussed Latimer's salary with the director of the agency. The director suggested $2,400 a year. Johnson covered his phone and called, "Make it $2,600," which Kleberg thereupon suggested. Latimer went to work with forty-five other people doing the same thing they were, but they all made $1,120 except the supervisor, who made $2,400, and Latimer, who made more than the supervisor.[4]

Eventually bad blood developed between Kleberg and Johnson. According to Sam Houston, who was moving into Lyndon's position in the office, a woman in Washington of whom Mrs. Kleberg was jealous wrote Lyndon a letter that fell into Mrs. Kleberg's hands, and from it the congressman's wife concluded, rightly or wrongly, that her jealousy was justified and that Lyndon was partisan to the woman who was vamping her husband. In any case, Mrs. Kleberg did turn against Johnson, telling her husband one day, "You'd better fire Lyndon or he's going to go back and run against you." Johnson, pressed on what happened, would say only, "I resigned."

Not yet five years out of Texas, Lyndon had already earned a sense of having participated in the reformation of the United States. While he had been with Kleberg, the conservative rancher had voted for the basic proposals of the New Deal—the AAA, the National Industrial Recovery Act (which included the NRA), the Tennessee Valley Authority, the Federal Housing Administration, the Securities and Exchange Act, social security, the Federal Power Commission. "I saw all the great reform legislation born," Johnson said.

Thirteen holding companies controlled seventy-five percent of the country's operating electric power companies, and "the big show" of 1935 in Washington was Sam Rayburn's hearings on his bill to stop the holding companies from milking their subsidiaries. Remembering this fight all his life, Johnson later said that although the corporate manipulators swore the regulation would kill them, "They all got richer than ever, but it kept them from swindling a bunch of widow women." Little wonder that briefing old law cases had bored him—he was headily involved in the actual struggles of the New Deal. "I saw," he said, "the businessmen hauled before the congressional committees, and I saw the Wall Street bankers with midgets on their knees."[5]

However, he had been a factotum. Now his time came to act in his own name. During the next few years he helped bring into some actuality the noblest hopes of his father and his grandfather for helping people in need. A war would end the New Deal (just as, when his turn came, a war would end the Great Society), but for these brief years in the thirties he was a true crusader.

---

33. "Always Concerned with Now"

Although enraging conservatives, the early New Deal left the poor and the jobless just about where they had been, and Long's appealing radio speeches for sharing the wealth, along with Dr. Townsend's pension plan and Father Coughlin's calls for nationalization, created among Rooseveltians a fear of a third-party challenge from the left in 1936. In his January, 1935, message to Congress, Roosevelt rushed to propose the measures of the second New Deal, among them the Works Progress Administration (the WPA), which Congress thereupon created to put men to work. By executive order in June, Roosevelt established the National Youth Administration (the NYA) to give students jobs to help them stay in school and to employ nonstudent youths in public works. There were to be state directors for the NYA, and Johnson, falling out with Kleberg, saw his next chance.

Malcolm Bardwell, learning from his boss, Congressman Maverick, that the new NYA chief, Aubrey Williams, was looking for a Texas director, gave the news to Johnson, who at once said, "I'd like that job." Bardwell conjectured that Johnson was eager for a chance to make friends in Texas preparatory to a run for the central Texas congressional seat of James Buchanan, who was getting old.

The two young men approached staff members of the two Texas senators, Morris Sheppard and Tom Connally, and Bardwell took Lyndon to Maverick and said, "Here's the man who wants the job." Maverick told Williams, and possibly FDR himself, that he was for Lyndon. Williams, running into Dr. Montgomery on the street in Washington, said he had selected another person, but Montgomery nixed the fellow and recommended Johnson. Then another quirk of circumstance helped Johnson. Senator Sheppard was considering Lyndon and a man from Port Arthur, Texas, who was known to a friend of the senator's daughter. Naturally Sheppard asked his daughter's friend about the Port Arthur fellow, and the young man replied, "Well, senator, I come from a part of Texas where if your neighbor down the road makes corn whiskey, you consider it his business and don't talk about it." As there were only two candidates for the job, Sheppard was for Johnson. Meanwhile Rayburn asked Senator Connally to ask FDR to name Lyndon and would not leave until Connally agreed to do it. Lyndon was in.[1]

Maverick mentioned to Bardwell how much Lyndon would be paid, but Bardwell hollered back, "Pay him a living wage!" Johnson said afterwards that every time Bardwell shouted "a living wage" the salary went up five hundred dollars. Maverick wrangled with Harold Ickes, then head of the Public Works Administration, "Aw, goddammit, Harold, give him $7,500," and Johnson later told Maverick, too, "Maury, every time you'd yell you'd get me another $50."

In August, 1935, still twenty-six, Johnson was named the NYA director for Texas and had his first encounter with Roosevelt. Briefing the new state directors in the White House, the president declared, "We have given you fifty million dollars. We are going to get action." After the ceremony he had Lyndon stay a moment and said something to him about Maverick's role in getting him the job. From then on, Johnson later said, Roosevelt "always kinda petted me." Sure of his course, Lyndon told Bardwell, "When I come back to Washington, I'm coming back as a congressman," and Bardwell didn't doubt it.

Setting up the Texas NYA, Lyndon horned in on the big-wigs as usual: he flew to Austin and beelined it for the state capitol to call on the pro-Roosevelt governor, James Allred, who promised to cooperate. At six o'clock one morning at the Post Office Café in San Marcos, over breakfast, Lyndon laid out his plans to his friends Sherman Birdwell and Jesse Kellam, and they agreed to get to work for him.

Leaving Bird temporarily at her father's home at Karnack, he wrote her, "It was more difficult to leave you last night than I had anticipated. I have learned to lean on you so much. . . . Never have I been so dependent on anyone—Never shall I expect so much of any other individual. . . . You do every day with your job what I want to do with mine and you know something of my ambitions.

"I enjoyed every minute with your daddy—Each visit I have only cements and confirms my first opinion—that he is truly a remarkable man—a strong character possessed with vision and sound judgment." (The tribute had an oddly political ring to it. Probably he knew Bird would show it to her father.)

In due time the Johnsons moved into the bank-side, university area Austin home of the Montgomerys, who were away, New Dealing in

Washington. Behind the house were a spring and a small natural amphitheater bordered by bamboo, with gardens at different levels. Bird's Aunt Effie came to live with them, and Bird had a full-time maid, who slept in a room in the garage. NYA headquarters were opened on the sixth floor of the gingerbread Littlefield building downtown. Lyndon, barging home for supper, often brought company, and Bird began a lifetime of cheerfully feeding unannounced guests.

The immediate task downtown was to get young people on the payroll so they could go to school that fall. "Put them to work, get them in school," Johnson kept saying. Within three years Harry Hopkins, the director of the WPA, was to supervise unemployment relief for fifteen million people. As Johnson told it, he had been on the job only a few days when a wire arrived from Hopkins asking, "How many people are you going to have working by next Saturday night?" Having been given little money for materials or the supervision of workers, Johnson proposed to state highway officials that the NYA would pay the salaries of fifteen thousand unskilled men if the highway department would do the rest. The officials agreed, and Johnson wired Hopkins back, "We will have 15,000 assigned."[2]

On the other hand, worried about being perceived in Texas as a big government spender, Johnson developed an image of himself as a most parsimonious humanitarian. When a young Texas liberal, Clay Cochran, called on him in his NYA office, Cochran was put off by the large picture of the conservative lobbyist Roy Miller hanging behind the desk and dominating the room. Luther Jones, who, with Willard Deason, lived in an upstairs room at the Johnsons' house and worked for the NYA downtown, said Lyndon's "big problem was he wanted to do something quick that would do some good, that would not lose money. His conferences were on this theme. . . . He was defensive about the idea of wasting money. There was another thing—he wanted something that would draw attention to him."

The roads of that time were narrow and often muddy, with bar pits on each side, and sometimes people who pulled over for a break were smacked into from behind. Gladys Montgomery, Dr. Bob's wife, had the idea of using the NYA boys to build "a little drive-off for trucks and migrants to pull off and sleep in safety." When she gave the idea to Lyndon, Jones said, *"instantly* he lighted up. You could do it quickly and it wouldn't cost money." The construction of rest parks alongside the roads, the "roadside parks," became the first statewide projects of the NYA boys in Texas.

The highway department furnished the trucks, materials, and supervisors, the NYA the labor, mostly Mexican-Americans and blacks because so many of them were school drop-outs. Once county officials had consented, Johnson would persuade farmers to give small plots of land along the roads. Then the boys cleared the brush, laid down curbed driveways, and built cement picnic tables, barbecue pits, and steps mounted over the fences to let people relieve themselves in the pastures. The parks are still one of the state's most pleasant and democratic features, and Gladys Montgomery's idea has spread across the country.[3]

During this period Lyndon was generous, expansive—in full flood. The editor of the Austin daily, visiting at the Johnsons' home, admired Mexican sandals Lyndon was wearing—Lyndon slipped them off and gave them to him. As Ben Crider remembered, Lyndon wrote him, "I got three million to spend. I know you're honest, I want you to come help me," so Ben became one of the Littlefield group, playing dominoes and spending the three million. Drawing the top staffer of the Texas labor movement into the NYA work, Lyndon made a valuable political friend. To a group of educators, he said of the 124,000 young people on relief in Texas, "We could starve them to death; we could send them to school; we could kill them through war," but obviously the best thing was to get them back to school or work.

While he was waiting to speak at a luncheon club in San Antonio, a member of the club said to him, "All these kids need to do is get out and hustle." Johnson had fresh in his mind some Mexican-American children he had seen rummaging through the garbage can at the back of a cafeteria, taking out grapefruit rinds, scraping off the coffee grounds, and gnawing on the rinds. "Right," he snapped to his well-dressed heckler. "Last week over here I saw a couple of your local kids hustling—a boy and a girl, nine or ten. They were hustling through a garbage can in an alley."

But he went only so far. According to Crider, "One of the first things that came up, they wanted a nigger on his NYA advisory board, and he said, 'I can't do it, the white people wouldn't serve with 'em.' He said Mrs. Roosevelt wanted it—but he didn't put a nigger on. . . ."

Lyndon's brother, although Kleberg's congressional secretary, was now also on retainer for the Klebergs' King Ranch as a public relations man, and when Lyndon returned to Washington to confer with NYA officials Sam could afford to take him out to eat at expensive restaurants. "Right smack in the middle of a fine steak dinner," according to Sam Houston, Lyndon "would ruin my appetite and make me feel guilty with a long recitation of statistics concerning the ill-housed and ill-fed people in his jurisdiction."

Luther Jones, living with the Johnsons in Austin, felt like Lyndon's brother and was excited and proud to follow him. "I always felt like we were making history," Jones said. "Everybody that worked with him was willing to let him lead—of course maybe he chose people who never fought him on anything. . . . I was acquiescent. . . . The guy would overwhelm you when you did argue with him."

Jones perceived that Lyndon was studying and learning, not from books, but from people. At breakfast every morning he was always talking about what was in the paper. "Never once—I can't *ever* remember this guy speculating about the future," Jones said. "He was always concerned with now, to an incredible degree."[4]

The NYA youths spruced up the old swimming hole at Barton Springs in Austin until it looked like a park. They built a playground in the black section of the city and a chapel at a women's college in Denton. In San Antonio they rebuilt a rundown Mexican section into the arts and crafts center, La Villita. At Bastrop they cut down trees, hauled them to sawmills and cut them into lumber, dried it in kilns, and built furniture with it for schools, courthouses, and other public places. They learned to be mechanics, wood and metal workers, seamstresses, book binders, dieticians. In Kenedy they repaired two hundred old school desks.

Perhaps one hundred thousand students were helped to stay in school by the money they earned in NYA jobs in Texas, and here it was that Johnson began using his public power covertly on behalf of blacks. When he had student job-money left over because white colleges had not used all their allotment, rather than return the surplus to the government he phoned black college presidents and offered it to them. Or he would get people to donate money for equipment for whites' programs and then apply the saving to the blacks' needs. On his way to Houston, he would stop at the Negro college just off the road and spend the night to see how they were doing. According to E. H. Elliott, the bursar of Sam Houston College for Negroes in Austin, Johnson would call him and ask, "You have any boys and girls out there that could use some money?" When sending Elliott his college's quota, Johnson would add, "I've got a little extra change here. Can you find a place to put it?" They could not have paid their faculty without Lyndon's help. Learning from associates that the same thing was happening at three other black colleges, Elliott felt that Johnson knew, if only because the white colleges had money left over, that the blacks needed it more. "It sorta sold us on him even before he ran for elective office."[5]

He was a harsh taskmaster. The way Birdwell felt, "You weigh 135 pounds, and the right guard against you weighs 260, and Johnson says 'Take him out'—he doesn't tell you *how.*" When Johnson concluded from a visit to a San Antonio project that the supervisor was permitting loafing, he left without a word and gave orders to shut it down. Irritated, while inspecting an agricultural resident center, that two beds were made up sloppily, he had the boys rounded up and lectured them on neatness.

"Johnson's recreation," said his publicity man, Ray Lee, was "enjoying the work." Standing before his workers with his hands dug into his pockets, Lyndon would say, "I got ex-lax in one pocket and aspirin in the other and I work seventeen hours a day. All I ask you to work is sixteen, and we'll get that boy on the streetcorner a job."

The first man to arrive in the office at the Littlefield headquarters, Willard Deason, had the mail from the post office sorted and on the desks before Johnson came in about eight. About twice a week Johnson, with Deason or Kellam, drove to San Antonio, where the NYA's fiscal affairs were handled. One day, after Johnson had been driving three of his supervisors in and around San Antonio for hours inspecting projects, one of the men in the back said to the fellow beside him, "Maybe we're not going to get to eat lunch today." Johnson said nothing, but he turned into the next drive-in and called out, "Eight hamburgers, four bottles of milk, and make it in a hurry." Getting back to Austin at nine at night, he would check by the office to see what had been going on.

The building electricity was shut off at ten-thirty, but, as Gordon Fulcher, a journalist who was close to Johnson, said, "He worked all night if it was necessary and his people worked all night." When the elevator shut down, they used the stairwell. The old pipes that had once been used for gas lamps were still in place, but there were no mantles or burners, so they would turn the gas on and light the end of the pipe. The flames flared high in the rooms.

Johnson was delighted when Eleanor Roosevelt inspected his headquarters and a girls' sewing room in Austin. With Birdwell she visited one of the roadside parks near Austin (some people were using it, and she thought it was wonderful). In the summer of 1936, Johnson saw a special chance for recognition when Roosevelt himself visited the Texas Centennial Exposition in Dallas. Gathering a bunch of his NYA workers at a point on Roosevelt's motorcade route between Fort Worth and Dallas, Johnson lined them up with their shovels at present arms and placed himself in front of them, straight and tall, saluting as the president passed. Roosevelt waved and threw back his head and laughed.[6]

From August, 1935, until the end of February, 1937, Lyndon Johnson was an inspired and inspiring administrator of a New Deal program that gave jobs to nearly thirty thousand young people, two-thirds of them students, and created various public works of lasting value. The NYA chief, Aubrey Williams, sent directors from other states to Texas to get ideas and said Johnson "did a beautiful job . . . one of the very best in the country. He fought for those kids to get them all he could, he even fought me to get things and money for them."

Later, Johnson would defend the NYA in the languages of conservative and Puritan values—schooling, hard work, independence. The program had helped keep young people in school "where they belonged" or paid them for work on useful public projects. "Not one dime" was spent except for work performed. "Something for nothing has not been tolerated." Youths had been denied the means to be self-supporting and independent, and the program had been "constructive, beneficial, American."

The NYA was, in fact, one of the New Deal's least controversial repair jobs on an economy that had broken down. The public works feature, which Johnson would never again advocate, was obscured between the down-home purposes of putting young people to work and keeping them in school. The pay was token, private business and labor were not competed with, and boys and girls were helped.

Johnson knew his work with the NYA would be convertible into votes—and why not? "It was a tremendous help to him," Birdwell said. Dr. Bob agreed: "We'd given him a little congeries of people in every county in Texas that would die for him."[7]

---

34. A Gentleman or a Congressman?

Lyndon was visiting his Uncle George in Houston when they read in the morning paper that James Buchanan, the congressman for central Texas, had died. While Lyndon was shaving George told him, "Son, I have $400 in the bank, and if you'll announce for Congress, I'll give you $400."[1] Although he was only twenty-eight, Lyndon wanted to go to Washington, and it was either now or much later—maybe never. An opening like this was a once-in-a-generation chance for anyone in the district who wanted to go to Congress. In one-party Texas the winner of the sudden-death special election, doing favors for constituents, reaping publicity, and accumulating seniority, would become almost unbeatable.

The year before the voters had handed Texas to Roosevelt by a margin of seven-to-one, and the month Buchanan died national events had given Johnson a perfect opportunity to identify himself as a Roosevelt loyalist. The Supreme Court had been canceling New Deal laws on the grounds that they were unconstitutional. Roosevelt proposed that Congress give him the power to expand the count with as many as six new justices, one for each sitting justice who was seventy or older (as a majority of the court were). Harold Ickes had berated the court in a speech in the Texas legislature, but among lawyers a convulsive reaction against "court-packing" was setting in, and some people were calling Roosevelt a dictator. Luther Jones, apprenticing in the law firm of Alvin Wirtz, happened to be in Wirtz's office when Johnson came in to talk about running. Jones said three decisions were made on the spot. Johnson would run; Lawyer Claude Wild, Sr., who had choreographed Governor Allred's first election in 1934, would be the campaign manager; and Johnson would support court-packing despite the anger of the lawyers. "I personally don't think Lyndon gave two hoots in hell about the court plan," Jones said, and "I believe Wirtz was opposed to this plan." What they knew was that Johnson could not win without the Roosevelt vote.

Wirtz was to become the most influential adviser in Johnson's first few years in office. In the Texas Senate, said editor-lobbyist Edmunds Travis, Wirtz was a conservative, "but he became a Rooseveltian. . . . I have a theory it was for material gain. . . . He was one man that Herman Brown would listen to. . . . He was Brown's political adviser—and he was Lyndon's political adviser." Brown was an anti-union contractor, in business with his brother George.

"You have been more like a father to me than a mere friend and adviser," Lyndon would soon tell Wirtz. "You have my blank check for anything and in any amount," Wirtz told Lyndon. Johnson later told an aide to President Truman that Wirtz was "my closest personal friend." "Ultimately," said Lyndon's man Ray Lee, the politician "just looked on Wirtz as his lawyer." When later the two of them had to act fast together or wanted to keep what they were doing out of any records, Wirtz in Austin, Lyndon in Washington, they went to great trouble to arrange in advance to telephone each other station-to-station.

Wirtz "could tell Lyndon something was silly," Lyndon's business ally, Ed Clark, said. "He molded him." For a time in 1939–40 Wirtz regularly reproached Lyndon for his "pacifism"—Colonel Charles Lindberg, Wirtz told Johnson, "is preaching your doctrine: just don't bother Hitler and Hitler won't bother you. . . . I have never agreed with you appeasal boys. . . ." When Truman advanced his civil rights program, Wirtz told Johnson that, playing "cheap politics," Truman evidently was hoping for "the support of Northern radicals, both black and white."

Johnson said his decision to run that spring of 1937 was made during a meeting with Bird and Wirtz in the Johnsons' two-story apartment at Four Happy Hollow Lane. Perhaps the poor boy from Johnson City was not certain he was running until Bird came up with the money. "She was going to call her daddy for money, if we went ahead," he explained. "We had $3,900 in baby bonds, but we needed much more."

Bird asked Wirtz if Lyndon could win.

"No, it's not likely," he said. But he added that it would cost ten thousand dollars to get anywhere.

"Well," she said, "if it's possible, I'd like him to have a chance."

She went to the phone and called her father in Karnack. "I was on the other end of the phone, my heart pumping the whole time," Johnson said. "She told him what we were thinking, that if we did go we would need $10,000 of the money her mother had left her." It was to be a loan.

"Honey," her father asked her, "couldn't you get by on five?"

"No, we've been told it must be ten."

"All right," he said. He would transfer ten thousand dollars to Lyndon's bank by the morning. "And," Johnson said, "I was at the bank at nine A.M. the next morning and there it was."

So Bird bankrolled Lyndon's first drive for power. Later he would grin and say, "Bird is the brains and the money in this family," and she would say, "Oh, darlin', " and lower her eyes.

Sunday morning Lyndon, accompanied by Carroll Keach, went to the state capitol to ask Governor Allred for his support. Keach, the first of a series of aides Johnson used as valets, waited outside in the reception room.

"How do you stand on the court plan?" the governor asked Lyndon.

"I'm for it," he replied.

That sent Allred off—the plan was upsetting the people, farmers were upset, the NRA had already been thrown out. Lyndon thought the governor was baiting him. "I won't tell you I'll support you," Allred said.

But, as they left the office and walked together into the reception room, the governor went over to a hat rack and took down a big Stetson. "Lyndon," he said, "wear this hat. This is my campaign hat, and every time I've worn it I've won." And he put it on Lyndon's head.

"The lucky hat" was all the young man needed. That day he started telling everybody Allred had given it to him—he was off and running. He began calling his friends to Four Happy Hollow to tell them he had not decided about running and to ask them their advice.

One of them, Dan Quill, had a girl waiting for him in San Antonio, so to bring matters to a head he exclaimed, "Lyndon, the only way you can ever get in Congress is to run for it. You can't get there if you don't." "Well," Lyndon said, "I'll just run for it." For the rest of his life Quill told about the wisdom he had laid on Lyndon as if it had caused him to run.

Malcolm Bardwell and his wife had saved fifty dollars to buy an electric icebox, but Bardwell left one of the meetings that Sunday to go home and tell her to get the money out of the hiding place. In another meeting upstairs, Wirtz promised five hundred dollars from a source he could rely on and altogether twelve hundred dollars was raised.

Friends of Dr. Montgomery heard that Tommy "the Cork" Corcoran, one of Roosevelt's brain trusters, had designated Montgomery as the president's choice to run. Dr. Bob, an electrifying speaker, had barnstormed for Roosevelt in 1936 and was well known in Texas as an advocate of publicly-owned utilities. Between twenty thousand and thirty thousand dollars was committed to his campaign, even though his wife Gladys did not want him to go into politics. While Montgomery was agonizing, Maverick told Johnson, "Let Bob fart around for forty-eight hours and let's see what he does."

Johnson said Montgomery "was the smartest man I ever met. He was a man of the people and a Populist. He was a revolutionist. . . ." Yet when Montgomery told Johnson he wanted to run for Congress, Johnson snorted, "you're crazy as hell." Johnson knew too well that Montgomery would compete with him for the Roosevelt voters.

In Washington NYA chief Williams, who did not want Johnson to leave the NYA, ran into Corcoran in the White House and asked him to tell Johnson not to run. Corcoran said he would. That Sunday Buchanan's widow agreed to run. This was serious, and at the Johnsons' the question became whether to try to bluff her out with an immediate announcement. A journalist friend of Lyndon's, Ray Lee, knowing that the light Sunday crew on the Austin paper might not accept a story turned in late, typed up an announcement. Johnson decided to let 'er rip and Lee took it down to the paper about six o'clock.

Next: Montgomery. "Ray Lee and Lyndon came out to the house," the professor said. "Ray told me they were just going to put it in the paper in the morning. I said 'O my God!' I just put it in tonight that *I'm* running.' They turned white." Dr. Bob let a few minutes pass, enjoying their consternation. Then Gladys told them he was kidding. Mark Adams, a New Dealer from Texas who had helped raise the money for Montgomery, said the economist decided not to run only when he heard that Lyndon had announced. According to Adams, "Montgomery said 'No, that would be two liberals in the race.' And we said 'an opportunist and a liberal.' "

By the time Corcoran called Johnson from Washington he had already announced. Mrs. Buchanan had wanted to announce in a Monday afternoon paper, but Johnson's statement was publicized that morning. Lyndon believed that Allred, attending Buchanan's funeral, also discouraged her by saying Johnson would win. For whatever reason, she backed out. Dizzied by the flashings of Johnson's guile, audacity, and timing, Montgomery and Mrs. Buchanan sank back into their natural timidities.[2]

The Sunday night after Lyndon's announcement was published, four cars drove up to the house where he and Bird lived on the second floor, and ten to twelve blacks piled out. They had come to tell him that they would get every black in the district to vote for him. The help he had given blacks getting through college was going to help him get to Congress.

The paramount issue was the court plan he "wholeheartedly" supported. He supported "unreservedly," too, the Democrats' 1936 platform, provided it was carried out "as interpreted by our great president."

Two young men who had attended the Sunday meetings at the apartment called on Claude Wild to ask him to manage the campaign. "Who the hell is Lyndon Johnson?" he asked them. When Lyndon and he met, Wild laid down his terms: "I'll call the shots and you do what I tell you to." This was the only one of Johnson's campaigns he did not run himself. "He said that whatever I asked, he would do," Wild said. "He had some misgivings, but he did them."

Within minutes after the arrival of the ten thousand dollars from Karnack, Wild was buying radio time. All Bird did in the campaign itself was scramble eggs, make sandwiches, and pack suitcases, but she was proud of coming up with the money. "For years," she said, "I carried in my purse the deposit slip from the Marshall National Bank—until it wore out!"

Johnson had a special advantage: the partisanship of the Austin newspapers. Charles Marsh, an honest radical who used cynicism like a flashlight, was owner and publisher of the *Austin American-Statesman* as well as the dailies in four or five other Texas cities, and he was for Lyndon from the first.

Marsh was a man of considerable, but hidden influence with the leading figures of the New Deal, including Franklin and Eleanor Roosevelt and Henry Wallace. When Wallace was nominated for vice-president in 1940, Marsh placed at his side, as political adviser, all-out New Dealer Harold Young, a lawyer in Odessa, Texas. A speech-writer for Wallace, Marsh called on FDR in his office freely. A timid man, not given to putting his name in his own newspapers or making speeches, Marsh wrote candid, discursive memoranda on politics and gave them to Young or attorney Creekmore Fath of Austin, who passed them on to the intended recipients. A progressive, Marsh once wrote Johnson that he believed capitalism would come to an end, but foretold the necessity for an American presidential dictatorship in 1940 because of Germany's industrial superiority to the European capitalist democracies.

Marsh and Herman Brown, the Austin contractor, had been in oil deals together since as early as 1934, and Young thought Johnson's connection with the Brown brothers was Marsh's work—"Marsh was their buddy," Young said. "Marsh was the big public power behind Johnson." Marsh was also (until 1941, when he sold his interest) a director and president of Richardson Oils, Inc., which gave Johnson a direct connection to oilman Sid Richardson. Marsh was so wealthy, he wrote himself a memo one year, "Arrange to make no money this year. By my carelessness this year I will have this $25,000 income tax to pay next year."

The publisher was quite candid in his partisanship for Lyndon, once telling the congressman that he would be taking a public opinion poll on his political prospects "(and print [it] if favorable)." And, said Young, "Marsh put big money on him" in his elections.

The 1937 campaign was a shotgun six-week affair with no runoff. Gene Latimer, assured by his superior in the FHA in Washington that anybody who asked why he was away would be given a fake reason, drove to Austin to lend a hand. Wirtz helped write the speeches. The aides closest to Johnson were Wild, publicist Ray Lee, and Keach, who drove the candidate around, "took orders off the back seat," and wrote the notes that would become newsy themes for releases or speeches.

There were five other serious candidates and three minor ones. All the major ones supported Roosevelt and four of them backed court-packing, but Johnson, calling his opponents "the Eight in the Dark," cast doubt on their loyalty to Roosevelt. "We were going on the theory," Wild explained, "that some of the vote would go for Roosevelt or anybody that he directed. Anybody that was sympathetic to him. That's the role he wanted; we figured that would win for him and let the others split up." Making his first speech from the porch of the family home in Johnson City with his very proud parents beside him, Johnson threw the charge of dictatorship back at the court and said, "I am for Roosevelt, the man, and his complete program; and the conscience of Lyndon Johnson."

The father of Lyndon's college sweetheart, Carol Davis, led the Blanco County opposition to his campaign with an accusation that if he was elected he would seek public ownership of the power companies. Johnson denounced Davis and his friends as enemies of the people, but as he spoke, he said later, he glimpsed Carol leaning against the back wall of the auditorium, wearing a white dress, her face pale and sad, and he veered off in mid-air, saying there were two sides and they were all honorable men.

As a speaker he was only fair, and at first his campaign dragged. According to one insider, Wild told the candidate, "You're going to have to throw a little dirt," but Johnson protested, "No, no, if I have to do that I don't want the office." After another sputtering week, Wild asked him, "Do you want to go to Congress or not? If you do, it's going to be necessary for you to throw a little dirt." "Well," Johnson said, "if it's absolutely necessary—let's mix up a little mud."

Wild's strategy was to pick a fight with each of the serious candidates, thereby getting the votes of their enemies in their own areas. The exception was one strong candidate, Merton Harris, whom they ignored because, as Wild said, "We didn't want to advertise him." For a campaign manager, Wild said, "There's no emotion and there's very little philosophy. . . . The adding machine is what counts with him." One of the candidates had had an office in a Washington hotel and sold stone to the government, "so we made a lobbyist out of him. And the one up here in Burnet, we found something on him; we made one of them an economic royalist." One candidate, C. N. Avery, was calling Lyndon "this young squirrel," so Lyndon went to saying that if Avery was elected people would find him, not in his office, but in the bar of the Shoreham Hotel.

Bird, the genteel southern lady, was surprised to hear her husband roughhousing his opponents and tried to elevate the tone of the thing. She told Wild she thought Lyndon was mudslinging, she was helping finance the campaign and she wanted her husband to be a gentleman. "Mrs. Johnson," Wild replied, "you're going to have to make up your mind whether you want your husband to be a congressman or a gentleman." She protested a while longer, but gave it up.

For his part, Johnson's plan was to work like hell. He told Bird, "Don't ever let me be in the house when there's daylight and keep the screen locked until dark," and he really did work until midnight, losing twenty-five pounds before the campaign was over. "He was a long, tall, lanky fellow, and slim," journalist Gordon Fulcher remembered, "and he took long strides and wore these bow ties and was always in a hurry and generally pulled his coat off and held it over his shoulder hanging down his back." On a country road he would vault a fence to shake hands with a rancher out in the field with his goats. Working Congress Avenue, the main street in Austin, he started at the south edge of town, accosting people on the sidewalk, crossing over, going into shops, "I'm Lyndon Johnson, I'm running for Congress," handshaking all the way to the downtown. A young man named Woodrow Bean, later a congressman and judge, said to himself, "That's a very egotistical son-of-a-bitch, but he's gonna go places, and if a man wants to get on, he'd better get on now." Bean got on.

Although the Austin dailies did not formally endorse anyone, Marsh turned them into Lyndon's harmonicas. "These papers went all-out for him," said Edmunds Travis, one of their earlier editors. Lyndon would make a speech in a little town, Wild or Lee would give the text to the boys at the paper, and they would just run it all—simple as that. Wild said there was "somebody inside there who was helping us," and there was, indeed—Fulcher, the chief editorial officer. Perhaps because he was spoiled by this partisanship, for the rest of his career Johnson abused journalists who were not servile.

His theme was Roosevelt, Roosevelt, Roosevelt. He exulted when Albert Sidney Burleson of Austin, Wilson's postmaster general, endorsed him as a Roosevelt man—Burleson told him, "I want you to be as strong for Roosevelt and the New Deal as I was for Wilson and the New Freedom." Billboards showed LBJ and FDR shaking hands. "Support the Man Who Stands With the President," said the campaign literature.

J. R. Parten, the liberal oilman who was chairman of the University of Texas board of regents, told Johnson court-packing was both wrong and poor politics, but Johnson knew that, whether it was right or wrong, it wasn't poor politics. He was pledging, really, to do whatever Roosevelt wanted. Considering the president's majority of ten million the preceding November, he said, he would be "stupid beyond words to make silly, petty, and insignificant reservations on the issues at hand."

Anyone less than one hundred percent for FDR was not good enough, Lyndon argued, because "enemies of the president" wanted either a Roosevelt-hater or somebody wishy-washy. Harris, a state assistant attorney general, was for FDR and court-packing, but Johnson did not acknowledge it. When Senator Houghton Brownlee, another candidate, condemned court-packing, Johnson accused him of "stabbing the president and the people in the back." Polk Shelton called Johnson a "me-too" candidate. "They all picked on me," Johnson said.

Wild's strategy worked not just at home, but in Washington. FDR's son Elliott warmly endorsed Johnson by telegram, and a mere kid from the hill country was able to quote columnist Drew Pearson writing that if he won the administration would "make heavy capital out of his triumph."

Blacks were thought to have no political power in those days. The New Deal paid their cause lip service, but in Texas they were niggers. Congressman Buchanan had been one of the hooded Klansmen marching down the street with robes on ("He had little feet—everybody knew!" Wright Patman said). But Johnson had a feeling for the blacks, and he broke custom to seek their votes openly. Bird remembered an example. After "the speakin' " in a little town, Lyndon shook hands with blacks. One of his advisers told him, "You better not do that, you might start a fight." He said he was going to anyway, and "there was some kind of disturbance about it," Bird said.

In Austin the blacks had a few leaders, a dentist, a journalist, a minister, a doctor, a few school people, and one morning, in the basement of a black church, Johnson met with them. There were no reporters—"it mighta been dangerous otherwise," E. H. Elliott, the bursar of the local black college, recalled. "He made a statement that there was some things he wanted to do that he couldn't do, and if we'd stick by him, 'I think I can help you.' " According to F. R. ("Friendly") Rice, later the principal of an Austin school, "He went on to tell that if he got to Congress he could do such things as recognizing the Negroes for their votes, we together could recognize their voting rights. He spoke of the hot lunch programs. He was very favorably disposed toward us, and he was askin' for our help." A black doctor, B. E. Conner, believed what the young man was telling them. "I'll never forget that meeting," Conner said. Friendly Rice said the blacks stayed with Johnson "ever since that meeting."

New Dealers perked up, too. "Everybody was excited," said Mrs. Jean Lee, an Austin liberal. "Here was somebody who could change things." In his public campaign Johnson supplemented his emphasis on Roosevelt with partisanship for farmers and working men, a promise to carry through pending dam-building projects, and a boast that he knew his way around the Washington bureaucracy. Although the unions were for him, he did not say much for them, simply lassoing them, along with "the struggling little business man," into his coalition. However, speaking to a group of workers he made one promise that has a certain elusive resonance. "Never," he said, "will I cast a vote which will cause a single American boy to spill a drop of his blood on foreign soil."

The district was mostly rural, and again and again he said "I was born and reared on a farm." As Kleberg's man he had helped farmers "refinance their loans and drive off greedy mortgagees"; he was all-out for the Triple A, soil and water conservation, a parity price system for farmers. Buchanan had obtained the government's commitment to build three dams that would turn the Colorado River basin above Austin into a little TVA, but Johnson claimed part of the credit for this because of his work with Kleberg, and he reasoned that, since he knew officials with "direct and intimate access to the White House," he was just the man to push the dams on through. As for the corporate dragons, "I will not have time to look after the power interests. I have never accepted a dime from a utility or special interst, and I never will."

He poor-boyed his way through the campaign, once throwing down onto a platform some kind of mortgage on his father's farm. When he was driven in a Pontiac four-door sedan to a funeral, rather than let people see the car he had the driver park three blocks away. Polk Shelton charged that lobbyist Roy Miller was backing Johnson with money and letters (not true, Johnson said much later), and in a debate at Smithville with Polk's brother, Johnson was accused of spending from fifteen thousand to twenty thousand dollars, some of it from sulphur and utilities interests, for a job that paid only ten thousand dollars a year. He answered that his campaign was financed by his own "meager savings." In chauvinist Texas it would not do for people to know he was running on his wife's money, but he later said that the bonds they had been saving came to $3,000 by 1937 and this went into the campaign, so there was probably some truth in his answer. Apart from the four hundred dollars from George, he said, there really were no donations; but an aide later said that people in south Texas got up "a kitty." Sulphur lobbyist Miller was a south Texan.

Johnson and Senator Brownlee were scheduled to have a debate, and more than a thousand people turned up in Burnet for it, but not Brownlee. "It won the election," Lyndon said. One night, after midnight, he went into the newspaper office in Austin, bragged to Fulcher about how well he was running, and suggested, "Why don't you get out and find out?" Fulcher and a reporter took a poll that showed Johnson and Harris leading. Johnson's "in" at the paper meant even more to him when the day before the election the banner headline proclaimed, "Lyndon Johnson Undergoes Emergency Operation for Appendicitis."

Finishing a speech at the courthouse in Austin, he had turned to Bardwell and said, "Sherman, stand close to me. I feel as if I'm going to faint," and that night he was taken to a hospital. Fulcher wrote him a note saying, in effect, "Go on and get operated on. The only thing you're going to have to worry about is what kind of tie you wear for your swearing-in ceremonies." Someone telephoned Dan Quill and said, "Well, he's sick; he has got acute appendicitis." "Operate on him," Quill said. "That'll get us more votes than anything else. He has fallen in the battlefield."

The thing looked faked and people said so. Lyndon, knowing they would, insisted that a brother of Brownlee's who was a doctor participate in the operation so that (as Johnsonian Paul Bolton, a journalist, was told later) "there would be no question about it being, you know, some put-up job or something." A country doctor, having called Johnson's family doctor to ascertain that the operation had actually happened, went up and down the streets of his town cussing "these sons of bitches" for saying it hadn't, thereby converting people to Johnson. "There wasn't any fake about it," Wild said. "He was sick."

But the timing was too neat. Biographer Clarke Newlon quoted an unnamed old friend of Johnson's, "I'm not sure how much of an emergency it was. Seems to me Lyndon had been complaining about that appendix for some time. But this sure was a good time to have it out —at least as far as the publicity was concerned." The final speech, which was to be broadcast on the radio, had been written probably by Ray Lee; Wild went to the rally and read it, saying Johnson had written it. "Oh," said Luther Jones of the operation, "I think it was real—but the way it was used! I remember how dramatic it was. Wild could make a better speech than Lyndon. Of course we were sorry he had the operation—but we were glad Mr. Wild was making the last speech."

On election day Quill was going to Washington, and down at the train depot Sam Fore, the Democratic editor, showed him a check (one thousand dollars it was, Quill thought) that President Roosevelt had sent down for the campaign. Governor Allred got on the train with Quill, and they heard spot announcements on the radio that Johnson was leading. Allred was delighted. No, no, governor, Quill explained, those are paid advertisements.

With thirty thousand votes cast, Johnson won with eight thousand, twenty-eight percent of the total. The next five candidates got sixty-nine percent among them, from seventeen to ten percent each. Merton Harris, the one Wild had feared the most and therefore had instructed Johnson to ignore, finished second with five thousand votes, ten points behind.

In his triumph Lyndon met Carol Davis one last time. Waking in his hospital bed, he saw her standing in the doorway in a flowered yellow dress. She had married a young banker who had pleased her father, Johnson said, "But here she was, looking more beautiful than I'd remembered." She told him how happy she was for him. She said she had defied her father's wish and voted for him. "I knew then that she was still in love with me," Johnson said. "But there was nothing left to be done about it."[3]

PART VII
Fast Shadow in a Power Plant

Yet, after all, let us acknowledge it wiser, if not more sagacious, to follow out one's day-dream to its natural consummation, although, if the vision have been worth the having, it is certain never to be consummated otherwise than by a failure. And what of that? Its airiest fragments, impalpable as they may be, will possess a value that lurks not in the most ponderous realities of any practicable scheme. They are not the rubbish of the mind. Whatever else I may repent of, therefore, let it be reckoned neither among my sins nor follies that I once had faith and force enough to form generous hopes of the world's destiny,—yes!—and to do what in me lay for their accomplishment; even to the extent of quitting a warm fireside, flinging away a freshly lighted cigar, and traveling far beyond the strike of city clocks, through a drifting snowstorm.

— Nathaniel Hawthorne, *The Blithedale Romance*

35. A Train Ride to Power

"Lyndon," his mother once told him, "if you must be a politician, at least be the best." Now she wrote him, "My darling boy, Beyond 'Congratulations, Congressman' what am I to say to my dear son in this hour of triumphant success? In this as in all the many letters I have written you there is this same theme: I love you; I believe in you; I expect great things of you."

On his way to those great things Johnson was never too proud to court an opponent there was a chance he could neutralize or win over. Three days after the election he had his people play up to Austin Mayor Tom Miller, who had opposed him. "I wouldn't have had the nerve," Quill said. In a three-hour session Lyndon himself completed his conquest of the mayor. It was a technique he used the rest of his life.

After Lyndon recuperated for a spell at the Taylors' plantation in East Texas, he and Bird returned to Austin and had dinner with the Allreds. The story is told in the Allred family that Lyndon put his arm around the governor's shoulder and said, "Jimmy, I couldn't have made it without you."[1]

Roosevelt's son Elliott had gone to Fort Worth to run the radio stations of the Texas State Network with the financial backing of Sid Richardson, who was already a major independent in oil, gas, and pipelines. As a Texas insider said, "Sid got in through Elliott and stayed friends with the Old Man." A bachelor, Richardson lived in the Fort Worth Club, and he and Amon Carter, the publisher of the *Fort Worth Star-Telegram,* would get on the phone direct to Roosevelt, telling him gamy jokes and making points.

That May in 1937 Roosevelt, aboard his official yacht with two destroyers in escort, was taking a ten-day fishing cruise in the waters off millionaire Richardson's private island on the Texas coast. For a week Roosevelt caught only kingfish, but on the ninth day he hooked and boated a seventy-seven pound silver king tarpon. When Allred suggested to Johnson that the president would like to see him upon disembarking to Galveston, Johnson eagerly agreed. Roosevelt "had met me a time or two," Johnson said, "but as far as I know he took no interest. . . . He asked me through Jimmy Allred to come join him in Galveston after the election. . . . I think he liked to see a young, vigorous, virile, hopeful person."

Driven to Galveston by Keach, Johnson waited at the dock with Allred and the city's mayor. As Roosevelt stepped ashore, a battery fired a twenty-one gun salute and the mayor called the president "the Pericles of the West" who was presiding over "the golden age of democracy." In front of the Hotel Galvez, the cameras grinding, Allred greeted Roosevelt, then yielded to Johnson so he could come beside the president and talk directly to him. Although Roosevelt had landed only one more tarpon, he was in good spirits. "Yesterday," he said, "one of our party caught a twenty-four-pound amberjack, and this morning that same fish weighed thirty-five pounds."

That night Johnson and Keach spent time with Elliott, and the next morning at Roosevelt's invitation Johnson rode on the presidential train to College Station. Johnson first went to the compartment of a reporter, rested there a little, and then went back to the president's car for a long visit with Roosevelt. The reporter believed from that day on that Johnson was preparing to be president. Serving in the White House three decades later, Johnson clearly remembered his talk with Roosevelt as the train clacked and swayed across the coastal plain.

In Europe Germany had quit the League of Nations, Hitler had rejected the Versailles Treaty and ordered universal conscription, his troops had reoccupied the Rhineland, Italy had invaded and annexed Ethiopia, and the civil war was bleeding Spain. Ambassador William C. Bullitt wrote Roosevelt from Paris that in Europe, "Everyone is spending every ounce of energy on preparing instruments of war."

In 1913 Roosevelt had been rewarded for supporting Wilson for president with his appointment as assistant secretary of the navy, and when war had broken out in Europe he had become a champion of military preparedness. Fishing out in the Gulf that spring of 1937, his thoughts may have returned often to the need for a stronger navy, and alone in the train compartment with this driving young man so eager to do whatever he wished, he assigned him on the spot to the cause of naval preparedness.

Knowing Roosevelt had served in the Wilson administration with Albert Sidney Burleson, Lyndon had brought along, to show the president, a paper sack on which Burleson had forecast Johnson's election. Johnson evidently also discussed with Roosevelt the idea of establishing a naval air base at Corpus Christi.

"You might be just the person I want to help out with Naval Affairs," Roosevelt told him. "We talked about the war when he was assistant secretary of the Navy," Johnson said. "He told me what committee I should go on. Hitler was going to take over the world. Garner was against some cruisers. He [Roosevelt] wanted somebody from Texas that would vote for a strong Navy." Roosevelt gave him the private phone number of Tom Corcoran and told him as soon as he got settled to call Tom and tell him they had discussed Johnson going on the naval affairs committee of the House.

At College Station Roosevelt told the three thousand members of the Texas A&M cadet corps that military spending was relatively inexpensive and was for defense, not for aggression. Thus Johnson's first personal experience of his hero in the thirties fixed firmly in his mind the cause of military preparedness.

Lyndon's old father was ailing from heart trouble, but he joined Rebekah in seeing his son off for Washington at the train station in Austin. "Son," Lyndon remembered his dad telling him, "measure each vote you cast by this standard: Is this vote in the benefit of people? What does this do for human beings? How have I helped the lame and the halt and the ignorant and the diseased? See if this vote is generally for humanity. . . . When you get ready to vote and you are in doubt, and there will be times when you are in doubt and you don't know whether to say yes or no, and they start calling the roll, just pass and wait until Wright Patman votes and then vote like he does, because I was his deskmate . . . and he always voted for the people." And Roosevelt, too: "Now you get up there, support FDR all the way, never shimmy and give 'em hell."[2]

"By the time Lyndon arrived in Washington," Tom Corcoran said, "the word had gone out: 'Be nice to this boy.' " On May 13, 1937, as the *Congressional Record* described the event, "Mr. Lyndon Johnson appeared in the Well of the House and took the oath of office," and Maury Maverick of San Antonio exclaimed, "Mr. Speaker, the gentleman just sworn in, Mr. Lyndon Johnson, supported the President's judiciary plan and was overwhelmingly elected!" and there was applause. Court-packing—already defeated in the Senate—was now a dead letter, but Franklin D. Roosevelt was still the president.

Fred Vinson, a member of the House ways and means committee, told Johnson, "Thank you for dinner at the White House last night." Roosevelt had invited him over and during the evening had let drop to him, "By the way, Fred, I wish you'd put that young man from Texas on the naval affairs committee." And it was done. "I never lifted my finger," Johnson said.[3]

To conservatives back in Austin, Johnson seemed a sychophant. "Right from the first," said editor Travis, "he had power, because he went over to the White House and told FDR he was there to serve him." But William O. Douglas, a member of the Securities and Exchange Commission at this time, said that because of the court-packing matter, Roosevelt "had a special feeling toward Lyndon." In less than three months the young man from the banks of the Pedernales River had announced and then consummated a relationship with the president of the United States.

"I had many breakfasts with him," Johnson said, "and even lunch with him—the day he fired Joe Kennedy." For one thing, he said, they used to talk about his grandfather's friendship with Sam Houston. The young congressman would find himself shuffled out of the president's office before he wanted to be, "but you weren't mad." His feelings that "this is the President" strongly impressed his wife. "I remember him, various times," she said, "talking about going down to see President Roosevelt, and how he would sometimes be propped up in bed with his navy cape around his shoulders, and how sometimes he would have lunch—just the two of them on a card table, with Missy LeHand going in and out."

Claude Wild said that Johnson, about the same age as Roosevelt's sons, "ran around with them. He could come in the back door just like they could, you know." Word seeped out that he had a special relationship with the president, and as Representative Manny Celler of New York said, this gave him a little extra clout. "He could always get to the President," Corcoran said, "and this information got around. He found other congressmen were asking him for favors; his prestige on Capitol Hill was sky high."[4]

Maverick, burly, belligerent, and a high-minded progressive, had become the leader of "the Young Turks," "the Neo-New Dealers" who saw that the New Deal was dying and fought to save it.

In 1935 Maverick, the spokesman for a group of at least thirty-four "mavericks" in the House, had announced their program of government ownership of all natural resources and monopolies vested with public interest, higher taxes on a graduated basis, farm debt refinancing at 1.5 percent interest and lower home-loan interest, and the "deprofitizing" of war. Maverick wanted a law that would "eliminate in advance any chance of profits" by merchants of war goods. Like John Kenneth Galbraith in the 1970s he wanted public ownership of munitions manufacturing, and he proposed a government-owned "central bank of issue" that would permit "the government of the United States—which belongs to the people—to finance itself."

The same month in which Maverick shouted his welcome to Johnson in the Congress, Walter Lippmann wrote that the San Antonian was "very representative indeed of the little group of bold and reckless men who have been setting the pace for the president in the past few months," and an article in the *Saturday Evening Post* identified him as the "guiding genius and general out-in-front man" for the bloc of forty or so where were demanding that the New Deal go forward. Their plan for 1937 included a job for every "willing worker." Maury Maverick was to the undeclared American populists of the thirties what Tom Nugent was to the Texas Populists when Lyndon's grandfather ran for the legislature as one of them.

"When I thought about the kind of congressman I wanted to be," Johnson told Kearns, "I thought about my Populist grandfather and promised myself that I'd always be the people's congressman, representing all the people, not just the ones with money and power." In fact, despite his long association with Maverick, Johnson turned away from him and his group. Maverick was fronting up to the president, telling him to forge new programs in the tempest of the conservative reaction, while Johnson was trying to serve Roosevelt.

According to Mark Adams, who was active in the Young Turks as a New Deal bureaucrat, Johnson never turned up at their meetings. Discussing that time with Maverick in his mind, Johnson spoke of "a trend away from what had been a prudent progressivism. We were not radicals, but progressives."[5] Whatever he meant exactly, what he did was work to obtain specific New Deal projects and benefits for his home district and his home people. Maury might march to a different drummer if he had to, but Lyndon's drummer lived at 1600 Pennsylvania Avenue.

Just at this time, Lyndon's flesh and blood bond to his Populist past snapped. In October, 1937, when he and Bird were in Austin, Sam Johnson had a heart attack. In the hospital he ordered Lyndon, "Get my breeches, because I'm going home." His son argued against it—they didn't have the medical facilities he needed in Johnson City. "Nope," Sam said, "I'm going home where they know when you're sick and care when you die." Liking the impersonal hospital no more than his father did, Lyndon gave in, helping his father dress; but he took him, not to Johnson City, but to his own Austin home at Four Happy Hollow. Sam had his son bring a radio into his room so they could hear Roosevelt make the case for a national minimum wage and call a special session that November. The old man's last ambition, to visit the gallery in Washington and see his son on the House floor, was not to be. He was the only person Lyndon ever saw die—he never wanted to see it again.

A hill-country woman who went to the funeral said Sam had owed everybody, and she heard men saying at the funeral, "Well, there went my $1,500," and "Yeah, I've got $1,000 in that, too." He had not been able to pay off a $3,500 homeowners loan, so "Mrs. Johnson got some money and paid it off," Lyndon said. "My father didn't leave anything."[6]

---

36. "They Called Me a Communist"

Lyndon and Bird began their twenty-three years of living back and forth between Washington and home base. They moved into the first of about seven Washington apartments they were to live in during the next five years. His salary was $10,000 a year, $833 a month, but, he said, Bird made them live on what was left after they paid her father $500 a month so they could retire the $10,000 they had borrowed. They kept Four Happy Hollow in Austin year-round, when in Washington renting it to friends. Bird had brought a black cook, Zephyr, into their household from the Taylors' home area at the Texas-Louisiana border. A little later Johnson, to help his mother with housekeeping and yard-work, hired Cleo Deaver, a black girl of fourteen who was pregnant and fortunately was married (he called her "Lucky").

From the time the Johnsons first arrived in Washington they frequented "Longlea," the plantation home of their friend, publisher Charles Marsh, in Culpepper, Virginia. "When you were with Charley Marsh," according to Martin Anderson, who jointly owned a Florida newspaper with him, "you were a part of his establishment," and this then included Colonel E. M. House of the Wilson years, oilman Sid Richardson, a Norwegian author, and a symphony conductor.

As always Johnson was all politics. His friends could not remember him going to a movie, a play, or a musical. He played a little golf or went swimming, but seldom hunting, and if he went fishing he didn't fish.[1]

Coming into his congressional office early, he would be gone most of the day, busy with his committee or the House, but he rode his staff by phone. As he had done for Kleberg, now for himself he insisted on the rule that all letters had to be answered in twenty-four hours. If people let him down he would hand out diplomas in the "I Cain't Do It Club." Birdwell, his first office manager, was so busy typing, he did not even enter the Capitol building his first three months at work. Except when trying to learn shorthand in a school, Birdwell worked from seven or eight in the morning till twelve or one at night.

Johnson not only wanted congratulatory letters sent to every high-school graduate in his district, the letters had to be personal, every one different so that no two graduates of the same school would get identical letters. To his key people back home he sent a farm yearbook and a government manual on horse diseases, scavenging extra copies from other congressional offices. "I imagine we filled a box car with those books, 'The Diseases of the Horse,' " said staffer John Koeniger.

Johnson had brought with him from the NYA a gifted, but hard-drinking researcher and writer, Herbert Henderson. Once this erratic fellow disappeared and Johnson had the FBI chase him down. Johnson then told Koeniger, "Now here's what I want you to do. He's indispensable. I want you to room with him. You're not to do any drinking, because if you do, he will." Like anyone who wanted to go on working for Johnson, Koeniger obeyed.

Johnson saw visiting constituents when he could, and during his first term a cowboy from Johnson City, Teamer Furr, stopped by. Furr had decided to ride a horse from Austin to New York City, delivering a letter from the mayor of the one to the mayor of the other. He trotted into Washington, staked out his horse, and called on his fellow townsman.

"Well, Teamer," Lyndon said, "what can we do for you?" "I'd like to meet the President," he said. Johnson called the White House, but Roosevelt was aboard his yacht for the weekend.

"Anybody else?" The vice-president would do. On the phone Mrs. Garner told Johnson, "You can always bring a cowboy to our office," so Johnson did. The vice-president from Texas, wearing his white hat, told Teamer, "I rode ninety miles one time in two days. I was sore after that. I had to eat my breakfast off the mantelpiece."[2]

With fellows like Garner leading the opposition, the reform period of the New Deal was ending. In 1937 only two important new laws were passed, the provision of low-interest loans to farm tenants and the creation of an agency for low-cost public housing.

Early on Johnson conspicuously displayed his fealty to Roosevelt. The president, frightened by a new recession and never a pump-primer as a matter of fixed policy, wanted to cut the budget, so he vetoed the continuation of veterans' term insurance. The House, which after four years as his yo-yo had begun to assert itself, overrode him, 372 to 13, but one of the 13 was Johnson. However, when FDR vetoed giving farmers low interest on land loans Johnson voted to override.[3]

Roosevelt's penny-pinching helped plunge the economy back to 1932 levels (unemployment increased by four million in the fall and winter of '37–'38) until Congress resumed spending for relief and public works. To prove that his White House access paid off, Johnson had to keep the federal money coming for the six dams that were being built on the Colorado.

Floods had ravaged the river valley three times since 1900, killing one hundred people, costing millions, and destroying a dam at Austin. In 1935 the Lower Colorado River Authority (the LCRA) had been created, and by the time Johnson took office the dams were forty percent done. Buchanan had been seeking five million dollars for Mansfield Dam when he died, and Johnson's number-one project was getting this money. "I said I would complete Buchanan and start Mansfield in 1937," he said. "What decided whether *I* made good or not was Mansfield."

Sam Rayburn, who had become the House majority leader earlier that year, had given Johnson and another new member of naval affairs some standard cautionary advice: "I want you two to keep your mouths shut on the floor. You won't know what the score is for a long time. Also remember, don't get involved with broad issues, because you have to get reelected; and if you get into the big issues, the voters will think you aren't taking care of your district's problems." Johnson had an oration prepared on behalf of the five million dollars, which was to be authorized in a work relief bill. Before he knew it they were two pages past the dam—the money was appropriated without a word said. From then on, Johnson said, "I'd try and say as little as I could." He associated all this with a remark Wirtz made, "I'd rather be a live congressman than a dead hero."

Johnson became almost indispensable to contractor Herman Brown as serious problems developed concerning his company's work on the Austin and Marshall Ford dams.

The Public Works Administration was "very definitely unfavorable" to the Austin dam because of previous LCRA cost overruns and excessive expenses, Johnson warned Wirtz shortly after the 1937 election. There was a conflict over new bond-issuing authority for the LCRA. In 1938 outside consulting engineers raised grave doubts about the engineering soundness of the project. There was a legal problem about how Austin would turn over the original Austin dam site to LCRA.

The feds regarded the fees LCRA paid to Wirtz's law firm as "way out of line." Wirtz's travel expenses, another Washington bureaucrat complained, were "unusually lavish." Johnson called signals for Wirtz in his struggle for his fees, which were a factor in Washington's growing skittishness toward the LCRA. By the end of the thirties Wirtz, having been paid fees and expenses of almost ninety thousand dollars by LCRA, was denied his request for an additional ten thousand dollars.

Johnson also swung into action when a serious issue arose concerning whether the Marshall Ford dam was "a federal project." Had it been found not to be, federal funding would have been jeopardized. Herman Brown sent briefs to his brother George and to Lyndon, arguing that it was. There was a hang-up about a reimbursable feature of the Marshall Ford contract.

At one point Johnson brought White House aide Tom Corcoran into play—Johnson and Wirtz met at a specified time at the White House. The bureaucratic hassles that enveloped Herman Brown were just what Johnson needed. Helping solve them one by one, he drew closer and closer to the Browns.

Although the appropriations for the dams had been sold at first as a flood control program, this was a trick to conceal the additional purpose, cheap public electric power. "That way," according to Ray Lee, "they could get the power people off their back." The dams, Johnson said, had several purposes, "but the most important . . . was electricity to replace the kerosene lamp." The five million dollars was not only for Mansfield Dam, but also for power turbines. As Lee explained their strategy, once the power was there, a rural electrical cooperative could be set up to distribute it.

The two private utility companies in the area, Central Power and Light and Texas Power and Light, did not believe they could serve rural areas profitably, so people even a mile or two outside Austin did not have electric lights, yet the companies also condemned the idea of rural co-ops and were suing to stop the whole Colorado project. Johnson became their political enemy.

He had been raised by the light of lanterns and cooked for on a wood-burning stove. He had seen his mother scrubbing clothes in a washtub. He knew the insides of outhouses. In 1935 only about one farm in ten had commercial electricity. In Johnson's area the farm people had a smokehouse for beef, sausage, and hams; for fresh meat they had to kill a chicken, go shoot some squirrels or rabbits, or catch some fish. When night closed in on them like a huge hand, they lit candles or lanterns or sat in the dark. Cheap electricity would change all that, making the night light and easing every day the one task that took the most work and time, getting your meals.

And Johnson was listening at this time to Dr. Robert Montgomery, the economist who had almost run for the job Johnson now held. The month before the Mansfield money was slipped through, Montgomery had laid out a formulation of the case against large corporations that was well designed to appeal to provincials like Johnson.

Texas, the good professor said, was the largest foreign colony owned by Manhattan. Among "foreigners" he included corporations of northern and eastern financial centers. In Dr. Bob's formulation, then, ninety-five percent of the state's electric power industry, eighty-three percent of the oil refineries, more than ninety-nine percent of the railroads, and all of the Texas-based worldwide sulphur monopoly were foreign-owned. The state's electricity rates were millions higher than they would have been if Texans lived in the Tennessee Valley, where power was publicly produced. Pipelines owned by non-Texans handled at least ninety-one percent of the state's natural gas production. Only the federal government was strong enough, Dr. Bob contended, to cope with this anomaly.

The dams and the power they would produce, called "the little TVA of the Southwest" by the *New York Times,* had socialistic implications.

Were private companies to be allowed to build the dams and pile up profits from the power generated from the publicly-owned falling water? Or would the government own the dams and sell the power cheaply to the citizens? Different companies could not compete to provide the electricity since you could not efficiently have two companies selling one river's power in the same areas. The case for the limited socialism called "public power" was plain, and Johnson knew and felt the sting of his position. "They hated me for these dams," he told me. "The power companies gave me hell. They called me a Communist." Still he went ahead, never failing to extract from the crunch every benefit he could.

A scene was staged at the White House for his home-town press, especially friend Marsh's Austin papers. "I came in and saw the president," Johnson said in the White House. "He called Jimmy Roosevelt in here and gave Jimmy a check, and Jimmy gave it to me." The reporters were assembled to be the audience for the scene on the White House portico: the president's son greeting an Austin delegation and presenting the five-million-dollar authorization to Johnson. WPA administrator Harry Hopkins was onstage, too, saying, "We are doing this for Congressman Johnson," who had been "fighting for this project." Back in Austin the newspaper headlined the story, "Johnson Awarded Five Million to Finish Colorado Work." People like Charley Marsh, producers of politics as a series of one-act plays, must have enjoyed this one. Later it was claimed that Johnson had persuaded Roosevelt to provide the money.[4]

---

37. Housing for the Poor, by Race

In some corporate board rooms resentment of Johnson's commitment to public power was sputtering like a snapped electric cable, but during this early period of his humanist crusading his first public conflict came over public housing.

In the 1920s a movement had begun in Europe to provide slum dwellers who could not afford private housing with publicly-owned or publicly-aided living quarters. In 1937 this movement reached the United States with the enactment of the Wagner-Steagall bill to have the federal government provide the poor with low-rent public housing through local agencies.

Johnson didn't just vote aye. He went to Austin, called together Tom Miller and his other local heavies, and said, "Now look, I want us to be first in the United States if you're willing to do this, and you've got to be willing to stand up for the Negroes and Mexicans." As Ray Lee remembered, "Tom got his shirt-tail to flyin' and the wheelers and dealers decided to go ahead with the thing."

Toward the end of the year the new U.S. Housing Authority awarded its initial aid for public housing to New York City, New Orleans, and Austin, Texas. Why Austin? "Because," said Leon Keyserling, then deputy administrator of the federal agency, "there was this first-term congressman who was so on his toes and so active and so overwhelming that he was up and down our corridors all the time. . . ."

Johnson called on Keyserling and said, "Lady Bird and I want you to have cocktails with us."—"How's that?"—"Well, we want Austin to be announced first."—"Well, why first? Mayor LaGuardia [of New York] might not like that."—"Well, it's first in the alphabet, isn't it?"

The three were announced simultaneously.

Johnson went before the city council in Austin just before Christmas, 1937. "We have some slums in Austin," he told them. "We ought to be progressive enough to remove certain eyesores." He argued there was a correlation between poor housing areas and juvenile delinquency, crime in general, and poor health, especially tuberculosis and syphilis. The next day the city organized a housing authority, Johnson himself naming two of the five members. By year's end the agency had applied for ninety percent federal funding of a half-million-dollar program to build 550 rooms that would be rented at three dollars to five dollars a room a month, but only to families whose incomes were not more than five times the rent. Washington approved in two weeks, giving Austin a first for the Southwest.

Johnson had warned of opposition by "selfish real estate interests." Waking with a start to what was going on, a past president of the Chamber of Commerce spoke up against the city going into the rental business, since, he said, every American has the right to say where he will live and "if his home is built of license plates, he still retains his independence." Governor Allred said the opposition was coming from people who had "forgotten what it is to be poor" and from people who owned slums. The Marsh papers ran stories about a "tin-can shack village" and families living in tents and the bodies of old cars, and Johnson made a walking tour through the city's slums on Christmas day:

"I found one family that might almost be called typical living within one dreary room, where no single window let in the sun," he said. "Here they slept, they cooked and ate, they washed themselves in a leaky tin tub after hauling the water two hundred yards. Here they raised their children, ill-nourished and sordid. And on this Christmas morning, there was no Santa Claus for the ten children, all under sixteen, that scrambled around the feet of a wretched mother bent over her wash-tub, while in this same room her husband, the father of her brood, lay dangerously ill with an infectious disease." Thirty years later

Johnson still remembered the squalor he saw that Christmas day, "five blocks a hundred families, an old man with TB, dying, a child of eleven . . . all of them Mexicans."

In a meeting attended, according to people's memories, by conservative realtors, Mayor Miller, Johnson, and others, the opposition was pincered. When one of the realtors would flail the socialistic plan, Johnson would point out how many slum units the man owned. Once again he was slugging back hard at the charge of socialism and unfair public competition with business. "The government is competing," he said, "with the shacks and hovels and hogsties and all the other foul holes in which the underprivileged have to live." At a meeting of several hundred at the courthouse he said one out of every six houses in the city had no running water, one out of five no lights, almost one out of three no bath—at that, the clubwomen joined the crusade. When a councilman bucked him he fought mean, telling a reporter the councilman "told me that he was for the housing project if it did not compete with his rent houses. . . ."

Austin's housing agency became the first in the country to complete and lease a unit under the 1937 Housing Act. Posing happily with five Mexican-American children in front of their new home in the project, Johnson said, "This country won't have to worry about isms when it gives its people a decent, clean place to live and a job, they'll believe in the government—they'll be willing to fight for it."

But the project had at least two serious flaws, each one in its own way a clue to the future.

The New Deal did not seek integration; the social crusaders of the thirties were content to advocate gains for the poor within segregated patterns. The first public housing in Austin came in three parts, Chalmers courts for whites, Santa Rita courts for Mexicans, and Rosewood courts for blacks.

The second problem was the scale of the reform, its size. Even after it was enlarged by a couple of hundred thousand dollars, the Austin project funded only "forty Mexican units, sixty Negro units, and eighty-six or more white units, with possible expansion of white units to be governed by the surplus," housing for not more than two hundred families in a city of fourteen thousand homes.[1]

---

38. Lighting Up the Farmhouse

Like Johnson, Sam Rayburn of north Texas had seen his mother doing the family washing in a tub and straining to read the Bible by a lamp. While Johnson was running the NYA in Texas, Rayburn was cudgeling the federal government into making thirty-five-year, two-percent loans for rural power systems that were to be run, preferably, by co-ops. Newspapers in his district called him a socialist. The president of Texas Power and Light asked a local banker how much it would take to beat him, and "when this banker told him it couldn't be done," according to Rayburn, "he said they had the money to do anything."

The farmers for sure did not have the money to get electricity without federal help. In Johnson City the Pedernales electric co-op had been denied a Rural Electrification Act (REA) loan because there weren't enough participants, so Johnson went himself into the field to solicit customers. For REA power to be economically feasible there had to be a certain number of people per square mile, and the population density in Johnson's district was less than half that required.

"I finally had to go all the way up to President Roosevelt," Johnson said. "I had been told that he liked to see pictures and drawings of ships and maps and things of that kind, so I had a big picture made of the dam, and a picture of the transmission lines that led from the dam to the big cities. . . ."

As Johnson later described what happened, he carried these three-foot pictures of Buchanan Dam and the power lines in to the president, and Roosevelt, sensing that his pet was about to ask a favor, studied them intently. "Great, wonderful, Lyndon!" he exclaimed. "I have never seen better or more marvelous examples of multiple-arch dam construction. It's real ingenuity." He went on and on about the engineering genius of their time, but his young friend listened, without interrupting, patiently.

Finally the president ran out of gab, fitted a cigarette into his holder, lit it up, and sat back.

"Now, Lyndon, now what in the hell do you want? Just why are you showing me all these pictures?"

"Water, water everywhere, not a drop to drink! Power, power, everywhere, but not in a home on the banks of these rural rivers!"

"What do you mean by that!" the exasperated Roosevelt demanded.

Johnson explained that although the people of his district had supported Roosevelt, they could not get power because of the density rule. Digging at the power trusts that had fought the New Deal, pleading for the impoverished farmer, he told the president how he and his brother had toted water from the well and heated it over a wood fire so his mother could wash the laundry; he cleaned again, for the president's imagination, the kerosene lamps.

Touched, Roosevelt rolled his wheelchair to a phone, telephoned John Carmody, the head of the REA, and asked him about Johnson's district. Johnson remembered Roosevelt saying into the phone, "What do you mean by density?" He waited while Carmody explained to him, and then he said, "Well, I don't know much about density, but I have seen those rivers, and I know those people, and in due time they're going to overcome that one handicap. There'll be ample people to pay that line out if you'll ever put it in, because those people are going to breed quickly." So put the line in anyway, the president said. Rule or no rule, it was done.[1]

In 1938 downriver farmers, who suspected correctly that the New Dealers were working harder on public power than on flood control, were enraged when the dams did not control a wild flood, and the power companies made the most of the situation.

The farmers of the flooded valley learned, in a mass meeting, that the Buchanan Dam site was such that the dam could be built high enough for the water to fall down through it far enough for power generation, but that the basin behind the dam was too small for controlling floods. Johnson always remembered, and with characteristic hyperbole, the roasting they gave him. "They said the dam hadn't been closed," he remembered. "I was almost burned at the stake. I was investigated, I was condemned. . . . The dam hadn't been finished—and they said it was a man-made flood and I caused it."[2] When he told them the dam would be made higher (even though at a cost of fifteen million dollars) they were somewhat mollified.

That fall, though, the Pedernales co-op received its first REA loan and went to work erecting 1,718 miles of line to convey electric power to 3,500 customers. From now on, Johnson exulted, farm women "can lay aside their corrugated washboards and let their red hot cookstoves cool off while they iron on a hot August afternoon. The farmer who has been dragging water out of a well with a bucket all his life can . . . get himself an electric pump to do the work. . . ."

Congressman Johnson of course had the run of the co-op based in his home town, and from now on, too, he began to cultivate a connection with antiunion contractor Herman Brown, a connection that became a politically lucrative liaison that would affect his entire career. Brown & Root won an $800,000 transmission line contract from the co-op.[3]

The struggle to establish the public power was, Ray Lee said, "a hard, mean, bloody fight, with Texas Power & Light at one end of the district and Central Power & Light at the other." Johnson said, "When we got our charter and formed our cooperative, outlined where we were going to build our line, overnight [the power companies] moved two hundred men in into a territory that had never seemed attractive to them before, but they built that line so that it would parallel ours when it was built.

"And a few days later we had a meeting with the president of the power company to try to work out some of the difficulties . . . and the conversation became strong and animated, and the discussions rather heated, and I kept trying to get some concession from the president of the power company that he wouldn't parallel our line, and finally in an outburst of emotion 'n irritation, I said,

" 'Well now we've tried to work with you for several months. We've waited many years to get lights in our homes, and now that we have the chance, you're going to deny us that chance, and I'm not going to try to reason with you any more, because you're so obstinate that I'm convinced it does no good, and so far as I'm concerned you can take a running jump and go straight to hell.'

"The board of directors and the farmers from the valleys and the ranchmen that heard that applauded my statement, and when we left the meeting room they all came over and shook hands and congratulated me and told me they were glad that their young congressman would stand up to the president of a big power company and tell him where to go. And I think there was almost unanimous approval."

But he had not talked with one person there, Alvin Wirtz, now the lawyer for the REA and the LCRA, and he wanted his approval more than anyone's. He went over to him and asked how he had liked his speech. Wirtz, looking at him cordially, said, "Well, I want to discuss it with you. Before you leave come by my office." In the office Wirtz led easily into what he had to say. He had been working to bring the power company president into the meeting for many months, and "There's one thing I must tell you and you might as well learn now," he said. "You conclusion wasn't very good. It's one thing to tell a man to go to hell. It's another thing to make a man *go* to hell. He doesn't want to *go,* and tellin' him to go's not gonna *make* him go. It took me months to get him here, and it just took you two minutes to bust up the whole meeting, and now I'll have to start all over again."[4] For the rest of his life Johnson, justifying compromise or chastening "the red-hots," told this story over and over.

The little towns had to decide whether to stay with the private companies or join with the rural co-ops and install municipally-owned power systems. Johnson crusaded in the little towns for public power. Remembering some of those speeches, Fulcher said that "in some respects he was a consummate actor. He would wheedle, he would cajole, he would pout, he would use logic, he would make a personal appeal, he would be lofty or humble, he would, upon occasion, throw a tantrum, he would be magnanimous and expansive or cold and distant. . . ." The REA won twenty-five of twenty-six municipal elections over Texas Power & Light. "I lost Columbus," Johnson said proudly. The power companies had to yield.

But once again an alligator from the swamps of ideology snapped at him: a circular was put out "that I was a communist," he remembered.[5]

In 1939 the Reconstruction Finance Corporation loaned the LCRA five million dollars to buy private utilities' properties, and two Texas companies sold to the LCRA, for that sum, electricity-producing prop-

AUSTIN STATESMAN

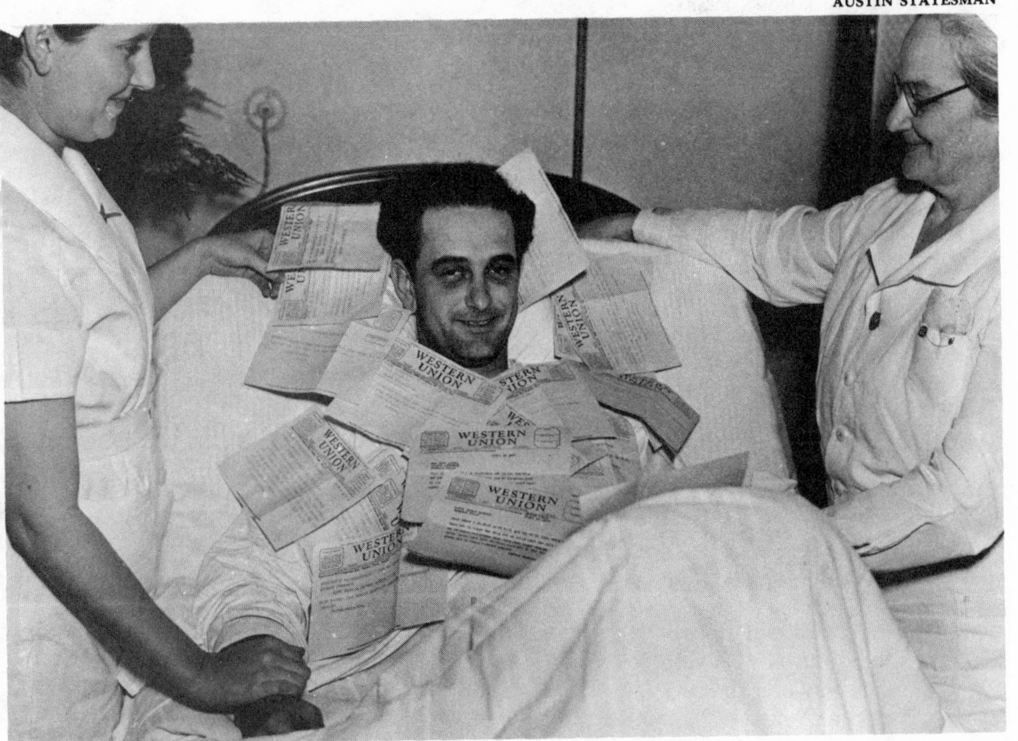

Johnson poses with congratulatory telegrams in his hospital bed after his 1937 victory for a congressional seat. A last-minute attack of appendicitis gave him dramatic publicity and extra votes.

Below left, Dr. Bob Montgomery, the liberal professor who almost but did not run in the election Johnson won. Right, the rich and powerful publisher Charles Marsh, a key man in Johnson's rise.

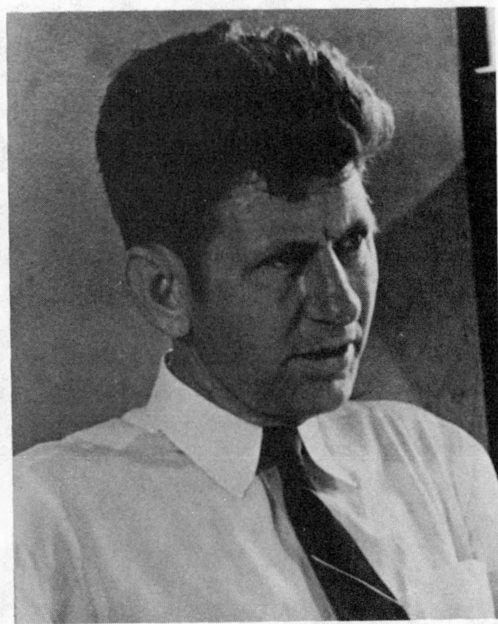

MONTGOMERY, JAMES DIBRELL

MARSH, JOHNSON LIBRARY COURTESY OF FRANK WOLFE

JOHNSON LIBRARY

President Roosevelt greets newly elected Congressman Johnson upon FDR's return to Galveston from a fishing trip. Governor Jimmy Allred of Texas stands between them.

Setting out for the Capitol for the first time since his election, Johnson kisses his father goodbye at the train station in Austin on April 27, 1937. Sam did not have much longer to live.

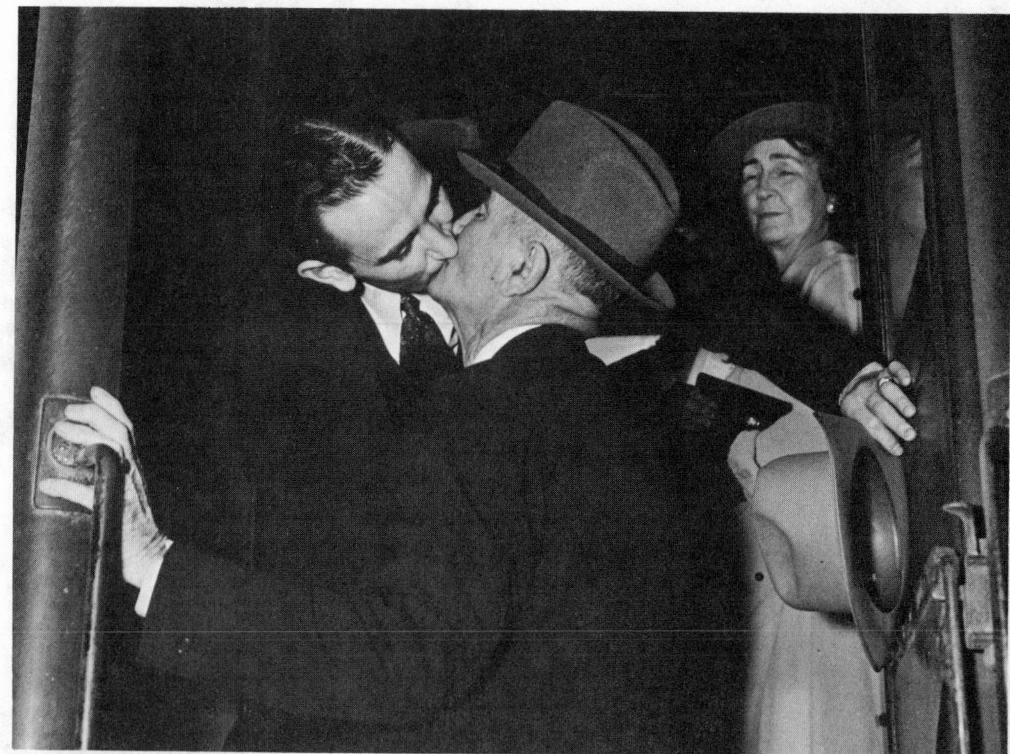

AUSTIN STATESMAN

NEAL DOUGLASS, JOHNSON LIBRARY

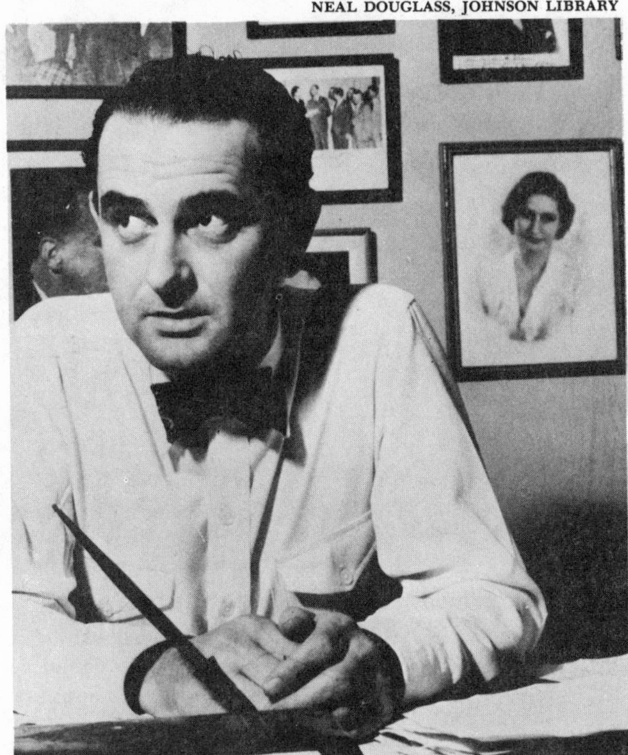

Johnson in his Washington office (a portrait of Lady Bird on the wall behind him).

Johnson visiting the Santa Rita public housing project in Austin in 1939.

JOHNSON LIBRARY

JOHNSON LIBRARY

At a harmony barbecue in Austin on June 7, 1940, left to right, lawyer Ed Clark, who helped Johnson make money and became his ambassador to Australia in the sixties; E. H. Perry, an Austin businessman; Herman Brown of Brown & Root, the company that funded Johnson's Senate race the next year; Johnson; Mayor Tom Miller of Austin.

Alvin J. Wirtz, Johnson's mentor and friend, making a speech during his term as undersecretary of the interior in the Roosevelt administration.

WIRTZ, BARKER HISTORY CENTER

erties that were expected to yield almost one million dollars a year in income. Roosevelt, in a letter to Johnson, said the agreement showed the companies could cooperate with a public power development "to the advantage of both themselves and the public." Announcing that in his district Texas Power & Light had been supplanted by LCRA with a resulting cut of thirty-seven percent in electric rates for homes and that Central Power & Light and LCRA had reached agreement in thirteen additional towns, Johnson sounded like Dr. Montgomery. "It gives me a great deal of pleasure," Johnson said, "to see a program which turns the profits of one of our greatest natural resources back to the people, instead of sending thousands upon thousands of dollars in profits from power consumption each year to the money centers of the North and East."

Counting pork-barreling, Johnson had wangled about seventy million dollars in federal projects for his district as the New Deal closed. Roosevelt invited him to become national administrator of the REA, but he declined. By 1946, he said, more than ten thousand homes in his district had REA power, although about as many still had none.[6]

Johnson also joined the New Deal initiative to require employers to pay a minimum wage. Maverick was pointing out that pecan shellers in San Antonio made an average $1.29 a week; it was said that Vice-President Garner was opposed to a minimum because he was paying Mexicans in his pecan groves in south Texas a dime an hour. Roosevelt's proposal called for only forty cents an hour and had as many exceptions as substance. Nevertheless, as Johnson remarked, "They said it was socialism, statism, communism, would wreck my political career, and would wreck the unions." He, like Maverick, had the pecan shellers in mind. "They said it was governmental interference, and it was. It interfered with that fellow that was running that pecan shelling plant. It told him he couldn't pay that little widow seven cents [an hour] any more. . . ."

When the bill was bottled up in a House committee only twenty-two southerners voted to force it to the floor for a vote, among them Rayburn, Maverick, and Johnson. The proposal, establishing a minimum wage and a forty-hour week and prohibiting child labor, became law in 1938.[7]

A change like this helped blacks and Mexican-Americans, but on legislation that could be recognized as pro-black Johnson seemed to be just another southern racist. For keeping minorities from voting, nothing was a more effective tool than the poll tax, and Koeniger said to Johnson in 1938 that, since it was going to be repealed, "Why don't you get in now and go in for that strong—introduce a bill in Congress?" Johnson replied that it was not the time. He liked to visit New Dealers Clifford and Virginia Durr in their home on the Virginia side of the Potomac, and once Virginia gave him hell for voting against repeal.

"Honey," he said, "I agree with you. You're dead right. But we haven't got the votes! Why don't you wait until we get the votes!"[8]

As long as he could not be seen helping blacks, though, he helped them. Evidently he told one biographer that when he learned New Deal agencies were making small loans to white farmers to buy seed and equipment, but not to blacks, he raised cain with the agencies, saying many of the blacks were just as good risks as the whites, and thereupon the blacks' applications began to be approved. Milo Perkins, assistant administrator of the Farm Security Administration, said "He was the first man in Congress from the South ever to go to bat for the Negro farmer."[9]

His instinct for power in perfect order, Johnson drew closer and closer to Rayburn, who was in line for the Speakership. "Mister Sam" both worried about his young protégé's frenetic pace and warned him against complaining of being tired or feeling sorry for himself. Garner, when Speaker, used to gather selected House members together for drinks and talk, calling this the "Board of Education." When Garner became vice-president, Rayburn, as majority leader, started convening his own "Board of Education" every evening, and Johnson was recognized, Patman said, as "Rayburn's special boy—Sam let it be known that only two House members had keys and didn't have to knock to gain admittance. I had one key; Lyndon had the other." Though the press continued to write about "the Board of Education," from the first Rayburn's boys called it "the Room."

Roosevelt wanted to expand the office of the presidency, create a Department of Social Welfare, and streamline and centralize the executive branch, and Rayburn became involved in fending off charges by conservatives that this would lead to presidential dictatorship. The day the House killed FDR's plan, Koeniger saw the discouraged Rayburn drop his head down and Johnson put his arm around him and pat him. The next year, though, the bill became law, giving the president a secretariat, six anonymous assistants, and the Bureau of the Budget and creating a social welfare department, named, to make it more palatable, the Federal Security Agency.[10]

In the fall elections of '38, behind closed doors, Johnson began raising political money from business interests, a black art that was to become a specialty of his. Robert S. Allen, a newspaperman who discovered him at the work, let him persuade him the endeavor was very confidential and so did not report it, although he told about it later. Someone, possibly Aubrey Williams or Corcoran, told Allen, "Lyndon's here." "He came up here," Allen said, "with about $120,000 or $150,000 in oil money." The purpose was to save Democratic House members from the reaction against court-packing and the whole New Deal.

Every few days Allen went to see Johnson, who was operating out of one or two small rooms on an upper floor in the Munsey Building on

E Street near Fourteenth, next to the National Theater. "I was telling him what I knew, and he told me about this race and that race and so forth." Contacting Democratic candidates and sending them money, Johnson "had set up his own National Democratic Committee." The usual contribution was two thousand or three thousand dollars, occasionally maybe five thousand dollars, in a day when that much money went a long way.

"He was in and out of the office," Allen said. "I think he had someone there, a secretary who took telephone calls, while he made flying trips here and there. . . . Who he helped and who he didn't help I don't know. Undoubtedly there [were] some criteria and I'm sure that one was their stand on the oil depletion allowance!"[11]

All the while Johnson was grinding down his staffers, as usual. Luther Jones told Maury Maverick, Jr., that "he had to get away from [Johnson]. He'd be devoured. He just left." Birdwell lasted as the top assistant only a year. He was replaced by Gene Latimer, who had a breakdown and was replaced in 1939.

The third top man in as many years had been an actor and the student president at the University of Texas, stacked books in a library for seventeen cents an hour in Johnson's NYA, and stuffed envelopes and ran errands in Johnson's 1937 campaign. Like Birdwell, for the first six weeks the new administrative assistant never set foot in the Capitol, shuttling back and forth between the Dodge Hotel basement and the office. Days he handled constituents and the phone, nights he wrote letters for Johnson. "I've answered as many as eighty letters a night on the typewriter after the office was closed," John Connally said.[12]

PART VIII
Defeat, and Then the War

. . . we all live in a moving stream, as surely as a catfish groping with its whiskers in the muddy dark.

— Loren Eiseley, *All the Strange Hours*

39. Ludlow, Munich, and Hitler

In 1938 Louis Ludlow, a congressman from Indiana, made a proposal that would have required a majority vote of the people before the United States could have made war in situations like Korea and Vietnam. Lyndon Johnson of Texas signed on as a sponsor of the plan.

The Ludlow amendment would have provided that, except for actual or immediately threatened attack on the United States or its possessions or attack by a non-American nation on any country in the Western Hemisphere, "the people shall have the sole power by a national referendum to declare war or to engage in warfare overseas." Johnson later characterized this as a plan "so that no President could take us into war until there was a referendum and a popular vote and a majority had voted for it," but in fact immediate self-defense and violations of the Monroe Doctrine were excepted.

Ludlow believed that, with the exceptions stated, the people who have to die in a foreign war have "an inherent right" to decide whether to fight it. "In the long sweep of history," he said, "this proposal will be vindicated," even though "years and even decades may intervene." Recalling George Washington's opposition to foreign entanglements, he quoted Benjamin Harrison, "We have no commission from God to police the world." Representative Hamilton Fish, New York, called Ludlow's plan "the greatest peace proposal before Congress during the eighteen years I have been a member." And it had a chance of passing, as President Roosevelt knew.

Maverick told Johnson he had received hundreds of letters supporting Ludlow's amendment, but none against it, so he had called up the White House. "Well, Maury," Roosevelt told him, "I feel this is one of the most dangerous pieces of legislation introduced, and I want it defeated by all means." Maverick replied, "Mr. President, that's good enough for me."

Johnson, having signed on as a sponsor, then backed down. "It took me a little time to realize and get my name off that petition," he told me in the midst of the Vietnam War. "Mr. Churchill helped some. Mr. Roosevelt helped some. Mr. Hitler helped some." He said he saw that Europe was going to be overrun, and "I had been informed that if this procedure had been required, there would have been eighty-five instances when the president had acted illegally in the past in protecting our own interest." He realized "that if we had to have an election and go through a campaign in this country every time that big decision had to be made, we would not have been protected."

When Ludlow forced the issue to a vote, a letter was read to the House from Roosevelt himself that the amendment would "cripple any president in his conduct of our foreign relations" and "encourage other nations to believe that they could violate American rights with impunity." Even with the president opposed Ludlow lost by only 209 to 188. Maverick later said he had persuaded enough liberals to change sides to defeat it, and Johnson was one of the liberals voting with him.[1]

"The rise of Hitler was something that Lyndon Johnson was keenly conscious of," Luther Jones said. "It frightened him."

A ruthless and demonic racist nationalist with a morbid sense of glory and total contempt for truthfulness, Adolf Hitler was bent on conquest by military violence. He told the duchess of Windsor in the fall of 1937, "Our buildings will make more magnificent ruins than the Greeks.' " He had invaded Austria, and he was sworn to destroy Czechoslovakia.

The British, dominated by Prime Minister Neville Chamberlain, were hoping to satisfy him and avoid war, to appease him, and during the last two weeks of September, 1938, Chamberlain went to him to beg for peace. For three hours on the evening of September 15, Hitler and Chamberlain talked alone in the dictator's study in Berchtesgarden. Although Hitler went into tirades, the Englishman thought him sane and was impressed both by his power and by his intolerance of opposition beyond a certain point. Believing Hitler's statement that all he wanted was parts of Czechoslovakia, Chamberlain personally agreed he should have them.

In the Munich Agreement, Chamberlain for Britain and Premier Édouard Daladier for France formally consented to the proposition that the Nazi army could march into parts of Czechoslovakia on October 1. Chamberlain, having extracted from Hitler a hatful of words about Britain and Germany never going to war again, returned to London and proclaimed "peace in our time." To his cabinet he explained in substance that his policy was appeasement of Germany to prevent a worldwide bloodbath, and millions thought he had achieved just that. Roosevelt, knowing the drift of the thing, had sent the prime minister the message when Munich was scheduled, "Good man"; after the agreement was reached delirious crowds celebrated in London and Paris. Part of Chamberlain's duty, after all, was to try to prevent war, and he did not know Hitler was lying.

As Hitler's troops occupied the ceded parts of Czechoslovakia, the Tory bulldog Winston Churchill and other members of Parliament proclaimed that this was not peace, but a disaster—Hitler would grab for more. Whoever turned out to be right would be a hero in history. Having cracked the shell of Czechoslovakia, Hitler swallowed the whole country like a raw egg. Betrayed, Chamberlain became bellicose and warned Hitler, No More. Britain guaranteed Poland against attack and when Hitler invaded Poland the war was on.

In the world that was devastated in the war which Chamberlain had tried to prevent, Munich became a myth in the form of a doctrine that an aggressor should never be appeased because he'll always want more. The myth was: Had Hitler been attacked, he would have been deterred. Munich came to mean appeasement, which came to mean negotiating instead of waging war against a distant aggressor. "No appeasement" became a mainstay of American policy in the cold war, Korea, and Vietnam.[2]

Lyndon Johnson was principally a domestic politician, and his foreign policy was neither subtle nor profoundly well-informed. From 1947 on his positions on international issues were dominated by the two words flashing across his mind, "Munich, Appeasement." Since Chamberlain was a dove and Churchill a hawk, Johnson would be a hawk.

Despite the events in Europe, politics continued as usual. While cultivating his relationship with Roosevelt, Johnson was also continuing to practice his guileful art of protégéship with other powerful men. He proposed that Roosevelt give a birthday party for Rayburn. Said Tommy Corcoran, "The President went for it, and Lyndon arranged it, brought Rayburn down to the White House on some pretext, and all the Texas [members] went with him. He even bought a big Texas hat for the President to give [Rayburn]. I couldn't figure out why he was doing all this. Then the papers came out the next day and there was Lyndon, standing right beside the President of the United States and Rayburn. That was the first time I really knew that an operator was loose."

Johnson also developed a "daddy" relationship with Carl Vinson, chairman of naval affairs. Johnson and his fellow committee member, Warren Magnuson, called Vinson "Admiral," and, said Magnuson, "We could get around him easily after the first few years—Lyndon more easily than I because he used me as a straightman and he had the southern syrup."[3]

In the committee meetings, Johnson said, "I sat . . . silently for more than four years," but Vinson put him on "the right subcommittees," aeronautical and ordinance, and, Vinson said, Johnson "supported every one of my efforts to strengthen our naval forces." This fit in well with FDR's program. With the election coming up in 1940, the president told a diplomat, "American mothers don't want their boys to be soldiers, so nothing really big can be done at present about expanding the Army. But the Navy is another matter; American mothers don't seem to mind their boys becoming sailors."[4]

As world war came closer Roosevelt had to make a decision that could cause or prevent corporate domination of the American system. Should the government let private companies fatten on war contracts and thereby dominate the postwar economy? According to Supreme Court Justice Hugo Black's sister-in-law, Black proposed to Roosevelt that the government take over the armaments industry, since clearly the government was going to have to fund it and the later implications of subsidized corporate power had to be considered. But Roosevelt, coping with the extensive resistance to getting into the war, told Black he could not fight Hitler abroad and the peace movement and the corporations at home all at once. He made the momentous decision: To pacify American business the defense effort would be profit-making.[5]

As a practical matter this meant that there would be politics in deciding what private companies got the big government contracts. Johnson participated in the discussions in the naval committee on behalf of the cause of getting an air base to train Navy cadets at Corpus Christi. On June 11, 1940, for the first time the government awarded a contract to private business on a negotiated basis rather than competitive bidding. On this same first day, a negotiated contract was signed for the construction of the 14,500-acre naval base at Corpus Christi. The job was given to Brown & Root, Inc., W. S. Bellows, a Houston contractor, and a California company. Almost nine thousand people were put to work on the $46-million job.[6]

Just as private business was beginning the war-long activity that was to produce a corporation-dominated government, Roosevelt also had to face the death of the New Deal. His attempt in the 1938 elections to purge his own party of reactionaries had failed, and as the decade ended, even though unemployment continued at between seven and ten million, Congress would not create enough public jobs to put people to work.

The rightists' revolt against Roosevelt in Texas had started in 1936 when historian J. Evetts Haley's "Jeffersonian Democrats" accused Roosevelt of fostering "a collectivist state" on the basis of "a blended communism and socialism." "Cactus Jack" Garner, who had literally held his nose and turned a thumb down on Roosevelt's court-packing, became the focus of anti–New Deal forces among the Democrats. Assuming FDR would not run for a third term, the Texans decided they wanted Garner for president or Rayburn for vice-president. Rayburn endorsed Garner, while Patman endorsed Rayburn as the leading darkhorse for president. Lobbyist Roy Miller opened up a Garner headquarters in Washington.

One day Jim Farley, the Democrats' chairman who also wanted to be president, realized, from a change in Roosevelt's way of saying he would not run again, that he would. Johnson had already shown that, forced to choose between Big Daddies, he would tag along with the biggest one. In mid-1939 labor leader John L. Lewis had called Garner a "labor-baiting, poker-playing, whiskey-drinking, evil old man," and Garner had demanded that the Texas delegation in Congress unanimously defend him in a resolution. FDR, who was tired of Garner calling him "Cap'n" and wanted him retired to his cactus patch, told Johnson he did not want the resolution passed, so in front of the Texas delegation and later in private argument with Rayburn, Johnson refused to sign. Then, in the spring of 1940, Johnson accepted a role in the Texas Third Term Committee for Roosevelt.

The Texas New Dealers—Maverick, Johnson, Tom Miller, both the Fergusons—stood fast for FDR, but both the state's members on the Democratic National Committee and three former Texas governors were for Garner. The fissure that now opened up between the Texas liberals and conservatives ran like a gash through Texas politics for the rest of the Johnson period.

Roosevelt dispatched Alvin Wirtz, who had become undersecretary of the interior, back down to Texas to lead the Third Termers against the Garnerites, who Wirtz said were "inspired by Wall Street bankers." Maverick and Johnson pitched in, too, and the Texas state convention at Waco was won for Roosevelt, but the day before delegates for it were selected FDR surprised Johnson. "I want you to see the Texas delegation goes for Garner," he told him.

"Mr. President, what are you talking about?"

"People are proud of their leaders," he said. "If I go in there and take the people away from their leader—I don't need those votes. I'd rather John Garner have the votes. I want to be magnanimous."

"I can't do it," Johnson said.

"You've got to do it," the president replied. He instructed him to tell the Garner forces, led by Rayburn, that the president had seen and approved a proposal that they could switch to him after the first ballot. ("He was a goddamn clever fella!" Johnson said in the sixties. "He makes all these boys around here now—well, look like kids.")

After some maneuvering Roosevelt asked Rayburn and Johnson together to send a public wire to Wirtz and the Texas party chairman declaring that the state convention should endorse the Roosevelt administration, back Garner as a favorite son, and resolve not to join the Stop Roosevelt movement. Rayburn refused, according to Harold Ickes, because he did not want to act on an equal footing with a congressman very much his junior, but Roosevelt had control over Rayburn's ambition. Ickes wrote into his diary that Roosevelt had treated the two Texans as equals "with the malicious intent of disturbing Sam Rayburn's state of mind." The wire went out, and Roosevelt told them they had been good little boys and had "papa's blessing."

Deal or no deal, Maverick, who was then mayor of San Antonio, plunged into the Texas convention openly favoring a third term and to hell with Garner. Maverick wanted to be national committeeman, but by the unsavory terms of the deal that was struck, the post went to a Garner leader. All this led to blows. By one account Mayor Miller knocked Mayor Maverick down, and Ed Clark, later to be the American ambassador to Australia, pinned Miller's arms to his sides to stop the fight.

The deal prevailed, with the Texas delegation instructed to vote for Garner on the first ballot. But Garner summoned Wright Morrow, a young oilman-lawyer in Houston, to the Garners' suite in the Washington Hotel, and told him, "I wanted you to put my name up as a candidate for the nomination. You'll have a hell of a time doing it. Let me tell you what's happened." Garner then continued to Morrow (as the latter recalled):

"You're not going to get many votes, because the man in the White House is a very attractive liar. He's a very personable man, but he doesn't tell the truth if it doesn't suit him. He will run, he'll be renominated, he'll be re-elected, and he'll remain in office until he dies, and you fellas'll be lucky if one of his sons doesn't succeed him."

Morrow replied it would be more logical for Rayburn to nominate him, but Garner said if either of them did they would have their political throats "cut wide open." At the convention Morrow did nominate Garner and Texas voted for him, but Roosevelt was renominated overwhelmingly.

Rayburn's hopes for the vice-presidency were crushed, too, perhaps in part because of another manifestation of the new Texas split, the candidacy of right-wing New Deal executive Jesse Jones of Houston for the same nomination. Johnson, as vice-chairman of the Texas delegation, played his only role at the convention by presiding at the Texas caucus on the subject. He refused to recognize a pro-Jones delegate who was jumping and shouting for recognition. Then, although Jones was telling the Texans FDR had chosen Henry Wallace and they should not themselves take a vote, Johnson took it and the Texans endorsed Rayburn, eighty-seven to seven. In the convention Rayburn dutifully nominated Wallace, but with a hint of a complaint.[7]

In contrast to Garner's old-fashioned contempt for Roosevelt's dishonesty, Johnson admired the president and emerged from the 1940 convention secure in his confidence. Although Johnson had crossed Rayburn to oppose Garner and had ruffled Rayburn again by standing equal to him in public, he had gained back some of that lost ground by presiding so partisanly for Rayburn at the Texas caucus. Yet Johnson had not gone all-out publicly against Garner as Maverick had, and that fall Roosevelt was able to tell him (as one rich Texas insider said) to get "some of that Texas oil money" for the general election.

According to columnists at the time, Rayburn and another House leader went to Roosevelt recommending Johnson be put in charge of the congressional campaign committee. "Sold," Roosevelt replied. "That was my idea, too. That boy has got what's needed." The next day, after breakfast with Roosevelt, Johnson went to work fifteen to eighteen hours a day in offices in the Munsey Building.

Johnson was telling Roosevelt that the prospect of congressional losses for the Democrats "gives me the night sweats at 3 A.M." Roosevelt informed an aide as the election approached that Johnson would be sending out money-raising letters, making no reference to the president. The congressman from Texas was experiencing first-hand the political wiliness of his model.

The chairman of the Democrats' congressional fund-raising told FDR that Johnson "has consulted me with reference to the selection of himself as the secretary of the Democratic National Committee." Hearing that this was not coming through for Johnson, Maury Maverick wrote FDR complaining, "this is a mistake."

Title or no, Johnson went to work raising money from his friends. George Brown sent a telegram to him in Washington November 19, "You were supposed to have checks by Friday from Woods, Malton, Shapiro, Cowin, Dahlstrom, and Wortham. . . ." Johnson responded, "All of the folks you talked to have been heard from. . . . I am not acknowledging their letters, so be sure to tell all these fellows that their letters have been received." (He meant, and Brown knew he meant, of course, that the money had come in.) In a postscript, Johnson added to Brown, "The thing is exceeding my expectations. The boss [FDR] is following suggestions and I'm extremely pleased."

John Connally and his wife Nellie were the key staffers in the effort. "When I went up there," said one Texan, "it was just a big empty space. Only things in there were John Connally and a typewriter." One report said Johnson and Rayburn collected about sixty-thousand dollars, but Harold Young, who talked to many Democratic candidates for Johnson, believed oilman Sid Richardson alone ponied up as much as one hundred thousand dollars. Richardson later told Charles Marsh, "I was the big factor in raising seventy thousand dollars" for the Democrats in 1940.

One can glimpse the illegitimacy and secrecy of the operation in a "personal and confidential" air mail, special letter Johnson wrote from the Munsey Building to Rayburn in Dallas late that October. "Paul has sent five," Johnson wrote cryptically. "I had hoped he would send five times that amount." Paul was not identified.

Under Roosevelt's supervision, Johnson funneled money to 150 Democratic candidates for the House, and instead of the Democrats losing ground, the Republicans lost six seats. On election night, Johnson phoned Roosevelt with reports of victories from across the country.[8]

In Europe, meanwhile, Czechoslovakia had been enslaved, Chamberlain had threatened war, Hitler had obliterated Poland, the British and French had declared war on Germany, Hitler had conquered Norway, Denmark, the Netherlands, Belgium, and Luxembourg, France fell, and the Nazis began bombing Britain. In Washington the Congress passed the first peacetime draft in American history and Lend-Lease to help the British. On February 13, 1941, the Johnsons went to their first dinner in the White House, an occasion honoring the Duchess of Luxembourg, and afterward were invited to see a movie, *The Philadelphia Story,* in Roosevelt's living quarters. Bird wrote in her diary, "I went to my first (will it be the last and only) dinner at the White House." The next month Johnson attended the dedication of the naval base in Corpus Christi, and the local paper ran a picture of the secretary of the navy, Texas Governor W. Lee O'Daniel with his wife and their daughter Molly, and Johnson. Molly had her hand around Johnson's elbow, but his forearm was not lifted to cradle it. Early in April, Senator Sheppard of Texas died.[9]

---

40. Red-Baiting for Herman Brown

Eight months before the United States was bombed into the Second World War, Lyndon Johnson made his first dash for the Senate. As Roosevelt's choice, he ran under the banner, "Franklin D. and Lyndon B.," but trying to offset the reaction against him as a New Dealer, he campaigned as a jingo instead. To counter another candidate, Congressman Martin Dies, who was the country's chief Red-headhunter, Johnson attacked labor unions as pinko in his first use of the noxious techniques that later came to be called McCarthyism.

As far as the voters could see, Johnson went in to talk to the president in the White House and emerged with typed copies of his announcement that he would run. However, according to a newspaper column by Joseph Alsop and a colleague, Johnson was reluctant to make the race and did so only after several long talks with Hopkins and Roosevelt. Johnson told the president he was still young, the field would be formidable and he did not want to embarrass the White House by losing; but Roosevelt replied that the administration needed votes in the Senate, he wanted Johnson to run, and he would help every way he could.

For a couple of days in advance of the staged White House scene, Johnson trumpeted the warlike themes he knew Roosevelt believed had become necessary. Proposing to compel business executives to work in the defense effort, Johnson demanded mobilization for war and condemned strikes by labor or capital in defense work. He gave his connection with Roosevelt the same martial snap: "I am proud that I enlisted in the cause and have worked with him since 1932. . . . We can trust and follow him."

It was the day after this that Roosevelt called him to the White House. Johnson said the president told him, "Martin Dies is going to be the next United States Senator, and he will be a disgrace to the United States and to Texas." Asking Lyndon to announce, Roosevelt assured him, "Jesse Jones will support you."

From Roosevelt's office Johnson strode to the White House steps and made his announcement to the press. The late Senator Sheppard, he told the reporters, had "supported President Roosevelt always," and so would he, "no matter what trials may face us."

Minutes later President Roosevelt held a previously scheduled press conference, and when the subject of Johnson's announcement predictably came up he said cagily, "Well, he told me that just about one minute before he told you." FDR gave his public blessing, but in his style of deceitful indirection that his Texas understudy was attentively absorbing. A reporter asked Roosevelt, "Would the White House endorse Johnson?" The *Washington Post* traced the president's weaving position:

"Of course it is up to the State of Texas to elect its own senator, said the politically aware President.

"He could not take part in a Texas primary, he said in apparent seriousness, nor could he take any part in Lyndon Johnson's election.

"All the President can say, said Mr. Roosevelt, is that Johnson is an old and very close friend of his.

"An outburst of laughter greeted his remarks." The *Dallas News* headline, "F.D.R. Picks Johnson to Defeat Dies," was the sum of it.[1]

Johnson showed his fellow House member Hale Boggs a poll saying he had only nine percent of the votes. "Well," Boggs commented, "I don't see how you can run under those circumstances." But Johnson was hopeful, and with reason. Roosevelt's wishes were the one dominant factor. Johnson moved up in the Texas poll from five-percent support before the two-act play at the White House to eighteen percent a month later and twenty-seven percent a week before the election. There were twenty-nine candidates in all, but Dies and Governor "Pappy" O'Daniel had to divide the anti-Roosevelt vote. The pro-Roosevelt state attorney general, Gerald Mann, was running, but the voters knew Roosevelt wanted Johnson.

The signals of this were everywhere. Wirtz resigned in Washington to join the campaign. When FDR declared a national emergency, Johnson wired him offering to return to Washington; FDR wired back suggesting he stay in Texas for the campaign, but adding, "Please return immediately after election." On a statewide broadcast Johnson read a "Dear Lyndon" letter from the president asking him to "come in and talk to me" about the pension problem when he got back to Washington. Harold Young, the Texan assistant to Vice-President Wallace, campaigned for Johnson on statewide radio, and Johnson read a letter from Wallace himself saying he would like to be with Johnson where he was campaigning in south Texas.

Speaking to a crowd packed into the concave city block of Wooldridge Park in Austin, Johnson shouted "A President Roosevelt comes only once in a century!" and used (with an interesting change) what Roosevelt had said publicly: "Just because the president's voice spoke about me as an old and trusted friend is no reason alone why Texans should vote for me. But a few words from President Roosevelt mean much to me, as one of the many in the work with him to beat Hitler back on his heels." His posters plugged "Roosevelt and Unity"—one bold advertisement said "Support Roosevelt and Johnson."

In a prevision of certain practices during the Watergate period, New Deal agencies and laws were used to help elect Johnson. He announced he had received a wire from President Roosevelt saying that he had signed the parity loan bill to assure farmers a certain income. On the basis of a telegram Johnson read in which the chairman of the Social Security Board in Washington promised that funds for the aged would reach forty dollars a month "if the state provides the additional funds," Johnson argued that Governor O'Daniel should stay in Texas to raise the needed funds.

Roosevelt, timing the ploy to hit as people were voting, gave Johnson an all-out, but backhanded endorsement. The absurd O'Daniel had proposed to Roosevelt that he create a Texas army and navy. As the voters were finally making up their minds, Roosevelt wired Johnson ostensibly for the purpose of spiking rumors that he had endorsed O'Daniel. The president also said he had read stories "seeking to make it appear that I have given some kind of endorsement to the plan proposed by the governor . . . to create a Texas army and navy. . . . My reply to the governor was intended to be merely courteous, thus avoiding calling the scheme preposterous, which it undoubtedly is."

The behind-the-scenes communications on file at the Roosevelt Library—Johnson to FDR, Wirtz to Jim Rowe of FDR's staff, Johnson to Charles Marsh (who was in Washington)—leave not the slightest doubt that the interventions from Washington were put-up jobs, conceived and drafted by the Johnson camp. Any Texas voter who didn't figure out that Roosevelt was for Johnson simply wasn't paying attention, and there was a boomerang. The *Dallas Morning News* spoke editorially of "Texans who regard the federal hierarchy's campaign in Texas as one of the most sinister occurrences in either Texas or national political history.[2]

Despite Roosevelt's declaration in the Oval Office, Jesse Jones did not support Johnson, perhaps because of Johnson's partisan presiding for Rayburn and against Jones the year before. But Roosevelt tried. During the campaign evidently he sent Jones a memo about Johnson and a week later wrote the banker asking, "What is the answer?" To Vice-President Wallace, FDR spoke contemptuously about Jones because he had not fought Governor O'Daniel.

As Roosevelt's boy now, a coat-tailer inviting progressives to get on *his* coat-tail, Johnson had the backing of most liberals and labor. In supporting him, said the Austin Trades Council, "we are but protecting our own interest." However, the progressive Jim Ferguson, who was close to Lieutenant Governor Coke Stevenson, wanted the governor sent to the Senate so Stevenson could become the governor—"We want O'Daniel so our man Stevenson will be governor," Ferguson told his secretary. The progressive oilman J. R. Parten was decidedly for Johnson, but few other oilmen were. Big business wanted O'Daniel, but there was another important exception: the Fort Worth tycoon and publisher, Amon Carter. Introduced to Carter, "Lyndon got right up in his face—talked to him thirty minutes, standing right up next to him, standing right there," said insurance executive Raymond Buck, who was a Johnson manager. "At the end of that time, Amon was *sold,*" and his big daily endorsed Johnson.[3]

The public did not know about an even more significant business convert to Johnson, antiunion contractor Herman Brown, who, with his brother George, ran the contracting and engineering firm of Brown & Root that had already received government contracts for the Pedernales co-op and from the navy for the Corpus Christi flight-training base. Just before he announced, Johnson had told the Texas legislature, "I have tried to make Texas navy-conscious. On the Gulf Coast millions are being spent for new shipyards." Campaigning, he said that twenty billion dollars would be spent on defense *in a few months* and promised that Texas would get much of it. Herman Brown knew what this meant for his company if his man won. Speaking of the 1941 campaign, Johnson told me flatly, "That was Brown & Root funded." The company helped most, he explained, in Corpus Christi and Houston, where they had headquarters.

The law prohibited corporate campaign contributions, of course. Shortly after the campaign a New York paper publicized reports that defense contractors had made large contributions to Johnson and as much as $300,000 had been spent in his race. *Life* said Johnson had "the most effective professional aid and a $250,000 chest which has enabled him to plaster the state with posters." However, fifteen years passed before the muckraker Drew Pearson broke the whole story with secret tax records given to him, evidently, by an early Daniel Ellsberg–type. Pearson had copies of about a thousand Treasury Department reports, letters, and exhibits in a tax investigation of Brown & Root's funding of the campaign. The tax people were bound by criminal law not to let out what they knew, but no one publicly denied Pearson's information.

IRS agents had discovered evidence of a false profit distribution by a Brown & Root subsidiary, Victoria Gravel Company, in the form of fictitious lawyer's fees to Edgar Monteith which Monteith passed on to Johnson as contributions. In a low farce of high politics, the subsidiary gave Monteith $12,500. Monteith distributed $10,000 of it as a profit between him and his partner, but then his partner transferred the $10,000 back to him and Monteith wrote checks against the sum, in undisclosed amounts, to pay campaign expenses.

An employee, paid $5,000 by Victoria Gravel, cashed the check and mailed half of it to Johnson's campaign headquarters. Another employee, receiving $2,500 from the subsidiary, deposited it in his bank, withdrew it the same day, and gave it to Johnson's campaign in Houston.

The tax agents uncovered suspicious bonuses paid by Brown & Root in the midst of the Johnson campaign. A purchasing agent was given $5,000 in two checks, a vice-president $5,000, an office manager $5,000, a secretary three checks totaling $9,500. The employees had all cashed the checks almost immediately, but could not show what they had bought with the money.

The agents also investigated large bonuses to Brown & Root officials shortly before or during the Johnson campaign: sums of $45,000, $25,000, $28,000, and $35,000 to four vice-presidents and $17,000 to the treasurer. The agents reported to Washington that although these bonuses were recorded as authorized in the minutes of a company meeting just after Christmas, 1940, before Senator Sheppard had died, there was evidence the minutes had been written afterward to justify withdrawals for the campaign. One of the vice-presidents admitted he made a cash contribution to Johnson, but could not remember the amount.[4]

Johnson also received campaign money from New Deal sources and from Sid Richardson. *Time-Life* estimated the total tab was half a million dollars or so. A Johnson man phoned to protest, but the reporter taking the call replied that they thought it actually was closer to $750,000 and could produce evidence Brown & Root had put in $100,000. That was the end of the protest.[5]

Although Claude Wild was again the campaign manager, John Connally did "the real work," according to Gordon Fulcher. Connally and Fulcher ghost-wrote speeches, with Charles Marsh helping. The publisher also flew Johnson about in his private plane. As usual Johnson himself campaigned day and night. When Dan Quill took him to a health club he fell asleep on the massage table (they let him sleep a couple hours).[6]

His speeches this year had two main themes, a hawkish position on war with Germany and his scourging of labor unions on the basis of the need for defense production and national unity.

"Appeasement" was already burned into his mind as a fixed and unchanging evil. The issue, he said in 1941, was "support of Roosevelt, against appeasement and in defiance of dictators." Six months before Pearl Harbor he said "This is not a European war. It is a world war—our war." Although Nye, Vandenberg, and "even some Texans" might gamble with democracy to win "the peace before death," not he.

As the opposite of appeasement, military preparedness became an invariant good in Johnson's politics. He told the voters he had backed Roosevelt in building a two-ocean navy, a fifty-thousand-plane air force, a two-million-man army.

Under the threat of war he adopted, too, a third slogan, unity and harmony, that made sense then, but became a dogma with him. "In unity there is strength," he said in 1941. "We must refuse to elect any man . . . who will in any way lend aid to discord, division, or disunity." When O'Daniel criticized Roosevelt as a back-slapping politician who couldn't run a peanut wagon successfully, Johnson snapped, "It must have comforted Hitler to hear the governor talk like that."

This ganglion of themes in 1941—opposition to appeasement, the need for military preparedness and national unity, and ruthless attacks on the patriotism of opponents—animated most of the rest of Johnson's career.

"If the day ever comes when my vote must be cast to send your boy to the trenches," he said, "that day Lyndon Johnson will leave his Senate seat to go with him." One piece of his campaign literature consisted entirely of this promise, the headline "We need courage like this," and a photograph of him and his mother. He said if he voted for war he would "go into the trenches with other soldiers."[7]

In the marshes of the fear of war and the lust for it, paranoia was the night-flower. O'Daniel, a sales-taxing corporation lackey who won his governship by campaigning on the Ten Commandments and the Golden Rule, announced that he had information on the activities of fifth columnists in Texas and, with flurries of associated rhetoric against labor racketeers and agitators, persuaded the legislature to prohibit threats of violence by labor organizers. (Strike-breakers' activities were not covered.) Dies charged that a secret, non-uniformed army, boring from within, had more people in it than the regular army. Johnson, open to the charge that he was a New Dealing socialist, tensed up. He knew what had happened to his friend Maury Maverick.

For his courage in trying to break new ground for the dying New Deal, Maverick was opposed and narrowly defeated in 1938 by a candidate who called him "a friend and ally of communism." Elected mayor of San Antonio the next year, Maverick gutsily authorized, on grounds of free speech, a Communist meeting at the city auditorium, but a mob of five thousand, ignoring tear gas and streams of water, broke up the meeting, smashed almost every window in the auditorium, and ripped up the seats inside. Efforts to recall Maverick failed. Indicted on charges of paying poll taxes for Mexican-Americans with outside union money, he was acquitted. But then, during the course of the 1941 Senate campaign, he was defeated for the second time in three years. With several weeks still to go in the Senate race, Roosevelt wrote Maverick's son that what his father stood for would prevail in the long run, and "The same thing is true about Lyndon Johnson. I hope he will win but even if he does not the things for which he stands will eventually win." Johnson, however, had no intention of standing for what might beat him.

In a curious lapse of memory, Johnson identified his father Sam with Maverick's bellicose idealism. During the trouble over the Communist meeting, Johnson told me, his father had said to him, "By God, he's right," and had told Maverick that not only should he let Emma Tenayuca, the beautiful young Mexican-American Communist leader in San Antonio, lead the rally, he should escort her to the stage. "I think it'll beat you, but I think you oughta do it," Johnson said his father told Maverick. But Sam had died two years before this. Whether the story was a mixed-up memory or a fantasy, by telling it Johnson was identifying his failed father with Maverick's defeated idealism.[8]

So, running against the head Red-baiter, Dies, and the head labor-baiter, O'Daniel, Johnson out-baited them both. Since the first record votes on the matter the year before, Johnson had been supporting the continuation of Dies's House committee on un-American activities. Dies had called the University of Texas a hotbed of communism, but finding no Communists there, apologized. Johnson, swiping him for this, said that the university, far from being "a factory grinding out communist comrades," was instead training "red-blooded Texas boys to command Navy ships."

As for the labor unions, Johnson told working people they should not strike in wartime, and "If there be subversive influences anywhere around you, deal with them as Texans deal with traitors"—a phrase that certainly suggested beating people up, perhaps killing them. Johnson said soldiers were wearing woolen uniforms in summer heat because of a coal strike. To the miners' leader, John L. Lewis, he said, "it is no longer . . . patriotic" to seek small advantages as war needs increased. "Strikes must cease!" That went for manufacturers, too, he said (but of course manufacturers were not striking). In a line that must have pleased Herman Brown, Johnson said, "Texas labor has been free of strikes and disturbances; free of radical leadership and membership." And he was quite ready to use troops to break strikes: "We're going to support the $21-a-month draft boy the president sends to open plane plants where communist agitators and radical labor leaders close them." He would uphold "the FBI as it ferrets out sabotage experts, traitors, and spies."[9]

He was almost silent on domestic issues. He supported parity income for farmers, national old-age pensions starting at sixty, federal provision for maternal and child care, low-cost electricity; but also, "We're going to keep politics out of medicine," and he would "always oppose the federal control of our oil resources." Basically he ran against Hitler. "I am a yes-man for everything that is American," he said. "I am a yes-man for everything that will aid in the defense of the Republic. I am a yes-man to the Commander-in-Chief, as every good soldier should be in time of war and national emergency."

Tough liberals blanched. To compete with O'Daniel's hillbilly roadshow, Lyndon put his own together, and Margaret Carter, a liberal in Fort Worth, attended "an unholy rally" for him at which the only thing worse than Kate Smith singing "You Are My Sunshine" was the candidate's speech. "I was appalled," she said. "There was nothing to it. It was the most banal sort of flag-waving speech." Disgusted by Lyndon's campaign, Otto Mullinax, a leading Dallas labor lawyer, fell out with him.[10]

Nevertheless, the campaign had its moments. Governor O'Daniel had to appoint an interim senator, but there is always a danger such an appointee will take it into his head to run for the office himself at the special election. O'Daniel played it so safe that his appointee, the eighty-seven-year-old son of Sam Houston, journeyed to Washington and promptly died. Then there was the large field, wild as a democratic fashion show—a radio minister known as the "voice of temperance," the secretary of the Texas Communist party, a long-bearded "Commodore," and a candidate who, instead of running, rocked, conducting his campaign from his rocking chair.[11]

In a special campaign edition of his home-town weekly, Johnson pulled his campaign together. Here was the picture of Roosevelt and Johnson shaking hands with the caption, "Old and Close Friends," here the claim that by wiring FDR asking him to sign a bill for farmers' price supports Johnson had "persuaded" him to sign it, here the text of FDR's wire to Johnson he need not return to Washington until after the election. "Strikes must cease!" The antiwar members of the U.S. Senate were seared as appeasers under the headline, "Nazis Given Aid, Comfort." Johnson was for "real action against fifth columnists and reds—not talk" and was quoted, "Fifth columnists, foreign agents, communists, fascists, proponents of every other ism but Americanism, must be wiped out, not just ridiculed and publicized." And if even that cry of the wolf-pack didn't pry the right-wingers away from O'Daniel and Dies, well, Johnson said it on out—he was "unalterably opposed to socialized medicine," and "I shall see that our present [oil] depletion allowances are preserved."[12] As the voters went to the polls in 1941 the New Deal candidate was campaigning against strikes, Hitler, Communists, and socialized medicine.

---

41. The Cagey Good Sport

Lyndon and his brother had worked with the south Texas political bosses, especially George Parr of Duval County, and one of the first things Johnson's manager in south Texas had done in the '41 Senate race was talk with the few men who controlled the border blocs, the leaders of the Raymond machine in Laredo, the Guerras in Starr, and Parr. On election night, with about fifteen thousand votes still out and Johnson ahead by fifteen thousand, John Connally said, four or five south Texas counties called in and asked, "Should we report our votes?" Connally said, "Yeah, bring 'em in." According to Sam Houston, "Lyndon called George to put all his votes in early so it'd look like he was leading." This was their mistake. "As soon as they all reported," Connally told me, "the opposition knew our total. The thing began to erode. . . . It was a question of the opposition *knowing.*"

On election night jubilation prevailed in the Johnson headquarters hotel, and Sunday the Texas Election Bureau manager said that barring a miracle Johnson was elected. With ninety-six percent of the vote in he led O'Daniel by about 5,000 out of 543,000 counted. The *Dallas Morning News* said he was "fairly certain of election." Dies had run a poor fourth, after Mann. People were so convinced Johnson was in that candidates for his seat in the House made their announcements.

But a few knew better. Sunday morning one of the governor's top aides, Jim Fritts, went to the mansion to help O'Daniel prepare for his regular Sunday morning radio broadcast. According to Fritts, as the two men were discussing Johnson's five-thousand-vote lead, "He said, 'Well that don't make any difference.' He said that Coke Stevenson had told him that he'd come out ahead."

Fritts told me later, "Coke Stevenson and his henchmen were stealing votes over in east Texas. Lyndon was stealing 'em in south Texas. Coke Stevenson's boys stole the most. That's a fact. I'm telling you the absolute fact. It was common talk." But, he added, "O'Daniel was no party to it."[1]

That Sunday afternoon Carroll Keach was fussing around alone in Johnson's headquarters when the phone rang. It was James Allred, by then a federal judge. "I'm in Silver City, New Mexico," he said. "I'm listening to the radio. They're stealing this election in East Texas!"

"Wait a minute, Judge Allred, I'll go get Lyndon," Keach said.

"No, I don't *want* to talk to him. I want to talk to you. These Ferguson people have sent these people fishing in East Texas, and they're going to steal this election from us."

Allred had Keach go tell Johnson what he had said. Johnson and his key staff conferred on the situation up in a hotel room. "Well, what can we do?" Johnson asked. "Can we do anything in South Texas? No—Duval's in, all the others are in. No, we have to wait to see what comes in from East Texas."

Johnson's guess was that the liquor interests, probably beer, which were opposed to O'Daniel because he was a dry, wanted him elected senator to get him out of Texas. Jim Ferguson was fist-in-mughandle with the beer interests. Johnson told me that Ferguson told Connally on the phone, "It'll take money to stop stealing in Dies's district," but that Connally was insulted and none was paid.

Monday O'Daniel reduced Johnson's lead to 77 votes, and in Tuesday's final count O'Daniel won by 1,311, less than half of one percent of the total for both men. Johnson, leaning on his arms draped around Keach and Sam Fore, said, "Well, Sam, I didn't know it would come to this, I didn't think it would get this dirty. But if this is the way you have to play, OK."

Johnson told me, "We thought Stevenson, Dies, and Jim Ferguson stole it." He said he won by five thousand votes, but was defeated "on a long count."

Sam D. W. Low, a Houston attorney active for him in the campaign, believed votes in Dies's east Texas counties had been switched from Dies to O'Daniel. Speculating, Low said, "I think that Mr. Coke went over to east Texas to where some of his very close friends and kinfolk [ran] the elections, saying Dies did not have much chance, but I don't want you to do anything irregular except hold out the vote until Monday, and if it's apparent Martin doesn't have a chance, count the Dies vote for O'Daniel and the O'Daniel vote for Dies."

Harold Young, the vice-president's aide, said, "There's strong evidence [Johnson] was fucked out of it by Coke, O'Daniel, and Dies. It's passing strange that Dies's early vote was big and then before it was all over O'Daniel starts getting that vote." Edmunds Travis, then an editor in Austin, said that when the late-reporting east Texas counties thought to be for Dies came in for O'Daniel, "there was a general feeling that Coke had done it."

There was pressure for an election contest, but Johnson certainly must have known what his outraged partisans did not: an investigation might turn up Brown & Root's scandalous contributions to him.

"We suspected, and we thought we knew the election was stolen," Sam Low said. "Lyndon came down, and it was a pretty sorrowful meeting. Some of his people were pretty violent about it. He said, 'Hell, we're almost in a war. Nobody ever gained anything from an election contest, we got beat, and we may think we got beat in an unscrupulous manner, but we probably can't prove it.—Anyway, I don't want an election contest.' "

Professor Greene told Lyndon they should challenge the returns, for he had a hunch they could catch the thieves. "You know what he said?" Greene remembered. "He just laughed and shook his head." His brother Sam Houston told me that, meeting Lyndon at an airport, "I asked him, 'Are you going to have it investigated?' We had spent twice what they had. He said, 'Hell, no, I hope they don't investigate *me.*' "

"A memory of Lyndon that I will always cherish," his wife said, "was the way he looked, walking away to catch the plane to Washington after his defeat had been announced. I still see him striding off, looking very jaunty, and putting extra verve into his step. His head was high, and he was stepping along real spryly."

According to Johnson, President Roosevelt, complaining that an election had been stolen from him, too, in 1928, sent in the FBI. In the White House Johnson offered to show me the FBI reports, but after saying sure, I indicated I did not want to see them, and he did not show them to me. Evidently on the basis of them, he said that a substantial portion of Dies's vote in his strong counties in the first primary was shifted to O'Daniel in the runoff. Phone calls had been made to every county clerk in Dies's district.

But even when the chairman of the Texas Democrats, an O'Daniel supporter, asked for an investigation, Johnson said no. He would play the good sport and hope it would help him when O'Daniel had to run for reelection in 1942. "I thought I could be elected the next year as a martyr," he told me.[2]

In Washington he kept right on playing it safe politically. One morning Harold Young picked up the *Washington Post* and read that Lyndon had voted to continue the appropriation for Dies's un-American activities committee. Later that day, seeing Lyndon, he said, "Listen, the *Washington Post* is slipping. They got you voting for the Dies committee."

"I did."

"You mean to tell me you voted for that son-of-a-bitch to get more money?"

"Yeah—I never claimed to be a liberal."

"Well," Vice-President Wallace's assistant said, "you sure fooled hell out of me—I went on statewide television and told people all over Texas. . . ."[3]

Johnson said the next few months were the most miserable in his life. Feeling rejected, he thought about going back to Texas to make money, giving up politics; but he just couldn't leave Washington. At least there he was still a congressman, and he felt that with war coming, "someone with all my training and preparedness was bound to be an important figure."[4]

Watching, watching, Johnson saw Roosevelt's problems, his mistakes —and his guile. One day Johnson was standing with several dozen Democratic members surrounding Speaker Rayburn as the House clerk read aloud an important new legislative request from the president. Members complained they had not known it was coming, it was awful, and so on. After they scattered, Rayburn told Johnson the president should give Congress more warning of what was coming, which Johnson took care to do when his turn came.[5]

After meeting the American president off Newfoundland August 9–12, 1941, Winston Churchill told his cabinet in London that Roosevelt was "determined that they should come in" to the war, but that "if he had put the issue of peace and war to Congress, they would debate it for six months." Churchill quoted FDR that "he would wage war but not declare it and that he would become more and more provocative. If the Germans did not like it they could attack American forces. . . . Everything was to be done to force an incident."[6]

The crisis in the House that month concerned extending the period of military service from a year to eighteen months. Johnson worked hard for the extension and said he proposed that a statement by Secretary of State Cordell Hull be brought to bear on the members, as it was. He associated opposition to the draft with young college editors and idealists who thought "munitions makers" and militarists wanted war. "Some cry out for appeasement," he told the House, "but there is a one-hundred-percent record of destruction and death in every attempt toward appeasement of the Axis powers." Later Johnson claimed he drummed up the one vote by which the extension passed—he exclaimed, "The vote was 203 to 202—that is when the fate of Europe is in doubt!"

Charles Marsh, in several communications, left us a study of Johnson in this year of his first bid for the Senate.

Recommending before the campaign "a month's radio and elocution work," Marsh wrote Lyndon, "Your voice high-tones under emotion. You will have to teach your throat better. You can't lose the

Johnson bellowing out his speech—his oratorical style was not elegant—at the rally in San Marcos, Texas, opening his 1941 Senate race.

AUSTIN STATESMAN

THE POLITICIAN IN ACTION Johnson running for the U.S. Senate in 1941, campaigning in east and north central Texas with a filling station worker, an equipment operator, a lumberyard worker, a welder, and, on the facing page, a mother and infant (who is taking his campaign card) and a farmer.

AUSTIN STATESM.

HOTOS

AP PHOTO

Lady Bird, Lyndon, and Lyndon's mother.

A snapshot of T. J. Taylor's grocery store in Jefferson, Texas, with a sign out front for Johnson's 1941 Senate race. Taylor, Lady Bird's father, loaned the Johnsons $10,000 for Johnson's first race in 1937.

JOHNSON LIBRARY

Johnson, hoisted onto the shoulders of two campaign workers, hails early returns showing him leading in the 1941 Senate race.

ACME NEWSPICTURES

AUSTIN STATESMA

John Connally (with the phone) and other campaign workers get the grim news: late returns did Johnson in. Losing and learning, Johnson bided his time until 1948.

AP PHOTO

Johnson returns to Washington.

emotion, but you must lose the high notes. Your gestures should be natural, but you must weed out about 50 percent. You have learned domination of slower and smaller people by pounding the table like a machine gun. . . . Gestures in speaking are for emphasis of meaning, not more determination and force beating a man down into saying yes or no."

Marsh knew his man, writing Gordon Fulcher to keep a close watch on Lyndon: "Get him to sleep every time you can, day and night. Keep the insignificant waiting. . . . See that his throat is sprayed night and morning. Watch him when he gets excited and you find him talking over-long on a small detail. Get him a rub-down every time you can before he goes to sleep. . . . Watching diet, see that he gets greens, salads, vegetables. . . . I don't think you will need to watch alcohol."

The campaign lost, Marsh warned Johnson to keep quiet about fellow Texan Tom Connally's sniping at him. Marsh was full of praise about Johnson's demeanor since losing the race: "The fact that you did no drinking and were able to keep your sense of humor and enjoy the days means very much. I liked your mind Saturday morning, because I saw that you see the significance of your selfless duty to be active regardless of victory or defeat. You have raised the ceiling of yourself. You may amount to something."

"What you need," Marsh also told Lyndon, "is a basic serenity of soul, and not a Saint Vitus Dance of self. You are old enough to enter the first class of old men's wisdom. It is called impersonality. Throw away all your looking glasses so that you may see."[7]

President Roosevelt, sitting in his wheelchair behind his desk in the Oval Office, told Johnson, "I want you to know that I have just accepted an invitation for you to keynote a national convention of young people in Louisville, Kentucky, and I have already prepared your speech for you."

"Fine, Mr. President, when is it and what do you say in your speech?" Johnson told me he replied.

Roosevelt said it was a call for young Americans to be as fanatical about democracy as young Nazis were about their system. Roosevelt was to speak after Johnson. The occasion was a convention of the Young Democrats.

"Every one of us," Johnson read in his speech to the YDs, "is a soldier in the heat of democracy's battle against the Nazi world." The country's defense program, he said, was endangered by "old men of yesterday." Then the president spoke, and with Europe in flames, Britain under siege, and Germany invading Russia, every word must have made an awesome impression on his young keynoter. Democracy, Roosevelt said, had to be defended world-wide against "the dark forces of despotism which would re-enslave the globe by turning back the clock of progress half a thousand years. . . . Across both oceans, on the oceans, and above the oceans, the struggle is one of armed forces, with the ghastly result of destruction and slaughter on a scale unparalleled in modern history. It had to be so. Against naked force the only possible defense is naked force. . . . Unfortunately, here, as abroad, there were and are appeasers and compromisers who contend for treaties with forces that make a mock of treaties," and what these people advocate, Roosevelt said, was "perilous to national security."[8]

Germany had been working through its embassy in Washington to encourage U.S. isolationists, paying for an advertisement in the *New York Times,* sending money for five U.S. writers who were to write pro-Hitler books. The day Roosevelt and his protégé were rallying the Young Democrats against disloyalty, Hitler was bullying his generals out of their desire to march on Moscow. Planning to crush Britain and Russia before taking on the United States, the dictator wanted Japan to attack, not the Americans, but British possessions in Asia. As winter came on he ordered his generals to take Moscow, but he was too late. Although his legions surrounded the city, subfreezing temperatures and the Russians, fighting to the death, stopped them twenty or thirty miles away.

On December 6 Russia counterattacked with one hundred divisions and drove the Nazis back. On December 7, Japanese dive bombers and fighter and torpedo planes sneak-attacked the American base at Pearl Harbor, sinking battleships and destroyers and killing twenty-three hundred servicemen. Roosevelt had been right. Congress declared war on Japan. Hitler declared war on the United States.[9]

---

42. In and Out of the War

Anyone who thought Johnson had promised he would quit Congress to go to war had underestimated his care with words. He had said not that he would quit, but that he would *leave.* Anyone who expected him to go "into the trenches" had been misled by his hyperbole. He knew he would not be a foot soldier: the year before his Senate race he had been commissioned a lieutenant commander in the Naval Reserve.

It stood to reason that as a protégé of Roosevelt's and a member of the naval affairs committee, he would go into Roosevelt's pet service. Charles Marsh helped him get the commission; Adlai Stevenson, who was then a young troubleshooter for the navy, said he secured it for the congressman. Johnson told Harold Young he had not trained a day to qualify for it.

"As a member of the Naval Reserve of the United States Navy,"

Johnson wrote Roosevelt the day after Pearl Harbor, "I hereby urgently request my Commander-in-Chief to assign me immediately to active duty with the Fleet." But neither of his two principal advisers showed, in their communications to him, the slightest expectation that he would stay in the war until it was over.

Afterwards it was often said that Johnson was the first congressman in uniform. As soon as war was declared he obtained an indefinite leave from the House, put on his hat, and reported to the navy for active duty as a congressman with the rank of lieutenant commander. Then he went over to the White House and told Roosevelt, "He said he understood, and told me goodbye," Johnson said. Roosevelt also assigned him to Undersecretary of the Navy James Forrestal. Foregoing his congressional salary, Johnson received only the three-thousand-dollars pay of his navy rank. Presumably at his insistence, his aide John Connally was also assigned to Forrestal, and for several months the two Texans did navy staff work in Washington.

At first Johnson threw his weight around a little carelessly. "I did not fully appreciate," he confessed, "that my uniform completely concealed my status as a congressman. The fact that I looked like any other junior officer, and that I was expected to salute my superiors, was called to my attention in a rather memorable fashion by an admiral. . . ."

Nine days after Pearl Harbor, Charles Marsh urged Johnson to announce he would not be a candidate for the Senate in 1942, and "This statement will cause people to make you a candidate." Wirtz wrote John Connally suggesting that he "send names that we could use in a 'spontaneous' movement to draft Lyndon for another term in Congress."

With Connally as his secretary, Congressman-Commander Johnson was transferred to San Francisco, assigned to the Office of the Chief, U.S.-New Zealand Navy Command, and put in charge of training navy employees in war production work. According to Young, Johnson spent time "laying up in very good San Francisco hotels" and having "a tremendous time" on duebills Marsh gave him. (Duebills are credit sheets for free lodging that hotels give newspapers as pay for advertising the hotels.)

Lady Bird ran her husband's congressional office, receiving no salary, but plenty of hectoring from Lyndon. Discussing letters to constituents, he wrote her, "see if you can't get out fifteen or twenty every day." She told him she was taking typing and shorthand in school. "Dear Bird," he wrote, "I hope you can hurry and finish your school because I feel if you could spend all day in the office, it wouldn't be long until we would be invincible. Think of the effect it would have if 2,000 of our best friends in the District had personal notes from you written at the rate of twenty-five a day for sixty days. I don't know how you are going to find time to do all this and still take the people to lunch that I want you to take, and see the people in the evening that you must see, but I guess with your methodical planning you can work it out."

Connally, tiring of Johnson's continuous talk of politics, suggested they drop south and visit a Hollywood movie studio. Johnson couldn't imagine why, so Connally admitted he wanted to see the picture-pretty blonde star, Lana Turner. "Who," Johnson asked, "is Lana Turner?"

Night after night Otto Crider of Johnson City, who had moved to California, spent time with Johnson and Connally in the hotel. "John, he bootlicked Lyndon," Crider said.

"Lyndon," Otto asked one night, "you gonna run for the Senate again?"

"No, I'm all through," Johnson said. He showed his friend a two-inch stack of wires he had gotten prematurely congratulating him on winning in 1941. "You know the county that beat me?" he asked.

"Sure!—Gillespie," Otto said. "The Germans were so damn worked up about the war."

"That's right!" Johnson said. Gillespie, the county of Johnson's birth, but populated mostly with Germans, had given him only 166 out of 1,922 votes.

Whiling away the time, the Texans pranked around. One night, Otto said, a Johnson crony—call him Jack Smith—joined them in a little revelry and got blotto. By the next morning Johnson had doctored up some pictures of Smith with some girls. When Smith woke up hung over, Johnson showed him one.

"You remember that?"

"Oh no—God, I don't," Smith groaned.

"You remember that one?" Johnson asked, showing him another one.

"Oh no—Oh, God."

"You don't remember climbing ou that telephone pole and threatening to jump off?"

"Oh, God, did I do that?" Smith cried. "Destroy those pictures—for God's sake don't let my wife see 'em!"

But none of this was making a war record, and Johnson decided he wanted to get into a combat zone. Bird has not released their correspondence concerning these weeks so crucial in his life. But politics was his life; he may have taken a private resolve that he cared enough about his career to risk death if necessary on behalf of it.

Johnson could stand for office in absentia, but neither Marsh nor Wirtz had this in mind.

"Get your ass out of this country at once where there is danger, and then get back as soon as you can to real work," Marsh wrote Commander-Congressman Johnson. "If you can't sell the Navy on ordering you out, you are not as good as I think you are. . . . And it [the work for Johnson in Washington] may be in Man Power; it may be in running the congressional campaign; it may be in the Congress, holding Rayburn's feeble hand. But, for God's sake, get going and quit talking."

On Feb. 23, 1942, Wirtz wrote Johnson—when he was holed up at the Empire Hotel in San Francisco—that Roosevelt's Pa Watson thought Johnson should be more active in Washington and that Wirtz had suggested his protégé be made an admiral.

He doubted, Wirtz told Johnson, that it would be advisable "for you to be called into the White House before summer and before you have some more active service. All of us have to do the things we can do, and we can't all be Roosevelts and MacArthurs."

Even at this point plans were being laid to justify Johnson's return from military service before the war's end. Wirtz said "Sam," presumably Speaker Rayburn, had told him he was thinking of suggesting to Roosevelt that he issue a general order discharging from active service all congressmen in the army and navy. "If the order is properly worded, it might have a good effect," Wirtz told Johnson, "but I do not think it should be done until after the primaries this summer and perhaps not until after the general election." Sam, Wirtz added, "is anxious to be helpful to you."

The war in the Pacific was going badly. With Roosevelt's beat-Germany-first policy limiting U.S. efforts in the Far East, the Japanese had conquered the Philippines and all of Malaya except Singapore. Advancing southward they had defeated the U.S. Navy in the Battle of the Java Sea. They had occupied Lae on the northern side of New Guinea, and their next objective, on the southern side, was Port Moresby, which they wanted to use as a staging area against the island continent of Australia.

"I was ready to go and whip the Indians," Johnson said. A week before U.S. bombers hit Tokyo, he set out for Washington. His brother said that when he saw him in Denver on the way, Lyndon said, "I don't want to stay home when our boys are fighting. I'm not doing a thing. . . . I want to go out and get into the thick of things. I'm going to Washington and see the Boss. He's got to get something done about it."

In Washington, Jonathan Daniels, assistant director of the Office of Civilian Defense who was soon to become a wartime administrative assistant to Roosevelt, met Johnson for a drink at the Carlton. Daniels remembered, "He came striding into the Carlton bar, then subsided into a relaxation apparently complete." Johnson made it clear that, although his talents for the war effort would best be used handling speakers and doing public relations for the government, he had to get into a combat area to further his political career. Daniels wrote on his engagement list after their meeting that Johnson "wants for the sake of political future to get into danger zone. . . ."

As they sipped their drinks, Daniels took Johnson's measure: "Immaculate in blue uniform with the two and a half gold stripes on his sleeves, he seemed still the rangy Texan. . . . He talked slowly with a tone that gave the impression that he was confiding completely to one whose attention he greatly desired. But there was no rest in his dark bright eyes. His mood altered easily. Slim and curly-haired, joking and laughing, he looked less like the conventional portrait of a congressman than the equally conventional picture of a movie actor in seagoing costume. I left him to go to realism in the White House."

Although Johnson's people were considering his running for the Senate in 1942 even when he was "away at war," Connally and Bird were convinced he could not win—he had already agreed to support ex-Governor James Allred. "All this spells Wirtz to me," Marsh wrote Johnson on May 21. Marsh told Roosevelt's Grace Tully that Allred could not beat Pappy O'Daniel and Johnson could, "from Dutch Harbor or Australia."

That May of 1942 a curious story from Washington appeared in a Dallas paper: the administration wanted to see Johnson in the Senate in place of O'Daniel, there was a movement in Texas to get Johnson's name on the ballot by petition, and if this happened, "it is expected that Johnson would say that if the people felt he could be of greater service in the Senate than in the Navy, he would make any sacrifice, even resign his commission." But if Johnson was considering this he decided quickly against it. The next day it was announced that on his way through Austin to the South Pacific, he had authorized putting his name on the ballot for reelection to the House. Connally, left the discretion to do as he decided and agreeing with Wirtz and Bird, filed Lyndon for re-election.[1]

In the White House Johnson had learned that Roosevelt was sending him to the Pacific with a group that would look into charges against General Douglas MacArthur. Forrestal had recommended that Johnson go, and "I was Forrestal's man," Johnson said. "I was . . . a very low-ranking set of eyes and ears" for FDR, he said.

Johnson flew to Australia in a vice-admiral's personal PB2Y-2 flying boat. During a pause in New Caledonia, Johnson ran into a pair of lieutenant colonels from the general staff, Samuel Anderson of the air force and Francis R. Stevens of the army, and the three discovered they were all on their way to see General MacArthur on related missions. General George C. Marshall had dispatched the colonels to get the same kind of information Forrestal wanted Johnson to get. The three of them agreed to stick together.

MacArthur was commander of the Southwest Pacific (Admiral Chester Nimitz commanded the rest of the Pacific). Driven out of the Philippines, MacArthur had established his headquarters at the southern tip of Australia, in Melbourne. On May 25 the three visitors arrived together at his office.

The army, navy, air force, and MacArthur were squabbling, and

MacArthur was not particularly pleased to see a naval officer who was a congressman as well. Walking up to Johnson, the general offered him a cigarette and asked, "What did you want to see me about?"

"I have a message from the president," Johnson replied.

To the two colonels MacArthur said, "There might have been a reason—" then swinging to Johnson he continued "—but God only knows what you're doing here!"

Pacing back and forth behind his desk, referring occasionally to a map, MacArthur gave the three visitors the big picture, awing them no little. The trio spent the next several days, escorted by a brigadier general despite their junior ranks, inspecting military installations. Then they began a plane trip up the east coast of the country to New Guinea, across to northwest Australia, and back to Melbourne.

A story Lyndon told Harold Young suggests that the lieutenant commander felt a certain hostility toward military brass who abuse subordinates. One night, during the three officers' inspections, Johnson and a general were waiting for a combat airplane that was being flown in from the states. They waited and waited, late into the night, and Johnson got very worried about the pilot's safety. Hearing at last the drone of an approaching plane, they rushed onto the airfield in Jeeps. The plane circled, dipped, and landed, and a young pilot emerged white as a sheet.

"Why, you ignorant, dizzy son-of-a-bitch," the general shouted, advancing on the boy, "you coulda wrecked $20 million worth of government property and caused us to lose the war!"

"Sir," the kid replied, "I'm so happy to be here."

However that general felt about the rookie pilot, MacArthur did not want to lose Roosevelt's congressman, and a general officer of the army was directed to keep Johnson "out of a bomber in which he was determined to fly over Japanese-held territory." In their 1964 book on the Johnson episode, *The Mission,* Martin Caidin and Edward Hymoff gave no details about this order, but Hymoff added from memory in 1975 that it was not in writing and came from MacArthur's headquarters, "which was a political as well as a military one."

In Townsville, on the eastern coast, the three inspector-observers stayed at a wooden frame two-story hotel. Colonel Anderson, who was a pilot, decided to go on a June 9 bombing raid on Lae, the Japanese base. Johnson said he would go, too. Probably the order from headquarters came into play when Brigadier General Bill Marquat and Major General Ralph Royce tried to dissuade Johnson. It *was* dangerous: on a recent mission over Lae five of six bombers had been destroyed, and the odds were one in four or five against making it back from a mission to bomb the place. But Johnson, who knew what was in his mind, told Marquat that he'd come to the Pacific to "see personally for the president just what conditions were like, and I cannot find out what they *are* like if I don't go along on this mission." Faced down by the reference to the president, the generals desisted. Colonel Stevens, remembering the agreement to stick together, said if Anderson and Johnson were going, so was he. A brigadier general at the airfield near Port Moresby, receiving a message from MacArthur's headquarters that a "very important congressman" would be arriving, arranged for the three emissaries to go on the mission to Lae.[2]

The objective was to get twelve B-26 Marauders, each one armed with six machine guns, past the defending Jap Zeros to bomb Lae. A group of B-17s was to go in first at a high level, then a group of B-25s was to go in at an intermediate level to draw Zeros into diversionary dogfights, clearing the way for the B-26s. In all twenty-seven planes were attacking, the B-26s taking off in the last of the three waves.

The B-26s, preparing for takeoff at Seven Mile Drome near Port Moresby, received an order to wait for some VIPs who were arriving, and since timing was vital the men were fuming. "I was sittin' on the side of the plane all pissed off," tailgunner Harry Baren told me. "Here comes a lieutenant commander—he was escorted by two generals. I knew damn well this was no lieutenant commander. Generals don't escort lieutenant commanders."

As Corporal Baren watched, Johnson boarded the *Wabash Cannonball.* After a few minutes he came back down to urinate, and just then Stevens got into the same plane. When Johnson approached again, Stevens grinned and told him to find another plane.

Johnson walked toward the *Heckling Hare,* where Baren was standing outside with the rest of its crew. To the pilot, Walter H. Greer, Johnson said, "I'd like to fly with you, Captain Greer." "Fine, sure, you can go," Greer said, and yelled to Baren to get a parachute for the guest. Johnson had left his aboard the *Wabash Cannonball.* Johnson then shook hands with the rest of the crew. Sergeant Claude A. McCredie took him to the bay where they were getting the bombs fused and ready for the mission, and Johnson showed intense interest.

"We were miles from the parachutes, and we didn't have any extra ones," Baren said. "But the Japanese never took any prisoners, a parachute didn't mean anything. I gave him mine." (The Americans weren't taking prisoners, either. "I was there eighteen months," said Baren, "and I've never heard of a Japanese prisoner. How could you take them?") Baren would now have to fly the mission without a parachute, but was convinced Johnson did not realize this and did not notice, during the mission, that Baren didn't have one. The chute was several inches too small for the Texan, so he had to fly the mission stooped over in the harness "like a hunchback," Baren laughed.

Johnson told Baren he was a congressman from Texas and had come out to see conditions firsthand.

"I think you're stupid," the tailgunner told him.

"What do you mean?" Johnson asked.

"Well, goddamn, do like everybody else does—wait until you get back and get it from intelligence."

"I want to see it for myself," Johnson replied.

"You're nuts," Baren said. "There's no milkruns. You're outa your goddamn mind."

Baren asked Johnson why he was wearing a uniform, since he was a congressman. "Oh," Johnson explained, "if I got shot down I would become a prisoner of war, not a spy."

When Johnson asked the men what was happening out there and what their problems were, Baren gave him another earful. "We're getting the hell beat out of us," he told him. "We go up with five planes—come back with three." They had no supplies, no parts, their bullets jammed their machine guns, their bombs were so old some of them didn't explode, their fighter planes were much slower than the Zeros and in short supply, their gasoline was rotten, and they had no refrigeration and no meat. They were ripping parts off crippled planes, making their own spare parts, and improvising stops on their machine guns so the guns would stop shooting off the rudders of their own airplanes. Baren let go about MacArthur, too—all the fighting men regarded him as "Dugout Doug," posturing and claiming that " 'Our casualties are light. . . . I shall return.' "

The men boarded the *Heckling Hare*—(under the pilot's window on the left side there was a painting of a rabbit reclining on a flying carpet, flipping bombs over the side)—and for the takeoff Johnson strapped himself in to the radioman's seat while the radioman-gunner, Corporal Lillis M. Walker, moved toward the two lower waist guns near the tail. The Nineteenth Squadron of twelve bombers ascended through an overcast, climbed over the Owen Stanley Range at fourteen thousand feet, and once clear of the peaks began a gradual descent to the bombing altitude.

Johnson was everywhere. He watched through a small window on the left side of the fuselage, squeezed between the pilot and copilot to look out through the windshield, and stood on a stool in the center of the fuselage to see through the bubble on top of the plane.

The weather had cleared, perfect for the day's work. After flying about an hour they spotted Lae off to their left, on a cove beside a river bisecting a valley.

Near the runway at Lae, eight Japanese pilots were posing for a photograph when the first alert sounded, so they reached their planes somewhat behind the first Zeros that had risen to reply. As the eight laggards took off they spotted two high-flying B-17s. Once airborne they joined the other Zeros in attacking five B-25s, but Saburo Sakai, the Japanese ace leading the laggard group of eight, then happened to look back and see "a group of specks." These, he figured, were the bombers coming in to hit Lae: the Zeros were attacking decoys. Sakai and seven other Zeros peeled away from the B-25s to attack the twelve incoming bombers.

In the B-26 Marauders the men at once knew the mission was fouled up. Two dozen Zeros coming at them had to mean the decoys hadn't worked. Some of the bombers went on in over Lae, some swerved to bomb Salamaua, the Zeros hammering them with machine guns and cannon shells.

According to Sakai's personal diary quoted by Caidin and Hymoff, the Japanese ace executed a brilliant aerial maneuver and at point-blank range cannonaded the *Wabash Cannonball,* which plunged into the ocean and exploded, killing Colonel Stevens and the crew. There, but for a call of nature, went Lyndon Johnson. Climbing back into position, Sakai wrote, "I saw one bomber begin to fall back. It was alone . . . trailing . . . a sure-fire target." He led seven more Zeros in pursuit of the straggler, which was the *Heckling Hare.*

About five minutes from Lae—"we could see Lae, we could see Zeros," Baren said—the B-26 carrying Johnson had suddenly lost power. Whether it was an engine or a generator is uncertain, but Greer had to shift into manual controls. Jettisoning its bomb load, the *Heckling Hare* made a diving turn away, pursued by the eight Zeros. The firefight lasted ten to fifteen minutes. Instead of flying straight ahead in a dive, the usual B-26 escape maneuver, Greer wove and skidded while diving. Sakai, trying the same maneuver that had brought down the *Wabash Cannonball,* found the *Heckling Hare* swerving left and jinking. He scored hits—none fatal—merely stitching holes in the wings and fuselage. As the seven other Zeros piled in, Sakai marveled at the prey's "wild skidding motions."

The Zeros pursued, Baren said, "like a bunch of dogs yapping at our heels," coming over and below, rushing ahead to come back in on curves. Firing from the tail, Baren said, "I know I hit one Zero—of course you couldn't follow it after that—other people said it went down." His was the only kill of a Zero made during the mission (another Zero was ditched).

Johnson watched the action from the bubble. Several times he worked back to the waist guns to watch as Walker crawled back and forth between the right and left guns to fire at the best targets. In the top turret the power failure had crippled the two guns; in the nose McCredie's single machine gun jammed. McCredie, moving back to man one of the waist guns beside Walker, saw Johnson in the radio compartment looking out the window at some Zeros. "There're three out there on the left," he said to McCredie. As the sergeant moved on past, Johnson grinned at him. "They were coming straight at us and firing! And this man was as cool as a cucumber," McCredie said later. Walker, moving to the radio to make sure that Seven Mile Drome would be clear to land, saw Johnson in the compartment, too, "just as calm as if we were on a sight-seeing tour," while bullets and shells were hitting the plane. A couple of Zeros came straight for them from the front, firing as they came. "Boy!" Johnson exclaimed to McCredie. "It's rough up here, isn't it." McCredie nodded. "You get kind of scared, don't you?" Johnson asked. "Always," McCredie replied. Johnson burst out laughing at him.

Suddenly, Sakai remembered realizing, eight Zeros were attacking one bomber while another ten behind them were bombing Lae and perhaps Salamaua. He led his pack back toward the action. Inside the *Heckling Hare* the relief was enormous. They settled down for the flight back to Port Moresby. None of them was hurt. Only the *Wabash Cannonball* had been lost.

Johnson said to Baren, "What a helpless feeling it is not to have anything in your hand." As the plane came in to land, he slipped off his borrowed parachute. "You know something?" he said to McCredie as they clambered down to earth. "I sure am glad to be back on this ground." To the crew as a group he gave his thanks, said, "It's been very interesting," and walked off. "He was," said Baren, "as cool as ice."

Among a group of officers watching the other bombers land, Johnson said, "You can have this place over here. You people really need some stuff to fight with." He watched as the crews scavenged one of the returned B-26s that had been crippled on the mission. Then he went to the base hospital and visited the wounded.[3]

His combat behind him, Johnson joined Anderson and other VIPs on a flight to the seaport of Darwin, inspected an air base, and set out (in a Flying Fortress named *Swoose,* for half-swan, half-goose) on a twenty-five-hundred-mile flight across the desert south to Melbourne and General MacArthur.

Blown off course by electrical storms, lost and running low on gas, they had to decide whether to parachute or try to land, and they voted, Johnson with them, to ride it down. As they lost altitude everyone but the pilots clustered in the tail—Johnson was holding onto the tailguns. The *Swoose* made a landing in the open not far from a ranch house, and some ranchers came up. According to the crew chief, Red Varner, Johnson shook hands all around and returned to the flight group saying the Aussies were real folks—the best damn folks in the world, except maybe Texans. "Pretty soon," Varner said, "he knows all their first names, and theyr'e telling him why there ought to be a high tariff on wool. . . ." But that night at a farmhouse Johnson suggested, between slaps at mosquitoes, that someone write a song dedicated to him and entitled, "I Wish I Were Still on Capitol Hill."

Perhaps Johnson's powerful friend in Washington heard what had been going on with him. Might General MacArthur have given his boss a report? Eight days after the mission over Lae, Roosevelt issued a directive that required members of Congress in military service to return to inactive duty, except those who wished to stay in uniform. That same day the exception was rescinded. Of the eight congressmen affected by the order, four resigned their seats and continued in uniform, but Johnson and three others elected to return to Congress.

Evidently there was some political hanky-panky going on. Bird wrote George Brown, the Johnsons' friend with Brown & Root, on July 3, 1942, six days before FDR released the directive to the press:

"You will be glad to know that Sam assured me on Wednesday that the orders about members returning, the phrasing of which was so objectionable, have been at Sam's urging changed. They are now quite alright." (Presumably, "Sam" was Rayburn.)

Perhaps one issue was whether the returning congressmen would quit the service outright. Jesse Kellam, Johnson's friend and NYA director, wrote him five days after FDR released the directive, "I think it is much better that you were recalled to Congress and put on the inactive list, rather than to have returned to Congress after having resigned a commission in the Naval Reserve." Many wanted him back in Washington, but, Kellam continued, "There are a good many people who . . . would think it all right for a congressman to give up his seat and to stay in active service."[5]

The day after the directive was written in its first form, Johnson and Anderson were summoned to MacArthur's office. The general did not appear to be pleased with Johnson. He could understand why Anderson, an air force officer, had joined the mission against Lae, but he was at a loss to understand why Johnson and Stevens risked their lives when they had no need to. Johnson repeated he could not prepare a personal report to the president by sitting in headquarters, but his explanation to MacArthur was also political.

In response to MacArthur, Anderson wrote me, "my recollection is that Johnson spoke up and said that many of the airmen on New Guinea knew that he was a congressman from Texas—that many were his constituents—and that he wanted to show them he would face the same dangers they *had* to face. As I recall, MacArthur said no more."

For another hour MacArthur listened to the two men's observations. As they prepared to leave he told them he had awarded the DSC posthumously to Stevens, and he awarded each of them the Silver Star. After several moments' silence, he added, "I have no medals to pin on you. The citations are not yet completed. But you can pick up some ribbons on your way out, through my outer office, and put those on."

None of the other crewmen who had gone down with *Wabash Cannonball* had received medals, other than Purple Hearts, yet Stevens had a DSC. On the *Heckling Hare,* the only man bemedaled was Johnson—not Greer for his brilliant flying, not Baren for getting his Zero, nor any of the others. Baren did not find out about Johnson's Silver Star until *The Mission* was published in 1964. "As far as we were concerned," Baren said, "why didn't *we* get Silver Stars? That was MacArthur. He was buckin'—Roosevelt woulda fired him. . . ."[6]

Time reporter Robert Sherrod, seeing Johnson in Sydney, asked him to deliver, to Sherrod's news colleagues in Washington, a long memo he had written that was in part somewhat critical of MacArthur. Sherrod was trying to evade the censorship. Johnson took the memo, but the journalists in Washington never received it, and later Sherrod asked Johnson what had happened. Johnson had opened and read it, and "It was too hot, so I put it in the toilet," he told Sherrod—who guessed he meant it was too critical of MacArthur, who had just given him the medal.[7]

Judging from its existence at the Johnson Library in Austin, Johnson kept a diary from May through July, the only time he is known to have done so. An "unofficial, transcript copy" is identified as "incomplete and of unknown origin," but tracks fairly well the handwritten diary in Johnson's script. Apart from the strange fact that Johnson wrote that the U.S. side over Lae shot down nine Zeros, some of it is interesting.

At one island where eleven hundred soldiers were stationed, Johnson found "Army food lousy. Army management about as bad. . . . Inadequate defense. No radar detector system. . . . Only 1 woman on island, wife 60 years old. . . . Only intercourse—social."

At Nournea, he recorded: "After visit with High Commissioner had lunch with Gen. Patch then on inspection of Island. . . . Plenty of prophylactics being used. . . . Natives very much like negroes. Work only enough to eat.—get 50¢ per day for Army work."

Someone he called "Miss Jesus" was much on his mind. Aloft, he recorded, "Thought of Miss Jesus all day." Again aloft, "Thought of Miss Jesus much." And as a plane took off one morning, he "thought of Miss Jesus plenty."

His account of the mission says nine Zeros were shot down, while his side lost a B-26 and a fighter, and "I lost my friend Steve."

Returning to Melbourne, he recorded that he had sent cables to Miss Jesus and hoped and prayed for an answer. The entry on the meeting with MacArthur says:

"Thursday, June 18: Saw MacArthur at 11:45 A.M. Very sad. Head down. Low voice, 'glad to see you two fellows here where three were last. It was a mistake of the head to go on combat mission but it did justice to your heart.' It was just what I would have done. I'm giving you Silver Heart. Gave Stevens DSC because he was your leader and gave his life—Such is war."[8]

Johnson meant, of course, the Silver Star, but he wrote the Silver Heart.

Wearing his ribbon, Johnson set his course back to the United States. He was hospitalized in the Fiji Islands for five days or so. Once he woke up delirious and heard someone saying, "You goddamn son-of-a-bitch,

I'll knock hell out of you!" and "He's gonna have an American doctor!" One morning he found an Alabama doctor bending over him telling him he had come down with a fever of 105 and had been brought to the hospital unconscious. The doctor, Johnson said to me, had had difficulty with the New Zealand doctors, and "Admiral Nimitz had sent him a message from Pearl Harbor to give his personal attention to me."

Flown homeward to Pearl Harbor, Johnson was ushered into Nimitz's office and told him his experiences. Since Nimitz was going to San Francisco he offered Johnson a seat on his plane, but the congressman opted to stay around the hospital at Pearl a few days. "The next day," Johnson said, "I picked up the paper and saw where Admiral Nimitz's plane had landed on a log in San Francisco Bay, and the plane had turned over and the lieutenant who had taken my seat had drowned."[9]

To save money during Johnson's absence from Washington, Bird had rented their house and moved into an apartment in Virginia with Connally's wife, Nellie, who was also replacing her husband in Johnson's office. After a few months Bird began living alone. Frequently in the middle of the night, usually about three or four in the morning, Gladys Montgomery, who lived on the floor beneath Bird, couldn't help but overhear, the windows being open, when Lyndon telephoned Bird from Australia. Bird would tell him what was going on in the office and in Texas and ask his advice on political matters; after a while she would say, "Good night, my love," and everybody would go back to sleep.

But now, after seven months, he was back; he returned to the House officially on July 17, 1942.[10] Allied offensives in the Pacific had been ordered, and late in July the congressman reported to Roosevelt during a breakfast meeting that lasted three or four hours.

Johnson told the president that the Zeros were superior to American fighter planes. Evidently there was also discussion about incompetent military brass (Baren had the impression Johnson was going to recommend MacArthur be thrown out). Johnson said later there was a shakeup and a new team was dispatched to the Pacific. Early the next month U.S. Marines attacked Guadalcanal in the first major Allied offensive in the Pacific, and by the early months of 1943 the Japanese lost the island and went on the defensive.

Johnson's report on his inspection tour must have been interesting and useful to the president, but insiders knew that, war or no war, something quite else was going on, too. As Roosevelt's aide Jonathan Daniels said knowingly, Johnson was "back from his politically essential plunge into the Pacific."[11]

43. Politics and Military Service

Johnson had risked his life to get a report for the president, but he certainly had not gone "to the trenches." After a brief and stagy tour as a VIP, he was provided, by the president who was his patron, a persuasive excuse to sit out the war in Washington. Yet his posturing as a battle-scarred veteran began immediately after his one combat mission and continued through his own presidency.

In the *New York Times* three days after the raid on Lae, he was quoted as saying that the men on the mission "are real Americans with real American courage." "I was robbed," the UP quoted him the same day. "When the generator of our plane burned out just as we neared the objective, the crew moaned. When the pilot said that we must turn back, those kids begged their skipper to continue. . . . They were heart-broken when he couldn't comply."

Two weeks later in a broadcast from Melbourne, heard in California by the CBS shortwave, he said, "Out here in the combat area I have seen some of our gallant Texans, under command of our own Texas admiral, Chester Nimitz, write pages in [the] record of the Pacific. I have seen the army of that matchless leader, General MacArthur, take it and give it out." When he returned to the mainland he wrote in a Texas newspaper that the Allied fighting men he had met "all had love of country in their souls, but only murder in their hearts for the enemy" and "are imbued with the spirit of Bowie and Crockett and Houston." For his constituents he dramatized his role in a few words suggesting more than one combat mission and a combat injury: "I lived with the men on the fighting fronts; I flew with them in missions over enemy territory. I ate and slept with them; and was hospitalized with them in the Fiji Islands. . . ."

His election opponents noticed the discrepancies. His 1944 adversary, Buck Taylor, rebuked "his failure to keep his promises to serve his country in the trenches beside the good soldiers he helped to send to those trenches." Hardy Hollers, his opponent in 1946, accused him of going to war "with a camera in one hand and leading his publicity man with the other." Hollers also said Johnson had used FDR's directive as "an excuse to return to an air-cooled fox-hole in Washington," breaking "a solemn promise to the people that if war ever came [he] would go to the trenches."

Yet as the years passed Johnson was not above continuing to glorify his wartime role. His 1948 opponent, "Calculatin' Coke" Stevenson, whose trademark-pose was sitting around puffing on his pipe, had sat out the war in Texas as governor. Against him Johnson spoke of "the horrors I experienced against the Japs in the Pacific"—unlike his opponent, "I didn't sit and puff my pipe when our country was at war. . . . I have seen the horrors of war. . . ." His 1948 campaign paper said he was "the only candidate with a fighting war record" and quoted his commanding officer, "an Admiral in the regular navy," saying of him "he is one of the bravest men I have ever fought with in my entire life."

In 1956, in an introduction for a flacky presidential campaign biography of Johnson written by a member of his staff, Johnson himself said, "I have read it and I like it," yet its account of Johnson's war service said falsely that the Japanese fighters had "knocked out" the motor of the "Heckling Hare."

If Caidin and Hymoff are correct, eight Zeros attacked the twelve Marauders and only one Zero was shot down by Allied planes on the Lae mission. Yet whipping up a crowd in Texas when he was running for president late in 1959, Johnson said, "I was with [the B-26s] in June, 1942, when they went into twenty Zeros. I saw fourteen of 'em go down in flames right in front of me. And a beardless boy with one motor gone brought us back to New Guinea—because he was a Can Do man."

Harry Provence's account of the mission for a 1964 campaign biographer typified the gloss put on the facts for the votes to be made. "On one flight in a Navy patrol bomber on which he was an officer observer," Provence wrote, "Johnson saw Japanese fighter-plane bullets knock out one of the bomber's engines and inflict gaping wounds on some of the crew members. The pilot barely managed to bring the crippled bomber back to its New Guinea base."

By letting such balderdash stand, Johnson earned the bitter attacks that ensued. A Johnson-hater said in a 1964 polemic that Johnson had returned from a brief tour with a citation and "left the dying to others." The 1964 Republican candidate for vice-president, William E. Miller, said that since FDR's directive meant "you could not be a congressman and in the service," Johnson "elected to be a congressman instead of a soldier" and "was back home again before the shooting had ever started." A Republican newsletter emphasized that no other person on the plane Johnson was in, not even the pilot, had received an award of any kind. Author David Halberstam wrote casually that Johnson's Silver Star was "one of the least deserved but most often displayed Silver Stars in American military history."

Every mile he traveled from Washington to San Francisco to Washington to Melbourne to New Guinea, to Melbourne, the Fiji Islands, Pearl Harbor, and back to Washington again, Johnson was a politician making a war record for words he would use in campaigns to come. Some voters caught on beforehand, and some later, but many were misled as he intended. He not only let falsehood pass for truth, he faked his record himself. Telling me about the mission over Lae, he said that when twenty Zeros attacked them, "it was like shooting fish out of the barrel." One of the two motors in Johnson's plane went out, and the

Zeros were boiling right past them, firing. Fourteen of the planes got the hell shot out of them. He saw Colonel Stevens's plane go down. He said that everybody who survived that mission got a Silver Star; everybody who died got the Distinguished Service Cross.[1]

---

44. Wartime in Washington

During the rest of the war, Johnson bought a house, laid the basis for his fortune by having Lady Bird acquire a radio station regulated by the federal government in which he was a congressman, turned against the New Deal, protected himself and Brown & Root from scandal, watchdogged the navy, intervened in the wartime bureaucracy for his constituents, and politicked. All this was quite a comedown for a boy wonder of the New Deal.

From time to time he invited friends like Drew Pearson and Ben Cohen to his home to see hand-camera movies he had taken in the Pacific. Whenever someone from Texas showed up in the movies Lyndon would point him out and say, "There's so-and-so from Austin," or "That's so-and-so from Beaumont." Cohen said to him dryly, "Lyndon, now why don't you just tell us the fellows who *aren't* from Texas? It would save you some time."

Johnson saw a heroic dimension in the Texanness of the Thirty-Sixth Division, which was fighting in Italy. In the *Congressional Record* he called attention to a news story that the first of the Americans on the beach "wore 'T-patches'—the patch for the division, the T for Texas. According to the account," he said, "these troops were untried in battle in this war, but when reporters asked why they were selected for this extremely important assignment the reply of the commanding officer was that they were from Texas. That, it appears, was considered explanation enough."[1]

As each month of the war passed, foundations of postwar corporate empires were being laid in defense contracting, and wartime Washington was crawling with lobbyists. According to one Texan, at Thomas Circle, George Brown of Brown & Root maintained an immaculate establishment with a housekeeper, a busboy, a cook, and always plenty of booze. "Everything was operated on the black market," according to this source. Reynolds Aluminum had a place a few doors away; a block from there Henry Kaiser's interests were looked after. Johnson was a regular at the B&R spread, and Pearson remembered him partying at Charles Marsh's mansion two and a half blocks from the Browns'.

Marsh also had "Longlea," the large estate at Culpepper, Virginia, and during the war (as well as before and after it), Johnson was out there often on weekends. So were Henry Wallace and his assistant, Harold Young. "It was one of the prettiest terraces in the world, in what looks like one of the prettiest valleys in the world, and a little river down there," Young said. There was horseback riding, and tennis; you could take fine long walks. Usually you would dress for dinner, except Sunday night, and gentry from all over Virginia came to the parties there. Young estimated that between 1941 and 1947 Johnson was out there two or three weekends a month.

On these weekends, Lyndon was no sparkling intellectual planning a better world. As the vice-president's assistant saw his back-sliding liberal friend, "He didn't amount to a shit, really, hell he was just along. He was no great strong light, I don't remember him saying anything great. He was a flatterer, a great flatterer."

Lyndon was sweet on Marsh's wife, Alice. "Lyndon would be sittin' out there flirtin' with her a little, and Lady Bird would be out there very distressed about her husband," Young remembered. One night Marsh, very drunk, complained to Young that Lyndon was trying to steal his wife. The publisher thought she would say she was going to the beauty parlor when she was really shacking up with the congressman. Just as Marsh was becoming most agitated about this Lyndon came in, and Marsh ordered him to get out of his house. OK, Johnson said, and he got his suitcase and left. Half an hour later he came back in, grinning. As he expected, Marsh had forgotten about ordering him out.[2]

Bird, after years of living in apartments, decided she was going to have a house of her own. She had had several miscarriages, and she passionately wanted the security of a nest, where she might have a better chance to have children and could feel she had a home. In a neighborhood a few blocks from Connecticut Avenue she picked out a two-story, eight-room white brick colonial with an attic and a basement. Believing Lyndon was jeopardizing their getting it by arguing too much about the price, she brought the subject up with him in their apartment while he was talking with John Connally. As if she had not said anything, Lyndon went on talking with his friend, and then she got mad.

"I want that house," she broke in on them. "Every woman wants a home of her own. I've lived out of a suitcase ever since we've been married. I have no home to look forward to. I have no children to look forward to, and I have nothing to look forward to but another election."

She stalked out of the room. Shocked, Lyndon looked to his friend. "What should I do?"

"I'd buy the house," Connally replied.

For $18,000, with Bird's Aunt Effie said to be making up the bulk of the down payment as an advance on Bird's inheritance, they bought it.

In 1944, after four miscarriages, the Johnsons' first daughter, Lynda, was born. She came early the morning of March 19, and Lyndon called Carl Vinson hollering "Hallelujah." A White House car turned up at the

Johnsons' house with a baby gift, a book about Roosevelt's dog Fala, which the president had inscribed "From the master—to the pup." With their second daughter, Luci, born in 1947, Bird always rejoiced about these years: "We bought a home in '42 and had a child in '44, and another child in '47, so the forties were good years."[3]

Jonathan Daniels laid his canny eyes on Johnson from time to time early in the war. On a Sunday before the 1942 elections Daniels went to a cocktail party the Johnsons gave. Senator Tom Connally of Texas came with his wife, a warm blonde who was the former wife of Senator Sheppard. Rayburn and Elmer Davis, director of the Office of War Information, argued whether Roosevelt should time his moves in the war to affect the election. Tommy Corcoran was there, and a recording was played on the Johnsons' radio-phonograph of "The Cork" singing "The Good Old Rebel," a ballad of an ex-Confederate.

A couple days after the party, talking with Daniels in Rayburn's hideaway office, Johnson analyzed Corcoran's fall from grace: his arrogance had cost him some friends, and when he began to get too much publicity, people high in the government feared he would grab the limelight of any show he got near. He had come to think the administration could not get along without him, and "You know," Johnson said, "anybody can get along without anybody."

On a winter day in 1942, a few weeks before Christmas, after visiting Johnson's hideout office, room 544 of the old House Office Building, Daniels scribbled impressions in his diary: "the green burlap and wood screen around the basin where the pretty blonde secretary in red mixed drinks and made coffee; dark-red steel filing cases; green figured carpet; black leather couch with red satin pillow on it; big red desk with congressman's feet on it; statuette of a fighting Irishman, labeled 'I'm Dimocrat'; photographs of politicians on the walls; hat stand with light-gray Texas hat on it; green steel wastepaper basket; monk's cloth curtains; scotch and soda bottles behind monk's cloth curtains and the bookcases."

This was a long way from the *Heckling Hare* just six months earlier. The two men talked about a bumbling bureaucrat . . . a ghost-written speech Johnson had given. As Daniels was leaving, Johnson gave him a photograph of himself inscribed "with affection and admiration," but Daniels would have been more touched if he hadn't seen the Texan take it from a pile of about a hundred prints, "which I presume will go to others for whom he feels equal affection and admiration."

By this time Johnson was a familiar among the men who stood at the commanding heights of government, and he was learning more and more about power in the salons, the corridors, and the hideaways of the Capitol. He watched, for instance, the ways Jesse Jones thwarted an order from Roosevelt. First Jones would ignore the order. If the president asked about it, Jones would say the matter was being investigated.

If the president asked again, there would be a report on it soon. If the president asked a fourth time, Jones would finally do part of what he had been ordered to do, but usually Roosevelt would not remember to ask that many times. Forrestal had learned to do the same thing. Johnson developed a light contempt for bureaucrats and a conviction that the president, while cooperating with Congress, has to dominate the executive agencies.

He was eager as always to cultivate the powerful. "There is something of the campus politician about him and a willingness to run in and do things which an older man might hesitate to do and which might not be accepted from an older man," Daniels wrote. When Assistant Secretary of War John J. McCloy went to the Capitol to testify, he received the impression that Johnson was "the white-haired boy amongst the Southern Democrats" so far as the White House was concerned. Working through the New Deal insider, Jim Rowe, Johnson had Tom Clark of Texas appointed an assistant attorney general, and during the war the two Texans took walks together almost every Sunday.

A real camaraderie developed between Speaker Rayburn and Johnson. When Rowe went to war his wife Elizabeth had dinner one evening with Rayburn, and she had taken off her shoes to dance. Rayburn told her, "I'm going to get even with this fellow Lyndon Johnson. You call him up and tell him you are in grave danger and want some protection." She called him. "Jim told me to be sure to call you if I got in trouble," she said. "I'm down here at the apartment of an old baldheaded man and he's got my shoes off and I don't know what he's going to get off next and I need help." Johnson told her he'd be right over, but Rayburn came onto the phone chuckling, telling him he was the swain. Johnson concluded the lady didn't need much help.

Daniels, knowing Johnson to be quick and handy, would take him in to see Roosevelt about politics and then leave him chatting about the forthcoming congressional elections with Marvin McIntyre, one of FDR's three secretaries. Learning that Roosevelt had offended Rayburn by failing to return a call, Johnson called the White House and FDR phoned the Speaker promptly.

Roosevelt asked Johnson to help with the 1942 congressional elections, but when Johnson went to see the president with Daniels, General "Pa" Watson, another FDR secretary, told them, "Make it snappy."

"I have nothing to talk with the president about; he wanted to see us," Johnson said.

Watson cut him. "The president hasn't anything to say to you, but you go in and speak to him, even if just for a minute." Then the general went into the president's office and returned to say FDR said he would see them later on.

Johnson strode out in a pique. McIntyre, upset, told Daniels that, although Johnson was "one of those thin-skinned Southern gentlemen,"

Watson had been clumsy, alienating a fellow who was important to Roosevelt in relating to, for instance, Rayburn. The next spring McIntyre was "trying to get Lyndon back in here," having him look over the invitation list for a smoker for new congressmen, and by the time Watson died a month before Roosevelt himself did, Johnson stood so well in the inner circle that Roosevelt's private secretary Grace Tully mentioned him as a possible successor to Watson.[4]

Circumstantial evidence indicates that Johnson used his influence in the executive branch to compromise the government's tax case against Brown & Root for its corporate contributions to his 1941 campaign. The tax people launched an investigation in mid-1942, but were called off when B&R complained. Early in 1943 they were told to proceed again, but to be "diplomatic." The evidence was strong, and Secretary of the Treasury Henry Morgenthau sent word that the investigation was to be "handled as any other case."

Certain messages without identifiable content may or may not fit in here. In the summer of '42, back from the war, Johnson wrote Connally, "Be extremely careful what you say to our friend about the fraud business. . . . Here recently I have detected a marked coolness, and I question the wisdom of our talking too much to one or two. . . ." That fall George Brown wired Johnson, "Understand the senator [presumably Wirtz] en route to Washington. Hope he will be able to make further progress on tax program. Herman and I both are interested in following through some of your ideas on this. . . ." Johnson wrote back he "thoroughly discussed the content of your wire with the senator. . . ." In another letter without any precise content, Johnson wrote Everett Looney, whose clients included the Browns, "I was glad to get . . . the tax data. . . . I am trying to ferret out now the way to get this into the proper hands. . . ."

On the first day of 1944, a special agent in charge of Texas and Louisiana told agents under him to be "extra tactful" because of complaints in Washington "relative to investigation of political donations." A memo extant in the Roosevelt Library shows that on January 11, Johnson phoned the White House that he was anxious to see FDR as quickly as possible—"He says it is not a 'Sunday School' proposition," Johnson was quoted to Watson. Two days later, on January 13, Johnson and Alvin Wirtz called on President Roosevelt. At 4:30 P.M. on the same day, the assistant secretary of the treasury telephoned Dallas saying that as a result of the meeting between Johnson, Wirtz, and the president, the assistant secretary had to be at the White House at ten the next morning and wanted a summary of the Brown & Root case teletyped to him by 9. It was. The company's tax liability, previously estimated at $1.1 million plus a fraud penalty of half a million, was settled for less than a fourth of the total, and proposals for prosecution were dropped.

When Drew Pearson, in 1956, gave Johnson a chance to explain the money B&R's Monteith had contributed to his campaign, Johnson said he had never heard of Monteith or received money from him. While candidly admitting to me later that B&R had funded the campaign, Johnson took up two lines of defense. The first was that Senator O'Daniel had stirred up the investigation (the implication being that it was just politics). Second, Johnson denied he and Wirtz had discussed B&R's tax crisis with Roosevelt. He thought they had talked about either public power or ditching Vice-President Wallace in favor of Rayburn. The charge that they talked about the tax case, he said, was completely untrue—Roosevelt would never let anyone talk to him on a tax matter. The information Johnson had about the case came, he said, from Wirtz after Pearson's stories appeared. Johnson also implied the issue was the company's depreciation schedule, not the 1941 election. About Pearson's conclusion that Johnson and Wirtz had talked with FDR about B&R's taxes, he said, "Pearson was told that wasn't true when he said it."

One can see why the columnist did not print a retraction. After giving Johnson's 1956 account of his talk with FDR, Pearson wrote: "However, Internal Revenue files are unequivocal. I have photostats of the messages sent from Dallas for the White House. Three days later a new revenue agent arrived in Dallas and shortly thereafter the Brown & Root tax case was ordered settled." Although he made quite a few errors in his time, Pearson could add two and two.[5]

By the time Helen Gahagan Douglas came to the House in 1944 from California, she saw that Johnson was one of the congressional elite, close to the committee chairmen who ran things. "You knew that he knew what was happening and when it would happen and how it would happen—not because he talked, I think he was one of the most close-mouthed men I ever knew. But it was his manner, and his sureness, and above all his friendship with the Speaker. His friendship with Sam Rayburn."

He never spoke from the microphone, she said, "except on rare, rare occasions. He didn't spend much time listening to others in the House. He usually voted and then left the chamber, loping off the floor with that great stride of his as though he was on some Texas plain. If he did remain, he looked the picture of boredom, slumped in his chair with his eyes half-closed. . . . Then suddenly he'd jump to his feet, nervous . . . restless, as if he couldn't bear it another minute. . . . Then he'd leave. He always gave the impression of someone in a hurry."

With FDR's liberal crusade aborted by the war, Johnson's liberalism faded, too. There are indications in Henry Wallace's diaries that Johnson, like "Dr. Win-the-War" Roosevelt himself, turned against the New Deal late in 1942. The vice-president wrote that Marsh told him Corcoran was working closely with, among others, Rowe, Supreme Court Justice William O. Douglas, and Johnson. Corcoran and Douglas arranged for Johnson to deliver a speech in Oregon that, Marsh told Wallace, kicked the New Deal into a cocked hat. "Apparently," Wallace concluded, "the Corcoran line is that the public is now tired of the New Deal; that they must be given something new."[6]

However, when Johnson was forced to choose between the ruling oil barons of his state and the war effort, he chose the war effort. Despite astronomical oil company profits, minions of the oil-producing states were then maneuvering through Congress, with help from Harold Ickes, a thirty-five-cents-a-barrel increase in the price of crude oil—half a billion dollars a year. The division was close, but there, voting against oil, was Lyndon B. Johnson. "It was an act of great courage," said price administrator Chester Bowles, who regarded Johnson as one of the major influences in turning Congress against the increase.[7]

Johnson's vote against this wartime windfall cost him some oil money in his next two campaigns. He had sided with the liberals in the first major conflict about oil during his career. Many a time he would hark back to this one vote to show that he was capable of opposing the oilmen. It was a point he needed to make since he never opposed them again.

As far as his constituents could tell, apart from his brief navy stint he spent the war waving the flag. They had a few glimpses of his work watchdogging the navy, but even there his subcommittee's reports were not published until after the war.

Of course he was keeping his fences mended at home. Preparatory to the 1944 election, in the fall and winter of 1943, he attended a war-bond rally in Johnson City, a chicken barbecue in Smithville, the Chamber of Commerce banquet in Taylor. He commended Russian stamina to the restaurant association in Austin, met with farmers in Georgetown, and spoke against inflation to the Austin League of Women Voters.

Home while boys were dying abroad, he developed a career-long habit of identifying himself with them by using their sacrifices to cudgel people into agreeing with his own positions. He told the farmers, "I am disgusted with any of you who bellyache about sugar rationing when only thirty-five miles from you at McCloskey's hospital are men who aren't even able to get their sugar up to their mouths."

The next year he spoke to a rally of the families of men and women in the war; in Austin he presented a Purple Heart to a World War I veteran and spoke to a VFW barbecue.[8]

Seeing the success of Senator Harry Truman's Senate committee that was watchdogging the war, Johnson persuaded his committee chairman, Vinson, to let him run a special subcommittee on the navy in the war and chose Donald C. Cook, a lawyer in a government agency, to run the staff. Soon after returning from the Pacific, Johnson made an inspection flight to the Aleutian Islands. In the spring of 1945, with other members of his committee, he made a twenty-eight-day tour of naval bases in Europe, North Africa, and the Near East. That summer, he and others visited an army-navy cemetery at the site of a battle in the Moroccan campaign. His subcommittee reported on the procurement activities and legal operations of the navy, its use of personnel, efficiency and working conditions in navy shore facilities, naval aviation training, draft deferments, and the disposal of surplus property. It was during this time that Brown & Root went into shipbuilding.[9]

Johnson's labor-baiting, so pleasing to Herman Brown, broke out again, this time in the context of his war work. He proposed "work or fight" legislation to require that war-work employers give draft boards the names of workers absent without justification, the boards then to decide whether to draft them. As Johnson saw it, war workers who loafed were aiding the enemy and deserved the contempt which one usually reserved for deserters. Absenteeism, he said, "sank forty-two Liberty ships" in one month (by causing that many not to be built) and deprived the country of 4,004 medium bombers in 1942 alone. Harold Young asked him, "What kind of a soldier will you get if you force him in as punishment?" "Well," Johnson said, "you got to keep guns being built, and tanks."

When, however, the CIO warned that antiunion employers might use the bill against union men, it was toned down to require merely that a worker's deferment request specify his absentee record and that war-work deferments be reviewed every six months in the light of absenteeism.[10]

Just as in his 1941 campaign Johnson had associated labor with Communist agitation, he now kept after witnesses before the naval committee about hiring people who—in Chairman Vinson's words—were "of subversive character." Vinson said the committee's legislation prohibiting defense contractors from employing such people was a result of Johnson's interest. With Rayburn's role obvious, Johnson was put on a hawkish twenty-three-man committee to plan postwar military policy that was expected to propose continued armed might and universal military training. Later Johnson said his subcommittee had studied the advance of communism in Africa and Europe in 1945.[11]

According to an official in charge of enforcing price control in Texas, Johnson intervened many times in enforcement cases on the theory that since he had supported the Office of Price Administration, the bureaucrats owed it to him to withhold enforcement against his friends. For instance, he intervened for poultry producers who were selling live poultry above the ceiling price. The wartime food administrator said Johnson called on him to get allocations beneficial to his constituents, but when refused, after pressing it again, would accept the adverse ruling. His reelection pending, Johnson sought higher prices for Texas egg producers.[12]

ACME PHOTO

Congressman-Lieutenant Commander Johnson is greeted by Brigadier General Martin Scanlon during Johnson's brief VIP tour of duty in the Pacific theater in 1942.

In a photograph released by Johnson's White House in 1966, Johnson is shown in General Douglas MacArthur's headquarters in June, 1942, pointing to New Guinea, where he had been on a bombing mission—his one combat experience of the war.

UPI TELEPHOTO

In March, 1942, Johnson struck these various campaign poses in his navy uniform. Evidently he had gone to a photographic studio and got carried away, running for office again in his mind before the war was four months old. He and his advisers considered his making a second Senate race in 1942 right up to the last minute, when John Connally filed him for reelection.

JOHNSON LIBRARY PHOTOS

About 1944, seated left to right, are Maury Maverick, Sr., of San Antonio, the leader of the Young Turks of the New Deal; actor Gene Autry, in uniform; Speaker Sam Rayburn; Herman Jones, an Austin lawyer and Democrat; and standing, Congressman Wright Patman, the Texarkana Populist, and Johnson.

JOHNSON LIBRARY PHOTOS

Johnson during a congressional inspection tour of Europe and North Africa on May 15, 1945.

Johnson's 1944 opponent, Buck Taylor, an anti–New Deal right-wing pamphleteer, was no threat, but in a campaign document, showing how adaptable his politics were to any appeal his opponent might have, Johnson put this out about himself: "The record shows that on twenty-seven major votes, [Johnson] supported the Democratic national administration *THIRTEEN* times, opposed it *FOURTEEN* times. Most of the votes against the administration were *FOR* bills to stop strikes, stop labor racketeering, stop the John L. Lewis dictatorship. *THAT'S THE RECORD.*"[13]

As the Roosevelt period neared its end one of Johnson's closest associates wrote down a cool assessment of the Texan. Generally, the friend said, Johnson looked out for and promoted himself. In 1940 he had quoted Roosevelt indirectly as saying he would make a good chairman of the Democratic National Committee because he was photogenic, and at other times he had spoken of himself as secretary of the navy or postmaster general. In 1944 he was saying, "Many people are asking me to become governor of Texas after Coke (Stevenson) quits." His friend thought Johnson lacked real brains, but had much energy and was a splended petty negotiator. He had made his district a model of the New Deal, had not wasted any money, and had not let the grafters ride him. The worst influence on him, the assessment claimed, was Corcoran, who had become a money-seeker.

Rayburn again wanted to be vice-president in 1944, but, the reaction against Roosevelt having settled into the Texas power structure, a rampaging band of "Texas Regulars" made the fourth term the major issue in Rayburn's state. When Senator Harry Truman told Rayburn he was going to nominate him for vice-president, "I thought he was going to hit me," Truman said. Johnson tried to persuade Governor Stevenson to back Rayburn, but Stevenson, probably influenced by the wealth of another Texas contender, Jesse Jones, would not commit himself. There was no way to paper over the split. Wirtz, hearing that Senator O'Daniel had been meeting with people who represented great wealth—the Pews, the Sinclairs, men from Standard Oil, Ford, Electric Bond and Share—believed that major industrial powers were funding a plot to deny Roosevelt the southern states.

In the Texas state convention of May, 1944, Wirtz and Johnson tried to stall off a split, but failed. Meeting in the Texas Senate chamber, the convention elected an anti-Roosevelt chairman by a vote of nine to seven. Wirtz moved for a party loyalty pledge for presidential electors, causing a near riot on the floor. When Johnson, visiting on the platform, prompted or whispered to the chairman, shouts were heard, "Get that yes-man off the platform," and "Throw Roosevelt's pin-up boy out of there." The pledge defeated, the liberals bolted across the Capitol to the House chamber, Johnson going with them, but then in a speech cautioning them not to go off "half-cocked."

Afterward Wirtz wrote Ickes that the country was in danger; that the business group's underlying purpose was to seize the government and set up a fascist state. Johnson said that the Texas Regulars had "secret, hidden goals" and were a rallying point for "all dissidents and die-hards, the Roosevelt-haters and the corporation lawyers, and those organizations trying to raise in Texas the ghost of intolerance."

But then Johnson, feeling heat from the money people, thought he had better quiet down. One key New Dealer said that Johnson stayed away from the Chicago convention rather than go and fight for Roosevelt. The votes there from Texas were split between the two competing delegations; the Texas conservatives then split, half for Roosevelt, half for Harry Byrd of Virginia. Of course Roosevelt won easily.

On the vice-presidency, Roosevelt let Wallace be shafted by indicating he would accept William O. Douglas or Truman, and the big-city bosses put Truman over. "Truman didn't have any delegates," Harold Young said. "They outsmarted us or outmaneuvered us." Returning to Texas, Rayburn told a local associate that but for the Texas split he would have been nominated vice-president. That would have made the Truman presidency the Rayburn presidency.

When it became clear that the presidential electors from Texas were not going to vote for Roosevelt, the liberals named a new slate pledged to FDR. As Roosevelt carried the country narrowly, Texas went for him 822,000 to Thomas E. Dewey's 191,000 and the Texas Regulars' 137,000.

That winter Roosevelt made it clear that the Texas revolt had finished Jesse Jones in Washington. At a cabinet meeting the president, saying that the best thing to do about Greece was give both sides plenty of ammunition and let them shoot each other up, looked at Jones and added that Greeks were a good bit like Texans, they liked to shoot each other.

For Johnson the Texas split had a serious meaning, too. Until 1944 he had not had to deal with an organized liberal movement in his state, but during the fourth-term fight liberals from different parts of Texas joined together on the basis of their ideological affinities. "It was the first time that we even got to know who the other liberals were," said Walter Hall, a progressive banker from Dickinson. "That was the beginning of the modern Texas liberal movement."[14]

And just in time. When the president addressed the Congress to open his fourth term, he had to speak from a seated position. The war was won, the New Deal was lost, and Roosevelt was dying. On April 12, 1945, about five in the afternoon, Rayburn called Truman to invite him to a meeting at the Room, and Truman walked on over, but before he could sit down among the half-dozen men already there, the Speaker told him Roosevelt's press secretary wanted him to phone at once. Truman did, and Steve Early told him to come to the White House immediately and go directly to Mrs. Roosevelt's suite. Truman, exclaiming "Jesus Christ and Andrew Jackson!" hastened from the Room. William S. White, learning from Rayburn that Roosevelt had died, ran into a stunned, disheveled Lyndon Johnson who reached out both his hands and cried out, "He's dead! He's dead!"

At thirty-six, Johnson was still regarded as one of Roosevelt's "Young Guard." He told his reporter-friend that like many others, he had conceived his first great desire for public office because of Roosevelt.

"The people who are going to be crushed by this," he said, "are the little guys—the guy down in my district, say, who makes $21.50 driving a truck and has a decent house to live in now, cheap, because of Mr. Roosevelt. . . . There are plenty of us left here to try to block and run interference, as he had taught us, but the man who carried the ball is gone—gone."

Johnson clamped his jaw over a white cigarette holder and said that when he heard of Roosevelt's death in the Speaker's office, "I was just looking up at a cartoon on the wall—a cartoon showing the President with that cigarette holder and his jaw stuck out like it always was. He had his head cocked back, you know. And then I thought of all the little folks, and what they had lost." Whatever you talked to Roosevelt about, whenever you asked him for projects for your district, "the only test for him was this: Was it good for the folks? . . .

"He was just like a daddy to me always; he always talked to me just that way. . . . They called the President a dictator and some of us were called 'yes men.' Sure, I yessed him plenty of times—because I thought he was right, and I'm not sorry for a single 'Yes' I ever gave. I have seen the president in all kinds of moods—at breakfast, at lunch, at dinner—and never once in my five terms here did he ever ask me to vote a certain way, or even suggest it. And when I voted against him—as I have plenty of times—he never said a word."

In this record we have of Johnson's reactions to the death of the hero of the New Deal, we can sense the younger man's grief, his admiration of his patron, and his desire to be another Roosevelt. A secretary with him said he would take no calls: "His grief was vast and he was crying tears." From time to time from then on, especially when he was declaiming without a text and his emotions took over, he returned to Roosevelt's achievements as a standard. In 1959, speaking of the New Deal before a crowd of Texas farmers and small-town merchants, he exclaimed, "We had the NRA, the WPA, the AAA, the CCC, the NYA, and a bunch of professors and a few of 'em were crackpots, probably more crackpots than we have now—but we had leadership—we had action—and a Republic was saved."[15]

The day after Roosevelt's death Johnson was asked by a secretary, "He's gone; what do we have now?" "Honey," he replied, "we've got

Truman. . . . There is going to be the damndest scramble for power in this man's town for the next two weeks that anybody ever saw in their lives."

Still following his own advice many years before to start at the president's office, Lyndon turned his attentions toward the new "Boss." In a letter to Truman ten days before Christmas, 1945, Lyndon wrote: "Dear Mr. President:

"—Because of your friendship through the years;

"—Because of your many kindnesses to me;

"—Because I want you to have the finest Christmas turkey the finest State in the Union can produce;

"—Because I look forward to your company and your counsel in the years to come;

"—Because of all these things, but mainly because *you're you,* there is a Christmas turkey at the Terminal Refrigerating and Warehousing Corporation at 4th and D Streets, S.W., Washington, D.C., left there for you by

"Lyndon."

Truman thanked him for the turkey and "your beautiful note to me." When Truman's mother died Johnson sent ten dollars to the public library of Grandview, the president's home town, only to have Truman write him back that Grandview had no public library.[16]

---

45. Roosevelt in History

During his twelve years as father in the American family, Roosevelt had governed, he had ruled. He transformed the presidency into the most dominant democratic office in the world. With programs that made the federal government partisan to labor unions, created stop-gap jobs and unemployment and disability insurance, shored up farm prices, underwrote home loans, imported the European innovation of social security for the old and widows, and gave small, but real benefits to the very poor, he deflected the desperation of the hungry and jobless during the depression. In the worst of world wars, he commanded, with Churchill and Stalin, the forces that crushed European and Japanese fascism, but left Eastern Europe hostage to the totalitarian Soviets and civilization hostage to nuclear nationalism.

Because Americans were still too provincial politically to understand the worldwide ideological currents within which Roosevelt was operating, he was perceived in his own country mainly as a liberal who was opposed to capitalism. To the contrary, he tried to give industry monopoly powers by legislation, he strengthened private banking with government insurance of deposits, and he strengthened capitalism's stock exchange by establishing new legal standards for corporate securities. While he did support the creation of some regional public electric power systems, he spurned the thoroughgoing structural changes in capitalism itself that were proposed by the Maverick group in the Congress. His refusals to lead in the directions the Young Turks proposed in 1935 and 1937 were the definitive moments. At the peak of his power, the president in charge of the greatest reform movement in the national history decided against organic changes in the Corporate Society, leaving small business and now the whole democracy disarmed against the giantism and overconcentrations of economic power that have ensued.

Roosevelt's New Deal was a fixing up of the Old Deal just enough to get it to work again—and just in time. In the long view of history, Lyndon Johnson's hero was an aristocratic conservative of the humane kind who, by somewhat liberalizing U.S. capitalism, strengthened it sufficiently for it to be able to resist the socialist surges that had already become the trend of the twentieth century. By the 1980s, with the Great Society being dismantled in the United States even as socialist problems and socialist reforms were preoccupying most of the rest of the world, Americans looking back could finally see more clearly what Roosevelt was, what he had done, and what he had not.

PART IX
Turning the Golden Key

The whole art of government consists in the art of being honest. Only aim to do your duty, and mankind will give you credit where you fail.

— Thomas Jefferson in *A Summary View of the Rights of British America,* 1774

46. The Congressman and the Radio Station

One of Lyndon's early supporters, liberal Austin lawyer Fagan Dickson, said that one day he and Alvin Wirtz did a bit of realistic headwork about the young congressman's career. Lyndon had no money of his own. He was not a lawyer; a congressman couldn't be a schoolteacher, too. The special interests would try to buy him in many ways. How could he get some money, an income that would give him security and independence from those special interests? "We've got to do something," Wirtz told Dickson, "to make Lyndon financially independent. He's got presidential possibilities, and we can't have him dependent on others for favors."

The idea they were working on was a radio station. These two canny New Dealers knew, of course, as Lyndon did, that the Federal Communications Commission, which decides who is permitted to own radio stations, would not fail to take note of Lyndon's regular line of work. The Congress created, and the Congress controls, the FCC. Nor could it possibly hurt that the Johnsons' good friend Clifford Durr was one of the commissioners.

The Johnsons' acquisition of radio station KTBC early in 1943 was their golden key. Lyndon and Bird obtained the station by combining his influence as a congressman and her ability to write out a check for the money that was required.

In 1937 Robert B. Anderson, a young Texas New Dealer, had been given permission to build the station with two associates. Evidently the money was put up by Dr. James G. Ulmer of Tyler, an anti-New Dealer, who was not identified in the company. The Anderson group asked the FCC to let them sell the station for fifty thousand dollars to a wealthy oilman, James M. West, who owned the *Austin Daily Tribune*, a conservative daily paper. Critically, the Anderson group told the FCC that a question about any silent partners did "not apply."

Early in 1940 the FCC revoked the license of the Anderson group on grounds that they had made "false and fraudulent statements and representations" about their financing. Commissioner George Henry Payne said they had no assets and Ulmer was to receive forty-four thousand dollars of the sale price and the Anderson group six thousand dollars—"for obtaining the license," Payne was told.

J. Evetts Haley, a historian and rancher who was oilman West's general ranch manager and dealt with Ulmer for him, related in his 1964 tract against Johnson that Ulmer had agreed to sell West KTBC for eighty-seven thousand five hundred dollars; that after the FCC revoked the station's license, Ulmer retained Alvin Wirtz to reverse the ruling; but that Wirtz, thus fully informed, then just dropped Ulmer, and Lady Bird Johnson applied to buy the station.

With Commissioner Payne moving to make the license revocation final, the Anderson group—specifying that they were eliminating any profit for Ulmer or themselves—entered into a new contract with West to sell KTBC to him for twenty thousand dollars, quite a comedown. The sale could not go through without FCC approval. A year later, by a split vote, the FCC ruled (in what Payne called a "backflip") that KTBC could stay in business, but stalled considering the sale to West. In 1942 West died, leaving an estate of seventy million dollars, and his son Wesley came into the contingent interest in KTBC under the twenty-thousand-dollar contract with the Anderson group.

In broad sketchings, Johnson summarized the deal to me. Bird had an inheritance of thirty-six thousand dollars at the time, and "That was what she bought the radio station with," he said. Wesley West had the option to buy it, a bank in Austin was trustee for this option, and through the bank Bird bought the station for $17,500 and the assumption of the station's indebtedness.

"Bird came to see me," Durr, the commissioner who was the Johnsons' friend, told me. She explained to him that she did not want to put all her inheritance into the station, but she wanted to know if he thought she should buy it. He told her, "I don't see why it wouldn't be a good investment." There was no skullduggery to it, Durr said—"Lyndon never had a thing to do with it."

There is no question that Bird bought the station. However, Lyndon was the main person in the inquiries and negotiations that enabled her to buy it, and he took an active part in its management, in drumming up advertising for it, and in events that decisively affected its growth and profit.

Neither did the fact that Bird owned the operation mean Lyndon did not profit from it. Under Texas community property laws, a wife retains as hers what she owns independent of her marriage, but any of her income becomes the joint property of her husband. Lyndon was personally enriched by the profits from their radio-TV business exactly as much as Bird was.

When James West had died, the estate's executor had told a hyper-conservative Austin businessman, E.G. Kingsbery, that the old man had wanted him to acquire a half interest in KTBC and to carry on with it and the *Tribune.* But before the FCC had approved this, Kingsbery said, Ray Lee, the Austin postmaster and Lyndon's speechwriter in his 1937 campaign, told him that Congressman Johnson wanted to see him.

Kingsbery had opposed Johnson in 1937, but in the summer of 1940 the wily congressman had taken a step intended, at the least, to neutralize Kingsbery in the future. Lee (who had become postmaster presumably upon Lyndon's nod) asked Kingsbery, "just out of a clear blue sky," Kingsbery said, if his son John would like to have an appointment to one of the military academies. Never having given this a thought, Kingsbery said he didn't know. Lee asked where John was—he was in summer school in Tucson—and whether Lee could call him and *ask* him if he wanted such an appointment. Kingsbery said all right, and that is how his son John went to Annapolis. "He knew there were two ways through to me, my family and money, and of those, the most important was my family," Kingsbery said. He regarded the play about his boy as Lyndon's way of preventing him from opposing him in the future.

It was near Christmas, 1941, when Lee told Kingsbery the congressman wanted to see him, and although Kingsbery regarded Johnson as a rubber stamp for Roosevelt, he called on him bringing him a gift of a quart of pure cream. Decades after it happened, Kingsbery recounted the meeting with gusto.

"I'd like to get in the radio station with you," Johnson told him. "I understand you own the station KTBC."

"Well," Kingsbery replied, "I don't really own it, but when Mr. West died he somehow left me half-interest in it and wanted me to get into the newspaper and radio business."

"I'm not a newspaperman, not a lawyer, and I might get beat sometime," Lyndon said. "I did have a second-class teachers' certificate, but it's expired, and I want to get into some business."

"Well," Kingsbery said, "I don't know, I understand that I'm to have a half-interest in this and a newspaper, and I'm supposed to help carry these on. But to pay my obligation to you, if you'll make your peace with the Wests I'll give you my half-interest. Furthermore, I understand the

Wests have an inheritance tax problem, and you might be able to help them out on that."

Johnson asked him, "Where can I get in touch with them?" Kingsbery told him.

During his conversation with Johnson, Kingsbery said, Mrs. Johnson was not mentioned. "I'm not sure I even knew there was a Mrs. Johnson," he told me.

By his obligation to Johnson, Kingsbery must have been referring to his son's appointment to Annapolis. The businessman explained that he had not actually owned anything to give to Johnson; all he had was an insider's right to acquire half the station, subject to FCC approval, and this right was what he gave.

This left the congressman with the problem of "making his peace" with Wesley West, and not only about Kingsbery; the West family owned the other half of the contingent right to buy KTBC from the Anderson group. Kingsbery said he understood that Johnson went to the Wests' ranch in Llano County, Texas, on December 23 or 24, 1941, and worked it out.

The late Charles I. Francis, the rich Houston attorney who was a friend of the Brown brothers and Wesley West, told me a revelatory episode.

"Wesley West had inherited it [KTBC] from his father. He sold Johnson that station," Francis said. "West told me one time George Brown told him Lyndon Johnson wanted to buy that radio station over there. He [Wesley West] said, 'I didn't *like* Lyndon Johnson, but by God I went over there, and he's a pretty good fellow. I believe I'll sell it to him.' "

Francis was regarded in Texas as a Johnson-connected person. Later he put together a government pipeline sale in which George Brown was a principal, and he was one of the lawyers who fought for Johnson in election fraud contests concerning the 1948 Senate election. But by the late sixties Francis was disillusioned with Johnson, and he said with a smile that he believed Lyndon "prevented anybody else from getting" FCC approval to take over KTBC. Francis added, "I think George Brown helped him buy it. . . . I think he put up some of the money to help him buy it." A good lawyer knows the difference between fact and opinion, and Francis acknowledged under questioning that he did not know these things, but coming from the insider he was, his opinions are part of the story.

Wesley West, recalling his part in the transaction, said he didn't want to buy the station, and he made the deal with Johnson because he didn't want to see Ulmer lose any more money and he thought it would be good for Johnson to learn how to meet a payroll.

Kingsbery, a devoted Republican, acknowledged, "I understood the station was bankrupt," but he remarked with inconsistent irony that this was how it came to pass that Johnson ended up "with what he called a defunct radio station that he ran into a fortune of twenty-five million dollars."

In the spring of 1942 the chairman of the FCC told the Anderson group that the commission was "placing in its pending files" all applications by newspaper interests (that is, such as the Wests) to acquire radio stations. Mid-way into his half-year stint in the navy, Lyndon had pulled it off. When he returned from the Pacific the contract for Bird's purchase was drawn. Her lawyer was Judge Roy Hofheinz of Houston; also acting for her was the Johnsons' old friend Wirtz, by then the former undersecretary of the interior. The musty FCC files contain Bird's handwritten note to Wirtz, dated January 2, 1943:

"Dear Senator Wirtz, I am enclosing a check payable to your order for $17,500 to cover my deposit under the contract with the owners of the radio station KTBC, and authorize you to execute contract in my name and make the deposit in my behalf. Best wishes, Claudia Taylor Johnson."

Wesley West relinquished the shaky option on KTBC only for the Johnsons. The Wests' lawyer told the American National Bank in writing that the Wests' commitments in the transaction were "conditioned upon the consumation [*sic*] of the sale to Mrs. Johnson as stated."[1]

The Johnsons had one more step: FCC approval. Rosel Hyde, an FCC staffer who was handling applications for permits and the assignment of channels, remembered Mrs. Johnson appearing in his office to inquire how she should proceed. Papers arguing on behalf of the transfer of KTBC to Mrs. Johnson recited her business acumen and placed her worth at that time at more than fifty thousand dollars. Much was made of her standing as Lyndon's wife.

"She is the wife," said one document filed with the FCC on her behalf, "of Lyndon B. Johnson, Congressman from the Austin, Texas, district, and she has recently served approximately a year as the secretary for the congressman. She is widely and favorably acquainted with the business and civic interests of the Austin congressional district, and the area of the district is almost identical with the primary service area of KTBC."

The FCC approved the transfer on February 16, 1943, seven months after Johnson's return from the Pacific. According to papers filed with the FCC, KTBC had liabilities of nineteen thousand dollars and accounts receivable of eight thousand dollars. In the middle of 1943 the station was moved to the Brown Building, which was owned by Herman and George Brown.[2]

At the outset, Johnson made a decisive move: he personally called on the head of CBS, William Paley, to seek CBS affiliation for his wife's station. As David Halberstam reports in *The Powers That Be,* Paley turned Johnson over to a young staffer, Frank Stanton, and the CBS people decided that KTBC would make a fine CBS station.

From the first year, Lyndon's role in getting advertisers for KTBC was active, wheedling, insistent. Although he had to know that the fact he was the seated congressman could not fail to get the attention of businesspeople, he threw himself into signing them up for ads as wholeheartedly as he ran for office.

In October, 1943, for example, Austin lawyer Ed Clark, working assiduously to get ads for the Johnsons' station, sent Lyndon in Washington the names of the key people in a hotel, banks, printing companies, clothes stores, a big Austin department store, a car dealer, an architectural firm, a sporting goods company, a funeral home, and a hardware store. Howard Butt owned a chain of grocery stores. "I am today writing to Corpus," Clark told Lyndon, "so that Howard Butt will contact the advertisers whose products he sells at his stores in Austin so that he will have an opportunity to get coverage here."

Clark also told Lyndon, as he had earlier wired Bird, that General Electric had made arrangements for a newscast to be heard on KTBC. "Thanks for the wonderful job on General Electric," Lyndon replied. "That's the most important thing that has been accomplished lately." The congressman wanted Clark to send him more lists, to send letters "for this and many other purposes." In 1944 Clark asked Lyndon to see a person to "help on the Dr. Pepper matter that we have in mind" and told him, "I hope you are pleased to have the 'We the People at War' Gulf program. . . ."

Jesse Kellam, the station manager, regularly wrote "Dear Bird and Lyndon" about station business. In 1946 and 1947, from his home address in Washington, Lyndon wrote Kellam, "The Cocoa-Wheat five times per week 15 minutes each time looks mighty good"; Kellam sent up the ad file on the National Biscuit Company.

Paul Bolton, KTBC's news director, wrote Walter Jenkins of Lyndon's staff asking for information about the anti-Semite Gerald L. K. Smith, adding: "And the fact that such a course [presumably a news story or comment on Smith] would please our Jewish advertisers, tell LBJ, is entirely incidental. . . . It might boost our stock to get sued for libel by him."

Network officials know that their privileges as mammoths astride the public airways depend on political decisions; here was a congressman who knew this, too. In 1947, concerning what Kellam described only as "A letter to CBS," Lyndon wrote him, "I will personally present the letter to CBS."

Lyndon himself wrote prospective advertisers from his Washington home, urging them to take ads. To KTBC staffer Willard Deason, to whom he sent copies of such letters, Lyndon wrote, probably about the time he was getting set to run for the Senate in 1948, "Now, Bill, I am convinced that we can put some permanent business on the books this week and next week if we will concentrate on a specific few. Last week none of our sales were really permanent, and the total sales for each person was very little more than his pay-check for the week. . . . I think we can and should sew up Ben Greig, Lawler, Prewitt, Schmidt, Yarings's, Red Arrow, Reynolds-Penland, and Swearingen-Armstrong in the next few days. Is there any chance of getting any Steck business?"

Jenkins was very much involved in KTBC business despite—or perhaps because of—the fact that people dealing with him knew he was close to Johnson. For instance, in 1952, when Johnson was the Senate Democratic whip, Jenkins made an ad-soliciting trip into New York and wrote letters thanking agency and network officials for the responses he received.

"We are pleased with the Kools and Viceroy spot order. . . ." Jenkins said in one of these letters. "We much appreciated the order for Crossley spots," he wrote another adman. To an agency he wrote, "Don't forget KTBC when General Foods gets ready to move into the Austin market." He thanked an NBC person for having "rolled out the purple carpet."

The KTBC operation had practical political uses for Lyndon, too. Bolton wrote speeches for Johnson upon request from Washington. The news director played a role providing a Texas publisher a draft done by Horace Busby of an article defending Johnson, in 1949, from election-theft suspicions. Bolton sometimes sent copies of his comments and stories on the air to Johnson.

Clearly, Lyndon was involved in KTBC up to his swiftly-cruising eyeballs. On his congressional letterhead, he inquired about a copyright that Bolton wanted for a program he had put on. He advised the station about complying with federal wage regulations.[3] The truth was, the congressman's wife owned the congressman's radio station. That was the way it was, and that was the way everyone understood it.

Johnson knew his position was vulnerable and he used every legalism he could to defend himself. In 1959, interviewing him in his plush offices as the Senate Majority Leader, I asked him whether he did not have a conflict of interest, being a congressman in a business so intimately regulated by the federal government.

"First of all," he said roughly, "I don't have any conflict of interest—all of that is owned by Mrs. Johnson and eleven or twelve others." In the second place, he said, he had never voted in Congress on any radio or television controversy. Third, Mrs. Johnson got her degree in journalism, and "she felt this was the way she wanted to invest her money." To criticisms that the Johnson stations had received lucrative advertising from firms getting government contracts and that his political position gave the stations an advantage in network affiliations, he replied,

"I have never received any funds or cast any votes in connection with it."

Nevertheless, William O. Douglas must have had his friend Johnson in mind, among others, when he said, "Even some members of Congress obtained (radio and TV) licenses for themselves or their families while in office—a practice that should be forever barred as being beyond the ethical line."[4]

---

47. The Brown & Root of the Matter

Franklin Jones, Sr., an iconoclastic lawyer in east Texas, used to say in the late 1950s, when speaking of his state's senior senator, "Well, now, let's get down to the Brown & Root of the matter."

In central Texas there was no oil in significant qualities. The railroads were not headquartered there. Lyndon cast his lot with consumers against the power companies. That left him, for his money base in politics, the construction business. He forged a politics-and-contracts partnership with Brown & Root that saw him through to the U.S. Senate.

The Brown brothers, Herman and George, poured money into Johnson's campaigns, won fat federal contracts in lines of work that paralleled his career, gave him a personal-political interest in higher military spending, and rooted his politics in their own antiunionism. For their part, they became nationally dominant builders and George became a tycoon in gas pipelines. Lyndon and the Brown boys rose from poverty to power together.

Lyndon's highly compromised liaison with Brown & Root tells more about the condition of democratic government than most textbooks do. What happened to Johnson has happened, in different permutations, to most American politicians, and what happened to Brown & Root was happening in different permutations (including the modern-day political action committees, or PACS) to most major American corporations. Corporate business needed political services; politicians needed corporate money. So politics went into partnership with business, and the New Deal was incorporated and militarized.

Herman and George had been his friends, President Johnson acknowledged to me—George, he said, was "sweet and gentle," and more progressive than Herman. But, Johnson said, "I never recommended them for a contract in my life," and there was not a single piece of paper anywhere in government records that would show that he did. "They never asked me to do anything for 'em." Once the firm got an eighty-million-dollar job in Houston "that I never heard of until they started telling me about it." Again he said, "Nothing in the record will show it." Brown & Root got ahead, he supposed, because they did the best work at the cheapest price.

But this was a most deceptive response.

In the first place, it would be a mistake to believe that the way these things must happen in the life of a skillful politician, the businessman comes in and says, "Congressman, there's a wad of dough to be made out of shipbuilding. Get me a contract and I'll take care of you." Rather, the politician and the businessman are friends; they have dinner together; they are mutually aware there is money to be made in, say, shipbuilding. Who gets the contract? A great deal depends on who knows what first; then there are the bureaucrats who make the discretionary decisions. Information is provided the businessman; perhaps an aide sees a bureaucrat. Nothing official or formal, but when the politician needs help, *he* has a friend.

As Admiral John J. Manning, former chief of the navy's Bureau of Yards and Docks, once said, the members of committees like Johnson's naval panel "get the first look at what we're going to do," and it would be natural for the politician to help his friends "just by telling them what's coming and by speaking to the right people, telling them that they're from Texas, that he knows the relevant factors such as the labor market and the material market." Or as J. R. Parten put this consideration more succinctly, "Lyndon might have told them [the Browns] where the work was. That's all."[1]

In the second place, if there is no "single piece of paper" showing that Johnson recommended Brown & Root for a contract, there are plenty of pieces of paper showing that he and his people were in effect lookouts for federal contracts for the firm in Washington.

As a young congressman Lyndon was open to alliances with businessmen for the time when he would need their money. A different Democrat, or the same Democrat in a different district, might have scrupled against a hog-tied alliance with the antiunion contractor, but Lyndon had little experience with unions, and he had his fields to plow. New Dealer or no, again and again he cast his antiunion votes, and by 1947 the alliance became common knowledge as his political identity changed from left to right before everyone's eyes.

Herman and George Brown were two of the seven children of a store owner in a small central Texas town of Belton. The boys chopped wood and did other chores common to the country life. Herman, the older of the boys by two years, drove a grocery wagon, tried college but quit, and then went to work in the Bell County engineering department, carrying a rod and checking building materials for two dollars a day when it didn't rain. After a year of that he switched to the outside, working for a contractor as a foreman for seventy-five dollars a month, paving streets in Belton. A year and a half later the contractor owed him a lot of back pay and gave him, instead, a few mortgaged mules and wagons. There were some fresnos, too, the scoop-shaped contrivances, with handles and a whiffletree, for moving dirt, one of which Lyndon had handled on the road gang as a boy.

Herman, finding himself a contractor, took as his first partner his brother-in-law, Dan Root.[2] When Root died in 1929 George came in, but they kept Root's name in the title. For a while in the depression the brothers had an outfit with no work to do. The only people with much money seemed to be the federal bureaucrats, and they were building dams. In 1936 Brown & Root won the contract to build the Mansfield Dam on the Colorado River, downcountry a way from them, near Austin. That was the one, George Brown has said, that made the difference between a small and a big operation. "They actually made their fortune," said George Fuermann, a columnist on the *Houston Post,* "as New Deal capitalists."

Right away a pattern appeared. Brown & Root got the contract on a low bid of six million dollars, but before the job was done the cost was twenty-five million dollars. There were new aspects, unforeseen developments, more that the government wanted done. But what about the low bid that had won Brown & Root the job ahead of the other contractors who had said it would cost more? Now you see it—now you don't.

While Herman was building up the business, George went to college —Rice, the Marines, then the School of Mines in Colorado—and one time explained how simple success really was. "We originally were roadbuilders," he said. "To be roadbuilders, you have to know about concrete and asphalt. You have to learn something about bridges. Once you learn these things, it's only a step, if you're not afraid, to pour concrete for a dam. And if you get into the dam business, you'll pick up a lot of information about power plants. Actually, when you break it down, each component of a new job involves things you've done before." If you're not sure how to do the new thing, team up with somebody who has done it before and watch them. "When we'd take on a big one," George said, "we wanted some company up in that dark alley with us."

The autumn before Johnson became a congressman in 1937, the Browns had a third-of-a-million-dollar contract clearing trees from the river basin for the uppermost lake on the Colorado and building a concrete wall for the dam there. Three or four miles downriver, about 350 workers for Morrison-Knudsen of Boise, Idaho, were digging and pouring concrete for another dam on the river. These two companies would team up later.

The congressman preceding Johnson in office had declared that the Mansfield Dam could cost no more than ten million dollars, but the foundation was to be large enough to make the dam higher later.[3]

There is no evidence of hanky-panky involving Johnson in the awarding of the contract for six million dollars' worth of work on it to Brown & Root in 1936.[4] Ground was broken for it before Lyndon had much real influence.[5]

When Johnson became a candidate he claimed that he had worked out of Kleberg's office "to get the work started" on the Colorado River project, which had to mean that he had been interested in it since before mid-1935.[6] The chairman of Johnson's advisory board for the Texas NYA was Alvin Wirtz, the general counsel of the river authority and the driving force within it. Nevertheless, the illiberal Herman Brown backed another candidate for Congress in 1937.

It was one of Johnson's lifelong tactics as a politician to try to win over his opposition into his camp. He worked ably in Washington for more money to build the Mansfield Dam higher, and he got it. That didn't hurt him any with Herman Brown. Herman's opinion of Lyndon must have taken another turn for the better in 1939 when his company received the contract to string 1,830 miles of electric lines for the Pedernales Electric Cooperative, Inc., headquarters Johnson City: that October Herman sent Lyndon a copy of a memo he wrote about getting this job.

One can trace the emergence of the Johnson-Brown & Root connection through communications that are stored in the Johnson presidential library. As if timorously, late in 1938, Bird sent George Brown's wife Alice a gift of some handkerchiefs. The ensuing spring George, while traveling on a train, handwrote a note to Lyndon asking what he might be able to learn about a group that had a contract for twelve hundred miles of roads for two hundred million dollars at cost plus ten-percent profit. "Hope you know," George closed this note to Lyndon, "how much I appreciate how much you have done for me and that I can return in my small way some of it in the future."

Later that month Lyndon wrote George lamenting that the economy crowd in the House had knocked out a one-hundred-thousand-dollar spending item in which George was interested, but by midsummer Lyndon was able to help deliver far more important government goodies to the Browns.

During his first talks with President Roosevelt in Texas in 1937, reportedly Lyndon discussed a naval air base for Texas. Many times later Johnson insisted he get the credit for arranging the location of the naval base at Corpus and the shipyards at Houston. As naval committee chairman Carl Vinson said, Lyndon "played a dominant role in setting up the naval air base in Corpus Christi, the naval air training station near Dallas, and shipbuilding facilities in southeast Texas—Houston and Orange."[7]

"I spent Saturday in Corpus and they are all pepped up over the prospects of the naval base," George Brown wrote sulphur lobbyist Roy

Miller, sending a copy to Lyndon. "Lyndon tells me that there is a very good chance of getting five million dollars for it this year," George added. Brown & Root, with a business partner, got the seventy-eight-million dollar contract to build the naval station.[8] (The final cost was closer to one hundred million dollars.)[9] A Corpus Christi banker (who cannot be named) said it was explained to him in Washington at the time that while the military had something to say about sites, actually the politicos had more influence on such matters and in this case the power was Vice-President Garner of south Texas.

In another copy of a letter he sent Johnson, George thanked a different Texas congressman for his help on the Marshall Ford appropriation bill, adding, "I am always doing work somewhere in your district and if there are any of your friends that I can at any time favor, please do not fail to let me know."

"I hope you know, Lyndon," George said in a note to him, "how I feel reference to what you have done for me and I am going to try to show my appreciation through the years to come with actions rather than words if I can find out when and where I can return at least a portion of the favors." Lyndon replied that both the letters George had enclosed were "very fine."

The Browns wanted a change order approving more money for their work on the Marshall Ford Dam, about which George wrote Lyndon this spring of 1939. He also told Lyndon that Brown & Root had decided to work together with W. S. Bellows, another contractor, on a navy project in Puerto Rico.

"Neither of us has so indicated to the Navy Department," George told Lyndon, "and [we] were of the opinion that we should wait until we got up to the actual time when they are ready to talk 'turkey.' What do you think of the idea? I was wondering if you can ascertain when the psychological time will be to come to Washington on this project."

Johnson all but consented to be the Browns' agent on federal contracts. "I'll do all I can to get you any information on the Puerto Rican project and will let you know when anything breaks," he wrote George. "You know how hard it is to get any dope in advance, but I'll have my eyes open. I'll probably wire you if I run into anything which seems likely."

As for the Marshall Ford Dam, George wrote Lyndon, "Our part of the five million dollars is something less than two million dollars, which is a nice bit of work, of course. I am happy that we have that back of us." George told Lyndon that Herman had just told him that the bureaucrat handling the dam though the Reclamation Department in Denver was working out the details of the change order, "and things are looking all right." In August, 1939, Johnson sent identical telegrams to George and Herman Brown saying:

"For your confidential information until announced by Department, Comptroller-General signed decision this morning at 11:30 approving use of change order 67 Marshall Ford as requested by Department. . . . I got decision sent by special messenger to Interior. . . . Will stay here until everything is cleared out and go order given."

Correspondence between Lyndon and the Browns was often oblique, concealing the substance of the matters they were discussing. For instance, in the fall of 1939 George assured Lyndon he would help "Senator"—evidently meaning Wirtz—by making a deal with "the Austin man." But the rest of this letter left none of its meaning to the imagination. George wrote Lyndon:

"In the past I have not been very timid about asking you to do favors for me and hope you will not get any timidity if you have anything at all that you think I can or should do. Remember that I am *for* you, right or wrong and it makes no difference whether I think you are right or wrong. If you want it, I am for it 100%."

Lyndon replied, "I wish I could dictate as sweet a letter as you wrote me. . . ." In the winter of 1940 Lyndon became closer to Herman, too, writing George, "I really enjoyed being with Herman this time. . . . We had a lot of heart-to-heart talks and, I believe, know each other a lot better. Knowing is believing, you know."

Keeping the Browns informed about other legislation affecting them, Lyndon wrote George that an item in the 1940 Interior Department appropriations bill would be subject to a point of order, but this would have limited impact. Less than a week later George suggested to Lyndon that he should run for the U.S. Senate when there was an opening. It was the next year when Brown & Root funded, as Johnson said, his 1941 Senate campaign.

Right after his 1941 defeat, when he was angling with Roosevelt for an appointment, Lyndon relaxed, for just a moment, his profound caution about the Browns. In a letter to George dated Nov. 5, 1941, Lyndon told him, "I will talk to Admiral Moreell as you suggest and do all I can." Moreell was the chief of the navy's Bureau of Yards and Docks and of its civil engineers.

The letter did not say what George wanted Lyndon to talk to the admiral about, but there may be a clue. B&R landed a fifty-eight-million-dollar contract to build an ammunition depot in Oklahoma. With Lyndon not yet returned to his office from the war, Bird wrote George Brown on July 3, 1942, "Congratulations! The navy certainly could not have done better on its ordnance depot at McAllister than you all. I am so happy you got it. I heard Thursday that an Oklahoma firm got it, but a later talk with Admiral Moreell confirmed that it was youall and he must know."

Another episode associated with Johnson's military stint makes it clear that even when he was attached to the navy, Johnson was looking out for the welfare of Brown & Root. With Lyndon in California, his man Connally was to have dinner the night of January 7, 1942, in Washington with "Mr. George" (as Connally called George Brown). Connally wrote Johnson from Washington two days later.

"I have just a few minutes ago," Connally told Lyndon, "been able to get hold of Peterson and the Way [War] Department, and he was very familiar with the Panama Canal and Mr. Raskaugh (I am not so sure about the spelling) who was seventeen million dollars under the bid which Mr. Brown placed. However, Peterson admitted that he didn't file a bond. . . . However, he spoke very highly of the man's ability and integrity. . . . He suggested that I call Madigan . . . to see if he knew anything further. I have put in a call for Madigan. . . . Of course, I will be very careful in my approach, even as I was with Peterson."

When Lyndon was doing his few months in the navy, George was in touch with him. "I talked to Lyndon about an hour the other night," George wrote Bird on March 20, 1942. "I am going to try to get up that way [Washington] real soon," he added to her. "When I do, I want a date with you for dinner and a dance." Back from the war by that fall, Lyndon wrote George from Washington, "Have done some more work on the McNutt thing. Will tell you about it when we talk." Paul McNutt was chairman of the War Manpower Commission.[8]

There were business dealings between the Johnsons and the Browns. After the 1941 election, Lyndon's Austin office was located in the brothers' Brown Building in Austin. KTBC had its offices in this building, too, until the station was moved to a corner of the street floor of the Driskill Hotel, another Brown property. Only when the station was prosperous enough to be moved to its own quarters in the sixties did the Browns cease being the Johnsons' landlords.[9]

Without saying who "they" were or whether his reference to "the Johnson Estate" in Austin meant acreage Lyndon had on Lake Austin, George wrote him in May, 1939, "I also understand while I was in Austin that they are about to complete the street improvement project on the Johnson Estate. . . . Also, was informed there has been no violation of regulations, ethics or policies, notwithstanding any of the ideas that the owner might have."

Something went on between Lyndon and George about a car. "I did not hear any more from your reference to the car," George wrote him in June, 1939. "I suppose you did not make up your mind. Louis' idea was that you would buy one and put a Washington, D.C. license on it. That way eliminating any question about where it came from and whom it came through. If you buy a station wagon, I will take it off your hands at your cost when you go back to Washington." Lyndon replied, "I have not yet made up my mind about the car."

Two weeks later George cited to Johnson prices on a radio and auxiliary loudspeaker, saying, "These prices are all less forty percent." Johnson wired him to hold up on that. Then, that October, 1939, Lyndon wired Herman Brown, "Be sure to mail car certificate to Covert Automobile Company." Six months later Connally sent Johnson apparently discounted prices on two cars that Johnson was interested in at the Covert dealership.

While Lyndon was away in the navy George Brown let Bird in on an investment. A proposal had been presented to him, in which he was investing, concerning production in Texas oilfields. "Write me what you think of this," he told her. "George," she replied, "this is such an involved and difficult thing for me to try to determine all by myself—I couldn't *begin* to tell you how much I appreciate your help." She said she would explain it to her Aunt Effie, and two weeks later she sent him Aunt Effie's name and address, the name of her bank, "and the amount she would like to invest."

A stream of gifts from the Browns to the Johnsons can be traced through the decade starting in 1948.

The Christmas after Lyndon was elected senator, George gave the Johnsons "the exquisite silver tray," which Lyndon told George he had opened before Christmas when Bird was away. The George Browns gave Lyndon a shotgun for his birthday in 1953. "I've used the 28-gauge nearly every day that I've been home and it has brought down many a dove," he wrote them. That year he also thanked the Herman Browns for a set of cufflinks. For Christmas, 1953, the George Browns gave the Johnsons two silver julep cups to add to their set and a salt shaker and a pepper grinder. Next Christmas the julep set was completed and the Browns also gave Lyndon a travel alarm clock. In 1956 the Herman Browns have him a brass bowl. Next year his birthday present was "little bulls with the rings in their noses," an ornament to wear. Then came a set of silver leaf ashtrays. The record shows that Christmastime, 1957, Lyndon gave George and Herman neckties.

As he did with other wealthy patrons of his, Lyndon often hunted with the Browns—a turkey shoot, or shooting doves at Fort Clark, the Browns' recreational hideaway. Johnson also made free use of the Browns' airplanes for trips back and forth between Texas and Washington. "I wonder," the Democratic majority leader wrote George Brown on December 15, 1955, "if you have a plane scheduled up East in the next week or ten days. If you do, I sure would appreciate your having someone let me know when it is scheduled to go." The same sort of thing at the 1957 holiday season is evidenced by Majority Leader Johnson's letter to Herman Brown on January 4, 1957: "You . . . can't imagine what a boon it was to all of us to be able to come back to Washington in such a comfortable manner. Many thanks to you for being so generous. You added another star to your crown and I'm going to try to see to it that you get your reward pretty soon." On another occasion Jenkins and his family traveled on a Brown plane.

There was also a comfortable hiring custom between the Johnsons and the Browns. In 1942, while running Lyndon's office, Bird wrote the superintendent of plant protection at Brown Shipbuilding to get a job for Lyndon's friend Walter Crider. He wrote her back, "As soon as Lyndon told Mr. George Brown that he wanted Walter to have a job Mr. Brown immediately set out to get him one," and the superintendent had put Crider on, which he said he was glad about, "because I know that whenever we call on Lyndon for anything he does everything in his power to help us. . . ."

Lyndon moved to fix up someone's brother-in-law in a letter to George in October, 1942. Lyndon said he had told Tommy Corcoran "we would fix up the brother-in-law with a timekeeping or some similar kind of job with the Brown boys in Texas. . . . I have already employed Jay Franklin's brother-in-law for you. I am not your employment manager. You did not authorize me to do it, but I did it anyway, and I hope you will confirm my action. If you can, please have your personnel man send me a wire . . . when and where the brother-in-law goes to work." (There is no reply in the file.)[10]

After Lyndon returned from the mid-Pacific in 1942, his political pull was highly useful in the Browns' shipbuilding. As a member of naval affairs subcommittees he looked into procurement activities of the Navy and watchdogged navy shipbuilding yards. Obviously a watchdog for the Congress could also be a birddog for the Browns.

The president of the Houston Chamber of Commerce at that period, Wright Morrow, recalled James Forrestal telling him in Washington in 1940 that "they were just giving contracts without hardly reading 'em." One day Brown & Root was notified that they had twenty-four hours to decide whether to take a lump-sum contract to build a shipyard outside Houston and deliver a specific number of ships by a specific date. As the *Houston Post* later said, "Nobody in the company had ever seen a ship built." Half a decade before, a six-million-dollar contract had thrilled George Brown. The company now embarked on building more than 350 submarine chasers, escort vessels, and infantry landing craft —multiplied millions of dollars' worth of work for which many a businessman would have been glad to fly to Washington, if there had been time. B & R helped build two ordinance works in Texas, too. By an inquiry to the War Production Board, Johnson facilitated Herman's getting permission to use a twin-motored plane to supervise B & R's war work.

Early in 1945, as the second-ranking member of the House naval committee, Johnson was appointed to a panel to study the armament and possible permanent U.S. ownership of Japanese-mandated Pacific Islands. ("Everybody recognizes," his chairman, Carl Vinson, said, "that we've got to have a defense ring beyond Pearl Harbor. . . .") One of these islands was Guam. In '46 the Browns won the Guam contract in accordance with government procedures. The initial award was for $21 million for a three-company venture. By 1950 the cost had reached $100 million; in 1955 it was still going on and the price had become $250 million. Increasing ten times the size of the original contract, the job lasted twelve years.[11] During the Vietnam War Guam was one of the important bases for American bombers.

Charles I. Francis, the oil and gas lawyer in Houston, and others saw the enormous profit possibilities in the private acquisition of the federal government's oil and natural gas pipelines after the war, and in 1947 Francis organized the Texas Eastern Transmission Company to buy them. He invited George Brown and others in, and the core group then raised enough money from other investors to buy the wartime Big-Inch and Little-Inch pipelines. Texas Eastern, in 1947, made the best bid to the War Assets Administration, $143 million, which was twelve million dollars more than the next highest. A competing group was represented by Johnson's shepherd in the meadows of the New Deal, Tommy Corcoran.

"Lyndon took no part in helping out with the original sale," Francis said. "I talked to Lyndon. He said, 'Charley, I can't do that. Tommy Corcoran is on the other side.' " Johnson, Francis says, did not take a hand—"Unless," Francis added, "there's something that I didn't know. George Brown and he were awfully close." Johnson's friend and project staffer, Don Cook, was the man, Francis remembered, who did all the necessary research for the Texas Eastern group.

The meeting place after World War II for the ruling Houston elite was suite 8F in the old Lamar Hotel downtown. There, George and Herman Brown met the other business powers of the city, ran the state's and their city's politics, and cut deals. George told a reporter that the turning point for the 8F crowd came when he, Gus Wortham, Francis, and the others in Texas Eastern bought the Big- and Little-Inch pipelines from the United States. "We just formed one corporation after another after that," George Brown said.

The purchase gave George Brown and his associates in Texas Eastern "3,182 miles of pipeline and 1,993 miles of valuable rights of way from Texas to the East Coast." The Big-Inch lines carried crude oil from east Texas as far north as Pennsylvania and over to New Jersey. The Little Big-Inch line carried refined petroleum products from southeast Texas to Little Rock, Arkansas, then parallel with the Big Inch to the East Coast. In 1947 these lines started Texas Eastern out from scratch for $143 million; by the time Johnson was president the company's properties were worth $1,468 million and its net profit for one year was $40 million. It had interests in more than one thousand oilwells and was pipelining crude and refined oil and products and natural gas from Houston to Boston—Oklahoma, Louisiana, Mississippi, Arkansas, Alabama, Tennessee, Kentucky, Missouri, Illinois, Indiana, Ohio, Michigan, Pennsylvania, New York, New Jersey, Connecticut, Rhode Island, and

Massachusetts. Chairman of the Board: George Brown. According to Francis, Brown & Root had made about $28 million on negotiated contracts with Texas Eastern in the first twelve years of the latter company's operation.

The Brown brothers carried on as war contractors, and their thrift and virtue were rewarded. They built, in the period of Johnson's career (either alone as Brown & Root or in joint ventures), roads, dams, generating plants, bridges, ships, tanks, oil, steel, and chemical mills, railroads, tunnels, atomic energy plants, ocean docks, navigation locks, offshore drilling rigs, ammunition depots, air bases, missile launching pads, radar distant-early-warning stations, and pipelines underground, overground, under the Arabian Gulf and over the Andes. Diversifying, like most American megabusiness, Brown & Root came to own hotels, oil and gas production, paper mills, mines, real estate, office buildings, and a dude ranch. A company was formed to handle the workers' insurance and another one to handle securities and another to handle oilfield hauling and another to handle salvage and, it was said, politicians.[12]

One welcome passenger in Johnson's helicopter in his 1948 Senate campaign was Frank "Posh" Oltorf, once a liberal state legislator who had become Brown & Root's Washington lobbyist. A dapper gentleman, Posh worked with the federal bureaucrats for his company. Established in the Mayflower, he was a key man—the friendly adjuster, the man who found out—in Brown & Root's Washington. Witty, ingratiating, quick to reach for the check, more than anyone Posh Oltorf came to represent, in his purposes and activities, Johnson's relationship with Brown & Root.

Lyndon told Posh that the Browns were like brothers to him. Posh thought Lyndon was closer to George than Herman. George was gentle and open-minded; Herman, Posh said, would consider others' views, but regarded his own as correct.

George ordered him, Posh said, "Never go on the Hill for any help" on contracts, and Posh said he never did. George's reasoning, Posh said, was that people would resent political influence. "When the Browns would come to Washington, of course," Oltorf said, "They would see Lyndon socially, but the old thing that he tried to get jobs for Brown & Root during the period that I was there was a myth."[13]

Johnson's Senate preparedness subcommittee helped expose a scandalous situation in the construction of five air force bases in French Morocco, North Africa. The military promised to straighten it out. Within two years, Brown & Root was engaged in a joint venture, building navy and air force bases in Spain.

Atlas Constructors, a group of five companies including Morrison-Knudsen, had the $300-million contract. The price tag had zoomed to $445 million; a major general said, "We were only receiving fifty cents worth of work out of every dollar we were spending." Improper asphalt mixes were causing the jet runways to be wavy and ridged. The chief of the Army Audit Agency called the job the "smelliest" in his thirty-five years' experience.

The investigation was opened by a House subcommittee. An army auditor said there had been kickbacks, conspiracy to increase prices, fees paid to get jobs, excessive drinking, loafing, and sleeping at work that resulted in the firing of a thousand employees in one day, and workers giving gifts in return for pay for time not worked. The House panel scheduled hearings, but then Johnson's Senate panel started its own and the House boys closed up. Lyndon had moved in.

The Texas senator quoted a high official that the program was "a major scandal" and demanded that the program be "cleaned up or closed down"—he'd "clean out some people" unless the Defense Department cleaned up the North African program. The secretary of the army promised to close it down if the reforms were not adequate. Even so, Johnson said additional "stringent" action might be necessary.

The defender of Atlas Constructors was John P. Bonny, head of the consortium and vice-president of Morrison-Knudsen. He denied fraud; they had done the best they could, he said. He made the mistake of agreeing "in general" that the investigators were "headline hunting" to promote Johnson for president, whereupon Johnson said, "I thank you," and added: "I think there has been some graft. . . . Unless there has been perjury, I think there has been fraud." Bonny apologized for what he had said. In its report the Johnson subcommittee said the North African "fiasco" had increased the cost of the bases by at least $120 million.

The subcommittee was an arm of the Senate armed services committee. That committee froze the spending of about fifty million dollars for the construction of air force bases at overseas sites pending a review by the president-elect.

Late in 1953 Johnson reported that the North African airbase project "is now in good shape." Two months later the navy announced that Brown & Root was one of the three companies that would build five air force air bases, one navy base, and some aircraft warning stations in Spain at an estimated cost—first phase—of $150 million. Construction men considered this (said the *Houston Post* later) "the most sought-after contract in recent history." By 1959 the cost had increased to $260 million. It turned out that the threesome—Raymond International and Walsh Construction Company, along with B&R—had to lay a 470-mile pipeline in Spain (all underground, for security from bombing) to fuel the bases, since a wing of B-47's would use more fuel in one afternoon than the Spanish railroads' tank cars could transport in a month. By completion the project, employing twenty thousand Spaniards and four thousand Americans, cost $360 million.

In 1955 a Brown & Root person told me that Lyndon would not have dared call the Republican administration to help the Browns get the contract in Spain—it would have "blown things sky high." They had been up all night before the contract award, worrying; he did not say who "they" were.

Just as Johnson started out his second Senate term, he named Isabel Brown, the liberal daughter of George Brown, to his staff as a research assistant. When he had his heart attack that summer he was visiting "Huntland," the George Brown estate in Middleburg, Virginia.

Life at this estate was very good indeed. A former staffer of Johnson's, Bill Brammer, told me of one evening there when the leader stretched out his legs before the roaring fire and mused on why the idealists, all full of piss and vinegar when they first arrive on the public scene, finally just forget about the poor folks—Here we are, he said, a good meal under our belts, a porter serving us drinks before the fire, and all this!

This *was* the reality of daily life for the Browns. Once Herman had two thousand dollars cash in his trousers pocket. The fact was not necessarily unusual; it became known because a maid had stolen it. Similarly, when Mrs. Herman Brown's jewel casket was stolen, the public was informed that it had contained nineteen loose diamonds; two turquoise necklaces, one containing 119 pearls; six pins, one with 32 fine Oriental pearls; eight pairs of earrings and ear clips, including one pair set with yellow Ceylon sapphires; three watches, one on a band set with seventy-four small diamonds; and nine rings, one of them set with four square diamonds, nine round diamonds, and nine Oriental rubies.

How much government work did Brown & Root do in these years? When a labor lawyer accused them of having held public construction contracts valued at three quarters of a billion dollars by 1950, Herman said the figure was too high. Four years later a PR man for the firm said it had done "a billion dollars worth of work for the Army and Navy." With companies splitting up the pie, one could not advance a ready guess, but there was the construction in Spain, a $200 million airbase job in France, and all the rest of it through the fifties. As of '57 B & R's share of the contract for French airbases was $55 million.

Five contracts, the largest one of them for $19 million, were given to Brown & Root by the army through the fifties for the machining of tank parts, the rebuilding of tanks, and "facilities." All during Johnson's period as the majority leader Brown & Root was doing little jobs, too, offshoots and spinoffs, for the military. For instance, in the three-year period 1956 to 1959 for the Army Corps of Engineers, apart from its extensive tank work the firm booked $4 million on ten separate jobs—building a rocket storage building, a boathouse, a bulkhead in Texas—exploring deep water off Maine, renting its dredge. Then, for the navy, three million dollars for mine defense structures off Florida . . . nine other contracts with "BuDocks" in a seven-year period. . . . It added up.

It *all* added up. Whether such facts as all these were pregnant, they were not virginal. As Charles I. Francis said, "I was close to the Browns. I just believe that Johnson helped them get contracts. I *know* he did, and I don't know it, either."[14]

Agitated by "the criticism that is going on about the oil companies having something to do with our foreign policy," George wrote Lyndon early in 1957, "I think this is the story that not only the oil companies, but also the oil importers, the steel industry, copper industry, aluminum industry, etc., must sell to our intellectuals. The intellectuals should be the first people to realize the importance of a partnership arrangement between our companies who are working abroad and our government, in order to keep us supplied with raw materials of natural resources to keep our economy from sinking."

It was, indeed, a partnership, the campaign contributions, the congressional look-out, the contracts, the appropriations, the telegrams, the investment advice, the gifts and the hunts and the free airplane rides —it was an alliance of mutual reinforcement between a politician and a corporation. If Lyndon was Brown & Root's kept politician, Brown & Root was Lyndon's kept corporation. Whether one concluded that they were public-spirited partners or corrupt ones, "political allies" or cooperating predators, in its dimensions and its implications for the structure of society their arrangement was a new phenomenon on its way to becoming the new pattern for American society.

Lyndon's friend Virginia Durr observed that he detested being the bond-servant of the "Texas power crowd." About having dinner with Lyndon, Wirtz, and the Browns, she said, "they really did act as if they owned him, very arrogant men, I thought." But taking stock in 1957, Lyndon wrote George, "I invariably find that my chief asset is that I have George Brown as a friend."

Allen Duckworth, the late political editor of the *Dallas Morning News,* liked to strew around tacks about the Johnson-B & R connection in his columns. In a story about Texans arriving in Atlantic City for the 1960 Democratic convention, Duckworth's readers were informed in a dependent clause that Brown & Root "rose and prospered on a track with Mr. Johnson." Duckworth just threw it into another story that "President Johnson's rise in politics has paralleled the rise in power of Brown & Root."[15]

That was the prevailing note, a brief remark, a chuckle, and back to the subject at hand. When Catholic John Kennedy and Johnson were running together in 1960 a joke hop-scotched around the parties in Texas and Washington that Kennedy had told Johnson, "Lyndon, when we get elected I'm going to dig a tunnel to the Vatican," and Lyndon had replied, "That's OK with me as long as Brown & Root gets the contract."

---

48. Texas New Dealers Break the Unions

The Brown brothers would not have any part of labor unions. Their dam-building for the New Deal was nonunion. So was their wartime airbase building, their shipbuilding, their remodeling of tanks. "Open shop," this was called. They said for the newspapers they would hire members of unions as well as nonmembers; in practice that meant nonunion.

If you were a Texas labor guy that Brown & Root was suing, Herman Brown was the depresser of wages all over Texas—he ran a sweatshop. If you were a liberal Houston columnist who wanted to get along in the private clubs among the Browns and their friends, the Brown boys were "two of the nation's most historically energetic open-shop operators. . . ." Were you laying it on the line, but mixing up the emotions for *Time?* Then Brown & Root was "one of the most actively anti-union firms in anti-union Texas." And if you were Hal Hazelrigg, the Browns' publicist—why, the space agency "just renewed our contract because they're so happy with us. One reason they're so happy with us is *because* of our labor policy. When a man is free to work at what he can do! There's no forty-bricks-a-day restriction in *our* company." But any way you said it, Brown & Root was antiunion.

The secretary-treasurer of the Texas AFL in the 1930s, Harry Acreman, complained to Secretary of the Interior Harold Ickes during the building of Mansfield Dam that Brown & Root was chiseling on a classification system by which workers were paid according to rated skills. "Ickes gave Brown & Root a pretty good working over," according to Acreman.[1] But the New Dealers did not require contractors to use union labor.

Johnson's connection with the Browns and his patriotic feelings during the war combined to produce his wartime toughness on unions. When he sponsored his "work or fight" bill in the House naval committee to draft absentees from their jobs, the Brown brothers were building ships for the navy.

Charging that goldbricking was "delaying construction of naval vessels," Johnson wanted to require that all navy contractors report absent workers to their draft boards, which would decide whether to draft them.[2] One worker in ten, Johnson said, was "the loafer, the inexcusable absentee, the slacker," committing an act of "disloyalty." The job, Johnson said, was "to disinfect our war plants of them—and our Selective Service has a very potent disinfectant for this type of vermin." To them "we say, 'The draft board will get you if you don't watch out.' "

Johnson proposed that each employer producing anything for the navy be required to give local draft boards the names of each worker "who has been absent from his employment without prior authorization by such employer," along with a statement of the circumstances. Each board could then decide whether to draft a worker who had been reported. Another member objected that military service "should not be used as a punishment," and the bill was not passed. Absenteeism was not even debated in the ensuing Congress.[3]

Johnson voted for a law against labor interference with trade and commerce by violence, threats, coercion, or intimidation, which became known as the Hobbs Anti-Racketeering Act. To Congressman Emanuel Celler of New York, the bill prohibited legitimate labor activity under the guise of curbing racketeering, and its provision of a twenty-year penalty for violations was in marked contrast to the powder-puff one-year penalty for violations of the criminal antitrust laws by businessmen. The bill passed better than two-to-one.

President Roosevelt was prepared to draft war-work strikers, but in 1943 he vetoed an antistrike bill that he said would prohibit political contributions by labor organizations. Literally 99.95 percent of the war work had gone forward without strikes, said the president. Johnson voted with the two-to-one House majority passing the bill over Roosevelt's veto.[4]

After the war the import of such events became clear. In Texas one of the tip-offs was the outcome of a strike by electrical workers at the Lower Colorado River Authority. For five years they had been appealing to the river authority to discuss with them their right to bargain collectively. The LCRA had refused, and the men struck in the fall of 1945. Power and water supplies were in danger of exhaustion; some towns passed the next night in darkness.

The official reaction was fury. Texas Rangers and police ordered the picketers to leave, which they did. The governor, Coke Stevenson, said anyone who "commits sabotage" where he's employed should not be "re-employed," and the LCRA fired ninety strikers. The river authority's manager said they had committed a "revolt against the state and a crime against society." The lieutenant governor said the National Guard should be called out if necessary. From Washington Lyndon Johnson wired the union:

"The public water supplies are involved. The sick in the hospitals are endangered. Farm products will spoil. . . . The people of my district will not countenance this action. I do not know the things in controversy, but I do know that Texans will not tolerate this stoppage or sabotage.

Johnson speaks easily during radio station KTBC's staff Christmas party in 1947. Lady Bird is at the left.

JOHNSON LIBRARY

About 1940, evidently at an airport, are, left to right, George Brown of Brown & Root, Johnson, an unidentified man, New Dealer Tommy Corcoran, and a fifth man who may be Herman Brown, George's brother.

JOHNSON LIBRARY PHOTOS

George, left, and Herman Brown shown during ceremonies at the Houston shipyards in December, 1942 (they had become shipbuilders).

You shall be assured of a fair hearing . . . but work must be resumed."

Work was resumed, by new workers. The union spokesman wired Johnson that apparently he placed "no responsibility on management." They had wanted to participate in decisions affecting their welfare; the river authority changed the conditions of their work by simple motion and without notice. "All we wanted," the strikers' man said, "was for them to meet with us . . . treat us like men instead of peons." Austin Mayor Tom Miller, and only he among the political actors, rebuked the authority for refusing to arbitrate the dispute. Jeff Hickman, who was to become the CIO's leader in Texas, said if the government could force men back to work, "it means we have just got through losing a war."[5]

The savagery of the official reaction meant that the New Deal's prize project in central Texas, built in large part by the antiunion Brown brothers, was run by antiunion Texas conservatives. By his harsh reaction against the strikers before he knew why they had struck, Johnson joined the Texas reaction against the unions.

With the war entirely over in 1946, the New Deal went upside down on labor union questions. President Truman was so inflammatory against strikers, the intervention of Senator Robert Taft, the upright Ohio Republican, was required to bring the Congress to its senses.

Truman asked for the power to draft strikers against government-seized plants, and the House (including Johnson) said sure, 306 to 13. Taft stopped this in the Senate. Then the Congress passed the Case bill, to which the unions angrily objected, and Truman vetoed it. He explained that while he had asked for legislation for the "reconversion period," the Case bill was for all time and covered the whole labor field (just as the Taft-Hartley law would the next year). Truman said in effect, this bill is antiunion; it would curb legitimate union activities. Although just more than a third of the House got itself together and sustained the veto, Johnson again voted in the union-curbing majority.[6] He was not following Truman as he had Roosevelt; something else was at work in him, probably the desire to be a United States senator by the birthday that had been foretold.

The New Deal's Wagner Act, passed before Johnson entered Congress, had positioned the government behind the right of workers to organize. The Taft-Hartley Act turned the government back toward a neutral stance; the National Labor Relations Board's machinery was retained for the protection of collective bargaining, but Taft-Hartley signaled a fundamental change in the federal posture, and Johnson voted for it.

Would the government be prounion, neutral, or antiunion in its letting of contracts for government work? If neutral, that would amount, in the real world, to favoring nonunion companies that could bid lower because they paid their workers less. Able to lower because of nonunion wages and practices, Brown & Root enlarged itself on government work at the expense of unionized firms. No matter whether New Deal, Fair Deal, Republican, New Frontier, or Watergate, the government never adopted an overall policy to prohibit the nonunion advantage (unless one considers as in effect pro-union the laws that require the payment of "prevailing wages" on federal construction jobs) with the result that nonunion companies could grow large in league with the government on the basis, in substantial part, of antiunion policies. In short, in and after World War II, the federal government shifted into an adversarial stance against unions while permitting a bidding advantage for nonunion firms.

By 1947 Brown & Root was so powerful in Texas, it led a many-aspected campaign against unions which made Texas one of the most antiunion states in the Union and the only major industrial state that has a law prohibiting workers from voting to be all-union. With their handyman Ben Ramsey, the lieutenant governor, running the Texas legislature, the Brown brothers were largely responsible for the enactment, from 1947 on, of the body of the state's antiunion laws.

The Texas "right to work" law, like similar laws elsewhere, denies unions and companies the right to negotiate a union shop, in which payment of union dues is required. In the *Reader's Digest,* Lester Velie wrote in 1953 of Herman Brown and his lobbyist Ed Clark in the Texas legislature: "At the last session, the Clark-Brown axis showed who's boss. They rammed through a law so drastic that no other state has one like it. The measure classes labor unions as monopolies, restricts them under Texas antitrust laws and imposes fines up to $1500 a day for violations. Neither the federal antitrust statutes nor the Taft-Hartley Act exposes unions to monopoly penalties. But the Texas legislature passed it two to one." Velie described Clark (later to become President Johnson's ambassador to Australia) as the boss of the legislature.[7]

There was a case to be made for Brown & Root's labor policy, and the company's PR man, Hal Hazelrigg, made it. If there was a piece of wire that needed cutting, he said, anybody at Brown & Root would cut it. You didn't have to wait until the guy whose union has jurisdiction over cutting wire could get to it. If a job using twenty welders closed up, "and ten of them are pretty fair hands as pipefitters—we do need pipefitters." This flexibility gave Brown & Root, he said, "teams of craftsmen who have worked with the same foreman, and they develop a hell of a competency, and we can go out and underbid on a contract *strictly* on the basis of superior efficiency."

When the labor lobbyists cased the first postwar Texas legislature early in 1947, Harry Acreman said, they found that the program of lobbying against labor was carried forward and financed largely by allies of Lyndon Johnson. Herman Brown and three lawyers who were synonymous politically with Johnson, Clark, Wirtz, and Everett Looney, were singled out for special condemnation by the Texas AFL-

CIO in 1947 because of the legislature's enactment of nine bills that were "viciously anti-labor." The executive secretary of the state labor organization told its annual convention that the "lobbying against labor was carried forward and financed largely by Mr. Herman Brown, of the Brown & Root Company," and three other parties. "Many of these anti-labor bills were written by Everett Looney, in former years an outstanding liberal and friend of labor, but his principles, evidently, were for hire. Mr. Brown personally attended every labor committee hearing in both House and Senate, and was usually ably supported by such counsel as . . . ex-Senator Wirtz, and had for his principal lobbyist, Ed Clark, a law partner of Mr. Looney. . . . Politics is being used in an attempt to destroy us."[8]

The lawyers for the union craftsmen then were Mullinax and Wells in Dallas. L.N.D. Wells, called "Nat," gave Brown & Root hell before the state labor convention in 1950. "Those waterboys for Brown & Root," he said—Ben Ramsey, Governor Allan Shivers, "the other minions of special privilege, don't allow you to have a closed shop."[9]

In the fall of 1950 Brown & Root filed a shotgun lawsuit against every AFL union in sight and some out of sight—the American Federation of Labor, the national building crafts, the Texas state federation and the state and Houston councils of carpenters, the thirty-three building trades councils in Houston, Austin, and Beaumont, and thirty-three local unions in Houston, twenty in Beaumont, and eleven in Austin. Brown & Root wanted almost one hundred thousand dollars in damages. The charge was that the union men had picketed Brown & Root job sites, a crime because they did it to carry out a conspiracy for a closed shop. Such an objective was, indeed, illegal in Texas: that had been seen to. This was the most sweeping lawsuit that has ever been filed against unions in Texas. The attorneys for Brown & Root were the Austin law firms of Powell, Wirtz, & Rauhut, and Looney, Clark and Moorhead.

When Wells accused B&R of paying low wages for work in sweatshops, New Dealer Wirtz retorted that the wages "are decent" and the sweatshop charge was "a myth that will be exploded." Everett Looney was the second leading attorney in the case. The Clark in the firm was Ed Clark. As the lawsuit dragged on another name appeared on Brown & Root's briefs, John Connally, a member of the Wirtz firm. Donald Thomas of Looney-Clark also toiled in the case for B & R. Connally had been Johnson's administrative assistant the year before; Thomas was to become Johnson's personal business lawyer.

Labor, justifiably, was bitter. Cross-examining Herman Brown in Houston, Wells said he and Brown & Root had "consistently undercut and attempted to destroy" union wage and working standards. The company alleged the unions used violence in organizing efforts. The judge in the case forbade fifty-six local unions and their councils from picketing Brown & Root, placing its name on any unfair list, or conspiring to force a closed shop on it. Appealing, labor charged that Brown & Root had discriminated against employees for union activity, refused to deal with unions, paid notoriously substandard wages, and campaigned for legislative and administrative repressions of the unions. When the case was finally settled by agreement, Paul Sparks, the secretary of the state AFL, said that Brown's only purpose had been "to tie up organized labor so that it couldn't interfere with his grabbing off government contracts."

The basis was here laid for the rancor and tangle of Texas Democrats for the rest of the decade during which Johnson was driving to become president. Since his wartime forays against absentee workers at the Browns' shipyards, Lyndon had continued voting antiunion; only two years before the Brown & Root lawsuit, the Texas AFL opposed his election to the Senate because of his vote for Taft-Hartley. It was impossible for anyone who knew what was what to resist regarding Lyndon Johnson as politically a party to Herman Brown's lawsuit against labor. He was in the same camp; he ran with these people. Perhaps, in fact, his self-interest had trapped him, but perhaps his self-interest was more important to him than his New Deal principles. When the suit was still going on, Wells went to Washington to try to lobby him for some amendments to the Taft-Hartley law, but Johnson never even returned his calls.

Texas liberals who thought Truman's election had meant more of the New Deal now felt crushed by wealth, political compromises, and a conservative judiciary. Contending at the next state labor convention that Brown paid fifty cents an hour less than the union scale, Wells declaimed: "I say it's unfair to get the most public work of any contractor in the state, and on every hour of that work for every man. . . . Herman Brown is reaching into the pockets of the working men and taking fifty cents an hour and adding it to his own millions. . . .

"You know," he said, "I'm pretty tired of that socialized millionaire, who is sucking at the public teat, if you please, who has made his millions from your pocket and mine in tax money, starting with a dam down here by Austin, most of the highway work in the state, political connections that gets him lots of federal work; that's your money and my money, our tax money. . . ."[10]

In May, 1951, Congressman Albert Thomas of Houston announced that Brown & Root would get a five-to-ten million dollar contract to machine heavy castings for about 1,500 World War II tanks. Before the summer was out the Department of Defense had earmarked forty million dollars for the program, and George Brown announced that a new plant would make tank hulls and turrets. The final cost of B & R tank work was about fifty-five million dollars. Cliff Potter, regional director of the National Labor Relations Board in Houston, said that while working on the tanks, Brown & Root fired some people who were trying to form a union and settled the ensuing complaint after the work was done and there was nothing left to organize. In its decision on the case, the NLRB ordered the company to hire back nine workers and give them back pay, and "upon the entire record of the case," to cease and desist from firing workers trying to get a union, interrogating them about the union, threatening them with reprisals, or putting their meetings under surveillance. The NLRB alleged that nineteen unionizers were fired, two union meetings watched, sixteen threats made, and six interrogations conducted. Generally speaking, the company admitted the surveillance and denied the rest. Disbelieving the company, the NLRB said it was affected by Brown & Root's "propensity for opposing the union by resort to unlawful measures." In the testimony it was charged that supervisory or management people said that anyone talking unionism would go and union supporters "had better get the fear of God in them." One supervisor pointed to a union button a worker was wearing and told him it was "a damn good way to get . . . run off." This was the situation on work paid for by the United States.[11]

A consortium of nine companies, including Brown & Root and their co-workers on the Colorado in 1936, Morrison-Knudsen, won a contract to build the forty-two-million-dollar Bull Shoals Dam in Arkansas. Struck by workers because of an alleged refusal to bargain, the consortium was ordered by the NLRB to reinstate fifty-six workers with back pay, and in 1953 a court ordered enforcement of the order. Brown & Root resisted; the dam was finished and reinstatement became an academic question. Findings, hearings, arguments ensued; a decade after the first court order the judges were talking about holding back pay for twenty-eight workers in trust and making awards to their survivors if necessary. The work was long over, and no one knew where all the workers were or who had died.[12]

In Lyndon Johnson's thousands of public pronouncements through this period, he is curiously elusive on the values and principles of union labor. During a speech he made as late as 1959 to the Texas labor convention, for instance, he promised labor "a fair shake," but refrained from philosophizing about unions.

Even as he moved into the Senate's Democratic leadership, his antiunion bias continued. In 1949 he voted for a flexible sixty-five-cent minimum wage, instead of seventy-five cents flat, which was what was agreed upon. He also voted to exclude from coverage about 250,000 retail employees. He opposed an effort by the Truman administration to knock out antistrike injunction provisions of Taft-Hartley. In 1951 and '52 he approved the importation of bracero labor from Mexico and opposed making it a felony knowingly to employ an alien illegally in the U.S. In 1952 he supported a Senate motion to ask Truman to invoke Taft-Hartley against the steelworkers, who were then striking. For the postwar conversion period he voted for unemployment compensation benefits, but by 1950 he was siding with state rather than federal jurisdiction over the program, and as the decade proceeded he opposed Senate liberals' proposals for higher and longer jobless benefits.

By the end of the fifties Johnson was a national politician, aspiring to become president through the nominating machinery of the Democratic party. Since he could not make it all the way to the White House on Brown & Root's antiunion barge, he began to arrange for other transportation. Brown & Root, however, had no such motive to change. During the Landrum-Griffin labor bill unpleasantness in 1959, for instance, B & R's publicist wrote Speaker Rayburn asking what the fuss was about since all the bill did was remove "gangsters and Gangsterism" from organized labor—"the evil elements who apparently control most of our labor unions."[13]

The Texas New Dealers joined Brown & Root in breaking the unions in Texas, and this was no small event in the postwar decline of the union movement in the United States.

PART X
Oscillations, Idealism, Reaction

The same Greek word stands for *stranger* and for *enemy.* Other human beings are traveling the same paths though out of sight.

— Roy Bedichek in a letter to Eugene George, Jr.

49. Toying with Prophecy

President Truman decided that rather than cut off Japan's supplies or, alternatively, lose the million lives an invasion might cost, the United States would drop the new atomic bombs on Japanese cities. In the squadron chosen for the work, the pilots vied for the honor of dropping the first bomb, and on August 6, 1945, Paul Tibbets's *Enola Gay* with a single bomb brought instant destruction and longterm agony to the citizens of Hiroshima. A few days later, without waiting for the warlords of Japan to react to the devastation of Hiroshima, the president authorized the destruction of Nagasaki by another, single, nuclear bomb.

In the Allies' victory, civilization survived, but the consciousness of being human could never be the same—the events of World War II ended the innocence of the species. The Nazis massacred two out of three East European Jews. Western democracies fire-bombed cities, and with only two of the new atomic bombs the United States killed or maimed the people of two great Japanese cities. From this war on, history was soaked in dread. People began to see that because of the new weapons, the leaders of the nuclear nations can kill us all.

These days, because of a phenomenon Robert Jay Lifton has called "psychic numbing," people will not think more than a minute or two about the abyss for the species that is waiting in the nuclear weapons. But in 1946 it was different; then it was thought that humanity could head off the holocaust. Johnson thought so, and what he said and did in his 1946 campaign comes down as a judgment, not only on his own career, but also on the human career since then.

Dr. Bob Montgomery, the liberal who almost ran for Congress the first time Johnson ran, had directed research during the war on determining bombing objectives in Europe and the Orient, but when he heard that the bomb had fallen on Hiroshima he resigned, "since there will be no more wars, or only one." He knew at once that an evolutionary maladaptation had occurred, and through him, Johnson understood, too. Montgomery returned to Austin and began making frightening speeches. One of them, Johnson said in 1946, "impressed me more than anything I have heard or seen with the immediate necessity for effective cooperation of all people and nations of the world, if we are to survive the atomic age."

With a head that seemed half again too large for his body, big ears, a big nose, eyebrows bushy as a magician's, an aggressive shock of wiry hair, Dr. Bob was a hypnotic person. On Hiroshima he was not the precise scholar, the sophist of alternative disasters, the awed and guilty Oppenheimer seeing God and death billowing high above the New Mexico desert. Dr. Bob was Jeremiah. "Now man has reached through the veil and seized the power of the gods," he said. "I could carry an atom bomb in a hollow tooth which would kill everyone in London." And he went on: "When we dropped those bombs on Japan we picked out the smallest cities in terms of civilian population. . . . We killed as few people as we possibly could. . . . That bomb over Hiroshima, we held it to explode five miles up. It pushed the earth down thirty-six feet in the center of the explosion.

"We're making bigger bombs now. Some say twenty thousand times bigger. That means that, if we exploded one of the new bombs five miles up, with one bomb we could kill every living thing from San Antonio to Waco. . . .

"Now we have this secret in our hands. We have this power of the gods. But how long will it stay ours? . . . Probably the thing we'd like to do is to kill off our enemies. . . . But the trouble is, if we fight once more, that's it. The next war will simply be the last war. There won't be any people left. . . .

"We've got to live in a brotherhood of man. I don't like the idea, either, of being brothers to Russians. And Africans, and Republicans. And some Democrats. But that's the way it is. . . . We've got to have peace. We probably have to have one world government. A United States of the world."[1]

This was prophecy. The trouble lay coiled in the differences between the prophet and the politician.

Awed, Johnson turned against professional anticommunism; he reversed his course. Three times he joined a hardy minority "not voting" on funding the House un-American activities committee and making it permanent. Finally, in May, 1946, on the issue of appropriating money to continue the work of the committee, he, with eighty others, voted no.[2] Inspired by Montgomery, Johnson's cause became peace and world brotherhood. But during the same critical first half of 1946, his actions betrayed an ambivalence in him so concealed it was almost invisible. He wanted to believe what he was saying, but in his nature, formed in the ideals of nationalism, honor, and courage, he could not.

To control atomic energy, he said later, "I was strong for the Baruch Plan." This was the U.S. proposal that, rather than all nations banning atomic weapons at once, the U.S. retain its atomic monopoly while Russia submitted to inspection during a phased discontinuation of making the atomic bombs—the plan that gave Stalin his rationale for building his. Secretary of State Dean Acheson said U.S. insistence (with Truman's approval) on "swift and sure punishment" of violators of agreement "meant certain defeat of the treaty by Russian veto." According to Stanford historian Barton J. Bernstein, the plan's provision that the U.S. would gradually make atomic secrets known to a UN authority "allowed the United States to go on making bombs, but barred the Soviets from such work," in effect requiring the Soviets "to sit back and trust the United States." The Soviets did veto the U.S. plan; the human race turned the atomic corner and set course for Armageddon.

Johnson may have gone much further than the Baruch plan at one point when he thought the press would not find him out. In a conference with women voters that Johnson may have thought would be off the record, one of the women told the press he had said the production of A-bombs should be controlled by an international body. She also said that he had heartily favored giving the secret of making the bombs to Russia and other countries that would be members of a control commission. "We've got to continue to get along with Russia," he was quoted. The local daily headlined the story, "Johnson Would Give Bomb to Russia." Facing an audience full of college students, many of them returned veterans, he deplored spreading distrust of Russia: "Those people who seek to breed hate and distrust may kill millions of their own boys."[3]

Yet in the first session of Congress after the war he cast his vote with the overwhelming majority to continue the draft into the postwar period, which was the first step in the postwar militarization of the New Deal. Speaking one way, he used his actual power in another, climbing into the cockpit with the Joint Chiefs of Staff to campaign for a seventy-group air force against the recommendations of Truman and Secretary of Defense James Forrestal that sixty-six would be sufficient. Forrestal, Johnson said, would drop orders for "the modern jet planes that air strategists think must be ready to cope with Russia if called on. . . ."[4]

One of his campaign flyers said he was "a pre-war believer in one world." He favored placing atomic weapons under a global agency and approved the U.S. offer to destroy its nuclear weapons or hand them over to an international agency. Unless the bomb was outlawed and procedures established to settle world disputes, he said, "civilization is going to be wiped out." In forty minutes forty planes flying over forty American cities "could wipe the heart out of a great nation." This is one world, he said that death-haunted year, "It's a place where a rocket bomb loaded with atomic energy can be fired from halfway around the world and wipe out Washington within a few seconds." Peace depended on relieving the starvation of "a half billion people," the choice was between "giving up a little bread or giving up blood." The atomic scientists had shortened the war, saving Allied lives, but now had become frightened, and should not we all be frightened, knowing we could not long keep the secret of the bomb? "Unless you people are determined to want peace more than bread and profits," he said in a little Texas town, "the next war will indeed by the war to end all wars." He said without equivocation that a strong United Nations meant yielding some American sovereignty.

But then, the other Johnson spoke. Should there be an international military? No, he was for "an Army and Navy strong enough to carry out our world war pledges, including our pledge to help the United Nations police the world." And what if nations, thus again fully armed, refused to be guided by the UN, as plausibly they would? We would be left then, would we not, with our military might and our pledge to help police the world. In his ideals and his deeds, his hopes and his programs, Johnson was characteristic of the postwar American liberals on war and peace. What he said was not enough to achieve what he wanted, and what he did was contrary to it.

But what Johnson had said was quite enough to give his right-wing opponent plenty of ammunition against him, and Hardy Hollers seized the opportunity. What was this fellow Johnson *saying?* Look at that newspaper headline, "Johnson Would Give Russians Atom Bomb Secret"! Johnson hastened onto the radio to say he "of course" opposed giving the bomb to "Russia, China, or any other nation," but then he seemed to plead for people to understand. After an A-war the world would be "mostly dead," he declared. Like the Colt pistol in the hands of a little man back in the days of his granddaddy, the bomb was "the great equalizer," cutting a big nation down to a little nation's size. "I propose to outlaw the bomb. The United Nations has got to work. It's our last chance," he said. The choice was between "terror and finally death" or a world in which "we use a God-like power in God-like ways" to cure disease, find oil, "put kernels as big as walnuts on your ear of corn and raise pigs which are three-fourths pork chops."[5]

Lyndon realized the situation, and he toyed with prophecy. Then, frightened more by the voice of yesterday threatening his self-interest than by the terror of the new times, he made confusion into a camouflage. He knew what was needed, but like the country he flinched.

50. "Enriched in Office"

Hollers, the son of a circuit-riding preacher, had assisted in the prosecution of German war criminals. He detested "lame-brained bureaucrats" and called Johnson "a silly boy" and "Little Lyndon." He was for housing for veterans, the REA, and soil conservation, but he wanted "to abolish strikes—I mean do away with them entirely" by giving the courts final authority in all labor disputes.

Not to be outdone, Johnson proposed to abolish collective bargaining. He had come out of the war firmly antiunion on the cutting-edge issues: among his farm constituents he cited his votes for the Smith bill, Truman's antistrike bill, and the Hobbs anti–labor-racketeering bill and to override Truman's veto of the Case bill. Although he opposed returning the employment service to the states, he voted with all the Texans to outlaw strikes against government-seized industries. But nothing more starkly exemplified his indebtedness to the Brown brothers than his proposal that a federal referee, responsible to no one, rule on labor disputes. During a referee's deliberations there could be appeals to the courts, but "no work stoppages," and for refusing to accept final court rulings, companies would be barred from interstate commerce and unions would be barred from collective bargaining.[1]

Antiunion, yes, but anti–big business, too! This was the last time Johnson would run as an antibusiness candidate. He saw big government as the people's bulwark against big labor and big business, both of them selfish and greedy; he favored keeping federal taxation as high as it was, and that year he voted to continue the OPA. Hinting he might have to be for federal aid to education, he said with a grin that if this made "the moneyed boys mad at me, so much the better, but I don't see how they could possibly do more to beat me than they already have." When in 1946 the Congress agreed to give the states the oil under tidewaters, he ducked the vote. He had not yet decided to be an oil-state politician, lock, whipstock, and barrel. The interests were out to get him, and maybe, he said, "we ought to call them PPP—powerful petroleum, powerful power companies, and powerful packers." He called them "the PUP," too—"packer, utilities, and petroleum backers of the opposition." Hollers, who did legal work for corporate clients, became "the candidate the PUP hired in 1944."

Homer P. Rainey, who had been fired as president of the state university by reactionary businessmen-regents, was running for governor on a platform of progressive taxation and state-administered humanitarianism, and Johnson's speeches this year also expressed a state-level liberalism that was not to recur in him. "In rich Texas," he said, "the per capita wealth is $654 compared with the national average of $861. There's further proof of the activities of that group which tried to beat Johnson in 1944, and are trying again in 1946—the same petroleum-utility-packer combine that has been milking Texas dry."

Proposing to federalize old-age assistance, thus taking it away from "that lobby group in Austin," he threatened to tax the rich to pay for it. "They ask," he said, "where will I get the money. I will put it this way: We will get it from those who have it; I know who's got it; they know I know it; and that's why they're scared of me." Empty bravado; but it made votes.

Polishing up his image as slayer of the oil dragon, he spoke not only of his refusal to vote for "Standard Oil's billion-dollar price increase bill," but he claimed credit for protecting the public interest by conducting a committee investigation of a contract concerning the Elk Hills naval oil reserves that an admiral had negotiated for the navy with Standard Oil. "While that investigation was under way," he said, "Standard Oil attorneys tried to whisper in our ears when we went down the corridors. Nevertheless, we made our report and we saved that land for the government. They didn't like me before and they liked me less afterwards."

Hollers, trying to depreciate Johnson's role in bringing electricity to rural homes, said that both the LCRA and the Pedernales co-op had been established before the 1937 election, but on this Johnson had him cold. The president of the Pedernales co-op reminded voters that before Johnson took office not one kilowatt had been produced by LCRA and there was not a single REA power line up in the district; Johnson had won federal funds for the work. Since 1937 in his district, Johnson said, half a million acres of farmland had been improved in soil conservation districts, and almost five thousand miles of electric lines had been built; 12,857 farms that before used coal-oil lamps and lanterns had been provided with co-op electricity.

Running, in his predominantly rural district, on the farmers' part of the new welfare state, he spoke also of farm-to-market roads, low interest on farm loans, crop insurance, and school lunches for farm children. He had voted for the federal school-lunch program even though an antidiscrimination rider, which he had opposed, had been attached to it.[2]

Hollers had a little more success when he suggested that Johnson was really the candidate of oil and the utilities. Wirtz, who wrote many of Johnson's speeches, was a lawyer for Humble, a subsidiary of Standard, and Everett Looney and Ed Clark, the two Johnson backers who were partners in a corporate law firm in Austin, represented Central Power and Light.[3]

But Hollers's lunge for the jugular was his charge that Johnson had "enriched himself in office." Never again, after this campaign, was Johnson free of the belief among many Texans that he used his public power to get money for himself. Editor Edmunds Travis believed that

Hollers blundered by making his charges. "If he hadn't, every sort of rumor would have been working for him. But when he brought it out, he had to prove it, and he couldn't." Nevertheless, Johnson never regained the St. George image most politicians cultivate.

Displaying folders he said contained evidence, Hollers alluded to "documented" charges "too hot to go on the air." Broadsiding, he said Johnson was "an errand boy for war-rich contractors and big-time lobbyists," seeking control of press and radio and "lending the authority of his job to enriching contractors and lobbyists, including members of his own family." Hollers implied a contractor had in some way paid for or financed Johnson's house and that Johnson illegally shared ownership of KVET, a new Austin radio station that his cohorts, including Connally, had formed. Suggesting that Johnson had also helped his own father-in-law get rich in the war, Hollers—as the Austin daily said—"asked insinuating questions regarding REA construction contracts and the priorities for a locker plant at Taylor."[4]

Johnson emerged this year as a master politician: 1937, 1941, 1944—he had learned. Cowboy actor Gene Autry was with him for twelve speeches. "Farmer" Jim Ferguson's daughter announced for him because he had never failed to visit the former governor during his illness. The GIs he had helped get terminal pay did not forget that.

Because of Marsh, he still had a hammerlock on the Austin dailies. "Mothers lifted up their children to receive a greeting, plainly displaying that to meet the congressman was an experience to remember," one story said. According to another one, Johnson shook hands in a little town schoolhouse as about one hundred citizens filed out past him and citizens were heard to say, "Thanks for my lights." "Thank you for my terminal leave pay." "Thank you for helping my sister and her children."

In Georgetown he said he would rather be an errand boy for Georgetown than for Standard Oil. The mayor of Granger, another small town, recalled that during the war he had tried to buy a fire truck for the town for $5,125, but shortages had delayed delivery, so Johnson got one for the town for $1,803. Johnson said he would rather be the errand boy who helped get the fire truck than the errand boy for Standard Oil.

And he was indefatigable as usual. Going into every store and talking with every man and woman, he visited many communities whose total vote would be no more than fifty. Inspired, a reporter for Marsh's paper wrote, "He did not pass up the one store and two women in Mahomet nor the highway chain crew on the country road." Watching him one morning in Austin, another set of Marsh's hands wrote: "His Stetson hat on the back of his head, and his seersucker coat over his arm, Johnson set out to see how many stores he could visit and how many hands he could shake. He started on Guadalupe near the Capitol, early in the morning. At noon he'd made it past Hemphill's Book Store deep up the Drag [the main street by the University of Texas] and an exhausted reporter who had trailed in the rear decided enough was enough. When last seen, Johnson was still going."[5]

Hollers, dazed by Johnson's political efficiency, at the last minute intuitively threw a haymaker. When he came back from the war, he said, "In my own district I found my own people with fear in their eyes and fear in their hearts . . . because they were afraid of the Johnson political machine. We were only one step ahead of the Gestapo system they had in Germany."[6]

Johnson won seven to three. As New Dealer Mark Adams said, "Hardy Hollers was just a small-scale Goldwater, and he lost on his own merits." But like Goldwater after 1964, Hollers never ceased believing he was right.[7]

---

51. The Policy of Secret War

Switching in the course of one winter from peace-seeking idealism to military anticommunism, Johnson the weathervane was only swinging with the new winds of the cold war, the manmade storm that swept the postwar world.

After the death of Roosevelt, Truman and his advisers had debated whether to take an accepting attitude toward the Soviet Union's domination of Eastern Europe as its sphere of influence or to declare some kind of war to deny the Soviets the buffer states they were determined to secure. Suddenly early in 1947 military anti-Soviet anticommunism became U.S. foreign policy.

As the cold war congealed, any hope of preventing a nuclear arms race went a-glimmering. The United States fought the Korean and Vietnam wars and, often unbeknownst to its people at the time, many minor ones.

In the 1960s in the West, a group of historians called cold war revisionists restored some perspective. A few sought to teach that Americans were the only villains, but when they were content to show the self-interests, misconceptions, and myths that misled both sides, they made sense. No one conceived the cold war, the statesmen just tumbled into it, wrote Henry Pachter: "There was no war plan and no concerted effort to achieve well-defined aims; no proof has been given that either Stalin or Truman was having designs for the destruction of the other's power."[1]

Unprepared to understand each other, each side feared the other—and fear without understanding easily becomes hatred. No simple moral, no simple national conflict, the cold war was a tragedy, but it was not a play on a stage, it led us to fields of corpses and vistas of loss. Only in retrospect could the costs be even approximated, and only in nuclear holocaust or an emergent world society can the books on the losses be closed. Stalin was in some sense mad, a tyrant who committed genocide against his own people; at best probably all the West could have done was wait out his regime. Instead both sides decided to fight all over the world and raced to arm.

President John Kennedy and Premier Nikita Khrushchev came to understand by 1963 that their nations' courses, seen as if intended, were insane, and with the nuclear test ban treaty of that year they started a cross-course. Although Johnson led Americans into the anti-Communist Vietnam War, he also laid some foundations for détente between the United States and Russia. Under the three ensuing presidents of both political parties the United States rushed openly into trade and friendliness with China and Russia. For a time in that afterlighting, the waste of the three decades seemed weird, history a pathological shrew. But then, suddenly under President Reagan, détente was abandoned, the nuclear arms race accelerated, and the United States plunged back toward a holy war with Russia.

Had Roosevelt lived, could he have found ways to avert the world's polarization? Shortly before his death he told Stalin that Soviet control of Poland would be unacceptable and generally agreed with Churchill that a firm, blunt stand should be taken with the Russians; at the same time, he urged minimizing the general Soviet problem, because most such things "straighten out." But Truman's course was confrontational from the outset. He dressed Molotov down within two weeks of Roosevelt's death. In May, Japan still undefeated, he shut off Lend-Lease, to Russia's loss. With the fate of Poland the provocation, the United States and Russia turned against each other bitterly. Russia's request for a six-billion-dollar credit for postwar reconstruction was ignored.[2]

Had U.S. relations with China taken a different turn, the most dangerous possibility, the emergent dogma that communism everywhere had to be Soviet and monolithic, would have been implausible. The State Department's best China hands had seen, as World War II ended, that the Communists under Mao Tse-tung were becoming stronger than Chiang Kai-shek's corruption-ridden Nationalists and had recommended, in various formulations, that the U.S. try to reconcile the two sides while keeping on good terms with the Communists. John Paton Davies, for instance, foresaw that the Communists would win and could become a force independent of Russia.

In the summer of 1944 Mao had told the U.S., "We do not expect Russian help. . . . China must industrialize. This can be done—in China —only by free enterprise and with the aid of foreign capital. Chinese and American interests are co-related and similar. . . . the United States would find us more cooperative than [Chiang]." In March, 1945, Mao proposed that the U.S., "the only country" fully able to help, give technical and capital assistance to China, which would not be ready for socialism "for a long time to come." Relations chilled violently in June, 1945, when U.S. diplomat John S. Service, who had been a U.S. representative in China, was arrested for having given copies of his reports to an editor of *Amerasia,* an event Mao took as a decisive turn in U.S. policy against the Chinese Communists. Yet even in 1946 Mao told General George Marshall, "Of course we will lean to one side. But how far we lean depends on you."

Truman's answer to these overtures, early in 1946, was the assignment of a military advisory group, initially more than three thousand men, to Chiang. In the Chinese civil war that was to rage from 1946 to 1949, Truman had failed to exploit an unmistakable opportunity to encourage independence from Moscow among the Chinese Communists.[3] The idea that communism had to be a single worldwide force directed from Moscow, that whenever it occurred in other nations it was merely Stalinist Russia in another disguise, was probably already set in his mind. In 1946, at Fulton, Missouri, he sat on the platform while Churchill, in the famous Iron Curtain speech, called for an alliance against Russia. That fall Truman's adviser, Clark Clifford, told him Russia sought "world domination" and the destruction of capitalist states and had to be foiled by military power.[4]

The Soviet takeover of Poland was the first focus of the cold war; Greece was the second. Stalin and Churchill had made a cold deal that Russia would take Rumania, Bulgaria, and Hungary, Britain would take Greece for the democratic side, and they would split Yugoslavia. In Greece a civil war broke out between friends of the reactionary monarchy and those resisting it, who were dominated by Communists. When Churchill used the British army against the rebels, Stalin kept his agreement, leaving Greece to England. By early 1947 it was clear that the monarchy was about to fall, and Britain informed Washington that it was withdrawing aid from Greece and Turkey and asking the U.S. to take over.

Six days later, at a meeting of congressional leaders called at the White House, Secretary of State Acheson said gravely that not since Rome and Carthage had there been such a polarization of world power. A Communist Greece, he said, might open up Iran and the Far East, Africa, and Europe to Soviet influence, and "we alone" could stop it.

Acheson supervised the preparation of Truman's address to Congress on the subject. Clifford wanted a passage lamenting the world trend away from free enterprise, but Acheson nixed that. Kennan opposed the sweeping, universalist meaning of the speech, but was overruled. Thus came into being, on March 12, 1947, the Truman Doctrine, which Truman regarded as second in importance among his official acts only to the use of the atomic bombs on Japan.

The United States, Truman told Congress, must "support free peoples who are resisting attempted subjugation by armed minorities or by outside pressures." This meant we would oppose the national revolutions we disapproved and would not accept violent change imposed on a nation from the outside. "We cannot allow," Truman said, "changes in the status quo in violation of the charter of the United Nations by methods such as coercion, or by such subterfuges as political infiltration." With this, Truman set American foreign policy on a course that would culminate in Vietnam.

The policy of unlimited intervention in the business of other nations bothered not only Taft isolationists, but also some liberals. Senator William Fulbright of Arkansas wrote later that the Truman Doctrine, elevating a distortion and simplification of reality to the status of a revealed truth, gave Americans a "faith" that "liberated us, like the believers of old, from the requirements of empirical thinking" and from "observing and evaluating the actual behavior of the nations and leaders with whom we were dealing." For the next two decades, Kennan said, U.S. foreign policy was bedeviled by people believing "that all another country had to do, in order to qualify for American aid, was to demonstrate the existence of a communist threat." Walter Lippmann wrote that U.S. policy would not be fully understood until historians explained how U.S. intervention in World War II was inflated into the Truman Doctrine committing the United States to "a global ideological struggle against revolutionary communism."

However it happened, it did happen. "The anti-Communist crusade," wrote Hans J. Morgenthau, "has its origins in the Truman Doctrine," with its assumption that the case for U.S. aid to Greece and Turkey had to be understood, not as rivalry between two great powers, "but as a struggle between good and evil, democracy and totalitarianism."

Historian Arthur Schlesinger, Jr., rejecting revisionists' conceptions of the Americans as anti-Communist ideologues, sees events within the U.S. government from 1941 to 1947 as a conflict between universalists hoping for world government (in a democratic form, of course) and sphere-of-influence theorists who wanted to accept major powers' domination of their own geographical multi-national spheres. While the Russians (and Churchill) thought only in terms of spheres of influence, most top American policy makers, excepting Henry Stimson, George Kennan, and Vice-President Wallace, were universalists. It was Wallace's opposition to the four hundred million dollars of requested aid for Greece and Turkey, Acheson said, that provided the "kiss of death,"[5] that is, the kiss that killed the opposition.

The new "Get-the-Reds" Lyndon Johnson appeared in May of 1947. Wallace, still pursuing the idealistic themes Johnson had tried out early in 1946, was scheduled into Austin to speak, but Johnson rushed onto the Senate floor to rescue his endangered Texans from the "false apostle," exclaiming, ". . . the forum for him and his appeasement doctrine is not before the clear-eyed, stout-hearted Texans. Rather, it is a sallow, deluded fringe that bores and scavenges like termites. . . . Texans have characteristics which prevent us from responding to the wiles of an appeaser." On aid to Greece and Turkey, Johnson said no one wanted war, but to halt totalitarian aggression, "some risk of war may be involved."

He applauded Ira Eaker, an air force general, for advocating the U.S. have the best air force in the world. More and more militarist, Johnson was given a seat on the joint committee on atomic energy and became the third-ranking Democrat on the armed services committee (which absorbed the naval affairs committee). Occasionally during armed services hearings he would set his wrist-watch alarm to call time on a witness he didn't like.

Once aid to Greece and Turkey passed (not without a fight: 287 to 107 in the House, 67 to 23 in the Senate), the American commitment was generalized to all of Western Europe. When Secretary of State George Marshall proposed that the U.S. help formulate and fund a program for European recovery, the Soviet Union was invited to benefit, too, but declined. The Marshall Plan was billed as "not directed against anyone, but against hunger, chaos, and poverty." However, it also marked the beginning of a conscious U.S. alliance with the French in their colonial war in Indochina. The classified Griffin Mission of 1950, for instance, said candidly that the U.S. aid to France was "of major assistance to the French in carrying the present load in Indochina." Although obvious to the Vietnamese, this truth was obscured from the view of American citizens.

Johnson favored the Marshall Plan for humanitarian reasons and to "keep Stalin from overrunning the world." Now that the Texan's bellicose rhetoric had broken loose nothing would stop it until the Vietnam War stopped him. "I am in favor," he said, "of letting Stalin know that he cannot run over the world and enslave us as vassals and impound our children as captives behind the Iron Curtain." Gone with the season were his warnings against spreading distrust that might lead to nuclear holocaust. Now he used fear of the atom bomb to justify an anti-Soviet military buildup. "Will an atomic bomb drop on New York and kill three million people before we get a strong foreign policy?" he asked. "We'd rather see the Communists stopped at the Mediterranean than to have to stop them at the Gulf of Mexico."[6]

The National Security Act of 1947 created a single, unified military establishment and a secret spy apparatus. Secret translegal and illegal covert operations around the world were authorized in a shell game that was played out under the black umbrella of this act.

The law created the Central Intelligence Agency and the National Security Council and authorized the NSC to order the CIA to do whatever the NSC told it to do, provided it was "related to intelligence affecting the national security." That much, and no more, the public knew. In December, 1947, the NSC, at its first meeting, secretly told the CIA to conduct covert operations abroad pursuant to U.S. foreign policy —operations that were to be concealed from public knowledge so that the U.S. could deny responsibility for them. Obviously "covert" meant secret from the citizens of the U.S. as well as everyone else. In 1955 a new NSC order told the CIA to counter, reduce, and discredit communism worldwide by covert activities related to propaganda, economic warfare, political action including sabotage, demolition, and assistance to resistance movements, and all activities compatible with the order.

Under Truman and Eisenhower, then, the United States government adopted a policy of secret warfare abroad in pursuance of foreign policy objectives. In the reality, as distinct from the rhetoric, this was the Truman Doctrine. And Lyndon Johnson, who when closer to the shock of Hiroshima had warned that breeding hate and distrust could kill millions of Americans, jockeyed for the front position in this dangerous new game.

On domestic policy his New Dealing days were over. "He told the press that "the term 'New Dealer' is a misnomer." He still believed in many of Roosevelt's causes, he said, specifying only water power, the REA, and all-weather roads. "But," he said, "I believe in free enterprise, and I don't believe in the government doing anything that the people can do privately."[7]

---

52. Running against the Reds and the Goons

His radicalism suppressed or well hidden, Johnson extended his 1947 turnabout into the most cynical period of his career, his next seven years of Red-baiting and reaction. In 1948 he ran for the Senate against Communists and labor unions and accepted and defended stolen votes to get in. However humanitarian his long-run purposes, he had steeled himself to say and do almost anything to get more power.

President Truman, having presented himself as a champion of the blacks just in time for the presidential election of that year, was hated in the South, so in April Johnson picked a public fight with him. The

FDR yes-man who had lost his Senate race in 1941 made his first move in 1948 by saying no to Truman.

Most of the eighteen hundred surplus war plants had been handed over to private buyers at bargain rates. Among the buyers, Johnson's political bankroller, George Brown, already had the government's natural gas pipeline safely in his hands. Johnson had cultivated the oilman, Sid Richardson, and it was mutual—for fun and talk, Richardson would fly the congressman down to his privately owned St. Joseph's island in the coastal Gulf. When the time came, Johnson helped Richardson purchase the government's carbon–black plant at Odessa, Texas, defending his rich friend's company against imputations of anti–trust difficulties in the transaction.

"We have helped" Richardson in the matter, staffer Walter Jenkins recorded, "on a number of occasions." The Department of Justice alleged that Richardson's carbon company had entered into deals with another carbon company in violation of antitrust laws. Jenkins put pressure for Richardson's cause directly on an assistant attorney general at the Department of Justice.

For $4.3 million, officially on Jan. 15, 1948, the War Assets Administration sold Richardson one of the largest plants the government had built during the war for military needs, 447 buildings on 426 acres of land, 50 miles of pipelines, housing for the employees, with a capacity of producing 45 million pounds of carbon black a year. For four million dollars, quite a buy. Then, to help Richardson make a go of it, Johnson advocated inside the government that carbon black be classified as a critical material and even stockpiled at Richardson's plant. It was natural that in Johnson's forthcoming campaign, one of Richardson's vice-presidents said to Jenkins, "I can assure you that (Richardson's) organizations will do all they can for Mr. Johnson's candidacy."

His patrons taken care of, Johnson called on Truman to review policy on disposing of the remaining three hundred plants. Truman suspended surplus sales for thirty days, but, Johnson carped righteously, "We shouldn't sell [industrial potential] to junk dealers today and ask Congress for more money to replace it tomorrow."[1]

Evidently Johnson at this time considered going into business himself rather than running for the Senate. Harold Young said a woman Johnson loved confided to Young that Johnson considered going into Wall Street, leaving Bird and taking up with the new woman. Johnson wrote his woman friend some notes along these lines, she told Young (when he was nominated for president she tore them up).[2]

By the story Johnson told me, he went to Texas to announce he would not run—he had no resources, he didn't want to stay in the House long enough to become Speaker, he didn't want to stay in politics at all. He said he wanted to go teach somewhere while Bird kept on with her radio business. "I told 'em all no, I wasn't running."[3]

One night at his home in Austin friends of his wheedled, taunted, and sweet-talked him, but adamant against running, he went to bed, leaving them arguing. They decided to run John Connally, and the next morning they asked Lyndon to help.

About four that afternoon, though, fifteen or twenty of Johnson's friends, people from his NYA days and the first Senate race, came in to urge him to run. He said they told him, "Governor Coke Stevenson will be our senator. There will be no future for us." Claude Wild, Sr., told him he could win—here was a so-called liberal who had voted *for* the Taft-Hartley antiunion law.

Johnson telephoned a few editors—Rhea Howard of Wichita Falls, Charley Guy of Lubbock, Millard Cope in Marshall, and Houston Harte, who had a chain of Texas papers—and all said they would support him, although a couple told him he couldn't win. He agreed he probably couldn't beat Stevenson, but "I thought, 'Well, it's probably the easiest way to end my career.' " He called Bird, catching her at a supermarket, and told her what he was thinking.

The Thursday on which he announced, a second time, for the Senate, the Austin paper, hawked at the corners downtown and looped into the yards of the slowly rousing citizenry, contained, in a column bearing his byline, his farewell speech to his fellow provincials. What he wrote foretold, opaquely, his presidency fifteen years later, his holy love to help the poor and holy hate to fight the wicked as all good Christians must:

"Eleven years ago, on May 13, 1937, . . . there was peace in the world . . . . It was a weak-kneed peace, true, propped up on fragile umbrellas of timid men who sought to buy security at the price of democracy's soul. . . . Americans still could go to bed at night and have no fears that a bomb might drop in their backyards before dawn. That luxury ended at Hiroshima when the first atomic bomb exploded. With that explosion a new era was born—the Atomic age. The power that ended the world's greatest war within 48 hours became ours to use, either to Christianize the world or pulverize it. Either we learn to live together, or we shall surely die together.

". . . The people of my district are not interested in war-making. They want atomic energy used to cure the sick, relieve us of drudgery, and raise our standard of living. That has been my goal as a congressman: To use the power we have to raise the standard of living for all —the people in my district, my state, my nation, and the world at large."

Here was Munich, here the awareness of Godlike national power, here the crusade to Christianize, to civilize, the world, here was the power to pulverize, and here was the will to help everyone everywhere. All the thirty-nine-year-old Lyndon Johnson left out that spring morning was the devil, and the devil was coming. Ten days later Johnson dedicated himself to the struggle against "the surging blood-red tide of communism."

As he tried for the Senate again, his resentment about 1941 was fresh in his mind. "I was urged to contest that result," he said now. "I tried to be a good sport. Lots of folks said they'd support me the next time, but the war intervened. . . . I know the fair-minded people of Texas will help me win that promotion to which I came so close before."

He did not add, but was thinking, that they wouldn't steal this one from him. Coke Stevenson had been one of the suspects in, and a major beneficiary of, the long count against him in 1941. When the election had made the governor the senator, the lieutenant governor, Stevenson, had moved up to replace the governor.

A right-wing west Texas rancher, Stevenson had served in Austin quietly through the war. He appointed reactionaries as regents to the state university. When Rainey, the liberal president of the school, was fired and ran for governor, Stevenson joined the gang-up against him. The governor's emblems were his pipe and his taciturnity. Announcing for the Senate, he advocated less government, lower taxes, segregated schools, "the complete destruction of the communist movement in this country."

A Houston oilman, George Peddy, announced next, orating about Russia's "bloody hands" and the need for state ownership of the tidelands oil. Incumbent Senator O'Daniel, bitter that Stevenson had not deferred to him, asked his people to back Johnson.[4]

For his opener Johnson chose Austin's downtown Wooldridge Park, the concave, grassy city block with a stage down in the middle. Two fiddle bands entertained the people, who spilled out onto the sidewalks. Johnson mounted the stage accompanied by his wife and mother, both of them dressed in white. Responding to the cheers, he threw his Stetson into the crowd. And then he condemned proposals for the equal opportunity laws he would later administer, stormed against civil rights bills he would later sign into law, blasted labor bosses he would later court, and pledged to fight the socialized medicine his medicare would later resemble.

Truman had proposed a federal law against lynching, a federal fair employment practices commission, an end to Jim Crow in interstate transportation, and protection of the right to vote. Johnson, his followers arrayed around him in Austin, called this program "a farce and a sham—an effort to set up a police state in the guise of liberty." He did not want any truck with it, at all: "It is the province of the state to run its own elections. I am opposed to the anti-lynching bill because the federal government has no more business enacting a law against one form of murder than another. I am against the FEPC because if a man can tell you whom you must hire, he can tell you whom you cannot employ."[5]

Although recalling his vote for Taft-Hartley, he said he was ready to oppose both unions and capital.[6] "I want no part of socialized medicine," he exclaimed—those charging the contrary (he said during the campaign) lied through "their valves of hate."[7]

Stevenson had spoken against "moving the Kimble County Courthouse to Washington," and Johnson construed this as opposition to government programs that helped farmers—price supports, good roads, electricity, soil and water conservation, access to markets abroad. "You don't take those problems to a man who can see no farther than the county courthouse," Johnson said. Local government could not very well combat hoof-and-mouth disease. "We had enough of do-nothing government back in the Hoover days, when cotton sold for a nickel, wheat for two bits, calves for three cents, and corn had to be burned for lack of a market." Hoover had believed "that 'constitutional government' gave every man, woman, and child the right to starve."[8]

By 1948 the income of the mineral industries in Texas, mostly oil, exceeded the combined income from farms and ranches; oilworkers, with their families, were about an eighth of the state's people. Yet with more than half of Texas oil produced by thirteen national companies, Texas was an even more abject "colony of Manhattan" than in the thirties when Bob Montgomery had first advanced the concept. Johnson, who in 1946 had sounded like a Populist David slingshotting the oil Goliath, now tapped under. With Truman claiming federal ownership of the oil under the seas offshore, Johnson joined the oil companies' fight for state control. He also proposed that the 27.5 percent oil depletion allowance (the industry's golden tax loophole) be made even bigger—guarded stories from Washington related that he was working in the bureaucracy to increase it.[9]

The two major issues of the Texas campaign of 1948 were who hated the Communists most and who the unions.

Head-hunter Martin Dies of Lufkin, when announcing he would not run for the Senate, had said that communism was the main issue, and certainly "our old vaudeville friend . . . 'me too Lyndon Johnson' " did not know about that. Peddy attacked Johnson for missing three votes on HUAC during the war and for voting against money for HUAC in 1946, against a 1946 proposal to investigate espionage, and against barring foreign relief to Soviet-dominated countries in 1947. Stevenson picked up the theme, accusing Johnson of "repeated votes . . . against measures designed to curb communism." Johnson retorted by citing the many votes he had cast for HUAC[10] and froze himself into a posture of militant, coercive anticommunism, glinting with aspersions upon anyone less bellicose than he was.

By an ingenious association of Stevenson's isolationism with communism, Johnson actually seized the anti-Communist offensive. Stevenson, hating government spending in principle, was not as enthusiastic as

Johnson about military spending, and with the club this gave Johnson, he assailed the charge that, being a New Dealer, he was soft on communism. Isolationists had opposed resisting Nazism, had they not? In 1948, Johnson argued, it was the same: isolationists now resisted opposing communism. The Chamberlains had appeased Hitler; now they appeased Stalin.

The argument posited a monolithic communism analogous to monolithic fascism. "Stalin is marching as Hitler marched—repeating chapter by chapter, verse by verse," Johnson said. Since military spending from 1938 to 1941 would have prevented Hitler's conquest of Europe, those who refused to support preparedness in 1948 were "the same stripe of isolationist who led us into two world wars."[11]

Starkly, Johnson painted the Reds as the enemy against which the U.S. had to re-arm. "The Russians understand only one language—the language of power." A seventy-group air force would "protect all Americans against communism." U.S. industrial and agricultural targets "will be the Pearl Harbors of the next war." If wanting an air force as big as Stalin's was warmongering, "then I'm a warmonger and proud of it." The U.S. needed "the world's greatest" air force and "the best atomic bomb that money can buy"—"We've got to have the best atomic bombs ready to be dropped first." The navy should be "adequate to any task." Every young man should take military training for six months.

". . . the state of our airpower is in crisis," he said in the Congress this spring. To produce the seventy groups "the Air Force experts" want, the U.S. needed six thousand new planes a year, he said, adding shockingly, "without superior airpower America is a bound and throttled giant; impotent and easy prey to any yellow dwarf with a pocket knife."[12]

Stevenson pointed out that Johnson was benefiting politically from the money there was to be made from militarism. Air Force General Eaker went to west Texas to insist on "no appeasement," military spending, and destruction of "the fifth column in this country" and to endorse Johnson. Stevenson said the Hughes Aircraft Company, for which Eaker worked after his retirement, was behind Johnson's "huge slush fund." A leader in the air power bloc in Congress and obviously allied with the aircraft companies, Johnson replied he was proud to be backed by the fellow "who led all our Air Forces overseas against Hitler."

Johnson saw and used the connection between war spending and prosperity—he got votes for being for guns, knew he was doing it, and wanted them. Helicoptering into San Antonio, which has army and air force bases, he called the city "the preparedness center of the world" and proposed that San Antonians lobby for more air power. "The president of a San Antonio retail store making a speech in Sioux City might determine the peace of the world," he said. He opposed "cutting planes and ships and cutting the Army" and said the election would determine whether there would be "war or peace" and "a Hoover depression or prosperity."

Stevenson suggested that Johnson was deliberately whipping up the fears in the people for his own profit. "They tell us another war is just around the corner. . . . We must—they tell us—be afraid," Stevenson said. "Is it possible they want to manufacture an 'emergency' based on fear in order to satisfy their greedy appetite for power and more power?"[13]

Johnson ran a labor-baiting campaign while Stevenson, by far the more conservative man, had to deny he was labor's candidate. The craft unions opposed Johnson because of his vote for Taft-Hartley, his antiunion tendencies in the war, and his ties with the antiunion Browns. Striking as always for any opportunity that opened up, Johnson censured his right-wing opponent as Sidney Hillman's gift to Texas.

When the Texas State Federation of Labor, endorsing Stevenson, said Johnson had "disqualified himself in the eyes of the working people" by supporting Taft-Hartley and the Case bill, Johnson accused Stevenson of making a deal in "a secret meeting with one of the big shots from Chicago" and asked if he had promised to help repeal Taft-Hartley. "A few so-called labor leaders" had not been able to make him their errand boy and "are now trying to stab me in the back," Johnson said. The labor people retorted that he was "the tool of special interest, caring nothing for the vast numbers of workers in this state."

Had Stevenson promised anything on Taft-Hartley? "No," said the secretary-treasurer of the labor group. "Personally he said to me it was a bad bill." Nevertheless, here was this New Dealer damning the unions, this right-winger ducking and feinting.

Johnson likened Stevenson to a yearling with "the labor boss brand" on his hip. Stevenson said Taft-Hartley was all right as far as it was needed to keep down a monopoly. A Johnson backer in Blanco County offered to shear Stevenson's goats free in return for a clear-cut statement on Taft-Hartley. Stevenson said a CIO blacklist did not contain Johnson's name. Johnson showed it was not a blacklist, but a voting record that graded him voting right four times and wrong six.[14]

Despite Johnson's brief war record, he painted himself as the veteran and Stevenson the stay-at-home. The political problem was how to hurt the sixty-year-old Stevenson as young enough to have been a slacker, but too old to be a senator. Well, Johnson said, Texans are "fed up with has-beens who want to sit things out," and "Texas is not going to send either an old man or an appeaser to the Senate." Why, Stevenson had opposed gasoline rationing when our "fliers were dropping into the Pacific with empty gasoline tanks," and "While our veterans were dying on the battlefield, he was mouthing about the sacrifices he had to make at home." Somehow the trick was done: Stevenson was an old slacker.

Like the abuse of his opponent, now also the use of dead boys to prove his own virtue recurred in Johnson's rhetoric. Stevenson was an isolationist, sounding like Chamberlain, and this was unacceptable to "Texans who remember the boys who died at Bataan because we couldn't defend the skies." Stevenson wanted to cut taxes; "It's either your boys' lives or tax rebates for the millionaires." Even the welfare issue could be turned into bleeding bodies. Stevenson had said, in opposition to feeding a man who won't work, "Our mothers were too smart to do that. When the tramp asked for a handout, they gave him an axe and showed him the woodpile. If he produced he was given food. Not otherwise." By implying that Stevenson's tramps were veterans, Johnson reaped liberals' indignation without defending welfare: Stevenson had "said, in effect, I'll give the tramps an axe and show them a woodpile—those 'tramps' who fought, bled, and died to hold back Hitler. . . ."[15]

Most politicians would have thought it laughable to paint a reactionary Texas rancher pink, but Johnson, in a wild and chilling burst of slander by alleged association, did just that. As the Alger Hiss case broke in Washington, the Senate race in Texas was taking shape as an early outbreak of the paranoid acrimony that poisoned political discourse in the United States for the next two decades.

Johnson had seen Red-baiting kill off Homer Rainey in 1946, and if he was going to get some of the same mud in the face, he was going to sling it out, too. Ten days before the 1948 election, over statewide radio, he laid into "big labor racketeers": "John L. Lewis, the coal mine dictator . . .; James C. Petrillo, who refuses to let our children record their fiddle playing, and Communist Harry Bridges." What were they up to? "These birds of a feather have flocked together in a united effort to defeat Lyndon Johnson, who refused to wear their Red feathers in his hat, and they are using Coke Stevenson as their silent Man Friday. . . . Lyndon Johnson voted for the Taft-Hartley anti-Communist law," while Stevenson had not said where he stood on "this measure that bans Communist control of labor unions" and had "refused to promise that . . . he will not repeal this law and return control of labor unions to racketeering Communist leaders who take orders only from Moscow."[16]

But if Johnson was willing to say almost anything, no matter how demagogic and damaging, to win, so was Stevenson. The governor linked Johnson to "Vito Marcantonio of the Harlem District," saying that they voted together on anti-Red issues. At the time Marcantonio's name meant "Communist" to many Americans, and, of course, Harlem meant "nigger" to racist white Texas voters. Stevenson said Johnson, with Marcantonio, opposed the investigation of "men who stole over 150 documents dealing with the defense of this country," opposed funding HUAC which had uncovered "the Communist spy ring in Washington," and opposed prohibiting aid to any country dominated by Russia except under strict supervision. George Peddy rushed in with a mud-pie, too, saying Johnson in 1946 favored appeasing Russia and would have "shared the atom bomb" with her.[17]

Meanwhile, outside of public view, the money men did their work. Wild, the oil lawyer, had the title of campaign manager for Johnson, but Connally has said he was the manager. The two of them, with Looney and Clark, were the key people. Connally raised money "from people who had it," as Wild said. Brown & Root helped again; while Stevenson had big oil, Johnson had Sid Richardson, the by now super-rich independent. Johnson played the poor boy, of course, calling attention to twenty-four "$300 billboards" Stevenson had along highways and to full-page ads for him in the dailies. "I'm thankful I don't have to have $1,100 advertisements saying I can't be bought," he added. In one of the fairy tales about campaign finance that were then the accepted thing, Johnson said at the end of the first primary that he had spent about $7,000 or $8,000. Stevenson told me later that two of his old-time backers in east Texas told him they switched to the other side because Johnson was paying them $1,000 each. Johnson ran up $30,000 in phone bills alone, according to a source inside the campaign.[18]

"Fractious and high-strung and a hard worker and driver," Johnson as usual outran everybody, campaigning eighteen hours a day; in sixty days he made 350 speeches. Walking up the steps of the high school in Robstown, he told his aide Cliff Carter he wanted to see every schoolchild in town. "Lyndon," Carter said, "we don't have *time.*" Glaring his man down, Johnson exclaimed, "Are we gonna join the Can't Do It Club right here on the steps of Robstown High School?"[19]

Coming up from behind,[20] Johnson didn't miss a trick. Voters in the vicinity of state prisons were worked on the issue of Stevenson's leniency in pardoning criminals. Johnson told Texas postal clerks a pay raise was coming. To reinforce the picture of himself as a war veteran, he used heroes and an amputee. Seven heroes endorsed him at one rally; at another he was introduced by a man who had lost a leg in France. Arriving in a town a few minutes after a casualty of the war had been reburied, he told a rally, "Private Jecemenek and a million other American soldiers would not have died in the last war had we been prepared."[21]

As the least conservative candidate, Johnson counted on Stevenson and Peddy splitting most of the conservatives, leaving him the FDR vote and some conservatives. He clicked because, in the pursuit of this strategy, he put Stevenson on the defensive about labor and military spending. But personal factors also had much to do with the outcome.

An estrangement between Stevenson and the still powerful Fergusons made a difference. "Farmer Jim" Ferguson had been kept waiting for two hours to see the governor. Ferguson told an aide one night he had invited Stevenson to come over and see them, the governor said he would, the Fergusons had dressed up for the governor's visit—and he didn't come. Following his principle of "Woo thy enemies," Johnson played up to the Fergusons despite their opposition to him in 1941. When Jim died in 1944 Johnson flew in from Washington for the funeral while Stevenson, as an aide said bitterly, "got in his goddamn pickup and went to Junction." Whenever Johnson was in town he called on the Ferguson women at their home, and "When leaving," one of the daughters said, "he would put his arm around Mamma and ask her if there was anything in the world he could do for her." Ma Ferguson did not forget. In 1948 she sent out five thousand letters rallying the Ferguson people for Johnson, and she made radio speeches for him. Ferguson aide Ghent Sanderford said Stevenson was "an ingrate. And they got their sweet revenge."

The newspapers in Dallas, Houston, and San Antonio favored Stevenson or Peddy, but Johnson's friend Marsh was the factor for Johnson in the Austin press, and the *Fort Worth Star-Telegram* backed him again, too. Mrs. Margaret Carter, a liberal activist in Fort Worth, said Johnson had helped Amon Carter, the publisher of the newspaper, get pulp he needed, and that Carter also wanted more airpower contracts for Fort Worth. About this time, she said, Brown & Root was hired to do a rather large repairing job on the streets of the city, and in 1949 John Connally was to leave Johnson's staff and go onto Sid Richardson's payroll. She saw a deal in these facts. Galveston insurance millionare Maco Stewart, angry that Stevenson had not reappointed him to a state board, paid half of everything that was spent against the governor in Stewart's county.

Some liberals in Texas trusted Johnson; some feared him. Despite what he was saying publicly, he converted the liberal banker Walter Hall, of Dickinson near Galveston. Hall's open advocacy of the liberal causes of the time had earned him notoriety and hostility among the conservatives. At this time American blacks were still totally oppressed, federal aid to education was regarded as a radical idea, and private doctors had total control of medical care. Alone with Johnson, driving him to a rally, Hall cross-examined him. Federal aid to education? "I believe in offering educational means to the youth of America by whatever means it has to be done!" Johnson exclaimed. Civil rights? "Whatever is necessary to see that a human being, black or white, gets educated or gets the vote, that's got to be done!"

"He did not go along on the civil rights anywhere as far as I did except on the ballot, which he contended was basic, if they got the vote their welfare would be assured," Hall said. Although opposed on the record to "socialized medicine," Johnson convinced Hall he believed "something had to be done." They shared extravagant enthusiasm for Roosevelt.

"On these humanitarian things," Hall said, "he was practical, but I was convinced that his heart was such, he would do these things. He convinced me he was sincere. . . . If he was attempting to snow me he did a hell of a good job." Convinced that because of necessary hypocrisy Johnson was a much better man than he sounded like, Hall "never did lose faith that if he could get to the place where he could, he would do as his heart dictated."

Mark Adams, the New Dealer from Texas, had been associated with Coke Stevenson for some time and sided with him against Johnson. Well left of center, Adams saw an analogy between the 1948 Senate election and the situation in Nazi Germany in the thirties when Hitler and General Kurt von Schleicher, the conservative chancellor of the Weimar Republic, were both bidding for the same powerful friends, but Hitler was also bidding for the mob. To Adams, both Stevenson and Johnson were conservatives, but Johnson was the more dangerous.[22]

---

53. "Son, They're All My Helicopters"

In 1948 Johnson campaigned across spread-out Texas in a helicopter. Whether an aviatrix friend or he himself thought of it first,[1] he had the brilliance and the audacity to do it.

The two-seater, model 47, was provided by Bell Aerospace Corporation, but Johnson announced his acceptance of the use of the machine and the services of a young Bell test pilot as if the donors were a group of "more than 100 veterans." For Bell, of course, Johnson's use of their novel whirlybird was good public relations and a political investment.

Flying Lyndon to the people, the pilot, Jim Mashman, set the weird-looking machine down on a softball field, a vacant lot beside a cotton gin, a high-school football field, a town park, an open-area space by the railroad tracks. When they landed on top of a building in a small city east of Houston, police had to direct traffic around the crowds—farmers came in from miles around to see. Lyndon was tagged "the Johnson City Windmill."

Jake Pickle, later to be a congressman, was the advance man, lining up the landing sites and the publicity. Four Dallas high-school kids who had been singing as a barbershop quartet were given matching shirts, a car with a loudspeaker on top, their meals, and one hundred dollars apiece, and while Johnson in the helicopter and the campaign motorcade leap-frogged along behind, the advance team would speed ahead, cruise around downtown attracting a crowd with their singing, lead people out to the landing site and keep them entertained until the drone of the copter reached their ears, yell "Here he comes"—and roar off to the next town as Johnson landed. Johnson promised the four boys, "Someday you'll sing on the steps of the White House."[2]

This, after all, was new—a politician was coming out of the sky in a helicopter. A kid named Bob Schieffer, growing up in suburban Fort Worth, was taken to see it by his mother. A great voice came down out of the sky, "This is your candidate, Lyndon Johnson, I'll be down to see you soon," then the roar, the hovering approach, and the great machine-bird landed at a vacant lot next to a fire-hall. Little Bob was terrified.

In east Texas a dozen cotton-choppers dropped their hoes and ran for the woods when the copter stopped dead in the air above them, but they hove to when they heard the voice from above, "Hello, down there. This is Lyndon Johnson, candidate for the U.S. Senate, dropping in to say good morning." As Lyndon flew from landing to landing one day in June, he leaned out of the plexiglas bubble at the front and waved to people down in Somerville, Lyons, Deanville, Dime Box, Smithville, Elgin, McDade, Hutto, and Round Rock. Coke Stevenson was addressing a crowd in north Texas when the Johnson City Windmill arrived overhead. "Lo and behold," Coke said, "it was Lyndon! I'd get the crowd assembled and he'd come and entertain 'em."

The machine also put down in Alice, the little south Texas town that would soon become the center of charges that the election was stolen for Johnson. Disembarking, Johnson was met by Ed Lloyd, the boss Democrat in the town, by Chief of Police Stokes Micenheimer, by Johnson's county manager Homer Dean—the local party boys. Standing in shirt-sleeves beside his helicopter, his microphone rig braced in front of him, he spoke and went on.

In Dallas, Lamar Holley represented an association of airplane dealers who sold small planes, and since Johnson was stressing the need for airpower, Holley and his friends arranged an escort of fifteen or twenty planes for the helicopter on a route above the highway loop girdling Dallas. Johnson was set down at a small field, where he spoke to a couple of hundred people. "It did work," Holley said.

In the five-week helicopter campaign Johnson, losing twenty-seven pounds along the way, made 370 landings. One Saturday alone he made seven "hoverings" and thirteen landings—he estimated that he spoke that day to fifteen thousand people.[3]

Bell Aircraft, which provided one of the two copters he used in '48, moved its entire helicopter operation to north Texas during the Korean War and became established as the world's largest builder of helicopters. By 1967 the Texas plant had eleven thousand employees producing two hundred helicopters a month, four-fifths of them military. That year Jim Mashman, Johnson's pilot in 1948, was an assistant vice-president of the firm and was still flying Johnson around the Texas area. After visiting a military base in late 1967, Johnson was walking toward a waiting helicopter among a group of them when a Marine colonel stopped him and said, "Mr. President, this is not your helicopter. Your helicopter is over there." "Son," Johnson answered, "they're all my helicopters."[4]

54. A Meeting in the Dark of Night

"I thought I'd lead into the runoff by 100,000 votes," Johnson said, but instead he trailed by almost that much: Stevenson led him 477,077 to 405,617, with the big margins in the cities. Peddy had another 237,195 votes. "It was so close," Johnson said, "I nearly had to get seventy or eighty percent of the votes that went to George Peddy."[1]

Election night, after a talk with his campaign workers, Johnson drove through a red light on the way home and went back to work. He decided to abandon the helicopter as too slow. Stevenson, striving to counter him on military spending, flew to Washington to confer with Forrestal and Senator Arthur Vandenberg on preparedness, so Johnson followed his foe into Washington, conferring with Forrestal, too, and issuing another bristling statement about the Russians.[2]

Oil-saturated dirt was dredged up. The *El Paso Herald-Post* reported that shortly after helping the major corporations try to pass a state sales tax, Stevenson had received a lump sum of twenty-one thousand dollars from the Magnolia Petroleum Company for leasing his ranches for oil in a county whose entire ten-year oil production would not cover a fourth of the sum.[3]

Despite his rhetoric against labor bosses, Johnson now met with CIO leaders in Jefferson County, a unionized area southeast of Houston. He made no promises, but said his doors would be open to them, and they split with the AFL and endorsed him. Texas CIO members probably voted for Johnson about two to one. The congressman from Beaumont, Jack Brooks, induced Johnson to get the lieutenant governor, Allan Shivers (who came from the county), on his side.[4]

During the runoff rural boxholders in the state received the "Johnson Journal," edited by Mrs. John Connally. Here Johnson told the farmers he "has not favored the CIO and the Political Action Committees of the American Federation of Labor which have always striven for labor dictatorship in the big cities to the detriment and harm of the Texas farmer and rancher."

Incredible attempts to associate Stevenson with Communists permeated the Journal. Stevenson had "dodged this anti-Communist labor law issue." "The big Northern labor unions, with their leadership which includes admitted Communists . . . , have aligned their forces against Lyndon Johnson and in favor of Coke Stevenson." Johnson himself was quoted, "These are the same Communists who would confiscate the farms of Texas and place Texas farmers under the lash of a commissar's whip, if they were given a free hand." One item in the Journal, "Stevenson Pardons Red," said Stevenson had pardoned "a well known Communist, CIO organizer and official . . . three months after the *El Paso Times* carried a picture showing him participating in Communist May

Day activities in Cindad Juarez." Another item sounded as if Joe McCarthy of Wisconsin, himself, might have written it. Under the heading, "Communists Favor Coke," the Johnson Journal said:

"The Communists, and many of them leaders in the big national labor unions which have endorsed and are supporting Coke Stevenson for the U.S. Senate, favor the election of isolationist candidates. . . . That's why the big shot labor bosses up North are trying to put Stevenson in office. . . . Wake up Texans! Don't let the Reds slip up on you by any such cunning plotting!"[5]

Thursday before the Saturday runoff, Johnson landed in Dallas in a private plane and stepped into Lamar Holley's new beige Ford convertible to lead a convey of cars downtown. Holley put back the canvas top so Lyndon could sit on the frame, "and he was so damn big, he broke it." Noontime traffic came to a stop as the procession, announced by the wailing sirens of the police motorcycles, passed under the Triple Underpass, turned up Main Street, and glided through the streets of the urban canyons, to city hall.

When they got to Johnson's hotel, Holley said, "He stuck out his big hand and said, 'Lamar, I want to tell you I think you are my kind of cattle and if there's ever anything I can do for you, win lose or draw, let me know,'" and turned on his heel and went in.[6]

Bird, on her way in a car with another woman to take part in the final radio speech, was bruised and shaken up when the car turned over twice. But, as Lyndon told many times later, she put her companion in a hospital, changed clothes, and made it to a reception in a town along the way and then to the broadcast, without even telling him about the accident.

The night before the election he told her, "Come on, honey, we're going home and spend the night at the ranch." "Oh no we're not," she said. "I'm going back to Austin and I'm going to get your mother, your sisters, your aunts, and your uncles, your friends, and your cousins, and I'm going to take the telephone book and I'm going to assign one of them all the A's, one of them all the B's, one of them all the C's, one of them all the D's, right through the Z's, and we're going to call and say, 'Won't you please go to the polls and vote for my husband?' 'Won't you please go to the polls and vote for my son?' 'Won't you please go to the polls and vote for my brother?'—or 'my cousin?'" And so she did.[7]

The mists of memories and the clouds of hearsay obscure a meeting that was held late one night in San Antonio in a pool of light made by the headlights of a circle of cars in Brackenridge Park, close to the San Antonio River. Reporter James McCrory was told by a county commissioner that Johnson, the commissioner, and several others, in this secret open-air session, agreed that only Boss Parr of Duval County could deliver the votes they needed from south Texas and decided that the commissioner would go south to see Parr, which he did.

The meeting did occur, according to James Knight, the pro-Johnson county clerk, and "We planned the South Texas boxes," but what actually happened down there, "Nobody'll ever know. It was quite an operation. It was put together by a master." But on another occasion Knight told me, "There wasn't anything to do with George Parr. They already *had* Parr—from the Roosevelt days." Johnson told me that although there was a meeting in San Antonio the night before the runoff, he did not remember anything in a park.[8]

He had lost San Antonio badly the first round, but in the runoff he united the city's warring factions—the Kildays and the Mavericks—behind him. Paul Kilday had defeated Maverick for Congress; when Maverick had become mayor he had fired Kilday's brother Owen as chief of police. Yet on the day of the runoff Johnson was driven through the Mexican section of town with Maverick on one side of him and Owen Kilday on the other.[9]

"The only time I ever took money from Lyndon Johnson," Knight told me, "was the day of the runoff. I took one thousand dollars and I got those in one-dollar bills because he, Lyndon Johnson, wanted to go around the polls. . . ." Knight accompanied Lyndon, and "Oh, when you go up there, why there's people standing around at the polls, they haven't had lunch and things like that—You happen to inadvertently put your hands in your pocket and give 'em a couple of dollars and move on, you understand. You take this and put ten, fifteen, twenty dollars and put this in the crowd and move over there and give 'em one dollar, two dollars. If the candidate personally gives the money, it has to be more. The price goes down immediately if somebody else but the candidate gives it to 'em, and the satisfaction is just as great. Don't misunderstand me, it's not a payoff or anything, because they've been standing there all day, drumming up votes, putting up posters. Five dollars for expenses or something like that. It was *costing* 'em that much money by the time they ate and bought two or three soda waters around the polls.

"That was the only time in my life that I ever took money off Lyndon Johnson."[10]

PART XI
Victory by Theft

We all pray to some god, but what happens has no name.

— Cesare Pavese, *Dialogues with Luecò,* translated by William Arrowsmith and D. S. Carne-Ross

55. The Cactus Fields of Boss Power

If one can stand the apparent irrationality of the decisive accidents of history, one may argue that the refusal of Texas Governor Stevenson to appoint a citizen named Jimmy Kazen to be the district attorney in Laredo, Texas, contributed to the American disaster in Vietnam. "We supported Jimmy Kazen for district attorney in Laredo because he was our friend," said George Parr. "Coke could have appointed him. But he didn't." Therefore, boss Parr said, the south Texas machine vote was switched to Lyndon Johnson and elected him senator. If he had lost he might have become a businessman instead of a president.

The original south Texas boss, James B. Wells, exercised his power from 1878 to 1920. Mexican nationals, let vote if they asserted they intended to become citizens, were imported by the hundreds for elections. The basis of the Parr family's power was laid in 1911 when four Anglos shot to death three Mexicans who had gone to vote in an election and Archer Parr sided with the victims. Wealthy Anglo farmers and ranchers resented the power of the bosses and their self-interested partisanship for the Mexican-American poor. In 1919, as a candidate of the Wells machine, Archer Parr was narrowly elected to office amidst charges of Mexicans voting by rote. When Wells died, Archer Parr became the boss; then Archer's son George succeeded to the role. Lyndon's father, Sam Johnson, Jr., knew all these things, worked the bosses to get the bloc vote, and passed along his know-how to Lyndon and Sam Houston.

Despite the intervention of Vice-President Garner for him,

George Parr was convicted of income tax evasion and served ten months in federal prison in 1936–37. The case involved charges of a twenty-five-thousand-dollar bribe "in a little black bag" and of protection money from gamblers, bootleggers, and whores. With reported help from Garner, Parr was paroled, but not pardoned, and he wanted a pardon. He applied in 1943, but Congressman Kleberg (the one Johnson had worked for) was not enthusiastic, and the pardon was denied. Parr helped beat Kleberg and, with the assistance of the new pro-Parr congressman, made a second try for the pardon. In 1946 President Truman pardoned him, enabling him to vote and hold office again.

George Parr had the power to elect in many counties. Favoring Stevenson during his three runs for governor, Parr delivered him, from Duval alone, majorities of 3,643 to 141, 2,936 to 77, and 3,310 to 17. A Stevenson man asked Parr for the bloc vote against Johnson, but there had been that Kazen snafu. And by one report Johnson and Connally had gone down to butter up Parr before the election.

A source who was completely inside Parr's circle, but who cannot be named, told me, "Lyndon came by for years," visiting Parr in his office in San Diego, Texas. When a secretary was sent around to the Windmill Café to bring in hamburgers, Lyndon always wanted them to "double the meat." Parr kept his home and his private life to himself, but Lyndon—and once his wife and little children—visited the boss in his office. *"For years,"* this source emphasized. On the telephone with Parr, Lyndon "would talk on and on and on," and to get back to his own life Parr, knowing Johnson was religious, would say something irreligious. Soon after Johnson would ring off.

As Harry Benge Crozier, an aide of Stevenson's, said, once Coke crossed the Kazens in Webb County he crossed Parr too—"the Webb County machine and Parr were pissin' outa the same quilt." Parr later told state Democratic chairman Robert Calvert, during a hunting trip on Parr's ranch, "My father supported [Stevenson]. I supported him after my father died. The time finally came when he had one little political appointment to give, and he gave it to our enemies. We just don't play ball that way."

In Starr, another boss county, Stevenson was hurt by his plan to locate a tuberculosis hospital next to the main city. Zapata County Judge M. B. Bravo, who worked with Parr and the Laredo bosses, had to work with the new district attorney the bosses didn't like. Stevenson had aroused the south Texas cactus fields of boss power against him. As election day neared, according to Bravo, "George Parr was calling up here. . . . very enthusiastically pushing for Lyndon."

E. H. Shoumette, the editor of a south Texas newspaper, said the machine of George Parr was more effective than New York's Tammany Hall at its best: "He manages to control the county in a number of ways, including the payment of funeral expenses for the needy, gifts of money to those who need help, promises of assistance in business matters, and fulfillment of those promises."

The poor people got some benefits from the system, just as did the poor in the French parishes of Louisiana who obeyed their local despots. Parr's deputies made the rounds reminding people to pay their poll taxes. Sam Houston, Lyndon's brother, told me, "I went down there for Kleberg once. If George Parr was for [a candidate], he was on the ballot first. They scratched all below the first name." Around Alice, Parr was quoted as saying, "I'll take the election—you take the election contest." Allan Shivers, whom Parr opposed, said of him, "If you had his support, you got 3,500 votes or 2,600; and if you didn't have it, you got 200. He could switch them around from one to the other just as easily."

George Parr denied that he controlled votes: "I pick the man and the people here vote for them. They trust me," he said. He was his own best defender. "Look out there in that bank," he said to William Bradford Huie. "See any Anglos? The Mexicans run the bank. . . . These people vote with me because I've been their friend all my life. My father was their friend. I spoke Spanish before I could speak English. I sit in their homes and talk with the old ones. My wife is Mexican. I live with these people, work with them, play with them. I go to chicken fights and bullfights with them. I bet on quarter-horse races with them. When they need a friend they come to me. I help them get born and help them get buried. I'm not like my churchified Baptist enemies. . . . they're too good to go to a Latin-American home. Well, I'm not too good." Delivering one-hundred-to-one majorities, he said, the Mexican-Americans in Duval "are a power in Texas." Otherwise, "we're nothing."

"The man did a lot of good," said the person close to him who cannot be named. "He went to the office every day to help people. People came not to give him anything, but to ask him legal advice. People voted for him because they appreciated him, because he had always done something for them—for my aunt, for my uncle, for my cousin, for my mother. Drugs, funeral expenses, education, you name it. He never drove people in like a herd like it said in the papers."

There was another way to look at it. With half a million dollars of Duval County money (which he later called a loan), Parr had bought a fifty-seven-thousand-acre ranch. His construction company got all the Duval County contracts. By 1948 he controlled banks in two towns and owned or had interests in about two hundred oil wells. He kept twenty-five good quarter horses and maintained a private race track that had automatic starting chutes and a judges' stand. His two-story Spanish mansion, hidden behind high walls in dusty San Diego, Texas, had a central patio, a swimming pool, fine grounds, servants' quarters, and a multi-car garage. Yet the Mexicans continued to live lives of wretched denial. Parr's county paid unskilled workmen sixteen dollars a week, and most of the people lived in pitiful shacks. The first requirement for his role as the *patrón,* giving the people small handouts, was the continuation of their relentless poverty.

"Well," said the member of his inner circle, "you can't make everybody rich."[1]

---

56. A Hinge of History

The county adjacent to George Parr's Duval was named for the original south Texas boss, Jim Wells. In Alice, the largest town in Jim Wells County, the big Mexican precinct was Box 13. The Box 13 election judge in 1948 was a savvy, handsome native of Mexico, Luis Salas, who had carried himself proudly ever since he rode with Pancho Villa in 1916. Luis would show you a photograph of his sister that Villa had signed on the back, and he had a picture of his brother with Villa and other men on horseback.

Homer Dean, Johnson's Jim Wells manager in 1948, said that before the runoff Johnson's lawyer-ally, Everett Looney of Austin, had many conversations with the Jim Wells boss, Ed Lloyd. Salas believed that although Lloyd decided which candidates for judge the machine supported, Parr ran the county. Parr called Lloyd "my lawyer."

Before the runoff Parr went over to Alice to see Salas. "Johnson made some agreement with Parr," Salas told me. "I know damn well he called George Parr about getting even with Coke Stevenson. That's why George came over here to see me." Parr didn't tell Salas that Johnson had called, but Salas believed it. What Parr had said, Salas would not tell.

Admittedly, Johnson's people were telling the south Texas bosses, "Hold back reporting your returns." Connally, remembering the mistake in 1941 when they let the opposition know Johnson's totals early, decided that this time the boss county votes would be kept quiet so the other side would not know how many votes they needed. Connally denies that votes were changed—all they did, he told me, was hold them back.

During the voting that Saturday in Box 13 a judge ordered Salas to let an election supervisor see each ballot as it was counted, but the tough Mexican refused. That night, a witness later testified, Salas went into the office of a newspaper the Lloyd family owned and reported Box 13 had gone for Johnson 765 to 60. These figures, telegraphed to the Texas Election Bureau in Dallas, were included in the unofficial returns. That same Saturday night reporter Jim Rowe of the Corpus Christi daily dropped by Box 13 because it was always the bellwether. To a couple of hundred people waiting outside, "Luis Salas came out and announced the returns," Rowe said. "He was just stating it publicly, and those within earshot could hear it," and again it was 765 to 60. Rowe also telephoned the Duval County chairman, who told him, "Yeah, I got it complete"—Johnson 4,197 to 38 for the whole county. (Stevenson rounded off the consequences of displeasing the Duke of Duval: "He just made it 100 to 1.") Presumably Johnson got these figures at once. "The South Texas counties—we knew the night of the election," Connally said.[1]

For the candidates the evening had begun quietly. Relaxing at his ranch, wearing a wrinkled khaki shirt, Stevenson led reporters into a grove of pecan trees alongside the Llano River and showed them how a camper washes his hands by holding a cup of water in his teeth and tipping the water out. Lyndon, Bird, and friends received returns out back on the lawn at 1901 Dillman in Austin. But as the totals came in, these stage-sets dissolved. By midnight Stevenson led by fewer than 2,000 out of 939,000 votes then counted, and he and Lyndon both knew this was another Texas election that could be stolen, 1941 all over again—one way or another.

As the closeness of the returns became clear that night, a source who was with Parr in San Diego, Texas, took a phone call for him from Johnson's headquarters in Austin. "They were looking for George, they were anxious for George. They said it was Lyndon Johnson's office. It was very important that they get hold of George," the source told me. When, later that same Saturday night, Parr was told about the call, he said, "Well, they can wait till tomorrow morning, because it's not that important."

Awake almost all night, Johnson rose with the sun for an eighteen-hour Sunday, and Stevenson, after three hours' sleep, drove from his home on the river to his Austin headquarters.[2]

Duval County gave out new figures that Sunday, adding 425 votes to Johnson's total, and by midnight he had a slight edge. Monday Stevenson took back the lead. Although Salas had given his totals for Box 13, Parr instructed him to hold back his official report. "You know," Salas told me, "they started making changes in the returns, coming in late, from Dallas, Fort Worth, and East Texas. That was when George B. Parr said to me, 'Well, you are going to be late, too.' "

A reporter covering Johnson day and night heard him "burning up the wires calling people" trying to get the votes in, but didn't recall his phoning south Texas. Did Johnson call Parr asking for more votes? The incoming Democratic chairman in Jim Wells, Harry Lee Adams, said, "You ask, you know, 'Well, did anyone actually call and say, 'We need some more votes'? 'Oh, yeah, I heard so-and-so say he was in the bank when the call came in.' But then they clam up."

Mrs. Dan Moody, the wife of the former Texas governor and a woman who hated Johnson, remembered former Texas Ranger Frank Hamer and her husband saying, in the Moodys' living room perhaps the Sunday afternoon after the election, that they had "impounded the telephone calls" and found that two calls had gone from Johnson's Austin home to Parr "in the middle of the fight . . . *before* they brought in those fraudulent votes." But such records were never made public.

A merchant in San Diego, the county seat of Duval, told a reporter he was sitting in his friend Parr's office when many calls from Johnson came in. A top political official in Duval told this same merchant that when the first calls began to come in while Stevenson was ahead, Parr replied that he had done all he could in Duval, but he'd go over to Alice and see what he could do there. The official told the source that Johnson was calling Parr "several times a day, saying Coke was ahead again."

I asked Johnson if he or any of his people had talked with Parr about Box 13. "We were in touch with every county in Texas," he replied, but "I never saw George Parr." This, obviously, was not an answer.

Salas had been given only about 600 paper ballots for Box 13, but finally reported 1,028 cast. The wife of a prominent lawyer in the Rio Grande Valley was used to fly a packet of election lists to Laredo. She was met at the plane, delivered the packet, and returned to Austin.

Connally said of Box 13, "I know nothing about it. Never went there." Charles I. Francis, the Houston lawyer who had helped George Brown get the government's pipeline, said Johnson "kept his fingers very closely on what *everybody* was doing" and that Francis saw Looney off on a flight to south Texas in Brown's airplane "when all those [votes] were switching back and forth." Homer Dean said Looney and Don Thomas, Johnson's business lawyer, came into Alice right after the election, but Thomas probably "after it was fixed." Later in Austin Thomas was said to have bragged that he had been down there disguised in work clothes.

"I know," said Dean, Johnson's Jim Wells manager, "that Looney and Ed Lloyd were in constant communication after the runoff the minute it became clear there was any trouble. As I recall there were some calls from somebody in Austin, and it was probably Everett, that's just a guess, either Sunday or Monday. Now who told who that they were stealing votes in East Texas and they had better add some down here—I'll never know. I suspect that's what was said—surely it was."

Sunday morning, Johnson's manager continued, "I heard, I guess it was from Ed Lloyd, that they were stealing votes in East Texas and that it was essential that we be sure that every vote was counted. It would be my guess that if there was any skullduggery done—and I believe there was—they justified it that they were fighting fire with fire. . . . The story around was that during the night Sunday, Monday, they took out Box 13, with Luis Salas, and added all those names and put in some ballots." Thus the returns were fixed: "I don't think there's any question that they added a bunch of names and votes," Johnson's county manager told me.

"It was two days after the election, when what happened down here happened," Luis Salas said. "But that's all I'm going to tell you."

John Cofer, one of the Austin lawyers close to Johnson, said he, Connally, and Alvin Wirtz knew Monday morning "that they had put a new certificate (of voting totals) in down in Alice." Who had phoned to tell them this? "Ed Lloyd told John [Connally]," Cofer replied, adding that Lloyd lived in Box 13 and "was devoted to Lyndon."

A basic decision was made then, Cofer told me in an interview in his Austin office. "Lyndon was just raisin' hell," Cofer said. "Wirtz asked my opinion. I said, 'Well, they stole it in '41 and I'd be in favor. Don't announce it until the recount.' " In favor of what? Cofer did not say, but in the context, the question had to be, Shall we accept the extra votes in Box 13, knowing they were surely stolen? Cofer indicated that they knew that morning they had it won in Box 13, although they were off a few votes because of other changes during that wild week. Unmistakably, too, from what Cofer said, Johnson was present and involved as the decision was made to take the stolen votes from Jim Wells and announce them after all the other votes were counted.

Meanwhile Johnson had the problem of preventing other returns from being shifted to Stevenson. H. Y. Price, a liberal politico in central Texas, heard inside the Johnson camp that they had tapped Stevenson's phone, and every time someone called the Stevenson headquarters and said that "We think we can pick up a few votes here," Johnson's people careened to the scene at eighty miles an hour to look over the officials' shoulders.[3]

As far as the public could see, by Tuesday Stevenson had won. The Election Bureau declared in effect he had won because he was leading by 349 votes with only 40 more ballots left to count.

The Johnson people, knowing from the same figures and their vote-shift in Box 13 that when Jim Wells was heard from Johnson would win, could not let the Tuesday impression stand, and Johnson counterattacked, all but saying Stevenson people were stealing votes and hinting Stevenson had stolen the 1941 election. The next day the "last" 40 votes came in and Stevenson's victory held—or so it appeared.[4] Thursday, apparently defying the facts, Johnson said he was "absolutely sure" he had won.

He knew, all right. The next day the Jim Wells officials, including Ed Lloyd, met in Alice and observed, as the county chairman said later, that compared with the Election Bureau's figures for Box 13, "there was a difference" of around 200 votes, and since they were satisfied that "there was no question there," they certified the new total. Between Saturday night and Friday 202 votes had been added, all but 2 of them for Johnson. The figures were changed from 765–60 to 965–62. This tiny alteration, coming, in consonance with John Connally's plan, after all the counting had stopped, reversed the result. Stevenson charged that he was robbed.[5]

The 1948 Senate election was a hinge of history, opening up for Johnson the Senate career that led him to the presidency. Schoolmarms who want to teach the way things are supposed to be, not the way they are, will not tarry long with their pupils over the implications. The career of a president rested on a foundation of theft.

"I think," I said when I first shook hands with Luis Salas in his little frame house in Alice, "I'm looking at the man who made Lyndon Johnson president of the United States."

"That's right, you are," he said.

"The election was stolen," he told me. In Box 13? "Yes." He felt sympathy for Coke. "That was a dirty thing we did to him," he said.

Before he died, he said, he was going to tell the story, in a book on his life. "People in town think I stole the election. And I didn't. I know who did, and how they did it, and when they did it." He had taken the rap? "That's right," he said. "I'm the only survivor, the only one who knows. All the rest of them are dead now."

He shook his head. "This American politics is worse than Mexican politics. American politics is run by hypocrites. Mexican politics is run by guns."

Before he died, Salas told the Associated Press that on the third day after the election, Tuesday, Johnson met with Parr, Ed Lloyd, Salas, and an Alice official in Parr's office in San Diego, Texas. This is how the conversation went, according to Salas:

Johnson: "If I can get 200 more votes, I've got it won."

Parr to Salas in Spanish: "I want you to add those 200 votes."

Salas said he would, and "When I left, Johnson knew we were going to take care of the situation."

Walter Jenkins said he was with Johnson all that day in Austin and it was impossible he could have gone south to Alice. Other Johnson people piled in decrying the story. A crack reporter, Bo Byers, said he was at Johnson's house in Austin from morning to night and such a trip was "highly improbable."[6]

---

57. Ballots Burning in a Dust Storm

The Texas Senate seat was stolen for Johnson. *Who stole it?* That was one question. In a recount, *would it have stayed stolen?* That was another one, posed by Johnson's contention that more fraudulent votes were cast for Stevenson than for him. Wasn't it really *fair* that the election was stolen for Johnson? Some thought so, since Stevenson had been a suspect and beneficiary when Johnson had a Senate seat stolen from him in 1941. Wasn't it *better* to let it be stolen for Johnson than to have Stevenson win? Leading Texas liberals, without any exceptions that have survived in the record, thought so. Possession is the first nine tenths of the law, and politics is the tenth.

By every legal stratagem available to him, Johnson obstructed any investigation of Box 13. He went into state court to prevent officials of Jim Wells County from changing the late-reported figures. In federal court he sought to stop a judicial investigation. He resisted a court-ordered examination of the ballots in the south Texas boss counties, including the ballots in Box 13. He alleged fraud in other counties he said would give him a majority even without Box 13—but he opposed judicial investigation of his own allegations. He was not going to stand back again. If votes were stolen for him, the other side had stolen more than his had—they'd stolen it from him in 1941 anyway, now it was his and he was going to keep it.

In and out of court the Stevenson partisans demanded to look at, simply to see, the records of Box 13. The new Democratic chairman in Jim Wells, Harry Lee Adams, asked that the man who had them, outgoing party secretary B. F. (Tom) Donald, produce them, and Donald refused to do it. The records were locked in the vault of the Texas State Bank, of which George Parr was the president and Tom Donald the cashier. The county party committee turned to the state party asking for an investigation on grounds that more than two hundred people had been shown as voting who did not.

Deciding to go to Alice himself, Stevenson ran into the Ranger Frank Hamer, who had been one of a posse of lawmen who had ambushed Bonnie and Clyde, and Hamer said, "Well, I'll just go down there with you." People told a Stevenson lawyer that if he was going down there he had better take a gun. Two Stevenson men, Kellis Dibrell and James Gardner, decided to go, too, and Dibrell decreed that they would not take guns—they would not even wear coats so everybody could see they were not armed.

When Stevenson's group arrived in Alice the town was vibrating like a beehive. By some reports, armed Parr men stood in front of the bank guarding it, but when the lone Ranger ordered them to get away, they did, and he took his stand, pistol in his holster, where they had been. Hamer did stand guard outside the door while Stevenson was inside trying to get the records. People stood around outside and across the street, watching.

"I'm Coke Stevenson," the former governor told Tom Donald, "and what I'd like to see is the tally sheet and other papers of the primary."

Donald called the county attorney to the bank and Stevenson repeated his request.

"No," said the county attorney.

"I thought they were open to the public," Stevenson told them. "Up in our country we do it that way—let anybody look at 'em."

"We don't do it that way," the county attorney replied.

Donald let Adams, the new county chairman who was a member of Stevenson's group, go back into the vault and look at the records, but told him he could not remove anything.

"I was alone," Adams told me. "He left me in there—had a call or something. I found that two hundred and some-odd names had been added to the end of the voters' list [in Box 13]. At the end there was a few over two hundred added to this list in a different colored ink and a different handwriting than the other, and I believe that they were alphabetically put down. I got around a dozen of the names, scattered through there. I was in a hurry—I was afraid they'd stop me. . . ."

Donald did indeed return from his phone call and tell Adams, "You've had plenty of time." Gardner made a few quick notes from the list before Donald asked him to stop. Gardner testified that all the names up to the name numbered 841 were written in blue ink, but all the roughly 200 names from then on were written in black ink. He also said the certification of the vote had been changed so that the total for Johnson, 965, had been changed from 765, with the top bar of the "7" altered into a loop to make it a "9". Dibrell said that from what they saw they concluded the last 200 names were written down in the same handwriting in alphabetical order.

Stevenson and his men left the bank and the town empty-handed, except for notes they had made in their hotel rooms.[1] Johnson obtained, from an Austin judge, an order telling the officials in Alice they could not change their election returns even if they found fraud. Johnson's petition charged Stevenson and others with a conspiracy to have some votes eliminated in Alice. "I only want the votes I got," Johnson said. But Harry Adams said this court order in effect told him, "Even if it was stolen, you're not to do anything."[2]

With both men claiming victory and skullduggery, the action shifted to the state Democratic convention that would have to certify one of them the winner. Midnight on Sunday before the Tuesday convention in Fort Worth, Democratic chairman Calvert ran into Vann Kennedy, the state party secretary. Kennedy smiled.

"Would you like to know who won the Senate race?" he asked.

"Well," Calvert replied, "I must confess I have a little curiosity about it."

"Johnson won it by eighty-seven votes."

"Is that so? Damn close."

The party secretary had added up the official returns, and Box 13 was the difference.

The party's executive committee, meeting Monday night, had to recommend whom the convention should certify as the winner. The vote was so close, every member mattered. One of them had a heart attack in the lobby of a hotel, and while he was lying prostrate on the floor Wirtz had him sign a proxy for Johnson.

As the meeting opened, "the whole atmosphere was tension," said Calvert, who was presiding. "The room was packed, absolutely packed, people standing around the walls." The debate was vicious. Johnson and Stevenson sat about ten feet apart, listening, Stevenson puffing on his pipe. "I'm here to prevent the stuffing of the ballot box," a Stevenson lawyer shouted. John Cofer declared, "You are not going to deprive [Johnson] of this election on the affidavits obtained from a few Mexicans." Ed Lloyd berated Stevenson's "goon squad."

The voting began. A proxy for Johnson was challenged; a notarized statement was produced. Johnson people were scouring the hotel for committee member Charles Gibson of Amarillo, absent because of a headache or a drunk or both. George Parr's sister, Mrs. Marie Thompson, perversely was for Stevenson, but significantly, she was not present, either. When the roll call ended Johnson was ahead by two—but a woman rose and switched her vote, causing a tie. Presiding, Calvert thought, "What about Mrs. Thompson? Do I call for her before I do anything about voting myself?" Stalling, still worrying, he was saved by the arrival of Charley Gibson. The crowd so packed he could not move through it, Gibson stood on a chair and called out, "What is it, Mr. Chairman—what are we voting on?" Told, he voted, and Johnson won twenty-nine to twenty-eight. Somebody pushed over the chair Gibson was standing on.

Ed Clark rushed down and threw his arm around Lyndon. From then on, Cofer said, "Ed Clark was on our side." Johnson, embracing the wobbly Gibson, said, "God bless you, Charley." Lyndon's brother, who claimed that he himself had found Gibson drunk in a bathroom soaking his head in the washbasin, said that afterward dozens of people claimed credit for producing him, and eventually Johnson solemnly thanked thirty or forty people for it.

After Calvert announced the result, a county chairman from east Texas sidled up to him and said, "By the way, I want to file an amended certificate. Stevenson got a good many more votes than we reported. Will you revise the vote?" "I tell you what," Calvert replied, "if you will revise the certificate, and put it under oath, for whatever consequences might be attendant to that action, I'll take it up with the committee." The man decided not.

A twenty-seven-member minority of the committee informed the convention that "palpable fraud and irregularities" had "undoubtedly produced" Johnson's eighty-seven-vote margin,[3] but Johnson had won the fight within the party. The committee vote, combined with the fact that on grounds of party disloyalty the pro-Truman liberals in control were determined to throw out large right-wing delegations that were favorable to Stevenson, gave Johnson an easy triumph in the full convention. Helping elect Truman and opposing the conservative Stevenson became, among the liberals, sufficient justification for siding with Johnson.

Bob Eckhardt, a CIO lobbyist (later a congressman from Houston), said, "Johnson was interested in preventing Box 13 from being opened, and we were interested in kicking out the Texas Regulars, and operating on a sort of deal of convenience, we controlled the convention. His major purpose was not to permit the opening of Box 13. It seemed much more important to a lot of us, including Maury Maverick, Sr., that there not be a bunch of [presidential] electors that could throw away the Texas votes," denying them to Truman.[4]

Thus it was that the state convention declared that Johnson won by less than one-tenth of one percent of the votes, 494,191 to 494,104. The delegates understood that George Parr was the man of the hour: he was asked to address them. Years later when Allan Shivers, then governor, was fighting Johnson, he charged that Sam Rayburn, presiding in Fort Worth, called Johnson and Parr to the platform, that Rayburn and Johnson put their arms around Parr, "And Mr. Sam Rayburn said, 'I present the hero of the Democratic Party in Texas, the savior of our cause.' " A delegate who happened to be seated behind the pro-Stevenson Potter County delegation while Parr spoke said, "Oh! you talk about people being incensed. There were some people in there, if they'da had a gun they'da shot him." A photograph was taken of Johnson and Parr, with a lot of lawyers crowding in.[5]

About a week later Calvert and former Governor Allred ran into each other in the lobby of an Austin hotel. "Now governor, tell me *really,*" Calvert said, "don't you think that somebody added 201 votes after the polls closed in Box 13 and cast 'em for Johnson?"

"Well," responded the man Johnson would soon restore to his judgeship, "I tell you one thing, the Stevenson people stole that election in 1941 with some east Texas counties so Stevenson could become governor when O'Daniel won, and if the Johnson people stole this one they were just getting things all squared up!" Allred told Calvert an FBI report proved the 1941 election had been stolen in three or four deep east Texas counties where the Ferguson people were strong.[6]

From the convention Stevenson dispatched a lawyer on an all-night drive to the east Texas ranch of T. Whitfield Davidson, a reactionary who sat on the federal bench in Dallas. Davidson, fussing around after rising at daybreak in accordance with his custom, read Stevenson's complaint and, at 6:25 A.M., wrote out a court order and scheduled a hearing. This kept the state from putting Johnson on the ballot.

To contest a state primary, why hadn't Stevenson first gone into state courts? "I defied him to do it," Johnson told me. "Why didn't he do it?" The answer, Johnson said, was that Stevenson knew that, since in state courts he could not have kept the case narrowed to Box 13, Johnson would have gained fifteen hundred votes in Archer County and more elsewhere. Stevenson told me his lawyers had convinced him that the primary involved a federal office and that the federal courts would take cognizance of "an invasion of my civil rights." One of his agents said that to use the state courts they would have had to start in Alice, which was "all Lloyd" (that is, all Johnson).

To Judge Davidson, Stevenson charged that Box 13 was stuffed, giving Johnson his margin, and that by faulty arithmetic Johnson had been given 106 illegal votes in Zapata. Later Stevenson charged Duval County with fraud on the face of it in giving Johnson 99.4 percent.

In a gleaming, high-ceilinged courtroom, filled with a hundred people, the gray-haired little Davidson presided over a two-day hearing. Stevenson had ten lawyers, Johnson eight; each side had an ex-governor. A feather in her hat, Bird sat with her husband. He looked toward Stevenson several times without drawing a return glance. After lunch, though, Stevenson, walking down the hall on his way to the men's room and passing Johnson on his way to the courtroom, raised a right hand in greeting. "Howdy," said Lyndon. Neither broke stride.

Mexican-Americans whom Adams had noted down among the last 202 voters in Box 13 swore they had not voted. The woman listed as having voted at the point where the ink changed color said she hadn't, either. One of the 202 lived in a different precinct. Another said he worked all night before the election and slept through election day. A twenty-one-year-old student among the 202 said that on the day of the election he was 190 miles away. In one affidavit, a Mexican-American who voted just before the ink changed color said he voted near closing time and did not see anyone else there. In a second affidavit, produced by Johnson's side, the same fellow said he'd signed the first one without knowing what it said because he was afraid.

Johnson figured that because of ballot frauds and other factors, even if the votes Stevenson challenged were thrown out Johnson would still win by 191 votes.[7]

Judge Davidson pleasantly offered to authorize an immediate inquiry into every county questioned, but the Johnson people replied they could not give time to it in the next few days.

Well, then, Davidson proposed, let's run the election over. The winner under these circumstances would probably serve only one term, the judge said. His idea was that both their names be put on the November ballot. He later remembered that, the lawyers drawn close to the bench, he said, "Gentlemen . . . you have here two men either of whom would serve with honor, but to let either of them go to Washington under a cloud would be unfortunate."

Stevenson agreed at once, but Johnson told the press no comment. "All of Lyndon's lawyers went into conference," Luther Jones (one of them) said. "I shall never forget the way Lyndon took over in that conference. He was firm. He directed that we stand up to the judge and fight. He said he would never yield to tyranny, no matter what its form might be, and that he regarded the judge's suggestion as nothing less than an unwarranted exercise of power." After lunch a lawyer gave Johnson's refusal.[8]

Finding "a prima facie showing of fraud" in Box 13, Zapata, and Duval that had been sufficient to elect Johnson, the judge ordered a trial and named two special masters to hold immediate inquiries in the three challenged counties and report back to him fast. Reporters and lawyers flocked to south Texas.[9] Johnson, seeing that Davidson was probably going to order Stevenson onto the ballot as the nominee, turned then to judicial and presidential politics at the very highest levels. Although the evidence on what happened next is sketchy, it is clear that from this point on, politics counted at least as much as law.

Johnson's many lawyers met with him in a Fort Worth hotel room to make plans. Throughout the day lawyer after lawyer theorized, spun stories, rambled on. Hearing that Abe Fortas was in Dallas, Johnson summoned him, and Fortas took charge. Hugo Black, one of the most liberal members of the U.S. Supreme Court, was the senior justice for the area that included Texas. Fortas's plan was to file a quick appeal to the federal appeals court and then go directly to Black. In two bounds of the kangaroo they could take their case from a right-wing judge to a left-wing one.

Like most people Johnson thought Truman could not win the presidency, in part because of his civil rights program was so hated by white southerners, but when Truman's train zipped into Texas Johnson saw a chance to get help.[10]

By one account, when the train stopped in San Antonio Truman talked with George Parr for half an hour. A source very close to Parr said the *patrón* visited with Truman in a hotel room during this stop, receiving important assurances, but did not travel north with the presidential party. Johnson joined the train in San Antonio and thereafter appeared on the back platform with the president. It would be impossible to believe Johnson did not tell Truman about Fortas's plan to go to Black.

There were allegations, *sotto voce,* that someone powerful spoke to Black in advance of his ruling. A Texas lobbyist with good Democratic connections said Speaker Rayburn called Black and told him to stay out of Texas elections, but when I asked Black about this, he flatly denied it. Wright Morrow, the Democratic national committeeman for Texas who was close to Judge Davidson, said, "Whit Davidson definitely believed that Truman or somebody spoke to Black and suggested he do it," while John Connally, Roy Hofheinz (later mayor of Houston) and Charles I. Francis were "said to have spoken to Black." Such suspicions, extraordinary for that period, showed how deep emotions were running.

Jack Carter, a member of the state party committee, said he saw that on the Truman train somewhere between Fort Worth and Bonham, Johnson became convinced he was in. In the morning Johnson had been gloomy, "a defeated man," but in Bonham he was the victor. "Something happened between Fort Worth and Bonham," Carter said.

The Truman party left the train in Bonham to visit Rayburn's well-kept, two-story board house five miles outside of town. Johnson worked the group, going around in a big Texas hat rounding up members of the state party committee to attend a meeting shortly before midnight under a big tree in Rayburn's back yard. So convened, the committee authorized a federal court action to stop the south Texas inquiries and dismiss Stevenson's suit. This action, taken in Johnson's emergency meeting right after the train ride with Truman, provided the legal foundation for Fortas's strategy.

A federal circuit judge said he could not stay Davidson's hand. After another foray into the circuit court, thirteen lawyers signed Johnson's motion for presentation to Black. The big names were former Interior Undersecretary Fortas, former U.S. Attorney General Thurman Arnold, former Assistant Secretary of the Interior Wirtz, and ex-Governor Allred.[11]

As Davidson's agents raced to complete their hearings in south Texas, Johnson's lawyers deployed themselves to obstruct the investigations. "When Lyndon stole that election there in south Texas," said Polk Shelton, the Austin lawyer who had run against Johnson in 1937, "I represented him in Duval and Zapata counties." And what did he remember? "Well, what I remember, I can't say. . . . I remember too much, I'll put it that way!"

In Zapata, Davidson's master was told there were no poll tax lists of voters because "the election judges knew everybody in the county." The county judge, M. B. Bravo, said he could not check the challenged arithmetic because one of the precinct returns was gone.

In Duval County the master ran into a Mexican dust storm or "I don't remember's" and "I don't know's." Only eight of the more than fifty witnesses called could even be found. The party chairman was "on vacation" and nine precinct judges and more than thirty other judges and clerks were out of town, or ill, or something. The county judge said he did not know the names of the precinct judges at Rosita, Realitos, Copita, Mindieta, Juahill, Freer, or Sejila. A lawyer who handled questioning at the Duval hearing, Joe Montague, told me that none of the precincts in the county had even filed returns with county officials.

For the main show in Alice, the home of Box 13, Coke turned up, puffing his pipe. Tom Donald, who had locked the Box 13 records in the vault at George Parr's bank, was traced to a hotel in Monterey, Mexico, from which there was no way to dislodge him.

That morning in Justice Black's office in Washington, Fortas, while deploring election fraud, argued that "for a federal judge to deprive a nominee of his rights is worse than for it to be done by some election judge in the Rio Grande Valley." For Stevenson ex-Governor Dan Moody argued the voters had been deprived of their civil rights by the fraud for Johnson. Black did not doubt the alleged fraud was covered by civil rights statutes. Wirtz told the judge, "They are trying to dress up a political contest in abstract phrases of the law." Black wondered why Stevenson had not gone to state court. Moody said no time. "What about the Senate?" Black asked.

Back down in Alice, with Donald gone Luis Salas took the heat. Where were his records of Box 13? He had made three copies, but his copy was lost. He had borrowed Donald's copy, but left it in his car one night when he went into Juan Flores's cantina and drank about half a dozen beers, "and when I come back they stole everything from the car." So the only copy not lost or stolen should have been inside Box 13. Learning that in Washington Black had just ordered the investigation stopped, Johnson's lawyers called for a halt in Alice, but the Stevenson people, arguing they had not been formally notified, dropped Salas and turned at once to Box 13 itself.

Actually it was a tin can. Its custodian had testified that after the election she had hidden it. Now Davidson's master ordered a federal marshal to cut the piece of baling wire that was keeping it closed. When the marshal hesitated, the master took the clippers and cut the wire himself. Inside the can were ballots, but no tally sheet and, worst of all, no poll list. Foiled! The investigators could not prove fraud without the list matching each voter to each ballot.

At two-fifteen that afternoon a wire arrived ordering the investigation stopped, and it was. Black said the issue was "whether a federal court should decide which man goes on the ballot." Johnson, moving left at once now that the moderates had no place else to go, hailed the ruling as a blow against the oil company lawyers who had been trying to deprive him of his victory.

That night Tom Donald, returning home from Monterey, said, "I understand someone was looking for me." The missing records were never found. They were seen by a lawyer in the offices of an Austin law firm closely associated with Johnson; possibly someone has preserved them all these years. Two party officials who might know what happened to them were Clarence Martens, the Jim Wells County chairman, and Tom Donald. "I'll be damned if I know," Martens told me. Donald, kind of kidding, said, "I might tell the story if I could make some money out of it—couple of million dollars, say."[12]

In Texas Democratic nomination meant election, and Johnson felt now that he was carrying forward his family's heritage, realizing his mother's ambition for him and making up for his father's failure.[13] He turned at once to helping raise money for Truman.

A meeting of Truman's finance committee early in October, 1948, in Washington, which Johnson attended, was held to raise thirty-nine-thousand dollars so Truman could make a radio speech in Pittsburgh. Johnson exclaimed, "I can't get a damn Texan who used to give $5,000 from every member of his family for Roosevelt to answer the damn phone!" Wright Morrow, the Houston oilman, was not a Truman man, but he was a party official, and he told Johnson he would put up ten thousand dollars if the balance of the thirty-nine thousand was raised. The next day an exuberant Johnson phoned Morrow that the rest had been raised and Truman was "absolutely thrilled."[14]

But Johnson himself faced a body politic poisoned by the stolen votes. The Democrats, already "socialists and nigger-lovers" to the rightists, now were thieves to boot. Lynn Landrum was the sharpest columnist in the most potent reactionary newspaper in the state, the *Dallas Morning News,* and in six columns in October, avoiding overstatement, Landrum coldly condemned Johnson as a man lacking honor, finally provoking him to passionate retort.[15]

When investigators from a U.S. Senate subcommittee tried to obtain the ballots in Duval County, it developed that the courthouse janitor had burned them a week before the law allowed it.[16] Despite Stevenson's pledge to support the nominee of the primary, he endorsed the Republican, calling Johnson the Democrats' "counterfeit nominee." Johnson name-called back: Stevenson was a turncoat without conscience, a poor loser, and a cry-baby, and as for "that oil-stained Jolly Roger" the Republican Senate nominee H. J. (Jack) Porter, he was the candidate of "pirates of privilege." Although the anti-oil crusader again, Johnson was still the chief anti-Communist, saying that when Russia decided she could attack the U.S. successfully, "she'll do it."

Johnson won two-to-one in the general election, but he received forty-eight-thousand fewer of the million votes that were cast than Truman did, and Porter received sixty-seven thousand more than Truman's opponent, Thomas E. Dewey. Johnson issued a bitter statement berating the mud-slingers, character assassins, and renegade Democrats, but concluding that everyone should join together for a unified nation.[17] Then as again, he simultaneously vilified his opponents and called for unity behind himself.

The janitor had burned the ballots in Duval; the Senate's investigators had wasted their time in Alice, too, learning (or so they thought) that all ballots cast in Box 13 were destroyed. Had the Republicans taken over the U.S. Senate that November, Johnson might have been, as columnist Arthur Krock wrote, "barred at the door," but the Democrats had control, the Senate investigating committee indicated that hearings would be "of no avail," and in 1949 the Senate's committees quietly approved Johnson's election. A grand jury in Alice, slamming the barn door with a horse-laugh, found that there was "complete lack of responsibility" in the handling of ballots in the August primary and recommended getting "new election boxes with good locks."[18]

When the *Dallas News* had called for an investigation of the election, Johnson had suggested the FBI do it. Fine, said the *News,* but not without remarking that the new U.S. attorney general, Tom Clark, was a friend of Johnson's.

A month later the *Dallas News* editorialized that Clark had "said there would be an investigation. The matter was turned over to an assistant and then to an assistant's assistant. Two months have passed and absolutely nothing has been done." The next day in Washington Alex Campbell, assistant attorney general, ordered an FBI investigation of the election in four unnamed Texas counties, according to an FBI statement.

Almost three decades later, shocked by the public statements of Luis Salas, the Johnson Library opened eight boxes of materials on the 1948 campaign. What these materials showed, mainly, was that the best that could be said of the FBI's performance in the case was that the investigation was muffed. At worst, it could be concluded that the FBI refused to look for evidence of the criminal offenses that must have been committed at Luis Salas's Box 13.[19]

---

58. Aftermaths and a Photograph

While some Stevenson people admitted stealing on their side, too, others never stopped crying "Thief!" and few of Johnson's men had the face to deny the theft in Box 13.[1] Johnson would disavow any wrongdoing, but he became known as "Landslide Lyndon," and he paid pained attention to what people said about the election long after it was over.[2] According to my source close to Parr, Johnson continued to go by San Diego to see Parr after 1948 and was even closer to him than before. Lyndon would communicate with Parr, this source said, through an officeholder from the South Texas area, who would then talk to Parr. Generally Johnson avoided doing favors for Parr or Lloyd, although he did several for Salas;[3] but there was one sequel to the election that seemed, for a time, to endanger Johnson politically.

Sam Smithwick, a deputy sheriff in Alice, heard that a radio commentator in the town, who had been crusading against a beer joint Smithwick owned, was going to mention one of Smithwick's children on a noon broadcast. The official sought the radio man out, drew a .45, and shot him dead. For this he got a life term in the state prison at Huntsville. Salas told me he received a penciled note from the imprisoned Smithwick asking him to ask Parr and Lloyd for help, but that when Salas showed Parr the note he refused to help. Salas pleaded for Smithwick. "Well, he did wrong," Parr said. "So did you! So did you!" Salas exclaimed, and from then on he had no more to do with Parr.

Two years later Smithwick wrote Coke Stevenson, giving him the names of two Mexican-Americans he said had told him, five days before he murdered the radio commentator, that they had been given the stolen Box 13 by a Mexican-American election official, whom Smithwick also named. Writing to the prison superintendent with the help of an inmate-aide, Smithwick informed Stevenson he had received the box from the two "and am quite sure that I can produce it if you are interested." He asked Stevenson to come to the prison to see him.

The letter, addressed to Stevenson at the State capitol and presumably rerouted to Stevenson's ranch, arrived when the former governor was away. "When I read it," Stevenson said, "I began making my preparations to go over there. I had left the ranch and got as far as Junction, when I got the information that he was dead." Three weeks after Smithwick had written Stevenson, he had been found hanging from his prison bars.

Stevenson released the letter and said his position that the election had been stolen from him "had been vindicated." Regarded as a probable candidate against Johnson in 1954, he said he thought the letter would help him win. Parr accused Stevenson of framing the letter to get ready to run. Salas told me Smithwick knew nothing about Box 13 and was just trying to get out of prison, and at the time of the incident Johnson implied the same explanation. In a statement from Washington the senator said, "I don't know what a convicted murderer might have done prior to committing suicide in an attempt to get released from prison," but Stevenson's disclosure of the letter was "a continuation of a fight by a group of disgruntled, disappointed people."

There was no evidence to prove that Smithwick was murdered. George Beto, later a director of the prison system, reviewed the records as he found them and became convinced that Smithwick killed himself by tying a towel to some bars and around his neck and slipping off his bunk, strangling himself. From what Beto could figure out, Smithwick had a game leg, had been "hearing voices," and was found hanged on a medical cell-row which the officials at the time said no other inmate could have penetrated.

Yet, the letter had been read by the authorities at the prison before it was mailed, and Stevenson seemed to take its contents at face value. Suspicions festered.

Parr had turned against the Texas governor, Allan Shivers, in 1950 when Shivers had refused Parr's request that he appoint Luther Jones, Johnson's friend, a district judge. Two years later Shivers, stirred to action by another murder in Alice, set the state's legal dogs loose on Parr, and the Duke of Duval was indicted on charges of income tax evasion and conspiracy to use the mails to defraud. None of the charges stuck.[4]

In 1956, when Shivers and Johnson were fighting each other for

JOHNSON LIBRARY

Johnson campaigns for reelection in 1946 with the assistance of cowboy singer-actor Gene Autry, left, and a band.

Texas Governor Coke Stevenson, called "Calculatin' Coke," who was Johnson's opponent in the historic 1948 Senate election.

EXPRESS-NEWS CORP.

In a daring innovation, Johnson campaigned for the Senate in 1948 by helicopter, gathering crowds in fields (as at Hillsboro, Texas, on June 23, 1948, top photo) and causing a commotion on the main street of another Texas town, unidentified, below.

ON THE FACING PAGE: Above, Johnson reclines on his couch in Austin as he receives returns in the runoff for the Senate in 1948. At left are staffers Mary Rather and Walter Jenkins. Below, Johnson and Lady Bird get some more returns, probably in the back yard of their Austin home.

AP PHOTOS

LUIS SALAS

PRECINCT
13
TEXAS-48
D
S 9565

Above, leaders in the George Parr machine pose with a Box 13 ballot box. President Johnson, after rummaging around in his wife's bedroom in the White House in 1967, showed the author this photograph, grinning broadly, but would not explain it or give it up. Later Luis Salas, the Box 13 election judge who admitted he doctored the returns, gave the author a copy of the photograph and said it was taken the day of the 1948 runoff primary, at Box 13 in Alice, Texas, before the polls closed. Left to right are police chief Stokes Micenheimer, Hubert Sain, Givens Parr (a cousin of George Parr), Jim Wells County Parr boss Ed Lloyd (steadying the ballot box on the nose of the car), and Barney Goldthorn. A copy of the picture is also on file in the Johnson Library.

An unidentified man seated with ballot boxes during the hearings on the 1948 Senate election in south Texas September 9–13, 1948.

JOHNSON LIBRARY

Inside President Truman's whistlestop train during the 1948 Texas Senate election crisis. Truman is striding toward Speaker Sam Rayburn, who is at the far right. Johnson is just behind Truman; next to Johnson, also standing, is Texas Governor Beaford Jester. Seated, second from the left, is Truman's attorney general, Tom Clark of Texas. Shortly after this train trip, events cascaded to confirm Johnson as the winner of the election over Coke Stevenson.

political control, "Shivers charged me with *murder,*" Johnson, with great incredulity, told me. Speaking from his four-poster bed late one night in the White House, Johnson said that Shivers had made a speech accusing him of Smithwick's murder, and in San Antonio "the reporters came running up to me saying Shivers had charged me with murder, and what did I have to say about it?" Obviously Johnson had dismissed the charge, but he did not say so, rather repeating indignantly, "Shivers said I was a *murderer!*" Shivers, shown this account of what Johnson said, told me, "I don't care to discuss it."[5]

So, Box 13 was a grievous subject with Johnson; yet he could laugh about it. That same night in the White House, rambling about other subjects in his bedroom, he thought of something suddenly and told me to wait a minute, he wanted to go find something to show me, it was in Bird's bedroom somewhere, maybe in the closet. He walked through the door connecting his room to hers, and I whiled away the time, five minutes, maybe ten, listening to the sounds of things being hefted around in the next room. He emerged beaming, he'd found it!—a photograph. He held it forward to me with a kind of pride: a picture of five men, all of them grinning, standing beside or sitting on the front fenders of an automobile of the forties, one of them balancing a ballot box marked "Precinct 13" on the rounded hood of the car, and another one —a Parr, I was pretty sure—apparently laughing tightly from some inner delight, such as a secret that he knows.

The president watched my face as I searched the photograph for its meaning. As I got it, I guess my amazement (particularly at his whimsy showing it to me) was funny to him, and he grinned at me with a vast inner enjoyment. I grinned back at him. Here these guys were, posing for a photograph that seemed to mean they were in on some secret about Box 13, and here *we* were, the president of the United States and I, grinning together with them, in his bedroom in the White House twenty years later.

I asked him to tell me who they were, what it meant, when it had been taken, where—but nothing, nothing, he would not say a word. He carried the picture back to its place in his wife's room. When I brought it up again the next day he smiled and talked of other things.

A few years after that I was talking with Luis Salas in his little house in Alice. Without telling him who had showed the photograph to me, I described it to him and asked him if he knew about it. "Yes, I know the one you mean!" he exclaimed, lighting up. Out back of his house there was a small bedroom-office, and for half an hour he rummaged about, finally finding a copy of the same photograph. He gave it to me. The fat man was the chief of police—Givens Parr was in it, too. Salas said it was taken the day of the 1948 runoff primary, at Box 13, before the polls closed.[6]

PART XII
Darting to the Top

This is the time to think what we are doing because, as soon as a war gets started, few people do any more thinking about anything except demolishing the enemy.... We have seen, in our most recent wars, how a divided and arguing public opinion may be converted overnight into a national near-unanimity, an obedient flood of energy which will carry the young to destruction and overpower any effort to stem it. The unanimity of men at war is like that of a school of fish, which will swerve, simultaneously and apparently without leadership, when the shadow of an enemy appears, or like a sky-darkening flight of grasshoppers, which, also all compelled by one impulse, will descend to consume the crops.

— Edmund Wilson, *Patriotic Gore,* 1962

59. "Rising on the Senate Floor"

What the politician wanted from the next six years was power in the Senate and reelection in Texas. Strolling as nonchalantly as he could into the cockpit of American political power, secretly he was insecure. Berated at home as a man of no principle because of his scuttled New Deal convictions and his stolen election, he turned to the southern lords of the all-white Senate for his next gains.

That December in Washington, Johnson heard about a twenty-year-old hustler from South Carolina, Bobby Baker, who had already become the Senate's "chief telephone page" and was in fact its chief staff tactician on legislative business. Phoning the prodigy, Johnson drawled, "Mr. Baker, I understand you know where the bodies are buried in the Senate. I'd appreciate it if you'd come to my office. . . ." When Baker came, the new senator did not waste words. "I want to know who's the power over there, how you get things done, the best committees, the works," and what about this senator, and that one? For two hours he interrogated Baker, who was impressed.

Johnson asked Baker to spread the word among national Democrats that he would be out of tune with them. ". . . my state is much more conservative than the national Democratic party," he said. "I got elected by just 87 votes and I ran against a caveman." To remain a senator he could not always vote with Truman, who was "about as popular as measles in Texas, and you'll waste your time trying to talk to me when I know it would cut my own throat to help him." He would vote for Taft-Hartley ("labor's not much stronger in Texas than a pop-corn fart"), against civil rights, and he would favor deregulating natural gas and state ownership of tidelands oil—"Frankly, Mr. Baker, I'm for nearly anything the big oil boys want because they hold the whip hand and I represent 'em. Yeah, I represent farmers and working men," but "the New Deal spirit's gone from Texas and I'm limited in what I can do." When Baker wondered if it was smart to spread such news about himself so soon, Johnson replied, "I know my own pasture better than my neighbor knows it."

The southerners were in control—"It was perfectly obvious in the caucuses that the southerners ran it," said another newcomer that year, Hubert Humphrey of Minnesota. Make a beeline to power—so Johnson had advised his cousin in college, so he had always done, himself. In the Senate, upon whom could he most shrewdly practice his art of protégé-ship? First there had been the college president, then Roy Miller, Kleberg, Maverick, Roosevelt himself, Speaker Rayburn, Chairman Vinson. The Senate was a new kind of challenge. A gentleman's club ruled by crusty hierarchs, each member fancying himself a figure in the nation's ruling set, this place would have to be conquered through its own tunnels and trap-doors of vanities, seniorities, and taboos.

"In the beginning," Humphrey said, "I noticed that he wasn't pushing. He was working his way into the apparatus." From the hour Lyndon was sworn in, Allen Ellender of Louisiana saw how he began to move into the influential group. "He knew whom to talk to. He knew who had a little influence. . . . Among the first he tackled for assistance was Richard Russell of Georgia," whom he had met at the Room. Sometimes after tippling there, Russell would go to supper at Johnson's. As Russell had visited Texas and had a good knowledge of Texas history, liking Lyndon came easily to him, but "I knew," Johnson said, "there was only one way to see Russell every day, and that was to get a seat on his committee. Without that we'd most likely be passing acquaint-ances and nothing more." With a recommendation from Vinson, Johnson won a seat on the armed services committee where Russell was the second-ranking Democrat. Having gained his new daddy's side, Johnson then courted him so shamelessly, the very transparency of it signified the competitive advantage of the newcomer who was willing to do it.

A bachelor who read a lot and drank alone, Russell's real home was the Capitol. Noticing that the Georgian took breakfast there and stayed late enough to have dinner across the street, Lyndon deliberately worked late, too, to be there to take some suppers with him. Sundays, all alone, Russell was glad to be invited to the Johnsons' for breakfast, lunch, or just to read the day's bulky newspapers. Soon he was taking most of his weekend meals with the Johnsons, and Lynda and Luci, coached to do so, began calling him "Uncle Dick."[1]

Not incidentally, Johnson had also chosen his major workload in the Senate to advance, not his policy purposes, but his career. On armed services he could be both a cat and a hawk. (As he would later say, on military preparedness he had learned under Vinson, but took his postgraduate work under Russell.)

The politician's antennae, vibrating to future throngs, may already have sensed he would eventually make a turn against racism. "Johnson did not consider himself a southerner, and he knew he could not be its captive," Humphrey said. He was "a Texan, enjoying the benefits of southern hospitality, southern power, southern support, but who carefully avoided the liabilities of being clearly labeled a southerner." Like the new senator from Tennessee, Estes Kefauver, Johnson shied away from the newly organized southern caucus, veering off from it after attending its first meeting. Truman told Kefauver of his satisfaction "that you and Lyndon are not permanently lined up with that crowd."

But Johnson's top staffer John Connally said his man was a conservative that year, "very much so," and "Walter George [also of Georgia] and Dick Russell were really his teachers." At the one meeting of the southern caucus he did attend he sided with Russell on strategy in fighting a proposed change in the filibuster rule, and a few days later Russell tipped off reporters that the newcomer from Texas would make a speech worth a story.[2] In this, his maiden speech, Johnson cocked his stances toward the future when he might need black votes to win the presidency and at the same time ingratiated himself to Russell and the whole southern bloc.

The Truman liberals had proposed that when two-thirds of the Senate so voted, debate would stop after another two hours. The filibuster issue was just what Johnson needed, a procedural dispute that was emotionally gaudy enough to package a cagily chosen mix of positions. The rules change would have helped prevent the white southerners from holding down the blacks the way they always had, teaming up and talking indefinitely. Nor was the reform academic: Truman's stiff civil rights bills were pending.

"Rising on the Senate floor" (as they say) for the first time, Johnson upheld "the freedom of unlimited debate in legislative chambers," condemned "mass-produced minorities," and worried about powerful presidents with large legislative majorities. But this, he alleged, did not ally him with "the strong and evil forces of racial prejudice" because blacks needed the filibuster, too, to prevent passage of "vicious legislation" against them.

He granted that filibusters had killed bills against lynching and the poll tax and for fair employment practices, but one by one he argued that these proposals had been well killed. Federal abolition of the poll tax would be unconstitutional; the states should do that. He detested lynchings as much as anyone, but still, he opposed the antilynching bill because it "would indict as killers men and women who never held a gun in their hands." As for Truman's Fair Employment Practices Commission (the "FEPC" then notorious throughout the South), he argued sophistically that "If the law can compel me to employ a Negro, it can compel that Negro to work for me" and thus "would do nothing more than enslave a minority." In short, "We cannot legislate love."[3]

It was a virtuoso speech, getting the job done while in effect apologizing to the liberals and the blacks for doing it. He sent out copies to liberal supporters in Texas and asked what they thought. Governor Allred commended him, but Banker Hall told him, "I'm sorry you think more of your right to talk without limit than of another man's right to vote."[4]

Characteristically, Johnson was not neglecting his constituents. In fact he organized his Senate office into a service station for them. Walter Jenkins headed the staff that included speechwriter Horace Busby and another top aide later, Warren Woodward. About this time Dorothy Nichols had a desk inside Johnson's office, the position of honor he had held with Kleberg. Alfred Steinberg, a writer who was close to Senator Tom Connally of Texas, heard that Johnson expected his employees to answer 650 letters and handle five hundred phone calls and about seventy visitors a day, the while dispatching, over a year's time, about 4 letters to each of eight thousand key supporters.

But an officeholder who was close to him believed that after the '48 campaign he had lost most of his folksiness. During the campaign he had invited a farmer to visit him in Washington, if he won. When early in his first year as a senator the farmer showed up and asked to see him, Johnson stuck his head out of his door, said hello, and slammed the door in the man's face.[5] He had told people what he thought would get him where he wanted to get, but now he was there and he was busy.

Sometimes Truman included Johnson in the whiskey-relaxed poker-playing weekends on the Potomac aboard the presidential yacht. Attending a celebration of Rayburn's birthday and Johnson's first year as senator, Truman chided Lyndon for bucking his administration, but Lyndon reportedly deflected him with a joke—he was loyal to the president just like the farmer who explained to the judge that the reason he'd beat his wife was she had cussed the judge.

The Johnsons also cultivated a tradition of being home every Sunday afternoon to politician friends who wanted to drop by. The conversation was politics—what was coming up, how who would vote—with the women just listening. Everyone had to stop talking for Drew Pearson's radio broadcast, after which the men talked about what he had said.

Rayburn was almost always there, sometimes Chief Justice Fred Vinson, sometimes Symington, often Senator Bob Kerr of Oklahoma. Late in the afternoon if Johnson wanted to go on with the talk he'd say, "Bird, go in and fix us something to eat," and she would.[6]

One of the things they had to talk about was Pearson's attacks on Kerr and Johnson for pushing the Kerr bill to exempt most natural-gas sales from federal regulation. Pearson called Kerr the busiest lobbyist on the Hill—a lobbyist for none other than himself, since he owned an estimated hundred million dollars worth of natural-gas reserves and had an annual gross income of twelve million dollars.

Pearson reported that Johnson, Kerr's "assistant lobbyist," had pounced on a critic of the bill in the Senate restaurant, only to be told natural gas was a monopoly that, without regulation, would jack up prices out of sight (it was estimated the bill would raise prices five hundred million dollars a year).

"Monopoly poof!" Johnson scoffed. "Aluminum is a monopoly. Steel is a monopoly. Automobile production is monopolized by a few companies. Natural gas doesn't have that kind of monopoly. There are many independent producers."

In one recent year, Pearson retorted, ten producers sold about half the gas used by the pipelines in the five southwestern gas states. The "independents" included companies owned by the majors; the four top producers had netted nineteen percent to twenty-eight percent profit. "It will be interesting to see," Pearson declared, "how much the two freshman senators will cost the nation's natural gas consumers." Other liberals were appalled, too. Doris Fleeson, the columnist, said the Kerr bill was "pro-interests, anti-consumer legislation of the type that Democrats for twenty years have successfully identified exclusively with the GOP." When Congress passed it, Truman vetoed it.[7]

But the consumer-oriented Democrats in the Senate felt like outsiders. "There was a little band of liberals over here, and they were looked down upon," Humphrey said—"We were looked upon as wild men, as dangerous radicals." Passing a group of southerners in the chamber one afternoon, Humphrey heard Russell say, obviously intending him to hear, "Can you imagine the people of Minnesota sending that damn fool down here to represent them?" "I was crushed," Humphrey said.

Through Johnson, Humphrey gradually became acceptable. Frequently Johnson invited him to his office for a talk and a drink; often Russell was there. Johnson also advised Humphrey to join the tightly knit southern group at lunch. Hubert saw that Lyndon knew politicians, "knew how to appeal to their vanity, to their needs, to their ambitions."[8]

60. Pre-McCarthy McCarthyism

There have been three convulsive reactions against the Bill of Rights: the period of the Alien and Sedition Laws at the end of the eighteenth century, the witch-hunts associated with World War I, and the McCarthy era from 1947 to the end of the Nixon presidency. Of the three the last was the most pervasive and the most momentous historically. In totalitarian systems the kind of paranoid nationalism called McCarthyism would have led to mass imprisonments and executions. In the American system, restrained by the commitment to free speech, it became a constitutionally limited demonism, ravaging and terrifying dissenters, firing and imprisoning some of them, but not murdering them. Nevertheless, as ideas and as fear it controlled American foreign policy during a critical quarter-century in the evolution of societies.

Like any fear, anticommunism can be rational or irrational, its uses fair or unfair. McCarthyism was the use of anticommunism for vicious effect against often unfairly-accused politicians and private persons. Although McCarthyism was anti-Communist, anticommunism did not have to be McCarthyism, but in the churned stream of events they became thoroughly mixed. Just as hate and fear of blacks was used in the South to label humanists as "nigger-lovers," McCarthyism was used nationwide to smear American progressives and their ideas as Communist. And more than this. During "those days of harsh attack," as Acheson called them, the American demonism limited the options of the highest American policymakers for the same span of years during which it was an unquestioned political commandment that communism in all its forms everywhere and forever was the same single and totally evil enemy.

Some of the people in power knew their independence of judgment was corrupted by the fear. George Mahon, a conservative congressman from west Texas, became chairman of the House military spending process in 1949—then the chairman of the entire House appropriations committee. Looking back, he said, "There was a time that any member of Congress would hesitate to vote against anything proposed by the Joint Chiefs of Staff because he might be subject to the charge of soft on communism. And the charge of being soft on communism was the kiss of death for a long period of years." What Mahon had the candor to admit, many, like Truman and Acheson, did not, but it was true, anyway. The test of policy became, not whether it was rational, humane, and patient, but whether it could be alleged to be "soft on communism." Most politicians automatically took positions that would shield them from that "kiss of death," and the few who were not afraid of being called Communist falsely were rendered ineffective. The psychological terror reigned throughout the American government and paralyzed the functioning of clear and ordinary intelligence in the formulation of American foreign policy.

Lyndon Johnson was shaped in pre-McCarthy Texas McCarthyism —it was a popular Texas game fifteen years before it became the national vogue. In the mid-thirties Johnson saw his mentor, Dr. Montgomery, fending off yahoo legislators investigating Communists at the University of Texas (finding nary a one, although some were probably there). A couple of years later, Johnson said, he himself was called a Communist for championing publicly produced, owned, and distributed electric power for his constituents. In 1939 Texas Communists asked Johnson's friend Maverick, then mayor of San Antonio, for permission to hold a meeting at the city auditorium. Maverick believed in freedom of assembly. He told his son that this one decision could end either his political or his spiritual life. He let them meet, anti-Communists attacked them, and Maverick, called an agent of Moscow by his opponent, lost office in the next election. The leader of the Red-hunts of the time, Martin Dies, came from Lufin, Texas, and in 1940 his House committee on un-American activities held hearings on subversion in the Southwest. Running against O'Daniel and Dies in the 1941 Texas Senate race, Johnson outdid Dies himself in baiting and abusing Communists, as we have seen.[1]

In this, Lyndon probably amused Roosevelt. During the thirties Roosevelt himself had been called a Communist his share of times, and so had some of his men. Just before the 1938 congressional elections, Dies had asked for an investigation of WPA and PWA and stated he would rid the government of such subversives as Hopkins, Ickes, and other "Communists and fellow travelers."

In 1939, during a Senate hearing in Washington on the confirmation of Felix Frankfurter for the Supreme Court, Frankfurter was asked if he agreed with his friend Harold Laski's doctrine as expressed in a book entitled *Communism.* Frankfurter had scruples against discussing his views, but the young Dean Acheson, in a whisper, passed on to him a senator's warning that he had best answer. Seeing the drift of things, Frankfurter replied emphatically that he had no truck with communism. The hearing room erupted into a pandemonium of celebration, and later, when Frankfurter told Roosevelt the whole story, "The president roared with delighted laughter."

This scene, prefiguring the personal responses of the Truman-Acheson Democrats to charges they were pinkos, taught one how to get through. One put out of one's mind the small, geometrical scruples and defended oneself—indeed, one played to the crowd. In private, one laughed at the yahoos—but not in public.

Though Senator O'Daniel, during the Second World War, berated the New Dealers for "their Communistic set-up," the U.S. and Russia were allies, and Johnson flirted briefly with voting against appropriations for HUAC (or abstaining on the issue); just as briefly he advocated sharing atomic secrets with Russia. But turning as Truman and the times turned, Johnson began berating Reds in the unions.

Enraged by a railroad strike in May, 1946, Truman had scrawled, in notes for a speech, "Let's hang a few traitors and make our own country safe for democracy!" That November he established his Temporary Commission on Employee Loyalty. Thirteen days after announcing the Truman Doctrine, he ordered that all 2.5 million federal employees undergo a new security test—whether they belonged to or had "sympathetic association with" any group "or combination of persons" that the U.S. attorney general labeled "totalitarian." This, the launching of what may be called, in retrospect, official McCarthyism, had to start, and did start, a witch-hunt that eventually ranged through the federal bureaucracy, 3 million members of the armed forces, 3 million employees of defense contractors, and state and local governments.

Vice-President Wallace became the first eminent victim. In November, 1947, presidential counselor Clark Clifford advised Truman that Wallace, as a third-party candidate, hoped to cause Truman's defeat in 1948 and inherit the Democratic party in 1952. To stop him, Clifford told Truman, "every effort must be made . . . to identify him and isolate him in the public mind with the Communists."

Lyndon, in his defense of the Truman Doctrine, had already stepped to the attack on Wallace. In the 1948 race, according to Harold Young, Wallace's former aide who was for Coke Stevenson, "Lyndon made speeches saying that Henry Wallace was a bad man and that Harold Young had visited with Coke (and I had had breakfast with him a few times) and that this proved Coke was a pinko—that was the real inference."

Speaker Rayburn joined in the fun, saying on behalf of Truman that the attempt of the Wallace third party to kill the Marshall Plan "has made it a Communist front, despite the good faith of the idealists who follow him," so that "On the right we have the party of privilege. On the left, the representatives of the Politburo. . . ." Yet once Senator Joseph McCarthy himself hit his stride, Truman would write Rayburn that "McCarthy and his crowd have almost ruined the morale of public employees"—as if Truman and his men had no responsibility.

In August, 1948, the Democrats should have begun to learn that their use of anti-Communist demagoguery, intended to protect them from the same demagoguery aimed at them, sanctioned its use and thus intensified their vulnerability to it. A *Time* senior editor, Whittaker Chambers, accused a Democratic diplomat, Alger Hiss, of having been a Communist. Hiss denied it, and Truman called the matter a "red herring." Representative Richard Nixon of California took the lead in the investigation and staged a public confrontation between the accuser and the accused. Hiss sued Chambers—Chambers produced the pumpkin papers—Hiss was indicted for perjury. The nation was agog.[2] Nor was the issue just a "red herring" to be tossed about for merely political reasons, as the exposure of the Cambridge-cell Soviet spy ring which infested the uppermost levels of British intelligence was soon to make painfully clear.

Joe McCarthy of Wisconsin was watching all these events, but he might have missed the meaning of the Democrats' excoriation of Wallace and the domestic political potentialities of the Hiss case; in 1949 the members of the Senate press gallery voted the junior senator from Wisconsin the worst member, mainly because he spent so much time boozing and talking to his bookies on the telephone. Conducting the Senate's observance of J. Edgar Hoover's twenty-fifth anniversary as head of the FBI, McCarthy's rhetoric was singularly free of the anti-Communist stress soon to become his trademark.[3] But four months before he launched his famous crusade, McCarthy received from his Senate colleagues, including Johnson of Texas, a model in anti-Communist character assassination.

---

61. The Crucifixion of Leland Olds

Secure by the spring of 1949 with the lords of the Senate, Johnson shifted his strategic attention back to the lords of his own state. The task was to dispel any doubts among the oil and gas barons that he was their agent. What would convince them? Events were converging into an antileftist witch-hunt. That year already the Hungarian Communists had imprisoned Cardinal Mindszenty for life, Mao had taken China. At home the first Hiss trial had ended in a hung jury, Judith Coplon had been convicted of stealing secret documents, and the trial of U.S. Communist leaders had begun in New York. In the Senate armed service committee Johnson had watched, but voted against, a vendetta tinctured with charges of communism against one Truman nominee.[1] When Truman renominated Leland Olds to preside over the Federal Power Commission, which regulated natural gas, Johnson saw his chance and took his method from the times. Turning against his party's president and setting aside, as if a discarded necktie, his own convictions about public power a decade before, he helped pillory a once socialist-minded official who still wanted the federal government to regulate natural gas prices.

In the twenties Leland Olds had been a labor editor for the Federated Press. A Roosevelt appointee on the FPC, he had saved consumers many millions of dollars in rate reductions and helped squeeze inflated values out of utility stocks. Federal regulation of natural gas, which began in 1938, was to inflame domestic politics into the 1980s. Oilmen like Hines Baker, the president of Humble (later Exxon), called such regulation the certain road to "full federal control of oil and gas production." Yet the alternative to regulation was letting producers and pipelines gouge captive consumers as much as circumstances allowed. The FPC controlled the pipelines, but had found that producers were spiking up the prices they charged the pipelines to take large profits, and Olds had led government into controlling the large producers' prices, too. In 1947 the Supreme Court had ruled that all gas sold in interstate commerce was subject to federal regulation, and when the Congress, the next two years, considered the Kerr and other bills to reverse this, Olds was an effective defender of regulation.

Billions were at stake in the Olds renomination. Tycoons in Texas, who could make or break Johnson for reelection, were watching his every twitch on the issue. George Brown, one of the Brown & Root brothers, was head of the natural gas lines he had bought from the government and turned into a bonanza. A Houston oilman worth hundreds of millions of dollars, Hugh Roy Cullen, pronounced, in outrage, that Olds "would establish 'social responsibility' in place of the profit motive. That is conclusive proof that he does not believe in our form of government." Johnson's man Connally was going to work as the political lawyer for another big-rich Texas oilman, Sid Richardson.

Johnson heard from his oil-and-gas buddy, Charles I. Francis, the lawyer for George Brown in the Texas Eastern deal. Francis wrote Johnson that Olds should be busted because of "his political views, and unjudicial temperament." Why should Truman punish the gas industry when Texas gave him his largest state majority vote "and is now rendering outstanding financial support to his party," Francis asked.

The real issue was profit, as Francis's letter to Senator Tom Connally of Texas (a copy to Johnson) showed. "Nothing is more important to the welfare of the natural gas industry in Texas" than that Olds be rejected, Francis wrote. "Olds . . . definitely believes . . . that producers should only earn 6% interest on the depreciated historical cost of their producing properties. Such is disastrous . . . to the gas industry. . . ." Johnson wrote Francis he would talk to Connally "about the Olds situation."

Far from reluctant to do the oilmen's dirty work, Johnson was eager to be of service—he sought the chairmanship of the subcommittee that considered the Olds nomination. In the hearing a south Texas congressman, John Lyle, took the smearpot in hand first, using fifty-four articles Olds had written a quarter-century before, from 1922 to 1929, to show that he had attacked the church, the schools, and the Fourth of July. Because Olds in the twenties had praised the practice in Russia of setting aside large estates as rest and recreation centers for workers and had suggested public ownership of railroads and the coal industry, Lyle charged that "he has reserved his applause for Lenin and Lenin's system."

Olds told Johnson's panel that he had never favored communism, that the New Deal had corrected many ills he had described in the twenties, and that on Russia he had changed his mind. When a witness, carried away by peer pressure, called Olds a Communist, Johnson said, "There is no testimony that Olds is a member of the Communist party or is disloyal to the United States."

But, using guilt by association, Lyndon did him in anyway. He asked Olds if he had addressed a meeting, sharing the platform with the Communist leader Earl Browder. When Olds replied he remembered speaking at the meeting, but not who the other speakers were, Johnson produced a 1924 copy of the *Daily Worker* reporting that Olds and Browder were the principal speakers. Johnson asked Olds if he rejected the positions he had taken in the articles in the twenties. "No sir; I do not," Olds replied, conceding, however, that changes in conditions "would lead me to write some of those articles in a somewhat different way today."

Reporters related that Edwin Johnson, the senator from Colorado, slipped Lyndon a note saying that the *Denver Post* was defending Olds, and Johnson replied by showing the Coloradan a letter Lyndon himself had written the same paper saying that Olds was in league with the "Marcantonio chore boys" and that Truman had nominated Olds to win support from the Communist-leaning American Labor party. Vito Marcantonio was the only congressman generally identified in the public's mind with communism.

In the *Washington Star* a columnist said the hearings had turned into "an inquisition. . . . Johnson and his committee colleagues put on a performance reminiscent of the House Un-American Activities Committee." From the White House Truman charged that "the powerful corporations subject to regulation," in opposing Olds, sought to dominate the commission created to regulate them.

In the *Dallas News* (which editorially was calling Olds "a fellow traveler"), Johnson complained about "smears in an effort to try somebody else," rather than Olds. To Truman, Johnson said the subcommittee was "shocked beyond description" by the views Olds expressed "some years ago" and did not believe that, "under our democratic capitalistic system," a person "holding such views" should regulate industry.

In the Senate debate James Murray of Montana estimated that the few large companies dominating the gas industry might have their holdings enhanced by sixteen billion dollars if federal control over field prices ended. Johnson of Colorado charged Olds with communism, radicalism, and "a warped mind." Senator Langer, scorning "these twenty-five-year-old charges," thought the case against Olds "smells strongly of oil."

Senator George D. Aiken, the high-minded Republican from Vermont, foresaw what was being unleashed. They had met in the Senate that night, he said, "to put the finishing touches on the career of a public servant. . . . I do not think that Mr. Olds is going to be hurt by those who would crucify him, but I think a great many other folk are going to be. I think the effects of what is being done here tonight will echo down far through the years ahead of us, and will continue to plague those who accuse him much longer than the echoes from Teapot Dome were heard. Certain public utilities of the country are out to destroy a man for performing his duty. I do not know of anything worse than that."

Minutes after Aikin yielded the floor, the major speaker against Olds stepped forward: the 1938 champion of public power for central Texas, Lyndon Johnson.

Thrice he called Olds "this man," holding him out to a sanitary distance, as with tongs. Using contemptuous sarcasm, sophistries, innuendo, and not only guilt by association but even guilt by environment, Johnson damned his prey as a fellow-traveler who wanted socialism for the oil and gas companies.

Knowing full well his service would be rewarded by those from whom he feigned independence, Johnson claimed that "Through eight elections, in twelve years of public life, I have been opposed by the oil and gas lobby," and he had seen none of these lobbyists at work against Olds. With Johnson fighting their battle for them, they had little work to do. Olds, Johnson alleged, had "a life-long prejudice and hostility" against the oil and gas industries. Olds's quiet statements that if he was not confirmed the FPC would not be as active in its regulatory effort, and that in one case the FPC staff had apparently fallen victim to "the continuous argument of the industry," became in Johnson's mouth his "snide and petty smears" and his attempt "to force the commission staff into a goose-step march." Johnson accused Olds of thinking "I am the law"—of wanting to confiscate the gas companies' property through "self-made law." Hardly granting at all Olds's view that the Supreme Court had indicated federal regulation should extend to the production of natural gas, Johnson converted his quarry's position into socialism: such regulation "would have constituted . . . nationalization" and Olds had sought to destroy the balance between regulation and "outright public ownership."

In 1924 Olds had supported the Progressive Bob LaFollette for president, but in 1928 he had favored the Republican Hoover, who, Olds wrote, was "the leader of progressive capitalism" and the trend "to a planned economic order with a responsible capitalist government integrated on a national basis." Olds had also written that Norman Thomas, the American Socialist, represented the British trend toward "progressive nationalization." Snipping and patching to twist, Johnson concluded that Olds "recommends a vote for Hoover and the planned economic order of Norman Thomas and progressive nationalization." From the yellowing writings of this Herbert Hoover socialist, Johnson seized on phrases approving "the elimination of competitive private capitalism," workers seeking "a worker government," and seeming to look forward to a time when "the profit system is superceded." Acknowledging that Olds had said he would express his views in a somewhat different way, Johnson shrugged this off as he rushed into calumny:

"I do not charge that Mr. Olds is a Communist. . . . I realize that the line he followed, the phrases he used, the causes he espoused, resemble the party line today, but the Communist tie is not the tie that binds Leland Olds's writings of the 1920's to his doctrine of the 1940s. . . . Leland Olds had something in mind. . . . when he chose to . . . plot a course toward confiscation and public ownership. . . ."

Was Joe McCarthy in the chamber as Johnson approached his climactic contumely? Probably: the Wisconsin Republican had answered both of that night's quorum calls. Olds chose "to travel with those who proposed the Marxian answer. . . . The company he chose, he chose of his own free will," Johnson said. "He spoke from the same platform with Earl Browder. He accepted subsidy from the so-called Garland Fund, a fund created and expended to keep alive Marxist organs and Marxist groups. The managing editor of Federated Press, under whom Leland Olds worked as industrial editor, was Carl Haessler, a notorious leader of party-line organizations who sat out World War I in Alcatraz as a seditionist. By the way: He was sent to Leavenworth, and was so dangerous that he was removed to Alcatraz. When he came out he joined with Leland Olds. Leland Olds knew who his friends were and what they stood for. . . .

"That is Mr. Olds as he is, as he was; the prologue to the future which he now seeks. Once more, let me repeat the words of Justice Black: 'Here we have a man in an environment which we know, and no man can honestly deny that he knows that environment creates the trend of thought and develops the bent of mind.' . . . It seems to me that the issue is clear-cut: . . . Shall we have a commissioner or a commissar? I leave the answer to the Senate."

That fixed him, all right.

Three of the Senate's leading liberals of that period, Humphrey, Wayne Morse of Oregon, and Paul Douglas of Illinois, led the defense of Olds. Answering Johnson, Douglas said, "Mr. Olds . . . stated that he was not at the present time and never had been a communist, that in his opinion the very theory of Russian communism represented the negation of democracy. . . . I have never heard that challenged. I am somewhat amused at the contradictory statements that in 1928 he held communist views and yet voted for Hoover for president." Yet the

Senate, including of course Joe McCarthy, rejected Olds, fifty-three to fifteen.

Joining in the political crucifixion of Leland Olds—driving in the nails himself—Johnson had used most of the tricks of what would come to be known as McCarthyism, and he nauseated some of his colleagues, but he had achieved his purpose—he had convinced the oilmen back in Texas that he was their man.

A spokesman for the Texas rural electric co-ops had endorsed the Olds nomination, and for this, speaking to the co-ops' convention a few weeks later, Johnson cudgeled them as if they were his schoolchildren. He suggested they adopt a slogan, "Stay out of the Red." He, not Olds, had been victimized by "the smear artists" who had pretended Olds was "a martyr being crucified by the big power companies and the big gas companies. . . . If Joe Stalin were nominated, I suppose his pals would try to arouse support by shouting that the power lobby was against him."[2]

Truman's own anticommunism had been used to kill off one of the most progressive of his own agents. His attorney general, J. Howard McGrath, as recently as April, 1949, in Washington, had charged, "There are today many communists in America. They are everywhere —in factories, offices, butcher stores, on street corners, in private businesses. And each carries in himself the germ of death for society." Little wonder, then, that when the oil companies found a "Communist" preventing them from charging what they wished for their natural gas, the senators removed him—and McGrath as early as 1951 hoped Johnson would become president.[3]

Joe McCarthy's Red-baiting began just as the Senate was busting Olds. In that same November of 1949, McCarthy attacked Cedric Parker, an ex-Communist journalist who worked for a Wisconsin newspaper that was severely critical of McCarthy. In a speech that November to a Young Republicans dinner, McCarthy tried out the theme of Communist infiltration into the State Department.

Then, three short months after the Senate rejected Olds, on January 7, 1950, during dinner at the Colony Restaurant in Washington, Joe McCarthy told his companions he needed a dramatic issue for his reelection campaign. After two subjects were toyed with and put aside, the late Father Edmund A. Walsh, author of books against communism and regent of the School of Foreign Service at Georgetown University, suggested communism in the world and as a source of subversion at home. "That's it," McCarthy said. "The government is full of Communists. We can hammer away at them."

One month later, in Wheeling, West Virginia, McCarthy stunned the nation by saying he had in his hand a list of 205 Communists who were working in the State Department and were known to Acheson.[4] He was talking through his hat, but for the time being that did not matter. The Truman Democrats' own demon had turned on them, and they were terrified.

But back home in Texas, the freshman senator had so improved his standing with his state's super-rich, one of them who was to become an ardent supporter of McCarthy, oil millionaire Hugh Roy Cullen, wired Johnson how disappointed he was to have read that he was supporting Truman. "You know my views about socialized medicine," Lyndon replied to the right-winger. "You know my views about the Kerr bill. You know my views about FEPC. . . . And you know that I have not hesitated to speak and work against [President Truman's] views on these subjects."[5]

---

62. The Senator Becomes a Rancher

"I kept coming back to this house—I guess I must have had a yearning to someday own it," Johnson said of the Martin place on the Pedernales up from where he was born. From the age of four, a poor cousin, he had walked up the river and played with his Uncle Clarence and his father's sister Aunt Frank, celebrated family reunions and holidays there. Now he wanted to own the place and be a Texas rancher as he advanced in politics.

"My aunt told me," he said, "she was in advancing years and poor health, and she was going to have to move in closer to where she could get treatment, and she wondered if I wouldn't buy the place."

But there was an obstacle—Aunt Frank's daughter-in-law, Lela Martin, had a substantial claim to it.

Clarence and Aunt Frank had agreed to will the place to their son Tom and Lela, his wife, provided Tom and Lela supported and cared for them until they died. Tom and Lela kept their part of the bargain for fifteen years, moving onto the place and putting their life savings into maintaining it. When Lyndon began to try to buy it, only Aunt Frank and Lela were still living, and with Miss Frank seventy-eight years old, Lela stood to get the place in due time. To help pay the ranch bills Lela had taken a job in Austin.

"There were just a lot of reasons why [Lela] had a right to the house," according to Lyndon's boyhood friend Payne Roundtree, and "she was really a fighter," but Lyndon wanted it and Miss Frank wanted to sell it to him.

Tom and Lela had paid the taxes on the place since 1934, but suddenly in January, 1949, for the first time, Aunt Frank paid them. She testified that a lawyer, Walter Linden, had come to her, "not knowing about anything," and asked about her finances. When he agreed to give her legal help without pay, she filed suit against Lela to establish her ownership of the place against Lela's claim.

Was Lyndon behind Linden? In the trial Lela was hostile to Miss Frank's attorney and apparently hinted broadly that Lyndon had put him up to what he was doing. Four days after Miss Frank had filed her suit, Linden had acquired a small mortgage on the place that Lela had been paying off, occasioning some discussion in the trial whether he had a conflict of interest as Miss Frank's attorney.

It did not seem fair that Lela and Tom had worked and saved to maintain a small ranch for fifteen years on the promise they would own it only to see it sold to Senator Lyndon Johnson. The jury found that they had been promised the place in consideration for caring for the old folks, and the judge held that while Aunt Frank had legal title, Lela had equitable title, possession, and control. However, on appeal a judge held for Aunt Frank because the promise to care for her until she died had not been performed as long as she was still alive. In her seventy-ninth year she was given clear title to the ranch and could sell it to Lyndon.[1]

Before going ahead, Lyndon had one more problem—his wife.

He laid his plans carefully. He and Bird, along with Secretary of the Air Force Stuart Symington and his wife, flew to Texas on what Bird thought was a pleasure trip. After visiting some luxury ranches they forded the Pedernales and, passing by an erosion ditch deep and big enough for an elephant to walk in, reached the little stone house, the Martin place.

"I almost should have foreseen it, because I think Lyndon was always heading back here," Bird said. "I wasn't intuitive enough to know it."

The place had badly deteriorated. "It reminded me of the Addams cartoons of the haunted house, you know," Bird said—"there were even actually bats up under close to the chimney up there. And Lyndon began talkin' to his aunt about buying it and getting her a more comfortable place in town to live, and I was aghast!—'How can you *possibly* do this to me?' " She saw at once the work she'd be in for. "I didn't like the idea one bit."

But Lyndon looked at the rundown old place and exclaimed excitedly, "Let's buy it!" He didn't tell Bird why he wanted it, "I just knew—and also he would get so enthusiastic when he would talk about it. He just said, 'I'll tell you what we can do!' and then he'd get launched on it, and my goodness, you really couldn't squelch that kind of enthusiasm that he had for it."

Perhaps borrowing three thousand dollars from banker Percy Brigham, the Johnsons bought the ranch for around twenty thousand dollars. Aunt Frank also received a monthly expense check and went to live in the Johnsons' house in Johnson City, which Lyndon reacquired after her death. A state senator who knew Lela said she felt that the ranch had been snatched away from her, but in 1964, when her cousin was president, all she would say to a reporter was, "We're good neighbors and I'm not interested in talking about anything that has happened." Perhaps at the sale in 1951 she received something in settlement, for she also said in 1964 that she had sold the property to Lyndon, and Bird was quoted, "we bought it from Lyndon's cousin in 1951," although in other accounts the Johnsons customarily said they bought it from his aunt.

Lyndon had a sense of humor about setting himself up as a rancher in his first year as a senator. Evidently he told one writer that Brigham warned him not to expect to pay off the ranch with profits from cattle, but added, "Now, if you're going to play cowboy and stomp in boots around the post office on Saturday, I'm not going to interfere." But Johnson knew that playing cowboy or not, he could strike a more impressive posture as a Texas politician rooted in the soil if he owned a ranch near where he was born. He invented circumstances to make it seem even more impressive, saying his grandfather had built the original house on the place, even telling me the ranch had been his grandfather's.

Settling in, the first thing he did was dam the river in front of the house. "You couldn't see the river," he said. "It had grown up in underbrush and shin-oaks and old weeds, sunflowers." Wirtz, sitting on the porch with him, suggested putting in a little dam not only to make a swimming and fishing hole and provide water for stock and irrigation, but also to serve as the base for a road across the river closer to the house than the crossing they had to use then. The dam, as Johnson said, "made a beautiful lake in front of our house." Some hill-country people cussed him for it, saying it was keeping water from reaching ranchers downstream. In retort his friend A. W. Moursund once told a reporter that the lake was partly fed by wells Johnson had dug, so he was actually furnishing water downstream.

That first fall Lyndon bought thirty-five Delaine sheep and had plans to buy thirty head of cattle. He had two hundred acres in winter oats. Bird had a tree surgeon come out to care for the ailing trees and went to work with the architect, the contractor, the carpenters. "You would be staggered if I told you how little it cost," she said. "But it enabled us to have a big comfortable house that meant a lot to him, to his spirit and his heart."

Indubitably, there was something stagy about Johnson as a rancher. "He created the hill country ranch as the proper home setting of a Texan in Washington," as the columnist Richard Wilson wrote. "Mr. Johnson is not intrinsically a Texas rancher, either in outlook or behavior. . . . He is seen in his real self in the midst of political strife and controversy in Washington. . . . He is like the ancient Romans. The historian Will Durant says they could not wait to get their country seats, but, once there, paced the atrium until they could leap into their chariots to return to Rome."[2]

---

63. Truman Turns Off Chou and Ho

Still a secondary senator on the make, Johnson in 1949 and the first half of 1950 entered into the consensus supporting U.S. actions that armed Western Europe, passed up a chance to encourage Chinese Communist independence of the Soviets, built the mass-annihilation hydrogen bomb, and armed the French against the Communist-nationalist rebels in Vietnam.

With Wallace out of the way, Truman proposed two kinds of foreign aid, the military buildup of the North Atlantic area and "Point Four," technological help for developing countries. From the first, American foreign aid was torn between anti-Communist and humanitarian purposes. As the Griffin Report said, the two elements "were interrelated, of course." In the reality, while token-size Point Four–type programs kept U.S. liberals supporting foreign aid, the anti-Communist smothered the humanitarian overview.

U.S. foreign policy was bottomed on arming other nations with the enactment, first in 1949, of the Military Assistance Program. Senator Arthur Vandenberg wrote his wife that the proposal would give the president "unlimited power" and "make him the number one war lord of the earth." To get it through, Truman dropped the section giving him extraordinary powers, and billions worth of arms began flowing from the U.S. into Europe.

Under the principle of collective security, the Senate adopted, eighty-two to thirteen, the North Atlantic Treaty Organization (NATO). The U.S., Britain, France, and nine other nations, 350 million people in all, agreed that an armed attack against any of them would be considered an attack on all of them and they would fight back together. Did the treaty mean, Acheson was asked at a Senate hearing, that the U.S. would be expected "to send substantial numbers of troops over there as a more or less permanent contribution . . ."? "The answer," replied the secretary of state, "is a clear and absolute 'No.' "[1] The historical answer was a clear and absolute Yes.

That same spring Mao's insurgent Communists captured mainland China. When Chiang collapsed, Truman said, "They wanted me to send in about five million Americans to rescue him, but I wouldn't do it . . . he was as corrupt as they come. I wasn't going to waste a single American life to save him." Despite knowing Chiang was no good,

Truman declined to join Britain in recognizing the new government of China, and his administration scorned or at least fumbled a dramatic appeal for help from Chou En-lai, a fact that was kept secret for twenty-nine years until it was discovered by historian Robert M. Blum.

On June 1, 1949, Chou sent the U.S. a request for economic aid to help rebuild China. The triumphant new Chinese leaders were divided between the relatively moderate faction for whom Chou spoke and a radical group that wanted an anti-American, pro-Soviet stance. Thus one more time, now as the victors, leaders of the Chinese Reds consciously offered the U.S. a chance to split them off from Russia.

Chou directed his message to the "highest American authorities on a top-secret level." The U.S. consul-general in Peiping, O. Edmund Clubb, wired Washington Chou's view that "U.S.S.R. cannot give aid which therefore must come from U.S.A. . . . Chou favors getting help from the U.S.A. . . . Liberals regard Soviet international policy as 'crazy.' . . . Chou feels . . . democratic China would serve in international sphere as mediator between Western powers and U.S.S.R."

State informed Truman, but expressed sharp skepticism about the message, and two weeks later, under Truman's order, a U.S. answer was drafted saying friendly relations could only follow "deeds" that would show friendship was possible. Even this dead-minded reply was never delivered. The same month both Mao and Chou invited the U.S. ambassador to visit Peiping, but while top U.S. officials debated over that, evidently the Chinese moderates decided the U.S. was hopeless: on June 30 Mao said in a speech he expected no help from the U.S. and China would lean toward Russia.[2]

In January, 1950, as Acheson told Churchill, the U.S. had come to believe there was a real possibility of inducing "Chinese Titoism." Apparently it had taken U.S. officials the six months after Chou's snubbed overture to figure this out. In any case, on January 10, Acheson admitted publicly, although indirectly, that there was a chance to split China off from the Soviets. In a speech, he said that Soviet pressure on China's four northern provinces would cause in the Chinese righteous anger, wrath, and hatred toward Russia, and it would be "folly" for the U.S. to deflect this hostility onto ourselves. He also defined the U.S. defense perimeter in Asia by drawing, in words, a line that excluded Taiwan, Indochina, and South Korea.[3]

But then, a month later, McCarthy went public with his Red-hunting charges against the State Department, Acheson, and, of course, Truman. The same Acheson who had watched while Frankfurter mollified prewar congressional Red-baiters now found himself called "the Great Red Dean" with his "crimson crowd." McCarthy berated the secretary, too, for sharing a platform in 1945 with Paul Robeson, Corliss Lamont, and Joseph E. Davies.

The preceding fall, State had received word that the Soviets had exploded an atomic bomb and could make a hydrogen bomb. If the U.S. saw this merely as a new stage in the arms race, there would be a geometrical increase in the horrors of weaponry. Kennan and J. Robert Oppenheimer argued inside the government that a try should be made for international agreements to head off "this fateful course." At that point the Soviets still had minimal ability to deliver nuclear weapons.

In that same January, 1950, Kennan wrote a memo to Acheson saying that it was "perfectly clear . . . that we were basing our defense posture on [nuclear] weapons, and were intending to make first use of them, regardless of whether they had been or might be used against us, in any major military encounter." Kennan proposed the United States publicly declare it would never be the one to use them first. Acheson did not pick up the point, and ten days later Truman decided the U.S. would develop the hydrogen bomb. The momentous result was the H-bomb race,[4] to which, a fortnight later, Lyndon Johnson made a prophetic contribution.

During a conference with Texas reporters, he said Russia was already two years ahead of the U.S. in guided missile work—if Truman's secretary of defense didn't get going on it, Congress might have to. "For push-button war," Johnson said, "we have neither the push nor the button." He raised alarms, too, about the inadequacy of the U.S. military establishment, strategic stockpilings, and military housing.[5]

Citizens hardly knew what was going on because "the fall of China" had ignited Republican attacks on what Senator Robert Taft of Ohio called "the pro-Communist group in the State Department." Appalled that "cookie-pushers" and "pinkos" were making foreign policy, the right-wingers were in fact making it themselves. Charles Yost, formerly the U.S. representative at the UN, has written, "It may be argued that it was McCarthy's all-too-popular persecution of those he claimed 'lost' China that drove John Foster Dulles, John F. Kennedy, and Lyndon Johnson into the morass of Vietnam." Their fear of being damned for 'losing' another country to communism was, Yost said, "in large measure a posthumous exercise of power by Joe McCarthy."

The National Security Council resolved on a fourfold increase in U.S. military spending. Kennan protested that too military an emphasis would hurt chances that diplomacy might end the cold war, but Acheson, again disregarding him, pushed for, and Truman initialed, NSC Paper 68, which said that (1) there would be conflict between the Communist and non-Communist worlds indefinitely and (2) the U.S. should think of arms costs in the range of 50 billion dollars a year. (Truman, however, ordered his secretary of defense to observe a 13.5-billion-dollar ceiling for 1951.) As a member of the armed services committee, Johnson was receiving top-secret briefings on the situation, and a reporter assigned to him at the time noted that he "favors total mobilization."[6]

Communist-nationalist rebels led by Ho Chi Minh had been fighting French colonial control of Vietnam since 1945, but the United States had stayed out of that, refusing French requests for troopships. After all, it was a straightforward case of colonial exploitation. But now, under attack from the Republicans and especially from McCarthy, Truman and Acheson reversed this policy. The first American intervention in Vietnam took the form of some kind of deal with France. Acheson wanted West Germany economically strong, while France feared a revived Germany. In exchange for French consent to increased West German steel production, or the assignment of twelve French divisions to NATO, or both, the U.S. agreed, at a cost of 2.3 billion dollars, to finance and arm the French in Indochina. As Hubert Humphrey said later, "our support of French colonialism in Indochina was a mistake begun by the Truman administration. . . ."

In Acheson's announcement of the new policy, the clue to what historian Carl L. Becker called an era's "unconscious preconceptions" was the inflexibility—the dogmatism—of Acheson's reasoning: "The United States Government, convinced that neither national independence nor democratic evolution exists in any area dominated by Soviet imperialism," would give the French economic aid and military equipment to help them defeat Ho. Vietnam was another Russian colony, just like China—Ho's nationalism was as meaningless as Mao's. Acheson admitted the theoretical possibility that Ho could become another Tito, Communist but independent of the Soviets, but argued, in cryptic cablespeak, "Question whether Ho as much nationalist as commie is irrevelant. All Stalinists in colonial areas are nationalists. With achievement of national aims (*i.e.*, independence) their objective necessarily becomes subordination state to commie purposes and ruthless extermination not only opposition groups. . . ." The language and logic could not have been more block-headed if McCarthy himself had composed it, as in a sense he had.[7]

In these eighteen months, the whole of Truman's elected term before the Korean War began, he and Acheson, hounded by McCarthy and the Republican right and both hounded and supported by "the bomber liberals" like Johnson, set the United States firmly on a militarist course based on the perception of communism as one world-wide monolith. We would help Europe re-arm, shun the Chinese Communists, build the H-bomb, quadruple military spending, and help the French subdue Vietnam.

As the historian Athan Theoharis wrote, "Because Americans were encouraged to expect victory as inevitable, owing to American purity, to Providence, and to Soviet perfidy and atheism, they were led to reject a policy of compromise and concession. The administration effectively equated restraint with appeasement and thereby discredited suggestions that a proper policy should rely on conciliation and not military strength." As Johnson argued while defending the allocation of thirty percent of the national budget to the military, for five years we had "held in check the most ruthless most sinister and evil dictator of modern times."[8] Stalin, mixed in the mind with Hitler, was this dictator, so how could we fail to rearm? Whether the postwar arms race might have been avoided, whatever Chinese Titoism diplomacy with the Chou moderates might have achieved, and whatever Vietnamese Titoism continued neutrality toward the French occupation might have achieved, history would never know.

---

64. The War of the Three Invasions

As World War II had jolted to an end, Russia was racing to get into the war against Japan, and the United States was calculating to keep her out. At the finish the Soviets occupied the northern half and the Americans the southern half of Korea, the peninsula stretching from China and Russia southward to within 120 miles of Japan. The country was partitioned along the thirty-eighth parallel, and in 1948 the UN formed the Republic of Korea in the south; at the same time a Communist state was established in North Korea.

Truman knew that the tyrannical leader of South Korea, Syngman Rhee, was just as corrupt as Chiang. According to Senator Tom Connally's friend Steinberg, the administration knew that Rhee ran a quasi-dictatorship, imprisoning or liquidating political opponents—his police slaughtering twenty-seven thousand left-wing Koreans in just two encounters. But Truman told none of this to Congress or the public, an omission that was critically important in the formation of American public opinion.

If the patched-together work *Khrushchev Remembers* was Nikita Khruschchev's bona fide memoirs, as it has come to be regarded, and if the Russian premier was to be believed, the North Korean leader, Kim Il-Sung, while conferring with Stalin in Russia, initiated the idea of invading South Korea. Kim believed the war could be won quickly —Rhee's government would collapse at once, he thought—and Stalin was inclined to agree. According to *Khrushchev Remembers,* Mao, consulted by Stalin, approved the invasion, too. They all thought that in a quick war the U.S. would not intervene. But before Kim acted, Stalin, telling Khrushchev "It's Kim Il-Sung's affair," withdrew Soviet advisers from the North Korean units so Russia would not be blamed. Kennan always believed that the Korean War was a civil one "and the term 'aggression' in the usual international sense was as misplaced here as it was to be later in the case of Vietnam."

One Sunday morning late in June, 1950, Acheson, in the State Department, phoned Truman, who was spending the weekend at his home in Missouri.

"What is it, Dean?" Truman asked.

"Mr. President, the news is bad. The attack is in force all along the parallel."

"Dean," Truman replied, "we've got to stop the sons of bitches no matter what."

North Korea's armies, outfitted by the Soviets, had attacked South Korea. Truman, preparing to send American troops into a war, made a conscious decision not to ask Congress for authorization to do it. Acheson said he feared "endless criticism," and Truman wanted, Acheson said, "no derogation of presidential power to send our forces into battle." Immediately after the UN Security Council condemned the attack and called on its members to assist South Korea, Truman sent in two divisions. Thus began—"on the sole directive of the President," as historian Allan Nevins wrote—one of the deadliest and costliest wars in American history. At the same time, Truman reversed U.S. policy on Taiwan, ordering the Seventh Fleet to prevent any attack on Chiang's island (and then giving Chiang military aid)—a step which Mao perceived as invasive.

The day after Truman acted, Senator Johnson of Texas wrote him commending "your inspired act of leadership," which he said "gives a new and noble meaning to freedom. . . . Having chosen this course, there is no turning back." "You will never know," Truman replied, "how much I appreciate your kind expressions in commendation of our decision. . . . That you so steadfastly approve of this course is highly gratifying to me."

At first public opinion, liberal to conservative, almost unanimously backed Truman. The American response was called "a police action," not a war; the UN sanctioned it. The rottenness of the Rhee government the U.S. defended was almost wholly unknown to U.S. citizens. The Reds had invaded their neighbors, they were bandits, we were stopping them. Taft protested properly that Truman had sent Americans into combat without the constitutionally required consent of Congress, but his was a lonely voice. With fifty-seven percent of the Americans polled believing this was the opening round of World War III, the people "rallied round the flag."[1]

As the U.S. intervention took effect, Kim Il-Sung's quick victory failed to develop. Truman told the National Security Council that the U.S. purpose in Korea was "to restore peace there and to restore the border," the thirty-eighth parallel (the "status quo ante"). Acheson said appositely that the U.S. was fighting in Korea "solely for the purpose" of restoring that boundary.

But then Truman's bellicosity—indeed, his will to counteraggression—supervened. Steinberg directly quotes his friend Tom Connally, who was a confidant of the president's: "Truman's real goal there was not to keep the Reds from taking over the Republic of South Korea, but as he said in a March 20, 1951, statement that he never made public, he wanted to establish 'a unified, independent and democratic state' in all of Korea—north as well as south." Steinberg also said that on October 2, 1950, Truman ordered his general in charge, Douglas MacArthur, to invade and conquer North Korea—this to convince the North Koreans that "aggression doesn't pay."[2]

Whatever the accuracy of that information, the harder record leaves no doubt that Truman authorized the invasion of North Korea, and perhaps Johnson, an insider in the Senate's military circle, sensed that this was ahead, because in mid-July he bugled the coming of Armageddon and seemed to be yearning for it. Korea, Johnson said, was "the first battle of a greater struggle" between communism and the West, and "We must accept this fact and understand what it means." The moment, he said, was more fearful than Pearl Harbor. To defeat the North Koreans he was quite ready, conditionally, for the United States to use the atomic bomb again: "I am sure we will use the atomic bomb—if and when it can be used to stem the tide of aggression. But we must remember the Kremlin has an atomic bomb, too." He called for all-out mobilization.[3]

During this national extremity Johnson moved, for the first time, into the magical and menacing garden of the presidential possibility. It was the Truman Committee, watchdogging the war effort against the Axis powers, that had established Truman as presidential timber. Seeing the potential even during that war, Johnson had tried, with only limited success, to play Truman's role on the House side. Now in one leap he landed in the shoes Truman had leapt out of that day in 1945 at the Room.

Senator Johnson proposed the creation of a preparedness subcommittee of the armed services committee. Russell favored Johnson for chairman, and on July 28, a little more than a month after the North Korean invasion, it was announced that Johnson would do it. As chairman of the watchdog committee, Johnson immediately advanced to the uppermost and most secret level of national leaders on military policy.[4]

When the Joint Chiefs of Staff proposed assumptions that would let MacArthur invade North Korea, a shocked Kennan urged Acheson to recognize that the balance of forces in the area clearly precluded our taking North Korea, neighbor to both China and Russia. Acheson paid no attention. Truman's secretary of defense told MacArthur he could "proceed north of the 38th parallel," and when MacArthur construed his orders as authorizing U.S. forces to go north, this was let stand. Chou warned that China "would not stand aside" if North Korea was invaded; China would "not supinely tolerate the destruction of its neighbor." The UN forces invaded anyway, abandoning the goal of restoring the status quo ante. What had begun as "a police action" had become an aggression of its own. MacArthur bombed bridges and planned his major drive to the Yalu River at the border with China. A meeting at State on November 21 was the government's last chance to stop MacArthur, but Acheson, knowing what might come, opposed changing the general's instructions.[5]

The next day Johnson, in Texas, said the U.S. should tell Russia "either you stop starting little fires around the world or else we will be willing to throw our might against your war-making capacity. . . . We are ready to face a showdown."[6] This sounded like an emerging will to destroy Russia's industry with atomic bombs.

Two days later, MacArthur launched his one-hundred-thousand-man offensive, and the Chinese, true to their warning, their counterinvading armies already massed in the North Korean mountains, attacked. Kim Il-Sung's aggression had become a war of the three invasions, and within four days the UN offensive met a crushing defeat. Goaded by McCarthy, misled by MacArthur, bugled onward by Johnson, and left oddly ignorant of Chinese troop movements by military intelligence, Truman and Acheson had made a hideous blunder. Americans were now fighting Chinese in battlefield combat.

Acheson recommended considering the bombing of China—("the bombing of Manchurian airfields and territory")—but only if necessary to save UN forces. As the rout continued Truman declared in a press conference that the use of the atomic bomb was always under active consideration. Britain's prime minister publicly insisted that the U.S. consult its allies before any such use and told Truman the U.S. had to negotiate with the Chinese Communists, recognize them, and admit them to the UN. The U.S. agreed to consult Britain before nuking China, in return for which Britain agreed to desist about U.S. policy toward Peking. But as Joe Goulden reports in *Korea, The Untold Story of the War,* secretly Truman had unassembled atomic bombs flown to the Far East and placed on a U.S. aircraft carrier stationed off the Korean peninsula.

In China itself Mao had mounted a campaign of murderous terror against those he regarded as his enemies. The number of people killed by 1951 has been estimated to have been as few as 135,000 and as many as 15,000,000.[7]

Two days after the UN began an evacuation of 105,000 troops and 350,000 tons of equipment and supplies from North Korea, Johnson said the U.S. was at war not only with Communist China, but with all the "resources behind the Iron Curtain." Again he seemed to lust for the real thing—how tragic it would be, he said, for the West to squander its manhood "in futile, indecisive little wars before the real enemy is engaged."

When Truman declared a state of emergency, Johnson demanded full mobilization—the government had thrown up a chicken-wire screen "instead of a wall of armed might." In the Senate he asked, "Is this our last hour? Is this the hour of our nation's twilight . . . before an endless night shall envelop us and all the Western world?" Bureaucrat David Lilienthal, seeing Johnson at a wedding as this nightmare of a year ended, said he looked like hell.[8]

Still, he had attended to his advancement in the Senate hierarchy. An opening had occurred when Lister Hill of Alabama, his relection jeopardized by whites' anger about Truman's civil rights program, quit as the Democrats' Senate whip. Bobby Baker urged Johnson to go after the job, and at first the Texan said, laughing, "You'll destroy me, because I can't afford to be identified with the Democratic Party right now."—Both the Senate majority leader and whip had been defeated in the last national election. But Johnson, with help from Senator Kerr and Baker, campaigned for the job, lining up votes while the other prospects did not, for Johnson already well knew that often it is not merit but audacity that determines the arrangements among us. "I kept leaking stories to the newspapers that Johnson had the inside track," Baker boasted. In the senators' minds Johnson was identified with oil, military spending, and the southerners' opposition to civil rights, so when he won in the caucus showdown among the Democrats, conservatives exulted. His admiring friend in the press, William S. White, called him "an outright antagonist of the civil rights plan" in whose election "the all-out Fair Dealers were outvoted nearly two to one." This was a victory for Russell and Kerr. Drew Pearson said Johnson was made the whip by southern reactionaries.[9]

MacArthur had demanded permission to blockade China, bomb her industrial capacity and use Chiang's army to invade South China. Clearly he, like Johnson, was ready to engage "the real enemy."

While Truman struggled to keep MacArthur leashed, Lieutenant General Matthew Ridgeway, who was in command of the Eighth Army, evacuated Seoul and withdrew U.S.-related forces to below the thirty-eighth parallel. The Chinese advance halted, Ridgeway began driving back up to the parallel. When China rejected a Canadian overture proposing that foreign troops be withdrawn, the U.S. (and later the UN), in a prime case of the one-sided use of language that seems to typify every war, branded Peking an aggressor. While China had invaded North Korea, obviously she was welcomed by her fellow Communists.

Suddenly, without so much as a by-your-leave to Truman, MacArthur offered to meet the Chinese commander-in-chief on the battlefield. That ended MacArthur's career: Truman fired him. A famous general and a presidential aspirant, MacArthur returned to an orgy of adulation and addressed a joint meeting of Congress. He thought the Joint Chiefs were with him, but during the Senate hearings on his dismissal he learned that presidents were still more powerful than generals.

Johnson regretted MacArthur's firing, but implied that the general had defied civilian authority and that this could lead to military domination. Otherwise Johnson's role was mainly a exchange with Acheson during the Senate hearing. Since Truman's conduct of the war was on trial, the Democrats wanted to show it was wise. One Republican criticism concerned the failure of U.S. allies to help in Korea.

"Mr. Secretary," Johnson asked Acheson, "can you comment here where our allies are helping us elsewhere? I mean Indochina."

"That's an excellent point," Acheson said. "The French have been fighting that battle since World War II."

In a series of questions, Johnson in effect asked MacArthur: if the U.S. pushed to the Yalu, "Are you going to have to keep a large number of men there to protect our position?" MacArthur avoided answering, whereupon Johnson told him that "When you present a positive program, such as you have presented," Congress had to provide the men required.[10] Had the new Democratic whip prevailed in his first major legislative sponsorship, every fit young man in America would have been called to military service.

The 1940 draft act had expired in 1947. The next year a twenty-one-month military obligation had been imposed on nonveterans between nineteen and twenty-six, but only thirty thousand were drafted. The law was to expire at the end of June, 1950, but after North Korea attacked, it was extended into 1951. The Pentagon, with Truman's support, proposed that every young man be required to serve six months' military training and eight years in the reserves—"universal military training," or UMT. A national coalition of alarmed opponents warned that such a permanent law would militarize the country.[11]

Johnson, made chairman of a subcommittee to prepare the UMT bill, was sensitive to the political dangers. He resisted the military's desire to extend tours of duty to twenty-seven from twenty-one months and wanted to delay the calling up of eighteen-year-olds until they were nineteen. He was suspicious of exemptions for most college students ("Where are we going to get our Army if we do that?").

Johnson introduced the administration's bill lowering the draft age to eighteen and providing that later on, when the military had time to gear up for it, every young man would receive at least four months' military training. While opponents warned of "permanent universal conscription" and "a great professional army on the Prussian model," Johnson was concerned with providing the military the men they wanted without taking eighteen-year-olds. To raise armed strength to 3,500,000 men, the Pentagon wanted 1,400,000 more. Convinced that the people were "genuinely disturbed about the drafting of eighteen-year-olds," Johnson proposed requiring that the Pentagon first take 4-Fs and married but childless nonveterans and only then eighteen-year-olds on the basis of those nearest nineteen going first. He announced an inquiry to find out how many women in the services could be reassigned to release "able bodied combat men" for dangerous service.

In the Senate debate, a limit of four million men under arms became an issue. Johnson's newly attained importance in military policy was manifest when he read into the record the opposition, to this ceiling, of the secretary of defense and the Joint Chiefs. It passed anyway, with Johnson and his mentor Russell voting against it.

Apart from institutionalizing a twenty-four-month draft, the law appeared to authorize UMT in the future, but Congress never implemented this.[12] The Korean War ground up so many fighting men, the military had to recall to duty large numbers of World War II veterans while students and fathers continued exempt. Men who had fought in World War II died in Korea while college men and fathers who had been too young for the world war were excused from Korean duty. In an effort to prevent such unfairness from recurring, a step far short of UMT was taken. The National Security Training Corps was created to provide a reserve of men with six months of training, and the six-month option did play a limited role, but with exemptions still in effect military duty continued to fall unfairly on some groups and not on others.[13]

---

65. Senator Strangelove

With American boys dying under the onslaughts of Asians, Johnson ascended into a Strangelovian transport of patriotism and military desperation he would not again approach for fifteen years. During the second half of 1951 he went all-out for a final showdown with the Reds.

To "the mad masters of the Kremlin," he said, the Korean fighting was "only a detail in the communist design for world conquest." Sure as sure could be, there would be a payday: "The inevitability of a showdown—a final test of strength between free men and slave men—may have been delayed; it has not been avoided. We may avoid total war," he said, but if not, hours after an attack on the U.S., American bombers would be over Moscow, each one carrying a bomb sixteen thousand times as powerful as the load carried by all of Doolittle's planes in the famous raid on Tokyo.

As Johnson was saying these things one night in Texas, a top-secret meeting was held in Washington between the secretary of defense and the chairman of the Atomic Energy Commission, increasing speculation that the use of atomic weapons in Korea was being considered. Soon after the Senate convened the next morning, Senator Henry Cabot Lodge of Massachusetts, a member of the foreign relations committee, advocated dropping tactical atomic bombs and firing atomic artillery shells in Korea if it could be done "efficiently and profitably." He presented an argument for first giving civilians "an ample time to evacuate" and then creating "a defensive line of atomic craters . . . across the Korean peninsula." That same day in Dallas, perhaps responding to the same top-secret stimuli as Lodge, Johnson threatened, in public, nuclear attacks not only on Korea, but also on Russia. To a jammed luncheon gathering of the business elite of Dallas, Johnson discussed the U.S. giving an ultimatum to Russia much as a sheriff might hope for a final shoot-out with Bonnie and Clyde.

The "police action" in Korea had served a purpose, Johnson said, by giving the U.S. time to triple its armies and double its air force and combat ships. In a display of the same logic that later led him into Vietnam, he said that failing to fight back in "calculated cowardice" could have won only "defeat, dishonor, and destruction."

But the time had come when the U.S. could not afford to be drawn into such "police actions" as Korea or perhaps later in Indochina, he said—that was "the course of battling a slave—and letting his master go scot-free."

In the spring, Iran, the buffer state between Russia and the Persian Gulf, had nationalized its British oil holdings; a progressive nationalist, Mohammed Mossadeq, had become prime minister; and the U.S. had cut off military aid. This was the context to Johnson's reference to Iran as he told his Dallas friends:

"We can go on fighting in Korea. We can probably handle another war in Indochina. We may even be able to take on a bout in Iran or Yugoslavia. But somewhere, sometime, something will snap." When it did, he said, the American people would demand a direct showdown with Russia. Unless those who plotted the destruction of our system changed their ways, he said, "it will come," and the United States will "crush this tyrant once and for all."

"It may take the form of an ultimatum . . . a warning to the communist commanders in North Korea—'make peace, quit stalling, or we will hit you with everything we have.'

"It may be a declaration to the communist conspirators of the world —. . . . 'At the first sign of aggression, at the first step you take over your boundary, we will smash you with whatever it takes to do the job.'

"It may be a declaration to the masters of the conspiracy themselves

—the men who sit behind the walls of the Kremlin—'We are tired of fighting your stooges; we will no longer waste our substance battling your slaves. . . . The next aggression will be the last. We will strike back not at your satellites—but you. We will strike back with all the dreaded might that is within our control, and it will be a crushing blow."

The Democratic whip knew what he was saying. "I realize full well," he said, "the awesome potentialities of this proclamation." A fast-rising new member of the American politico-military leadership was clearly implying that because of actions by smaller Communist nations, the U.S. well might initiate a nuclear strike against Russia.

Two weeks later in west Texas he called for Armageddon. "Someday, somewhere, someway," he said, "there must be a clear-cut settlement between the forces of freedom and the forces of communism. It is foolish to talk of avoiding war. We are already in a war—a major war. The war in Korea is a war of Soviet Russia."

And then, in February, 1952, in a newsletter bristling with italics, he advocated, without qualification, a nuclear attack on Russia if any Communist forces anywhere committed any act the U.S. regarded as aggression. "We should announce, I believe," he said, "that *any* act of aggression, *any*where, by *any* communist forces, *will be regarded as an act of aggression by the Soviet Union. . . .* If *any*where in the world—by *any* means, *open or concealed*—communism trespasses upon the soil of the free world, *we should unleash all the power at our command upon the vitals of the Soviet Union.*"

In the event, then, of any aggression by any Communist state or any civil rebellion behind which U.S. officials thought they saw the Russian hand, the United States should lob its atomic bombs into the Soviet Union, even though this would kill hundreds of millions of human beings there and, by retaliation, in the United States, blighting civilization for generations or forever. Two years earlier the Republican secretary of state, John Foster Dulles, declared that the U.S. should depend for its defense "primarily upon a great capacity to retaliate instantly by means and places of our own choosing." Now the Senate Democratic whip, who was a future president, advocated all-out nuclear retaliation against Russia whether the offending force was Russia herself, a small Communist nation, or even a native rebellion.[1]

Wild and dangerous though this was, it was hardly wilder or more dangerous than President Truman's own apocalyptic thoughts, recorded, apparently for his eyes only, in his handwritten private journal.

Johnson of course had private time with Truman. Judging from Truman's appointment books, the Texan was with him alone in the Oval Office five or more times before 1952. The month before Johnson's bellicose newsletter, and two weeks before Truman's first private entry on eliminating Moscow and Peking, the senator saw Truman half an hour at the president's request. Truman might have shared his thoughts on the Korean War with the chairman of the hawkish Senate watchdog committee.

Be that as it may have been, the president who had already used atomic bombs on Japan considered ordering all-out attacks on the Soviet Union and China if they did not fold up the Korean War. Unbeknownst to the American people until 1980 when historian Francis L. Loewenheim first reported on it, Truman wrote on Jan. 27, 1952:

"It seems to me that the proper approach now would be an ultimatum with a 10-day expiration limit, informing Moscow that we intend to blockade the China coast from the Korean border to Indochina, and that we intend to destroy every military base in Manchuria by means now in our control—and if there is further interference we shall eliminate any ports or cities necessary to accomplish our purposes.

"This means all-out war. It means that Moscow, St. Petersburg, Mukden, Vladivostok, Peking, Shanghai, Port Arthur, Darien, Odessa, Stalingrad and every manufacturing plant in China and the Soviet Union will be eliminated."

The Korean War ceasefire talks in Panmunjon, begun in July, 1951, were going nowhere, and in a handwritten May 18, 1952, memorandum, Truman said, as if addressing the Chinese and the Soviets directly:

"Now do you want an end to hostilities in Korea or do you want China and Siberia destroyed? You may have one or the other; whichever you want, these lies of yours at this conference have gone far enough. You either accept our fair and just proposal or you will be completely destroyed."[2]

---

66. The Invisible Vice-Presidential Candidate

Johnson spent 1952 darting through the political underbrush, stalking the vice-presidential nomination, hell-bent for the White House.

Truman, coming up for a second term, but plagued by petty scandals among his gift-laden cronies and blamed for the dreary and bloody war, was acutely vulnerable to attacks from the southern Bourbons who hated his civil rights program, and as the year opened Johnson was blasting him as if the Senate Democratic whip was the natural-born enemy of the Democratic president. In Texas, Johnson said a "day of reckoning" was coming for grafters who sold America's birthright for a mink coat. In an interview for his state's arch-rightist daily he saw no chance for the passage of any of Truman's Fair Deal legislation.[1]

This was not a senator preparing to fight for his president's reelection, but neither would Johnson take Truman on. Estes Kefauver, the drawling trust-buster from Tennessee, had captured the country with his Senate crime subcommittee hearings, while Johnson, with his watchdog committee, had not; and it was Kefauver who went forward against the war-weakened president. In the New Hampshire primary (in a prevision of the event that would knock Johnson out of the White House sixteen years later), Kefauver trounced Truman, and two weeks later the humiliated president said he would not seek reelection.

In the ensuing primaries listing candidates or pledged delegate candidates, Kefauver outpolled Richard Russell nine to one and Adlai Stevenson, the governor of Illinois, forty-two to one. Another poll showed Estes a three-and-a-half-to-one favorite over Adlai among the Democrats. But all this only made the Tennesseean worse poison to the Democratic bosses he had alienated by exposing Democratic ties with mobsters. Just one senator, Paul Douglas of Illinois, endorsed him. "Lyndon didn't like Estes Kefauver," Lyndon's brother said, because "Estes was getting more publicity than Lyndon and both of 'em wanted to be president—hell, that was all there was to that."

Once Roosevelt's protégé, Johnson now actively favored Russell, the arch-conservative segregationist, for the presidency. This was the year the Georgian thought he had a chance. Lyndon was beholden to Russell, as Senator Joseph Clark of Pennsylvania said, and he still needed the Georgian's patronage in the Senate. Texas oilman Sid Richardson, who favored Russell, had taken on John Connally as his political lawyer. And since Allan Shivers, the labor-baiting Texas governor and a potential candidate against Johnson in 1954, was for Russell, too, Johnson saw a chance to both mollify and finesse a powerful figure in his future.

But the main thing, if the columnists, Evans and Novak, had it right, was a secret pact between Russell and Johnson. Even after he had served in the White House, Johnson advised a Texas politician that the only way he could reach the presidency was through the vice-presidency. Many times Johnson said no southerner would be elected president. An Austin newsman who knew Johnson well wrote that he "hopes for the vice-presidential nomination in 1952." By the pact between Russell and Johnson, the Texan would do all he could to help nominate the Georgian for president, but that failing, as Johnson expected it to, the powerful Georgian would then do all he could to help Johnson be nominated for the vice-presidency. Johnson even had a floor manager picked out for the Russell-Johnson team. In the opinion of George Reedy, who was close to Russell, the Georgian was cultivating Johnson because he believed he was the only southerner who might be elected president.[2]

In 1952, for Texas politicians tidelands oil was the big issue. The coastal states, especially Texas, Louisiana, and California, wanted title to the oil off their coasts under the submerged plains of the continental shelf. Off California the shelf could be drilled as far out as 20 miles—off the Gulf states, 70 to 140 miles. The oil companies figured they would make higher profits if the states, rather than the federal government, owned the oil and conducted the leasing. Truman, however, believed the oil belonged to the country, and in 1945 he vetoed a bill giving it to the states. After the Supreme Court ruled that the U.S. had "paramount rights" 3 miles out, the words "tidelands oil" began rolling off the tongues of the southern statesmen as smoothly as "southern womanhood." Johnson joined with the tidelands senators in proposing another quitclaim bill for the states. The political strategists of business in Texas sensed an issue here that might swing the state Republican—Truman was taking oil-leasing revenues away from Texas schoolkiddies.[3]

Tom Connally, the senior senator from Texas, and a member of Congress since 1917 and chairman of the Senate foreign relations committee, came up for reelection this year, too. His opponent was the Texas attorney general Price Daniel, who was prepared to use the tidelands issue against him. Senator Connally told a writer that Shivers was behind Daniel and Johnson had promised Shivers to back his choice. Tom Connally thought it less likely that Lyndon had knuckled under to Shivers than that he simply wanted to stop being called the junior senator from Texas. When a group on whom Connally relied for support told him he was finished, rather than try again he retired. Johnson promptly pledged his support to Daniel.

Johnson had written Truman in 1951 that the prospect of federal leasing of the tidelands was "shocking to me" and would be "an unthinkable display of contempt for Congress and for the states." Where Lyndon's letter said, "The people of Texas are sorely disturbed," someone put a heavy "x" over the word "Texas," maybe the president himself, because the feisty Missourian retorted to Johnson, ". . . I labor under the opinion that Missouri is just as much entitled to Tidelands as Texas, California, or Louisiana, and if I can help it as President of the United States, I'm going to see that the whole United States profits from the national ownership of Tidelands oil."[4]

Since the split in 1944, the Texas Democrats had divided into progressive and conservative camps. In 1952 the liberals suspected that the business Democrats, steamed up about tidelands oil and aligned with racists who were steamed up against civil rights, would betray the party by switching to the Republicans after the national convention. The Dixiecrats (in Texas named "Shivercrats" after the governor) favored Russell for the nomination. The loyalists generally favored Kefauver.

With Shivers berating the "socialist philosophy creeping into Democratic councils," the anti-Truman forces won control of the state convention in San Antonio. Maury Maverick, leading the liberals, proposed that all delegates pledge to support the party's nominees, but was declared out of order. The great curmudgeon led the liberals out of the hall, leaving the Shivercrats there. The rumpers marched a mile through the rain to Maverick's beloved La Villita, a Mexican village that had been restored by the New Deal, and selected a rival set of delegates pledged to support the nominees.[5]

The Democrats' national convention in Chicago would have to decide whether to seat the Shivercrats or the Mavericks. According to Walter Hall, chairman of the Maverick delegation, Truman, in a letter to Maverick, vowed he would see the Mavericks seated, but the liberals also heard that Russell had threatened a bolt if the Shivercrats weren't seated. By one report Johnson shepherded Shivers around Washington to let him make the case for his delegation. In Rayburn's office in the Capitol, Hall told the Speaker that Shivers was going to bolt and support the Republicans.

"Walter," Rayburn replied, "I can't believe the governor of Texas would tell an unadulterated lie. He sat in that chair you're sitting in and told me . . . that no matter what happened, he would not bolt the party."

"Mr. Sam," Hall replied, "I think he's lying."

Years later Shivers said he told Rayburn that "we could not pledge that we would vote for whoever the nominee was—and would not!—that as of that time we had no intention of *not* supporting the nominee—always had and hoped we always would."[6]

At Chicago, Kefauver led in the pre-convention delegate count, Russell was a good second, Adlai Stevenson a poor fifth. Jesse Jones, the New Dealer who had backed Dewey in 1948 and was publishing the *Houston Chronicle,* ordered his reporters and editors in Chicago to start a boom for Rayburn, who encouraged their efforts.

Rayburn, however, was to preside over the convention. Sources agree Johnson escorted Shivers to Rayburn's suite at the Blackstone Hotel to discuss the problem of which Texas delegation would be seated. Bringing Shivers and Rayburn together, Johnson was helping the Dixiecrats against the Roosevelt-Truman Democrats of his own state. In the meeting, Rayburn thought Shivers said he would support whoever was nominated, but again by Shivers' account he made no commitment.[7]

According to Herman Talmadge, then governor of Georgia, Johnson was "working diligently" to get Russell the nomination. The Shivercrats were seated, leaving the Texas liberals outside. In the presidential balloting Kefauver led on the first and second ballots. With Truman's sudden backing, Stevenson won on the third; but all three times Texas voted for Russell. Kefauver believed the Democrats' will had been thwarted by Truman and other Democratic bosses.[8]

A Johnson lawyer who spent time in Senator Russell's suite during the convention said the Georgian and Johnson were very close there, and now it was time for Russell to pay up on his part of the deal. According to Sam Houston Johnson, Russell and Rayburn went to Stevenson and advocated that Johnson be chosen as the vice-presidential candidate. ("I know it," Sam Houston said, "because Lyndon told me.") Lyndon knew Adlai would not beat the likely GOP nominee, General Dwight Eisenhower, but figured that the second spot would build him toward 1956, Lyndon's brother said. As Sam had it, Adlai gave Russell and Rayburn the impression he would accept Lyndon as his running mate. But Stevenson—and perhaps Truman—decided No. Perhaps Johnson's anti-Trumanism and support of the segregationist Russell was too much for them.[9]

After the convention Shivers journeyed to Illinois to discuss tidelands oil with Stevenson. Contrary to advice from Johnson that he shilly-shally, Stevenson told Shivers he was for federal ownership. Giving this as the reason, Shivers led the fall Texas Democratic convention into an official endorsement of Eisenhower-Nixon, betraying the party in whose name he was governor. Rayburn had been taken in and Johnson had helped it happen. Rayburn, his later friend Booth Mooney said, "felt that Shivers had lied to him and betrayed him."[10]

Hunkering down with his thoughts about his own race in 1954, Johnson did little to help carry Texas for Stevenson. "Well, Sam Houston," he asked his brother, "why should I be for him? Goddammit, he promised Rayburn and Russell he'd put me on the ticket and then he didn't do it. And he couldn't have gotten it without Rayburn and Russell and me. And then—goddamn fool—he let Allan Shivers go up there and trap him on tidelands. What do you want to do, crucify me?" Besides, as Anna Rosenberg Hoffman, who was an honorary chairman for Stevenson, said of Johnson, "He didn't like Adlai. Adlai just wasn't his kind of man."

The second sentence of Johnson's lukewarm endorsement of his party's nominees stated he disagreed with Stevenson on "our Texas tidelands." Shivers, actively leading the Eisenhower campaign in the state, said later Johnson talked to him "about his position and what he was going to do in it and what effect it might have on his '54 race." By one report, when Stevenson asked Johnson to introduce him in Texas, Johnson asked Shivers if doing it would hurt him with the conservatives. Shivers told him he had to do what Stevenson asked. Johnson asked if Shivers would protect him on it, and Shivers said he would.

Johnson agreed to introduce Stevenson, but said that Amon Carter, the Fort Worth publisher, phoned him and "asked me—no, he didn't, he *told* me—not to do it." Lyndon's brother thought John Connally had prompted Carter to make the call.

When the Stevenson campaign train entered the state, Johnson went aboard quietly and looked up Senator William Fulbright of Arkansas, who was close to Stevenson. "Bill," Lyndon said, "I'm sorry, but I can't campaign for Adlai in Texas. It would hurt my reelection chances." Fulbright erupted—cussed Johnson out—named him a renegade—and may have threatened to oppose him as Senate Democratic Leader.

Introducing Adlai in Fort Worth, Johnson spoke as glowingly of him as he would be expected to, and he also made a state radio broadcast for the ticket, but as much as he could he held back. Ralph Yarborough, the Texas Populist who had just run against Shivers for the governorship (losing two to one), believed that Johnson, aware that his big oil backers Richardson and Clint Murchison were for Eisenhower, hid out at his ranch until Stevenson's presence in the state forced him to make a minimum effort. Hank Brown, a labor leader who later became president of the Texas union movement, worked two months for Stevenson in San Antonio and thought they could have won Texas, "but we didn't do much. The literature always came late and the campaign was always late and we had very little to do it with. . . . Johnson took a beating, among many of us," for doing so little. As Shivers himself observed, Johnson did not *stump* for Stevenson. Drew Pearson nicknamed Johnson "Lyin' Down Lyndon," saying he made only two speeches for Adlai. Johnson was storing up ill-will from the liberals of his own state as if he had never had any connection with the progressive cause.[11]

While Yarborough and Maverick went down fighting Shivers in 1952 and Stevenson went down fighting Eisenhower, Johnson improved his position among the conservatives for his reelection in '54, and even though his undercover play for the vice-presidency had come to naught, before the year ended he took into his hands more power than any other Democrat in the country except Rayburn.

---

67. Truman in History

President Truman's popularity had plummeted at the end of his term because of the bloody Korean War and the corruption in his administration. By the late fifties and early sixties, the human costs of the war were forgotten because they were so painful and the corruption was forgotten because it was so trivial, and Truman was ranked, especially by liberal historians, among the great presidents. He had stymied world communism; launching the American part of the cold war and then going into Korea, he had given Stalin his come-uppance. And he had a compassionate program, too.—That was the gist of the judgment.

His Fair Deal was largely ignored in this assessment; having failed, it was forgotten. He should have been credited for carrying on the directions of the New Deal, especially for initiating the proposal for national health insurance, and for being the first American president to propose broad reforms to protect the rights of minorities. When medicare and civil rights proposals became law under Johnson, Truman's contributions here came to be better appreciated.

In the longer retrospect his failures could be seen better, too, and they exceeded in historical importance the ground-breaking proposals of his Fair Deal. By instituting internal, governmental witch-hunting, he set the official example—an example swiftly turned against him by his fellow Democrat Johnson in the Olds case and then against the country itself in what came to be called McCarthyism. Despite rhetoric about economic aid for the poor nations, the Truman Doctrine quickly became global, militaristic adventurism and, by 1954, secret warfare, as well. The Truman-Acheson administration may have bobbled a real chance to develop Chinese Communist independence from the Soviet Union and abandoned neutrality toward the French colonialists of Indochina. President Truman's pledge of U.S. support for the French against Ho Chi Minh was this nation's first plunge down the chute to the Vietnam War. Then the Truman-Acheson administration waged war on North Korea without a declaration of war by Congress. Perhaps the U.S. should have gone in, but only with a declaration by Congress, and not so far in. Having presented and justified the Korean War as a police action to restore the boundary to what it was before North Korea invaded, Truman consciously transformed it into a military drive into and up North Korea toward the very border of China, an aggression only less obvious than the North Koreans', provoking the Chinese counterattack that should have been expected as a consequence of such folly. Then, in 1952, with what seriousness we do not know, President Truman considered, at least in his own mind, destroying the Chinese and Soviet societies.

In the history of civilization (transcending that of nations), people's first use of nuclear weapons against each other was a signal event unlike any other. President Truman's stature in the broadest ranges of history will also express the cumulative judgment on his ordering that the two U.S. atomic bombs be dropped upon two unwarned Japanese cities.

His justification was that, in so doing, he ended the terrible war and avoided the necessity of invading Japan, an invasion in which a million people might have been killed. A final Allied invasion of the Japanese islands would, or at the least could have been obviated by an economic blockade, forcing the submission of the Japanese before the certain alternative of their starvation. Truman's order resulted in the deaths of several hundred thousand civilians and lingering injuries for uncountable others. Hiroshima and Nagasaki also deprived the human race of the chance to ban these planet-stunning weapons before any nation had used them. In an epoch already hideously disfigured by the Soviets' Gulag Archipelago and the Germans' racist genocide, the Americans' unnecessary use of the atomic bombs against Japanese cities was a tragic and momentous error, a deed without vision that defines the meaning of the Truman presidency in the fullness of time.

---

68. Gut Politics in the High Grass

Just at dawn the morning after the 1952 election, the vote-counting showed that Jack Kennedy, the playboy scion of the Joseph P. Kennedy clan, had defeated Henry Cabot Lodge for a seat in the United States Senate. The prize was still glistening in the early light when the call from Texas came—Johnson extending his congratulations. Turning to Larry O'Brien, Kennedy said, "The guy must never sleep." How could he when he knew that the Senate majority leader, Ernest McFarland of Arizona, had lost to a department-store owner named Goldwater?

Bobby Baker was beckoned out of law class in Washington to take a call from Johnson at the ranch.

"It looks like you're the new leader," Baker told him. "All you've got to do is convince one man and you're home free."

"You're talkin' about Dick Russell," Johnson said.

Russell had the allegiance of half or more of the forty-seven Democrats in the new Senate, but Baker surmised the Georgian would not want to be the leader himself. According to Sam Houston, Lyndon told Baker to get Burnett Maybank of South Carolina, Baker's sponsor in the Senate, to call Russell and urge him to take it, but if Russell said no, to reply, "Well, it has to be Lyndon." Baker first persuaded Maybank to wire Johnson a pledge of support should Russell decline—then Baker spread news of the wire. When, during Maybank's call to Russell, Russell did decline and Maybank said it had to be Lyndon, Russell replied, "Well, yes." Johnson himself phoned Russell and proposed that the Georgian take over. (At the least, as Sam said, Lyndon wanted to be "on the inside.") "I'll do the work and you'll be the boss," Johnson told Russell. No, Russell said—you be it. OK, Lyndon said, if you'll move your seat in the Senate to right behind mine.

Darting like a fox, Johnson phoned Shivers now and told him Russell had told him he didn't want to be the Democratic leader and would support Johnson for it. "What do you think about it?" he asked the governor who had just carried his state for Eisenhower.

"I think it's great. You ought to do it. Do you think you can get enough votes?"

"I think I can," Johnson said. "The only thing that bothers me—this position is open because [McFarland] has just been defeated. And the one before him . . . was defeated while he was Majority Leader. And I don't want to take this position and then get defeated in my next election!"

This was gut politics in the high grass. One can imagine Johnson, head cocked to one side, eyes squinting, hand on his hip, Shivers clamping his lips together, thinking quickly. As a right-winger Shivers would want the newly conservative Johnson running the Democrats' business in the Senate to check the "wild-eyed liberals" there. More specifically, Johnson as the Democrats' leader would help consummate the cause over which Shivers had supported Eisenhower: state ownership of the tidelands. But now, here on the telephone, Johnson was asking him—the very man who was in a position to replace him or help clobber him for reelection in a year and a half—for assurance that he wouldn't do it if Johnson took the Democrats' leadership. Shivers replied at once:

"Well, I don't think you run that risk. I think you ought to take it because you know how to do the job, and you'll do a great job and be a great service to the country, to Texas to have its own senator in that position."[1]

This was a critical moment. The party of Roosevelt and Truman, the New Deal and the Fair Deal, was passing into the hands of congressional and state-level politicians who were entailed in compromised liaisons with—or were themselves agents of—major corporate interests. In Johnson's call there was a webbing of pure shrewdness. A deal was implied, a potential foe finessed. Most likely Johnson would have gone for the leader's job with or without Shivers' approval. But as much as any other single event, this talk between them signified the massing power of the corporations, of which the politics of the coming period was only a function.

Though the Republicans had carried Texas by only three votes out of a hundred, Johnson decided to back President Eisenhower on the issues much of the time. Further to impress conservative Texans he decided to bring into his office, as his "executive assistant," Booth Mooney, who had done much of the brainwork for Coke Stevenson's 1948 race against him.

Late in 1952, one morning at eight o'clock, Mooney, responding to an invitation, called on Johnson in Austin, and for the rest of the morning the senator talked "nearly nonstop." The thrust of it, according to Mooney, was that "about half the voters of Texas were against him. He had to make a dent in that large body of citizens before 1954, when he would be up for re-election, and he knew I could help him do it. . . . He, Johnson, was not really the all-out-New-Deal-Harry-Truman-liberal that many Texans believed him to be. He wanted to—he must—project a more conservative image. If he was elected Democratic floor leader, he would have an opportunity to lead his colleagues in support of the Republican president when matters affecting the general welfare—and

WIDE WORLD PHOTOS

The swearing-in: Senator Arthur Vandenberg, R.-Mich., swears in new senators in the class of 1948, left to right, J. Allen Frear, D.-Del., Johnson, Paul H. Douglas, D.-Ill., and Robert S. Kerr, D.-Okla. Johnson promptly joined with Kerr in sponsoring legislation to free natural gas producers from federal price controls, with the estimable liberal Douglas leading the opposition.

ACME NEWSPICTURES

Johnson was included in President Harry Truman's stag parties on the presidential yacht. The two are shown on the yacht with a presidential adviser.

DENNY HAYES, DALLAS TIMES-HERALD

Texas Governor Allan Shivers was a likely candidate against Johnson in 1954, but Johnson went to work ingratiating himself to the right-wing Shivers. Johnson grins as Shivers speaks at an open house at Walker's Austex Chili in Austin in the fall of 1950.

General Eisenhower and Johnson during a Senate committee hearing on February 2, 1951.

INTERNATIONAL NEWS PHOTOS

EXPRESS-NEWS CORP.

In the early fifties the Johnsons bought "the big house" up the river that had belonged to Johnson's aunt and uncle, Clarence and Frank Martin, placing Lyndon's own family in the position of poor relations. The front of the ranch-house of what then became known as the LBJ Ranch.

Left, Lyndon and Bird at the ranch. Right, Lyndon rings the dinner bell.

EXPRESS-NEWS CORP.

EXPRESS-NEWS CORP.

UPI PHOTO

Johnson kisses Speaker Sam Rayburn's bald pate on Rayburn's seventy-sixth birthday in 1952.

Johnson and Governor Adlai Stevenson of Illinois talking at a Democratic dinner in New York City in February, 1951. Johnson, who did not like Stevenson, worked in 1952 for the nomination of Senator Richard Russell of Georgia for president. When the Democrats nominated Stevenson, Johnson laid low, but endorsed his party's nominee.

TOMMY WEBER, JOHNSON LIBRARY

ACME NEWSPICTURES

Left to right, Senators Johnson, Wayne Morse, the maverick from Oregon, and Richard Russell of Georgia.

Governor Allan Shivers of Texas, left, and Johnson conferring on a buggy during a western party in the fall of 1951. Johnson was ingratiating himself both to Russell, one of the leaders of the southern bloc that ran the Senate, and to Shivers, whom Johnson feared might run against him for reelection to the Senate.

W. FRANK EVANS

Senators Johnson and Russell on the second or third day of January, 1953. With Russell's nod, Johnson was elected leader of the Senate Democratic minority—which became the majority in the 1954 elections, making Johnson the boss of the Senate.

UNITED PRESS ASSOCIATIONS

especially the welfare of Texans—were at stake." Dazed by Johnson's "thick flattery, urgent persuasion, appeals to my patriotism, and hints that many men who worked for him went on to high-paying jobs in private industry," Mooney said OK.[2]

After Russell endorsed Johnson for leader other senators followed suit. Senator-elect Kennedy pledged his support. Fulbright and Drew Pearson, sore about the noncampaign for Adlai in Texas, "did a little maneuvering" against Johnson, Pearson said, and Senate liberals decided to oppose him. Sam Houston claims he provoked a policy writer for the *Dallas News* into writing that if Johnson didn't get it the wild-eyed Humphrey would, after which Jesse Jones and Amon Carter phoned and urged Johnson to try for it.[3]

Lyndon romanced Humphrey with a promise he'd be his "ambassador to the liberals," a plan to modify the Senate seniority rule, and a hint about a seat on foreign relations. Baker told Hubert seductively, "I wouldn't be surprised if he brought you into the leadership circle." When, even so, Humphrey backed the liberal Murray of Montana for the job, Johnson told him he was foolish to think his man would get many votes. When Humphrey tried to bargain with him, Johnson snapped, "I'm through wastin' my time. Get over there and get your eight votes and get humiliated." In the caucus Johnson won handily; whether Murray received eight or three, Humphrey moved to make it unanimous.[4]

The liberals organized as Americans for Democratic Action, the ADA, who watched national politics all the time, sensed what had befallen the party of Roosevelt and Truman. Their magazine said Johnson, making book with the southern conservatives and facing Dixiecrat Shivers for reelection in 1954, would be of little help to northern Democrats who had to seek election then and in 1956: "His support for the oil lobby and the beef trust and his opposition to civil rights and the regulation of natural gas will hurt the Democrats in their efforts to build a record on which to go to the people in coming elections."[5]

PART XIII
In the Wider View

Thank God our time is now when wrong
Comes up to face us everywhere,
Never to leave us till we take
The longest stride of soul men ever took.
Affairs are now soul size.

— Meadows in "A Sleep of Prisoners," by Christopher Fry, 1957

69. The Politician as Predator

After the laissez-faire era, corporations became predators on the public. "Tit for tat," in the Johnson Period, politicians, using the public's delegated power and tax money, became predators on the corporations.

Johnson's own career exemplified what happened. His cynical attitudes about money power and about political money, borne out through his affinities for responsively cynical associates, were part of the long fall of the democracy, including the Democratic party, into cooptation and de facto corruption.

In the American ideal, yeoman farmers and city-dwelling citizens govern themselves intelligently, considering the issues and the candidates and then electing their representatives. The reality, an odious farce contrasted to the beauty and wisdom of the ideal, is the principal source of the alternating alienation and cynicism among the waves of the arriving young. When you promise to show a boy a mansion of many gardens and take him, instead, to a whorehouse, he wonders about you.

The transition from laissez faire to the politician as predator began with the perception, by many men in many similar situations, of a new opportunity. Some of the chieftains of corporations (and, in variant special situations, the corrupt leaders of some unions, notably the teamsters, as well) saw that government as their hidden partner was just the thing to give them safety as they rolled on toward more bigness and wealth. All one had to do was accept selected politicians into de facto partnerships. All these politicians had to do was make their personal decisions to use their public power for their secret partners' private profit and welfare, the while contriving convincing cover stories, such as national preparedness or loyalty to their state's dominant industry or free enterprise or workers' welfare or the "American way."

The men of private business power know that official favors have enormous dollar value. Anticipating, from their inside knowledge of its necessity, the governmentalization of the economy, they use the predatorial politicians to aim the government's golden funnel into their own domains. Many ways are easily found to reward the sleepers on the public's political juries. These sleepers, selling their bureaucratic influence and inside knowledge and either selling or renting out their impact on public debate and policy, receive from every secret side favors, huge sums of money, and publicity for their careers. The money is usually, but not always, called campaign contributions.

As Darwin might see this process, some of the chieftains of corporations and government organized the citizens' tax funds, authority, and purchasing power into a latticework of catwalks from which the citizens can be preyed upon.

Government in the public's name sets and enforces, or fails to enforce, the conditions and minimum standards of commerce and gives or refuses to give business specific permissions, properties, tax monies, and contracts. To the chieftain of the corporation, the truly powerful chieftain in government is a threat: he holds the levers that manipulate the corporation's access to credit, resources, productive processes, and even the citizens whose purchases are the golden coin. The government chieftain can be either a clever friend or a devastating enemy because of government's general authority over commerce and its givings or refusals of nods and favors to corporations or entire industries.

The predatorial politician, like a bank robber who is also the bank teller, often partially controls the record on which he is judged. In granting media licenses and controlling various conditions of production, the government uses subjective judgments that are not always susceptible to effective challenge. In tax fraud, antitrust, and many regulatory areas, government agencies refuse the public substantial knowledge in order to protect the corporations and individuals that are charged. The fat military contracts often are let on the basis of tangled, vague, and amorphous factors. Political influence is inherent, as organic to the process as wind currents to gliding. Politicians, from bureaucrats to presidents, knowing when they are using their public authority in order to direct profit toward a chosen corporation, may transact such business orally. The telephone is quick and personal and usually leaves no record.

In Johnson's case, he began without money of his own, living off his teacher's and then his federal salaries. His development as a predatorial politician involved three fairly distinct forms. For his first leg up he used his wife's money and his public power to get wealth for his family and thus for himself through the radio-television business. He used his public power to get or protect wealth for business which in turn got campaign money and publicity to him. He used his public power to get campaign money and publicity from business to other politicians who in *their* turn helped him increase his public power. In sum, he built his own engine of public and private power by using his public power to obtain, protect, or provide special advantages.

Because a government-using politician needs to conceal from the public the processes by which he is getting rich and reelected, the secrecy and deceit for which Johnson became notorious as president also characterized every important step in his business career. As a one-time member of his circle said, there were "false fronts everywhere." Nevertheless, his three forms of predatory politics—Government to Self, Government to Business to Self, and Government to Business to Other Politicians to Self—were irregular in their emergence, but clear in their cumulative reality. By about 1958 his mature employment of these forms had evolved into a compound system for producing power and wealth from politics that in its range, professionalism, caution, and cynicism was unlike anything known before in the American democracy.

He applied this system mainly in four areas: government construction, sometimes under cost-plus-profit contracts that are government-guaranteed gain and literally reward inefficiency; government-licensed radio and TV stations and the network affiliations and advertising from the business community on which, once licensed, such stations depend; the oil industry, subsidized by hundreds of billions of dollars worth of the citizens' taxes and its profits further enhanced by whatever government policies on prices, supply limitations, leasing practices, drilling rights, and imports best serve in the shifting situation; and the aerospace industry, underwritten and expanded by government policy decisions that have multibillion-dollar meanings for the Corporate Society.

Specializing, one after another, in these four areas—government construction, the broadcast media, oil, and aerospace—Johnson got political profit from the first, personal profit from the second, and intensified political profit from the third, and after the Sputnik uproar of 1957 and his space hearings the ensuing year, he hit the political predator's jackpot, the wary but opportunistic support of a broad selection of major corporations as their chieftains realized that he was working full-throttle from his positions of power in the Senate and the Democratic party to achieve government-funded conditions of commerce that would enrich them. His methods cohered just as he and his group in the government stepped onto the escalators that rise to the summits of political authority. Finally he became the presiding political profiteer of "the President's Club" and a fascinating group of sub-chieftains and agents who moved fluidly in and out of government and corporations. After three decades of deploying his public power for personal or political profit, he was a multimillionaire ranging through his personal domain of mass-media stations, banks, ranches, a dummy corporation, and a foundation, and he was the president of the United States—not just the chief politician, but in certain intimations the chief among the chieftains, the predator upon whose decisions and orders the luck and lot of the others waited and for the time being depended.[1]

Much then went askew, but the new patterns and Johnson's own case clearly raised the question whether, as in Darwin's survival of the fittest, democracy can survive powerful systems of both economic and political predators. If the "partnership" of government and the corporations, of which Johnson was the most successful agent and Richard Nixon a bolder, but cruder one, is consummated within hollowed-out democratic forms, it can result in a new kind of fascism—one with a democratic form.

As fascism is usually conceived in Europe, it is the ruling of a people by a merger of government and big business. The predatorial politician, whose banal motive is his own power and wealth, has now acquired an historically important role as the principal agent in the impending debasement of the world's foremost experiment in democracy. In the Johnson Period, we are dealing not merely with more episodes of American politicians using their public standing for corporate interests. Now we must deal with the prospect (which some believe is already the reality) that the two kinds of predators, the corporate and the political, will join their techniques and interests together so thoroughly, the United States will become the Incorporated Democracy, its rulers periodically still chosen in elections, but in elections that present the people only carefully pre-limited options and are then dominated by the themes and devices of the conspiracies between the corporate and political predators.

---

70. The Confrontation

From the international point of view, Johnson had advanced himself dramatically in American politics by leaping wholeheartedly into the forefront of the anti-Communist crusade that has dominated American foreign policy since World War II. Not until too late in his own presidency did he seem to have serious second thoughts about his leadership in the Confrontation.

The anti-Communist crusade was a reaction against the "Second

World," the bully-states whose peoples were being kept under control by the murderous repression of their liberties. In these same years, in the "Third World," impoverished peoples who had never before mattered much to Western civilization became aware of their condition and its contrast to life in the developed nations. Their violent experimentations, liberations, and oppressions exposed the once-revolutionary United States as itself counterrevolutionary on a world scale. Three reform presidents, Truman, Kennedy, and Johnson, Democrats all, worked to advance social justice in the United States, but proved themselves no less counterrevolutionary abroad than the contemporary Republican presidents.

During the postwar gloom in the United States, communism was perceived as four threatening evils. Prevailing only in police states, it repressed civil liberties and scorned political democracy. Uniting the state and the economic system, it scorned free enterprise and privately owned mega-corporations. Its leaders and nations were atheistic. Its military strength was a fourth and major menace. These four evils were taken to be aspects of a monolithic Communist world, a single adversary that could not vary from nation to nation and was controlled from Moscow.

In the Soviet Union, and after 1949 in China, the United States was perceived as the prime historical evil, capitalism in a nation. Political democracy was the trick by which the rich kept their power, and civil liberties were sham and window-dressing: democracies permitting capitalism were assumed to be ruled by the capitalists. The Soviets and the Chinese naturally then perceived American military strength as a summarizing menace, and the Soviets saw the U.S. and NATO nuclear bases ringing their country as capitalist encirclement. To the murderous and paranoid Stalin, opposition from fascist and democratic nations was all basically capitalist hostility to Soviet Russia.[1] However, the presence of large Communist parties in France and Italy and the willingness of first Britain and then France to deal with Communist China altered the Eastern perception of the Western block as monolithic earlier than the mirror-image of the Communist powers was shattered in Western minds by unmistakable events.

The Communists, committed to totalitarian repression as a means to industrialization and economic justice, failed to understand, or at least failed to acknowledge in practice, that human rights exist and are insisted upon quite apart from the specious arguments that corporations are entitled to unlimited economic liberty. Their minds numbed by Marxist doctrine that capitalism is doomed by internal contradictions and that the workers, becoming more and more miserable, will revolt, Communists only slowly accepted the political stability of democratic welfare capitalism and the comparatively much higher standards of living—despite the fixed relative distribution of the wealth—among

Americans. Righteously opposed to the manifold evils of capitalist exploitation, Communists overlooked the beneficences without which welfare capitalism would not long survive. Needing a nemesis to distract their consciences from their own police states, they shut their minds against the good in the Western system.

Likewise, the West. Neither Russia nor China had democratic traditions (February to October in 1917 did not make a tradition in Russia), yet Westerners tried to cast aside these historical boulders as if they were pebbles. Neither in the West was weight given the truism that once people anywhere decide they can improve things only by violently overthrowing corrupt ruling aristocracies, the denial of these aristocracies' liberties at least for a period of time is the revolutionary purpose. Western attitudes also quite broadly denied Communists the good in their motivations and achievements—the production of more material goods and their distribution more fairly among their peoples, to whatever extent this may have been achieved as and where it has been. Justly enraged by Stalin's and Mao's murderings of millions, but also mind-blinded by the terrors of McCarthyism at home, Americans disallowed the good achieved by Communist systems and rejected any posture of patience concerning the evolution of such systems toward more liberty.

Both sides made the same mistake about the other, a mistake of insufficient understanding. Good people who are Communists are not evil because they are Communists, they are good people who are involved in a different conception of good. And Communists failed to penetrate their own demonology to see the corollary for good people who are capitalists. This logical mistake, this intolerance, was the cause of everything that went wrong. With Stalin on one side and intemperate men in power on the other, perhaps there was no help for it.

The zealots of both sides were by definition crusaders. Christianity and Communism are equally devoted to the scourging of devils and the doing of good. The more zealous the believers on both sides, the more they were inclined to demonism. Whoever in the East might question the Confrontation was faced with murder or confinement to the Gulag Archipelago—fates that were administered to many millions of Russians for far less reason or no reason at all. Whoever in the West might lack sufficient zealotry to celebrate the Confrontation was likely to go along with it anyway because of devotion to human rights and democracy. Idealists of both sides believed that, as John Foster Dulles said, the conflict was "primarily a moral struggle."[2] Here were the ingredients of a holy war in what was principally a disagreement over how to modernize.

The two opposed systems, sitting behind their nuclear weapons and their moral screens, were hidden from each other also by the perceptions that dominated the means of communication in each. State ownership of the media in the East was all-smothering. In the West the media were constrained by the Truman-McCarthy psychological terror and the media's perhaps unconscious administration of the prevailing limits of political discussion. This was a very different phenomenon, but the overall effect was, for quite some time, nearly as unhealthy.[3]

Consider what happened to cautionary views when they were advanced. Henry Wallace let domestic Communists get close to him, and that was the end, not only of his career, but also of the argument of that time for peaceful coexistence. In a different process, an argument advanced by even such an Establishment stalwart as Senator Robert Taft, the Ohio Republican, could disappear into the velvet void outside of the mass media.

Six months into the Korean War, Taft declared into the teeth of the alarmist rhetoric, "I do not myself see any conclusive evidence that they [the Russians] expect to start a war with the United States. . . .

"I do not believe it is at all clear that the Russians contemplate a military conquest of the world. In the first place, I believe they know it is impossible. It would take them at least a hundred years to build up their sea power and get across the seas."

The *New York Times* asked the Democratic whip of the Senate, Lyndon Johnson of Texas, for comment. "Yes," he replied. "Well, I seem to recall that Senator [William E.] Borah of Idaho said something in the spring of 1939 to this effect: 'I have better sources of information than the State Department, and I am sure there is not going to be any war in Europe.' " The four-inch *Times* story on Taft's momentous dissent concluded with the reporter's informational advisory: "World War II opened in September of 1939."

Stalin *was* the leader of the Communist bloc of nations, save only the singular Yugoslavia. North Korea's invasion seemed to be possibly a part of a larger plan. Like Hitler, Stalin had engaged in political conquests and set up localized tyrannies modeled after his own. But was it Stalin's purpose to assault the West militarily? That was the operative question. In Greece he had kept his deal with Churchill and let Britain defeat the local Communists. "Stalin never broke his word to me," Churchill told C. L. Sulzberger. "We agreed on the Balkans. I said he could have Rumania and Bulgaria; he said we could have Greece (of course, only in our sphere, you know). He signed a slip of paper. And he never broke his word. We saved Greece that way. When we went in in 1944 Stalin didn't interfere." In 1952, when the Korean War was almost two years old, Truman's new ambassador to Russia, George Kennan, called on the president and recorded in his diary, "He [Truman] indicated that he shared my views as to the motives and principles of behavior of the Soviet leaders, and had never believed that they wanted another great war." Apparently Stalin was doing what Russian leaders had often done, securing Russia's sphere of influence. Now it is clear that the emergence of Communist China in 1949, which the U.S. cold warriors greeted as a Soviet event, was profoundly Chinese. It does appear, in retrospect, that the arms race based on the Confrontation was a Great Mistake. As Kennan wrote in 1956, "The image of a Stalinist Russia poised and yearning to attack the West . . . was largely a creation of the Western imagination, against which some of us who were familiar with Russian matters tried in vain, over the course of years, to make our voices heard."

Once the mistake was committed (as in Johnson's retort to Taft and the way the *Times* treated it), ideologues on both sides were free to wage the War of the Great Abhorrence, the democratic hate of communism versus the Communist hate of capitalism. Errors based on fears not free of guile became tragedy rooted in competing ideals.

To social idealism in the United States, the Confrontation dealt a painful wound. "Counterrevolutionary America"—the very idea was stunning. In his brilliant if faulted essay under that title in *Commentary* in 1967, economist Robert Heilbroner alluded to the mass executions and repression under communism, but argued that the overriding problem of modernization is time, the need for haste, because people are suffering and dying in the absence of change.

"No one is now toting up," he wrote, "the balance of the wretches who starve in India, or the peasants of Northeastern Brazil who live in the swamps on crabs, or the undernourished and permanently stunted children of Hong Kong or Honduras." Heilbroner's point is that in such situations, failing to change the social structure kills, just as a revolution kills. Once the deaths that are caused or permitted to continue by aristocracies and oligarchies are admitted into what Heilbroner called "the calculus of corpses," the whole subject is transformed, and his thesis can be seen to be substantially true: the cause of unrest in the Third World is not communism, but poverty and oligarchy.

It is likely, Heilbroner said, that development "will require policies and programs repugnant to 'our way of life,' that it will bring to the fore governments hostile to our international objectives, and that its regnant ideology will bitterly oppose capitalism as a system of world economic power." Does it follow, he asked, that the United States is therefore counterrevolutionary? "It must be said aloud," he concluded, "that our present policy prefers the absence of development to the chance for Communism—which is to say, that we prefer hunger and want and the existing inadequate assaults against the causes of hunger and want to any regime that declares its hostility to capitalism. . . . Is the United States fundamentally opposed to economic development?"

The policy of opposing revolutions around the world, wrote Hans J. Morgenthau, "surrenders to communism the sponsorship of revolution everywhere. Thus the anti-communist crusade achieves what it aims to prevent: the exploitation of the revolutions of the age by the Soviet Union and China."[4]

"Revolution in the twentieth century," said Lyndon Johnson's friend and critic, Supreme Court Justice William O. Douglas, in 1961, "means much more than rebellion against colonial regimes. In vast areas of the world it means revolution against feudalism." One finds "very, very few countries" that are not under political and economic oligarchies. "Many areas in Africa, Asia, and South America are distinguished by the monopolies in land ownership. A few families often own an entire country. In some nations a group of landlords who are favorites at court or who support the dictator in power own most of the wealth. In nation after nation the bulk of the people are sharecroppers of the worst kind. They live on a subsistence level. They have no doctors, no first-aid centers, no schools. Sons inherit only the debts of their fathers." Yet, "in the American witch-hunt that followed World War II the word 'revolution' became almost subversive. . . . We let the Communists preempt the field. . . . We lost our pride in 'revolution' as an American concept and identified it largely with communism. . . . The Dean Achesons who staffed our State Department stood firmly against Indonesian independence. . . . The Henry Cabot Lodges who manned the United Nations stood resolutely against independence for Morocco or Algeria or Vietnam. By the mid-twentieth century we had become members of a rather plush club whose members wore Homburgs, who were highly respectable, and who stood for the status quo."[5]

What the United States government did during the second half of the Johnson Period—actively, secretly, with guile and military force, and at first unbeknownst to the American people—was oppose the Third World movements for modernization. Despite tokens, like Point Four and the Peace Corps, by which citizens were reassured about humanistic purposes abroad, the most powerful free country in history, frightened by what it saw happening in the Second World, allied itself with the rich and cynical oligarchies of the Third one in actions that kept suffering masses poor, disorganized, and helpless. And Lyndon Johnson, the Texan rising to take control of the Democrats in the United States Senate, bought it all.

---

71. From Self-defense to Global Combat

As much as any other leading politician of the period, Johnson was preoccupied with military hardware and military policy. He projected himself as a specialist in the military. His well-placed ally in the press corps, William S. White of the *New York Times,* wrote in mid-1950, "The Texan has specialized in military legislation during his thirteen years in Congress and has always been close to the military establishment"; the *Times* routinely called Johnson "a congressional specialist in military affairs." Serving on the naval committee of the House, its committee for postwar planning, and the Senate armed services committee, presiding over the Senate's preparedness subcommittee, he became in effect a political general.

Johnson knew well throughout the fifties that in supporting the military, he was short-changing the kind of federal spending for social and educational programs that he advocated later for his Great Society. In his patriotic alarm early in the Korean War he even said outright, "We must not permit the tax money which could go for defense to be depleted by unjustified demands for government programs . . . which do not contribute to our survival."

His doctrine of military strength was rooted in the simple idea of national preparedness for self-defense. Before World War II, the American debate on war and peace harked back to George Washington's hostility toward foreign entanglements. Self-defense meant essentially defense of the national body, the territory of the United States. Johnson's affection for the homely examples of self-defense arose in this period. "If you let a bully come into your front yard," he was still saying late in his life, "the next day he'll be up on your porch, and the day after that he'll rape your wife in your own bed."[1]

From the first Lyndon was closely identified with President Roosevelt's hostility toward isolationism and appeasement. Running for the Senate at Roosevelt's request in 1941 meant in effect running as an advocate of American participation in the war in Europe.

It was the lesson of Munich that dictators do rise who are wholly without scruple or honor and that the only way to cope with them is to prepare to fight. If you do not, they take you for a weakling and a fool and crush you. Churchill had been right. For Americans, the Japanese attack on Pearl Harbor made the matter even simpler: we had to defend ourselves. During the first dark years of Johnson's career in public office the United States was engaged in the necessary use of force to defend itself against violent aggressors.

After the defeat of Germany, in the United Nations charter, the United States committed itself to the doctrine of international self-defense, the idea that nations must defend *each other* against aggression. In practice, because of the great-power veto at the UN, this meant little at first, but the principle was established and accepted at San Francisco. It was named "collective security." The country's first leap in doctrine from the unarguable right of self-defense, at first the new idea seemed to be just a logical extension of the old one. It was reassuring, as we entered the postwar period, that the UN charter was still firmly grounded in defense against aggression—that is, in self-defense.

In retrospect little may seem more calamitous in world history than the accident that as the United States emerged from World War II

Russia was ruled by a murderous tyrant. Stalin had widened his rule in Europe and his influence in Asia, Poland had nationalized her basic industries, even beloved Britain had nationalized coal and railways, Hungary and Romania were taken over by the Soviet Union, as was the very country whose dismemberment was sanctioned by the Munich Agreement, Czechoslovakia. It looked like the thirties all over again, except for the one salient fact that Stalin's troops were not marching on the West. Collective security became embodied in the NATO Pact which held that "an armed attack against one or more of [the twelve signatory nations] in Europe and North America shall be considered an attack against all." The Warsaw Pact nations faced off against NATO, and self-defense was regionalized.

Tirelessly after the war, Johnson drummed out again the prewar theme, Be Prepared, the Boy Scout axiom scored in a few basic variants until it became a jungle beat, we must pre*pare,* we *must* prepare, we must *prepare!* But now this rhetoric had a heavier burden. Americans had to be persuaded to prepare, not to defend themselves and their territory, since this was not under attack, but to fight in wars that would occur entirely elsewhere.

The rhetorical shift was subtle and seemed, at first, all right. For instance, Johnson said in the fall of 1947, "If it becomes necessary to stop aggression, we must act promptly and boldly. . . . The United States is now in a position of world leadership where it must act affirmatively to preserve peace. . . . Eternal and international vigilance is the price of our liberty at home."

But the next year he said atomic power had become "ours to use, either to Christianize the world or pulverize it." We had to be prepared, and now there was just one way to be really prepared, with atomic bombs. As chairman of the watchdog committee during the Korean War, Johnson badgered and bullyragged the services. But by never bringing into doubt the extent or the purposes of the military and by championing universal military training and the keeping of men under arms without a ceiling on their number, he in effect became the senator from the Pentagon. He of course knew that he had chosen for his main arena a subject of maximum publicity and minimum controversiality—doubters and critics could be damned as pinks and isolationists. He had incorporated military preparedness into his own political future, and as he achieved the leadership of the entire Senate, the unarguable rhetoric of self-defense shaded ever more profoundly into the highly arguable rhetoric of making the United States the policeman of the world.

The ideal of a United States of the World lay curled in Johnson's mind from way back, as perhaps it lies curled in the imagination of the country itself. "Our ancestors have built a democratic country," he had told the Texas legislature in 1941. "I believe the time is approaching for the birth of a democratic world—a world with common ideals—a world without barriers. . . . My hope and belief is that the same undying courage, the same love of freedom, the same unconquerable spirit which raised the flag of independence over Texas, one day will raise it over a democratic world."

But how was this lovely world to be achieved? Eleven long years later, six months into the Korean War, the same Johnson proclaimed, "We are at war. . . . We may be at war for 10 or 20 years more. . . . First, above all else, we must evolve a long-range, overall global plan of strategy for the war to which we are now committed. . . . We, not Russia, must decide where we shall fight and where we can fight."

The dream of a democratic world had become a strategy for global combat. Questioning General MacArthur after Truman broke him, Johnson said, "There is a school of thought which believes that we should confine the bulk of our ground forces to the continental United States and that we should provide other nations with nothing but sea and air support in the battle against communism." MacArthur responded with evasion. Pressing home the meaning—giving the answer he wanted from the general—Johnson continued, "Then you would not favor legislative straightjackets that would place a limitation on the number of ground troops that could be supplied?" MacArthur ducked again, but Johnson, in his own career, enacted the answer that he wanted.[2]

The global American presidents, from Truman to Reagan (possibly excepting Carter), have sought to use the awesome power vested in them to teach and convert the world. Truman, Kennedy, Johnson, and Nixon, all of them acting without once asking the people's Congress for a declaration of war, supplied American men by the tens of thousands in this endeavor. National preparedness for self-defense having become national preparedness for collective security, the postwar doctrine then evolved, under the global presidents, into the idea of national power to protect. To protect what? No longer just Americans and the national territory. To protect us from communism, of course. To protect "the free world," the dictatorship in South Korea, "American interests abroad," the shah of Iran, "the national interest," the dictator Somoza, "every nation's sacred right of self-determination," the dictatorship in South Vietnam, "the United States and our allies," the military junta in El Salvador. Under the open-ended doctrine of national power to protect, the United States protects anything far enough right of center in the world that the administration in power decides to protect, and that is quite a change, indeed, from national preparedness for the self-defense of the United States. Through time, in complex mixings of many considerations, motives, and interests, there has been a sleight of hand to it, a magic, a trick. Step by rhetorical step, the American people were misled and misused by right-wingers, jingos, geopoliticians, corporations with interests abroad, and militaristic presidents.

There were alternatives to this. Truman's Point Four and the Marshall Plan were the kind of foreign aid that, had it been persistently applied to the needs of the underclasses in the Third World, would have been the democratic system's most effective answer to the police states, an answer at once humanitarian and illustrative of the abundance of the West. As Johnson himself said at the outset of the Marshall Plan, humanitarian foreign aid was an attempt "to wage peace," justified as "the Christian thing, the humanitarian thing." He added, "By sending food, by sending financial aid, by sending faith abroad, we contest with the evil [of communism] in a battle for peace. If despair is replaced by faith, if desolation is replaced by construction, if hunger is answered by good . . . we shall be victors."

Official American approval or tolerance of left-wing, but potentially democratic revolutions would have helped democracy to emerge more frequently than did the deployment of the might of the United States in support of local dictators and despots. Nor did the global presidents heed the insistence of scholars and diplomats that some revolutions deemed Communist in the Pentagon and corporate board rooms were also essentially nationalist and could have been tolerated on the perception that their successes would intensify the rivalries among the Communist nations.

Diplomat-scholar George Kennan counseled a combination of patience and moral suasion. ". . . whoever said 'no war' was obliged," he wrote, "to suggest how the seemingly insoluble conflicts of outlook and aspiration that divided the United States and the Soviet Union were ever to find a tolerable issue. And to this my answer was: change—gradual, peaceful change—the sort of change to which no man and no government was immune—plus a positive example."[3]

Economic aid instead of armaments; a world view tolerant of democratic socialism; a distinction between monolithic, imposed communism and nationalistic revolutions; in the hardest cases, persuasion and patience—these were alternatives. How they were all crushed in the quiet struggles between the Athenians and the Spartans inside the American government is a story to be told, but rising fast among the Spartans and ultimately the first among them was the Democratic majority leader from the Pedernales River, Lyndon Baines Johnson.

---

72. Undeclared World War III

World War II rolled into World War III, which has been fought without declaration on local battlefields since 1950 and continues in 1982, a war around the world that has already lasted longer than the somewhat similar Thirty Years' War of the seventeenth century.

Although World War II discredited fascist capitalism, World War III has been humanity's first thoroughly ideological world war. Broadly, it is a war between totalitarian socialism and democratic welfare capitalism. Partisans of the Soviet-led side see their cause as the war for social justice; partisans of the American-led side see their cause as the war for civil liberty. Neither side concedes the enemy its cause. The totalitarians stress the economic foundations of personal liberty; the democrats stress the progress in free countries toward social justice; but the zealotry on each side proceeds from the head-to-head worldwide confrontation between justice and liberty. In all of the conflicts national loyalties have been at least as important as this chasm of zealotry, but the national interests tended to organize themselves either on one or the other side of that chasm, and in this way the ideological conflict crystallized into the actual war. Caught askew in the middle ranges of the embattled earth, the nations of democratic socialism and those of vestigial fascist and military capitalism have arrayed themselves first on one, then the other, but sometimes on neither, side.

World War III is the violence incident to the evolution of the human species toward a social form or social forms that can foster justice and liberty in ethically satisfying harmonies. While variant mixings of the conflicting systems appeal to the intuition as a solution to the war, actual historical and class-power conditions in many different countries have prevented the achievement, without violence, either of enough justice or of enough freedom to correct the underlying conditions of the war.

"The Cold War" lasted five years, from the end of World War II to the outbreak of the Korean War. Applied to events later than mid-1950, the cold war is a misnomer that has misled the world's population about the realities of the sporadic but very hot worldwide war that has continued now for nearly a third of this century.

One place the fire will go out, continuing there as a smouldering, then fire breaks out at another place, then another. Because the fighting has been local (that is, merely national or regional) and has often been covert, people living during this period have not usually understood that this is a world war. In general, concentrations of fighting have been perceived as separate wars in national arenas, when in fact they were just battles in the world war. Perhaps people who understand the nature of nuclear weapons have been so frightened about them, they have not wished to know that the world is at war. Since Hiroshima people have been thinking, too, that the next world war would be the detonation of the earth; with that expected, battles in local nations seemed small cheese. There was one kind of psychological wisdom in this general blindness. With cataclysm possible and, within the span of a few decades, probable, World War III, misperceived as merely a series of local wars, was almost a relief, instead of a continuous demoralizing terror. But just as there is enormous danger in the prevailing general psychological denial of the terminal horror of nuclear weapons, there is enormous danger in the failure to perceive accurately a worldwide reality that can at any time explode into a nuclear holocaust.

The peculiar character of World War III—battles that appear to be local—is caused by the nuclear weapons. This is the only way World War III can be fought without destroying at least half the species. Even so, on a number of occasions the war could have become nuclear. In the late 1940s some Americans and others wanted a preventive war to destroy Chinese installations with nuclear weapons. In 1952 President Truman considered all-out nuclear attack on Russia and China. In May, 1953, author Joe Goulden has ascertained, the National Security Council approved atomic bombing China; Eisenhower's Secretary of State sent word to Chou through Nehru that unless the Korean War ended, the U.S. would bomb China and had perfected nuclear artillery shells. In 1962, in the world's closest brush with terminal holocaust, the crisis over Soviet missiles in Cuba almost escalated into a nuclear exchange. These matters became known on the American side as a result of freedom of communications in the West; on the Soviet side such events are kept from the public at the whim of its masters.

Détente, which began to emerge with the nuclear test-ban treaty in 1963 and gathered strength and its name in the 1970s, was the euphemism used to describe openings for peace and trade. Détente was a vague phrase that worked because it was so difficult to discuss ending a world war that had not been declared. The increasing hostility between China and Russia and the proliferation of nuclear weapons among nations suggest that World War III could be supplanted by a war between Russia and China or could roll on into a nuclear World War IV caused by single-nation provocations that would not themselves necessarily be perceivable as aspects of World War III. But it is likelier that, unless there is a general peace—that is, a détente—the present World War III will explode into a nuclear World War IV.

Not all the military fighting since 1950 has been part of World War III, but most of it either has been part of the war or has become involved in it. The great engagements of the war so far were the battles of Korea and Vietnam. Although both sides attained some of their objectives in Korea, neither won there. In Vietnam the United States learned its limits in local engagements far from its shores; totalitarian socialism won. In other nations far from Russia and the United States, but usually armed and advised by one or the other side, many other battles have been and still are being fought. Although religion is a dominant source of disagreement in the Middle East, the skirmishes there are nevertheless profoundly involved in the general war because of the importance of oil and Israel to the West.

In the main, the new worldwide ideological violence from the left and the right—kidnappings, hijackings, blackmail, bank robberies, bombings, shootings, coups, and government or government-sponsored murder, variously called terrorism, repression, proletarian justice, and law and order—explode from the same causes and are just another of the forms in which World War III is raging below the threshold of nuclear holocaust.

Dean Rusk, the secretary of state in the Kennedy-Johnson years, regarded Vietnam as part of one worldwide action that also included the earlier military activity against Communist threats in Iran, Greece, and Korea. Columnist Marquis Childs wrote in 1965 that Rusk "sees all these efforts as part of a single pattern and he lists the casualties in Korea and now in Vietnam and the Dominican Republic—a total over 160,000—as part of the cost of this policy."

During President Johnson's triumphal-style visit to Korea, an American reporter said to Rusk that it was too bad Truman never got to take his bows in Korea. Rusk agreed with feeling.

"When are you going to have a show like this in Saigon?" Rusk was asked.

"I don't know, it'll be a long haul; but we will, we will," he said. And as the secretary of state walked away he turned, shook his finger, and added, "And off the record, someday there's going to be a Bay of Pigs Avenue in Havana, too!"

Speaking in Thomas Jefferson's Rotunda at the University of Virginia in 1977, Rusk stated, "We have taken more than 600,000 casualties since World War II in the name of collective security." He added, "We put up 90% of the non-Koreans in Korea, 80% of the non-Vietnamese forces in Vietnam."[1]

As the consummate militaristic politician of the period, Johnson understood that he was participating in what he took to be a war. He said in 1950 that the Korean War was "the first battle of a greater struggle," and "we must accept this fact and understand what it means." In Korea, he said, we were at war not only with China but also with all the "resources behind the Iron Curtain." The Korean battle over, Johnson continued in this view. During the discussions in Washington concerning U.S. actions to intervene against revolutionaries in Guatemala, he said the U.S. should go on "the offensive" against "soft spots in the communist system." To a Texas reporter he said the U.S. had to go on a "diplomatic offensive through measures short of open war." He carried his sense of this conflict with him into the White House, where he said in 1964, "More than 20 years ago I was in the war, and for more than 20 years I have been in the Cold War. I saw Harry Truman . . . meet the Communist guerillas in Greece and Turkey and win. I saw Dwight David Eisenhower, with the help of Lyndon Johnson as the Democratic Leader, meet them in the Formosa Strait and win. . . . And I saw John Fitzgerald Kennedy win in the Cuban missile crisis."[2] But by the end of his time in the White House, sobered by the awesome horror that a nuclear war would be, Johnson was hoping for an opening to Russia—the Soviet invasion of Czechoslovakia aborted his intended venture in that direction.

In one of its strangest events, however, former President Richard Nixon declared World War III after he left office. In a 1980 book, *The Real War,* Nixon, sounding very much like the Johnson of the early fifties, wrote:

"During all of my presidency we were engaged in a 'war' with the Soviet Union. . . . We are at war. . . . World War III began before World War II ended. . . . World War III has gone on now for a third of a century, since those closing days of World War II. . . .

"World War III has proceeded from the Soviet seizure of Eastern Europe, through the communist conquest of China, the wars in Korea and Indochina, and the establishment of a western hemisphere outpost of Soviet power in Cuba, to the present thrusts of the Soviet Union and its allies into Africa, the Islamic crescent, and Central America. . . .

"Korea and Vietnam were battles in the war, as were the coups that brought Soviet satellite regimes to power in places as remote as Afghanistan and South Yemen. So, too, have been the struggles to keep Communist parties from taking control in Italy and Portugal, and to contain Castro's export of revolution in Latin America.

"World War III is the first truly global war."

Détente, as Nixon saw it, was a tactic in the war, not an attempt to end it; the opening to China was a thrust in the war. In 1980 Nixon discussed current events on the assumption that World War III was in progress. ". . . in World War III," he wrote, "there *is* no substitute for victory."[3]

The Johnson of the early fifties and the post-presidential Nixon rhetorically declared World War III because national preparedness had lost its credibility as a theme—it will not cover what has been wreaked in its name. Declaring World War III, Nixon took the ultimate rhetorical step to persuade the Americans once again to ratify whatever military spending and whatever military adventures President Reagan and his successors might wish to undertake. But the same objective considerations that permit one to understand that World War III is in progress can lead either to jingoistic outcry for victory or sobered hope for a détente that means peace among the nuclear powers.

Whether World War III has been in progress is a question, not of fact, but of interpretation and decision. People may differ on the same facts. One could still argue that there was no Hundred Years' War—that there had been only a long series of battles interrupted by two treaties and many truces, and yes, a civil war in France. The dukes and kings alive from 1337 to 1453 could hardly have known, in the course of those events, that they were fighting in a Hundred Years' War, and when historians say that they were, this is only an exercise of judgment and opinion. One can see, though, an analogy between the Hundred Years'

War, a profitless struggle between the two emergent nations of France and England over territory and titles, and the present struggle between Russia and the United States fighting world-around over territory and entitlements.

There is even more similarity between World War III and the Thirty Years' War of 1618–1648, a series of battles beginning in Germany, between the armies of Protestant princes (themselves divided over creedal matters) and the armies of Catholicism, with frequent foreign interventions and warfare all over Europe. Each engagement was dominated by its own local details, but in the end one could see the continuing nature of the one war, France and its Protestant allies arrayed, in battle after battle, against Catholicism and the House of Hapsburg in Spain and Germany. Although political, the Thirty Years' War was primarily religious and in that sense ideological: the chief issue was religious freedom, as now, from our Western point of view, the chief issue is political freedom.

The Hundred Years' War just petered out. Neither side "won," but both France and England survived and in that way won. For the West to prevail in World War III as France and Protestantism did in the Thirty Years' War, one would have to visualize both the democratic and the Communist systems continuing in an uneasy peace without war, neither imposing its authority on or extinguishing the other. Surely this kind of an end to World War III is what is intended by those who see détente as the cooling down and eventually the ending of the war.

But if, as Nixon says and in the White House President Reagan may seek to enact, there is no substitute in World War III for victory, then there is no substitute for nuclear holocaust, either, because one cannot plausibly imagine either the United States or the Soviet Union accepting military defeat and occupation of their homeland without resorting to nuclear arms.

As Lyndon Johnson schemed to achieve the vice-presidency, the position from which he believed he had the best chance for the presidency, he all but declared that the United States was at war with Russia, and he rallied the majority of the Senate Democrats behind the militaristic program which the Republican hawks desired. After decades more of secret and open warfare in many far corners of the world, former President Nixon declares the World War III which the Truman-Acheson-Johnson Democrats, for the American side, inaugurated. Far from having subsided as a result of "the lessons of Vietnam," the misconceived American crusade once again controls the White House and therefore the Pentagon. If the holocaust comes and if there is still a human history, the global American hawkery of the Johnson Period will be understood as a principal cause of World War IV.

Acknowledgments

For fellowships that have assisted me in this work, I thank the Rockefeller Foundation and the National Endowment for the Humanities.

For helping me obtain teaching situations in which I could interact with faculty and students concerning the Johnson Period, I thank Fred Schmidt, Richard Lyon, George Hendrick, and Roger Shattuck, and their institutions, UCLA, Hampshire College, the University of Illinois, and the University of Virginia.

I thank the Ossabaw Island Project in Georgia and Mrs. Eleanor Torrey West for granting me sanctuary on the island for a time during my closing of the present volume.

I acknowledge with thanks the cooperation of the many people who generously granted me interviews, including the late President Johnson and his gracious wife, Lady Bird Johnson, and many of the Johnson people. I acknowledge with gratitude the value of the work of the writers of many books, articles, and studies on Johnson and public affairs during the Johnson Period, who are credited in the notes, of course. I thank public servants who provided government information; the conductors of the valuable oral history interviews at the Johnson and Kennedy libraries; many helpful and dedicated librarians, especially those at the Johnson, Kennedy, and Rayburn libraries, but also at other libraries in Washington, D.C., Frederick, Md., Austin and San Antonio, Texas, and elsewhere; officials at the Democratic and Republican national committees and the Republican party of Texas for granting me access to their files, and colleagues in news organizations for granting me access to their morgues and files; those who have extended me other special research assistance, including the Roosevelt and Truman libraries; and those who have read parts of this work in manuscript, although the finished work is of course entirely my responsibility.

At the Johnson Library I wish to thank specifically Harry Middleton, Charles Corkran, Mike Gillette, and archivisits Tina Lawson, Nancy Smith, Claudia Anderson, Linda Hanson, and Bob Tissing, audiovisual archivist Phil Scott, and interviewers Joe Frantz, David G. McComb, Paige E. Mulhollan, Thomas Harrison Baker, Stephen Goodell, Dorothy P. McSweeny, and others. At the Kennedy Library I thank Will Johnson and Joan Hoopes, research archivists, and Martin F. McGann and Barbara L. Anderson, and at the Rayburn Library, H.G. Dulaney.

To my former wife, Jean Dugger, and our two children, Gary and Celia Dugger, I owe extended thanks. I appreciate the services performed for me by Mrs. Anton Myrer of McIntosh and Otis. Patricia Blake, I thank for valuable suggestions she made upon her reading the manuscript as I was concluding it with her indispensable encouragement. I thank particularly also my friend at colleague at the *Texas Observer,* Cliff Olofson, and others who have helped me during this venture, giving strength to a friend who may do good work: Bob and Mary Sherrill, Willie Morris, Lisa Brunet Hazel, Lawrence Goodwyn, Ruth Ellinger, Keith Stanford, Walter Morrison, and my other colleagues at the *Observer,* present and past.

I come to a full stop to thank Eric P. Swenson, my editor at W. W. Norton. He has never wavered in his support of this work, despite the time that I have taken to deliver it to him. He is a gifted, high-minded editor of profound integrity and my friend, as well. He and his colleagues, sustaining by their work the success of a distinguished and independent publishing house, are among the small group of citizens likewise engaged who must be listed on any inventory of the resources we have in our country for the creation of a peaceful world suffused with both justice and liberty.

To others at Norton who have helped me specifically, I also express my appreciation: chairman George Brockway, copy editor Josepha Gutelius, typist Jane Freeman, designer Marjorie Flock, production manager Andrew Marasia, art director Hugh O'Neill, and Jeannie Luciano, Fran Rosencrantz, and others.

Anyone undertaking a "life and times" becomes so generally indebted to so many journalists, scholars, writers, actors in events, witnesses, workers, relatives, friends—to so many people—that all one can do in return is hope that one can make a gift that will be well received. I told Lyndon Johnson that I intended to write a work about him that would be fair, accurate, and worthy of the attention of serious people. If I am doing that, then this volume itself is my real thanks to everyone who has helped me write it.

NOTES AND SOURCES

BIBLIOGRAPHY

INDEX

PRINCIPAL ABBREVIATIONS USED IN THE NOTES

AA *Austin American*
AAS *Austin American-Statesman*
AP Associated Press
AS *Austin Statesman*
CCC *Corpus Christi Caller*
CCCT *Corpus Christi Caller-Times*
CCT *Corpus Christi Times*
CR *Congressional Record*
DMN *Dallas Morning News*
FDRL Franklin Delano Roosevelt Library, Hyde Park, N.Y.
Harper's Ferry tapes The tape-recorded materials on Lyndon and Lady Bird Johnson held by the National Park Service at Harper's Ferry, West Virginia
JL Lyndon B. Johnson Library, Austin, Texas
LaBJ Lady Bird Johnson
LJ Lyndon Johnson
NYT *New York Times*
PP *Public Papers* of the Presidents, Lyndon B. Johnson, 1963–1969
RBJ Rebekah Baines Johnson
RD Ronnie Dugger
RL Sam Rayburn Library, Bonham, Texas
SAE *San Antonio Express*
SAEN *San Antonio Express-News*
SAN *San Antonio News*
SHJ Sam Houston Johnson
SLPD *St. Louis Post-Dispatch*
TL Harry S. Truman Library, Independence, Missouri
UP United Press
UPI United Press International
WP *Washington Post*

Notes and Sources

In these notes, books and articles are cited by reference to the last name of the author and the first word or two of the title of the book or article. For the full citation, please see the author's work listed in the Bibliography.

As mentioned at the outset, reference numbers that are italicized in the text refer the reader to notes that add information other than sources; reference numbers that are not italicized lead to notes that give sources only.

Sources given within parentheses in the notes apply to information immediately preceding them in the notes.

When I have felt that a reporter did an unusually good job on a newspaper story being cited, I have given the name of the reporter along with the newspaper.

Johnson's public papers for Nov. 22, 1963, through the end of that year occupy the first 105 pages of the first of the two volumes in which the papers for late 1963 and the year 1964 were published. In the short citation here devised for *The Public Papers of the Presidents, Lyndon B. Johnson* (which is *PP* and the year), the citation *PP 1963* refers to the first 105 pages of the first of those two volumes. (On the other hand, *PP 1965,* for example, refers simply to the two volumes of Johnson's papers for that year.)

Prologue: The Man in the Special House

1. Lash, *Roosevelt,* p. 277.
2. Johnson made a similar, although qualified remark to Hubert Humphrey. Then-Senator Humphrey was having dinner with the Johnsons at the Elms, their Washington home, the Tuesday night after the assassination of President John Kennedy on Friday, Nov. 22, 1963. "He had a portrait of Diem in the hallway," Humphrey wrote, "and as we passed it he said, 'We had a hand in killing him. Now it's happening here.' "

   I interviewed Johnson in the White House on Dec. 13 (two sessions), 14, and 16, 1967, and on Mar. 23, 1968. At the time he was off the record, but I could use what he told me without attributing it to him. When I asked at the first if I could make notes, he said "I want you to." Telling me his father's last words, he said, "I wouldn't want it to be quoted that way" and asked me to change it slightly. Relating a minor episode that might have had diplomatic reverberations if published, he told me not to take it down in my notes; he told me something having to do with Vietnam that he said was "secret" and not to be published. It was quite clear that what he told me, with exceptions he stated, could be published at the time, but not attributed.

   I decided that after Johnson's death

what he had said to me, no longer news, was history and could be quoted directly and attributed to him. I never, in a news story, quoted anything he told me, although there is precedent for the conclusion that after a certain period of time this would be acceptable journalistic practice.

In 1969 James Reston of the *New York Times* printed direct quotations from "a private talk" he had had with Johnson in the White House in 1964, and Ted Lewis directly quoted many of Johnson's off-the-record remarks to him in the White House. In 1970 Hugh Sidey of *Life* directly quoted aspersions Johnson had cast on Humphrey and Nixon in 1968. In 1971 Joseph Kraft attributed to John McNaughton, a defense official under Johnson who had just been killed, a remark Kraft had published without attribution in 1966. Also in 1971, Edward T. Folliard, in the *Washington Post,* directly quoted remarks Johnson made to him off the record in 1965 (at which time Folliard had written an account of the interview, without calling it an interview or using quotation marks).

Reporter Neil Sheehan has said to me informally that there is an unwritten rule of sorts that after six months pass, an off-the-record interview goes on. I would think that might depend on the subject and the circumstances, but speaking of Tom Wicker of the *New York Times* and me, Robert Semple, another *Times* reporter, said to me in 1972, "The Wicker-Dugger statute of limitations has run on everything Johnson has said as president because he's hovering over all that stuff and putting out his own version of events. The statute has run out."

Tom Johnson of the Johnson White House press staff sat in for some of my interviews with Johnson. (He told me he regarded my questions as the toughest asked and Johnson as more responsive to such questions than in any interviews Tom Johnson knew of.) I told Tom Johnson in 1973 that I regarded what Lyndon Johnson had told me in 1967 and 1968 as on the record, and Tom Johnson replied, "Oh, I think so."

Interviews, LJ (Dec. 13, 14, 16, 1967, and Mar. 23, 1968), and on this note, Humphrey, *The Education,* p. 265*n*.; Interviews, Robert Semple, Tom Johnson; James Reston, *NYT,* Dec. 28, 1969; *Newsweek,* Feb. 3, 1969; *Life,* Dec. 11, 1970; *WP,* July 8, 17, 1971.

1. The Preacher and the Cowboy

1. Newlon, *L.B.J.,* pp. 113–114; William McGaffin, *CCCT,* March 6, 1960.
2. Clarke Newlon was shown, for his 1964 book on Johnson, "The Mother's Book," which, Newlon wrote, was never loaned and was shown only with Johnson's permission. Johnson had given me a part or all of this book in the late 1950s. Newlon, writing from it in detail, reported the parts about black slaves held by Johnson's antecedents, but when Johnson had the book published during his presidency the references to the slaves were gone.

   Miller, *Lyndon,* p. 5; *CR,* April 11, 1956; Newlon, *L.B.J.,* pp. 232, 233, 236, and cf. RBJ, *A Family,* pp. 107, 108, 115; Turner, "Texas and the Far West," as cited in *The Shaping,* Williams, ed., pp. 171–73; Martin, *The People's,* p. 93 *n,* citing *Preliminary Report of the Eighth Census,* Table I; Interviews, LJ (Dec. 1967); Turner, *The Frontier,* p. 16; *Texas Almanac for 1858,* pp. 65–66, . . . *for 1859,* p. 169; and . . . *for 1861,* p. 190. On the colony of blacks ten miles from Blanco, see *AA,* Nov. 5, 1972.
3. Ruth Schumm of the *Dallas Morning News* reported after an interview that Rebekah Johnson believed the Wilson in her father's name, Joseph Wilson Baines, might be traced back to a signer of the American Declaration, although she was not sure.

   Johnson's mother came from a German family named Hoffman that left Europe in 1848.

   Johnson told Bela Kornitzer his mother prepared the album in 1954, four years before she died. On the dustjacket of its later published form there is a statement that she prepared it as a Christmas present for Lyndon. He had his heart attack in 1955.

   Showing the original album to Kornitzer, Johnson broke up with emotion as he read aloud this sentence from his mother to him: "May this ancestral history be of interest as a record of the lives that have gone into the making of your life, afford you further understanding of the traits of mind and heart which are your inheritance, and inspire you to greater heights." The inscription to him, of which this was a part, was not included in the later published version.

RBJ, *A Family,* pp. 112, 99, 143; Adams, *Texas,* vol. III, p. 167; Provence, *Lyndon,* p. 22; Kornitzer, "President"; *DMN,* June 22, 1954; Interviews, LJ (December 1967); *PP 1963,* p. 98. The Kornitzer interview occurred before Johnson became president; other than that the time is not given. On the album and its inscription, cf. Newlon, *L.B.J.,* pp. 217–36.

4. Johnson remembered on one occasion that when he was a boy, his father told him about his ancestors who had lived in Georgia. "He said that grandpa told them that they could stay here and go up in the world, or they could leave and go to Texas." (*PP 1964,* p. 652.)

As reporters he has taken to the little cemetery down from his birthplace know, he had a strong sense of the riverbank where his forebears had walked before him. A month before the 1964 campaign ended, his mind turned home. "On election night," he said in Illinois, "I am going to be at my little ranch home on the banks of the Pedernales, down the road from where my mother, my father, my grandfather, my grandmother, my great-grandfather and great-grandmother are buried." A few days before the election he spoke of being, on election day, "at my little library room down at the Pedernales where my grandfather and grandmother and mother and father and uncles and cousins and aunts are all buried on the banks of that little river." (*PP 1964,* pp. 1240, 1513.)

In Georgia during that campaign he said, "My roots are deep in Georgia." In Memphis he called for an end to "the color line across our opportunity" as a man who "has spent all of his life and cast his every vote in Texas, and is the grandson of two Confederate veterans."

"So many of my ancestors come from Kentucky," he said at the courthouse in Louisville, "that I can sing 'My Old Kentucky Home' with almost as much feeling as you. My dad's mother was born in Russellville in 1849. I hve some real Kentucky blood in my veins. My great-great-grandmother, Phoebe Ann Desha, was the sister of Joseph Desha, a former governor of the great state of Kentucky, and she also had a brother who was a congressman from Kentucky at the same time, and also a brother who was a congressman from the State of Tennessee.

"My great-great-grandfather, John Huffman, farmed in central Kentucky until 1851. He was the first man to breed shorthorn cattle in Texas, and he introduced the Sir Archer breed of horses to . . . Kentucky."

Speaking in Tennessee, Johnson said, "Sam Houston was governor of Tennessee before he came to our state and became president of Texas."

(*PP 1964,* pp. 1449, 1408–9, 1269, 635, resp.)

In an argumentative context he made use of his Anglo-Saxon origins. Speaking in 1964 for the liberalization of the immigration laws (which was later accomplished in his term) he used his and others' forebears from Western Europe as defensive coloration: "President Roosevelt, with a good Dutch name. . . . President Truman, with a good English name. . . . President Eisenhower, with a good German name. . . . President Kennedy, with a good Irish name, proposed that the law be changed. And now a president, Lyndon Johnson, with an English name, and with an Irish name, and with German and Scottish and French forebears, proposes this law be changed." (*PP 1964,* p. 1244.)

2. From the Alamo to Khe Sanh

1. Johnson said his mother had a copy of the painting in which the figures were numbered (Bunton, he thought, was No. 27). The painting, *The Surrender of Santa Anna,* by William H. Huddle, hangs in the Texas state capitol in Austin. Interview, LJ (Dec. 13, 1967).
2. Travis, the Alamo commander, late the preceding month had sent out a message to "the people of Texas and All Americans in the World" saying he would never surrender or retreat and asking that people "come to our aid with all dispatch." On March 3, too late, Travis sent to the convention where Bunton was a message that

closed with the words, "God and Texas —Victory or Death."

3. A first sergeant in Capt. Robert M. Coleman's company of Mina Volunteers from the Mina Municipality (Bastrop, Tx.,) John Bunton was transferred for the Storming of Bexar Dec. 5–6, 1835, to the company of Capt. John York, a leader of expeditions against the Indians. In 1853 Bunton was issued Bounty Certificate 1244 for 320 acres of land in appreciation of his role in the siege of Bexar. He was a delegate from Mina to the convention of 1836; then he served in the army from March 28 to May 12 of that year. Also in 1853, he was issued Donation Certificate 484 for 640 acres of land on account of his part in the battle of San Jacinto. He served in the Congress of the Republic of Texas in the late 1830s. He is buried in the state cemetery in Austin.

   On Bunton in general, Kemp, *The Signers,* pp. xii, xx, xxii, xxiv–xxv, 36–38, and 72; Dixon and Kemp, *The Heroes;* Cf. Ray, *Austin Colony,* p. 345. On Bunton's wife, *The New Yorker,* Jan. 23, 1965. On his first fighting against Indians, Thrall, *The People's,* p. 134.

   On the storming (or siege) of Bexar (or San Antonio), *The Handbook of Texas,* vol. I, p. 154. For the statement Bunton was with Milam in this siege, I have relied on two details. According to Bunton's obituary in the *Galveston News* Sept. 5, 1879, "He was with Milam at the storming of the Alamo. . . ." His receipt of a land grant because of his role at San Antonio also argues he participated in the siege.

   On the convention of 1836, Gray, *From Virginia,* pp. 107, 108, 121, 126; Ralph Steen, *The Handbook of Texas,* vol. I, pp. 494–95.

   The text of the declaration and the names of the signers of the Texas Declaration of Independence may be found in the *Texas Almanac,* e.g., in the 1964–65 edition, pp. 56, 58.

   There is a large literature on the Alamo and San Jacinto. People outside Texas can have little idea how these two battles and the associated events dominate the Texas public schools' conception of Texas history.

   By the long-accepted story, all the Alamo defenders died fighting. However, a lieutenant colonel in Santa Anna's army, Jose Enrique de la Pena, kept a diary which was translated into English for a book published in 1975. According to him, seven captives were taken before Santa Anna, who ordered their executions. De la Pena wrote that he then saw the men around Santa Anna fall upon the captives with swords. The diary was disputed by Texans; its translator, Carmen Perry, seemed skeptical that the story of the seven who surrendered would be accepted. "We prefer to live by legend," she said. *AA,* Sept. 10, 1975; *Daily Texan,* Sept. 12, 1975.

   On Bunton at San Jacinto, Dixon, *The Men,* p. 109. See also "List of All the Men in the Texas Army at the Battle of San Jacinto," *Texas Almanac for 1859,* p. 162. Bunton was not among those listed on the "Return of killed and wounded," given as a part of this list. The quote from Billingsly is given in Dixon and in an old clipping reproduced in RBJ, *A Family,* facing p. 120.

4. *College Star,* April 18, 1928, cited in Pool et al., *Lyndon,* p. 124.
5. Herndon and Weik, *Herndon's Life,* pp. 221–26.
6. See, e.g., *PP 1967,* pp. 176 *ff,* 225.
7. Interview, LJ (Dec. 13, 1967); *PP 1966,* p. 404; Butterfield, "Clara Driscoll"; Ryder-Taylor, *History,* pp. 93–94; Pool et al., *Lyndon,* p. 26.
8. The reporter of the 1928 story did not give his source for the account; it may have been Lyndon's pretty sister Rebekah, whose picture was run with the story, the picture's caption saying she wanted to be a reporter. Although this story indicated there was resistance to the bill's passage in the House, it passed the House 101 to 9 and the Senate 24 to 0.

   The 1937 handbill said Johnson's father was "one of the signers of the bill for purchase of the Alamo grounds for the state."

   Clara Driscoll became Democratic national committeewoman from Texas in the thirties, and in 1941 she was listed as making the largest contribution to Johnson for the Senate, $5,000.

   Dick McMurray, *AAS,* Dec. 2, 1928 (cf. *DMN,* Jan. 11, 1964); Handbill, Barker History Center, UT-Austin; *DMN,* June 27, 1941; *AA,* June 27, July 30, 1941.

9. Interview, LJ (Dec. 14, 1967); Halberstam, *The Unfinished,* p. 25, and cf. Sidey, *A Very,* p. 212.

10. When George Christian, his press secretary, told Johnson what he had said at Camp Stanley, Johnson denied it. "I said no such thing. I didn't have any grandfather at the Alamo," he said. Christian said the president refused to believe he had said it. Christian concluded that "he got his tongue twisted in the emotion of the moment."

    Lisagor, "Lyndon"; Sidey, *A Very,* p. 151; *PP 1965,* pp. 1069–70, 1333; *PP 1966,* pp. 759, 1287, 1443–44; *PP 1968,* p. 702; Interview, LJ (Dec. 14, 1967); *SAE,* Oct. 3, 1967; Joseph Califano, *WP,* May 30, 1974; Christian, *The President,* pp. 219–20; see Wise, *The Politics,* pp. 27–31.

11. Johnson did also say that one of his forebears had died at the battle of San Jacinto. When Doris Kearns asked him about his statement in Korea about his great-great-grandfather, he replied, "The fact is that my great-great-grandfather died at the Battle of San Jacinto, not the Alamo." Of course that particular forebear had not been at San Jacinto. Kearns's discussion of this contretemps does not mention Bunton, who fought at San Jacinto, but did not die there. Kearns, *Lyndon,* p. 15.

12. *AA* (AP), Nov. 12, 1967.

    In her book on neuroses of leading male politicians in the modern American era, N. C. Clinch asserts that "Johnson . . . saw Vietnam as his own personal chance to become an Alamo-like hero in the full American mythic tradition." Clinch, *The Kennedy,* p. 208.

13. Johnson recited to me the first two stanzas of "The Defence of the Alamo," by Joaquin Miller, that are given in the text. (Perhaps you can imagine my astonishment.) The remaining five stanzas are cast in the same heroic tone. Stevenson, ed., *Poems,* p. 357. Cf. Johnson's partial recitation in Lisagor, "Lyndon."

14. Hoopes, *The Limits,* pp. 211–14.

15. Heren, *No Hail,* p. 181; Sidey, *A Very,* p. 240.

16. Sidey, "Deep."

3. Indians and Communists

1. Berlandier, *The Indians,* esp. pp. 41–42.
2. Webb, *The Texas,* pp. 243–44; *Southwestern Historical Quarterly,* vol. 58, p. 6.
3. Speer, *A History,* pp. 2, 12, 15, 20, 35.
4. Sibley, *Travelers,* pp. 73, 75, 59; Gregory and Strickland, *Sam, passim.*
5. Winfrey and Day, eds., *The Indians,* vol. IV, pp. 326–29; Speer, *A History,* p. 51; Wilbarger, *Indian,* p. 643 (Pemberton Press ed.). (Wilbarger relied on hearsay.)
6. Henderson Shuffler, an historical writer, did a good deal of checking on this story and became convinced it happened.

   "I approached that one with a great deal of caution, simply because it was too apt," he said. Mrs. Johnson first mentioned it to him, and her press secretary got more details from the family and passed them on to him. "They had enough accurate detail—they did know it was the Felps family, they did know the gal was a school-teacher," Shuffler said. "They had it spelled Phelps and the Indian papers had Felps—I don't know which is correct." The Johnsons lived near where the scalpings happened, Shuffler added.

   Harper's Ferry tapes; Interviews, LJ (Dec. 14, 1967), Henderson Shuffler; cf. Bishop, *A Day,* pp. 178–79, and Sidey, *A Very,* pp. 21–22.
7. As Texas historian Shuffler noted, there is no specific evidence that Johnson's grandmother was endangered by the Indians. It is just a story that is told. RBJ, *A Family,* pp. 70–71; cf. *NYT,* April 20, 1964, and *DMN* (AP), Nov. 3, 1965; see *National Observer,* Nov. 22, 1965.
8. Interview, Tom Crider.
9. Joseph Hall, ed., "Horace"; see also *AS,* Aug. 20, 1960.
10. Sibley, *Travelers,* pp. 75–76, 185–86.
11. Hunter, ed., *The Trail,* pp. 362–67.
12. RBJ, *A Family,* p. 23; Jenkins III, ed., *Recollections,* pp. xvi, 145, 183–87, 192–98, 262–63.
13. Opening the peace conference with the Indians on the San Saba at noon, Meusebach addressed them through an interpreter, proposing three articles for the treaty:

    "1. My countrymen have the permission to go and travel where they please, and no harm must be done to them, but you must protect them everywhere. On the other hand, your people can come to our wigwams and cities without fear and can go wherever they please and shall be protected.

"2. You and the chiefs, and your people will assist us and report to us, when bad men and redfaces of other tribes steal our horses or intend other felonies, and we shall do the same, when you are attacked.

"3. I am going to send men with the thing that steals the land [compasses], as the red men call it, and will survey the whole country of the San Saba . . . so that we may know the boundaries where we can go and till the soil. And if you are willing after consultation with your warriors, to make this treaty, then I will give you and your squaws many presents, or equal them with the white pieces of metal, that we call dollars, and give you as many as one thousand and more of them. . . .

"If we agree on this treaty, I shall go and fetch the presents and will sign the treaty solemnly, at the latest when the disk of the moon has rounded twice."

Biesele, *The History,* pp. 184–90, citing *Meusebach's Answer to Interrogatories.*

14. Muesebach's predecessor as commissioner-general of the German colonists, Prince Carl of Solms-Braunfels, wanted to keep them apart from the other settlers on the frontier and sought to perpetuate his aristocratic privileges in Texas. Meusebach renounced his baron's status before he came.

    The Germans spoke, of course, a different language, or accented English. By early 1847 Fredericksburg's main street was two miles long, but had only about fifty dwellings along it, mostly huts made by ramming poles into the ground, packing the framework against the weather with clay and moss, and covering over the roof with dry grass.

    In the twentieth century the Germans became mainly Republicans in traditionally Democratic Texas. Then the state became two-party.

    Roemer, *Texas,* pp. 21–22, 154, 218, 228–29, 241–242; Biggers, *German,* pp. 42–44; King, *John,* pp. 54, 55, 59, 60–63, 115, *passim;* see Sibley, *Travelers,* pp. 97, 99, 114, 164–66, *passim.*

15. RBJ, *A Family,* p. 75, illustration before p. 67; Interviews, LJ (Dec. 13, 14, 1967); Allen Duckworth, *DMN,* Dec. 14, 1963; "The Hill Country," an NBC Special.
16. "Know the difference between a Texas Ranger and a Sheriff?" Johnson asked some journalists he was guiding through his boyhood home. "When you shoot a Ranger, he just keeps comin' on." *PP 1964,* pp. 1162–63; Sidey, *A Very,* p. 22.
17. The University of Texas Press, which published Webb's book, received Johnson's introduction for it from the White House between April 2 and May 26, 1965.

    Webb, *The Texas,* pp. x–xi, 233–75; Letter, Frank Wardlaw to RD; *The Handbook of Texas,* vol. II, pp. 125–26.

4. From Deer Creek to Pleiku

1. Although Ball did not say so, he may have been quoting Johnson when he said the bombing after Pleiku was justified as "giving tit for tat." Ball put the phrase in quotation marks, without saying who had said it. (Johnson said to me in 1967 that if your daughter is raped it's tit for tat.)

    PP 1964, p. 1230, and see pp. 926, 965, 1285, 1511; *PP 1965,* pp. 153–54, and see p. 449; Interview, LJ (Dec. 16, 1967); Draper, *Abuse,* pp. 63–64, 73; Ball, *The Discipline,* pp. 319–20; *NYT,* Feb. 7–10, 10, 12, 13, 15, 24, 26, 1965; *Houston Chronicle,* early Feb., 1965; *Houston Post,* Feb. 9, 1965; *SAE,* Feb. 8, 1965.

2. Berlandier, *The Indians,* pp. 34, 67.
3. Webb, *The Texas,* p. 261.
4. Sonnichsen, *I'll,* pp. xv–xvi, 258–59.
5. *AA,* June 24, 1955; RBJ, *A Family,* pp. 117, 74.
6. RBJ, *A Family,* pp. 70–71.
7. Interview, LJ (Dec. 13, 1967).
8. By the Blassingames' written account, Callahan and three friends rode up to the house, and "The row quickly commenced; fire after fire was heard. Blassingame was shot at several times; several balls were shot into the house

amongst mother and the little children; one ball came very near hitting mother."

John Speer wrote that Callahan had fired Calvin Blassingame, this leading to Calvin's father making "some unjust and damaging remark about Callahan's family," about which Callahan was told. Speer said Callahan's group went to the house to talk things over, only to be fired on without warning.

A jury ruled the Blassingame men were "shot by a company of men unknown to the jury."

W. S. "Mallheel" Johnson was the second man killed, and one Thomas Johnson is named in the Blassingames' appeal as one of the Callahan group who escaped unhurt. The existence of two groups of Johnsons, one in the Blanco Valley and another in the Pedernales, would seem to make it likely that the Johnsons in the Callahan-Blassingame dispute were not forebears of Lyndon Johnson.

Kemp, "A Blanco County Tragedy"; Goar, "Bloody Times"; Speer, *A History,* pp. 7–10; see *Record of Southwest Texas,* pp. 373–74.

9. Elliott, "Union Sentiment."
10. See Holden, "Law."
11. The issue of the courthouse was finally settled in favor of Johnson City by 15 votes out of 1,001 cast in the last of three elections on the subject.

    Moursund, *Blanco,* pp. 210–11; *The Handbook of Texas,* vol. I, p. 918, and see vol. I, p. 172; Speer, *A History,* p. 67; Interviews, LJ (Dec. 14, 1967), Emmette Redford; see Nevins and Commager, *A Short,* pp. 326–27.
12. The 1941 account emanating from the Austin bureau of the *Dallas Morning News* said:

    "One of the strangest political situations in modern Texas history is shaping up in this, the Tenth Congressional District, though it had its exact counterpart of 50 years ago.

    "There promises to be another contest between a Johnson and a Martin unless Representative Lyndon Johnson is again a candidate for the United States Senate.

    "Tom Martin, former legislator and ex-serviceman with a brilliant overseas record, a first cousin of Johnson, said Monday he positively will be a candidate for Congress from this district regardless of who runs.

    "In 1892, Sam E. Johnson, grandfather of both men, ran for the legislature on the Populist ticket against his son-in-law, Clarence Martin, Democrat, father of Tom Martin. Clarence Martin defeated his father-in-law, but suffered a serious stab wound in a public speaking at Twin Sisters, Blanco County."

    Interviews, LJ (Dec. 13, 1967), SHJ; *DMN,* Nov. 27, 1941.
13. *AA,* July 16, 1946.
14. Sonnichsen, *I'll,* pp. xv–xvi, 258–59.

5. Johnsons on the Chisholm Trail

1. Goodwyn, *The South,* p. 84; RBJ, *A Family,* pp. 70, 87; Newlon, *L.B.J.,* p. 229.
2. Speer, *A History,* pp. 39–40.
3. Goodwyn, *The South,* p. 81.
4. Johnson made these remarks during tapings at Harper's Ferry. Later he also described the trail drives for Kearns.

    Harper's Ferry tapes; cf. Kearns, *Lyndon,* pp. 28–29.
5. Hunter, ed., *The Trail,* pp. 362–67.
6. Hall, ed. "Horace."
7. This account, from a contemporary newspaper, may be more reliable than Johnson's memory that the man's name was Berry Roebuck. In 1967 Johnson told me he heard, when he was running for Congress his first time, that the old man had gotten into a cane fight with another man who had said some hard things about Johnson. Seeking out his defender—Berry Roebuck—Johnson was told that when Roebuck (then eighty-nine) had been nine, he had gone up the trail for Sam and Tom, and they had brought back down "a sack of gold." *AA,* Sept. 6, 1946; Interview, LJ (Dec. 14, 1967).
8. Speer, *A History,* p. 20.
9. Bode, "Back Home."
10. Lyndon Johnson said in 1949, "Johnson City was founded by my grandfather and named after him. There were only Indians there then. I guess the old gentleman named the place after himself." Johnson's mother said the Johnson brothers "established head-

quarters at Johnson City" in the late 1850s. In a handbill for Johnson in his 1937 campaign, it was stated, "His grandfather, Sam Johnson, was one of the first white settlers in Blanco County, and for him Johnson City was named." Elizabeth Carpenter, Mrs. Lyndon Johnson's press secretary, was quoted in 1964, "His grandfather founded Johnson City, you know. . . ." UPI reported in 1965 that Johnson City was "the town built by [Johnson's] grandfather . . . in 1853."

By 1860 J. L. Moss lived "on the Provost place, near where Johnson City now stands," and it was "the Moss place near Johnson City" that the two Johnson brothers bought in 1867. Johnson City was surveyed and established in 1879—the Johnson brothers' success in the cattle business and prosperity in the area had meanwhile ended—by a nephew of the Johnson brothers who had worked for them and got Sam's land in the early 1870s. Specifically, in 1872–73, James Polk (Jim) Johnson, nephew of Tom and Sam, acquired title to the land that first Tom, then Sam, had owned, and it was 1879 before Jim Johnson laid out the town of Johnson City.

SLPD, Feb. 27, 1949; RBJ, *A Family,* p. 70; handbill, Barker History Center, UT-Austin; Young, "The LBJ"; *WP* (UPI) Oct. 28, 1965; Goodwyn, *Democratic,* pp. 19–20; Speer, *A History,* pp. 18, 48, 51, 57–58; Moursund, *Blanco,* pp. 210–13. For other examples of the statement that Sam Johnson, Sr., founded the town, see Healy, "The Frantic," and Shannon, "Lyndon."

11. My account of the Johnson brothers' careers as cattlemen, derived mostly from John Moursund's careful study of the tax rolls, differs in ways from the story earlier gathered together by Johnson's mother. Before the Civil War, according to her account, Sam and Tom were pasturing cattle and had established ranch headquarters in the log cabin and rock barn. According to Moursund, Jack (Andrew Jackson) Johnson, one of Johnson's great-uncles, settled on the Pedernales in 1859. Jack paid his poll tax through the war years; the records indicate he owned livestock through the same period. Moursund conjectured Jack returned to east Texas in the latter part of 1865. Tom (Jesse Thomas) Johnson, the other great-uncle in this story, and Sam Ealy Johnson, Sr., his brother and Johnson's grandfather, visited Jack in 1859, but not, Moursund believed, for long. The names of Tom and Sam were on the tax rolls for 1861 and 1862, but not 1863; in 1864 Tom paid his poll tax and owned considerable livestock. Tom had enlisted as a private in the company of Texas State Troops for Blanco County and served eight days in 1864; twenty-seven years old at the time, he paid his poll tax in the county in 1864 and 1865. In 1865 he owned cattle, horses, and sheep. In 1871 Tom owned the 640-acre Fentress grant, twenty-five horses, and 1,010 cattle and had a total worth of $16,992. The next year he had 1,200 cattle; he had sold the Fentress tract to Sam and bought another 640-acre tract and his total stated worth was down to $6,640. In 1873, for tax purposes his property was worth $180; in 1875, nothing.

Sam appeared on the tax rolls in 1870 owning 960 acres, 290 cattle, and ten horses, with a total worth of $4,210. In 1871 he rendered, as his total worth, $1,200, the value of 320 acres he still owned. His name disappeared from the rolls in 1872.

RBJ, *A Family,* p. 70; Moursund, *Blanco,* pp. 208–14, 217, *passim.* On the size of the Johnsons' cattle pens and the area from which cattle were driven to them, Interview, LJ (Dec. 13, 1967).

My authority that the trails the Johnsons used included the Chisholm is Lyndon Johnson, who said his grandfather and great-uncle drove cattle up the Old Chisholm Trail ("The Hill Country," an NBC special). The Chisholm Trail in its inception extended from San Antonio to Abilene, Kansas, about 800 miles. Cattle herds began going up from Texas in 1867. In 1889, under the pressures of immigrants and homesteaders who were fencing range, the drives ended. (Ridings, *The Chisholm,* pp. 5, 15, 570–71, 27.)

12. Bob Barton, Jr., was told the story of Sam, Sr.'s fight by Edwin Nivens of Buda on condition Barton not print it while Nivens was alive.

Bob Barton, Jr., *Onion Creek Free Press,* Oct. 3, 1981, and Interview, Bob Barton, Jr.; RBJ, *A Family,* p. 71.

6. A Populist Johnson Runs for Office

1. Nugent's remarks and the Populists' platforms were published in *Southern Mercury,* the publication of the Farmers Alliance of Texas.

   Nugent received 380 votes in Blanco County, the Republican Clark 352, and Hogg 214. Apparently the Populists' strength in Blanco was doctrinal, because Marion Martin, Nugent's running mate for lieutenant governor, got 385 votes there.

   According to the *House Journal* for 1893, Clarence Martin was a fairly active member the first five weeks of the session, but did not attend thereafter.

   The *Blanco News* report was reprinted in the *Hays County Times;* evidently the campaign meeting being reported took place a week or several before the November election. I am indebted to Bob Barton, Jr., editor of the *Onion Creek Free Press,* for this item.

   Interview, LJ (Dec. 13, 1967); Martin, *The People's,* pp. 21, 25, 41, 25–57, 69, 142, 210–11, *passim;* Smith, "The Farmers' "; Goodwyn, *Democratic,* pp. 33–34, 113–53, 167, 213, 244, 285, 328–33; *Southern Mercury,* Oct. 6, 1892; *Biennial Report of the Secretary of State, 1892,* Blanco County returns in the general election of 1892; *Members of the Legislature,* Texas, pp. 154, 156; *Hays County Times,* Nov. 4, 1892, reprinting the report from the *Blanco News.*

7. Like Father, Unlike Son

1. Interviews, LJ (Dec. 13, 1967), LaBJ, SHJ, Otto Lindig (JL); Provence, *Lyndon,* p. 29; Singer and Sherrod, *Lyndon,* pp. 95–96; RBJ, *A Family,* p. 25; Pool et al., *Lyndon,* pp. 21–30, *passim;* Moursund, *Blanco,* p. 217; a confidential source.
2. Harper's Ferry tapes.
3. President Johnson's recollection of Bailey's division of the legislature into rogues and honorees was very slightly off. According to the *Austin Tribune* the morning after Bailey's speech, he proposed to have the separate pictures of the members framed in two groups, one being the "Roll of Honor," the other the "Rogues' Gallery."

   For a feeling of the rhetoric of the time, the passion of the issue, and the primitivism of such feuds, here is part of what Hilton R. Greer wrote in the *Tribune* the morning after Bailey's victory in the legislature:

   "He proposed—he, the Most Immaculate, the Supreme High Dictator of Texas Politics—to . . . see that few, if any, who had the manhood to oppose him should ever hold public office in Texas again. . . . Let the senator beware! . . . [T]he senator himself will lie for all time in the trench that he has made."

   In an editorial celebrating the American Constitution, Lyndon wrote as a college student: "Occasionally a Joe Bailey may be found who devotes time and thought to the study of the constitution and who rises rapidly, not only in the legal profession, but in the political life of our nation."

   Acheson, *Joe,* pp. 139–82, 212–32, 237; Cocke, *The Bailey,* pp. vi, 2, 4–5, 119–22, 146–48, 174–77, 205–26, 215, 219, 631–33, 643–47, 680, 725–35, 942–43; *PP 1965,* p. 835; Interview, LJ (Dec. 13, 1967); *AA,* Nov. 21, 1967; Pool et al., *Lyndon,* pp. 29, 60; Steinberg, *Sam Johnson's,* p. 10, and see Steinberg, *Sam Rayburn,* pp. 14–18; SHJ, *My,* pp. 29–30.

8. A Frontier Baptist Mother

1. *AA,* Nov. 17, 1955; Interview, Emmette Redford.
2. Sidey, *A Very,* pp. 12–13; Interview, SHJ; *San Marcos Record,* May, 9, 1930, cited in Pool et al., *Lyndon,* pp. 175–76; Jones, *The Life,* Vol. 1, p. 5, citing Sigmund Freud, *Gesammelte Werke* (London: Imago, 1940–1952), Vol. 12, p. 26, and Letter, R. B. Downs to RD; Ruth Schumm, *DMN,* June 27, 1954, and *DMN* (AP), Nov. 23, 1963; Elizabeth Carpenter, *AA,* June 24, 1955.
3. However, Johnson took a (somewhat formal) position contrary to my interpretation: "My Daddy and my dear Mother were equally affectionate, equally considerate with their children. . . . I looked at them with equal respect and cherished them with identical love."

The late Virginia Durr, who knew and admired Rebekah, discounted the view that she was so important. "I think all this crazy stuff about his mother being the dominating influence in his life is so exaggerated," she said. "He had a great respect for his father. And I think he had that sort of respectful attitude toward older men."

The quotations from Lyndon about his mother in these passages are from my interviews with him except the remark about a special feeling, which is from Schreiber and Long; impulses and moderation, from Carpenter; and a saintly woman, from Kornitzer.

Flora Schreiber and Stuart Long, *AAS,* Oct. 16, 1971; Pool et al., *Lyndon,* pp. 51, 56; Interviews, LJ (Dec. 13, 14, 1967), Charles Boatner (JL), George Reedy (JL); Elizabeth Carpenter, *AA,* June 24, 1955; Kornitzer, "President"; William McGaffin, *Fort Worth Star-Telegram,* June 25, 1964; Miller, *Lyndon,* p. 25.

4. Johnson was fully aware of his great-grandfather's career and held forth about it while he was president.

   Texas Historical and Biographical Magazine, 1891, pp. 159, 480–85; William Neal Ramey, *Texian Annual,* 1886, vol. 2, no. 17, pp. 231–32; *Baptist Standard,* Jan. 20, 1965; see RBJ, *A Family,* pp. 91–97, and *PP 1964,* p. 419.

5. Mrs. Houston had told Baines that others had tried to put the old man's mind at ease so he could join their church, but had not succeeded. Here is a fuller account of Baines's argument:

   "Bro. Baines . . . explained the passage as referring the Corinthians not to the violation of a law affecting their relation to Christ and governing their Christian existence or being, but their relation to the law of the ordinance and its proper observance as affecting their well-being, happiness, and usefulness as Christians. That to eat worthily was to observe the proper form of the ordinance, and to eat unworthily was to not do so, for which the Corinthians were rebuked."

   Houston "looked very reasonable" and said he would read the chapter carefully. "The result was that he . . . was baptized. . . . Nov. 19, 1854."

   The chapter that was in question must be the eleventh of 1 Corinthians, in which Paul rebuked the Corinthians. After Houston was Baptized he still had his doubts. "I know," he wrote his wife in 1856, "that I am a sinner. . . ."

   AA, Nov. 17, 1955; *Texas Historical and Biographical Magazine,* 1891, pp. 361–62, 483; see 1 Corinthians 11: 1–2, 18–22, 27, 29, 34; Shuffler, *The Houstons,* pp. 27–28.

6. The letter from Houston to Baines, Sr., was published in Houston's collected writings. A framed copy of the text hung on a wall at the Johnson Ranch, and Mrs. Johnson was quoted that if the house caught on fire the letter was the first thing she would save.

   Johnson said that in 1857, "My great-grandfather, my mother's grandfather . . . brought General Houston—San Houston—into the Baptist Church and General Houston made him a loan of $300 at 8 percent. And so four or five years later he sent him the note and asked him to renew it because there hadn't been anything paid on it."

   The Writings, Williams and Barker, eds., vol. VII, p. 32; Marie Smith, *WP,* Dec. 22, 1963, and cf. *Houston Post,* Nov. 1, 1964; *PP 1965,* p. 227.

7. RBJ, *A Family,* pp. 76, 79, 78, citing the *Baptist Tribune,* Dec. 13, 1906.
8. Stambaugh and Stambaugh, *A History,* p. 145.
9. In a commencement talk in 1886, Joseph Baines said school teachers, being "quasi-public" officers, should "never be independent of the People." (*Texas Review,* July, 1886, pp. 767–68.)

   During his tenure as secretary of state, Joseph Baines was a ghost writer for Governor John Ireland of Texas, or so Rebekah Johnson told her son. (Interview, LJ, Dec. 13, 1967.)

   RBJ, *A Family,* pp. 29, 79; Hall, ed., "Horace"; Anita Brewer, *AS,* Dec. 16, 1964; *Baptist Standard,* Jan. 20, 1965.

10. Compare, however, Lyndon's mother's account of her father's financial failure with Lyndon's to Kearns: ". . . in 1904 . . . he lost all his money in one disastrous deal. It killed him." Kearns said Johnson associated this sudden failure with idealism and naïveté. To me, Johnson regularly associated his father's failure with his father's idealism, but not his maternal grandfather's.

    RBJ, *A Family,* pp. 28–30, 67–69, 76–77; Kearns, *Lyndon,* pp. 20, 22, 40 *n.* 4; Ruth Schumm, *DMN,* June 27, 1954; Charles Mohr, *NYT,* Dec. 26,

1964; Waugh, "The Boyhood"; Interviews, *LJ* (Dec. 13, 1967), SHJ, Otto Crider, Ghent Sanderford, Otto Lindig (JL), Josefa Baines (Mrs. W.E.) Saunders (JL); Baines, *Pioneering,* pp. 15–16; cf. also Pool et al., *Lyndon,* pp. 31–33.

9. "A Sharp, Compelling Cry"

1. Rebekah said the attending physician was Dr. John Blanton. Apparently the doctor did not arrive until after the baby was born.

   Rebekah described the house as a "rambling old farmhouse," but Lyndon later said the place had three rooms, and a photograph showed it to be small.

   Harvey Jordan, who came to own the land on which the house stood, tore down the original birthplace in 1945 or 1946 and used the lumber to build a small tenant house. About 1964 Johnson bought a two-acre tract with a small building on it from Jordan, had the building torn down, and had a reconstruction of his birthplace erected.

   W.C. Linden was district attorney in Blanco County in the late 1890s.

   RBJ, *A Family,* pp. 17–18; Interviews, Jessie T. Hatcher (JL) and Otto Lindig (JL); *PP 1964,* pp. 650, 689, and *PP 1965,* p. 150; Pool et al., *Lyndon,* p. 50; Jack Keever, *SAEN,* Oct. 31, 1965; *Time,* June 22, 1953; see Steinberg, *Sam Johnson's,* p. 12. On the reconstruction, *Houston Post,* May 21, 1964; *SAEN,* Dec. 28, 1963; for a piece based on the incorrect impression that the reconstruction is the original birthplace, see *Time,* July 27, 1970. On W. C. Linden, Speer, *A History,* p. 73, and Pool, et al., *Lyndon,* p. 24. On Rebekah's dislike of Martin, Interview, SHJ.
2. RBJ, *A Family,* first page of illustrations after p. 32; Charles Mohr, *NYT,* Dec. 26, 1964.
3. Interview, LJ (Dec. 13, 1967); Steinberg, *Sam Johnson's,* p. 14.
4. Interviews, Otto Crider and Mrs. Virginia Durr; Singer and Sherrod, *Lyndon,* p. 96; Mooney, *The Lyndon,* p. 32; *Texas Co-Op Power,* Mar. 1954, a reprint from *Progressive Farmer.*
5. RBJ, *A Family,* p. 19; *PP 1964,* p. 420; LaBJ, quoted by Winzola McLendon, *WP,* May 14, 1965.
6. Interview, LJ (Dec. 13, 1967)
7. Harper's Ferry tapes and Sidey, "The Private Preserve."
8. Provence, *Lyndon,* p. 30; RBJ, *A Family,* p. 19; Pool et al., *Lyndon,* p. 51; *PP 1965,* pp. 228; 413; Interview LJ (Dec. 13, 1967); NBC, "The Hill"; cf. Miller, *Lyndon,* p. 9.
9. Kearns, *Lyndon,* pp. 24–25; NBC, "The Hill."
10. Kearns, *Lyndon,* pp. 33, 22–23.
11. Johnson told Kearns these memories while they stood at the doorway to what he said had been his parents' bedroom in his birthplace home. Kearns, *Lyndon,* pp. 19–20.
12. The ranch house stands on land granted to Rachel Meals of Georgia in 1845. William Meier of Germany bought the land in 1882 and that year built a one-room log cabin on it, Mrs. Lady Bird Johnson's history reports. About 1894 or 1895 a one-room, but two-story rock house was built. The Martins bought it with 350 acres on June 22, 1909, for $9,500. At that time the house consisted of the stone living room, a pantry, a kitchen and dining room, a screen porch, and a summertime kitchen and eating place. In 1912 several rooms were added.

    LaBJ, "The Story"; Harper's Ferry tapes.
13. The story that his grandfather announced Lyndon would be a senator the day Lyndon was born was told by, among others, Lyndon. "The story goes," he said, "that the day I was born my grandaddy saddled up his biggest gray mare, Fritz, and rode into town, looking as proud as if he had won the Battle of the Alamo singlehanded. He announced to everyone that a U.S. Senator had just come into the world. It was kind of a joke with my playmates as I was growing up. But I guess the idea sort of rubbed off. I did want to become a senator. . . ."

    Interview, LJ (Dec. 13, 1967); RBJ, *A Family,* pp. 18–19; Singer and Sherrod, *Lyndon,* p. 87; and for other instances of the recurrences of the story, see Pool et al., *Lyndon,* p. 50; Mooney, *The Lyndon,* p. 8 (and p. xx); *CCCT,* March 6, 1960.
14. Interview, LJ (Dec. 13, 1967); Harper's

Ferry tapes; RBJ, *A Family,* p. 18 and illustration on third page following p. 32; LaBn, "The Story"; Kearns, *Lyndon,* pp. 33–34.

15. Johnson told this memory to Kearns, who speculated that it "may, instead, have been a dream or even an aggressive fantasy against both his mother and the unborn child she was carrying." Johnson told her that later his mother confessed to him she'd been afraid her fall had hurt the child in her womb. Although in his story Johnson said the baseball had knocked his mother off balance, Kearns did not see how a boy of five could throw a ball hard enough "to knock an adult woman to the ground." She found Rebekah's fear that the foetus had been hurt almost incredible, and she suggested Johnson had her step in the way to shift guilt from himself.

    Kearns, *Lyndon,* pp. 26–27.
16. *PP 1966,* p. 442; and Kearns, *Lyndon*, p. 67.
17. The Johnsons' home in Johnson City was built in 1886. Lyndon's parents bought it after he was born.

    Interviews, SHJ, Mrs. Jessie Hatcher (JL); *WP,* May 24, 1966; see Pool et al., *Lyndon,* p. 51.

10. The School and the Churches

1. Interviews, Tom and Otto Crider, Emmette Redford, Gene Waugh, LJ (Dec. 13, 1967), Otto Lindig (JL), Ben Crider (JL); a confidential source; Newlon, *L.B.J.,* p. 26; Sidey, *A Very,* p. 10.

11. Poems, Curls, Hymns, and a Rabbit

1. According to his friend Horace Busby, later on Johnson, seeking sympathy from the compassionate types, "constructed for himself a past which he believed would transform him into a weak, even a pitiable figure," but in fact, Busby said, Johnson's youthful friends "insist he was disabled not by parental deprivation, but by parental indulgence, which left him 'spoiled rotten.' "

    Interview, LJ (Dec. 13, 1967); SHJ, *My,* p. 25; Harper's Ferry tapes; confidential source; Horace Busby, *WP (Book World),* June 6, 1976.
2. The account of little Sam shuttling from his father's to his big brother's side to keep them warm comes from the book Johnson's brother later wrote. Kearns, psychologizing about the practice, called it "this peculiar game of power and convoluted sexuality."

    Newlon, *L.B.J.,* p. 28; SHJ, *My,* p. 10; Pool et al., *Lyndon,* p. 51; Provence, *Lyndon,* p. 30; Waugh, "The Boyhood"; Kearns, *Lyndon,* p. 37; *PP 1966,* p. 388; see *WP,* May 24, 1966, and *NYT,* Dec. 24, 1965. For a variant story that Lyndon broke his leg jumping from the barn in a corncob fight, see Miller, *Lyndon,* p. 19.
3. Interview, C. S. Kinney.
4. Interview, LJ (Dec. 14, 1967).
5. Interviews, Otto Crider, C. S. Kinney, and Ghent Sanderford; Waugh, "The Boyhood." For Ben Crider, *contra,* on Rebekah not charging, see Miller, *Lyndon,* p. 14.
6. Johnson told me that after his curls were shaved off, he was kicked off the platform, but perhaps this was hyperbole. For the poem he learned, see p. 34.

    PP 1967, p. 121; Interview, LJ (Dec. 14, 1967); Lisagor, "Lyndon"; RBJ, *A Family,* p. 19 and illustrations after p. 32; Kearns, *Lyndon,* p. 25.
7. *NYT,* Mar. 14, 1965; RBJ, *A Family,* third and fifth pages of illustrations after p. 32; a confidential source.
8. Pool et al., *Lyndon,* p. 51; Singer and Sherrod, *Lyndon,* p. 95; cf. *PP 1967,* p. 909.
9. Waugh, "The Boyhood"; Newlon, *L.B.J.,* p. 28; see Steinberg, *Sam Johnson's,* p. 19.
10. Interviews, Otto, Ben, and Tom Crider; RBJ, *A Family,* p. 20; Steinberg, *Sam Johnson's,* p. 19.
11. As an example of the Baptist orthodoxy of his mother's family, Johnson once remarked, of his mother's grandfather's election to represent the southern Baptist convention and selection to preach one of its annual sermons, "If that doesn't prove he was orthodox, nothing will."

    Interviews, LJ (Dec. 13, 1967), Tom Crider; *PP 1964,* pp. 418–20, 1294; *PP*

1965, pp. 1016, 593; *PP 1966,* p. 491; SHJ, *My,* pp. 33–34; *Pioneers in God's Hills,* pp. 63–64; cf. Kearns, *Lyndon,* p. 31.

12. Kearns, *Lyndon,* p. 25.
13. Robert B. Semple, Jr., *NYT,* Nov. 9, 1966; *AA,* Aug. 24, 1969; Interview, Ben Crider; Carpenter, "Lyndon"; Steinberg, *Sam Johnson's* p. 16; confidential sources.
14. Interview, LJ (Dec. 13, 1967) and LJ, *The Vantage,* p. 425; RBJ, *A Family,* pp. 69, 73; SHJ, *My,* pp. 11, 12. On Eliza, cf. Kearns, *Lyndon,* pp. 31–32.
15. Interview, Payne Roundtree; *PP 1964,* pp. 1263, 1276.
16. Pool et al. *Lyndon,* pp. 54–55; Kearns, *Lyndon,* pp. 38–39; Steinberg, *Sam Johnson's,* p. 17; a confidential source.
17. *AA,* July 11, 1948; Provence, *Lyndon,* p. 32; Jack Keever, *SAEN,* Oct. 31, 1965; *PP 1964,* pp. 1457–58; Pool et al., *Lyndon,* pp. 52–53. See, for a variant form of the story about the cotton-picking contest, Steinberg, *Sam Johnson's,* pp. 18–19.
18. Lyndon's later college teacher and mentor, Professor H. M. Greene, said, "He watched that old man [his father], and saw, and that's where he got his political savvy."

    Interviews, LJ (Dec. 13, 1967), Tom Crider, John Fritz Koeniger, H. M. Greene; Provence, *Lyndon,* p. 31; RBJ, *A Family,* p. 21; Pool et al., *Lyndon,* pp. 57–58; Bishop, *A Day,* p. 89 cf. Steinberg, *Sam Johnson's,* p. 26.
19. Interviews, Payne Roundtree, Otto Crider; Breazele, "Hye and the Mighty"; Pool et al., *Lyndon,* p. 53 and see pp. 52, 54; *PP 1965,* p. 1094; see Bishop, *A Day,* p. 179. For an account of the donkey-riding with variant details, see Steinberg, *Sam Johnson's,* p. 19.
20. Interviews, Ben Crider, John Fritz Koeniger; LJ quoted by Elizabeth Carpenter, *AA,* June 24, 1955, and speech by LJ in Snyder, Tx., Nov. 12, 1959; Waugh, "The Boyhood"; T. A. Price, *DMN,* June 30, 1941; RBJ, *A Family,* p. 9; cf. Singer and Sherrod, *Lyndon,* p. 97.
21. *PP 1968,* p. 936.

12. Siding with Another Grafter

1. Interview, LJ (Dec. 13, 1967); Harper's Ferry tapes.
2. Interviews, Ben Crider, Reverdy Gliddon, SHJ; Mooney, *The Lyndon,* p. xxi; Pool et. al., *Lyndon,* pp. 24–25.
3. Interview, LJ (Dec. 14, 1967).
4. Ferguson's secretary Ghent Sanderford had a lively pro-Ferguson perspective, and he provided me with the original form of an article he wrote in 1955, "The Ferguson Era, 1914–1944," from which I have drawn perspective and information. A persuasive case can be made that the Fergusons were the last liberals in the Texas governor's mansion in this century. It is said in Texas that Gov. James Allred, who succeeded Mrs. Ferguson in 1936, was the last liberal governor the state had, and he did support and administer the New Deal in Texas, but Allred was not as tuned in to the common people as the Fergusons.

   Interview, Ghent Sanderford; Pool, *et al., Lyndon,* p. 35.
5. *Record of Proceedings,* pp. 11–16, 670–75, 680–83, 714–32, 749, 778; Pool et al., *Lyndon,* pp. 35–36.

13. A Resolve at Recess

1. Lyndon said he was twelve when the family moved back to his grandfather's farm, but Sam Houston believed that he dated the move exactly at January, 1919, when Lyndon was ten, and in the text I have followed Sam Houston.

   The boy in Lyndon's story was named Alton Hodges.

   Waugh, "The Boyhood"; Jack Keever, *SAEN,* Oct. 31, 1965; Interviews, SHJ, Otto Lindig (JL); Mooney, *The Lyndon,* p. 32; Johnson on "The Hill Country," an NBC Special; Seth Kantor, *Fort Worth Press,* Mar. 8, 1964; Harper's Ferry tapes.
2. Interviews, Wright Patman, Ben and Otto Crider, LJ (Dec. 13, 1967), Emmette Redford; Singer and Sherrod, *Lyndon,* p. 96; Steinberg, *Sam Johnson's,* p. 3; RBJ, *A Family,* pp. 24–25, 27; a confidential source.
3. Sam Johnson's defense of the Germans moved his son when he was presi-

dent. Welcoming foreign-language newspaper publishers to the White House during his 1964 campaign, the president remembered "when some sought to turn against those from other lands" and his father had said "No."

Interviews, LJ (Dec. 13, 14, 1967), R. E. Thomason (JL); Pool et al., *Lyndon,* pp. 36–41, 45, 57, *passim;* Kearns, *Lyndon,* pp. 36–37; *CR 1941,* vol. 87, pp. 1992–94; *PP 1964,* pp. 924–26 and *PP 1968,* p. 873.

4. Steinberg, *Sam Johnson's,* p. 30; news item, undated.
5. Pool et al., *Lyndon,* pp. 55–56; SHJ, *My,* pp. 6–7.
6. Sidey, *A Very,* pp. 16–17.
7. *Brenham Banner-Press,* June 10, 1946; Jack Keever, *SAEN,* Oct. 31, 1965; *CR 1946,* vol. 92, p. 8188; Newlon, *L.B.J.,* p. 116.

14. Lyndon's Father Fails

1. Reconstructing the conversation between Sam and Rebekah, I relied on accounts of it from Lyndon and Sam Houston Johnson. Both the boys could have been present, but Lyndon was the older, and I have not used some of the more colorful lines in Sam Houston's reconstruction. For Rebekah's last retort, bringing into play Neff's being a Baptist (which comes from Sam Houston's account), there is additional support in Lyndon's telling of the story to Elizabeth Carpenter. "Mama was serving supper," Lyndon said, "and she spoke up. 'I'll tell you where that Neff vote came from. It came from me. I've got too much Baptist in me to vote against Pat Neff.' " (In this latter version Neff had received only one vote in the Johnsons' box.) Sam Houston erroneously placed the election in 1916; it was 1920.

   Interview, LJ (Mar. 23, 1968); SHJ, *My,* pp. 32–33; Elizabeth Carpenter, *AA,* June 24, 1955; see Gantt, *The Chief,* p. 271, *passim.* On Neff, see Neff, *The Battles,* pp. 305, 307, 310. On Rebekah Johnson's food, see *Houston Chronicle* (AP), May 14, 1965. (She also made turkey dressing Lady Bird Johnson said was the best she ever tasted.)
2. *PP 1964,* p. 1298; Mrs. Birge Alexander quoted in *WP,* May 14, 1965; Waugh, "The Boyhood"; Interviews, Emmette Redford, Ben Crider (JL), Charles Boatner (JL), Mrs. Jessie Hatcher (JL), a confidential source; Sidey, *A Very,* p. 150; William McGaffin, *CCCT,* March 6, 1960; Mrs. O. P. Bobbitt quoted in *The State* (Columbia, S.C.), Dec. 7, 1966, and *Dallas Times-Herald,* Dec. 8, 1966; "The Hill," NBC; Lauren Lane, *AS,* Jan. 23, 1973.
3. Pool et al., *Lyndon,* pp. 22, 26, 39–40; Interview, Wright Patman; Steinberg, *Sam Johnson's,* pp. 27–28.
4. Interviews, LJ (Dec. 13, 1967), Otto Lindig (JL); Harwood and Johnson, *Lyndon,* p. 23; *Brenham Banner Press,* June 10, 1946; *CR 1946,* vol. 92, p. 8188; Harper's Ferry tapes; see Nevins and Commager, *A Short,* p. 419.
5. Harper's Ferry tapes; Waugh, "The Boyhood"; *SLPD,* Feb. 27, 1949; Interview, SHJ.

15. *The Boy Turns Away*

1. Interviews, Ben Crider, SHJ; Carolyn Patrick, *DMN,* May 14, 1965; Kearns, *Lyndon,* p. 24; SHJ, *My,* pp. 10–11; confidential sources.
2. Alfred Steinberg quoted an unnamed politician saying that Sam Johnson ran around with rich lobbyists, especially Roy Miller of Texas Gulf Sulphur, and "was thrilled to be in contact with anyone rich." Sam did get to know Miller, a fact that became important when Lyndon wanted to get a job as a congressional secretary.

   Interview, LJ (Dec. 13, 1967); Pool et al., *Lyndon,* pp. 39–44; Steinberg, *Sam Johnson's,* pp. 29–30.
3. Lyndon Johnson also told Hugh Sidey that the Klan threatened his father and did violence to some friends of the Johnsons', but Lyndon did not tell the story his brother Sam Houston did about waiting on the porch with shotguns.

   When Sam was in the legislature Governor Pat Neff was a "friendly neutral on the Klan," but in 1924

Ma Ferguson, running on an anti-Klan ticket (and supported by Sam), won. As governor she got an anti-mask law passed and the Klan wilted.

During Johnson's presidency four Klansmen were arrested and charged with violating the civil rights of Mrs. Viola Liuzzo, who had been murdered on a lonely road in Alabama. President Johnson called the names of the accused from the White House, all but convicting them, so vehemently did he attack the Klan:

"Mrs. Liuzzo . . . was murdered by the enemies of justice who for decades have used the rope and the gun and the tar and the feathers to terrorize their neighbors. They struck by night, as they generally do, for their purpose cannot stand the light of day.

"My father fought them many long years in Texas and I have fought them all my life . . . their loyalty is not to the United States of America but instead to a hooded society of bigots."

He even compared them to "the terrorists in North Vietnam."

Interviews, Wright Patman, LJ (Dec. 13, 1967); *CR,* Mar. 23, 1953, a speech by Patman; Bill Porterfield, *Houston Chronicle,* April 2, 1965; Sidey, *A Very,* p. 109; SHJ, *My,* pp. 30–31; Barron, "LBJ Smile"; *AAS,* Mar. 27, 1965; McKay, *Texas,* pp. 129–37, 156; *PP 1965,* pp. 332–33; Kearns, *Lyndon,* p. 230; and see White, *The Professional,* p. 60, Baker, *The Johnson,* p. 200, and Steinberg, *Sam Johnson's,* p. 28.

4. Interviews, Edmunds Travis, Harry Benge Crozier, LJ (Dec. 13, 1967); Singer and Sherrod, *Lyndon,* p. 96; Pool et al., *Lyndon,* p. 57; Harwood and Johnson, *Lyndon,* p. 23; *PP 1964,* p. 286; *PP 1963,* p. 103, cf. *PP 1964,* p. 577.
5. Mooney, *The Lyndon,* p. xxi.
6. Interview, LJ (Dec. 13, 1967).

16. Bootleg Wine and Berry Vines

1. Interviews, LJ (Dec. 14, 1967), Otto Crider, Emmette Redford, SHJ, John Fritz Koeniger; *PP 1964,* p. 562; Newlon, *L.B.J.,* p. 29; confidential sources.
2. Interviews, Emmette Redford, Otto Crider.
3. Johnson used this story to show that the nation should arm: "The chances are," he said, "the bully would never have picked on this quiet boy in the first place if he'd known what was going to happen."

   Singer and Sherrod, *Lyndon,* pp. 204–5.
4. Jack Valenti heard Johnson tell this story to Secretary of State Dean Rusk during a meeting in the White House Situation Room on June 5, 1964. Defense Secretary Bob McNamara and McGeorge Bundy were also present. The officials had been discussing the situation in Laos and South Vietnam. Upon finishing the story about the collapse of the gang attack on the teacher, Johnson added, "What I am saying is if I have to turn back [in Indochina] I want to make sure I am not in too deep to do so." Valenti took this to mean Johnson did not want to provoke reprisals from China or Russia and have the U.S. too deeply involved to turn back. Perhaps Johnson was also thinking of his 1954 position on Vietnam, when he asked Eisenhower and others what allies would go in with the United States to save the French garrison at Dien Bien Phu. (None manifestly would; a decision was taken against intervention.)

   Valenti, *A Very,* p. 134.
5. SHJ, *My,* pp. 15–16, and interview, SHJ.
6. Winzola McLendon, *WP,* May 14, 1965; *PP 1964,* p. 727; see Miller, *Lyndon,* pp. 28–29.
7. Mooney, *The Lyndon,* pp. xx, 14; White, *The Professional,* p. 64; Pool et al., *Lyndon,* p. 54; Interview, Ben Crider; *PP 1965,* p. 1057.
8. Interviews, John Fritz Koeniger, Otto Crider, John Fritz Koeniger; Newlon, *L.B.J.,* p. 221; confidential sources.
9. Newlon, *L.B.J.* p. 26; Geyelin, *Lyndon,* p. 93; Interview, Tom Crider.
10. Interview, Emmette Redford; *AA,* Aug. 16, 1971; Shearer, "Can."
11. Interviews, Otto Crider, John Fritz Koeniger.
12. *PP 1964,* p. 727; RBJ, *A Family,* ninth page of illustrations after p. 32 (*contra,*

on the size of the class, Newlon, *L.B.J.*, p. 221); Pool et al, *Lyndon,* pp. 64–65; White, *The Professional,* p. 62 ("too thin to throw," etc.); *WP,* May 14, 1965.

13. Peter Lisagor (CDN), *Fort Worth Star-Telegram,* Mar. 21, 1965, and cf. Amrine, *This,* pp. 119–20; Kearns, *Lyndon,* p. 40; Newlon, *L.B.J.,* p. 221.

17. "I Felt on My Own"

1. In telling about this trip, Johnson did not go into his ragging of Summy, saying only that when they stopped for the night beyond Van Horn they dug a hole with their hands to bury their money. Payne and Otto remembered that they had gotten as far west as Sheffield, Texas, not Van Horn, when the cowboys invited them into the poker game. Otto said that, rather than one of them sleeping on their money, each of them buried what he had in a different place.

   My only source on the roles of Lyndon's parents in this matter is Sam Houston Johnson, who was in Johnson City with them after Lyndon left. According to Sam Houston's book, the boys evaded the sheriffs looking for Lyndon by driving at night until they got out of Texas, but this does not jibe with what the boys on the trip said.

   Interviews, Payne Roundtree, Tom, Ben, and Otto Crider, LJ (Dec. 13, 14, 1967), and John Fritz Koeniger; SHJ, *My,* pp. 20–24; *PP 1964,* pp. 726, 1293, 1319, and *PP 1965,* p. 408; *Washington Evening Star,* Nov. 23, 1963; T. A. Price, *DMN,* June 30, 1941.

2. Johnson told me he returned with his Uncle Clarence, but that conflicts with what he had apparently told the AP earlier. The AP reported, " 'The trip back home was the longest I have ever made,' Mr. Johnson said. It was accomplished by walking and hitchhiking. He was away for several months." The story that he hitchhiked home and had been gone only several months was repeated widely.

   Interviews, LJ (Dec. 14, 1967), John Fritz Koeniger Jessie Hatcher (JL); SHJ, *My,* pp. 23–24; Kearns, *Lyndon,* pp. 42–44; Baker, *The Johnson,* p. 65; Pool et al., *Lyndon,* p. 65; Provence, *Lyndon,* pp. 32–33; *PP 1964,* pp. 642, 726, 1293, 1319, and *PP 1965,* p. 408; Carpenter, "Profile"; *SLPD,* Feb. 27, 1949; *Washington Evening Star,* Nov. 23, 1963; T. A. Price, *DMN,* June 30, 1941; see also Steinberg, *Sam Johnson's,* pp. 32–33.

18. Working and Helling Around

1. *PP 1964,* p. 726; Interview, LJ (Dec. 13, 1967).
2. As president, Johnson said he worked "on a highway crew for a dollar a day" and "started out at a dollar a day."

   The employment records of the Texas Highway Department were researched for an article in the Texas highway magazine on Johnson's highway work and yielded somewhat vague information. The records were not clear on when Johnson did this work, although an official said "we believe it was sometime between 1922 and 1925." Lyndon's sister Rebekah thought he had worked "part-time or during the summers" and his brother thought the time of this could have been 1924. Ben Crider told me that he and Lyndon had worked on the roads upon their return from California, but this would not preclude Lyndon's having worked for his dad earlier, too, perhaps in the one month between his graduation and departure for California. However, since Lyndon worked in Robstown in the summer of 1923 and graduated from high school in May, 1924, left for California early in July of that year, and was gone for 20 months, the bulk of his work on the highways had to be upon his return from California and before he entered college in February, 1927.

   J. W. Puckett, the engineer who, according to the Texas highway magazine, fired Lyndon, died in 1952.

   Johnson's statement that he caused his parents grief in his late teens was made in 1964: "I think I would have made my parents happier if at 16 or 18, or even 20, I had conducted myself to the same high standards of morals as my daughters apply to themselves now."

   Interviews, Ben and Otto Crider, Emmette Redford, and SHJ; Nation,

"A Rendezvous"; *The Texas Almanac for 1867,* p. 110; *PP 1964,* pp. 543–44, 568, 1319; Newlon, *L.B.J.,* pp. 21, 30–31; Sidey, *A Very,* p. 15; Mooney, *The Lyndon,* pp. 14, xx; Baker, *The Johnson,* p. 64; *SLPD,* Feb. 27, 1949; Robert B. Semple, Jr., *NYT,* Nov. 9, 1966; a confidential source.

3. Johnson told me this story at the height of the Vietnam War. "Now that was pretty good psychology, wasn't it?" he asked. "Damn right," I replied. Ben and Otto Crider remembered the incident, too. John Koeniger heard a variant in which the boys were drinking bootleg wine, and after the wreck Lyndon left home and took a job rather than face his father, but Koeniger was not present. In another variant Johnson told Kearns, the uncle lived in New Braunfels, not San Antonio. I have followed what Johnson told me and the Criders.

   Interviews, LJ (Dec. 13, 1967), Ben and Otto Crider, John Fritz Koeniger; cf. Kearns, *Lyndon,* p. 38.

4. There is an apparently variant account of the circumstances of Lyndon's decision to go to college. His mother wrote that the day he came home ready to go was a cold afternoon after a particularly unpleasant day on the highway gang.

   In Johnson's own later account to Kearns of deciding to go to the capitol and talk about big ideas, he said he "saw it all before me" on the way back from California.

   Sam Houston Johnson wrote that after his big brother set out for San Marcos, Sam Houston heard their father call the president of the college in San Marcos and say "we want to be sure he gets everything he needs. And if there's any expense involved, please bill me directly."

   Newlon, *L.B.J.,* p. 21; Provence, *Lyndon,* p. 33; *Time,* June 22, 1953; T. A. Price, *DMN,* June 30, 1941; *PP 1963,* p. 48; *PP 1964,* pp. 1319, 1356, 1428; *Washington Evening Star,* Nov. 23, 1963; SHJ, *My,* p. 26; Kearns, *Lyndon,* p 44; another source.

   By one account the sum of Lyndon's loan was $25, but most sources say $75. Johnson approved a book that said it was $75 (but the same account said erroneously the bank was in Johnson City). In a 1937 campaign flyer for Johnson there was a statement that when he enrolled he had less than $20 in his pocket (presumably after paying the fees).

   When Johnson was a young congressman, Brigham helped him buy the first tract of what was to become the LBJ ranch. Through the years Johnson kept an account at the Blanco bank of which Brigham was president. In 1965 Johnson called on Brigham in a Blanco rest home; when Brigham died the next year Johnson made a flying trip to Texas for the funeral.

   William Chapman, *WP,* Oct. 9, 1966; T. A. Price, *DMN,* June 30, 1941; *AA,* July 9, 1946; Mooney, *The Lyndon,* p. 15; Bell, *The Johnson,* p. 86; Steinberg, *Sam Johnson's,* p. 35; Interview, *LJ* (JL: *McKay); "He Gets Things Done," Johnson campaign flyer, 1937; Steele, "A Kingmaker"; Time,* June 22, 1953.

19. Start at the President's Office

1. Pool et al., *Lyndon,* pp. 67–89, 100–101, *passim;* Interview, Alfred H. Nolle; Letters, LJ to Alfred H. Nolle, and D. R. Russell to RD; Carolyn Patrick, *DMN,* May 14, 1965, Lyndon's letter to his grandmother dated Feb. 2, 1927, has been on display in JL. On Johnson's later visit to the boardinghouse he lived in as a freshman and the preservation of this house, see *Houston Chronicle,* June 13, 1965, and *AA,* June 6, 1965, and Aug. 11, 1966.
2. Pool et al., *Lyndon,* pp. 90–91; Provence, *Lyndon,* p. 34; Singer and Sherrod, *Lyndon,* pp. 99–100; cf. Kearns, *Lyndon,* p. 45.
3. RBJ, *A Family,* 12th page of illustrations after p. 32; Kearns, *Lyndon,* p. 70.
4. "I worked on the telephone line from San Marcos to Blanco," Johnson once said. He also practice-taught in a San Marcos high school at $55 a month.

   AA, Dec. 6, 1963, Nov. 10, 1967, Jan. 24, 1975, and 1946 (otherwise undated clipping); T. A. Price, *DMN,* June 30, 1941; Pool et al., *Lyndon,* pp. 99–100; Newlon, *L.B.J.,* pp. 32–33; Steele, "A Kingmaker"; Letter, D. R. Russell to RD; Sam Kindrick, *SAEN,* Jan. 11, 1964; *Houston Post,* Nov. 1, 1965; *PP 1965,* pp. 417, 535, 1028, 1105; Provence, *Lyndon,* p. 35; *SLPD,* Nov. 8, 1965; Interviews,

Ben Crider, Emmette Redford, LJ (Dec. 13, 1967); Kearns, *Lyndon,* p. 47.

5. *SAEN,* Jan. 14, 1964; Pool *et al., Lyndon,* pp. 97–98.
6. Kearns, *Lyndon,* p. 56.
7. Pool et al. established that there was no substance to newspaper reports that Johnson had written stories about the national convention in Houston in advance of it and then used them to talk his way in.

   Interview, Alfred H. Nolle; Pool et al., *Lyndon,* pp. 127–28.
8. Johnson's first item in the *College Star* of Mar. 23, 1927, an essay he had written in a class in the sub-college, said "Thinking is not popular," but is good to do. He appeared as associate editor first on the June 8, 1927, masthead; his title became assistant editor June 22 and associate editor again Aug. 17. Some of the editorials listed as written by Johnson in a pamphlet entitled *"The College Star,* The Student Editorials of Lyndon Baines Johnson, 1968, compiled by James Benson and Anthony Sisto," are not signed by Johnson in the issues of the newspaper, although from internal evidence it would seem that at least some of them were his. Pool, Craddock, and Conrad also attribute editorials to Johnson that were not, as they appeared in the paper, identified as his. In these latter cases, I have said that Johnson probably wrote them.

   College Star for 1927, esp. Mar. 23, June 8, 22, July 1, Aug. 3, 10, 27; *The Pedagog* (the student annual), 1927, p. 258; Pool et al., *Lyndon,* pp. 112–36.
9. The spoof of Johnson in the 1928 *Pedagog* found its way into a memorandum between Republican policymakers during the 1964 presidential campaign. A GOP researcher, calling attention to the spoof, asked, "Can Lyndon have *ever* been a person of *any* integrity at *any* time in his life?"

   Provence, *Lyndon,* p. 35; Pool et al., *Lyndon,* pp. 74–75, 100, 101, 125–26 (italics supplied in the story of Lyndon and Ava); Interviews, Ethel Davis, H. M. Greene, Alfred H. Nolle; *AA,* Nov. 17, 1955; *Time,* May 21, 1965; *PP 1964,* p. 1607; *PP 1965,* p. 1105; Singer and Sherrod, *Lyndon,* p. 100; *Pedagog,* 1928, p. 302; memorandum, Lance Tarrance to Peter O'Donnell and others; a confidential source.

   On getting close to leaders, cf. Miller, *Lyndon,* p. 33.
10. Interview, H. M. Greene, Elmer Graham (JL); *Pedagog,* 1928, p. 138; Pool et al., *Lyndon,* pp. 101–2; RBJ, *A Family,* 16th page of illustrations after p. 32; Greene quoted in Sherrill, *The Accidental,* p. 163*n.*; *Houston Post,* May 31, 1965.
11. Interviews, LJ (Dec. 14, 1967) and Alfred H. Nolle; Pool et al., *Lyndon,* pp. 102–11, *SAEN,* Jan. 11, 1964; SHJ, *My,* pp. 26–27; cf. Kearns, *Lyndon,* pp. 49–50.

20. "He Was after Everybody"

1. Johnson later said both that he was superintendent of the Cotulla school and principal of it, but in the context it is clear that he meant he was the principal.

   Daniel Garcia told the story of his getting a whipping from Johnson in 1964 on the CBS-TV show, "I've Got a Secret." As he walked off the television stage he was called to the phone to talk with President Johnson, who asked him, "Tell me—does it still hurt?" "Oh, no, Mr. President," he answered, I treasure the memory." Johnson had him to the White House.

   Interviews, LJ (Dec. 14, 1967), Mrs. Elizabeth Johnson; *PP 1965,* pp. 227, 286, 535, 538; *PP 1966,* p. 1348; *PP 1967,* p. 603, and cf. *PP 1967* p. 956; *PP 1968,* pp. 1139, 1202; *WP,* Jan. 9, 1964; Steinberg, *Sam Johnson's,* pp. 46–47; Ronnie Thompson, AP story from Cotulla, datelined Mar. 18, 1965.
2. LJ, *The Vantage,* pp. 74–75; Interview, LJ (Dec. 14, 1967); *PP 1965,* pp. 88–89, 229–30; Newlon, *L.B.J.,* p. 36; Pool et al., *Lyndon,* pp. 142–43; Miller, *Lyndon,* p. 39.
3. I have this story in two versions, from a speech Johnson made in 1965 and one of my interviews with him. I have combined these accounts, which are consistent except for the exact words of the dialogue Johnson re-created in the different tellings. *PP 1965,* pp. 535–36; Interview, LJ (Dec. 14, 1967).
4. Interview, Mrs. Elizabeth Johnson; Newlon, *L.B.J.,* p. 36; a confidential source.
5. Steinberg, *Sam Johnson's,* p. 48.

6. In 1960 Juan Gonzalez turned up working for Johnson for president.
   RBJ, *A Family,* 8th page of illustrations after p. 32; on Gonzalez, Geyelin, *Lyndon,* p. 24; Singer and Sherrod, *Lyndon,* p. 101; Davidson, "Texas."

21. Taking Over in College

1. *College Star,* June–Aug., 1929, esp. June 12, 26, July 10, 17, Aug. 14.
2. Ma Ferguson (Mrs. Jim Ferguson) ran as an anti-Klan candidate for governor and was elected in 1924; in 1926 she was defeated for reelection by Dan Moody. These are the campaigns to which Johnson was referring in his spiel to Barron. Mrs. Ferguson tried again in 1930, losing, and in 1932, winning, but by then the Klan was no longer the issue that it had been in the twenties.
   Barron, "LBJ"; McKay, *Texas,* pp. 129–37, 156, 209, 239.
3. Interviews, LJ (Dec. 14, 1967), Ben Crider, Willard Deason (JL); Pool et al., *Lyndon,* pp. 102–11; *AA,* Dec. 6, 1963; Newlon, *L.B.J.,* pp. 33–34; cf. Kearns, *Lyndon,* pp. 50–52.
4. Pool et al., *Lyndon,* pp. 96, 98–99; Davidson, "Texas"; Tom Johnson, *AA,* Dec. 6, 1963; Sam Kindrick, *SAEN,* Jan. 11, 1964.
5. Pool et al., *Lyndon,* pp. 91, 96, 123, 144, 176; Interview, Alfred H. Nolle.
6. Roger Greene, *Milwaukee Journal* (AP), Jan. 18, 1955; Interviews LJ (Dec. 13, 1967), Alfred H. Nolle, and Ben Crider; Sam Kindrick, *SAN,* Jan. 11, 1964; *PP 1965,* p. 818; see Pool et al., *Lyndon,* p. 91.
7. Interview, H. M. Greene; Pool, et al., *Lyndon,* pp. 95–96; *AAS,* April 22, 1956.
8. Kearns, *Lyndon,* pp. 67–68; Interview, *LJ* (JL: McKay).
9. A confidential source.
10. *PP 1965,* pp. 195–96.
11. Johnson did not remember the date at Henly, but Hopkins said it was early summer, 1930, and Lyndon's mother said it was when Lyndon was still in college. (He graduated that August.) Hopkins served in the Texas House of Representatives in 1929–30, was nominated for the Senate in July, 1930, and was elected that November.
    Lyndon's mother is the source of the fact that his father told him to get up and make a talk. "He did, standing in the back of a truck, and it was a good speech even if it was impromptu," she said.
    Johnson gave me the first two sentences of his speech. He gave Harry Provence the gist of the speech and his retort about hunters from Austin shooting cows.
    I followed the dialogue between Hopkins and Johnson as Hopkins recreated it for me. Hopkins gave this variant of the exchange to Emmie Craddock:
    Hopkins—"Lyndon, why did you volunteer this speech for Pat Neff?"
    Johnson—"I couldn't let it go by default, Pat Neff once gave my daddy a job, and I couldn't let him down."
    Hopkins told me Johnson did not help him until after he graduated, which is slightly different from the account in Pool et al.
    Interviews, LJ (Mar. 23, 1968), Welly Hopkins, and Charles Schnabel; *AA,* Nov. 17, 1955; Pool et al., *Lyndon,* pp. 164–66; Provence, *Lyndon,* pp. 37–38; cf. Kearns, *Lyndon,* p. 69.
12. Johnson was a member of the student welfare council (which met with the dean of students on matters of student welfare), a literary society, an honorary social science fraternity, and the business administration club. He was secretary of the Schoolmaster's Club, president of the Press Club and its delegate to the state college press association, and worked on the yearbook staff. His last year he was elected a "senior legislator" of his class.
    Pool et al., *Lyndon,* p. 91; Singer and Sherrod, *Lyndon,* p. 100; *SAE,* April 14, 1966; *SAEN,* Jan. 11, 1964; *Pedagog,* 1930, esp. pp. 37, 226, 235; *AA,* Jan. 24, 1973; RBJ, *A Family,* 11th and 13th pages of illustrations after p. 32; Interview, Wally Hopkins (JL).
13. Kearns placed the Davis family in Kerrville; my information places them in San Marcos.
    Sam Houston Johnson's written account of a fight over a girl he called Carol Davis placed her erroneously in Johnson City. He said in an interview he had meant the story to be placed in San Marcos. His additional account of the breakup between Lyndon and Carol has to be qualified in the light

of this confusion, although presumably Lyndon told his little brother what happened, and Johnson's account of the breakup to Kearns is in substantial agreement with SHJ.

Dean Nolle, for his part, added, "Of course, this is gossip, but I wouldn't say it if I didn't believe it had basis in fact."

I tried to talk with the former Carol Davis (long since married to Harold Smith), but her sister, Ethel Davis, said Mrs. Smith was too ill to be interviewed.

Kearns, *Lyndon,* pp. 57–58; Interviews, Alfred H. Nolle, Ethel Davis, SHJ; SHJ, *My,* pp. 17–19, 29; cf. *PP 1964,* pp. 724, 1329.

22. Teacher on the Run

1. Ghent Sanderford, Jim Ferguson's private secretary during Ma Ferguson's first term as governor in 1924–25, said that not Jim Ferguson, but Lon Smith, a railroad commissioner, got the job for Sam Johnson. A state legislator, Roscoe Runge, said he got the job for Sam, according to Crozier.

   Johnson's comments to me about his helping his family were less self-serving than his remarks to Kearns on the same subject.

   Interviews, LJ (Dec. 14, 1967), Ghent Sanderford, Harry Benge Crozier; RBJ, *A Family,* p. 25; Provence, *Lyndon,* pp. 35–36: cf. Kearns, *Lyndon,* p. 55.

2. Johnson told quite a different story: that notified the Houston job was open, he wired Houston that he was obligated to stay in Pearsall, but that word of the Houston offer reached the superintendent, who recommended he accept the offer. I have followed the superintendent's account.

   Johnson received a check for $67 for services rendered at Pearsall. He said his salary there was $175 a month, which might indicate he worked less than two weeks. He said he was "a principal at Pearsall," but apparently he was the vice-principal.

   In 1965 he said, "I became principal of a Houston school and they paid me $265 a month—and that is when I left and came to Washington," but according to my information he made substantially less than $265 a month at each of his three teaching jobs and was not the principal in Houston.

   PP 1965, pp. 418, 535, 1028; *Houston Post,* Nov. 1, 1965; Pool et al., *Lyndon,* p. 149; Barron, "LBJ"; a confidential source; Interview, LJ (JL: McKay).

3. The debate topic that year was "Resolved, that a substitute for trial by jury should be adopted." When Johnson left, his debaters had good card files, and under his successor as coach the next year they won first in the state.

   The school newspaper at Sam Houston High, the *Aegis,* might have been interesting to consult, but the principal, W. H. Powell, told a person inquiring on my behalf that the back issues were burned in the fifties by a janitor who had found them but would not yield them up.

   Interviews, Luther E. Jones, Jr. (RD and JL), Miss Jessie Roy, Mrs. Roy Dealey, LJ (JL:McKay), Gene Latimer (JL); Pool et al., *Lyndon,* pp. 149–58; *Interscholastic Leaguer,* Feb. 1964; Letters, Luther E. Jones, Jr., to Eric Goldman and Victor Emanuel to RD; *PP 1964,* p. 686; Alsop, "The New"; see Singer and Sherrod, *Lyndon,* p. 101 (erroneously stating Johnson was referring to his own career as a debater).

4. Interviews, Byron Parker and Miss Jessie Roy, LJ (JL:McKay); *PP 1964,* p. 418; Steinberg, *Sam Johnson's,* p. 700.

5. The candidate was Edgar Witt, who won in 1930 and was reelected in 1932. It was Mrs. Bill Kittrell who explained the south Texas feature of Johnson's participation. Kittrell more blandly said, "I got him [Lyndon] to make the rounds, shaking hands with the men on the street, explaining the issues to the farmers in the field, patting babies on their heads. Well, sir, we won, hands down, in a district we had given up as lost."

   Davidson, "Texas"; Interview, Mrs. William H. Kittrell; Singer and Sherrod, *Lyndon,* p. 103; *Texas Almanac, 1931,* pp. 241, 255, and *1933,* p. 271. Letter, Welly Hopkins to Roy Miller, JL: LBJA Sel. Names, box 19 (Hopkins fdr.).

6. Interviews, LJ (Dec. 14, 1967), *LBJ,* Miss Jessie Roy, Mrs. Roy Dealey, Byron Parker, Michael Spampinato, Welly Hopkins (JL); *PP 1965,* p. 418; Pool et al., *Lyndon,* pp. 145–49, 151.

7. Byron Parker, a teacher at Sam Hous-

ton who was close to George and Lyndon Johnson, said George told Lyndon to campaign for Kleberg and Lyndon did so. An old-timer who cannot be quoted told me he saw Lyndon carrying posters at a rally for Kleberg in this election. Lyndon read and approved a book in which it was stated that he had made speeches and worked with the voters for Kleberg in 1931, and Dan Quill, the San Antonio politician, said Lyndon worked in Corpus for Kleberg. However, Senator Welly Hopkins stated that Lyndon was busy with his debaters and did not campaign.

Interview, Byron Parker; Interview, Daniel J. Quill, (JL); Mooney, *The Lyndon,* pp. 17, xx; Pool et al., *Lyndon,* pp. 167–69, 172; Nicholas C. Chriss, *AAS,* Dec. 12, 1977.

Kleberg made a speaking tour of Blanco County and carried it with 234 votes to 160 for other candidates. On this election, see *CCCT,* Nov. 13–25, 1931.

8. Johnson told me Welly Hopkins had recommended him to Kleberg. Lady Bird said Hopkins recommended Lyndon to Miller, who helped him get hired. Ghent Sanderford said Alvin Wirtz proposed Johnson to Kleberg. Robert Jackson of Corpus Christi, aide to another Texas congressman, said, "He was hired by Roy Miller. I know it for a fact."

   Interviews, Richard T. Fleming, Luther E. Jones, Jr., Robert Jackson, LJ (Dec. 14, 1967), LaBJ; SHJ, *My,* pp. 43–44; Pool et al., *Lyndon,* p. 172; a confidential source.
9. Pool et al., *Lyndon,* p. 159 (quoting Helen Weinberg), 172; *AA,* Dec. 27, 1966; Interviews, Mrs. Roy Dealey, Malcolm Bardwell (JL); Henderson, *Maury,* p. 61; Letter, LJ to Luther E. Jones, Jr.; Kearns, *Lyndon,* p. 70; see film, *The Journey.*

23. Pioneers, O Pioneers!

1. Geyelin, *Lyndon,* p. 21.
2. Austin was celebrating its centennial. "Surely no celebration of a Texas anniversary would be complete," Johnson had opened the quoted passage, "without a fitting remembrance of the magnificent contribution of the Catholic Church to the pages of its history." Letter, Johnson to Austin Catholic Centennial Committee.
3. *PP 1964,* p. 1307.
4. See, e.g., Robert M. Jackson, writing in *Dallas Times Herald* (AP), May 28, 1961.
5. *AA,* May 29, 1961.
6. *PP 1966,* p. 34.
7. Transcript, *The Machinist,* Nov. 18, 1967.
8. Turner, *The Frontier,* pp. 269–73.
9. *PP 1966,* pp. 616–617.

24. Two Patriotic Cowboys

1. *PP 1966,* pp. 927–28.
2. Interviews, LJ (December, 1967); Kearns, *Lyndon,* p. 35.
3. *PP 1965,* p. 10.
4. Roosevelt, T., *Addresses,* pp. 124–27; Watterson, *History,* pp. 109, 113–14, 137; Andrews, ed., *The Autobiography,* pp. 26–30, 58–59, 64–65, 119–20, 135–38, 270, 272–73, 353–55.
5. Burns, *Roosevelt,* pp. 24–25; Gunther, *Roosevelt,* pp. 155, 203, 207–12.
6. Sully's life-span was 1783–1872, Stuart's 1755–1826. The Roosevelt by Shoumatoff is dated 1966.

   When Johnson was seated in his rocking chair before his coffee table-console (with parallel divans forming an aisle before him toward the fireplace), he faced the Roosevelt.

   See *PP 1967,* pp. 67, 115–116.
7. Bishop, *A Day,* p. 207; *PP 1965,* p. 380. *DMN,* May 27, June 3, 1944; *AA,* June 2, 3, Nov. 9, 1944.
8. McKay, *Texas,* p. 223; Jon Ford, *SAE,* July 11, 1954; *AAS,* June 27, 1944, June 27, 1954, see Wise and Ross, *The Invisible,* chap. 11, and Horowitz, *The Free,* chap. 10.
9. *Dallas Times-Herald* (AP), May 29, 1961; *Houston Post,* Sept. 23, 1962; *DMN,* Dec. 12, 1962; *SLPD,* dateline Sept. 8, 1962.
10. Months later Johnson was still saying that his plane had "never landed in any country on any continent where we were met by any person that wouldn't like to trade places with us."

    PP 1964, pp. 289, 1514.
11. *PP 1964,* pp. 214, 1457, 148, 170, 1476, 1512; *PP 1965,* p. 247; *PP 1966,* p. 899.

25. The Politician as Western Hero

1. Interviews, LJ (Dec. 1967); Halberstam, *The Unfinished,* p. 25; *Houston Post,* Nov. 12, 1964; Wright Patman's Newsletter, Jan. 19, 1967.
2. Stegner, "History."
3. At his ranch in 1959 Johnson spent quite a bit of the lunch-table conversation explaining, to Allen Duckworth, then the political editor of the *Dallas Morning News,* how he had helped develop the Texas-shaped steaks. Several people had told the Senate majority leader that it couldn't be done, so he took it up with Harry Akin, operator of a string of cafés in Austin (and later the mayor of the city). Akin solved the problem with a cookie mold.

   Allen Duckworth, *DMN,* Nov. 9, 1959.
4. Lorraine Barnes, *AA,* July 27, 1946.
5. Quoted by Margaret Mayer, *AA,* July 25, 1948. See also *AA,* May 23, June 26, 1948, and *DMN,* July 4, 1948.
6. *DMN,* May 26, 1937, May 7, 1954, Aug. 10, 1959; *AA,* Aug. 28, 1948, Sept. 23, 1953 (AP), Dec. 16, 1957, Oct. 19, 1959; Speech to the Senate Mar. 9, 1949, a reprint, Government Printing Office; LJ's newsletter, in the *Uvalde Leader News,* Oct. 29, 1953; Geyelin, *Lyndon,* pp. 16, 113; *PP 1964,* pp. 117, 923, 1180, 1479, and *PP 1965,* pp. 476, 488, resp.; *PP 1967,* p. 652 (and cf. *AA* (AP), June 26, 1967).
7. *Houston Post,* Nov. 5, 1964; *AA,* Nov. 16, 1964; Sidey, *A Very,* p. 21; Kraft, *Profiles,* p. 11. "Edward P. Morgan and the News," ABC (Radio), July 13, 1966.
8. Harry Rolnick, president and chairman of the board of Byer-Rolnick Hat Corp. in Dallas, said Johnson paid for the hats, too, about $20 each wholesale; non-statesmen could buy similar models for between $17 and $100. Rolnick was quoted about the "Lone Star": "This hat signifies that the wearer is used to rough going and that he handles it well."

   Sidey, *A Very,* p. 150; *DMN,* May 20, 1963, May 23, 1967; *Houston Post,* July 17, 1961, Aug. 25, 1962, and April 28, 1963; Chalmers Roberts, *WP,* Dec. 28, 1963; Interview, Harry Rolnick; "LBJ's Lids," *Texas Magazine,* July 3, 1966; *Newsweek,* April 10, 1967; *SAE* (NYT News Service), Mar. 25, 1964.

26. Honor, and the World in Ruins

1. But here is the fuller quotation: "So, our hope and our purpose is to employ reasoned agreement instead of ready aggression; to preserve our honor without a world in ruins; to substitute if we can understanding for retaliation.

   "My most fervent prayer is to be a president who can make it possible for every boy in this land to grow to manhood by loving his country, loving his country instead of dying for it."

   PP 1964, p. 417.
2. Letter, Rayburn to C. C. Miller, Sept. 19, 1956; Sorenson, *Kennedy,* p. 670; Draper, "Israel."
3. Just think, Johnson said, "What would happen to ANZUS, to SEATO, to NATO, and to all these other countries that we have given our solemn word and our sacred honor that we would stand by them, if they saw us defaulting on one note, running out on one commitment, and tearing up one contract? If we will not be true to our word in Vietnam with a nation of 14 million, how can a nation of a million and a half across the seas expect us to keep our contract there?"

   PP, 1966, pp. 519, 691.
4. *NYT,* Nov. 27, 1966, and remarks by Walt Rostow and Richard Goodwin at a meeting of the U.S. Student Press Assn. in Washington, D.C., Feb. 4, 1967.
5. Rostow, "L.B.J.," and see *NYT,* Nov. 27, 1966.
6. *PP 1965,* pp. 410, 749, 1149, 485; *PP 1966,* pp. 37, Mark Twain, *Life on the Mississippi,* cited in Wilson, *Patriotic,* pp. 444–445.

27. The Nationalization of Courage

1. Weintal and Bartlett, *Facing,* p. 71.
2. *AA,* May 8, 1947, Aug. 4, July 21, 1948; *DMN,* Aug. 17, 1948; Roberts, *LBJ's,* p. 180; a confidential source; Geyelin, *Lyndon,* p. 13; *PP 1964,* pp. 795–96, 1301; *PP 1965*, pp. 456, 487, 752, and *PP 1966,* pp. 535, 620, 684, 691; Kearns, *Lyndon,* pp. 253; Interview, H.M. Greene; See Weintal and Bartlett, *Facing,* p. 76.

28. Myth-Norms and Maladaptations

No Notes.

29. God Visits the President

1. Concerning the references to God's direct relationship with men, see Genesis 5:22–24 and 6:13–21, Exodus 20:21–22, 34:4–6, Job 38–42.
2. On this same occasion, Johnson proposed that in Washington, where there are monuments to Lincoln, Jefferson, Washington, to many statesmen and soldiers, the country's religions should join together and build "a fitting memorial to the God who made us all," an interfaith center of prayer. Mrs. Johnson joined in the singing of "What a Friend We Have in Jesus."

   PP 1964, pp. 261–63; Marie Smith, *WP,* Feb. 6, 1964.
3. *PP 1966,* pp. 617–18.
4. Speaking to students at Ohio University on May 7, 1964, Johnson said, "I know as surely as God gives us the right to know what is right that you will succeed."

   AS, Jan. 3, 1944, and *PP 1964,* p. 632.
5. *PP 1963,* p. 63.

   In his State of the Union speech early in 1964, he said "our ultimate goal is . . . a world made safe for diversity," omitting the reference to God. (*PP 1964,* p. 116.)

   "From our Jewish and Christian heritage," he said to newspaper editors as president, "we draw the image of the God we sow. Our God is still a jealous God, jealous of his righteousness, jealous of his mercy, jealous for the last of the little ones who went unfed while the rich sat down to eat and rose up to play. . . .

   "These are the stakes, to make a world in which all of God's children can live or to go into the dark. . . ." (*PP 1964,* p. 485.)
6. See, e.g., *NYT,* Nov. 9, 1964, July 3, 1965, Sept. 12, 1966 (UPI), Nov. 28, 1966; *WP,* Mar. 2, 1964 (AP), Nov. 1, 1966; *AA,* May 13, 1968.
7. Attracted to Catholicism perhaps because her friend Beth Jenkins was a Catholic, Luci was baptized at Saint Matthew's Cathedral in Washington on July 2, 1965. She said that five years before then, "I, like all young people, began to question, and I began to wonder. I found my answer in the church." When she was confirmed in 1966, Archbishop Patrick O'Boyle reportedly presided.

   Interview, Willie Day Taylor (JL); *NYT,* July 3, 1965, and Aug. 26, 1966; *CCCT,* Aug. 6, 1966.

   The ring Luci put on husband Pat Nugent's finger at their wedding was inscribed, "Together through Christ, L.J. to P.N. 8–6–66." (Margaret Mayer, *AA,* Sept. 7, 1966.)
8. *DMN,* Dec. 7, 1963; *Houston Post* (AP), July 5, 1965; *AA,* Sept. 23, 1968; Robert Semple, Jr., *NYT,* July 31, 1965; Bishop, *A Day,* p. 182.
9. Sidey, "Beyond."
10. *PP 1964,* p. 420; Oscar Griffin, *Houston Chronicle,* Jan 1, 1966; Bishop, *A Day,* pp. 182, 88; Singer and Sherrod, *Lyndon,* p. 234, quoting from *I Believe in Prayer,* L. M. Brings, ed., Minneapolis: Denison.
11. *WP* (AP), undated, reporting a mass performed by Archbishop Patrick O'-Boyle in Saint Matthew's Cathedral in Washington, D.C.; *SAE,* Sept. 7, 9, 1967.
12. *Newsweek,* July 20, 1970; Sidey, *A Very,* p. 31; Interview, LJ, Dec. 14, 1967.
13. Concluding his inaugural address, Johnson said, "For myself, I ask only, in the words of an ancient leader: 'Give me now wisdom and knowledge, that I may go out and come in before this

people: for who can judge this thy people, that is so great?' " (*PP 1965*, p. 74.)

God replied to Solomon's prayer: "Because this was in thine heart, and thou hast not asked riches, wealth, or honour, nor the life of thine enemies, neither yet hast asked long life; but hast asked wisdom and knowledge for thyself, that thou mayest judge my people, over whom I have made thee king: Wisdom and knowledge is granted unto thee; and I will give thee riches, and wealth, and honor." (2 *Chronicles* 1:9–12.)

The AP pointed out this context and added: "Solomon, whose name means peaceful, ruled for about 40 years over a period of great prosperity and peace for his nation, avoiding aggression and reaching pacts of concord with neighboring countries." (*SAE*, (AP), Jan. 21, 1965.)

For the detail that Graham suggested the prayer from King Solomon, I have relied on Edwin Martin of Copley News Service. *DMN*, April 22, 1965.

14. *PP 1964*, p. 1221, and see *PP 1965*, p. 374; *Houston Chronicle*, Jan. 21, 1965; Andrew A. Yemma, a UPI dispatch from Austin on Jan. 24, 1973; Fiske, "The Closest"; Frady, "The Use." See also, Frady, *Billy*.
15. I had a sharing of ideas with Dr. Barclay, pastor of the Central Christian church, in his study in Austin Feb. 9, 1968. The analysis in the paragraph to which this note refers is my own.

    Graham's self-description is from Lauren Lane, *AS*, Jan. 25, 1973.
16. Interview, LJ (Dec. 14, 1967); Frady, "The Use"; Lauren Lane, *AS*, Jan. 25, 1973.
17. Graham's opening quotations from Jesus about sending fire and a sword are from Luke 12:49 and Matthew 10:34, respectively. Jesus said on these occasions, in fact, even more than Graham quoted.

    "Suppose ye that I am come to give peace on earth?" Jesus said. "I tell you, Nay, but rather division: . . . The father shall be divided against the son, and the son against the father; the mother against the daughter and the daughter against the mother." See Luke 12: 48–51, 53, 56.

    In the passage from Matthew, Jesus also said, "I came not to send peace but a sword. For I am come to get a man at variance against his father, and the daughter against her mother." See Matthew 10:8, 11, 14–15, 34–39.

    Johnson's Biblical passage is at Isaiah 40:31.

    PP 1966, p. 192; *WP*, Feb. 18, 1966; cf. Fritchey, "The Issue."

    At the 1968 prayer breakfast, Johnson said religious belief is often, as in Vietnam, "a call for a very great sacrifice" and that while we can "never be so arrogant as to claim God's special blessing for America," we can hope that "in His eyes we have helped to make possible a new vitality of the human conscience . . . throughout the world." *U.S. News & World Report*, Feb. 12, 1968.

    In 1979 Graham said in an interview that he had been wrongly portrayed as a supporter of the Vietnam War. "I don't ever recall making a statement supporting the Vietnam War or being against it. I just didn't take a position," he said. (*SAN*, Aug. 7, 1979.) My point in the text is that he provided Johnson important support in a military-apocalyptic context when Johnson was embattled politically over the wisdom of his actions in the war.
18. *SAN*, June 17, 1968; Mary Bishop, *SAE*, Oct. 4, 1977.
19. Erwin Knoll, Newhouse National News Service dispatch, May 12, 1967.
20. A report about the Middleburg, Virginia, dinner party first reached me through Tristram Coffin, the independent Washington author and journalist, who had heard it from Mrs. Edwards. I asked Coffin to provide me a letter on the matter, and he obliged, writing to me that according to his information, the Austrian Ambassador told Mrs. Edwards:

    "I have been quite perplexed by a conversation with your president, and don't quite know how to report it to my Government, as I must. Perhaps you could explain it.

    "At a recent diplomatic function the president sought me out and spoke to me for an hour and a half in his very concentrated way. He said he had been very attracted to the Catholic Church by his daughter, Luci, a convert, and was even considering becoming one himself. Did I think this wise? I replied this was a matter [on] which I would not attempt to advise one in his high position; it was a matter of individual faith.

    "He told me that his daughter had

taken him to Saint Dominic's Church in [southwest] Washington and he had prayed with 'the little monks,' as he calls them. 'I knelt and prayed so damn long my knees ached,' he said, but when he returned to the White House he was amazed and given faith because his prayers were answered. The bombers went out and returned without a loss.

"Later in the conversation the president asked me if I thought it probable that the Divine Spirit might come down and visit a modern head of state and give him counsel. I replied that I was inclined to doubt this. The Church had records, which it believed were valid, of heads of state some time past receiving visitations, but none had occurred in modern times. The president replied, 'Oh, but you are mistaken. He comes and talks to me. At three-thirty in the morning.' "

This ended Coffin's 1968 account to me of what Mrs. Edwards had told him. (Recalling the matter again a decade later, Coffin then said Johnson had asked, "Mr. Ambassador, do you have any records of a modern chief of state being visited by God?" and when told no, continued, "Well, you've got one now. He comes and speaks to me about two o'clock in the morning—when I have to give the word to the boys, and I get the word from God whether to bomb or not.")

Coffin's account varies in interesting details from what Mrs. Edwards told me directly. The text, of course, follows the primary source. Coffin was the source of the suggested explanations, getting a message to the Vatican, or simply hyperbole.

Dr. Lemberger is dead now.

In early 1968, Johnson told Jack Anderson concerning Vietnam, "I pray about it. But it's hard to know what God wants you to do."

Letter, Tristram Coffin to RD; Interviews, Congressman and Mrs. Don and Clyda Edwards, Dr. Ernst Lemberger, Tristram Coffin, and Mrs. Clyda Gugenberger (the former Mrs. Edwards); Anderson, "The Many."

30. Signing Letters with Bleeding Hands

1. Letter, LJ to Luther E. Jones, Jr.; Interviews, Richard T. Fleming, R. E. Thomason (JL), Robert Jackson; *PP 1965,* p. 698; *PP 1967,* p. 1069; Knippa, *The Early,* pp. 10–11.
2. Kearns quoted Johnson that there was one bedroom at the end of the corridor in the basement of the Dodge, and all the tenants used it. This does not match Jackson's memory. Johnson told Kearns that to meet and size up the other young men on the floor, the first night he took four showers in the floor's one bathroom; the next morning, for the same reason, he washed his face and brushed his teeth at ten-minute intervals five times. Sometimes, weaving memories into a similitude of the solidity of the past, one cannot make sense of everything that is remembered.

   Interviews, Robert Jackson, (RD and JL), Carroll Keach, Luther E. Jones, Jr., Gene Latimer (JL), Marvin Jones (JL); Letters, LJ to Luther E. Jones, Jr.; Newlon, *L.B.J.,* pp. 46, 50; Mooney, *The Lyndon,* p. 19; Steinberg, *Sam Johnson's,* p. 69, and Steinberg, *Sam Rayburn,* p. 159; Kearns, *Lyndon,* pp. 72–73; Houston Harte, *Washington Evening Star,* Dec. 15, 1963; *CCC,* Sept. 16, 1964; Schreiber, "First Years"; see Knippa, *The Early,* pp. 11–12.
3. Williams, *Huey,* pp. 559–61, 582–93, 650–86, 709–23; *PP 1964,* p. 1285, and cf. *PP 1965,* p. 195, *PP 1966,* p. 1145; Interviews, LJ (Dec. 14, 1967), Robert Jackson; Kearns, *Lyndon,* p. 92.
4. *PP 1965,* p. 480.
5. *PP 1965,* p. 480; Williams, *Huey,* pp. 613–23.
6. Speech by LJ in Snyder, Tx., Nov. 12, 1959, and cf. *PP 1964,* p. 449; see *Encyclopaedia Britannica,* 1974, "Bonus Army."
7. Interview, Robert Montgomery (JL).
8. The two young men who called on Young with Johnson were Chris Dixie and Creekmore Fath, both later figures in Texas liberalism.

   I have an account of Johnson's visit to the Fores from a well-qualified confidential source. However, in this version of the story, Johnson called on the Fores on his way to see Kleberg about becoming his secretary in 1931. Knippa had it direct from Fore that the episode occurred when Johnson and Kleberg called on Fore during Kleberg's 1932 campaign. I have followed my confidential source on some details of the episode, but Knippa on when it happened.

Kleberg won every county except, oddly, Blanco, in 1932.

Knippa, *The Early,* pp. 26–27, 30; Interviews, Harold Young, Ben Crider, and a confidential source; Pool et al., *Lyndon,* p. 173.

9. Interviews, Carroll Keach, Robert Jackson, Gene Latimer (JL), Dr. Robert Montgomery, Luther E. Jones, Jr., LJ (Mar. 23, 1968); Knippa, *The Early,* pp. 15–19, 37–38; Newlon, *L.B.J.,* p. 46; Weintal and Bartlett, *Facing,* p. 132; *Denton Record-Chronicle,* June 21, 1964.
10. Interview, William S. White (JL); Steinberg, *Sam Johnson's,* p. 71, and *Sam Rayburn,* p. 159.
11. Interviews, Robert Jackson, Gene Latimer (JL), Luther E. Jones, Jr. (RD and HL), Dan Quill (JL), Ben Crider (JL); Letter, Luther E. Jones, Jr., to Eric Goldman; Newlon, *L.B.J.,* pp. 45–46, 50; Knippa, *The Early,* pp. 28, 34–36.
12. Interviews, Robert Jackson, Robert Montgomery; speech by LJ in Stephenville, Tx., fall, 1959; Burns, *Roosevelt,* pp. 163–65; Freidel, *Franklin,* pp. 196, 198, 202; *NYT,* Dec. 1, 1964; cf., *PP 1964,* p. 546, *PP 1967*, pp. 115, 621–22.
13. Johnson told me he heard Dirksen relate a story about a black woman and her stockings during the AAA debate in 1933 and much later baited Dirksen by offering to remind him of the story. Dirksen had said No, thanks.

    "Nobody here seems to know what the bill is about," Dirksen said during the 1933 debate. "I realize it is not up to expectations. I think it is a good deal like the stockings that the Negro lady bought down here in Washington. They did not fit, and she took them back. The clerk said, 'What is the matter? Do not they come up to expectations?' She replied, 'Lawdy, boss, they do not even come up to my knees.' [Laughter.] I think that is the way with this bill. . . ."

    Interview, LJ (Dec. 14, 1967); *CR 1933,* vol. 77, p. 753. (The word "Negro" was not capitalized in the *Congressional Record.*)
14. Interviews, LJ (Mar. 23, 1968), Luther E. Jones, Jr., Carroll Keach; Newlon, *L.B.J.,* pp. 46–47; *PP 1966,* pp. 608, 1142.
15. President Roosevelt later liked to tell the story of Johnson's takeover of the "Little Congress," and columnists retold it.

    According to Alfred Steinberg, Kleberg paid Johnson $3,900 a year at first, cut him back to $3,000 on Mar. 1, 1932, restored him to the original figure the next May 1, and then cut him back to $3,050 the next year.

    Interviews, Robert Jackson, Gene Latimer (JL), Luther E. Jones, Jr., LJ (Mar. 23, 1968); Drew Pearson and Robert S. Allen, a 1941 column (otherwise undated); Newlon, *L.B.J.,* pp. 49–50; Williams, *Huey,* pp. 676–79; SHJ, *My,* p. 48; Steinberg, *Sam Johnson's,* pp. 67, 78; Miller, *Lyndon*, p. 58; Considine, " 'A President . . .' "; Steele, "A Kingmaker"; William Shannon, *New York Post,* May 31, 1956; *Washington Evening Star,* April 18, 1933; *Washington Herald,* April 28, 1933.
16. Interview, Luther E. Jones, Jr.; Letter, Luther E. Jones, Jr., to Eric Goldman, April 6, 1965.
17. A confidential source, who said that he was present; Interviews, Luther Jones (JL), Creekmore Fath, Edmunds Travis, Mary Rather (JL).

31. Suddenly, Courtship and Marriage

1. Interview, SHJ.
2. Leslie Carpenter wrote that Lyndon and Lady Bird met Sept. 4, 1934. Bird gave the timing I have used, although she added that neither she nor Lyndon was sure of it.

    Nan Robertson reported, "Right after breakfast, he proposed." However, Bird said that "before the day was over, he'd asked me to marry him," although they had not yet known each other twenty-four hours.

    Johnson's awareness of the impressiveness of the King Ranch may be indicated by an invitation he probably wrote for Kleberg to a barbecue and agricultural exhibit there. The meal announced was son-of-a-bitch stew, red beans, rice, skillet bread, and cabrito, all to be served at the tail-gate of an old-fashioned chuck wagon. After the meal Kleberg was to show the guests two herds of beef cattle of a breed originated at the ranch.

    Lyndon and Bird thought they had lost their marriage license, but the county clerk, having no address for them to mail it to, had pinned it to the page in the official book on which their marriage was recorded. Quill, finding it there, gave it to them, framed, on their thirtieth anniversary.

After Johnson became president, Quill said the Johnsons had never paid him for the ring, and a few months later Quill met with Johnson.

"Come here, Dan," Johnson said. "I read in the *New York Times* where you said I never had paid for that wedding ring."

"Well, that's the truth, you haven't."

"Well, you ought not to say those things."

"Well, just pay me"—and Quill put his hand out.

Johnson reached his hand into his pocket—but he never took it out. "And he still owes me," Quill said.

According to the records at Georgetown University, Johnson matriculated in law school there on Sept. 17, 1934. The date of his withdrawal is not shown in the records, but the dean of the law center in 1977 stated, on the basis of conversations with Johnson's classmates, that he withdrew shortly after he enrolled.

Excerpts from correspondence between Lyndon and Bird were released by Mrs. Johnson in 1977 for use in a tribute to her on her sixty-fifth birthday at the Johnson Library. I made notes on this correspondence during the ceremonies. Subsequently a transcript was provided, and I have relied on it.

Interviews, LaBJ, LJ (Dec. 14, 1967), Otto Crider, Malcolm Bardwell (JL), Daniel J. Quill (JL and RD), Harold Young; Robertson, "Our New"; Schreiber, "First Years"; Smith, *The President's,* pp. 38–44; Bishop, *A Day,* (evidently quoting LJ without attribution), pp. 36–37; White, *The Professional,* p. 73; Kearns, *Lyndon,* p. 80; Mooney, *The Lyndon,* pp. 21, xvii, xx; Newlon, *L.B.J.,* pp. 51–53, 56; Steinberg, *Sam Johnson's,* pp. 80–81, 82, 89; Nan Robertson, *NYT,* Nov. 18, 1964, and also *NYT,* May 14, 1965; *Washington Star,* June 17, 1954; *AA,* Nov. 18, 1964; Davidson, "Lyndon"; "A National Tribute," (JL); movie, *The Journey.* See also, Provence, *Lyndon,* pp. 44–45; SHJ, *My,* pp. 41–42; Carpenter, "The Whip."

On Johnson and the King Ranch: The letter of invitation was initialed "RMK LJ" and an associated form letter was initialed "RMK J." The date of the barbecue was Nov. 3, 1933. Letter, Richard M. Kleberg to G. F. Newheuser.

On Johnson in law school: Interview, Luther E. Jones, Jr.; Newlon, *L.B.J.,* pp. 45, 55; speech by LJ, New York City, Oct. 12, 1963; Letter, David J. McCarthy, Jr., to RD.

32. Favors, and a Falling Out

1. Interview, LJ (Dec. '67); Schreiber, "First Years"; Newlon, *L.B.J.,* pp. 54, 206; *PP 1965,* p. 34; Provence, *Lyndon,* p. 46; Smith, *A President's,* p. 57; *AA,* Nov. 3, 1948.
2. Interview, Carroll Keach; Williams, *Huey,* pp. 850–51; *PP 1964,* p. 1126, 1285; *PP 1966,* p. 1745.
3. Since the events in question happened forty years ago and no formal charges were filed, there would be no point in identifying the man in trouble or elaborating on the case against him.

   In a wire from Washington to the man in trouble Feb. 16, 1935, Johnson said that "counsel here suggests you sign no statements of any kind."

   When, on July 12, 1935, the man in trouble paid the reduced legal fee, he sent Johnson a copy of his letter to the lawyer accompanying the fee.

   This account is based on documents made available to me for inspection and quotation by John Jenkins, proprietor of the Pemberton Press in Austin.
4. Interview, Gene Latimer (JL).
5. During World War II George Parr, the south Texas political boss, set out to defeat Congressman Kleberg, believing he had been responsible for Roosevelt's not giving Parr a pardon on a criminal conviction. Kleberg's friends resented that Johnson did not come to the assistance of his former employer as Kleberg lost to John Lyle of Corpus Christi. In 1948, running for the Senate, Johnson complained of "the bloc vote in a box behind the locked gates of the King Ranch where not one single vote went to Johnson." In 1964 Robert Kleberg, Richard's brother, supported Goldwater for president

against Johnson. Cong. Richard Kleberg's widow told me in 1970, with bitterness, "I don't think you'd be interested in my opinion of Mr. Johnson."

Interviews, SHJ, Maury Maverick, Jr., Mrs. Maury Maverick, Sr., LJ (Dec. 14, 1967), Mrs. Richard Kleberg; Knippa, *The Early,* fig. 1; Steinberg, *Sam Rayburn,* pp. 125–29; *PP 1964,* pp. 449, 563; *DMN,* Sept. 7, 1948; *The Newsletter,* Aug. 28, 1964.

33. "Always Concerned with Now"

1. Johnson credited Maverick and Senators Sheppard and Connally with having a hand in his appointment.

   Sheppard's daughter's friend was Doyle Willis, who became a member of the Texas legislature. Willis worked against Johnson in the 1948 election and said Johnson blocked him for a federal judgeship.

   Schlesinger, *The New,* p. 9; Henderson, *Maury,* pp. 78–82; Interviews, Malcolm Bardwell (JL), Maury Maverick, Jr., Robert Montgomery (JL), LJ (May, 1959, and Mar. 23, 1968); Knippa, *The Early,* p. 52; Steinberg, *Sam Johnson's,* pp. 93–94; Davidson, "Texas." On the Willis episode, Letter, James Rowe to RD, corrected in details by Letter, Willis to RD.
2. Interviews, Sherman Birdwell, LaBJ; "A National Tribute," JL; Schreiber, "First Years"; Newlon, *L.B.J.,* pp. 58, 59, 150–51; Provence, *Lyndon,* p. 47.
3. Interviews, Luther E. Jones, Jr.; Mrs. Gladys Montgomery, Sherman Birdwell, Ray Lee; Letter, Clay Cochran to RD.
4. Interviews, Luther E. Jones, Jr., Ben Crider, Wallace Reilly, Welly Hopkins (JL); Provence, *Lyndon,* p. 48; Knippa, *The Early,* p. 58; LJ, "A Helping Hand"; Newlon, *L.B.J.,* p. 62; SHJ, *My,* pp. 49, 51; *PP 1964,* p. 1553.
5. Interviews, Sherman Birdwell, O. H. Elliott; Kearns, *Lyndon,* p. 231; Newlon, *L.B.J.,* pp. 61, 63–64; *NYT,* Dec. 1, 1964; Bill Davidson, "Lyndon."
6. In Ray Lee's recollection, Mrs. Roosevelt's inspection visit must have been 1935 or 1936. She came down later, too, when Johnson was in Congress.

   I reviewed the story about Johnson and the NYA youths on Roosevelt's motorcade route with Johnson, and he enjoyed the memory.

   Interviews, Ray Lee, Sherman Birdwell, Gordon Fulcher, LJ (Dec. 1967), Willard Deason (JL); Newlon, *L.B.J.,* pp. 61–62, 65; Knippa, *The Early,* pp. 78–79; Provence, *Lyndon,* pp. 47–48; see Steinberg, *Sam Johnson's,* p. 98.
7. According to a Johnson campaign flyer in 1937, at the end of his tenure with NYA more than 19,000 students, in addition to another 10,000 who were not in school, had been given jobs. ("He Gets Things Done," Johnson campaign flyer, 1937; see also, *NYT,* Dec. 1, 1964, *Brenham Banner Press,* Mar. 9, 1937, and movie, *The Journey.*)

   Aubrey Williams made his comment in a letter to Sam Rayburn endorsing Johnson for president. (Interview, Dr. Robert Montgomery, and Letter, Aubrey Williams to Sam Rayburn, RL.)

   When Johnson went to Congress Jesse Kellam succeeded him as Texas NYA director. Under Kellam, in "resident projects," girls lived in cooperative circumstances while they were taught personal hygiene and how to type, cook, sew, wash dishes, and use surplus commodities. Mrs. Montgomery said that in old houses all over Texas, with aging couples acting as supervisors, girls made their clothes out of tow sacks and contrived furniture out of orange crates. Periodically the girls went home for two weeks for a break and also (or so the planners intended) to teach their parents some of the things they were learning. (Interview, Mrs. Gladys Montgomery.)

   In his later defense of the NYA, "Here," Johnson continued, "is how NYA dollars are spent:

   "John Jones is a boy 17 years old. He cannot go to school unless he finds a job. If he goes into the labor market . . . he will compete with someone out of work. . . . His school, participating in the NYA program, tells him to go on with his classwork and it will permit him to earn, say, 25 cents an hour doing useful work about the campus or in the school offices at hours which do not conflict with his studies. . . .

   "Here is Mary Smith, who has finished high school and wants to go to college to train herself for some special profession or calling. Her family is too poor to send her. . . . The college gives her an NYA job, taking her out of the labor market and permitting her to train. . . .

"Now we come to Bill Kelly, who is through school. He wants to go to work. If he enters the general labor market as an untrained, unprepared worker, he not only has a poor chance to establish himself in life, but he becomes a competitor. The NYA gives him a job. It is a job on a public project which is not only useful in itself but will permit Bill to learn the rudiments of a trade or profession. . . ."

(CR 1939, vol. 84, pp. A2338–39; see T. A. Price, *DMN,* June 30, 1941.)

For other remarks Johnson made when president on his NYA period, see *PP 1966,* pp. 405, 923, and *PP 1967,* pp. 103, 515.

By the end of 1943 under NYA, more than 2,100,000 students had earned $169 million while in school, and almost 2,700,000 young people out of school had been paid almost half a billion dollars for work. (Newlon, *L.B.J.,* p. 59.)

The Civilian Conservation Corps had been established to employ youths in conservation work. Two days after Pearl Harbor Johnson introduced, with Roosevelt's approval, a bill to consolidate the NYA and the CCC into the "Civilian Youth Administration," this to be done "in the interest of economy, efficiency, and national defense." That was that. (*NYT,* Dec. 10, 1941.)

34. A Gentleman or a Congressman?

1. Johnson told Kearns that he was staying in a seedy hotel in Houston, there to receive and escort the director of the Kansas NYA, a woman, on a tour of his NYA operation in Texas. They were walking through a park when he saw a newspaper lying open on a bench and its headline that Buchanan had died. That moment, his mind started churning; he could not keep his mind on his visitor: he kept thinking that this was his district and his chance.

   An account in *Time* magazine followed what Johnson told me, but varied in details. Richard Fleming, a friend of George Johnson, also said George told him of his urging Lyndon to run.

   It is plausible to suppose that both events substantially happened, but only one of them could have been his first learning about Buchanan's death.

   Interviews, LJ (Dec. 14, 1967), Richard T. Fleming, Mary Rather (JL); *Time,* June 22, 1953; *PP 1964,* p. 408; Kearns, *Lyndon,* pp. 85–86.

2. Creekmore Fath, one of Montgomery's young New Deal friends, said he went to Washington and, with Corcoran's assistance, raised $30,000 for Montgomery. Adams understood that $20,000 had been committed when Montgomery said no. Adams worked for Walton Hamilton's cabinet committee on price policy in 1935 and subsequently with the Farm Security Administration.

   Beginning in the spring of 1935, the Supreme Court had struck down the New Deal's Railroad Retirement Act, the National Industrial Recovery Act, a farm mortgage act, the AAA, labor provisions of a coal conservation act, a municipal bankruptcy act, and the New York minimum wage law.

   In reference to Jones's opinion that Johnson did not care about the court-packing plan he was supporting, in 1954 the U.S. Senate passed an amendment to bar future packing of the Supreme Court and Johnson voted aye, but said nothing.

   Johnson is my source for his discussions with Bird and Wirtz in the three-person meeting on running, along with some further remarks he made to Kearns on the matter. Luther Jones told me he took the $10,000 check to the bank, but I have followed Johnson to Kearns on that point. Johnson is also my source on the dialogue he had with Allred in the governor's office, and it was Johnson who said to me that he told Montgomery "You're crazy as hell."

   Birdwell said the persons present at the meeting at Four Happy Hollow (which he left to get the $50) were the Johnsons, Wirtz, Ray Lee, Kellam, and himself. Those attending the meeting that lasted into the mid-afternoon were probably the Johnsons, Wirtz, Sam Fore of Floresville, Denver Chestnut of Kenedy, Quill, and Lee. Quill said Welly Hopkins might have been there, but did not specify Lee. Lee specified only the Johnsons, Wirtz, Fore, he himself, and one other person he could not remember.

Maury Maverick, Jr., remembers his father's telling him that Johnson lacked money to get to Texas from Washington to announce, whereupon Maverick, Sr., called John L. Lewis, who provided a couple hundred dollars from United Mineworkers' Union sources. However, Johnson announced in Austin.

By one account, Allred, the contractor Herman Brown, and Charles Green, chief aide to Charles Marsh, the publisher of the Austin daily, met at Marsh's home to choose a candidate and agreed on Johnson. A difficulty with this is that Johnson told me Brown did not back him in 1937.

Johnson's brother Sam Houston said he had a role persuading Johnson to announce in order to forestall Mrs. Buchanan from doing so. He said he told his brother: "Don't go waiting on her. That's just some damned stallin' tactic. . . . You go on ahead and announce right away. The minute Mrs. Buchanan knows she's got opposition, she won't get in. Hell, Lyndon, she's too old to campaign."

Interviews, Creekmore Fath, Mark Adams, LJ (Dec. 13, 14, 1967, and Mar. 23, 1968), Robert Montgomery, Luther E. Jones, Jr., Ray Lee, Carroll Keach, Sherman Birdwell, Daniel Quill (JL), Robert S. Allen (JL); Letter, Luther E. Jones, Jr., to Eric Goldman; Burns, *The Lion,* pp. 230–33, and see pp. 361–62; Blum, *From the Morgenthau,* vol. 1, pp. 327, 329; Knippa, *The Early,* pp. 93–94; Schreiber, "First Years"; Keams, *Lyndon,* p. 86; SHJ, *My,* p. 54; Newlon, *L.B.J.,* p. 72; *NYT,* May 12, 1954; and see Johnson's discussion of the court-packing plan at *PP 1964,* p. 684. On Wirtz, Interviews, Harold Young, Edmunds Travis, Ray Lee; Harrison, "Lyndon"; Letter, LJ to Matthew Connelly, TL, Sel. Doc., Pres. Psl. File; JL, Wirtz papers, box 6, Johnson-psl. fdr., LCRA papers, box 26, Gnl. Info. USG LJ 1937–38 fdr., and LBJA Sel. Names, box 36, A.J. Wirtz 1938 and 1944 fdrs.: Letters, LJ to Wirtz, Wirtz to LJ (five), and Tgms., LJ to Wirtz, Wirtz to LJ (two); and see, *NYT,* Jan. 3, 1940. On the $10,000 from Bird's father, *cf.* Singer and Sherrod, *Lyndon,* p. 122; Schreiber, "First" and "Lady"; Smith, *The President's,* pp. 58, 137; Steele, "The Kingmaker."

3. The two young men who visited Wild to ask him to be Johnson's campaign manager were Sam Fore and Denver Chesnut.

When the election was called, newspaperman Stuart Long was working for International News Service at the state capitol with Vann Kennedy, who was close to Allred. Long remembered some conversations about getting Allred to call the election quickly for Johnson's benefit.

The stories about Wild and Johnson discussing throwing mud, and about Johnson insulting Avery and Avery's retort, come from John Fritz Koeniger, a member of Johnson's Washington staff, who was told them by Herbert Henderson, who had been with Johnson in the NYA and in 1938, after the election, went to Washington as a publicist and speechwriter for Johnson. Koeniger related these stories after Henderson was dead.

Hollis Frazer, a young man Johnson had helped get elected to the legislature and who had then replaced Johnson as speech teacher at Sam Houston High when Johnson went with Kleberg, worked in the 1937 campaign supervising campaign workers.

Johnson's meeting with black leaders in Austin occurred, by the memory of Dr. Conner, in the basement of the old Huston-Tillotson College administration building, not the church where Elliott and Rice said it was.

The general themes of Johnson's 1937 campaign are illustrated by a campaign poster for him that said: "Support the Man Who—Stands with the President and for the People; Has Helped Hundreds of Farmers and Working Men; Understands Departmental Routine of Washington; Will Carry Colorado and Brazos Projects Through; Capably Administered His Part of the Roosevelt Program for Texas."

A note on the campaign's financing: When, with Montgomery out of the race, Creekmore Fath had gone back to Tommy Corcoran for money for Johnson, Corcoran, knowing nothing about Johnson, had said no. Evidently, judging from the check from FDR that

Quill saw, the administration came around.

The final returns: Johnson 8,280 (27.6%); Merton Harris 5,111 (17.1%); Polk Shelton 4,420 (14.8%); Sam V. Stone 4,048 (13.5%); C. N. Avery 3,951 (13.2%); Houghton Brownlee 3,019 (10.1%); Ayers K. Ross 1,088 (3.6%); Edwin Waller 18 (.1%); Stanley S. Smith 12.

Interviews, Luther E. Jones, Jr., Claude Wild, Sr. (JL), LaBJ, Stuart Long, J. R. Parten, LJ (Dec. 14, 1967, and Mar. 23, 1968), John Fritz Koeniger, Edmunds Travis, Gordon Fulcher (JL), Carroll Keach, Woodrow Bean, Mrs. Roy Dealey, Gene Latimer (JL), Allan Shivers (JL), Mrs. Jean Lee, Polk Shelton, Wright Patman, O. H. Elliott, F. R. (Friendly) Rice, B. E. Conner, Creekmore Fath, Ray Lee (JL), Anna Rosenberg Hoffman (JL), Clifford and Virginia Durr (JL), Daniel Quill (JL); Knippa, *The Early,* pp. 102–105, 122–23, 129, 141, 152–55, 158, 169–170, and table IV; Provence, *Lyndon,* p. 53; Newlon, *L.B.J.,* pp. 66, 68; Keams, Lyndon, pp. 58, 231, and cf. p. 87; *NYT,* Mar. 7, April 11, 1937; *AA,* Nov. 2, 1964; *AS,* Sept. 25, Dec. 29, 1936; *Brenham Banner Press,* Mar. 1, 3, 6, 11, 15, 16, April 3, 6, 1937; *PP 1965,* pp. 34–35; Steele, "A Kingmaker"; Schreiber, "First Years"; poster on file in Barker History Center, UT-Austin. On Marsh, Interview, Harold Young; JL, Marsh papers, box 1, H.A. Wallace 1941 fdr., box 2, LJ and LBJ 1941 fdrs., box 7, Chas. E. Marsh 1942 fdr., box 22, S.W. Richardson fdr., box 27, Oil a/c 1936 fdrs. (2); see Davidson, "Texas," and Singer and Sherrod, *Lyndon*, p. 126.

35. A Train Ride to Power

1. Allred had called on Johnson when he was in the hospital in Austin. The date of the Johnsons' dinner with the Allreds was April 26, 1931.

   Jon Ford, quoting Johnson on what his mother told him about being the best, *SAE,* Oct., 1959; Letter, RBJ to LJ, undated, JL; Interviews, Daniel Quill (JL), Carroll Keach (JL), and a confidential source; *AA,* April 14, 26, 1937; Diary of Joe Betsy Allred, entries for April 11 and 26, 1937, provided by Letter, Mrs. Dave Allred to RD; Letter, Dave Allred to RD; Miller, *Lyndon*, p. 75.
2. *CR 1937,* vol. 82, p. 354; *PP 1964,* pp. 150, 1579; Kearns, *Lyndon,* p. 89.
3. FDR had "met" Johnson in the NYA group called to the White House in 1935. Johnson believed FDR had heard him speaking over a Texas radio station before their train ride together, but FDR's fishing trip occurred weeks after the election had ended.

   Roosevelt's yacht arrived in Galveston May 11, 1937. The mayor of Galveston was Adrian F. Levy. A scale from a tarpon Roosevelt caught was mounted and displayed, dated May 8, 1937, at the Tarpon Inn at Port Aransas and could still be seen there in the eighties.

   Bullitt's letter to Roosevelt was written in the fall of 1936.

   "When you come down to it," Roosevelt said at College Station, "we are not paying a high price for national defense," only 10 or 11% of the cost of government compared to 30 to 50% in Europe. "We know another thing—that our preparation is honestly made for defense and not for aggression."

   Interviews, Claude Wild (JL), LJ (May, 1959, and Mar. 23, 1968), Welly Hopkins (JL), and confidential sources; *NYT,* May 12, 1937; *AA,* May 11, 1937; *AAS,* Aug. 22, 1948; *The Journey,* a movie (JL); Bascom N. Timmons, *Houston Chronicle,* Nov. 24, 1963; Bullitt, *For the President,* p. 187; Singer and Sherrod, *Lyndon,* pp. 129–30; Steinberg, *Sam Johnson's,* pp. 118–21; *CR 1937,* vol. 81, p. 4508; Henderson, *Maury,* p. 135; Newlon, *L.B.J.,* pp. 72–73; see White, *The Professional,* pp. 89–90.
4. Marguerite (Missy) LeHand, Roosevelt's personal secretary, had a strong influence on Roosevelt.

   When Johnson was besieged with criticism as president he recalled that Roosevelt, likewise beset, used to invite him for lunch because he was so loyal a supporter.

   Interviews, Edmunds Travis, LJ (May 1959), LaBJ, Emmanuel Celler (JL), Claude Wild, Sr. (JL); Douglas, *Go,* p. 327; Newlon, *L.B.J.,* pp. 72–73; Anderson, *The Presidents',* pp. 57–59; Hugh Sidey, *Life,* Nov. 17, 1967.
5. Henderson, *Maury,* pp. 78–82, 153–60;

Kearns, *Lyndon,* p. 91; Interviews, Mark Adams, LJ (May, 1959).

6. "Although there was not a labor union in the legislative district he represented," the local paper said of Lyndon's father, "he consistently led and supported the legislative program sponsored by Texas labor unions. . . . Mr. Johnson was widely known because of his progressive liberal stand on all matters of state legislation."

The date of Sam Johnson, Jr.'s death was Oct. 23, 1937.

Interviews, LJ (Dec. 13, 14, 1967), SHJ, a confidential source; *PP 1964,* p. 1495; Harper's Ferry tapes; Singer and Sherrod, *Lyndon,* pp. 240–241; RBJ, *A Family,* p. 26; Schrieber, "First"; *AS,* Oct. 24, 1937; cf. Kearns, *Lyndon,* pp. 89–90 (but this is wrong on where Sam died).

36. "They Called Me a Communist"

1. By one account the Johnsons moved ten times between 1937 and 1942; Bird told me they had about seven apartments.

   Lyndon told me Bird made them live on $250 a month, which he said was left after the $500 loan repayment.

   According to Steinberg, Bird's Aunt Effie was living with them about half the time and "paid many of their bills." Steinberg also quoted a friend of Bird's that Bird would pick up empty milk and soda-water bottles in the street and collect the deposits on them.

   Interviews, LaBJ, LJ (Dec. 14, 1967), Gordon Fulcher (JL); Letter, Martin Andersen to RD; Steinberg, *Sam Johnson's,* pp. 121–22; Larry Springer, *AA,* Jan. 30, 1973; see, Smith, *A President's,* p. 83, and Singer and Sherrod, *Lyndon,* p. 127.
2. Interviews, Sherman Birdwell, John Fritz Koeniger; *Houston Chronicle,* Aug. 28, 1962; see Steinberg, *Sam Johnson's,* pp. 153–56.
3. Johnson later cited his vote to override as a defense against the accusation he was an FDR "yes-man." The veto of the farmers' interest bill was overridden, 260 to 98.

   Rauch, *The History,* pp. 290–93; *CR 1937,* vol. 81, pp. 5165, 7132, *passim;* see Mooney, *The Lyndon,* p. 50, and Steinberg, *Sam Johnson's,* pp. 129–30.
4. Buchanan's role in the continuing effort for the LCRA appropriations was shown in a story late in 1936 saying he was seeking an additional $5.5 million for Mansfield Dam. "One of the first allotments by the Works Progress Administration 18 months ago," the story said, "was $20 million for the Lower Colorado program. A contract was signed recently for about $5 million worth of work on the Mansfield dam, but Buchanan said the additional amount would be needed. . . ."

   The private utilities' lawsuit, filed by Texas Power & Light Company and other companies, sought to enjoin federal funding of the then-$20-million Colorado River project and another such development on the Brazos River (east of the Colorado in Texas) for which $30 million had been appropriated. In a parallel case the U.S. Supreme Court upheld the right of the PWA to make loans to cities for public electric works, and the Texas suit was dismissed by agreement. This left the LCRA free to sell power to public agencies and to build power lines.

   Montgomery's blast at eastern capital was published as a guest column in the student newspaper at the University of Texas in Austin. A copy of the column can reasonably be presumed to have come to Johnson's attention.

   The claim that Johnson had "persuaded" FDR on the $5 million was made by the president of the Pedernales Rural Electric Co-Operative (headquartered in Johnson City) during a radio speech on behalf of Johnson's reelection to the Congress in 1946.

   On LCRA, see press release, Federal Emergency Administration of Public Works, PWA, May 3, 1937; "General Information concerning the Colorado River Project, Texas," U.S. Bureau of Reclamation, July 1, 1938; *AAS,* Jan. 7, 1973. On the bureaucratic hassles, JL: LCRA papers, box 26, G.I.F. USG Johnson 1937 and 1937–48 fdrs., box 25, G.I.F. Adm., Wirtz fdr., box 27, G.I.F. Adm., Wirtz-Compensation fdr., LBJA Sel. Names, box 36, Wirtz 1937, 1938, and first 1939 fdrs., box 37, Wirtz 1940–42 fdr.: Letters, C. McDonough to LJ, A.J. Wirtz to Carl Farbach and

LJ (eleven), LJ to Wirtz, E H. Foley to Roy Fry, C. McDonough; W.S. Gideon to Frank W. Kuehl, Claude E. Hamilton Jr. to Powell, Rauhut & Gideon, Powell Rauhut & Gideon to Claude E. Hamilton, and Tgms., C. McDonough to LJ, A.J. Wirtz to LJ, LJ to A.J. Wirtz (three). On LCRA in the recent period see also "The Story of Five Years" and "Years of Progress," both published by the LCRA.

Interviews, LJ (Mar. 23, 1968), Ray Lee, Gordon Fulcher (JL); Harper's Ferry tapes; *AA*, Dec. 2, 22, 29, 1936, July 22, 1937, Jan. 12, 1938, and July 9, 1946, and see *AA*, May 1, June 1, and Nov. 16, 1937; *AS*, July 21, 1937, Jan. 11, 1938; *NYT*, July 25, 1939; Sylvia Porter, *Houston Post*, Dec. 20, 1964; *CR 1937*, vol. 81, p. A1289; Steinberg, *Sam Johnson's*, p. 139; Montgomery, "Texas"; Sidey, *A Very*, p. 17; *PP 1967*, p. 623.

5. Haynes Johnson, *WP*, Jan. 24, 1973.

37. Housing for the Poor, by Race

1. Johnson had voted, of course, for the Wagner-Steagall bill that put the federal government in the business of providing the poor low-cost housing. It passed Aug. 18, 1937. (*CR 1937*, vol. 81, p. 9293.)

   Johnson said his two members of the five-member Austin agency were Wirtz and Edgar Perry, Sr.

   Johnson distributed questions and answers on the federal housing program in his district, and he stressed that the program paid its own way out of revenues. "It is in no sense . . . a public leech," he said.

   John Fritz Koeniger, who was hired for Johnson's staff while the two of them drove around Johnson City together over the year-end 1937–38 holidays, recalled Johnson saying over Austin radio that if he had to, he would return to the city and name the names of slum owners. "It was a threat," Koeniger said. Johnson told me he called the name of one landlord who fought him on the issue. Perhaps he was speaking of Simon Gillis, the city councilman he quoted to the paper saying the program was all right if it did not hurt his interests, or perhaps he was referring to something he said at the small meeting of conservative realtors, Miller, and others.

   Johnson made a radio speech describing his Christmas Day walk in the slums in March, 1938. The first project opening occurred in mid-1939.

   Interviews, Ray Lee, Leon Keyserling (JL), LJ (Mar. 23, 1968), Harmon Hodges, John Fritz Koeniger, Guiton Morgan; *CR 1937*, vol. 81, p. 9293; *CR 1938*, vol. 83, pp. A1251–52; *AS*, Dec. 23, 1937, Jan. 19, 25, 1938, and Mar. 4, 31, 1938; *AA*, Dec. 25, 30, 1937, Jan. 11, 13, 19, 20, 24, and Mar. 1, 2, 18, 1938, and Mar. 10, June 26, 1939; William Shannon, *New York Post*, June 1, 1956; see *PP 1967*, p. 513, and *PP 1968*, pp. 1192–93.

38. Lighting Up the Farmhouse

1. This story was told by Johnson with slight variations on different occasions. My account of it is drawn from Johnson on the Harper's Ferry tapes, his account as reported in Sherrod and Singer, and his account for *Look* magazine.

   In Singer and Sherrod, Carmody is identified as a power commissioner. In the Harper's Ferry and *Look* accounts, the density rule is described as three homes per square mile of transmission line; in the third version, the rule is three people per square mile.

   Steinberg, *Sam*, pp. 127, 130–31; Sylvia Porter, *Houston Post*, Dec. 20, 1964; Harper's Ferry tapes; Singer and Sherrod, *Lyndon*, pp. 132–33; Davidson, "Texas"; Newlon, *L.B.J.*, p. 73.
2. *NYT*, July 31, 1938, and cf. *AA*, July 9, 1946; Interview, LJ (Mar. 23, 1968); *PP 1965*, p. 751, pp. 623, 875.
3. Sylvia Porter, *Houston Post*, Dec. 20, 1964; Newlon, *L.B.J.*, p. 74; *AAS*, July 23, 1939.
4. Johnson told me this story, but his telling of it on the Harper's Ferry tapes was fuller and more amusing. I have generally followed the Harper's Ferry version except for his discussion of his desire for Wirtz's approval. (I took one liberty with the Harper's Ferry version, inserting the word "you" so that Wirtz told Johnson, ". . . it just took you two minutes to bust up the whole meeting." My basis for this was John-

son's statement to me that Wirtz told him, "It took me two months to set up this meeting, and you broke it up in two minutes.")

Interviews, Ray Lee, LJ (Dec. 14, 1967); Harper's Ferry tapes.

5. Interviews, Gordon Fulcher (JL), LJ (Dec. 14, 1967, Mar. 23, 1968).
6. In 1941 Johnson said that rural homes in Texas using electricity had increased from 11,000 to 100,000.

He favored from his first years in office federal funds for highways, college buildings, harbor improvements, city sewers, and the like. To GOP critics of the Public Works Administration he retorted that the agency created "useful, permanent, heavy public works" and relieved unemployment.

AA, Jan. 3, Sept. 2, 1939; *AAS*, Sept. 17, 1939; *AS*, Aug. 7, 1939; *NYT*, July 25, 1939; *Houston Press*, Sept. 19, 21, 1939; Drew Pearson and Robert S. Allen, *DMN*, 1941 (otherwise undated); *CR 1939*, vol. 84, p. A2627; *CR 1941*, vol. 87, p. 9501; *CR 1946*, vol. 92, pp. 1320, A1065; Letters, Franklin D. Roosevelt to LJ, LJ to FDR (FDRL).

7. As one prominent Texas labor official said of this time, "There was no antilabor going on in Washington in those days."

Johnson, when the NYA director in Texas, had helped get a labor man, A. J. Reinhard of Fort Worth, on the board of the Lower Colorado River Authority. (The board was organized in 1935.)

The minimum wage bill was called the Fair Labor Standards Act. The House labor committee bottled it up, whereupon Johnson joined the successful attempt to force it to the floor by petition. By a vote of 216 to 198, the House killed it for the year. In May, 1938, the House passed it, 314 to 97, and subsequently the conference report on the final bill also passed, 291 to 89. Johnson voted for the bill at these various stages.

Johnson in 1963 and 1964 faultily characterized the circumstances associated with the petition movement in the House.

On LCRA, "Years of Progress," LCRA; a confidential source.

On minimum wages, Henderson, *Maury*, pp. 146, 173; Steinberg, *Sam*, pp. 149–50; *CR 1937*, vol. 82, pp. 1834–35; *CR 1938*, vol. 83, pp. 7449–50, 9266–67; *PP 1963*, p. 21; *PP 1964*, pp. 573, 656, 1254, 1265, 1363; *PP 1967*, p. 117; see Rauch, *The History*, pp. 305–7, Steinberg, *Sam Johnson's*, p. 130, and Miller, *Lyndon*, pp. 82–83.

8. Interviews, John Fritz Koeniger, Clifford Durr.

As the House passed a bill to make lynching a federal crime in 1940, Johnson voted with the southerners against it. In 1943 the House had a clear vote on outlawing the poll tax in the seven poll-tax states, and had the House had its way (which of course it didn't) this would have been done: the vote was 265–110. Johnson voted no, as he did again in 1945, when the vote was about the same. (*CR 1940*, vol. 86, pp. 253–54; *CR 1943*, vol. 89, p. 4889; *CR 1945*, vol. 91, p. 6003.)

9. Interview, Mrs. Ida Bloom; Newlon, *L.B.J.*, pp. 76–77; Mooney, *The Lyndon*, p. 35.
10. Steinberg, *Sam Johnson's*, pp. 134–35; Steinberg, *Sam*, pp. 146–49; Interview, John Fritz Koeniger.
11. Allen told me, "He came up here with about $120,000 or $150,000 in oil money," but was vaguer in his Johnson Library interview, saying Johnson had come up with a campaign fund of one or two hundred thousand dollars, "undoubtedly oil money." He told me there were two small rooms in Johnson's disbursing office; he told the Johnson Library there was one.

Once Johnson knew Allen had caught on, "his interest," Allen said, "was to keep me from writing anything. . . . He made it very clear this was all very confidential, and that's the way I kept it until after the election. . . . I wrote nothing about it at the time . . . and as far as I know no other newsman knew about it."

Allen expressed a qualified approval of Johnson's operation, saying: "Undoubtedly there was some eyebrow-raising about where the money came from, and there probably [were] some of the so-called 'lefties' or 'out-and-outers' who said the oil people were buying themselves some insurance. But . . . it was within the bounds of political propriety. . . ."

Interviews, Robert S. Allen (by RD and JL).

12. Interviews, Maury Maverick, Jr., Gene Latimer (JL), John Connally; Crawford and Keever, *John B.*, p. 41.

39. Ludlow, Munich, and Hitler

1. Johnson voted with his chairman, Carl Vinson, for the naval authorization bill of 1938 against attempts to cut it back. The next year he was voting with Vinson on fortifying the island of Guam and buying a larger navy; he opposed cuts in military spending. Johnson's vote remotely might have been decisive in the passage of the Bloom amendment to the Neutrality Act (the act had passed before Johnson came to Congress). The Bloom provision, which in effect gave Roosevelt a freer hand in aiding the countries that were to become our wartime allies, was saved from recommittal by a vote of 196–194, with Johnson in the majority; then it was passed. He joined the House majority fighting off attempts to limit the president's power to send arms to our allies-to-be; he voted to repeal the arms embargo. (*CR 1938*, vol. 83, pp. 3767–68; *1939*, vol. 84, pp. 1843–43, 5262–63, 7723, 8512–13, and vol. 85, pp. 1343–44, 1389.)

   The draft was established on Sept. 7, 1940; Johnson's vote for it (the margin was 263–149) is at *CR 1940*, vol. 86, pp. 11754–55. Cf. Newlon, *LBJ*, p. 80.

   Johnson told Kearns he realized Hitler could take over America while the referendum was being held, and he felt so silly he rushed to take his name off the resolution.

   In 1924, the Democratic and the Progressive party platforms had endorsed a popular referendum on war —"except in case of actual or threatened attack," the Democrats added; "except in cases of actual invasion," said the Progressives' plank.

   In the 1970s, right-wing Congressman John Rarick of Louisiana proposed an amendment that, except in case of actual or threatened attack on the country or the hemisphere, the only way war could be declared or warfare engaged in overseas would be by a national referendum.

   CR 1938, vol. 83, pp. 275–83, A207, A1052–53; Interviews, LJ (Mar. 23, 1968), John Fritz Koeniger (who was present in Johnson's office when Maverick related his conversation with Roosevelt to Johnson); LJ's remarks to foreign journalists in 1968, provided by Letter, George Christian to RD; Henderson, *Maury*, pp. 172–173; Kearns, *Lyndon*, p. 329; Schlesinger, *The Imperial*, pp. 97, 301.
2. Interview, Luther Jones, Jr.; Bullitt, *For the President*, p. 230; Colvin, *The Chamberlain*, pp. 146–73; Eubank, *Munich*, pp. viii, 128–230, 263–64, 295–300; Shirer, *The Rise*, pp. 357–420.
3. Steinberg, *Sam Johnson's*, pp. 135, 137; Letter, LJ to Sam Rayburn, *RL*.
4. *PP 1965*, p. 372; Interview, Carl Vinson (JL); Murphy, *Diplomat*, p. 69.
5. Interview, Mrs. Virginia Durr.
6. By Johnson's account of the discussion in the committee, Admiral Ben Moreel had told him he thought the base should be at Corpus, and Johnson had asked three questions, but each time Vinson had cut him off for bothering the committee with local matters. Johnson became angry. "Mr. Chairman," he said, "I have been on this committee four years and I think that on a matter which concerns a member as this concerns me in my district, in my area of the state, I think I am entitled to ask at least four questions, one a year." "Well," Vinson said, "that's all right, you asked three, and you got one more to go."

   Construction of the base began in July, 1940, and it was dedicated in March, 1941.

   CCCT, Mar. 9, 11, 12, 13, 1941; *PP 1965*, pp. 372–73.
7. J. Evetts Haley, (later the author of a tract against Johnson,) was chairman of the "Jeffersonian Democrats of Texas," who condemned FDR's "wanton" spending for "a false humanitarianism" and supported Landon and the Republican platform in 1936.

   The chairman and secretary of the Texas Roosevelt Third Term Committee, Tom Miller and Edward Clark, respectively, urged that Rayburn and Johnson be chairman and vice-chairman, respectively, of the Texas delegation to the national convention. I have construed this as Johnson's acceptance of a public role for Roosevelt.

   The Garner leaders included Myron G. Blalock and Mrs. Clara Driscoll, the Texas members on the Democratic National Committee, and former Governors Pat Neff, W. P. Hobby, and Ross Sterling.

Johnson is my source for the conversation between Roosevelt and him about letting Garner have the Texas votes. Johnson said Roosevelt told him to tell the Garner forces that Roosevelt had seen a wire from Johnson that the Garner people could change to Roosevelt after the first ballot and had approved it. This might indicate that Roosevelt first intended that Johnson alone send the wire advocating the deal and only later included Rayburn.

The account that Miller knocked Maverick down appeared in the *Austin Tribune,* which was pro-Garner. The AP passed along several versions of the altercation, in none of which was Maverick reported knocked down. Miller said Maverick had insulted him, so he hit him.

Morrow said Rayburn was supposed to introduce him at the national convention, but did not. "When I went to the microphone [to nominate Garner]," Morrow said, "you never heard such boos and hisses and jeering. This went on the whole time I was speaking. It was a 17-minute speech, but it took 30 minutes for me to deliver it."

Elliott Roosevelt was to nominate Jones for vice-president, but backed out. Jones had been appointed to the Reconstruction Finance Corporation by Hoover in 1932 and later had been simultaneously Roosevelt's secretary of commerce and federal loan administrator. After having a conflict with Henry Wallace in 1945 in which Roosevelt sided with Wallace, Jones returned to Houston and was overheard saying that maybe the Democratic party should be buried. He owned the *Houston Chronicle* and three big hotels—in all, almost a fifth of Houston's downtown real estate—and had interests in banking, insurance, and investment companies. He set up a foundation with $20 million in assets. Although his government paychecks, covering thirteen years, came to more than $100,000, he refused to cash them.

Garner, after swearing in his successor Wallace, took the train to Texas and never returned to Washington. In 1960 he endorsed Johnson for president.

Interviews, LJ (Mar. 23, 1968), Wright Morrow; Burns, *Roosevelt,* pp. 294, 369–70, 417; Evans and Novak, *Lyndon,* pp. 11–12, citing Michael C. Janeway, "Lyndon Johnson and the Rise of Conservatism in Texas," thesis, Harvard, 1962; Steinberg, *Sam Johnson's,* pp. 145, 147–48, and Steinberg, *Sam Rayburn,* pp. 160–61; Dorough, *Mr. Sam,* pp. 292–93; Ickes, *Secret,* vol. 3, p. 168; Fuermann, *Houston,* pp. 77–85, and Fuermann, *Reluctant,* pp. 36–37, 102; see SHJ, *My,* p. 62, and cf. Little, "The Congressional," thesis, p. 133; documents, Jeffersonian Democrats, "Jeffersonian Democrats of Texas" and "To Democrats"; mimeographed announcement of the Garner for President Committee in Dallas, April 15, 1940; *Official Report, Democratic National Convention, 1940,* pp. 138, 183, 190, 226; *Paris* (Tx.) *News,* Aug. 23, 1939; *Memphis Commercial Appeal,* Aug. 13, 1939; *AA,* May 28, 29, 1940, and Nov. 8, 9, 1967; *AS,* May 26, 28, 1940; *Austin Tribune,* May 28, 1940; AP story May 16, 1940, datelined Austin (RL); *NYT,* April 15, 16, 30, 1940; see, on Johnson and Jesse Jones, *CR 1939,* vol. 84, p. 2960.

8. Maury Maverick, Sr., wrote Rayburn on Oct. 5, 1940, that he understood Rayburn favored making Johnson "secretary of the party." Maverick said this should be done to keep a lot of Democratic congressmen from getting beat.

A variant account of Johnson's meeting with Roosevelt on this matter quoted Johnson, "Mr. President, let me do it my way with no interference. Give me 'carte blanche' to handle the Texans and the rest of the party members." Roosevelt, by this account, responded by extending his hand and saying, "Good luck."

Johnson came to the attention of political columnists Drew Pearson and Robert S. Allen, as well as Joseph Alsop and Robert Kintner, because of his 1940 money-raising. Alsop and Kintner reported that Tommy Corcoran had sponsored Johnson in the White House, giving him access to James Rowe, FDR's administrative assistant, and many other younger New Dealers. Roosevelt had become worried about the congressional elections, they wrote, and Johnson, chosen as FDR's agent on the problem, collected with Rayburn the sum of about $60,000 "chiefly from anti-Roosevelt Texas Democrats who would not give money to be spent on the President but were glad to finance Democratic House nominees."

Interviews, John Connally, Harold Young; Drew Pearson and Robert S. Allen, *DMN*, a column, my copy of which is dated only 1941; "Highlights in the Life of Lyndon B. Johnson," Citizens for Johnson National Committee, July, 1960; Joseph Alsop and Robert Kintner, *New York Herald-Tribune*, Nov. 26, 1940; Letters, LJ to Sam Rayburn (RL) and Maury Maverick, Sr., to Sam Rayburn (RL); Tgm., Edwin M. Watson to Edward J. Flynn (FDRL); Letters, LJ to Franklin D. Roosevelt, FDR to LJ, Pat Drewry to FDR, Maury Maverick, Sr., to FDR (FDRL); Memo, FDR to "Mac" [presumably Marvin McIntyre] (FDRL); JL: LBJA Sel. Names, box 12, 2nd. George Brown fdr.: Tgm., George Brown to LJ, Letter, LJ to George Brown; Singer and Sherrod, *Lyndon*, pp. 143–44; *NYT*, 1942, otherwise undated (on Johnson's role as party secretary); a confidential source.

9. Lady Bird gave Lyndon, for their wedding anniversary in 1968, a copy of her diary entry for Feb. 13, 1941, bound in a folder.

   AA, Nov. 18, 1968; *CCCT*, Mar. 9, 11, 12, 13, 1941.

40. Red-Baiting for Herman Brown

1. The *Dallas Morning News* quoted Roosevelt directly, ". . . everybody knows that I cannot enter a primary election. . . . all I can say is that Lyndon Johnson is a very old, old friend of mine." The *News* reported that Johnson was "the well-branded administration candidate, and it generally is admitted that the administration has picked him for the one purpose of defeating" Dies.

   Interview, LJ (Dec. 14, 1967); McKay, *Texas*, p. 353; Joseph Alsop and Robert Kintner, *DMN*, May 17, 1941; *NYT*, Ap. 20, 1941; *CR 1941*, vol. 87, p. A1994, and see *DMN*, April 22, 1941; *WP*, April 23, 1941; *DMN*, April 23, 1941.
2. Interview, Hale Boggs (JL); *DMN*, April 25, June 6, 17, 19, 27, 28, 30, 1941; *NYT*, June 28, 29, 1941; Johnson's 1941 campaign posters and ads, Barker History Center, UT-Austin; Tgms., LJ to FDR and Charles Marsh, FDR to LJ (four) and W. Lee O'Daniel, A.J. Wirtz to James Rowe (FDRL); Memos, White House (on phone message from Tom Corcoran), James Rowe to FDR (FDRL).
3. Elliott Roosevelt, ed., *F.D.R.*, vol. II, pp. 1159–60; Blum, ed., *The Price*, p. 107; resolution, Austin Trades Council, Austin, Tx., May 2, 1941; Interviews, Ghent Sanderford, J. R. Parten, and Raymond Buck.
4. The major listed contributors ($5,000 each) were Clara Driscoll and E. S. Fentress, publisher. Johnson's wife was listed at $2,500, and four others were listed as having given more than $1,000, none of them George or Herman Brown.

   Pearson's information about the 1941 campaign needs be relied upon because the Internal Revenue Service rejected inquiries on statutory grounds.

   "I regret," an IRS publicity man wrote to me in 1959, "I am unable to furnish any information relating to the Federal income tax status of Brown & Root, Inc., or George and Herman Brown of Houston for the years 1941 to 1943. Federal tax law—Section 7213 of the Internal Revenue Code of 1954—provides criminal penalties for unlawful disclosure of information concerning any taxpayer's income return. . . ."

   Pearson's series of columns on this subject appeared in the *Washington Post* and many other newspapers. They were subjected to a lot of editing.

   On the aspect of the case involving Edgar Monteith, Pearson quoted a federal agent writing from Dallas May 13, 1944:

   "It is quite obvious that Monteith aided and abetted Brown & Root, Inc., and Victoria Gravel Co. in showing that political contributions for which he was the conduit were attorney's fees. This would make his income tax fraudulent. . . .

   "I seriously doubt that he was afraid of incriminating himself in connection with his own tax liability, but believe that he was afraid he might be involved in a conspiracy in connection with the evasion of taxes by Brown & Root, Inc., and Victoria Gravel Co."

Interview, LJ (Dec. 14, 1967); *CR 1941*, vol. 87, pp. A1992–94; *DMN*, June 22, 1941; *Life*, June 30, 1941; *AA*, June 27, July 30, 1941; *New York Herald-Tribune*, July 5, 1941; Walter Hornaday, *NYT*, July 6, 1941; Drew Pearson, *WP*, Mar. 25, 1956, et seq.; Drew Pearson, *Texas Observer*, Mar. 28, 1956; Letter, Larry George to RD.

5. A confidential source.
6. Interviews, Gordon Fulcher, Daniel Quill; Provence, *Lyndon*, pp. 65–66.
7. *DMN*, May 4, June 17, 20, 21, 22, 24, 27, 1941; *Johnson City Record-Courier*, June 2, 1941; Johnson campaign literature, Barker History Center, UT-Austin; a film, *The Journey*.
8. McKay, *Texas*, pp. 349–50; Henderson, *Maury*, pp. 176–77, 214–16, 228, 231; *DMN*, July 26, 1938, Aug. 8, 27, Oct. 17, Dec. 6, 8, 1939, May 28, 1941; Interview, LJ (Dec. 13, 1967).
9. There were no record votes as the House approved the appropriations for the Dies committee in 1938 and 1939. In 1940 and 1941 Johnson was among the majorities of 344 to 21 and 354 to 6 approving the committee's continuation. In 1942 he was in the service during the vote on the subject. By 1943, 94 members of the House opposed Dies going on with his work, but 302 voted otherwise, Johnson among them.

   CR 1938, vol. 83, p. 8638, *1939*, vol. 84, p. 1291, *1940*, vol. 86, pp. 604–5, *1941*, vol. 87, pp. 899, A1994, *1943*, vol. 89, pp. 809–10, and see 111–12; *DMN*, Mar. 15, April 4, June 18, 22, 25, 1941.
10. McKay, *Texas*, p. 354; Letter, LJ to Austin Trades Council: *DMN*, June 18, 25, 1941; Interviews, Margaret Carter, Otto Mullinax.
11. McKay, *Texas*, pp. 344–45; *Time*, May 5, 1941; *NYT*, June 29, 1941.
12. *Johnson City Record-Courier*, June 2, 1941.

41. The Cagey Good Sport

1. Interview, Jim Fritts.
2. On Sunday, June 29, Johnson led 167,-471 to O'Daniel's 162,910, with returns from all 254 Texas counties, 116 complete. The Associated Press said Johnson's victory "was indicated." The final unofficial count on Tuesday, July 1, gave O'Daniel the victory by a margin of 1,095. By the official canvass the results were O'Daniel 175,590, Johnson 175,279, Mann 140,807, Dies 80,653.

   Time quoted Johnson: "That's the ball game. I thought it was a curve ball, but the umpire called it a strike. Let's play again some day." Johnson later told Bob Considine, "I had won . . . but the victory didn't take. They kept counting the votes until the Wednesday after the election. If they had stopped Tuesday I would have gone to the Senate." (Johnson was a day off here.)

   "I'll show you the FBI reports if you want me to," Johnson told me in the White House. My first reaction was delight—what a source! "I'd be very glad to see them," I told him. But something checked me then (it was at least irregular and maybe frightening that the president would show a reporter raw FBI reports), and I added, "I'll be going to see Coke Stevenson and I'll ask him everything needs asking. . . . of course I couldn't ask him about anything I couldn't see officially." That was that.

   The state party chairman, E. B. Germany, requested that the U.S. Senate committee on privileges and elections investigate. Johnson said, "I believe all the candidates in this Senate race are honest. I am making no charges of any kind, requesting no investigation, and preparing no contest." At that point Senator Tom Connally of the committee in question said there could be an investigation only if formal complaints were lodged.

   Interviews, J. C. Looney (JL), SHJ, John Connally, Allan Shivers (JL), Carroll Keach, LJ (May, 1959, and Dec. 13, 14, 1967), Sam D. W. Low, Harold Young, Gordon Fulcher (JL), Edmunds Travis, Harry Acreman, H. M. Greene; *DMN*, June 30, July 9, 1941; *AA*, Aug. 30, 1948; *NYT*, June 30, July 1, 2, 15, 1941; McKay, *Texas*, p. 365; *Texas Almanac 1943–1944*, pp. 259–60; *Time*, June 22, 1953; Bob Considine, "A President"; SHJ, *My*, p. 72; "A National Tribute," JL.
3. Interview, Harold Young.
4. Kearns, *Lyndon*, pp. 93–94.
5. LJ, *The Vantage*, pp. 447–48.

6. Quoted by John P. Roche, *WP,* Jan. 22, 1972, from secret minutes of the British cabinet that had been released, and see Loewenheim, ed., *Roosevelt,* pp. 152–55.
7. William S. White is the source of a report that Johnson said he advised Roosevelt to have Hull make a statement. In White's interview for the Johnson Library, he quoted Johnson that Roosevelt had responded, "Why would you do that, Lyndon?" and Johnson had said Hull, a former member of Congress, was held in enormous respect. In a book, White told a variant story in which Johnson persuaded Rayburn to ask Hull to make the appeal.

   PP 1967, p. 277; Interviews, Carl Vinson (JL), LJ (Mar. 23, 1968), William S. White (JL), Chalmers Roberts (JL); *CR 1941,* vol. 87, pp. 6938–39, 7074; White, *The Professional,* pp. 94–95; JL, Marsh papers, box 2, LJ and LBJ 1941 fdrs.: Memo, Charles Marsh to LJ, Letters, Marsh to Gordon Fulcher, Marsh to LJ.
8. *PP 1965,* p. 149; *NYT,* Aug. 22, 1941.
9. See Shirer, *The Rise,* pp. 749–50, 793–900.

42. In and Out of the War

1. Johnson in 1967 remembered the importance of the difference between the words "resign" and "leave." Repeating the wording of his promise for me, he gave it as, "If I ever send your boy to war, I will leave my seat and go with him."

   Johnson was commissioned in the navy on Jan. 21, 1940.

   A navy biography of him dated or released 1960 said he "was ordered to the Office of the Chief of Naval Operations, Navy Department, Washington, D.C., for instruction. . . ." and Caidin and Hymoff concluded from this that he was receiving training in Washington, but Johnson is my source that he and Connally were doing staff work for Forrestal.

   Singer and Sherrod said that Johnson made the statements to his brother in a letter; Mooney said the statements were made to Sam Houston Johnson in person, and in an interview Sam Houston Johnson said it was in person.

   Alvin Wirtz said he told Johnson, as the latter was passing through Austin, that petitions signed by more than 22,000 voters asking his name be placed on the ballot for reelection had been forwarded to his Washington office. "It was at my suggestion," Wirtz said, "that he signed and acknowledged the statements, in the form of applications." The petitions were signed by 27,581 voters. Johnson was reelected in 1942 without opposition.

   Connally told Merle Miller Johnson left him two filled-out applications, one for senator and one for reelection to the House, and Connally decided on his own to file the latter.

   Interviews, LJ (Dec. 13, 1967), Harold Young, Malcolm Bardwell (JL), Otto Crider, Gordon Fulcher (JL), SHJ; *PP 1965,* p. 492; Severeid, "The Final," and see Muller, *Adlai,* p. 49; Caidin and Hymoff, *The Mission,* pp. 16–17, 19, 23; Mooney, *The Lyndon,* pp. xx, 45, 46; Newlon, *L.B.J.,* p. 86; *Texas Almanac 1943–1944,* pp. 259–60; Singer and Sherrod, *Lyndon,* pp. 156–57; Daniels, *White,* pp. 28–29; Miller, *Lyndon,* pp. 121–22; Healy, "The Frantic"; *NYT,* Dec. 12, 1941, Sept. 21, 1964; *DMN,* May 13, 14, 1942; a 1946 Johnson campaign pamphlet; movies, *The Journey, A National Tribute*; Letter, LJ to FDR (FDRL); JL, Marsh papers, box 2, LBJ 1941 fdr., box 4, Memos, Texas campaign 1942, box 3, Johnson, Lyndon B., 1942 fdr., and LBJA Sel. Names, box 37, A.J. Wirtz 1940–42 and 1942 fdrs.: Letters, Charles Marsh to LJ (four) and Grace Tully, A.J. Wirtz to John Connally, LJ, and A.J. Wirtz, LJ to FDR, Memos, Marsh to LJ (two), Tgm. or cable, Marsh to LJ; *FWST,* Sept. 14, 1947.
2. On May 30, 1942, MacArthur's headquarters announced that Johnson had arrived in Australia and conferred with MacArthur. Johnson "had been on duty in San Francisco and later Auckland, N.Z., with Vice Admiral Robert L. Ghormley, head of United States naval forces in the South Pacific," a *New York Times* story said. (The plane in which Johnson flew to the Southwest Pacific was Ghormley's.)

   Harold Young is my source of Johnson's account (to Young) of MacArthur's greeting to Johnson May 25.

Interviews, LJ (Dec. 13, 1967, Mar. 23, 1968), Harold Young; Caidin and Hymoff, *The Mission,* pp. 21, 32–50, 78–80, 96–97, 118–19, 124–25; Letter, Edward Hymoff to RD; Newlon, *L.B.J.,* pp. 88–90, 92; *NYT,* June 12, 1942.

3. The Associated Press, the United Press, and the *New York Times* agreed, in stories a few days after the June 9, 1942, mission over Lae, that the *Heckling Hare* had dropped out and turned back. The AP said the cause was "engine trouble"; the *Times* said "mechanical trouble." On how close to Lae the *Heckling Hare* was when it turned back, the *Times* said only that it had turned back "without reaching its target," the AP said "before reaching" the target. None of the news stories said anything about Zeros firing on the plane, and Johnson, in a long quote in the UP story (cited partially in the succeeding chapter of the text), did not mention having come under fire.

   In 1964 the *Times* suggested that its 1942 story on the episode might have been censored. "Remember," wrote Edward Hymoff, co-author of *The Mission,* in 1975, "when the Lae mission occurred . . . there were not that many war correspondents abroad, public information officers were limited in number, and communications were bad."

   In a radio report in Texas that summer, Johnson left the impression that his plane had been caught in cross-fire, but did not say so. He told Texans that two hours after take-off, "Jap Zeros intercepted us. Most of our squadron of bombers were hit with fire from the Jap Zero cannon. The plane in which Anderson was riding was repeatedly hit. My pilot, a flight leader, quickly dived his crippled plane out of formation because of mechanical trouble. The plane in which a Colonel Stevens was riding and all the crew were shot down."

   Anderson was in a different wave and could not attest to what happened to Johnson's plane.

   Back in Washington that summer Johnson told Harold Young about the incident, but did not, Young said, say that the *Heckling Hare* had been fired on. Young thought the later stories that it had been were "a lot of bullshit."

   The Marauders were officially credited with thirteen kills, but only one Zero was shot down and another ditched in the sea, according to Caidin and Hymoff. In a curious passage, they wrote that the thirteen kills were indicated in "whatever official records still exist—and these are not in the archives of the United States government." By letter Hymoff stated that he and Caidin "had *no* help from the White House, LBJ, or the military" in putting together their book on the mission. ". . . there was absolute silence from the White House. Nobody would talk to us. [George] Reedy never returned my many phone calls."

   The crew of the *Heckling Hare* were Capt. Greer, the pilot; Flight Sgt. G. A. McMullin of the R.A.A.F., copilot; Lt. Billy B. Boothe, navigator; Sgt. McCredie, bombardier; Cpl. Walker, radio-man gunner; Pfc. Marshall, top turret gunner; Cpl. Baren, engineer-tailgunner. Greer died in Louisiana in 1944 in the crash of a B-29. McMullin was lost in action in the Pacific the same year. Caidin and Hymoff discussed the air battle with friends of Greer and McMullin, especially Gerald L. Crosson, a close friend of Greer's, as well as with McCredie, Walker, Baren, and possibly Marshall. The authors also quoted Sakai, the Japanese ace, extensively.

   The Lae mission was carried out by the 19th Squadron, 22d Bomb Group. James N. Eastman, chief of research at Maxwell Air Force Base in Alabama, informed me, "The histories of the 22d Bomb Gp for the time period in which you are interested are extremely sparse, and do not include data on any missions. No histories of the 19th Bomb Sq exist for that period."

   Caidin and Hymoff, *The Mission,* pp. 114–68, 179, 201–2; Letters, Edward Hymoff, Samuel E. Anderson, and James N. Eastman, Jr., to RD; Interviews, Harry Baren, Harold Young; Tom Cheatham, *Houston Chronicle* (UPI), May 10, 1966; *WP* (AP), June 12, 1942; *AA* or *AS* (UP), datelined "Somewhere in Australia," June 12, 1942; Byron Darnton, *NYT,* June 12, 1942, and *NYT,* Sept. 21, 1964; *Chicago Sun,* July 27, 1942; cf. Robert Buckhorn, *AA* (UPI), Mar. 1964, and Newlon, *L.B.J.,* pp. 92–97.

4. Lee Van Atta, an International News Service story datelined June 14, 1942,

from United Nations Headquarters in Australia *(AA* or *AS);* White, *Queens,* pp. 266–67; Interview, Harry Schreiber (the navigator on the *Swoose*); Newlon, *L.B.J.,* pp. 98–100; Caidin and Hymoff, *The Mission,* pp. 187–89.

5. The date of the directive was June 17, 1942. The exception was rescinded on the same day at the suggestion, the AP understood, of Secretaries Stimson and Knox. Roosevelt gave reporters the text of the directive July 9. One senator and seven congressmen were affected.

   As Johnson saw it, "I had been ordered out of uniform and back to Washington by my commander-in-chief." However, Johnson's election opponent in 1946, Hardy Hollers, said that he was informed in a communication from the Library of Congress dated May 22, 1946, that after Roosevelt's directive, Congressmen Baumhart and Secrest of Ohio, Van Zandt of Pennsylvania, and Will Rogers, Jr., of California resigned their seats and continued in the armed forces.

   Roosevelt refused to extend his directive to state legislators. Speaker Rayburn wired the president on the matter, and early in January, 1943, Roosevelt replied that "constant attendance to duty" was required in the land and naval forces, the war and navy departments refused extended furloughs or leaves "except in cases of extreme emergency," and those departments thought letting state legislators have prolonged absences was "inadvisable." However, he added, state legislators could get honorable discharges for the purpose of performing their legislative duties. This put the political burden of evading service on the politician, as Roosevelt's directive concerning members of Congress did not appear to do.

   NYT, July 10, 1942; *DMN,* July 18, 1942; *AA,* Nov. 6, 1942; Letters, LaBJ to George Brown, J.C. Kellam to LJ (JL, LBJA Sel. Names, Brown and Kellam fdrs,); Letter, Franklin D. Roosevelt to Sam Rayburn, *RL.*

6. Baren, for other missions, received a Distinguished Flying Cross and an Air Medal.

   Johnson's citation said that he, "in order to obtain personal knowledge of combat conditions, volunteered as an observer on a hazardous aerial combat mission over hostile positions in New Guinea. As our planes neared the target area, they were intercepted by eight hostile fighters. When, at this time, the plane in which Lieutenant Commander Johnson was an observer developed mechanical trouble and was forced to turn back alone, presenting a favourable target to the enemy fighters, he evidenced marked coolness in spite of the hazards involved. His gallant action enabled him to obtain and return with valuable information."

   Newlon, *L.B.J.,* pp. 100–102; Caidin and Hymoff, *The Mission,* pp. 190–91; *NYT,* Sept. 21, 1964; Tom Cheatham, *Houston Chronicle* (UPI), May 10, 1966; Interview, Harry Baren.

7. Letters, Robert Sherrod to RD, along with a copy of a draft chapter Sherrod wrote on his conversations with LJ.
8. "World War II Diary," typescript and handwritten original, JL.
9. *Time* later said Johnson had pneumonia, but he told me it was some kind of fever. He said he was unconscious for five days and was in the hospital at Suva, Fiji Islands, a week.

   Interview, LJ (Dec. 13, 1967), and Harper's Ferry tapes; *AA,* Nov. 6, 1942; *Time,* July 27, 1942; a 1944 Johnson campaign pamphlet; see Caidin and Hymoff, *The Mission,* pp. 192–93.

10. Newlon, *L.B.J.,* pp. 206–7; Schreiber, "First"; Smith, *A President's,* p. 61; Letter, Zeake W. Johnson, Jr., to RD.
11. *Time,* July 27, 1942; Drew Pearson, *DMN,* Aug. 6, 1942; Interviews, LJ (Dec. 13, 1967) and Harry Baren; Daniels, *White,* pp. 33–34.

43. Politics and Military Service

1. Byron Darnton, *NYT,* June 12, 1942; AP from San Francisco datelined June 28, 1942 (*AA* or *AS*); *Houston Post,* July 24, 1942; "A Report to YOU from your representative in Congress, Lyndon B. Johnson" (which can be dated 1942–1945 because it contains the words, "once this war is won"); *AA,* July 27, 1946, and July 3, 1948; *Johnson Journal,* Aug. 1948, p. 1; Mooney, *The Lyndon* (1956 ed.), pp. viii, 57; speech by LJ, Stephenville, Tx., Nov. 1959 (which I

covered); *Houston Chronicle,* Aug. 1964 (an AP dispatch from Olean, N.Y., quoting William Miller); *Republican Congressional Committee Newsletter,* Sept. 4, 1964; Sidey, *A Very, pp.* 142–43, 153; Interview, LJ (Dec. 13, 1967); Halberstam, *The Best,* p. 449, and see The Unfinished, p. 25.

44. Wartime in Washington

1. Interview, Drew Pearson (JL); *CR 1943,* vol. 89, p. A5133.
2. Interviews, Drew Pearson (JL), Harold Young, a confidential source.
3. Schreiber, "First"; Smith, *A President's,* p. 50; Bishop, *A Day,* p. 40; *PP 1964,* p. 646; *NYT,* April 13, 1945; a movie, *The Journey.*
4. Daniels, *White,* pp. 44–50, 54–55, 72–74, 98–99, 137, 272–73, and see p. 77; Interviews, Tom Clark (JL), John J. McCloy (JL); Abell, ed., *Drew,* p. 401.
5. As Johnson described the Brown & Root tax case to me, the issue was the company's depreciation rate on equipment. Nine years was the standard period, but the company was using the equipment in question on a twenty-four-hour shift and had claimed three years. The net of it was, Johnson said, that the government paid B&R something back.

   William Shannon wrote, in the context of Pearson's columns, that "Johnson denies that the purpose of the meeting [with Roosevelt] was to discuss Brown & Root's problems."

   Drew Pearson, *WP,* Mar. 25, 1956; Drew Pearson, *Texas Observer,* Mar. 28, 1956; Interview, LJ (Dec. 14, 1967); William Shannon, *New York Post,* June 3, 1956; JL, LBJA Sel. Names, Letters, LJ to John Connally (box 15, Connally fdr. 2) and Everett Looney (box 25, Looney fdr. 2); Tgm., George Brown to LJ (box 12, George Brown fdr. 2); Memo, "ld" to Gen. Watson (FDRL).
6. Marsh told Wallace that Johnson had showed the speech to him and said it had been approved by Douglas. Wallace believed the group's plan was to make Douglas president on a program somewhat to the right of the New Deal. Beginning in 1943, Roosevelt shifted right, siding with Jesse Jones in a shakeup that stripped Wallace of much authority.

   Interview, Helen Gahagan Douglas (JL); Blum, *The Price,* pp. 138–39, 226–29, *passim.*
7. *CR 1944,* vol. 90, pp. 5537–38, 5700–3, 5919–20; Bowles, *Promises,* p. 533; and see Evans and Novak, *Lyndon,* pp. 5–6.
8. *AA,* Aug. 12, 15, 22, Dec. 22, 23, 29, 30, 1943, and Oct. 13, 1944; *AAS,* Jan. 2, 1944.
9. Interview, Carl Vinson (JL); *DMN,* Aug. 20, 1942, May 15, June 25, 1945; *AA,* May 13, June 25, 1945, April 4, 1946; *AS,* June 15, 1945; see Evans and Novak, *Lyndon,* pp. 15–16; Sidey, *A Very,* pp. 153–54; Newlon, *L.B.J.,* p. 104; Janeway, "Johnson."
10. Interviews, Harold Young, Carl Vinson (JL); *NYT,* Feb. 24, Mar. 4, 7, 9, 18, 1943; *AA,* Jan. 28, 1944; Newlon, *L.B.J.,* pp. 105–6.
11. Interview, Carl Vinson (JL); *AA,* Mar. 30, 1944; *DMN,* July 3, 1948; on Vinson himself see Evans, "The Sixth."
12. As Johnson later explained the matter concerning egg prices, Swift and Company, operating under a government contract, tried to force the price the company paid producers down from 30 to 15 cents a dozen, but he persuaded the federal agencies to set the price at 26 cents and cancel the packers' contracts if they paid less.

    The remarks of Lester C. Boone, who had been in charge of enforcing OPA food regulations in a six-state area including Texas, took the form of a wire to Johnson's 1946 election opponent, Hardy Hollers. The wartime food administrator quoted was Marvin Jones.

    Interview, Marvin Jones (JL); *AA,* Mar. 21, April 21, 1944, and July 9, 1946, and *Brenham Banner Press,* July 15, 1946; a confidential source.
13. Taylor, who called his pamphlets "Buck Taylor's Middle Buster," was sixty. Johnson was thirty-four.

    The capitalization was in the original campaign document, entitled "A Report to YOU from your representative in Congress, Lyndon B. Johnson," and datable by a reference to Johnson's war service and the words, "once this war is won."

    Johnson won, 26,454 to Taylor's 11,-393.

    DMN, May 27, July 4, 1944; the

named document, Barker History Center, UT-Austin; *Texas Almanac 1945–46,* p. 537.

14. The dropping of Wallace from the 1944 ticket was momentous for the postwar period, but Wallace's amateurism as a politician did not help his cause much. Young said that one night when the fight for delegates for the vice-presidential nomination was on, Wallace was talking at length with professorial types while politicians who controlled delegates cooled their heels outside. "Get rid of these shitheels," Young told the vice-president, "and let's talk to some of these people with delegates." "OK," Wallace said, and they did. Later that night Wallace asked Young, "Harold, what's a shitheel?"

    Interviews, Harold Young, R. C. Slagle, Robert Calvert, Walter Hall; *NYT,* May 24, 1944, Oct. 12, 1948; *AA,* May 21, 23, 24, June 2, 3, 1944; *AS,* May 23, 1944; *SAE,* May 24, 1944; *DMN,* May 24, June 3, 1944; *Time,* Oct. 21, 1957; McKay, *Texas,* pp. 434–38, 445; David et al., *Presidential,* vol. 3, p. 332; Blum, *The Price,* pp. 412, 422, *passim; Official Report, Democratic National Convention, 1944,* pp. 16, 10103–7; Letter, Sam Rayburn to Clara Driscoll; a confidential source.

15. Carroll Kilpatrick, *WP,* May 23, 1971; White, *The Responsibles,* p. 31, and *Majesty,* p. 13; Miller, *Plain,* pp. 197–98; *NYT,* April 13, 1945; Interview, Dorothy Palmie Alford (JL); speech by LJ at Stephenville, Tx., Nov. 1959 (which I covered).

16. Interview, Dorothy Nichols (JL); Letters, LJ to Harry Truman (two), Truman to LJ (two), TL, Sel. Doc., Pres. Psl. File.

45. Roosevelt in History

No Notes.

46. The Congressman and the Radio Station

1. Under the 1943 agreement, Ulmer had been replaced in the situation by W. M. Roberts of Tyler, or so it appeared from the documents. What had become of Ulmer's interest, just how Roberts was involved, was not clear. Roberts made statements in Tyler, but not on the record. From other sources it appeared that Ulmer and Roberts were associated in the KTBC enterprise, although Ulmer was on the scene in Austin while Roberts had stayed in Tyler. Ulmer put off reporters who tried to interview him on these matters.

    The instrument by which Bird acquired KTBC, dated January 18, 1943, began: "Memorandum of agreement between A. W. Walker, Jr., R. A. Stuart and R. B. Anderson, for convenience called 'Sellers,' and Claudia T. Johnson, for convenience designated 'Buyer'. . . . " The Anderson group agreed to sell all their stock in the KTBC company to Mrs. Johnson for the $17,500, but the bank was to distribute the money—in four different sums to the estate of J. M. West, Professor Walker of the Anderson group, W. M. Roberts of Tyler, and the bank. The $6,000 that went to the bank, the largest sum, happened to be the same sum Commissioner Payne had been told a couple of years earlier was to have been paid to the Anderson group for getting the original license for Ulmer.

2. Interviews, Fagan Dickson, Clifford Durr, Charles I. Francis, LJ (May, 1959, and Dec. 14, 1967), E.G. Kingsbery, Rosel Hyde, J.C. Kellam, and cf. Clifford Durr (JL); the files and records on KTBC examined at the Federal Communications Cmsn. in Washington, D.C.; Haley, *A Texan,* pp. 60–66; Louis Kohlmeier, *Wall Street Journal,* March 23, 24, 1964; Chesly Manley, *Chicago Tribune,* Oct. 25, 1964; John Barron, *Washington Evening Star,* June 9, 1964; RD, "The Johnsons'."

3. Concerning Busby's draft of an article defending Johnson from election-theft suspicions, the publisher for whom it was being prepared was Houston Harte, head of the Harte-Hanks newspaper chain, but the record I have seen is not clear that the draft was actually sent to Harte.

    Halberstam, *The Powers,* pp. 439–40; JL, LBJA Sel. Names, box 11 (Birdwell folder), box 12 (Bolton folder), boxes 14, 15 (Clark folders), box 20 (KTBC, Deason folders), box 22 (Kellam folder): Letters, LJ to Ed Clark, LJ to Jesse Kellam (two), Kellam to the Johnsons (two), Kellam to Walter Jenkins, Jenkins to Kellam, Paul Bolton to Jenkins, LJ to Willard Deason, Jenkins to Bill Kennedy, Jenkins to Bob Tatum, Jenkins to Tom Carson, Jenkins to George Frey, LJ to E.M. DeGuerin, Sherman Birdwell to LJ, LJ to Birdwell, Jenkins to LJ, all between Oct. 30, 1943, and Aug. 16, 1954, as described in the text.

4. Interview, LJ (May, 1959); Douglas, *Go,* p. 409.

47. The Brown & Root of the Matter

1. Harrison, "Lyndon."
2. Brown & Root was incorporated on July 2, 1929, with a capital stock of $200,000. The first three directors were Herman Brown and his wife, Margaret Root Brown, and George Brown. Herman Brown paid in $155,000, his wife $30,000, George Brown $10,000, and W. A. Woolsey $5,000. By 1936 the directors were the Brown brothers, Woolsey, and a fourth person. The two Browns and Woolsey were the only directors of the company as of December 28, 1942.

   These facts are taken from information Texas law requires corporations to file with the secretary of state's office.

   Everett Collier, *Houston Chronicle,* Dec. 18, 1950; *Houston Post,* Nov. 16, 1962.
3. Interviews, Hal Hazelrigg, George Fuermann; *Business Week,* May 24, 1957; *AA,* Sept. 10, Dec. 4, 1936; *AS,* Sept. 25, 1936.
4. The Bureau of Reclamation of the Department of Interior, an official thereof advised me in 1959, is required to advertise for bids, open them publicly, and award the contract to the lowest responsible bidder complying with conditions of the bid.

   "Because our contracting procedure is strictly governed by law, political influence cannot affect a contract award," this official said. ". . . most of the political effort on reclamation work is directed toward authorizations and appropriations for projects."

   While this may be arguable, the figures are persuasive. Mansfield Dam was built in two stages, the low-dam and the full-height stages. Brown & Root-McKenzie Construction Co. bid $5,781,235, compared to Utah Construction's $5,909,049 and W. E. Callahan's $7,332,496 on the low dam; Brown & Root-McKenzie bid $3,137,495 to Al Johnson's $3,353,649 on a phase of the full-height dam, and in these two cases B&R-McKenzie got the contract. But B&R-McKenzie bid higher than a competitor on another phase of the full-height dam and lost out on that.

   Letters, Grant Bloodgood, Asst. Cmsr. and Chief Engineer, Bureau of Reclamation, Department of the Interior, Denver, Colo., to RD, with bid documents enclosed, and Alfred R. Golze, Asst. Cmsr., the same agency, Washington, D.C., to RD.
5. Notice was received in Austin that the Department of the Interior had approved the contract with B&R-McKenzie to build the Mansfield Dam early in December, 1936. The dam was still a $10-million flood control project at this point. About 1,500 to 1,700 workers were to be employed, compared to the 350 men by then working for Morrison-Knudsen on the Inks Dam upriver from the Mansfield site. Herman Brown, president of B&R, announced that ground was to be broken for the Mansfield Dam early in January, 1937 (*AA,* Dec. 4, 1936.) Congressman James Buchanan died Feb. 22, 1937.

   The Mansfield Dam was built near the Marshall ford and was called the Marshall Ford Dam at first. It was given its present name in 1941.

   Cf. Evans and Novak, *Lyndon,* p. 9. The statement there that Alvin Wirtz and Johnson saw to it that the contract for a dam in Johnson's district went to the Browns would seem to be predicated on the idea that it was awarded after Johnson became a congressman. It was awarded before then.
6. An advertisement for Johnson in his 1937 campaign contained the statement: "When the Colorado River project first came to Washington, Johnson's help as a secretary who could get things done was enlisted by those trying to get the work started." *Brenham Banner Press,* March 24, 1937.

7. Johnson's 1941 Senate campaign called attention to the fact that "defense construction is now underway" at both the Corpus and and Houston sites. (A campaign poster, "Roosevelt and Unity," on file at the Barker History Center, University of Texas, Austin.) In Booth Mooney's semiauthorized book on Johnson (who wrote in a preface to it that he had read and liked it), Johnson was given more credit than anyone for the location of the base at Corpus and was said to have guided the Roosevelt administration in designating Houston and Orange as sites for shipyards. (Mooney, *The Lyndon,* p. 36; cf. Newlon, *L.B.J.,* p. 140.) Mooney's source could have been a *DMN* story June 22, 1941, in which the reporter wrote after talking with Johnson, "His was the Texas hand that guided the administration" in designating the shipyard locations, but it's likelier that Johnson was the source of both reports himself.

   AAS, July 23, 1939; *AA,* Aug. 22, 1948; on Vinson, Interview, Carl Vinson (JL). On correspondence, see the next note.
8. *Houston Post,* Nov. 16, 1962; *Houston Chronicle,* Dec. 18, 1950; Fuermann, *Houston,* pp. 152–53; and, all following from JL, LBJA Sel., boxes 12 and 13 (George and Herman Brown fdrs.) and box 15 (Connally fdr.): Memo, Herman Brown to J.E. Van Hoose, and Letters, Gene Latimer, Jr., to Mrs. George Brown, George Brown to Roy Miller (copy to LJ), John Connally to LJ, George Brown to LJ (seven), LJ to George Brown (seven), George Brown to LaBJ (two), LaBJ to George Brown (two), and identical telegrams, LJ to George and Herman Brown, all between April 16, 1939, and Sept. 25, 1942, as described in the text.
9. Interview, Mary Rather (JL), and see *Variety,* Nov. 25, 1959.
10. JL, LBJA Sel. Names, boxes 12 and 13 (Geo. and Her. Brown fdrs.), box 15 (Connally fdr.): Letters, George Brown to LJ (six), LJ to George Brown (six), LJ to the George Browns (three), LJ to Mrs. George Brown (two), John Connally to LJ, LJ to the Herman Browns, LJ to Herman Brown (three), Walter Jenkins to Herman Brown, George Brown to LaBJ, LaBJ to George Brown (two), and Tgm., LJ to Herman Brown, all between May 27, 1939, and Nov. 3, 1958, as described in the text.
11. Interview, Wright Morrow; *AA,* Jan. 24, 1945, and see *AA,* April 6, 1946; *Houston Chronicle,* Sept. 17, 1946, Feb. 8, 1950, Sept. 18, 1955; *Houston Post,* Nov. 16, 1962; see *Houston Press,* Nov. 17, 1962.
12. Letter, Harold D. McCoy (Interstate Commerce Cmsn.) to RD; Interview, Charles I. Francis, and see Interview, J.R. Parten (JL); *Houston Post,* Jan. 29, 1967, and see *Houston Post,* Nov. 16, 1962; Hurt, "The Most"; Texas Eastern Transmission Corp., 20th annual report, 1966; JL, Sel. Names, Wirtz fdr., Letters, Alvin Wirtz to LJ, LJ to Wirtz.

    Three years after the pipeline sale to Texas Eastern, the Senate preparedness subcommittee, of which Johnson had just become chairman, denounced the munitions board, the highest supply agency in the Department of Defense, for disposing of military surplus with "less prudence than they would display in operating a charity bazaar." The panel urged that the board disapprove from then on all sales of industrial facilities capable of war production, except where the sale or lease of them was the only alternative to keeping them idle a long time. (*NYT,* Nov. 22, 1950.)
13. Interview, Frank (Posh) Oltorf (JL).
14. *NYT,* Jan. 27, 31, Feb. 28, March 4, 19–22, May 8, Aug. 25, Sept. 28, 29, Dec. 29, 1952, and see *NYT,* Feb. 20, 1953; *AA,* May 8, 1952, Nov. 7, 1953; *Fort Worth Star-Telegram,* Nov. 15, 1950, Jan. 12, 1954; *Houston Chronicle,* Oct. 11, 1961, Nov. 16, 1962; *DMN,* Jan. 10, 1955; *Houston Post,* Dec. 11, 12, 1951, Aug. 4, 1957; *Houston Press,* April 1, 1954; *Business Week,* May 25, 1957; Letter, Warren E. Young (Navy Bureau of Yards and Docks) to RD, and Letter and enclosure, Col. B.A. Saholsky (an Army procurement officer) to RD.
15. JL, LBJA Sel. Names, box 12 (Geo. Brown fdrs.), Letters, George Brown to LJ, LJ to George Brown; Letter, Virginia Durr to RD; Interview, Charles I. Francis; *DMN,* Aug. 18, 1960, June 21, 1964.

48. Texas New Dealers Break the Unions

1. Interview, Harry Acreman.
2. *DMN,* Feb. 17, 1943.
3. *CR 1943,* vol. 89, pp. A829, 1079, 1118–19, 1416. The index to the *Congressional Record* for 1944 does not mention absenteeism, about which many entries were indexed in 1943.
4. The Smith-Connally Act, S. 796, titled the "War Labor Disputes Act," prohibited strikes at government-operated war plants. Since the president had emergency power to seize war plants, this meant war-work strikes could be prohibited by the president. The House passed S. 796 238 to 136 and overrode the veto 244 to 108. The Senate overrode also, and the bill became law.

   On the other hand, Johnson went along as the House approved overtime pay for government workers.

   CR 1943, vol. 89, pp. 3201, 3230, 4001, 5392, 6487, 6548–49.
5. *AS,* Oct. 1, 3–5, 13, 1945; *AA,* Oct. 2–5, 9, 13, 1945.
6. This year Johnson also voted for the anti-Petrillo act "to prohibit certain coercive practices" affecting radio broadcasting. Although there was no record vote, Johnson said in the course of the 1948 campaign that he had favored it.

   CR 1946, vol. 92, pp. 1566, 5762, 6674–78.
7. Velie, "Do."
8. Interview, Hal Hazelrigg; *Proceedings 1947, Texas State Federation of Labor,* pp. 118–20.
9. *Proceedings 1950, Texas State Federation of Labor,* pp. 117–18.
10. A story in the *Houston Chronicle* called it "probably Texas' biggest labor-management lawsuit." There has been nothing like it since.

    A Texas appeals court found that the temporary injuction was not invalid, "it appearing that these union activities are in violation of Texas statutes outlawing the closed shop and secondary boycott."

    The same court also stated:

    "We find no evidence that appellee [Brown & Root] is engaged in a campaign to flout the labor laws or to destroy labor organizations. . . . There is little, if any, evidence that appellee does not maintain excellent working conditions." Its safety record, the ruling indicated, was 31% better than average.

    "There is some evidence," the court continued, "that in all instances appellee does not pay union wages to employees of the same classification. Appellee explains that this is due to the kind of construction work performed by it, which is heavy construction . . . and that in this type of construction carpenters, electricians, plumbers and other craftsmen need not have or exercise as great skill as is required in the construction of buildings, and that less skill being required less wages are paid."

    Attorneys for labor in the case were Mullinax, Wells, and Ball, Marion C. Ladwig, Creekmore Fath, Robert Eckhardt, Dixie & Ryan, W. A. Combs, and Combs, Brown & Brock.

    For Brown & Root the attorneys were Powell, Wirtz & Rauhut, John B. Connally, Ben H. Powell, Jr., A. J. Wirtz, Looney, Clark & Moorhead, R. Dean Moorhead, and Donald S. Thomas, all of Austin.

    Texas Federation of Labor vs. Brown & Root, Texas Court of Civil Appeals, Third Supreme Judicial District, no. 9984, Feb. 6, 1952 (Labor Relations Reference Manual, vol. 29, pp. 2467–76); *Houston Chronicle,* Oct. 3, 17, Nov. 9, 20, 1950, and April 17, 1951; *Fort Worth Star-Telegram,* Nov. 15, 1950, Jan. 7, 1952; Interview, L. N. D. Wells; *Proceedings 1952, Texas State Federation of Labor,* pp. 91–93.
11. The tank contract was reported to be the subject of a Department of Justice investigation in 1954, but Brown Booth, a B&R spokesman, said the only investigation he knew of was a routine final audit.

    Brown & Root, Inc., and International Union, United Automobile, Aircraft, and Agricultural Implement Workers of America (UAW-CIO), Case No. 39-CA-322, June 8, 1955, *Decisions and Orders of the National Labor Relations Board,* vol. 112, pp. 1068–80; *Houston Chronicle,* Jan. 20, May 15, Aug. 1, 1951; Neil McNeil, *Houston Press,* April 1, 1954; Interview, Cliff Potter; Letters, Frederick Curley and George L. Hawkes to RD.
12. Ozark Dam Contructors was the name of the consortium that got the con-

tract; under the name of Flippin Materials Co., the same nine companies got the contract to provide crushed stone aggregate for the dam. Morrison-Knudsen used union labor (Brown & Root did not). Trade unions struck on Dec. 3, 1948. A finding that Ozark had refused to bargain collectively was made by the NLRB on Oct. 13, 1949, and by the Court of Appeals for the Eighth Circuit on July 5, 1951. In 1952 the NLRB held that a list of employees in effect had been discriminatorily denied reinstatement; Ozark and Flippin resisted enforcement, and in 1953 the St. Louis Court of Appeals, Eighth Circuit, granted enforcement as to Ozark, but denied it as to Flippin. In 1958 there were hearings; in 1960 an examiner's recommendations; in 1961 an NLRB order; in 1963, a court decision about holding some of the back pay in trust.

For a general statement of the case and detailed citations, *NLRB v. Brown & Root, Inc., et al.,* U.S. Court of Appeals, Eighth Circuit (St. Louis), No. 14,680, Jan. 4, 1963, 52 Labor Relations Reference Manual, pp. 2115 *et seq.*

13. Brown Booth's letter to Rayburn was written on the Houston letterhead of "Post Office Box Three," Brown & Root's, on April 11, 1959. Apparently Rayburn did not reply. (RL.)

    On Johnson's labor record, see Dugger, "Johnson's."

49. Toying with Prophecy

1. I entered the University of Texas as a freshman in 1947 and was a student of Montgomery's in several courses, so I heard his speeches on this subject several times. What he said never left me. Even when his statements were incorrect, which they sometimes were, his hyperbole rang true. He announced the new world, or the end of everything.

   Paul Bolton, the news director of the Johnsons' KTBC, heard Montgomery make the quoted speech and reported it on radio with profound alarm. ". . . he is preaching salvation, yours and mine," Bolton said. ". . . if he doesn't convince you that we must have a brotherhood of man, he'll certainly do what he did to that luncheon club today. He'll scare the living hell out of you." Johnson put Bolton's report of the speech into the *Congressional Record.* Later in his 1946 campaign he said he had heard this fellow say he could "put into his hollow tooth" enough atomic energy to wipe out London.

   For a summary of the events leading up to Hiroshima and accounts proving the pilots in the atomic squadron were jealously competing for the honor of dropping the first bomb, see Dugger, *Dark Star, passim.*

   For Montgomery's speech, *CR 1946,* vol. 92, pp. A827–828. On Montgomery himself see *Daily Texan,* Oct. 18, 1945; *AAS,* June 6, 1948, Aug. 27, 1967.

2. In 1945 Congressman Rankin of Mississippi sought to make the House committee on un-American activities permanent, and 40 members, among them Johnson, were "not voting." By a vote of 208 to 186, un-Americanism became the officially assigned business of a standing committee of the House. Later that session Johnson had again joined the abstainers on giving the committee some money.

   In 1946, on the question of asking the Speaker to certify the committee's report concerning the refusal of the head of an "anti-fascist" organization to yield up records, the no votes dwindled to 4, but the "not voting" position became almost a cause with 88 members, including Johnson, so recorded. In April Johnson abandoned the nonvoters (who still numbered 82) and voted to cite 16 of those antifascists for contempt of Congress. The posse grew. The Dies committee had already compiled a card-index system of more than a million separate cards about "un-American activities and . . . people engaged in un-American activities," and the Wood-Rankin committee was becoming even more zealous. The librarian of Congress came under attack; a congressman said a Communist group was trying to raise money to beat him back home. For the moment Johnson had had all he could take and on the question of appropriating $75,000 to HUAC, on May 17, 1946, he voted no. With 108 not voting, the appropriation passed, 240 to 81.

   CR 1945, vol. 91, pp. 15, 1857; *1946,*

vol. 92, pp. 2752–53, 3772–73, 5209–24.

3. Interview, LJ (Dec. 14, 1967); Acheson, *Present,* pp. 154–5, cf. McLellan, *Dean*, pp. 73–82; Coit, *Mr.,* pp. 560–608; Bernstein, "New"; *AS,* Jan. 9, 1946, *Daily Texan,* Jan. 19, 1946; see Yost, *History,* p. 130.
4. Why was the 1940 draft extended? Because, said the congressman handling the bill, "it is believed by the officials of the War Department, and of the Army . . . that it is necessary . . . in order to tide us over, so to speak, the period of transition from war to peace, and pending the solution of many grave problems that are now under consideration by diplomats and statesmen representing our government." When asked what U.S. military commitments were, the sponsor could not answer, but, he said, we had to stay in Germany, Japan, and Korea until the recent enemies were wholly subdued. In short, it was done; the pattern was set.

   On the topic of the seventy-group air force, Johnson said, "In the name of heaven, if [the Joint Chiefs] say we should have 70 modern groups, why not recommend that?"

   CR 1946, vol. 92, pp. 3585, 3588, 3713; *Daily Texan,* April 23, 1946; see *AA,* July 5, 1946.
5. *Brenham Banner-Press,* June 14, July 22, 1946; *AA,* July 9, 12, 13, 17, 18, 20, 1946; *CR 1946,* vol. 92, pp. A3170–71.

50. "Enriched in Office"

1. Johnson's antistrike proposal has to be considered as a whole to see that it would abolish collective bargaining. It was reported by the Austin newspaper:

   ". . . Johnson declared he favored the use of a federal referee similar to the setup for a referee in bankruptcy. Under such a plan, differences between management and labor would be referred to the referee who would make his decision. Either side could appeal to federal courts and if necessary to the Supreme Court, but meanwhile there would be no work stoppages. In the event the referee's decision was upheld on the appeal and either side refused to abide by the ruling, punitive action would follow.

   "In the event the manufacturer balked, the government would prohibit that corporation from indulging in interstate commerce.

   "Should a labor union balk at the decision, the union's privilege, now provided for by statute, to determine its own bargaining agent would be withdrawn.

   "Johnson advocated that such referees be appointed for life at a salary of $10,000 in each federal judicial district and that the referees be responsible to no one."

   I have drawn the conclusion that if, in the event of a strike contrary to such a referee's decision, the union is denied the right to choose its own collective bargaining agent, collective bargaining has been abolished.

   Texts of speeches by Hardy Hollers in 1946; *Brenham Banner Press,* July 15, 1946; *AA,* Jan. 9, May 28, June 28, 1946.
2. *AA,* Feb. 24, Mar. 27, July 2, 8, 9, 12, 19, 1946, Sept. 18, 1947, *AS,* July 21, 1946; *Brenham Banner Press,* June 10, 1946; *CR 1946,* Vol. 92, pp. 10660, 10745.
3. *Brenham Banner Press,* July 22, 1946, and other sources.
4. See note 1, chapter 69.

   Brenham Banner Press, July 11, 18, 1946; *AA,* July 27, 1946; Interview, Edmunds Travis.
5. Interview, LJ (Dec. 14, 1967); *AA,* July 2, 11, 12, 20, 23, 24, 1946.
6. Interview, Edmunds Travis; *AA,* July 16, 27, 1946.
7. The final vote was Johnson 42,980, Hollers 17,782, and a minor candidate 2,468. (*Texas Almanac,* 1947–1948, p. 403.)

   Hollers stated his opposition to Johnson for president in 1964 on a "Doctors for Goldwater" statewide TV program in Texas. Speaking after the Walter Jenkins affair, Hollers compared Johnson to "Hitler and his crew of very curious people" and said the civil rights act of 1964 gave the president "all the power A. Hitler ever had." Another speaker on this program said Hubert Humphrey was a Socialist, that Johnson was "pretty much branded with the same brand," and that socialism and communism were about the same. (Texas TV, Oct. 28, 1964.)

51. The Policy of Secret War

1. Pachter, "Revisionist."
2. Francis L. Lowenheim, *NYT,* Mar. 27, 1972; Horowitz, *The Free,* p. 31; R. Lasch, "How"; Schlesinger, *The Crisis,* pp. 78–110; cf. Truman, *Memoirs,* vol. I, pp. 108–9, and see pp. 255, 263–64.
3. Davies, "The China"; testimony of Allen S. Whiting, a former State Department official, before the Senate Foreign Relations Committee, June 28, 1971, excerpted in *WP,* July 1, 1971; Schram, *Mao,* pp. 231, 238, 242–45.
4. Anderson, *The Presidents',* pp. 122–23; see, Horowitz, *The Free,* cf. Revere, *Waist,* p. 27.
5. McLellan, *Dean*, pp. 107–19, 274*n.;* Acheson, *Present,* pp. 215–25; Kennan, *Memoirs, 1925–1950,* pp. 311–14, 319–22; Schlesinger, *The Crisis,* pp. 78–110; R. Lasch, "How"; Graebner, "The Cold"; Geyelin, *Lyndon,* p. 71; Fulbright, "In Thrall"; Morgenthau, "Globalism."
6. Johnson's rhetoric as he locked on the armor of a Cold Warrior shows he understood the implications. "The only thing a bully understands," he said, "is force, and the one thing he fears is courage. In making this assertion, I disavow the demagoguery of a jingo. I repudiate the tactics of a warmonger. I want peace. But human experience teaches me that if I let a bully of my community make me travel back streets to avoid a fight, I merely postpone the evil day. Soon he will try to chase me out of my house."

   Acheson, *Present,* pp. 222, 226–30; McLellan, *Dean,* p. 132; Hayes, *The Beginning,* pp. 3, 62; Burns, ed., *To Heal,* p. 20; *AA,* May 8, Aug. 1, Sept. 30, Oct. 23, 24, Dec. 26, 1947; *CR 1947,* vol. 93, pp. 10578, A3200; *CR 1949,* vol. 95, p. 10807; Evans and Novak, *Lyndon,* pp. 19–20.
7. Church, Tower et al., *Alleged,* p. 9; LJ to AP, April 23, 1947, quoted in Sherrill, *The Accidental,* p. 109.

52. Running against the Reds and the Goons

1. *NYT,* April 6, 7, 9, 1948, and see Drew Pearson, *DMN,* April 28, 1948.; JL, LBJA Sel. Names, box 31, Sid Richardson fdr.: Letters, LJ to Sid Richardson (four), Walter Jenkins to W.F. Matheny (two), Glynn Stegall, Matheny to Jenkins, Waldemar A. Von Schoeler, Memos, Don Cook to LJ, Jenkins to LJ, Tgm., LJ to Matheny.
2. Interview, Harold Young; see Mooney, *The Lyndon,* pp. 55–56.
3. Johnson remembered this hesitancy quite differently for Kearns: his work in the House and his money-making having become routine, he felt something missing from his life, but feared at first to run for the Senate because if he lost, his House seat would be gone, too, and he could not bear the thought of losing everything.

   Interview, LJ (Dec. 14, 1967); Kearns, *Lyndon,* p. 100.
4. Provence, *Lyndon,* pp. 76–77; Interview, LJ, (Dec. 14, 1967) and see Singer and Sherrod, *Lyndon,* pp. 175–76; *AA,* May 13, 1948, and see *AA,* June 23, 29, Aug. 28, 1948, and McKay, *Texas,* pp. 27, 114, 167, 169–70; on O'Daniel, a confidential, authoriative source.
5. Old-line Democrat Sam Rayburn, the House Speaker and Johnson's mentor, took an even harder segregationist line in 1948. In a letter that year Rayburn wrote, " . . . I have voted in this Congress against federal repeal of the poll tax law. I am against the so-called federal anti-lynching law. I have been opposed to the Fair Employment Practice Commission and still am and shall vote against it and against any bill that has any tendency towards crippling our segregation laws or any other part of the program that has to do with, in what I consider, interference of our local rights." Letter, Sam Rayburn to R. H. Cochran.

   In the main, Johnson desisted from repeating his position on these issues during his Senate campaign. In December, elected, he waffled back toward certain civil rights, if the state provided them. "I favor repeal of the poll tax, but not by the federal government," he said then. "I will never vote for it in Washington. And the same goes for the federal anti-lynching law and the FEPC." *DMN,* Dec. 8, 1948.
6. "Americans believe," Johnson said in his opener, "it's still possible to sit at a conference table and work out differences. Both the John L. Lewises and the reactionary labor-baiters must be

subject to the law. Neither side must be allowed to ruin our country."

7. "In 1941," Johnson said, "I repudiated any such socialistic doctrine [socialized medicine] and . . . since then I have worked for the doctor-recommended plan of building hospitals." He was for more doctors and nurses, too; more public health work; higher old-age assistance.

   He had introduced a bill, and then warmly supported another one, providing federal aid for constructing hospitals. "Before the Congress starts talking about socialized medicine," he said in this context in 1946, "we ought to get enough doctors to take care of our people." *CR 1946,* vol. 92, p. A2154.
8. Steinberg, *The Man,* p. 303; *DMN,* May 23, July 10, 1948; *AA,* May 26, June 23, 1948.
9. Johnson's proposal was that on discovery wells, the depletion allowance be increased to 30%. In Washington late in July, 1948, he was reported urging the creation of a committee to be headed by a Texas railroad commissioner that would advise on increasing the depletion allowance to stimulate wildcat drilling.

   Sakowitz, "The 1948," thesis; *DMN,* July 9, 15, 29, 1948; *AA,* July 29, 1948.
10. Johnson answered, "I have voted to support the investigations of the House un-American activities committee with these specific votes: January, 1939, February of the same year, again in 1940 and on down through the years, in 1941, 1943, and on numerous other subsequent years including the year 1948." He said the vote Stevenson criticized was against an appropriation for HUAC that was unnecessary because the committee had not used up its preceding appropriation.

    McKay, *Texas,* p. 183; *DMN,* July 20, Aug. 17, 25, 1948; *AA,* Aug. 19, 1948.
11. *AA,* April 21, July 3, 1948.
12. Johnson also said, "If Joe Stalin knows we're armed and ready for him, he won't try anything," but did not think the U.S. could stay out of war "if Stalin thinks we are weak."

    Truman and Secretary of Defense James Forrestal did not think seventy groups were needed for the air force. The 1948 appropriations bill provided a fifty-nine-group air force.

    AA, Mar. 26, April 18, May 5, 11, July 3, 11, 18, Dec. 7, 1948; *DMN,* July 4, Aug. 20, 27, 1948; *CR 1948,* vol. 94, pp. 2882–3.
13. On military spending and prosperity, as on many issues at one time or another, Johnson expressed variant opinions. In 1953 he said, "I do not believe in using the defense effort for so-called pump-priming."

    AA, May 5, July 23, Aug. 19, 1948; *DMN,* July 22, 1948; McKay, *Texas,* pp. 191, 205, 229, 234; speech, LJ, May 24, 1953 (text).
14. *DMN,* June 25, Aug. 13, 17, 27, 1948; *AA,* June 24, Aug. 6, 13, 18, 26, 1948; *Proceedings, 1948, Texas State Federation of Labor,* Fort Worth, June 21–25, 1948; McKay, *Texas,* pp. 225; Interview, Harry Acreman; *El Paso Herald-Post,* Aug. 10, 1948.
15. McKay, *Texas,* p. 212; *DMN,* July 18, 1948; *AA,* July 21, Aug. 5, 6, 1948.
16. *DMN,* Aug. 18, 1948; McKay, *Texas,* p. 208.
17. McKay, *Texas,* pp. 191, 205, 229; *AA,* Aug. 24, 1948.
18. Interviews, John Connally, Claude Wild, Sr., Coke Stevenson; *AA,* July 28, Aug. 24, 1948; another source.
19. Interview, Claude Wild, Sr.; other sources.
20. A poll in the week before Johnson announced showed that Stevenson was first, Johnson second in public esteem, compared to less support for Dies and O'Daniel. With the field shaped up, Stevenson led Johnson more than two to one, but by late June Johnson had cut the margin to ten points, and by July Johnson was shown barely leading with 42% to Stevenson's 39% and Peddy's 16%. *AAS,* May 6, 1948; *DMN,* June 20, 1948; *AA,* July 23, 1948.
21. The seven heroes were Merrill Connally, a twice-wounded Marine sniper and John's brother; a survivor of a Japanese prison camp; an airman shot down in a Flying Fortress; a pilot who flew thirty-five bombing missions; a submarine man; a soldier wounded at Salerno; a Fort Worth man shot down over Italy and captured by the Germans. The private who was reburied in the town El Campo was named Rudolph J. Jecemenek.

    AA, June 12, 29, 1948; *DMN,* July 3, 10, Aug. 18, 1948.
22. Interviews, Ghent Sanderford, Mrs. Margaret Carter, Walter Hall, Mark Adams; Nalle, *The Fergusons,* pp. 256, 262; McKay, *Texas,* pp. 213–18; Letter, Walter Hall to RD. On von Schleicher, see Shirer, *The Rise,* pp. 3, 150–52, *passim.*

53. "Son, They're All My Helicopters"

1. According to Booth Mooney, the aviatrix Jacqueline Cochran, a friend of Johnson's, played a role as the campaign opened. Once again Johnson's ailments had come to his aid for a campaign: shortly after his opening speech he had developed a kidney infection, and Cochran had flown him to the Mayo Clinic in Minnesota.

   Mooney, *The Lyndon,* p. 59.
2. My source, Paul Mansfield, at seventeen was the oldest member of the quartet. The boys had been singing on WFAA in Dallas, but they lost the spot because of their work for Johnson. Mansfield never sang at the White House.
3. Letter, Paul Mansfield to RD; *AA,* about June 1 (undated) and June 16, 25, 27, July 18, Aug. 4, 1948; *DMN,* July 18, 24, 1948; *Time,* June 28, 1948; *AAS,* May 25, July 25, 1948; and Margaret Mayer, *AAS,* June 27, 1948; Bob Schieffer, a CBS correspondent, on CBS Jan. 24, 1973, and letter, Schieffer to RD; Interviews, Coke Stevenson, Lamar Holley, Claude Wild, and one other; McKay, Texas, p. 213.
4. Interviews, Jim Mashman, Bob Lichten; *WP,* Nov. 20, 1967.

54. A Meeting in the Dark of Night

1. Interview, LJ (Dec. 14, 1967); *Texas Almanac,* 1949–1950, pp. 218, 459.
2. *AA,* July 25, 31, Aug. 1, 3, 1948; *DMN,* July 27, 1948.
3. *El Paso Herald-Post,* Aug. 9, 10, 1948.
4. Letters, W. Don Ellinger to RD, George W. Cowart to RD, Jack Brooks to LJ (RL).
5. "Johnson Journal," Aug. 1948, "Editor . . . Mrs. John Connally, published by friends of Lyndon Johnson . . .".
6. Interview, Lamar Holley; cf., *DMN,* Aug. 27, 1948.
7. There are minor discrepancies in the tellings of Bird's roles in the campaign, mostly having to do with their timing.

   Smith, *A President's,* p. 140; *PP 1964,* p. 1488; Newlon, *L.B.J.,* p. 207; Interview, LJ (Dec. 14, 1967); *AAS,* Aug. 29, 1948.
8. McCrory said the commissioner (whose name I am omitting because of the confusion surrounding the available information) told him the meeting occurred close to the river at the bridal path in Brackenridge Park and that he did, indeed, go on the mission to south Texas. Knight said the meeting occurred at Olmos Park, at Franklin Fields.

   Interviews, James McCrory, James Knight, and LJ (Dec. 14, 1967).
9. Interviews, Maury Maverick, Jr., and Malcolm Bardwell.
10. Knight told me this in the fall of 1975. I had just asked him again about the night meeting in the park in 1948. He gave a short answer and then, without explanation, launched into the remarks quoted. He died in 1976.

55. The Cactus Fields of Boss Power

1. I benefited especially, preparing for this account about the south Texas bosses and for related reportage later in this book, from the generosity of James Rowe, who permitted me to read his unpublished manuscript about the subject. Other sources: Schendel, "Something"; *Houston Press,* Sept. 7, 1948; Bryson, *The Social,* thesis; James Rowe, *CCCT,* Sept. 9, 1948, quoting E. L. Shoumette; Wick Fowler, *DMN,* Oct. 31, 1948; Huie, "Murder"; Interviews, James Rowe, Harry Benge Crozier, Robert Calvert, M. B. Bravo, A. J. Vale, Allan Shivers (JL), Bob Mullen, SHJ; a confidential source; and see, Williams, *Huey,* p. 273.

56. A Hinge of History

1. The Corpus Christi newspaper for which Rowe worked (or at least the edition on microfilm) did not report, the morning after the election, any figures from Box 13 or Jim Wells County, but Rowe's testimony is specific.

   Throughout my account of the 1948 election controversy, a basic source is the full court record on file in the Fort Worth federal courthouse, which will not again be cited, *No. 1640 Civil, Coke R. Stevenson v. Tom L. Tyson, Vann*

M. Kennedy, and Lyndon B. Johnson.

For the opening passages of this chapter, additional sources are: Interviews, Bob Mullen, Luis Salas, John Cofer, Homer Dean, John Connally, C. W. Price, James Rowe, Coke Stevenson, and two others; *Alice Daily Echo,* July 25, 1948; *CCCT,* Aug. 29, 1948; Rowe's unpublished ms.

2. A confidential source; *AA,* Aug. 29, 30, 1948.
3. Salas denied in official proceedings he had given out the 765 to 60 total. I spent time with him twice in 1970 and again in 1975. He received me gently and generously. He was cagey with me, but seemed to want to tell me enough to establish some part of the truth. I liked this old revolutionary immensely.

He said everything quoted to me directly except his remark of sympathy for Stevenson, which he said to my companion on the trip to Alice in 1975, who told me about it.

Concerning the unnamed merchant's reports of Johnson calling Parr, I am not authorized to specify the reporters' documents from which this information is drawn, and I could not locate the merchant to reinterview him.

I tried to question Ed Lloyd without success. "I wonder if I might come talk to you about 1948?" I asked him. "Well, I don't have a thing in the world to say about it," he replied, giving a little laugh. My attempts to interview George Parr and his nephew Archer were also unsuccessful.

My source on the woman flying election materials to Laredo, a source who was on the inside of the Johnson group, said the woman probably did not know what was in the packet. I located her in the Rio Grande Valley on Nov. 20, 1969, and she said, "Whatever it was was private, and it had nothing to do with Lyndon Johnson."

The election official who handed out the election supplies in Alice, B. M. Brownlee, testified before Judge T. Whitfield Davidson (see later) that he had given precinct 13 only about 600 ballots, fewer than 60% of the total reported cast.

Cofer sort of let his information slip one day. He was remembering that he had formed the opinion that Ed Clark, in the law firm with Everett Looney, had not voted for Johnson. "That was Monday morning," Cofer added, "before Ed knew what John Connally and Alvin Wirtz and I knew—that they had put a new certificate (of voting totals) in down in Alice." Thus occurred the only confession on the record that the Box 13 vote-change was known in the uppermost counsels of Johnson's camp as it was happening.

Interviews, Bo Byers, Harry Lee Adams, LJ (Dec. 00, 1967), Mrs. Dan Moody, Homer Dean, Luis Salas, John Cofer, Charles I. Francis, H. Y. Price, Ed Lloyd, Polk Shelton, and others; *AA,* Sept. 23, 1948.

4. "Late yesterday," Johnson said in his statement, "I was told that there were telephone calls to a west central Texas county, urging that at least 200 votes be sent in as a correction. We telephoned our men in that area and they assured us the correct vote was already in. But at 1:30 o'clock this morning our men telephoned that there had been a mistake, and there was a net gain of 225 for Stevenson.

"Last night we were told that a Gulf Coast county had been asked to deliver another 100 votes. We are now advised that a revision has been reported showing this county has made a 'mistake' of 87 votes in favor of Stevenson; and another county in the same vicinity sent in a revision of 23 in favor of Stevenson.

"Up to now, I'm sure that all of the mistakes have been honest mistakes, but nevertheless, Stevenson has been kept in the running by those mistakes. . . .

"In 1941, I lost this office by 1,311 votes, and I was counted out on Wednesday. In 1941, the same men were involved. I lost the senatorial race by 1,311 votes and Coke Stevenson won the governorship by 1,311 votes."

The Saturday after the voting Johnson again spoke of 1941, when, he said, "after leading by more than 5,000 votes for several days last minute returns defeated me . . . and made Coke Stevenson governor." In this statement Johnson used the words, "Remembering 1941. . . ."

AA, Sept. 1, 1948; *AAS,* Sept. 5, 1948; *CCCT,* Sept. 1, 1948.

5. The Texas Election Bureau had reported on Monday that Jim Wells County had gone for Johnson 1,786 to

769. The officially confirmed Jim Wells total was 1,988 to 770. After a week of see-sawing totals, the *Austin American* headlined the switch, "LYNDON SWINGS BACK INTO LEAD BY 17 BALLOTS/Jim Wells County Puts Lyndon Ahead."

Stevenson named the four boss counties he had in mind: Jim Wells, Duval, Starr, and Webb. All except Webb figured directly in subsequent investigations conducted by the federal court in Fort Worth.

AA, Aug. 29–Sept. 5, 1948; *CCCT,* Sept. 3–4, 1948; cf. *NYT,* Aug. 29–Sept. 3, Sept. 5, 1948; *DMN,* Sept. 7, 8, 1948. There is a detailed account of the vote seesawing also in McKay, *Texas,* pp. 237–239.

6. "He (Salas) only said one thing new," Walter Jenkins told me. "That Johnson was with them," I ventured. "Right," Jenkins replied. "And I *know* that wasn't true. I was with him all that day."

I studied through the 5,000 pages of material on the 1948 election that the Johnson Library released. Apart from the draft of a statement by Johnson, undated and never before released, denying knowledge of vote fraud in Jim Wells County, the main interest in the materials was the light thrown on the FBI's role. For my report on this at the time, see the *Texas Observer,* Sept. 23, 1977.

Interviews, Luis Salas, Walter Jenkins; James W. Mangan, Associated Press, *e.g.* in *CCC,* July 31, 1977, and ensuing press comment for several months; Dugger, "Up."

57. Ballots Burning in a Dust Storm

1. Stevenson gave me the dialogue at the bank that I have directly quoted.

Stevenson said that only he and Hamer had gone to the bank together; that Dibrell and Gardner had called on Donald there beforehand. However, at the time of my interview with Stevenson, his memory was shaky. Other witnesses, the contemporary news accounts, and subsequent court testimony generally agree that the Stevenson people went to the bank in a group. Jim Rowe reported the next morning that the members of Stevenson's party were Adams, Dibrell, and Hamer. Adams told me Gardner was there; Gardner testified in court later in the year as a person who had been present. Another witness was reported to be a precinct chairman in Alice. The county attorney was Homer Dean.

Writing sixteen years later, Clyde Wantland, a conservative with sources in the Stevenson camp, re-created the scene in front of the bank as a showdown out of the old West:

"Across the narrow, dusty street five riflemen, trailing Winchester carbines, at the ready, lolled casually in skirmish formation in front of a feed store. Directly before the bank door a dozen or more seasoned fighters, armed with pistols, stood calmly in a half-moon circle."

By Wantland's account, Stevenson and party, escorted by Hamer, approached:

"Captain Hamer waved the Stevenson men to a halt. He stepped forward a few paces to make sure he was recognized. The veteran Ranger Captain was known to every gunman there. He was respected as a stern, inflexible officer who never gave an order until he was prepared to enforce strict and prompt obedience.

"He surveyed slowly, almost casually, the groups on both sides of the street. Then, he crossed over to the riflemen, pointed down the street and spoke just one word—

" 'Git.'

"The captain stood motionless as the five men mumbled angrily and cursed audibly. Presently the mumbling ceased; the riflemen cradled their carbines, with the muzzles lowered, and departed down the street precisely as ordered. . . .

"The Captain crossed back and faced the group before the bank. When the talking and mumbling had quieted down, the Captain spoke just two words—

" 'Fall back.'

"With a minimum of hesitation, the order was obeyed, and a path was cleared to the bank door. Tom Donald opened the door, and Captain Hamer beckoned Gov. Stevenson's men to approach and enter. He took his place in the door and forbade others to enter."

John Cofer said that in the subsequent hearing in federal court, "We proved that was not true about the alphabetical," the alleged alphabetical listing of the last 200 or so names on the poll list. I found no such proof in the court record of the hearing, but neither did witnesses testify there to this feature of the alleged fraud.

Interviews, Coke Stevenson, Harry L. Adams, John Cofer, and others; Dibrell's statements in Jim Rowe's unpublished manuscript on Parr; *CCCT,* Sept. 11, 1948; *DMN,* Sept. 12, 1948; *AAS,* Sept. 12, 1948; *AA,* Sept. 23, 1948; Clyde Wantland, *The Texas Argus,* spring, 1964.

2. The district judge who issued the order, Roy Archer, told me that Everett Looney, Johnson's lawyer in the matter, "wanted a temporary injunction to prevent the destruction of the ballots," but this description of what Archer did does not jibe with the order he actually issued. Adams, in Alice, provided me a photostat of the telegram sent him on Sept. 1, 1948, from Helen Sellers, the clerk of Archer's 126th district court in Austin, prohibiting Adams and the other party officials from eliminating "any votes on the ground of illegality or irregularity" or filing returns showing any result other than the disputed late returns that gave Johnson 200 more votes than the unofficial Saturday night returns.

One of the people accused in Johnson's petition was former Ranger Frank Hamer. In 1949 Hamer charged Johnson with false swearing in the Austin litigation in accusing Hamer of going to Jim Wells County and "by threat and intimidation" attempting to have the voting results changed. The day the affidavit was filed, a Travis County grand jury no-billed Senator Johnson on the charge.

Stevenson tried to get a judge in Alice to order a recanvassing, but the judge there said no, too.

CCCT, Sept. 5, 1948; *DMN,* Sept. 12, 23, Oct. 31, 1948, Oct. 21, 1949; *AA,* Sept. 7, 11, 14, 1948; *WP,* Oct. 21, 1949; *Daily Texan,* Oct. 21, 1949; Interviews, Roy Archer, Harry L. Adams; Letter, Harry L. Adams to RD.

3. The woman who changed her vote was Mrs. Seth Dorbandt of Conroe. Rhea Howard of Wichita Falls cast the challenged proxy for Mrs. Clifford E. Deaton of that city.

Charles Gibson's story, told to Relman Morin of the AP, was that Gibson had developed a killing headache and had left the committee meeting to look for an aspirin. When he returned, Johnson's friends were yelling at him to go vote.

Mrs. Margaret Carter of Fort Worth heard one of the other versions, based on the idea that Gibson was drunk in his room. She said Bill Kittrell of Dallas sobered him up enough to put him under a shower and get him down to the meeting.

The east Texas committee member who proposed to revise his returns in Stevenson's favor was Thomas Y. Abney of Harrison County. Calvert explained what was said to me. Abney's contemplated revision would have given Stevenson 140 votes, enough to elect him.

Interviews, Robert Calvert, Creekmore Fath (on the scene in the hotel lobby), Wright Morrow, John Cofer, Mrs. Margaret Carter, one other; *NYT,* Sept. 14, 1948; Allen Duckworth, *DMN,* Sept. 14, 1948; *AA,* Sept. 14, 1948; Relman Morin, AP from Amarillo, undated; excerpt of an interview, Mrs. Clifford E. Deaton, James V. Alred Collection (provided the author by David Allred); SHJ, *My,* p. 77; cf. Provence, *Lyndon,* pp. 82–83.

4. When Johnson called New Dealer Creekmore Fath of Austin the day before the Fort Worth convention of 1948, it had been, according to Fath, "Creek, buddy, pal, how are you?—he'd love me dearly, he knew all I could do for him, he'd never forget it—all that." To Fath it was not a matter of who had stolen what, but of Johnson versus the reactionary governor who had leased his land to the oil companies. "Sure!" he told Johnson. "Between you and Coke Stevenson, I'm in." At an earlier county convention at which Fath had presided, he had recognized a black to speak and had been denounced as "a nigger-lover" by a certain virulent racist, who now confronted him in the state convention hotel lobby and pulled a knife. They were separated by two men, one of them George Parr. A little later Johnson went up to Fath, put his arm around him, and said, "I heard about

you almost gettin' knifed for me."

The struggle to extract pledges of party loyalty from the right-wing presidential electors had been going on well before the convention. Calvert had wired the twenty-three Texas electors, who had been pledged by the spring state convention to support the national Democratic ticket, demanding they promise to do so. In Fort Worth he told leaders of rightist delegations from Houston and Fort Worth that if they refused to pledge to support Truman, he would help throw them out of the convention. Nevertheless, they so refused. They had clearly won their county conventions, 1,209 to 508 in Houston and 2 to 1 in Fort Worth, but Governor Beauford Jester and his agent Calvert were saying that no matter who had won the county conventions, delegates would not be seated in Fort Worth unless they pledged to Truman.

As the convention opened Calvert ruled the Houston delegation could not vote on their own seating. "They were just a bunch of Republicans—that was the issue," he said. The Houstonians were booted on out, 1,349 to 734; the convention threw out the Fort Worth rightists, and Dallas anti-Trumanites left the convention floor, too. These big-city delegations were then replaced with pro-Truman, and pro-Johnson, people. The Fort Worth rightists, who had made the convention arrangements, angrily carted out every chair, table, typewriter, and adding machine in the hall. Former Governor Allred had to take the microphone and have hats passed so the equipment could be replaced. But the liberals had taken over the state party, and the convention's canvassing committee showed the meaning of this for Johnson, a 28 to 4 vote for certifying him, which the convention then did overwhelmingly.

When I asked Stevenson what he thought of the convention, he laughed.

5. Vann Kennedy, the secretary of the state party, was loyal to Stevenson and would not sign the papers certifying Johnson as the nominee. Cofer, wheedling and cajoling him, said "It was like trying to get a widow woman to sign a mortgage."

   I have not found the photograph of Johnson and Parr, but Cofer said "I saw it taken. I was standing back of the photographer. . . ." On the other hand, my confidential source close to Parr says he did not go to the Fort Worth convention.

   Interviews, Creekmore Fath, Bob Eckhardt, Robert Calvert, LJ (Dec. 14, 1967), Everett Morgan, Jr., John Cofer, a confidential source; *AAS*, Aug. 1, 1948; *AA*, Aug. 3, 6, 14, 15, 16, 1948; *DMN*, Sept. 16, 1948; McKay, *Texas*, p. 239; cf. Arthur Krock, *NYT*, Sept. 26, 1948.

6. Interview, Robert Calvert.

7. In a contest concerning a local office in Brown County a judge had ruled that much of the balloting had been illegal and void, cutting down Stevenson's statewide total by 468 votes. In Galveston County, a grand jury had reported indications of fraud, including, Johnson charged, "transfer of votes from one precinct to another, votes by parties unknown, 'tombstone votes,' and votes by prostitutes who had left the city; and [Stevenson] received practically all of said illegal votes." The Dallas County party chairman was Coke Stevenson's cousin, and the Johnson people said this cousin had made five corrections in the returns in favor of Stevenson.

   In Dallas there were five changes in the returns, but not all of them favored Stevenson. According to the *Dallas Morning News,* the voting machines produced a complete total on election night. A few days later the figures were added again and Stevenson gained about 250. The next day they were re-added and Johnson gained back 200. In copying down that total, someone made a 9 instead of a 7 and Johnson was given 2,000 more votes than he had. The official certificate corrected that error, and the final returns were certified, without protest from Johnson leaders, on Sept. 4.

   In an exculpatory Sept. 6 speech, Johnson had hinted in an inexplicit way at other irregularities favoring Stevenson:

   "They [Stevenson partisans] were strangely silent about the bloc vote which gave my opponent a 30,000-vote lead coming out of three big cities. You didn't hear of the Kenedy County bloc vote where only eight votes were in the Johnson column. You weren't told of the bloc vote in a box behind the locked gates of the King Ranch where not one single vote went to Johnson, nor of the box that came in Tuesday in another county where Johnson's vote was zero. Nobody has asked for an investigation of the Panhandle county where I got just twelve votes or from the River Oaks box of Houston where Stevenson got eight out of every ten votes cast."

As to Brown County, after Davidson's investigation was halted (see later), a court of circuit appeals upheld the invalidation of 1,272 ballots there because of a contest over county judge, giving Johnson, as of the press reports at that point, 466 more votes.

8. The lawyer told Davidson that Johnson replied: "I received a majority. . . . I have a legal right to the nomination. . . . To voluntarily barter away that right would be to stultify myself and result in a betrayal of the Democratic Party and the Democratic voters. . . ."

   In the closing arguments, John Crooker, speaking for Johnson, dripped with constitutionalist sanctimony, speaking of "encroachment of the federal powers in Texas," "this fair nation," "the rights of the sovereign states." Closing for Stevenson, ex-Governor Moody said, "There was corruption. Somebody's been stealing votes. There's something wrong when they won't let a candidate examine the records."

9. While I was discussing 1948 with Johnson, he called Judge Davidson "this old son-of-a-bitch."

   Interviews, John Cofer, T. Whitfield Davidson, LJ (Dec. 14, 1967), Coke Stevenson, another; Letter, Luther E. Jones to Eric Goldman; *DMN,* Sept. 5, 7, 14, 16, 21, 22, 23, 26, 1948 (including work by reporter Allen Duckworth); *AA,* Sept. 3, 22, 23, 30, Oct. 1, 1948 (including work by reporter Margaret Mayer).

10. The *Dallas Morning News* proposed an investigation, and Johnson suggested the FBI do it, with consequences discussed later in the text.

11. Fortas said Wirtz called him into the planning meeting in the Dallas hotel. Luther Jones said Fortas telephoned into the meeting, whereupon Johnson "made Abe come to the hotel."

    Interviews, Abe Fortas (JL), Tom Clark (JL), Wright Morrow, Charles I. Francis, Jack Carter, Mrs. Margaret Carter, Creekmore Fath, confidential sources; *DMN,* Sept. 4, 28, 29, Oct. 28, 1948; *AA,* Sept. 19, 25, 26, 28, 1948; *Daily Texan,* Sept. 28, 1948; *NYT,* Oct. 30, 1948; Steinberg, *The Man,* p. 325; Schendel, "Something"; Letters, Luther Jones to Eric Goldman and Hugo Black to RD. On Truman, cf. Dorough, *Mr. Sam,* p. 406, and *AA,* Nov. 5, 1948.

12. Montague, the lawyer at the Duval hearing, said in 1967, "We've got a president that stole an election."

    The transcript of the Alice hearing is inconclusive on whether all the boxes were opened before the investigation was cut off by Black's orders, and the contemporary press reports appear to be in conflict.

    The custodian of the box, Mrs. Juanita Hulsey, said it was brought in not sooner than thirteen days after the election, and she had hid and kept it. Evidently Salas designated two boxes as probably the ones used in precinct 13. Dawson Duncan of the *Dallas Morning News* said neither was the one pointed out by Mrs. Hulsey. Both the boxes Salas pointed out were opened, but not Mrs. Hulsey's box. Duncan indicated the master meant to open Mrs. Hulsey's box the next day (but the investigation ended that afternoon). The AP reported that two boxes thought to be from precinct 13 were opened and it turned out that one was from precinct 13, one was not. But the AP also reported that, with the assistance of a local locksmith, the master opened "all" of the Jim Wells boxes without locating the missing records.

    Justice Black stated in a letter that he had invited the press to attend the hearing on the Texas election in his office. In his ruling, he said, "It would be a drastic break with the past, which I can't believe Congress ever intended to permit, for a federal judge to go into the business of conducting what is to every intent and purpose a contest of an election in the state. It is impossible to believe that a federal court could go into a state and suspend the orderly process of an election."

    The day after Black's ruling, a state official wired each county judge that the state Democratic party had certified Johnson as the nominee and "he is entitled to have his name printed on the official ballot for the General Election. . . ."

Stevenson asked the entire Supreme Court to throw out Black's ruling, and the court responded with a curious equivocation. Refusing Stevenson's request, the court nevertheless also denied Johnson's requests that it order Davidson's proceedings stopped and issue an order similar to Black's. By this time, Oct. 5, however, Johnson's name had already been ordered onto the ballot and Davidson had called off his investigation. Stevenson's later attempt to get a hearing on his charges of fraud before the high court did not succeed.

Interviews, Polk Shelton, M. B. Bravo, Joe Montague, LJ (Dec. 14, 1967), Clarence Martens, B. F. (Tom) Donald, and one other; *DMN*, Sept. 28, 29, Oct. 5, 6, 1948 (including work by reporter Walter Hornaday); *AA*, Sept. 26, 28–30, Oct. 6, 1948; *NYT*, Sept. 29, 30, Oct. 5, 6, Dec. 18, 1948, and see Arthur Krock, *NYT*, Oct. 3, 1948; James Rowe's unpublished manuscript on Parr; Letter, Hugo Black to RD.

13. Musing in the White House over the legend in his family that the day Lyndon was born his grandfather had bragged he would be a senator by the time he was forty, President Johnson said, "That was a pretty good prediction, wasn't it?"

    Johnson was forty on Aug. 27, 1948, the day before the runoff primary, and in a radio speech before the voting, he said, "You know life begins at forty, and I hope to be the next junior senator when I am forty years and one day old." Since nomination was tantamount to election, he made it, and this may have then become the basis for the legend about what his grandfather said.

    Interview, LJ (Dec. 13, 1967); *DMN*, Aug. 27, 1948.
14. Interview, Wright Morrow.
15. "It is a strange thing," Landrum wrote in the *News*, "that men who are otherwise honorable will steal, lie, and commit almost any felony short of murder —all in the name of party loyalty or under cover of party membership." The people "are pretty nearly compelled to assume that the election was stolen," and Johnson, "demanding for himself the fruits of a stolen election," was "not worthy to be senator." The charge was not that he stole the election, but that his majority was made with untrue returns and he was "willing to profit by ballots never cast for him." Usurping the will of the people is "the blackest of all political crimes. . . . Mr. Johnson wants his senatorial toga, stained or not."

    Landrum continued, "Now there is a difference between being the innocent beneficiary of fraud and being the insistent beneficiary of fraud." If Johnson would call for a complete investigation all would say "Here, indeed, is a man of honor," but instead, "He has fought every legal effort" to get a fair count. "He actually demands that false votes be recorded and counted in his favor."

    Infuriated when a Republican official in Duval County was told that the Duval County courthouse janitor had burned the ballots there a week before a statutory date after which such burning was allowed, Landrum wrote an open letter to Johnson:

    "It is now a question of honor. . . . In counties on which you rely for your slender margin, evidence is being burned, subpoenaed witnesses are hiding from investigation, and the stain of scandal is on the run-off outcome. . . . Will Lyndon Johnson take a nomination which is stained by fraud so great and so criminal that the perpetrators leave the country or burn the evidence? . . . [F]orego the nomination by your own free will while there is yet time. You can vindicate your honor."

    Stung at last to answer, in a letter to the *News* Johnson avoided any mention of Box 13. Five times in his reply he laid his troubles to "the Johnson haters." The burning of the ballots, he said, was no proof of fraud, and nowhere had fraud in Duval been alleged except in "the biased and polluted columns of the *Dallas News,*" which had been well called "the scarlet woman of Texas journalism." Stevenson had gotten Duval's votes before—why hadn't the *News* cried foul then? "What about the burning of ballots in Navarro County?" What about the altered returns in Dallas, the 2,000 illegal votes in Galveston, Stevenson's illegal majority in Brown County, and other dubious returns? Johnson had challenged Stevenson to file his contest in the state courts, but Stevenson had refused. "I could not file a suit for a recount because I was the winner." So it was Stevenson who did not want an investigation of the facts. The *News*'s "sinister purpose" was to persuade Johnson to surrender his office "to your oilicrat, Republican candidate," and he would not do it.

Lynn Landrum, *DMN,* Oct. 3, 15, 18, 22, 27, 29, 1948; Johnson's reply, *DMN,* Oct. 31, 1948.

16. According to J. Evetts Haley, George Parr, at a time when he was with Duval County Democratic Chairman T. C. King, received a frantic phone call from Johnson about the burning of the ballots. "George," Haley wrote that Johnson told Parr, "don't burn those ballots. It'll be a reflection on me." But Parr shouted back: "To hell with you. I'm going to protect my friends." I found the same story in the research file of a major news organization, attributed to a source inside Parr's camp.

NYT, Oct. 28, 1948; *AA,* Oct. 29, 1948; Haley, *A Texan,* p. 45; a confidential source.

17. Johnson defeated Porter, 702,985 to 349,665. Truman defeated Dewey in Texas, 750,700 to 282,249.

DMN, Oct. 3, 1948, seriatim, and Oct. 31, 1948; *AA,* Oct. 23, Nov. 2, 3, 1948; *WP,* Oct. 14, 1948; McKay, *Texas,* pp. 242–44; on Johnson's remark about war with Russia, cf. *DMN,* Oct. 23, 1948.

18. In October, 1948, the chairman of the Senate elections subcommittee ordered the impounding of ballots in Jim Hogg, Starr, Jim Wells, Duval, and Zapata counties (all south Texas boss counties), but had been informed that the key records in Duval and Box 13 had been destroyed "before the arrival of the investigators." Johnson countercharged that irregularities favoring Stevenson had occurred in eight other counties.

Senate investigators gathered up the available ballot boxes from Jim Wells, Zapata, and Starr counties and evidently carted them to Washington. On the last day for seizing records before the law permitted them to be destroyed, Johnson asked the Senate to impound "all ballot boxes in all counties." His Republican opponent Porter noted that this proposal came at a "late hour."

Stevenson sent three communications to the Senate rules committee alleging fraud. The first, in October, 1948, contained copies of more than 1,000 pages from court records showing irregularities in the election. In January, 1949, Stevenson outlined his position in a telegram to the committee. A third message was sent in February. Each time Stevenson asked to be notified if other material was necessary. In July, 1949, the committee upheld Johnson's election and said the action was final. The decision was essentially legalistic, based on the finding that Stevenson did not pursue his remedy, outlined at state law, of filing an election contest in state court. The committee said a full recount would have been necessary for it to arrive at its own conclusion about the true outcome, and virtually all the ballots had been destroyed in accordance with state law.

In September, 1949, Johnson received a report of the Senate subcommittee on privileges and elections that he was duly elected. Senator Francis J. Meyers, chairman, told Johnson the three senators on the panel had unanimously concluded that "no basis whatsoever existed for contesting your election. On the contrary, only minor irregularities, common to every election, . . . were discovered. . . . No evidence has been disclosed which would support Stevenson's allegations." This report did not mention Duval County or Box 13.

AA, Oct. 27, 1948, July 28, 1949; *NYT,* Oct. 28, 29, 1948; *WP,* Oct. 28, 1948, July 28, 1949; *DMN,* Oct. 27, 1948, Jan. 14, 1949; McKay, *Texas,* pp. 245–46; Arthur Krock, *NYT,* Oct. 10, 1948. See Interview, Carl Hayden, (JL) in which Hayden incorrectly remembers that the rules committee of which he was a member had conducted a full recount.

For general purposes on the 1948 election scandal, cf., Schendel, "Something"; *U.S. News & World Report,* April 6, 1964. For a partisan, anti-Johnson, and in aspects unreliable account, see *The Texas Argus,* April, 1962, and spring, 1964, issues.

19. See Dugger, "Up."

58. Aftermaths and a Photograph

1. Ex-Governor Dan Moody was given to saying in the fifties that Johnson belonged in the penitentiary instead of the Senate. One of Stevenson's lawyers, C. C. Small, was still saying in the sixties, "It was just a straight-out steal of the damned election." In J. Evetts Haley's 1964 anti-Johnson paperback, the election was a robbery and Parr a criminal, and Johnson had made a frantic call to Parr that resulted in the stuffing of Box 13.

   Connally told me, "All of the conversation about fraud and so forth was ridiculous." "There wasn't much doubt about it," ex-Wallace aide Harold Young said. "They were his boys doing it." The 1948 manager in Houston for Johnson, Sam Low, recalled, "The race was against the very man we thought stole it in '41—I doubt there were any holds barred."

   In the early fifties Creekmore Fath was drinking coffee in Austin with the town's mayor, Tom Miller, who was drinking milk. "Tom," Fath said, "who won the election in 1948?" Miller bubbled in his milk, put it down, and said, "They were stealin' votes in east Texas. . . . We were stealin' votes in south Texas. Only Jesus Christ could say who actually won it." As Fath saw it, "they must've stole more than we stole, that's all." Johnson's manager in Galveston County in 1948, Walter Hall, thinking over everything that happened, said "this was probably the most corrupt election in modern Texas politics."

   A journalist reported that Parr told him, "Assuming that Box 13 was stuffed —and it is generally conceded that it was—it didn't happen in my county. . . . My friend Ed Lloyd was running Jim Wells County then. He would have to be the man to tell someone to do that." But Parr told another reporter he had not said these things.

   Interviews, John Connally, C. C. Small, Sam D. W. Low, Creekmore Fath; Haley, *A Texan,* pp. 27, 28, 33, 53; Letter, Walter Hall to RD; Jack Donahue, *Houston Press,* April 28, 1953; James Rowe's unpublished manuscript on Parr.

2. When I asked Johnson about the 1948 election in 1959 he went on a tear as if by gusty rhetoric he could blow the subject away. Had he or his people phoned Parr on the returns? No, "Parr didn't have anything to do with that election." The Stevenson people "tried to steal the '48 election like they stole the '41 election. Our people felt we were elected by three to four thousand votes. We got each county chairman, each chairman, to sign and swear. . . . They questioned several counties and we questioned several counties. . . . [Senator] Bill Jenner had 'em tear the lock off the ballots and put 'em in a tow sack and bring 'em up here. The vote [in the Senate committee] was 13 to nothing. The grand juries took 'em—had all the ballots—and the grand juries made formal reports."

   Eight years later Johnson was still saying that Stevenson's past reliance on the south Texas bosses made his indignation a laugh. And Johnson tried to narrow the issue to the accuracy of a reporter: a newspaperman said, from what he heard that Saturday night, the votes were cast one way, but the figures from the Jim Wells officials simply did not agree. I again asked Johnson if he had called Parr, and he gave the nonanswer that is in the main text.

   Sensitive about Box 13, he let people know he was listening. One night in the late fifties reporter Jim Rowe, speaking to not more than twenty people at a Unitarian fellowship, was asked if Johnson had stuffed the ballots in Box 13. "You can't blame Johnson for that," Rowe answered. "But some of his friends sure did." About three months later a Johnson operative told Rowe, "the senator appreciates what you said about him."

   Interviews, LJ (May, 1959, Dec. 14, 1967), Ralph Lowry; Letter, James Rowe to RD.

3. Avoiding the implications of becoming Parr's man in Washington after 1948, Johnson said Parr never asked him a favor and he never granted him one—oh, except once Parr asked him for some Kentucky Derby tickets. A railroad had sent Senator Earle Clements some, so Johnson had some sent to Parr. Homer Dean, Johnson's manager in Jim Wells in '48, said that, although Johnson, acting through Fortas, did favors for Parr after 1948, actually he "kinda shunned us.

Ed Lloyd got very bitter about it."

Salas asked Johnson for help getting a friend into medical school in 1949. Johnson wrote the school, was told the boy's score was far too low, and wrote Salas that he expected him to tell him if he could do anything further for the boy. Salas's son Edmundo was wounded in Korea in 1951, and Salas asked Johnson to get him back in the country at once. Johnson's aide Walter Jenkins wired Salas that the army had been asked "to see if it is possible for Edmundo to be evacuated to the states immediately." (Though Edmundo could have been flown back, he decided to stay with his buddies in the hospital in Seoul.)

Salas also tried to get help from President Johnson. A friend of Salas's sons, called a "goddamn Mexican," hit a postal official, and Salas called on Johnson. Salas, who was prejudiced against blacks, was piqued when Johnson sent in "a nigger from Dallas" to investigate and nothing was done. Salas turned Republican.

Interviews, LJ (Dec. 14, 1967), Luis Salas, a confidential source; telegram, Walter Jenkins to "Louis Salas."

4. The murder that figured in Shivers launching his drive against Parr was widely publicized. The leader of the anti-Parr party in Jim Wells County, Jacob S. Floyd, was warned by a Parr lieutenant that he was going to be murdered, and as they talked Floyd's son, mistaken for the father, was shot down and killed. Fingerprints found on the murder weapon were traced to a Mexican national, Alfredo Cervantes, and its ownership to Mario Sapet, a deputy sheriff at $400 a month under Parr. A jury gave Sapet ninety-nine years in prison. Cervantes evidently vanished into Mexico.

(Reporter William Bradford Huie wrote in 1961 that Cervantes "was hired to kill by Texans to whom Vice President Lyndon B. Johnson is indebted" and quoted Jacob Floyd that Cervantes could be extradicted from Mexico only if President Kennedy asked that he be.)

The tax case against Parr was dismissed. In the mail case, involving charges against Parr and others, Parr was sentenced to ten years, but the conviction was thrown out by the Supreme Court. Percy Foreman, a famous lawyer hired to defend the Parr group, said, "There were 454 indictments returned against 109 people. Not only did not one of them serve one day in jail, but none of them was ever mugged or fingerprinted."

Huie, "Murder in Texas"; James Rowe, unpublished ms. on Parr; *SAE*, Mar. 20, 1964; *SAEN*, Oct. 2, 1964.

5. According to a reliable anti-Parr source, former Representative Bob Mullen of Alice, Smithwick's murder of Mason had nothing directly to do with the 1948 election. Mason was a crusading kind of radio man and had made some statements on the air about Smithwick's daughter that had offended him, and this, Mullen said, was what led to the killing.

Like the AP news story at the time, the copy of Smithwick's letter on file with the AP in Austin omits the meat of the letter in which Smithwick named the persons he accused. Two and three-fourths lines of the letter in the AP's files are X'ed out. I have the text of the letter and here omit only the names. (The last-named person is a principal figure in the Box 13 dispute.)

Huntsville, Texas
March 23, 1952

Mr. Coke R. Stevenson
Capitol Building
Austin, Texas
Dear Sir:

You probably do not remember who I am but I am the fellow who got in trouble in Alice over killing Mr. Mason, something that I regret very much and I am now serving a life sentence in the Texas Penitentiary.

I am writing you in regard to the 1949 election in Jim Wells County when you were running against Lindon Johnston as you recall the election box with all the votes disappeared, and that is the main cause of my trouble with Mr. Mason as he was on one side and I was on the other.

On June 24, 1949 five days before I got in trouble I arrested [name] the son of [name], and [name],the son of]name], and from them learned that [name, with a job identification,] and a bossom friend of Mr. Mason's, had stolen the box and gave it to them to dispose of, but I recovered the box from them and am quite sure that

I can produce it if you are interested. . . .

If it would be possible for you to come to Huntsville Prison to visit with me at your earliest convenience, I would like to go into this matter in detail with you. . . .

Respectfully yours,
Sam Smithwick, #11826

My only source for Shivers accusing Johnson of murder is Johnson, since Shivers would not be interviewed for this book and I have not seen any newspaper story referring to the accusation. Were my unconfirmed source on the point anyone but Johnson, I would not write it here. Johnson told me about it late the night of Dec. 14, 1967, while reminiscing about the 1956 fight for control in Texas. I told him I had never heard that Shivers had said this. He replied, Well, it happened. Shivers refused to discuss it with me on Feb. 24, 1982.

Associated Press files, Austin, Texas, including a copy of the Smithwick letter and undated 1952 AP dispatches from Junction, Tx., and Washington, D.C.; a full copy of the Smithwick letter made by the late Harry Benge Crozier, close associate of Stevenson's, from the original shown him by Stevenson; *Houston Press,* May 28, 1952; Interviews, Coke Stevenson, George Beto, Luis Salas, LJ (Dec. 14, 1967, although probably past midnight, and so Dec. 15); and Bob Mullen; James Rowe, unpublished manuscript on Parr.

6. Interviews, LJ (Mar. 23, 1968), Luis Salas.

59. "Rising on the Senate Floor"

1. Baker, *Wheeling,* pp. 34, 40–41, 51; Interviews, Hubert Humphrey, Allen Ellender, Tom Clark (all JL); Kearns, *Lyndon,* pp. 103, 105; Newlon, *L.B.J.* p. 117; Baker, *Wheeling,* p. 42, and cf. Busch, "Senator."
2. Interviews, Hubert Humphrey (JL), John Connally; Humphrey, *The Education,* p. 163; *PP 1964,* pp. 402–3; Gorman, *Kefauver,* pp. 66–67; *Time,* Mar. 17, 1958.
3. Although Johnson's 1949 speech was hostile to civil rights in the time and place, some of his remarks are interesting in the light of his later career:

   "I realize that we of the South who speak here are accused of prejudice, that we are labeled in the folklore of American tradition as a prejudiced minority. I would point out, though, that prejudice is not a minority affliction; prejudice is most wicked and most harmful as a majority ailment. . . .

   "The civil-rights question brings into play all those strong and evil forces of racial prejudice. Perhaps no prejudice is so contagious or so dangerous as the unreasoning prejudice against men because of their birth, the color of their skin, or their ancestral background. Racial prejudice is dangerous because it is a disease of the majority, endangering minority groups. . . . The Negro . . . has more to lose by the adoption of any resolution outlawing free debate in the Senate than he stands to gain by the enactment of the civil-rights bills as they are now written. . . .

   "I, like all other citizens, detest the shameful crime of lynching. . . . Within the past 20 years new generations of Texans have reached maturity free of the ingrained hatreds and prejudices which beset their forebears."

   Speech, LJ, "Unlimited Debate."
4. Letter, James V. Allred to LJ; Interview, Walter Hall, cf. Interview, Walter Hall (JL).
5. John Connally returned to Texas to practice law in October, 1949, and Jenkins replaced him as Johnson's administrative assistant.

   Interview, Dorothy Nichols (JL); Mooney, *The Lyndon,* 1964 ed., p. 65; *AA,* Nov. 24, 1948, Feb. 6, 1949; *DMN* Oct. 9, 1949; Steinberg, *Sam Johnson's,* pp. 276–79; on the farmer's reception, a confidential source.
6. Evans and Novak, *Lyndon,* pp. 47–48; Steinberg, *Sam Johnson*'s p. 298; Interview, Mrs. Lloyd Bentsen (JL).
7. *DMN,* Feb. 14, 1950; Drew Pearson, *DMN,* Mar. 15, 29, 1950; Doris Fleeson, *DMN,* Mar. 30, 1950.
8. Interview, Hubert Humphrey (JL); Humphrey, *The Education,* pp. 124–25.

60. Pre-McCarthy McCarthyism

1. Acheson, "Memories"; George C. Wilson, *WP,* as published in *AA,* Dec. 22, 1969; Interview, Maury Maverick, Jr.; *AA,* July 8, 1940.
2. The letter from Truman to Rayburn, dated Aug. 15, 1950, said, "[Senator Harry] Byrd and his crowd have succeeded in effectively ruining the efficiency of the government while McCarthy and his crowd have almost ruined the morale of public employees. That may be patriotism and economical but I have my doubts about it."

   Sherwood, *Roosevelt,* pp. 104, 138–39; Acheson, *Morning,* pp. 201–11; McKay, *Texas,* pp. 157–58; Anderson, *The Presidents',* pp. 114, 119–20; Horowitz, *The Free,* p. 100; Goulden, *The Superlawyers,* p. 85; Interview, Harold Young; *Democratic National Convention,* 1948, *Democracy,* pp. 123–126; Letter, Harry Truman to Sam Rayburn.
3. Engelmayer and Wagman, *Hubert,* p. 22; *CR 1949,* vol. 95, pp. 5941–43. On the Soviet spy cell in England, see, e.g., for recent phases of the matter, *The Observer* (London), Nov. 8, 1981; *Times* (London), Nov. 7, 10, 1981; *Telegraph* (London), Nov. 8, 1981.

61. The Crucifixion of Leland Olds

1. That spring of 1949, Senate conservatives on the armed services committee opposed Truman's nominee to be chairman of the National Security Resources Board, Mon C. Wallgren. Statements that Wallgren was not a Communist were part of the controversy. The committee tabled the nomination seven to six, but Johnson voted with the minority against tabling.

   Senate Committee on Armed Services, *Nomination; NYT,* Mar. 15, 1949; Letter, Charles B. Kirbow to RD.
2. The next year Johnson implied that senators who differed with him on the Kerr bill to prevent federal regulation of gas prices had embraced Olds's philosophy against free enterprise: "I am truly shocked that some senators will so quickly embrace the philosophy after so completely rejecting the man."

   Later he turned sheepish about the Olds episode. At a luncheon with Clyde Ellis of the national electric co-ops, Johnson said to Ellis, as Clay Cochran, who was present, recalls, "you and I always been good friends, except for that Leland Olds deal. You got pretty mad at me didn't you—slugging himself with more drinks—(Ellis nods grimly into his plate—he always ate frantically until done—) Yeah, you figured I was wrong, but I don't think so. I gave him every chance in the world didn't I, Clyde? I offered over and over that if he'd deny that radicalism of his I'd vote for him, didn't I Clyde? (Yeah. . . .) But he wouldn't do it, so I just didn't have any choice, did I?"

   When I asked Johnson about the case when he was the Senate Democratic leader, he spun out an account the public record does not support. Olds, before his committee, was asked, Johnson said, "if he still entertained opinions that the churches ought to be destroyed, the schools should be destroyed, and communism was the only salvation to us. He had only said these things in his youth, but would he repeat 'em or retract 'em? He just looked up defiantly and said, 'I repeat 'em," and the committee voted unanimously against 'im. . . ."

   (Johnson's subcommittee unanimously rejected Olds; the full committee voted against him, ten to two and the Senate *53 to 15.*)

   Johnson also told me in 1959, "It was never proven or argued that he was a Communist, but the views that he expressed were such that" he was rejected; and he was for, among other things, "public ownership of all the basic industries." (The record does not support that, either.)

   Harris, "The Senatorial"; Sherrill, *The Accidental,* pp. 155–65; Engler, *The Politics,* pp. 115–19, 125, 338–39, 361; Evans and Novak, *Lyndon,* pp. 26, 36–37; Ryskind, *Hubert,* pp. 155–56; Caute, *The Great,* p. 48 UP wire service copy dated Sept. 29, 1949; *DMN,* Oct. 5, 1949; AA, Oct. 26, 1949; *CR 1949,* vol. 95, pp. 1858, 14357–85; Interview, LJ (May, 1959); letter, Clay Coch-

ran to RD, and letters, JL: LBJA Sel. Names, box 12, George Brown fdr., and box 18, Francis fdr., Charles I. Francis to LJ (two) and Tom Connally, LJ to Francis.
3. Athan Theoharis, "The Rhetoric of Politics," in Bernstein, ed. *Politics,* pp. 214–15; *AAS,* Mar. 18, 1951.
4. Rovere, *Senator,* pp. 122–23.
5. JL, LBJA Sel. Names, box 16, Cullen fdr., Letter, LJ to Hugh Roy Cullen.

62. The Senator Becomes a Rancher

1. The agreement between Clarence and Miss Frank Martin, on the one hand, and Tom and Lela Martin, on the other, was made in 1935. Clarence Martin died in 1936. Tom and Lela cared for Miss Frank from then on, moving onto the Martin place in 1940. According to Payne Roundtree, Tom drank too much, and Lela supported both him and Miss Frank and kept the place up, too. By one report Lyndon had tried to get Tom to sign the place over to Aunt Frank so she could sell it to Lyndon, but Tom, who disliked Lyndon (and had considered running against him in 1942), would not. In 1948 Tom died. In his will he left Lela the Martin place, "said land being in the name of my mother, which she has given me to become my own after her death."

   In the trial Lela produced evidence that she and Tom had spent $40,000 on the place. "I thought I was improving my property," she said. Miss Frank alleged in effect that she had earned her keep by keeping house; that they had sold the crops and given her no part; that the improvements they had made were for their own benefit and comfort.

   Barred from the house by a court order for a time, Lela claimed that Linden and his wife moved in with Aunt Frank and sorted through Lela's papers. "Naturally," she said, "it looked like a well laid scheme" to keep her away and give Linden the chance to go through her and Tom's papers. "That is the gist of this lawsuit. It is not between me and Mrs. Martin," Lela said. The lawyers did not ask her what she meant.

   In a family letter in December, 1948, Lela had written, "I handle all my business through a lawyer, I don't do like the Johnsons and seek cheap free advice." Asked "who are the Johnsons you refer to," she said, "None specifically," but not Miss Frank. Walter Linden, of course, was giving Miss Frank free legal help.

   The 1935 agreement, if written, was what lawyers call a bilateral executory contract. The appeals court judge, giving Miss Frank clear title, specified that Lela was free to sue for damages.
2. Harper's Ferry tapes; Court of Civil Appeals, Fourth District of Texas, No. 12081; *SAE,* April 27, 1950; Interviews, Payne Roundtree, LaBJ, LJ (Dec. 13, 1967); Montgomery, *Mrs.,* pp. 44–45; deed records of Gillespie County for Mar. 5, 1951, and of Johnson City for Mar. 7, 1951; Smith, *The President's,* p. 207; Bishop, *A Day,* p. 175; Provence, *Lyndon, p.* 88; Chalmers M. Roberts, *WP,* Dec. 28, 1964; Thomas W. Ottenad, *SLPD,* Dec. 26, 1963; *Fredericksburg Standard,* Nov. 14, 1951; Richard Wilson, in *DMN,* May 17, 1966; confidential sources.

63. Truman Turns Off Chou and Ho

1. Acheson, *Present,* pp. 264–65, 283, 285, 307–13; see Nevins and Commager, *A Short,* pp. 509–11; Hayes, *The Beginning,* p. 5.
2. The Chou overture of 1949 was turned up by Blum, a diplomatic historian at the University of Texas, in 1978. The State Department had been delaying release of the volume containing the information; Blum broke it open under the Freedom of Information Act.

   A correspondent of the United Press in China, Michael Keon, reported to U.S. officials in Peiping that he had talked to Chou and had been asked to deliver the message. Clubb advised State that it was either a bona fide message or a ploy to get the U.S. to strengthen China so that China could better help Russia against the U.S. But our ambassador to China counseled, "We must be careful not to overplay our chance while also taking full advantage of it." With Acheson in Paris at a lengthy meeting, Acting Secretary of State James Webb gave Truman a memo taking note of some recent signs of Chinese Communist moderation toward the West, but concluding that there was "no sign that the change is permanent, much less genuine." Truman ordered Webb "to be most careful not to indicate any softening toward the Communists but to insist on judging their intentions by their actions." Clubb was in effect prohibited from giving the reply verbally: he was to give it in writing on plain paper without signature or designation of its source. Blum speculates, on Clubb's inability to make the delivery, that he might have been able to do it verbally, had he been permitted to, or that Chou may been found out by the radical faction and had to disavow the whole thing.

Miller, *Plain,* p. 283; Blum, "The Peiping." Blum's book, *Drawing the Line, The Origin of the American Containment Policy in South Asia,* was scheduled for spring, 1982, publication by W.W. Norton.

3. In his Jan. 10, 1950, speech to the National Press Club, Acheson defined the U.S. defense perimeter as running from the Aleutians through U.S.-occupied Japan and the Ryukyu Islands to the Philippines.

Historian Samuel F. Wells, Jr., has called attention to the often-neglected section of Acheson's speech alluding to the Soviet pressures on northern China as "the single most significant, most important fact, in the relation of any foreign power with Asia." Outer Mongolia, Soviet-dominated since 1921, had declared its independence from China in 1945. Acheson mentioned Outer Mongolia, Inner Mongolia, Sinkiang, and Manchuria, citing, as to the latter, the Soviet-run Far Eastern Railway. Negotiations in progress as Acheson spoke resulted in the end of Soviet control of the railway and Soviet evacuation of Port Arthur in Manchuria.

McLellan, *Dean,* p. 321; Wells, "The Lessons."

4. The exact nature of Acheson's response to Kennan's memo, if any, is not known. "I cannot remember," Kennan wrote, "that this paper was ever seriously considered or discussed. Nor can I recall what was the reaction to it of the Secretary of State."

Caute, *The Great,* p. 46; Kennan, *Memoirs, 1925–1950,* pp. 471–76; see Bernstein, "New."

5. *DMN,* Feb. 14, Mar. 9, 16, 1950; Mooney, *The Lyndon,* 1964 ed., pp. 68–69.
6. Yost, *History,* pp. 148, 168; Acheson, "Memories"; McLellan, *Dean,* pp. 270–72; Horowitz, *The Free,* pp. 259–60; Wells, "The Lessons"; David Botter, *DMN,* April 31, 1950.
7. Halberstam, "How"; Chester Bowles, *WP,* Aug. 15, 1971; Humphrey, *The Education,* p. 315; McLellan, *Dean,* p. 260.
8. Athan Theoharis, "The Rhetoric of Politics," in Bernstein, ed., *Politics,* p. 213; *AAS,* May 28, 1950.

64. The War of the Three Invasions

1. Steinberg, *Sam Johnson's,* p. 302; Talbott, trans. and ed., *Khrushchev* (vol. 1), pp. 367–70, and cf. Barnet, *Roots,* p. 274, Hoopes, *The Devil,* p. 101, and Schram, *Mao,* pp. 261–62; Miller, *Plain,* pp. 272–73; Acheson, *Present,* pp. 404, 414–15, 420; Nevins in *New York Herald-Tribune,* 1964, pp. 12–13, but cf. McLellan, *Dean,* pp. 281–82; Letters, LJ to Harry Truman, Truman to LJ, TL, Sel. Doc., HST Ofcl. File; see Wiltz, "The Korean."
2. Kennan, *Memoirs,* 1925–1950, p. 488, and see Stanley Karnow, *WP* in *AA,* Nov. 26, 1969; Horowitz, *The Free,* p. 130; Steinberg, *Sam Johnson's,* pp. 310–11, 316; Goulden, *Korea,* p. 234.
3. *AA,* July 19, 1950; *DMN,* July 19, 1950.
4. Mooney, *The Lyndon,* 1964 ed., p. 71; White, *The Professional,* p. 108; Steinberg, *Sam Johnson's,* pp. 303–5.
5. McLellan, *Dean,* pp. 282–91; Horowitz, *The Free,* pp. 132–33 Goulden, *Korea,* p. 238.
6. *AA,* Nov. 23, 1950.
7. McLellan, *Dean,* pp. 293–300; Schram, *Mao,* pp. 266–68; Goulden, *Korea,* p. 416–17.
8. McLellan, Dean, p. 301; *NYT,* Dec. 13, 1950; Sherrill, *The Accidental,* p. 217, 223; Mooney, *The Lyndon,* 1964 ed., pp. 70–71, 78–79; Lilienthal, *The Journals,* vol. 3, *Venturesome,* p. 46.
9. Baker, *Wheeling,* pp. 59–60, and see

Steinberg, *Sam Johnson's,* p. 317; *Time,* Mar. 6, 1964; William S. White, *NYT,* Jan. 3, 1951; Abell, ed., *Drew,* p. 246, and cf. Evans and Novak, *Lyndon,* p. 43.

10. Johnson's statement on MacArthur's firing:

"While I regret what the Commander-in-Chief deemed to be the necessity for General MacArthur's removal, I realize it is essential that civilian control over the military be maintained. If one general were permitted to defy civilian authority, then other generals, good and bad, could do the same; we might soon find ourselves obeying the order of the military in all that we do. That is not in accordance with the traditions of our freedom."

McLellan, *Dean,* pp. 302–18; Miller, *Plain,* pp. 298, 300; *DMN,* April 3, 1951; Halberstam, *The Best,* p. 120; Goulden, *Korea,* pp. 529–30.

11. Graham, "The Universal"; Fliegel, "Forgotten."
12. *NYT,* Aug. 31, 1950, Jan. 17, 18, 19, 30, Feb. 11, 12, 15, Mar. 8, 1951; *DMN,* Feb. 14, 1951; *AAS,* Feb. 25, Mar. 18, 1951; Haynes, *The Awesome,* pp. 86–87.
13. The civilian-majority National Security Training Commission proposed the reserve corps, made up of young men trained for six months and obligated for another seven and a half years of reserve liability. Johnson supported this on behalf of veterans unfairly called up for Korea. In 1955 the Reserve Forces Act provided for annually training a reserve corps of up to 250,000 men between seventeen and eighteen and a half, but only 50,000 signed up the first year, probably because of the total eight-year obligation. In 1957 the Pentagon cut the reserve term to three years and opened the corps to every draft-eligible man who had not received his draft notice. Since this gave a young man a more meaningful choice between two years and six months in active service, the "six-month hitch" then played a more significant part in military manpower.

(Edgar Shelton, who had been a staffer on the Johnson preparedness subcommittee, was executive director of NSTC; I was his assistant for writing and research.)

NYT, Feb. 9, Oct. 30, 1951, April 28, 1952, June 11, 1955; Graham, "The Universal"; National Security Training Commission, *Twentieth; CR 1951,* vol. 97, pp. 2052–53.

65. Senator Strangelove

1. Johnson's Dallas ultimatum speech was delivered to a luncheon sponsored by that city's Chamber of Commerce, the Dallas Citizens Council (the city's ruling elite), and other business groups.

Asked for comment after Dulles proclaimed his doctrine, Johnson repeated some of his 1951 statements and said he still believed them.

DMN, July 10, Oct. 11, 12, 1951, Jan. 26, 1954; *Fort Worth Star-Telegram,* Oct. 23, 1951; *AA,* Oct. 11, 25, 1951; *NYT,* Oct. 12, 1951; *Dallas,* October, 1951; Sherrill, *The Accidental,* p. 224.

2. Johnson saw Truman in the Oval Office usually either alone or in company with other members of Congress. By 1951 he was sometimes attending meetings with Truman as a Democratic leader in the Senate. The half-hour conference at Truman's request occurred Jan. 14, 1952.

Truman's private thoughts were of course at variance with his publicly expressed opposition to a preventive strike against China or Russia. When asked about the memoranda by the *New York Times,* W. Averell Harriman, a special assistant to Truman in 1952, said he had never discussed the subject of the memoranda with Truman, and Dean Rusk, then assistant secretary of state for Far Eastern affairs, said the diary entries were counter to everything he knew about Truman.

Dr. Bob Ferrell, a Truman scholar at the University of Indiana, said about these two memos: "I think the president was simply, oh, he was mad, he just simply wrote it down and forgot about it. He never did anything about it. It was just on the top of his head, and he was mad. He wasn't gonna drop a bomb on anybody, he was too smart for that."

TL, Sel. Doc., Pres. Appointment Bks.; *NYT,* Aug. 3, 1980, quoting Francis L. Loewenheim, *Houston Chronicle,* Aug. 3, 1980; Interview, Bob Ferrell.

66. The Invisible Vice-Presidential Candidate

1. Johnson said he wanted foreign aid cut out entirely. But he predicted that legislation securing oil under the continental shelf to the states would be passed over the expected Truman veto.

   DMN, Jan. 5, 1952, and Walter C. Hornaday, *DMN,* Jan. 9, 1952.

2. Sam Houston Johnson said to me, "Lyndon wasn't for Stevenson, he was against Kefauver." George Reedy wrote that Johnson this year favored Stevenson as a way to head off Kefauver. This was Johnson's private, realistic position, as distinguished from his public, active one.

   "I was not a delegate to the 1952 convention," Johnson explained later. "Had I been, I would have voted for Senator Russell until it was apparent he could not be nominated, and then I would have supported Governor Stevenson."

   John Connally, confirming Johnson's support of Russell, said, "I was for Russell more than Johnson was," meaning, apparently, even more than Johnson was. But as Senator Clinton Anderson said, Johnson in 1952 was "very heavily involved with Dick Russell." Johnson arranged for the Texas publicist Booth Mooney to work in Washington for Russell's nomination.

   The Washington writer Douglas Kiker reported a "theory" that Russell, believing he could win the nomination in 1952, was so shocked when he lost, he gave up hope of national office and transferred his ambition to Johnson.

   Interviews, SHJ, Clinton Anderson (JL), Joseph Clark, John ConnallyStuar Long (JL), George Reedy (JL); Letter, LJ to *RD,* June 1, 1959; Evans and Novak, *Lyndon,* pp. 226–27; a confidential source; Reedy, *The Twilight,* pp. 150–51; Kiker, "Russell"; see Gorman, *Kefauver,* pp. 74–155, and cf. Abell, ed., *Drew,* p. 221. On Johnson's advice to Texas Lt. Gov. Ben Barnes about getting to be president through the vice-presidency, Marianne Means, *AA,* undated (1969).

3. See Engler, *The Politics,* pp. 86–92.

4. Daniel was elected to the Senate with reported contributions exceeding $100,000. Among his financial backers were the Houston oil multimillionaire Hugh Roy Cullen ($5000), the president of El Paso Natural Gas Company ($1350), and Houston oil operator George Strake ($250).

   Mooney, *LBJ,* p. 22; Steinberg, *Sam Johnson's,* p. 325; *Houston Press,* Mar. 6, 1956; Letters, LJ to Harry Truman, Truman to LJ, TL, Sel. Doc., HST Ofcl. File; Interview, Price Daniel (JL).

5. David et al., eds., *Presidential,* pp. 333–45, and see, e.g., *DMN,* Aug. 31, 1958.

6. Hall is certain his conversation with Rayburn occurred before the convention in the Capitol in Washington. The meeting is not to be confused, then, with a later one at the convention (see the text).

   Interviews, Walter Hall (by RD and JL) and Letter, Hall to RD; Interview, Allan Shivers (JL); see Steinberg, *Sam Johnson's,* pp. 326–27, and *Sam Rayburn,* pp. 272–74.

7. Drew Pearson reported that Johnson took Shivers to Rayburn's room and "told Sam that Allan could be trusted." By Bob Sherrill's later account, Johnson "persuaded the old man that Shivers could be depended on to stay true blue to the party." Creekmore Fath said Rayburn later told him, "As I remember it, that Shivers was going to support the nominees." But Shivers said, "I made no commitment to support the nominee and he made no commitment to have my delegation seated. I told Mr. Rayburn . . . that I had always supported the party but that I would not promise to do so in this case regardless of whether we were seated or not."

   Addressing the convention, Shivers did not pledge to support the nominees regardless, but said he had come "hoping to find the platform and the nominee that all the Democrats can join behind for a victory in November. . . . Coming here as one who wants to help keep the Democratic Party united . . . we don't want to be forced out. We came here with good intentions." He pledged to put the national nominees on the ballot in Texas as the nominees.

   Interviews, Walter Hall, Creekmore Fath; Drew Pearson in a column dated May 22, 1956, place of publication uncertain; Sherrill, *The Accidental,* p. 98; Kinch and Long, *Allan,* p. 216; Collier,

"Rayburn"; Democratic National Convention, 1952, *Official Report*, pp. 136–46; see Steinberg, *Sam Rayburn*, pp. 272–74, and *Sam Johnson's*, pp. 326–27.

8. Interview, Herman Talmadge (JL); Democratic National Convention, 1952, *Official Report*, pp. 456, 484, 538; see Gorman, *Kefauver*, pp. 131–55.
9. Interviews, SHJ, Charles I. Francis; cf. Schlesinger, *A Thousand*, p. 52, and Evans and Novak, *Lyndon*, pp. 226–27.
10. David et al., eds, *Presidential*, pp. 346–47; Interview, Booth Mooney (JL).
11. According to James Rowe, Jr., Johnson was "somewhat cross about (Stevenson's) stand on Tidelands Oil because he thinks he unnecessarily gave Shivers a weapon to beat Johnson over the head in Texas."

Johnson's statement of endorsement continued: "The fact Governor Stevenson is wrong on this [tidelands] issue does not automatically make General Eisenhower right on all other issues. Texans once left the Democratic Party to help the Republicans elect Herbert Hoover. Our people suffered many years because of this desertion. . . .

"A Republican victory would not assure our retaining our tidelands. Texas has more to lose by deserting our Democratic colleagues from inland states who have fought by our side on tidelands. . . ."

Two days later Stevenson wrote Johnson, "I am most grateful for your support in Texas and I can only do this job step by step as I see it according to my best lights and let the chips fall where they may, with the hope, forlorn perhaps, that people will at least give me the credit for sincerity. You have heartened me." (Johnson brandished this letter in 1959, implying that it proved Stevenson's gratitude.)

Introducing Stevenson, Johnson called him "a square shooter . . . who looks us in the eye—and keeps his hands above the table," who stood by his convictions at cost of personal gain, "more than a fighter—more than an honorable man . . . a tested statesman, an administrator of unquestioned ability." Singer and Sherrod have him saying of Stevenson publicly, "We have a new leader. I won't discuss the wisdom of the choice, but he is our leader." Newlon has Johnson in Austin calling Stevenson "the greatest improvement that could be offered by any party to the voting public," a phrase also found in materials Johnson's staff showed me.

Shivers, discounting Johnson's effort for Stevenson, added, "Johnson introduced Stevenson at Fort Worth, maybe some other place—maybe San Antonio . . . but I don't think he made any other speeches." In 1959 Sam Houston Johnson, evidently sic'ed on me by Lyndon on the question of how many speeches he made, said the total was "no less than 40." Johnson's staff provided a list of Johnson's "activities . . . in behalf of" the ticket listing twenty-eight items, nineteen of them stops, during a three-day tour with Congressman Patman in tiny east Texas villages like Pattonville and Redwater and three in Missouri and Arizona.

Johnson wrote me that he had announced at the convention he would "heartily support" Stevenson and that, with his Aug. 28 statement, "I think I was the first public official in Texas to announce" for the ticket. Rayburn, the state manager for the ticket who made speeches and worked in the headquarters, later claimed Johnson, too, did all he could. "Lyndon," the Speaker wrote, "made several speeches for the ticket in 1952 and I know he made at least one statewide broadcast." Johnson's friend William S. White alleged ludicrously that Johnson "met Stevenson at the state line and campaigned all across Texas with him."

That year Shivers beat Yarborough in the gubernatorial primary 834,000 to 488,000. In the general election, in which all the Texas statewide Democratic candidates save one ran as both Democrats and Republicans, Allan Shivers, Democrat, defeated Allan Shivers, Republican, 1,376,000 to 468,-000. Eisenhower beat Stevenson in Texas 1,103,000 to 969,000, a 3% margin (nationally Eisenhower's 34-to-27-million margin exceeded 5%).

Interviews, SHJ, Ralph Yarborough, Allan Shivers (JL), Anna Rosenberg Hoffman (JL), LJ (May, 1959), Hank Brown (JL), Drew Pearson (JL); Letters, Adlai Stevenson to LJ (Aug. 30, 1952), LJ to *RD* (June 1, 1959), Sam Rayburn to J. W. Potter; LJ statements of Aug. 28 and Oct. 17, 1952, provided by LJ staff, "Activities of Senator Lyndon Johnson in Behalf of the National Democratic Presidential Candidates in 1952"; *Adlai,* p. 652; Evans and Novak, *Lyndon,* pp. 227–28 (cf. Steinberg, *Sam,* pp. 277–78); Mooney, *LBJ,* p. 18; Coffin, *Senator,* p. 119; Singer and Sherrod, *Lyndon,* p. 211; Newlon, *LBJ,* p. 123; White, *The Professional,* p. 45.

67. The War of the Three Invasions

No Notes.

68. Gut Politics in the High Grass

1. The dialogue between Johnson and Shivers was provided by Shivers; the interpretation is my own.

   O'Brien, *No,* pp. 37–38; Baker, *Wheeling,* pp. 60–61; Interviews, SHJ, Allan Shivers (JL); Evans and Novak, *Lyndon,* p. 52.
2. Mooney, *LBJ,* pp. 10–13, 16.
3. "LBJ," CBS, Jan. 27, 1972; Interview, SHJ, cf. LJ, *The Vantage,* p. 3, and SHJ, *My,* pp. 83–85.
4. Evans and Novak, *Lyndon,* pp. 55–56; Baker, *Wheeling,* pp. 61–62; Interview, SHJ, and cf. SHJ, *My,* pp. 85–86; cf. also Steinberg, *Sam Johnson's,* pp. 340–41.
5. Johnson favored beef price decontrol, which occurred early in 1953. (The ADA's aside on this topic exaggerated its importance.)

   William S. White wrote that Johnson was "about half-way between the right-wing Southerners and the 'regular' Northern Democrats, with powerful Southern backing." Cabell Phillips wrote in the *Times* that Johnson was "sagely a 'Russell' man whenever the chips go down between the Northern and Southern wings of the party." Stewart Alsop wrote that Johnson became Leader because of Russell's backing.

   ADA World, quoted in *DMN,* Dec. 30, 1952; *DMN,* Feb. 5, 1953; William S. White, *NYT,* Jan. 3, 1953; Cabell Phillips, *NYT,* Jan. 11, 1953; Alsop, *The Center,* p. 303.

69. The Politician as Predator

1. I discussed with Johnson various radio-TV, real estate, ranch, banking, and other political-financial matters in which he was involved. However, this being a volume in which my main policy focus is on foreign policy, I will be taking up Johnson's business affairs in detail in the next volume, which will be focused mainly on domestic issues.

70. The Confrontation

1. See Kautsky, "Myth."
2. Goold-Adams, *John,* p. 287.
3. See, e.g., Chomsky, "Ideological," and *contra,* John Leonard, *NYT,* Feb. 5, 1979.
4. *NYT,* Jan. 6, 1951; Sulzberger, *The Last* p. 304; Kennan, *Memoirs: 1950–1963,* p. 107; Horowitz, *The Free,* p. 23, quoting Kennan; Heilbroner, "Counterrevolutionary"; Morgenthau, "Global."
5. Douglas in Boulding et al., "The U.S." (see "Miscellaneous").

71. From Self-defense to Global Combat

1. *NYT,* July 13, 1950, Nov. 7, 1951; LJ, speech, undated, c. December, 1950; Kearns, *Lyndon,* p. 95.
2. LJ, guest columns in *AA,* Aug. 17, 1947, and May 13, 1948; LJ's address before Texas legislature, text in *CR 1941,* vol. 87, pp. A1992–1944; *CR 1951,* vol. 96, pp. 16458–60; William S. White, *NYT,* May 6,1951.
3. *CR 1949,* vol. 94, pp. 4066–67. Kennan, *Memoirs: 1950–1963,* p. 103.

72. Undeclared World War III

1. Goulden, *Korea,* pp. xxv–vi, 628–31; Marquis Childs, *SLPD,* June 12, 1965; Dean Rusk, speech, University of Virginia, April 7, 1977 (which I covered). I am not at liberty to give my source concerning Rusk in Korea.
2. *AA,* June 19, 1950, Oct. 25, 1951; *NYT,* Dec. 13, 1950; *AAS,* May 30, 1954; Jon Ford, *SAE,* July 11, 1954; *PP 1964,* p. 1370.
3. The idea that World War III has been under way may have been expressed first in the American press in articles and statements made by Alexander Solzhenitsyn in 1975 and 1976. The Nobel Prize winning writer and Russian expatriate wrote in the *New York Times* in 1975:

   " . . . World War III has already happened. . . . It ended this year—with the free world soundly defeated.

   "World War III began immediately after World War II . . . as the cowardly pens of Roosevelt and Churchill . . . signed away Estonia, Latvia, Lithuania, Moldavia, Mongolia, condemned to death or to concentration camps millions of Soviet citizens, created an ineffectual United Nations Assembly, and finally abandoned Yugoslavia, Albania, Poland, Bulgaria, Rumania, Czechoslovakia, Hungary, and East Germany. . . .

   "Trying to avoid World War III at any price, the West permitted it, allowed it to devastate and enslave twenty countries, and to change the face of the earth. . . . World War III has already taken place and has ended in the West's defeat."

   Acknowledging Solzhenitsyn's venturings on the topic, right-wing global strategist Brian Crozier, in a 1978 book, developed the idea that World War III began in 1944 and was continuing as he wrote. When, two years later, Nixon set forth his views on the subject, he quoted Crozier.

   These declarations have been all but discounted because they came from three right-wingers who were animated by the purpose of arousing the West to act much more forcefully worldwide against what they perceive as worldwide Communist aggression. (Despite his preeminent and indispensable writings on Stalin's Gulag Archipelago, in the American political context Solzhenytsyn has had an indisputably right-wing influence.)

   In 1978, whether influenced by Solzhenitsyn's statements I do not know, I formulated the outlines of my own thoughts on World War III. The acknowledgment that it is being waged is dangerous; for instance, Crozier argues that because of the war, civil liberties may be repressed as in wartime. But the failure to deal with the truth is, I believe, even more dangerous.

   Aleksandr I. Solzhenitsyn, *NYT,* June 22, 1975; Crozier, *Strategy, passim;* Nixon, *The Real,* pp. 2, 4, 9, 17–19, 279, and on World War III being in progress, see also pp. 45, 228–29, 242, 295, 299.

Bibliography

Books and Theses

Abell, Tyler, ed. *Drew Pearson Diaries, 1949–1959.* New York: Holt, Rinehart and Winston, 1974.
Acheson, Dean. *Morning and Noon.* Boston: Houghton Mifflin, 1965.
———. *Present at the Creation: My Years in the State Department.* New York: W. W. Norton, 1969.
Acheson, Sam Hanna. *Joe Bailey, The Last Democrat.* New York: Macmillan, 1932.
Adams, Frank Carter. *Texas Democracy: A Centennial History of Politics and Personalities of the Democratic Party, 1836–1936,* 4 vols. (No further publishing information available.)
Adams, Henry. *The Education of Henry Adams.* New York: Modern Library, 1918.
Adler, Bill, ed. *The Kennedy Wit.* New York: Gramercy, 1964.
———. *More Kennedy Wit.* New York: Citadel, 1965.
———. *The Johnson Humor.* New York: Simon & Schuster, 1965.
Aiken, George D. *Senate Diary January 1972–January 1975.* Brattleboro, Vt.: Stephen Greene Press, 1976.
Alsop, Stewart. *The Center: People and Power in Political Washington.* New York: Harper & Row, 1968.
Amrine, Michael. *This Awesome Challenge: The Hundred Days of Lyndon Johnson.* New York: Putnam's, 1964.
Anderson, Clinton P., with Viorst, Milton. *Outsider in the Senate, Senator Clinton Anderson's Memoirs.* New York: World, 1970.
Anderson, Jack, and Blumenthal, Fred. *The Kefauver Story.* New York: Dial Press, 1956.
Anderson, James E.; Brady, David W.; and Bullock III, Charles. *Public Policy and Politics in America.* North Scituate, Mass.: Duxbury Press, 1978.
Anderson, Jervis. *A. Philip Randolph: A Biographical Portrait.* New York: Harcourt Brace Jovanovich, 1973.
Anderson, Patrick. *The Presidents' Men: White House Assistants of Franklin D. Roosevelt, Harry S. Truman, Dwight D. Eisenhower, John F. Kennedy and Lyndon B. Johnson.* Garden City: Doubleday, 1968.
Andrews, Wayne, ed. *The Autobiography of Theodore Roosevelt.* New York: Scribner's, 1958.
Anonymous. *Pioneers in God's Hills, A History of Fredericksburg and Gillespie County. . . .* Austin: Von Boeckmann-Jones, for the Gillespie County Historical Society, 1960.
Anson, Robert Sam. *McGovern: A Biography.* New York: Holt, Rinehart and Winston (paper), 1972.
———. *"They've Killed the President!" The Search for the Murderers of John F. Kennedy.* New York: Bantam (paper), 1975.
Ashman, Charles. *Connally: The Adventures of Big Bad John.* New York: Morrow, 1974.
Austin, Anthony. *The President's War: The Story of the Tonkin Gulf Resolution and How the Nation was Trapped in Vietnam.* Philadelphia: Lippincott, 1971.
Bailey, Thomas A. *Presidential Greatness: The Image and the Man from George Washington to the Present.* New York: Appleton-Century, 1966.
Bainbridge, John. *The Super-Americans: A Picture of Life in the United States, As Brought into Focus, Bigger than Life, in the Land of the Millionaires—Texas.* Garden City: Doubleday, 1961.
Baines, Huffman. *Pioneering the Telephone in Texas: A Half Century of Experiences.* Evidently privately printed, 1955.
Baker, Bobby, with King, Larry L. *Wheeling and Dealing: Confessions of a Capitol Hill Operator.* New York: W.W. Norton, 1978.
Baker, Leonard. *The Johnson Eclipse: A President's Vice-Presidency.* New York: Macmillan, 1966.

Ball, George W. *The Discipline of Power, Essentials of a Modern World Structure.* Boston: Little, Brown, 1968.
Barber, Richard J. *The American Corporation: Its Power, Its Money, Its Politics.* New York: Dutton, 1970.
Barnet, Richard J. *The Economy of Death.* New York: Atheneum (paper), 1969.
———. *Roots of War.* Baltimore: Penguin (paper), 1972.
Beal, John Robinson. *John Foster Dulles: A Biography.* New York: Harper and Row, 1957.
Beard, Charles A. *President Roosevelt and the Coming of the War, 1941.* New Haven: Yale University Press, 1948.
Bell, Jack. *The Johnson Treatment: How Lyndon B. Johnson Took Over the Presidency and Made It His Own.* New York: Harper & Row, 1965.
Berlandier, Jean Louis. *The Indians of Texas in 1830,* ed. John C. Ewers, trans. Patricia Reading Leclercq. Washington, D.C.: Smithsonian Institution Press, 1969, illus.
Berle, B.B., and Jacobs, Travis Beal, eds. *Navigating the Rapids 1918–1971: From the Papers of Adolph A. Berle.* New York: Harcourt Brace Javanovich, 1973.
Bernstein, Barton J., ed. *Politics and Policies of the Truman Administration.* Chicago: Quadrangle (paper), 1970.
Bernstein, Carl, and Woodward, Bob. *All the President's Men.* New York: Simon & Schuster, 1974.
Berrigan, Daniel. *Absurd Convictions, Modest Hopes, Conversations after Prison with Lee Lockwood.* New York: Random House, 1972.
———. *America is Hard to Find.* Garden City: Doubleday, 1972.
Berrigan, Daniel, and Coles, Robert. *The Geography of Faith: Conversations between Daniel Berrigan, when underground, and Robert Coles.* Boston: Beacon, 1971.
Bhatia, Krishan. *Indira: A Biography of Prime Minister Gandhi.* New York: Praeger, 1974.
Bidault, Georges, trans. Sinclair, Marianne. *Resistance: The Political Autobiography of Georges Bidault.* New York: Praeger, 1965.
Biesele, Rudolph Leopold. *The History of the German Settlements in Texas, 1831–1861,* Austin: Von Boeckman-Jones, 1930.
Biggers, Don H. *German Pioneers in Texas,* Fredericksburg: Fredericksburg Publishing Co., 1925.
Billington, Monroe Lee. *The Political South in the Twentieth Century,* New York: Scribner's, 1975.
Bishop, Jim. *A Day in the Life of President Kennedy.* New York: Bantam (paper), 1964.
———. *A Day in the Life of President Johnson.* New York: Random House, 1967.
Blair, Joan, and Clay, Jr. *The Search for JFK.* New York: Berkley Publishing, 1974.
Blair, Leon Borden, ed., intro. Johnson, Lyndon B. *Essays on Radicalism in Contemporary America.* Austin: University of Texas Press, 1972.
Bloom, Lynn Z. *Doctor Spock: Biography of a Conservative Radical.* Indianapolis: Bobbs-Merrill, 1972.
Blum, John Morton, ed. *From the Morgenthau Diaries,* vol. 1, *Years of Crisis: 1929–1938.* Boston: Houghton Mifflin, 1959.
———, ed. *The Price of Vision: The Diary of Henry A. Wallace 1942–1946.* Boston: Houghton Mifflin, 1973.
Bohlen, Charles E., with Robert H. Phelps. *Witness to History, 1929–1969.* New York: W. W. Norton, 1973.
Boller, Paul, Jr. *Quotemanship, the use and abuse of quotations for political and other purposes.* Dallas: Southern Methodist University Press, 1967.
Bowles, Chester. *The Coming Political Breakthrough.* New York: Harper & Brothers, 1959.
———. *Promises to Keep, My Years in Public Life 1941–1969.* New York: Harper Colophon (paper), 1971.
Boyd, Malcolm. *As I Live and Breathe: Stages of an Autobiography.* New York: Random House, 1969.
Bracht, Viktor, trans. Schmidt, Charles Frank. *Texas in 1848.* San Antonio: Naylor, 1931.
Brackman, Arnold C. *The Communist Collapse in Indonesia.* New York: W. W. Norton, 1969.
Bradlee, Benjamin C. *Conversations with Kennedy.* New York: W. W. Norton, 1975.
Brammer, Bill. *The Gay Place.* Boston: Houghton Mifflin, 1961.
Brandon, Henry. *The Retreat of American Power.* Garden City: Doubleday, 1973.
Brauer, Carl M. *John F. Kennedy and the Second Reconstruction.* New York: Columbia University Press, 1977.
Briggs, Vernon, Jr. *Chicanos and Rural Poverty,* Baltimore: Johns Hopkins University Press, 1973.
Briggs, Vernon M.; Fogel, Walter; and Schmidt, Fred H. *The Chicano Worker.* Austin: University of Texas Press, 1977.
Brock, Clifton. *Americans for Democratic Action.* Washington, D.C.: Public Affairs Press, 1962.
Broder, David S. *The Party's Over.* New York: Harper & Row (paper), 1971.
Brooks, John. *The Great Leap, The Past Twenty-five Years in America.* New York: Harper & Row (paper), 1966.
———. *The Go-Go Years.* New York: Weybright and Talley, 1973.
Brown, Stuart Gerry. *Conscience in Politics, Adlai E. Stevenson in the 1950's.* Syracuse, N.Y.: Syracuse University Press, 1961.

Bryson, Bill. *The Social Basis of South Texas Bossism,* thesis, Harvard University, Mar. 1969.
Bullitt, Orville H., ed. *For the President: Personal and Secret, Correspondence Between Franklin D. Roosevelt and William C. Bullitt.* Boston: Houghton Mifflin, 1972.
Burdick, Eugene, and Wheeler, Harvey. *Fail-Safe.* New York: McGraw-Hill, 1962.
Burns, James MacGregor. *Edward Kennedy and the Camelot Legacy.* New York: W. W. Norton, 1976.
———. *John Kennedy: A Political Profile.* New York: Avon (paper), 1959, 1960.
———. *Roosevelt: The Lion and the Fox.* New York: Harcourt, Brace & Co., 1956.
———. ed. *To Heal and to Build: The Programs of Lyndon B. Johnson.* New York: McGraw-Hill, 1968.
———. *Uncommon Sense.* New York: Harper & Row, 1972.
Buss, Claude A. *The Arc of Crisis.* Garden City: Doubleday, 1961.
Byrnes, James F. *All in One Lifetime.* New York: Harper & Brothers, 1958.
Caidin, Martin, and Hymoff, Edward. *The Mission.* Philadelphia and New York: Lippincott, illus., 1964.
Califano, Joseph A., Jr. *A Presidential Nation,* New York: W. W. Norton, 1975.
———. *The Student Revolution: A Global Confrontation.* New York: Norton, 1970.
Carpenter, Liz. *Ruffles and Flourishes.* New York: Pocket Books (paper), 1971.
Cater, Douglass. *Power in Washington: A Critical Look at Today's Struggle to Govern in the Nation's Capital.* New York: Vintage (paper), 1965.
Carter, Jimmy. *Why Not the Best?* New York: Bantam (paper), 1975.
Casey, William Van Etten, and Nobile, Philip, eds. *The Berrigans.* New York: Praeger, 1971.
Casserly, John J. *The Ford White House: The Diary of a Speechwriter.* Boulder: Colorado Associated University Press, 1977.
Caute, David. *The Great Fear, The Anti-Communist Purge Under Truman and Eisenhower.* New York: Simon & Schuster, 1978.
Chase, Harold W., and Allen H. Lerman, eds. *Kennedy and the Press.* New York: Crowell, 1965.
Chester, Lewis; Hodgson, Godfrey; and Page, Bruce. *An American Melodrama: The Presidential Campaign of 1968.* New York: Dell (paper), 1969.
Christian, George. *The President Steps Down: A Personal Memoir of the Transfer of Power.* New York: Macmillan, 1970.
Church, Frank, and Tower, John et al., foreword Clark Mollenhoff. *Alleged Assassination Plots Involving Foreign Leaders: An Interim Report of the Select Committee to Study Governmental Operations with Respect to Intelligence Activities, United States Senate, with additional, supplemental, and separate views.* New York: W. W. Norton, 1976.
Clark, Kenneth B., and Hopkins, Jeannette. *A Relevant War Against Poverty: A Study of Community Action Programs and Observable Social Change.* New York: Harper & Row, 1968, 1969.
Cleaver, Eldridge. *Soul on Ice.* New York: Dell (paper), 1968.
Clecak, Peter. *Radical Paradoxes, Dilemmas of the American Left: 1945–1970.* New York: Harper & Row (paper), 1973.
Clinch, Nancy Gager. *The Kennedy Neurosis.* New York: Grosset and Dunlap, 1973.
Cloward, Richard A., and Pliven, Frances Fox. *The Politics of Turmoil, Essays on Poverty, Race, and the Urban Crisis.* New York: Pantheon, 1974.
Cocke, William A. *The Bailey Controversy in Texas.* San Antonio: The Cocke Co., 1908, 2 vols.
Coffin, Tristram. *The Armed Society, Militarism in Modern America.* Baltimore: Penguin (paper), 1964.
———. *Senator Fulbright, Portrait of a Public Philosopher.* New York: Dutton, 1966.
Coffin, William Sloane. *Once to Every Man: A Memoir.* New York: Atheneum, 1977.
Cohen, Richard M., and Witcover, Jules. *A Heartbeat Away, The Investigation and Resignation of Vice President Spiro T. Agnew.* New York: Viking, 1974.
Coit, Margaret L. *Mr. Baruch.* Boston: Houghton Mifflin, 1957, illus.
Coles, Robert, intro. Kennedy, Edward M. *still hungry in america.* New York: World, 1969.
Colson, Charles. *Born Again.* Old Tappan, N.J.: Chosen Books, 1971.
Colvin, Ian. *The Chamberlain Cabinet.* New York: Taplinger, 1971.
Conaway, James. *The Texans.* New York: Knopf, 1976.
Condon, Richard. *The Manchurian Candidate.* New York: McGraw-Hill, 1960.
Cooke, Alistair. *A Generation on Trial, U.S.A. v. Alger Hiss.* New York: Knopf, 1950.
Cook, Fred J. *The Corrupted Land, The Social Morality of Modern America.* New York: Macmillan, 1966.
———. *The Nightmare Decade, The Life and Times of Senator Joe McCarthy.* New York: Random House, 1971.
Cormier, Frank. *LBJ, The Way He Was.* Garden City: Doubleday, 1977.
Cowan, Paul; Egleson, Nick; and Hentoff, Nat. *State Secrets, Police Surveillance in America.* New York: Holt, Rinehart, and Winston, 1974.
Cowles, Fleur. *Friends and Memories.* New York: Reynal and Co., Morrow, 1978.
Coyle, David Cushman. *Ordeal of the Presidency.* Washington, D.C.: Public Affairs Press, 1960.
Crawford, Ann Fears, and Keever, Jack. *John B. Connally, Portrait in Power.* Austin: Jenkins Publishing Co., 1973.
Crouse, Timothy. *The Boys on the Bus.* New York: Random House, 1972, 1973.

Crozier, Brian. *De Gaulle.* New York: Scribner's, 1973.
———. *Strategy of Survival.* New Rochelle, N.Y.: Arlington House, 1978.
Cutler, John Henry. *Ed Brooke.* Indianapolis: Bobbs-Merrill, 1972.
Daniels, Jonathan. *White House Witness, 1942–1945.* Garden City: Doubleday, 1975.
David, Lester. *Ted Kennedy, Triumphs and Tragedies.* New York: Grosset and Dunlap, 1971, 1972.
David, Paul T.; Moos, Malcolm; and Goldman, Ralph M., eds. *Presidential Nominating Politics in 1952, The South.* Baltimore: Johns Hopkins Press, 1954.
Davis, Kenneth S. *A Prophet in His Own Country: The Triumphs and Defeats of Adlai E. Stevenson.* New York: Doubleday, 1957.
———. *The Politics of Honor: A Biography of Adlai Stevenson.* New York: Putnam, 1967.
Davis, Nuel Pharr. *Lawrence and Oppenheimer.* New York: Clarion (paper), 1969.
Dayan, Moshe. *Story of My Life, An Autobiography.* New York: Morrow, 1976.
Deakin, James. *The Lobbyists.* Washington, D.C.: Public Affairs Press, 1966.
Dean III, John W. *Blind Ambition, The White House Years.* New York: Simon & Schuster, 1976.
Divine, Robert A., ed. *Exploring the Johnson Years.* Austin: University of Texas Press, 1981.
Dixon, Sam Houston. *The Men Who Made Texas Free.* Houston: Texas Historical Publishing Co., c. 1924.
Dixon, Sam Houston, and Kemp, L.W. *The Heroes of San Jacinto.* Houston: Anson Jones Press, 1932.
Domhoff, G. William. *Who Rules America?* Englewood Cliffs, N.J.: Prentice-Hall (paper), 1967.
Dorough, C. Dwight. *Mr. Sam.* New York: Random House, 1962.
Douglas, Paul. *In Our Time.* New York: Harcourt, Brace and World, 1967.
Douglas, William O. *Go East, Young Man, The Early Years, The Autobiography of William O. Douglas.* New York: Random House, 1974.
Draper, Theodore. *Abuse of Power.* New York: Viking (paper), 1968.
Dubofsky, Melvin, and Van Tine, Warren. *John L. Lewis, A Biography.* New York: Quadrangle, 1977.
Dugger, Ronnie. *Dark Star, Hiroshima Reconsidered in the Life of Claude Eatherly of Lincoln Park, Texas.* New York: World, 1967.
———. *Our Invaded Universities: Form, Reform, and New Starts.* New York: W. W. Norton, 1974.
Dunne, Gerald T. *Hugo Black and the Judicial Revolution.* New York: Simon & Schuster, 1977.
Eban, Abba. *Abba Eban: An Autobiography.* New York: Random House, 1977.
Eisenhower, Dwight D. *The White House Years, Mandate for Change 1953–1956.* Garden City: Doubleday, 1963.
———. *The White House Years, Waging Peace 1956–1961.* Garden City: Doubleday, 1965.
Eisenhower, John S.D. *Strictly Personal.* Garden City: Doubleday, 1974.
Eisenhower, Milton S. *The Wine Is Bitter, the United States and Latin America.* Garden City, N.Y.: Doubleday, 1963.
Engelmayer, Sheldon D., and Wagman, Robert J. *Hubert Humphrey, The Man and His Dream.* New York: Methuen, 1978.
Engler, Robert. *The Politics of Oil, A Study of Private Power and Democratic Institutions.* New York: Macmillan, 1961.
Eszterhas, Joe, and Roberts, Michael D. *Thirteen Seconds, Confrontation at Kent State.* New York: Dodd, Mead, 1970.
Eubank, Keith. *Munich.* Norman: University of Oklahoma Press, 1963.
Evans, Rowland, and Novak, Robert. *Lyndon B. Johnson: The Exercise of Power.* New York: New American Library, 1966.
Evers, Charles, ed. and intro. Halsell, Grace. *Evers.* New York: World, 1971
Fall, Bernard B. *Hell in a Very Small Place, the Siege of Dien Bien Phu.* Philadelphia: Lippincott (paper), 1967.
———. *Last Reflections On a War.* New York: Doubleday, 1967.
Faulk, John Henry. *Fear on Trial.* New York: Simon & Schuster, 1964.
Finer, Herman. *Dulles Over Suez.* Chicago: Quadrangle Books, 1964.
Fischer, George, ed. *The Revival of American Socialism, Selected Papers of the Socialist Scholars Conference.* New York: Oxford University Press (paper), 1971.
Flemmons, Jerry. *Amon, The Life of Amon Carter, Sr., of Texas.* Austin: Jenkins, 1978.
Frady, Marshall. *Wallace.* New York: World, 1968.
———. *Billy Graham, A Parable of American Righteousness.* Boston: Little, Brown, 1979.
"Free," Aliases Meteskey, George, Hoffman, Abbie. *Revolution for the Hell of It.* New York: Dial Press (paper), 1968.
Freidel, Frank. *Franklin D. Roosevelt, Launching the New Deal.* Boston: Little, Brown, 1973.
Fuermann, George. *Houston: Land of the Big Rock.* Garden City: Doubleday, 1951.
———. *Reluctant Empire.* New York: Doubleday, 1957.
Fulbright, J. William. *The Arrogance of Power.* New York: Random House, 1966.
———. *The Pentagon Propaganda Machine,* New York: Liveright, 1970.
———. *Annals of an Abiding Liberal.* Boston: Houghton Mifflin, 1979.

Gantt, Fred. *The Chief Executive in Texas, A Study in Gubernatorial Leadership.* Austin: University of Texas Press, 1964.
Geyelin, Philip. *Lyndon B. Johnson and the World.* New York: Praeger, 1966.
Gold, Gerald, ed. *The White House Transcripts, Submission of Recorded Presidential Conversations to the Committee on the Judiciary of the House of Representatives by President Richard Nixon.* New York: Bantam (paper), 1974.
Goldman, Eric F. *The Tragedy of Lyndon Johnson.* New York: Knopf, 1969.
Goldston, Robert. *The American Nightmare, Senator Joseph R. McCarthy and the Politics of Hate.* Indianapolis: Bobbs-Merrill, 1973.
Goldwater, Barry. *Where I Stand.* New York: McGraw-Hill (paper), 1964.
Goodwin, Richard N. *Triumph or Tragedy, Reflections on Vietnam.* New York: Random House, 1966.
———. *The American Condition.* New York: Bantam (paper), 1975.
Goodwyn, Lawrence. *Democratic Promise, The Populist Movement in America.* New York: Oxford University Press, 1976.
———. *The South Central States.* New York: Time, Inc., 1967.
Goold-Adams, Richard. *John Foster Dulles, A Reappraisal.* New York: Appleton-Century-Crofts, 1962.
Gore, Albert. *Let the Glory Out, My South and Its Politics.* New York: Viking, 1972.
Gorman, Joseph Bruce. *Kefauver: A Political Biography.* New York: Oxford University Press, 1971.
Goulden, Joseph G. *Monopoly.* New York: Putnam's, 1968. *Meany.* New York: Atheneum, 1972.
———. *The Superlawyers, The Small and Powerful World of the Great Washington Law Firms.* New York: Dell (paper), 1971, 1972.
———. *The Best Years 1945–1950.* New York: Atheneum, 1976. *Korea, The Untold Story of the War.* New York: Times Books, 1982.
Graubard, Stephen R. *Kissinger: Portrait of a Mind.* New York: W. W. Norton, 1973.
Gray, A. C. *From Virginia to Texas, 1936, Diary of Col. William F. Gray, giving details of His Journey to Texas and Return in 1935–1936 and Second Journey to Texas in 1937.* Houston: Dillaye & Co., 1909.
Green, George Norris. *The Establishment in Texas Politics.* Westport, Conn.: Greenwood Press, 1979.
Gregory, Jack, and Strickland, Rennard. *Sam Houston with the Cherokees, 1829–1833.* Austin: University of Texas Press, 1967.
Griffith, Winthrop. *Humphrey, A Candid Biography.* New York: Morrow, 1965.
Gruening, Ernest. *Many Battles, The Autobiography of Ernest Gruening.* New York: Liveright, 1973.
Gunther, John. *Roosevelt in Retrospect.* New York: Harper & Bros., 1950.
Halberstam, David. *The Making of a Quagmire.* New York: Random House, 1965.
———. *The Unfinished Odyssey of Robert Kennedy.* New York: Bantam (paper), 1969.
———. *Ho.* New York: Random House, 1971.
———. *The Best and the Brightest.* New York: Random House, 1972. *The Powers That Be.* New York: Knopf, 1979.
Haldeman, H.R., with DiMona, Joseph. *The Ends of Power.* New York: Times Books, 1978.
Haley, J. Evetts. *A Texan Looks at Lyndon, A Study in Illegitimate Power.* Canyon, Tx.: Palo Duro Press (paper), 1964.
Hall, Gordon Langley, and Pinchot, Ann. *Jacqueline Kennedy: A Biography.* New York, Signet (paper), 1964.
Harrington, Michael. *The Accidental Century.* Baltimore: Penguin (paper), 1966.
———. *Toward a Democratic Left, A Radical Program for a New Majority.* New York: Macmillan, 1968.
Hartley, Robert E. *Charles H. Percy, A Political Perspective.* Chicago: Rand McNally, 1975.
Harvey, Frank. *Air War-Vietnam.* New York: Bantam (paper), 1967.
Harwood, Richard, and Johnson, Haynes. *Lyndon.* New York: Praeger, 1973.
Hatfield, Mark O. *Not Quite So Simple.* New York: Harper & Row, 1968.
Hayes, Samuel P., ed. *The Beginning of American Aid to Southeast Asia, The Griffin Mission of 1950.* Lexington, Ma.: Heath Lexington Books, 1971.
Haynes, Richard F. *The Awesome Power, Harry S. Truman as Commander in Chief.* Baton Rouge: Louisiana State University Press, 1973.
Heilbroner, Robert L. *The Future As History, The historic currents of our time and the direction in which they are taking America.* New York: Harper Torchbooks (paper), 1959, 1960.
Heller, Walter W. *New Dimensions of Political Economy.* Cambridge, Ma.: Harvard University Press, 1966.
Henderson, Richard B., foreword Frantz, Joe B. *Maury Maverick, A Political Biography.* Austin: University of Texas Press, 1970.
Heren, Louis. *No Hail, No Farewell.* New York: Harper & Row, 1970.
Herman, Edward S., and DuBoff, Richard B. *America's Vietnam Policy, The Strategy of Deception.* Washington, D.C.: Public Affairs Press (paper), 1966.
Herndon, William H., and Weik, Jesse W. *Herndon's Life of Lincoln.* Cleveland: World, 1930.
Hersh, Seymour M. *My Lai 4, a report on the massacre and its aftermath.* New York, Vintage (paper), 1970.
Hess, Karl. *In a Cause That Will Triumph, The Goldwater Campaign and the Future of Conservatism.* Garden City: Doubleday, 1967.

Hickel, Walter J. *Who Owns America?.* Englewood Cliffs, N.J.: Prentice-Hall, 1971.
Higgins, Marguerite. *Our Vietnam Nightmare.* New York: Harper & Row, 1965.
Hilsman, Roger. *To Move a Nation, The Politics of Foreign Policy in the Administration of John F. Kennedy.* Garden City: Doubleday, 1967.
Hirsch, Richard, and Trento, Joseph John. *The National Aeronautics and Space Administration.* New York: Praeger, 1973.
Honan, William H. *Ted Kennedy, Profile of a Survivor.* New York: Quadrangle Books, 1972.
Hoopes, Townsend. *The Limits of Intervention.* New York: McKay (paper), 1969.
———. *The Devil and John Foster Dulles.* Boston: Little Brown, 1973.
Horowitz, David. *The Free World Colossus.* New York: Hill and Wang, 1965.
Hughes, Emmet John. *The Ordeal of Power, A Political Memoir of the Eisenhower Years.* New York: Atheneum, 1963.
———. *The Living Presidency, The Resources and Dilemmas of the American Presidential Office.* New York: Coward, McCann & Geoghegan, 1972, 1973.
Humphrey, Hubert H. *The Cause Is Mankind, A Liberal Program for Modern America.* New York: Praeger, 1964.
———. *The Education of a Public Man, My Life and Politics* [ed. Norman Sherman]. Garden City: Doubleday, 1976.
Hunt, E. Howard. *Undercover, Memoirs of an American Secret Agent.* New York: Berkley, 1974.
Hunter, J. Marvin. *The Trail Drivers of Texas.* New York: Argosy-Antiquarian Ltd., 1963.
Hyman, Sidney. *The Lives of William Benton.* Chicago: University of Chicago Press, 1969.
———. *Marriner S. Eccles, Private Entrepreneur and Public Servant.* Stanford, Ca.: Graduate School of Business, Stanford University, 1976.
Ickes, Harold, *The Secret Diary of Harold L. Ickes.* New York: Simon & Schuster, c. 1953.
Jaworski, Leon. *The Right and the Power.* Pleasantville, N.Y.: Reader's Digest Press, 1976.
Jenkins III, John Holmes. *Recollections of Early Texas, The Memories of John Holland Jenkins.* Austin: University of Texas Press, 1958.
Johnson, Haynes, and Gwertzman, Bernard M. *Fulbright, The Dissenter.* Garden City: Doubleday, 1968.
Johnson, Lyndon Baines. *The Vantage Point, Perspectives of the Presidency, 1963–1969.* New York: Holt, Rinehart and Winston, 1971.
———, intro Stevenson, Adlai E. *A Time for Action, A Selection from the Speeches and Writings of Lyndon B. Johnson, 1953–1964.* New York: Atheneum, 1964.
Johnson, Mrs. Lyndon Baines. *A White House Diary.* New York: Holt, Rinehart and Winston, 1970.
Johnson, Nicholas. *How to Talk Back to Your Television Set.* Boston: Little, Brown, 1967.
Johnson, Rebekah Baines, intro Johnson, Lyndon Baines. *A Family Album.* New York: McGraw-Hill, 1965.
Johnson, Sam Houston, ed. Lopez, Enrique Hank. *My Brother Lyndon.* New York: Cowles, 1969, 1970.
Johnson, Walter, ed. *The Papers of Adlai E. Stevenson,* Vol. IV, *"Let's Talk Sense to the American People," 1952–1955.* Boston: Little, Brown, 1974.
Jones, Ernest. *The Life and Work of Sigmund Freud.* New York: Basic Books, 1953–1957, 3 vols.
Kahin, George McTurnan, and Lewis, John W. *The United States in Vietnam.* New York: Dial Press, 1967.
Karp, Walter. *Indispensable Enemies, The Politics of Misrule in America.* New York: Saturday Review Press, 1973.
Katz, Harvey. *Shadow on the Alamo, New Heroes Fight Old Corruption in Texas Politics.* Garden City: Doubleday, 1972.
Kearns, Doris. *Lyndon Johnson and the American Dream.* New York: Harper & Row, 1976.
Kefauver, Estes, with Till, Irene. *In a Few Hands, Monopoly Power in America.* New York: Pantheon, 1965.
Kemp, Louis Wiltz. *The Signers of the Texas Declaration of Independence.* Houston: Anson Jones Press, 1944.
Kennan, George. *American Diplomacy 1900–1950.* New York: Mentor (paper), 1963. *Memoirs: 1925–1950.* Boston: Atlantic Monthly Press, 1967. *Memoirs: 1950–1963.* Vol. II. Boston: Atlantic Monthly Press, 1972.
Kennedy, Robert F., ed. Lowi, Theodore J. *The Pursuit of Justice.* New York: Harper & Row (paper), 1964.
Kennedy, Rose Fitzgerald. *Times to Remember.* Garden City: Doubleday, 1974.
Khruschev Remembers, intro. Edward Crankshaw, trans. and ed. Strobe Talbott. Boston: Little, Brown, 1970. *Khruschev Remembers, The Last Testament,* intros. Edward Crankshaw, Jerrold Schechter, trans. and ed. Strobe Talbott. Boston: Little, Brown, 1974.
Kinch, Sam, and Long, Stuart. *Allan Shivers: The Pied Piper of Texas Politics.* Austin: Shoal Creek, 1973.
King, Irene Marschall. *John O. Meusebach, German Colonizer in Texas.* Austin: University of Texas Press, 1967.
Kistiakowsky, George B., intro. Maier, Charles S. *A Scientist at the White House, The Private Diary of President Eisenhower's Special Assistant for Science and Technology.* Cambridge: Harvard University Press, 1976.

Kluckhohn, Frank L. *The Inside on LBJ.* Derby, Conn.: Monarch (paper), 1964.
———. *Lyndon's Legacy.* Derby, Conn: Monarch, (paper), 1964.
Knebel, Fletcher, and Bailey, Charles. *Night of Camp David.* New York: Harper & Row, 1965.
———. *No High Ground.* New York: Harper & Row, 1960.
———. *Seven Days in May.* New York: Bantam (paper), 1963.
Knippa, Edwin William, Jr. "The Early Political Life of Lyndon B. Johnson, 1931–1937," unpublished thesis. Southwest Texas State College, Aug. 1967.
Koskoff, David E. *Joseph P. Kennedy, A Life and Times.* Englewood Cliffs, N.J.: Prentice-Hall, 1974.
Kraft, Joseph. *Profiles in Power.* New York: New American Library, 1966.
Kuehne, Cyril Matthew. *Hurricane Junction, A History of Port Aransas* (Texas). San Antonio: St. Mary's University, 1973.
Kunen, James Simon. *The Strawberry Statement: Notes of a College Revolutionary.* New York: Random House, 1968.
Landau, David. *Kissinger: The Uses of Power.* Boston: Houghton Mifflin, 1972.
Lash, Joseph P. *Roosevelt and Churchill—1939–1941: The Partnership that Saved the West.* New York: W. W. Norton, 1976.
Lee, R. Alton. *Truman and Taft-Hartley.* Lexington, Ky.: University of Kentucky Press, 1966.
LeMay, Gen. Curtis E, with Smith, Maj. Gen. Dale O. *America Is in Danger.* New York: Funk & Wagnalls, 1968.
Lilienthal, David E., intro Commager, Henry Steele. *The Journals of David E. Lilienthal.* 5 vols.: vol. 1, *The TVA Years 1939–1945* (1964); vol. 2, *The Atomic Energy Years 1945–1950* (1964); vol. 3, *The Venturesome Years 1950–1955* (1966); vol. 4, *The Road to Change 1955–1959* (1969); vol. 5, *The Harvest Years 1959–1963* (1971). New York: Harper & Row, 1964–1971.
Lincoln, Evelyn. *Kennedy & Johnson.* New York: Holt, Rinehart, and Winston, 1968.
———. *My Twelve Years with John F. Kennedy.* New York: David McKay, 1965.
Lippman, Theo, Jr. *Senator Ted Kennedy.* New York: W. W. Norton, 1976.
Lippmann, Walter. *The Cold War, A Study in U.S. Foreign Policy.* New York: Harper & Brothers, 1947.
Little, Dwayne L. "The Congressional Career of Sam Rayburn," thesis, University of Cincinnati, 1963.
Loewenheim, Francis L.; Langley, Harold D.; and Jonas, Manfred, eds. *Roosevelt and Churchill, Their Secret Wartime Correspondence.* New York: Saturday Review Press/E.P. Dutton, 1975.
Long, Edward V., foreword Humphrey, Hubert. *The Intruders, The Invasion of Privacy by Government and Industry.* New York: Praeger, 1967.
Lubell, Samuel. *The Hidden Crisis in American Politics.* New York: W. W. Norton, 1970.
Lucas, Jim G. *Dateline: Viet Nam.* New York: Award House, 1966.
Luskin, John. *Lippman, Liberty, and the Press.* University, Ala.: University of Alabama Press, 1972.
MacPherson, Myra. *The Power Lovers, An Intimate Look at Politics and Marriage.* New York: Ballantine (paper), 1976.
Maguire, Jack, ed. *A President's Country, A Guide to the Hill Country of Texas.* Austin: Alcalde Press, 1964.
Malraux, Andre, trans. Kilmartin, Terence. *Anti-Memoirs.* New York: Bantam (paper), 1970.
Manchester, William. *The Death of a President, November 20–November 25, 1963.* New York: Harper & Row, 1967.
———. *Portrait of a President, John F. Kennedy in Profile.* New York: MacFadden (paper), 1964.
Mankiewicz, Frank. *Perfectly Clear, Nixon from Whittier to Watergate.* New York: Quadrangle, 1973.
Marchetti, Victor, and Marks, John D., intro Wulf, Melvin L. *The CIA and the Cult of Intelligence.* New York: Dell (paper), 1974.
Marris, Peter, and Rein, Martin. *Dilemmas of Social Reform, Poverty and Community Action in the United States.* New York: Atherton, 1969.
Martin, Harold H. *Ralph McGill, Reporter.* Boston: Little, Brown, 1973.
Martin, Joel Bartlow. *Adlai Stevenson of Illinois: The Life of Adlai E. Stevenson.* Garden City: Doubleday, 1976.
———. *Adlai Stevenson and the World: The Life of Adlai E. Stevenson.* Garden City: Doubleday, 1977.
Martin, Roscoe. *The People's Party in Texas.* Austin: University of Texas Press (paper), 1970.
Masani, Zareer. *Indira Gandhi, A Biography.* New York: Crowell, 1975.
Mayer, George H. *The Republican Party 1854–1964.* New York: Oxford University Press, 1964.
Mazlish, Bruce. *Kissinger, The European Mind in American Policy.* New York: Basic Books, 1976.
McCarthy, Abigail. *Private Faces/Public Places.* Garden City: Doubleday, 1972.
McCarthy, Eugene J. *The Hard Years, A Look at Contemporary America and American Institutions.* New York: Viking, 1975.
———. *The Year of the People.* Garden City: Doubleday, 1969.
McCord, William. *Mississippi: The Long, Hot Summer.* New York: W. W. Norton, 1965.
McGaffin, William, and Knoll, Erwin. *Anything but the Truth, the Credibility Gap—How the News Is Managed in Washington.* New York: Putnam's, 1968.
McGovern, Eleanor, with Hoyt, Mary Finch. *Uphill, A Personal Story.* Boston: Houghton Mifflin, 1974.

McKay, Seth Shepard. *Texas Politics, 1906–1944, With Special Reference to the German Counties.* Lubbock: Texas Tech Press, 1952.
———. *Texas and the Fair Deal.* San Antonio: Naylor, 1954.
McKinney, R. Kay. *LBJ . . . his home and heritage.* San Angelo, Tx.: Anchor Publishing Co., 1964.
McLellan, David S. *Dean Acheson, The State Department Years.* New York: Dodd, Mead, 1976, illus.
McNamara, Robert S. *The Essence of Security, Reflections in Office.* New York: Harper & Row, 1968.
McPherson, Harry. *A Political Education.* Boston: Little, Brown, 1972.
Melman, Seymour. *The Permanent War Economy, American Capitalism in Decline.* New York: Simon & Shuster, 1974.
Miller, Merle. *Plain Speaking, An Oral Biography of Harry S. Truman.* New York: Berkley Publishing Corp., 1973, 1974.
———. *Lyndon, An Oral Biography.* New York: Ballantine (paper), 1980.
Miller, William "Fishbait," as told to Leighton, Frances Spatz. *Fishbait, The Memoirs of the Congressional Doorkeeper.* Englewood Cliffs, N.J.: Prentice-Hall, 1977.
Millis, Walter, with E.S. Duffield, eds. *The Forrestal Diaries.* New York: Viking, 1951.
Mills, C. Wright. *The Power Elite.* New York: Oxford University Press, 1956.
Milton, Henry A. *The President Is Missing!* New York: Banner (paper), 1967.
Mintz, Morton, and Cohen, Jerry S. *America, Inc., Who Owns and Operates the United States,* New York: Dell (paper), 1971.
Montgomery, R.H. *The Brimstone Game, Monopoly in Action.* New York: Vanguard Press, 1940.
Montgomery, Ruth. *Mrs. LBJ.* New York: Holt, Rinehart and Winston, 1964.
Mollenhoff, Clark R. *Despoilers of Democracy.* Garden City: Doubleday, 1965.
Mooney, Booth. *The Lyndon Johnson Story.* New York: Farrar-Strauss, 1956, 1964.
———. *LBJ, An Irreverent Chronicle,* New York: Crowell, 1976.
———. *Mister Texas, The Story of Coke Stevenson.* Dallas: Texas Printing House, Inc., 1947.
Moursund, John Stribling. *Blanco County Families for One Hundred Years.* San Antonio, Tx., 1958.
Muller, Herbert J. *Adlai Stevenson, A Study in Values.* New York: Harper & Row, 1967.
Murphy, Robert. *Diplomat Among Warriors.* Garden City: Doubleday, 1964.
Myrdal, Gunnar. *Challenge to Affluence.* New York: Pantheon, 1962.
Nalle, Ouida Ferguson. *The Fergusons of Texas.* San Antonio: Naylor, 1946.
Neary, John. *Julian Bond: Black Rebel.* New York: Morrow (paper), 1971.
Neff, Pat. *The Battles of Peace.* Fort Worth: Pioneer Publishing, 1925.
Nessen, Ron. *It Sure Looks Different from the Inside.* New York: Playboy Press, 1978.
Nevin, David. *Muskie of Maine.* New York: Random House, 1972.
———. *The Texans, What They Are—And Why.* New York: Morrow, 1968.
Nevins, Allan, and Commager, Henry Steele. *A Short History of the United States.* New York: Modern Library, 1956.
Newfield, Jack. *Robert Kennedy, A Memoir.* New York: Dutton, 1969.
Newlon, Clarke. *L.B.J., the Man from Johnson City.* New York: Dodd, Mead, 1964, 1966.
New York Herald Tribune (ed. not listed). *1964 Presidential Election Guide.* New York: Whitney, 1964.
Nixon, Richard. *The Memoirs of Richard Nixon.* New York: Grosset & Dunlap, 1978.
———. *The Real War.* New York: Warner Books, 1980.
Novak, Michael. *Choosing Our King.* New York: Macmillan, 1974.
Oberdorfer, Don. *Tet!* New York: Doubleday, 1971.
O'Brien, Lawrence F. *No Final Victories, A Life in Politics—From John F. Kennedy to Watergate.* New York: Ballantine (paper), 1975.
O'Donnell, Kenneth P., and Powers, David F., with McCarthy, Joe. *"Johnny, We Hardly Knew Ye," Memories of John Fitzgerald Kennedy.* Boston: Little, Brown, 1972.
Perkus, Cathy, ed., intro. Chomsky, Noam. *COINTELPRO, The FBI's Secret Political War on Political Freedom.* New York: Monad Press (paper), 1975.
Pilat, Oliver. *Drew Pearson, An Unauthorized Biography.* New York: Pocket Books (paper), 1973.
Pool, William C.; Craddock, Emmie; and Conrad, David E. *Lyndon Baines Johnson, The Formative Years.* San Marcos: Southwest Texas State College Press, 1965.
Porterfield, Bill. *LBJ Country.* Garden City: Doubleday, 1965.
Prochnau, William W., and Larsen, Richard W. *A Certain Democrat, Senator Henry M. Jackson, A Political Biography.* Englewood Cliffs, N.J.: Prentice-Hall, 1972.
Provence, Harry. *Lyndon B. Johnson, A Biography.* New York: Fleet, 1964.
Purdy, Anthony, and Sutherland, Douglas. *Burgess and MacLean.* Garden City: Doubleday, 1963.
Purvis, Hoyt, ed. *The Presidency and the Press.* Austin: Lyndon B. Johnson School of Public Affairs (paper), 1976.
Ramey, William Neal, on George Baines, Sr., in *Texian Annual.* 1886.
Rank, Hugh, ed. *Language and Public Policy.* Urbana, Ill.: National Council of Teachers of English Committee on Public Doublespeak, 1974.
Rather, Dan, and Gates, Gary Paul. *The Palace Guard.* New York: Warner (paper), 1975.

Rather, Dan, with Herskowitz, Mickey. *The Camera Never Blinks, Adventures of a TV Journalist.* New York: Morrow, 1977.
Rauch, Basil. *The History of the New Deal.* New York: Creative Age Press, 1944.
———. *Roosevelt from Munich to Pearl Harbor.* New York: Creative Age Press, 1950.
Ray, Worth S. *Austin Colony Pioneers.* Austin: published by the author, 1949.
Reedy, George. *The Presidency in Flux* New York and London: Columbia University Press, 1973.
———. *The Twilight of the Presidency.* New York and Cleveland: World, 1970.
Reich, Charles A. *The Greening of America.* New York: Random House, 1970.
Ridgeway, James. *The Politics of Ecology.* New York: Dutton, 1970.
Ridings, Sam P. *The Chisholm Trail.* Guthrie, Okla.: Co-Operative Publishing Co., 1936.
Roberts, Charles, intro, Salinger, Pierre. *LBJ's Inner Circle.* New York: Delacorte Press, 1965.
Roemer, Ferdinand, trans. Mueller, Oswald. *Texas with particular reference to German immigration and the Physical Appearance of the Country.* San Antonio: Standard Printing Co., 1935.
Rogow, Arnold A. *James Forrestal, A Study of Personality, Politics, and Policy.* New York: Macmillan, 1963.
Roosevelt, Elliott, ed. *F.D.R. His Personal Letters 1928–1945.* New York: Duell, Sloan and Pearce, 1950, 2 vols.
Roosevelt, Theodore. *Addresses and Presidential Messages of Theodore Roosevelt, 1902–1904.* New York: Putnam's Sons, 1904.
Ross, Lillian. *Adlai Stevenson.* Philadelphia and New York: Lippincott, 1966.
Roszak, Theodore, ed. *The Dissenting Academy.* New York: Random House, 1967, 1968.
Rovere, Richard. *Senator Joe McCarthy.* New York: Harcourt, Brace, 1959.
———. *Waist Deep in the Big Muddy, Personal Reflections on 1968.* Boston: Atlantic Monthly Press, 1968.
Rowen, Hobart. *The Free Enterprisers, Kennedy, Johnson and the Business Establishment.* New York: Putnam's, 1964.
Ryder-Taylor, Henry. *History of the Alamo and of the Local Franciscan Missions.* San Antonio: Nic Tengg, Inc., c. 1936.
Ryskind, Allan H., *Hubert, An Unauthorized Biography of the Vice President.* New Rochelle: Arlington House, 1968.
Sakowitz, Robert T. "The 1948 Texas Senatorial Campaign and the Crisis in the Democratic Party," thesis, Harvard University, 1960.
Sale, Kirkpatrick. *Power Shift, The Rise of the Southern Rim and Its Challenge to the Eastern Establishment.* New York: Random House, 1975.
Salinger, Pierre. *With Kennedy.* Garden City: Doubleday, 1966.
Schandler, Herbert Y. *The Unmaking of a President, Lyndon Johnson and Vietnam.* Princeton, N.J.: Princeton University Press, 1977.
Schell, Jonathan. *The Time of Illusion.* New York: Vintage (paper), 1976.
———. *The Village of Ben Suc.* New York: Vintage (paper), 1968.
Schlafly, Phyllis. *A Choice Not an Echo.* Alton, Ill.: Pere Marquette Press (paper), 1964.
Schlesinger, Arthur M., Jr. *A Thousand Days, John F. Kennedy in the White House.* Boston: Houghton Mifflin, 1965.
———. *The Bitter Heritage, Vietnam and American Democracy 1941–1966.* Boston: Houghton Mifflin, 1967.
———. *The Crisis in Confidence, Ideas, Power, and Violence in America.* New York: Bantam (paper), 1969.
———. *The Imperial Presidency,* Boston: Houghton Mifflin, 1973.
Schoenbrun, David. *The Three Lives of Charles de Gaulle.* New York: Atheneum, 1966.
Schorr, Daniel. *Clearing the Air.* Boston: Houghton Mifflin, 1977, illus.
Schrag, Peter. *The End of the American Future.* New York: Simon & Schuster, 1973.
Schram, Stuart. *Mao Tse-tung.* Middlesex, England: Penguin Books (paper), 1972.
Serling, Robert J. *The President's Plane Is Missing.* New York: Doubleday, 1967.
Shadegg, Stephen. *Barry Goldwater: Freedom Is His Flight Plan.* New York: Fleet, 1962.
Sheehan, Neal; Smith, Hedrick; Kenworthy, E.W.; and Butterworth, Fox. *The Pentagon Papers as published by* The New York Times. (Based on investigative reporting by Neil Sheehan, written by Neil Sheehan et al., with eds. Gerald Gold, Allan M. Siegal, and Samuel Abt.) New York: Bantam (paper), 1971.
Sheridan, Walter, intro Schulberg, Budd. *The Fall and Rise of Jimmy Hoffa.* New York: Saturday Review Press, 1972.
Sherrill, Robert. *The Accidental President.* New York: Grossman, 1967.
———. *Why They Call It Politics, A Guide to America's Government.* New York: Harcourt Brace Javanocich, 1972.
Sherwood, Robert E. *Roosevelt and Hopkins, An Intimate History.* New York: Harper & Brothers, 1948.
Shirer, William L. *The Rise and Fall of the Third Reich, A History of Nazi Germany.* New York: Simon & Schuster, 1960.
Shuffler, R. Henderson. *The Houstons at Independence.* Waco: Texian Press, 1966.

Sibley, Marilyn McAdams. *Travelers in Texas, 1761–1860.* Austin: University of Texas Press, 1967.
Sidey, Hugh. *John F. Kennedy, President.* Greenwich, Conn.: Crest (paper), 1964.
———. *A Very Personal Presidency, Lyndon Johnson in the White House.* New York: Atheneum, 1968.
Singer, Kurt, and Sherrod, Jane. *Lyndon Baines Johnson, Man of Reason.* Minneapolis: Denison, 1964.
Sirica, John J. *To Set the Record Straight: The Break-in, the Tapes, the Conspirators, the Pardon.* New York: W.W. Norton, 1979.
Slater, Jerome, intro. Morgenthau, Haus. *Intervention and Negotiation, The United States and The Dominican Revolution.* New York: Harper & Row, 1970.
Small, William J. *Political Power and the Press,* New York: W. W. Norton, 1972.
Smith, Marie. *The President's Lady, An Intimate Biography of Mrs. Lyndon B. Johnson.* New York: Random House, 1964.
Solberg, Carl. *Riding High, America in the Cold War.* New York: Mason and Lipscomb, 1973.
Sonnichsen, C.L. *I'll Die Before I Run, The Story of the Great Feuds of Texas.* New York: Harper & Brothers, 1951.
Sorenson, Theodore C. *Kennedy.* New York: Bantam (paper), 1965.
Speer, John W., ed. Armbruster, Henry C. *A History of Blanco County.* Austin: Pemberton Press, 1965.
Stambaugh, J. Lee, and Stambaugh, Lillian J. *A History of Collin County, Texas.* Austin: Texas State Historical Association, 1958.
Steinberg, Alfred. *The Man from Missouri, The Life and Times of Harry S. Truman.* New York: Putnam's, 1962.
———. *Sam Johnson's Boy, A Close-Up of the President from Texas.* New York: Macmillan, 1968.
———. *Sam Rayburn, A Biography.* New York: Hawthorn, 1975.
Stern, Philip M. *The Great Treasury Raid.* New York: Signet (paper), 1965.
Stevenson, Burton Egbert, ed. *Poems of American History.* Boston and New York: Houghton-Mifflin, 1908.
St. John, Robert. *Eban.* Garden City: Doubleday, 1972.
Stormer, John A. *None Dare Call It Treason.* Florissant, Mo.: Liberty Bell Press (paper), 1964.
Sulzberger, C.L. *An Age of Mediocrity, Memoirs and Diaries 1963–1972.* New York: Macmillan, 1973.
———. *The Last of the Giants.* New York: Macmillan, 1970.
Talbott, Strobe, trans. and ed., intro. Crankshaw, Edward. *Khrushchev Remembers,* Boston: Little, Brown, 1970, illus.
Taylor, Maxwell D. *Responsibility and Response.* New York: Harper & Row, 1967.
terHorst, Jerald F. *Gerald Ford and the Future of the Presidency.* New York: The Third Press, 1974.
Thayer, George. *The War Business, The International Trade in Armaments,* New York: Avon (paper), 1969.
———. *Who Shakes the Money Tree?* New York: Simon & Schuster, 1973.
Thomas, Helen. *Dateline: White House.* New York: Macmillan, 1975.
Thomson, Charles A. H., and Shattuch, Francis M., *The 1956 Presidential Campaign.* Washington, D.C.: Brookings Institution, 1960.
Thrall, Homer S. *The People's Illustrated Almanac, Texas Handbook and Immigrants' Guide, for 1880.* . . . St. Louis, Mo.: Thompson & Co., 1880.
Truman, Harry S. *Memoirs.* Vol. I, *Year of Decisions;* Vol. II, *Years of Trial and Hope*. Garden City: Doubleday, 1955.
Truman, Margaret. *Harry S. Truman.* New York: Pocket Books (paper), 1974.
Tugwell, Rexford G., and Cronin, Thomas E., eds. *The Presidency Reappraised.* New York: Praeger, 1974.
Turner, Frederick Jackson. *The Frontier in American History.* New York: Holt, Rinehart and Winston, 1963.
Valenti, Jack. *Ten Heroes and Two Heroines and Other Writings by the Houston Post Columnist.* Houston: Premier Printing Co., 1957.
———. *A Very Human President.* New York: W.W. Norton, 1976.
Vestal, Bud. *Jerry Ford, Up Close, An Investigative Biography.* New York: Coward, McCann & Geoghegan, 1974.
Walton, Richard J. *Henry Wallace, Harry Truman, and the Cold War.* New York: Viking, 1976.
Ward, Barbara. *The Rich Nations and the Poor Nations.* New York: W.W. Norton (paper), 1962.
Warren, Sidney, ed. *The American President.* Englewood Cliffs, N.J.: Prentice-Hall (paper), 1967.
Watterson, Henry. *History of the Spanish-American War.* New York: The Werner Co., 1898, illus.
Webb, Walter Prescott, intro. Frantz, Joe B. *Divided We Stand, The Crisis of a Frontierless Democracy* University [of Texas] Co-Op (undated), orig. pub. 1937.
———. *The Great Plains.* New York: Grosset & Dunlap, 1931.
———, intro. Toynbee, Arnold J. *The Great Frontier.* Austin: University of Texas Press, 1964.
———, intro. Johnson, Lyndon B. *The Texas Rangers.* Austin: University of Texas Press, 1965.
Webb, Walter Prescott, and Carroll, H. Bailey, eds. *The Handbook of Texas.* Austin: Texas State Historical Association, 1952, 2 vols.
Weintal, Edward, and Bartlett, Charles. *Facing the Brink, An Intimate Study of Crisis Diplomacy.* New York: Scribner's, 1967.

Whaley, Richard J. *Taking Sides, A Personal View of America from Kennedy to Nixon to Kennedy.* Boston: Houghton Mifflin, 1974.
White, Theodore H. *The Making of the President 1960.* New York: Pocket Books (paper), 1961.
———. *In Search of History, A Personal Adventure.* New York: Harper & Row, 1978.
White, William S. *Queens Die Proudly.* New York: Harcourt, Brace and Co., 1943.
———. *The Taft Story.* New York: Harper & Brothers, 1954.
———. *Citadel: The Story of the U.S. Senate.* New York: Harper & Brothers, 1956.
———. *Majesty and Mischief, A Mixed Tribute to F.D.R.* New York: McGraw-Hill, 1961.
———. *The Professional: Lyndon Baines Johnson.* New York: Crest (paper), 1964.
———. *The Responsibles.* New York: Harper & Row, 1972.
Whitman, Alden, and *The New York Times. Adlai E. Stevenson: Politician, Diplomat, Friend.* New York: Harper & Row, 1965.
Wicker, Tom. *JFK and LBJ, The Influence of Personality Upon Politics.* New York: Morrow, 1968.
Wilbarger, J.W. *Indian Depredations in Texas.* Austin: Hutchings Printing House, 1889; Austin: Pemberton Press edition, 1967.
Williams, Amelia W., and Barker, Eugene C. eds. *The Writings of Sam Houston, 1813–1863.* Austin: University of Texas Press, 1942, 8 vols.
Williams, T. Harry. *Huey Long,* New York: Bantam (paper), 1970.
Williams, William Appleman. ed. *The Shaping of American Diplomacy.* Chicago: Rand McNally, 1956.
———. *The Tragedy of American Diplomacy.* Cleveland: World, 1959.
Winfrey, Dorman H., and Day, James M., eds. *The Indian Papers of Texas and the Southwest, 1825–1916.* Austin: Pemberton Press, 1966, 5 vols.
Winter-Berger, Robert N. *The Washington Pay-Off, An Insider's View of Corruption in Government.* New York: Dell (paper), 1972.
Wise, David, and Ross, Thomas B. *The Invisible Government,* New York: Random House, 1964.
———. *The Politics of Lying, Government Deception, Secrecy, and Power.* New York: Vintage (paper), 1973.
Witcover, Jules. *85 Days, The Last Campaign of Robert F. Kennedy.* New York: Ace (paper), 1969.
Wolfskill, George, and Hudson, John A. *All But the People, Franklin D. Roosevelt and His Critics, 1933–39.* Toronto: Macmillan-Collier-Macmillan Canada Ltd., 1969.
Woodward, Bob, and Bernstein, Carl. *The Final Days.* New York: Simon & Schuster, 1976.
Yarmolinsky, Adam. *The Military Establishment, Its Impact on American Society.* New York: Perennial (paper), 1973.
Yost, Charles W. *History and Memory.* New York: W. W. Norton, 1980.
Young, Whitney M., Jr. *Beyond Racism, Building an Open Society.* New York: McGraw-Hill, 1969.
Zeitlin, Arnold. *To the Peace Corps, With Love.* Garden City; Doubleday, 1965.

Articles

(Including some occasional publications and interviews in the form of articles)

Abel, Lionel *et al.*, "Liberal Anti-Communism Revisited," Symposium, *Commentary,* Sept. 1967.
Acheson, Dean. "Memories of Joe McCarthy," *Harper's,* Oct. 1969.
Alexander, Herbert E., and Meyers, Harold B. "The Switch in Campaign Giving," *Fortune,* Nov. 1965.
Alsop, Stewart, "Who Will Be the Democrats' Candidate?" *Saturday Evening Post,* "The New President," *Saturday Evening Post,* Dec. 10, 1963; "Johnson Takes Over: The Untold Story," *Saturday Evening Post,* Feb. 15, 1964.
Amrine, Michael, "Hubert Horatio Humphrey," *Progressive,* April, 1960.
Anderson, Jack, "The Many Sides of Lyndon Johnson," *Parade (Fort Worth Star-Telegram),* Mar. 3, 1968.
Anderson, Patrick, "The New Defense Secretary Thinks Like the President," *NYT Magazine,* Jan. 28, 1968.
Anonymous, "LBJ: The Theme is Unity, Achievement," *Democratic Digest,* Aug. 1960.
Anson, Robert Sam, "A parallax view of history," *New Times,* July 26, 1974.
Bagdikian, Ben H., "The New Lyndon Johnson," *Saturday Evening Post,* Feb. 24, 1962.
Bailey, Thomas A., "Johnson and Kennedy, The 2,000 Days," *NYT Magazine,* Nov. 6, 1966.
Ball, George W., "Slogans and Realities," *Foreign Affairs,* July 1969.
Barber, James David, "Analyzing Presidents: From Passive-Positive Taft to Active-Negative Nixon," *Washington Monthly,* Oct. 1969.
Barron, George P., "LBJ Smile Won Him Job," *SAE,* Jan. 30, 1966.
Bernstein, Barton J., "New Light on the A-Bomb Race," *Nation,* Sept. 16, 1978.
Bird, John, "Lyndon Johnson's Religion," *Saturday Evening Post,* Mar. 27, 1965.
Blum, Robert M., "The Peiping Cable: A Drama of 1949," *NYT Magazine,* Aug. 13, 1978.
Bode, Winston, "Back Home," *Southwest Review,* Autumn 1966.

Boller, Paul F., Jr., "LBJ and the Art of Quotation," *Southwest Review,* Winter 1966.
Boulding, Kenneth, "The Many Failures of Success," *Saturday Review,* Nov. 23, 1968; "In the Money," *NY Review of Books,* Sept. 12, 1968.
Brammer, Bill, "Call to Greatness Muffed by Mr. Mitty," *Texas Observer,* Feb. 28, 1955; "To Hell With the Facts," *Texas Observer,* April 11, 1955; "President Glooey," *Texas Observer,* Jan. 10, 1963; "Mencken and Minnesota Fats," *Texas Observer,* Oct. 18, 1968; "Apocalypse Now? A Sensitive Sounding of Today's New Youth," *Texas Observer,* Nov. 1, 1968.
Breazeale, George, "Hye and the Mighty," *Texas Parade,* June, 1968.
Broder, David, "Consensus Politics: End of an Experiment," *Atlantic Monthly,* Oct. 1966.
Brodie, Fawn, "Hidden Presidents, Looking through their memoirs for involuntary truth," *Harper's,* April 1977.
Busch, Noel F., "Senator Russell of Georgia," *Reader's Digest,* Dec., 1966.
Carpenter, Leslie E., "The Whip from Texas," *Collier's,* Feb. 17, 1951; "Lyndon Baines Johnson, Profile of a President," supplement to *Dallas Times-Herald,* Feb. 1964.
Carpenter, Liz, "The Serene Widowhood of Lady Bird Johnson," *McCall's,* July 1973.
Cater, Douglass, "Lyndon Johnson, Rising Democratic Star," *The Reporter,* Jan. 20, 1953; "The Trouble in Lyndon Johnson's Back Yard," *The Reporter,* Dec. 1, 1955; "The Hard-Won Destiny of Lyndon Johnson," *The Reporter,* Dec. 19, 1963.
Chavez, Cesar, "Sharing the Wealth," *Playboy,* Jan. 1970.
Chomsky, Noam, "Ideological Conformity in America," *Nation,* Jan. 27, 1979.
Clifford, Clark, "A Viet Nam Reappraisal," *Foreign Affairs,* July 1969.
Collier, Everett, "Rayburn for President? A Footnote to the 1952 Election," *Texas Quarterly,* Winter, 1966.
Conroy, James, "Record Arms Budget Marks 'Generation of Peace,'" *Newsletter of the Democratic Left,* June 1974.
Considine, Bob, "'A President Has Damned Few Friends'—LBJ," *This Week,* Aug. 25, 1968.
Danzig, David, and Feild, John, "The Betrayal of the American City," *Commentary,* June 1968.
Davidson, Bill, "Texas Political Powerhouse . . . Lyndon Johnson," *Look,* Aug. 4, 1959; "Lyndon Johnson . . . Can a Southerner Be Elected President," *Look,* Aug. 18, 1959.
Davies, John Paton, Jr., "The China of John Paton Davies," from his book, *Dragon by the Tail* (New York: W. W. Norton, 1972), *Intellectual Digest,* July, 1972.
Deakin, James, "The Dark Side of L.B.J.," *Esquire,* Aug. 1967.
DeWeerd, Harvey A., "Strategic Decision Making: Vietnam, 1965–1968," *The Yale Review,* June 1978.
Draper, Theodore, "Israel and World Politics," *Commentary,* Aug. 1967.
Drew, Elizabeth, "Autumn Notes—II," *New Yorker,* Mar. 18, 1974.
Dugger, Ronnie, "What Corrupted Texas?" *Harper's,* Mar. 1957; "The Johnsons' TV Interests," *Texas Observer,* Dec. 18, 1959; "Johnson's Record—I," "The Johnson Record—II," and "Johnson of Texas: A Summing Up," *Texas Observer,* June 3, 10, and 24, resp., 1960; "Before We Shall Cheer," *Progressive,* May 1964; "As Mike Mansfield Was Saying—" *Progressive,* May 1968; "Up and at 'em on Box 13," *Texas Observer,* Sept. 23, 1977; "To a Novelist Dying Young—Laureled Writer, Johnson Adviser, Bill Brammer OD'd on the '60's," *Washington Post,* June 18, 1978.
Elliott, Claude, "Union Sentiment in Texas, 1861–1865," *Southwestern Historical Quarterly,* vol. 50, pp. 463–64.
Evans, Rowland, Jr. "The Sixth Sense of Carl Vinson," *The Reporter,* Apr. 12, 1962.
Evans, Rowland, and Novak, Robert, "Report," *Atlantic Monthly,* Oct. 1967.
Fairlie, Henry, "Thoughts on the Presidency," *The Public Interest,* Fall 1967.
Feifer, Jules, "LBJ in Caricature," *Harper's,* Feb. 1968.
Ferry, W.H., "The Unanswerable Questions," *Center Magazine,* July 1969.
Fischer, John, "The Kennedy Era: Stage Two, A Forecast," *Harper's,* Feb. 1962.
Fiske, Edward B., "The Closest Thing to a White House Chaplain," *NYT Magazine,* June 8, 1969; "Praying with the President in the White House," *NYT Magazine,* Aug. 8, 1971.
Fliegel, Dorian J., "Forgotten History of the Draft," *Nation,* April 10, 1967.
Frady, Marshall, "The Use and Abuse of Billy Graham," *Esquire,* April 10, 1979.
Frank, Jerome D., "The Great Antagonism," *Atlantic Monthly,* Dec. 1958.
Frantz, Joe B., "Kennedy and Johnson: The Senatorial Years," *Proceedings,* Philosophical Society of Texas, 1967, pp. 22–34; "Opening a Curtain: The Metamorphosis of Lyndon B. Johnson," *Journal of Southern History,* Feb. 1979.
Fritchey, Clayton, "The Issue (and Some Miscellaneous Trimmings)" *Harper's,* May 1966.
Fulbright, J. William, "In Thrall to Fear," *New Yorker,* Jan. 8, 1972; "The Wars in Your Future," *Look,* Dec. 2, 1969.
Gass, Oscar, "The Political Economy of the Great Society," *Commentary,* Oct. 1965.
Gelb, Leslie, "The Pentagon Papers and *The Vantage Point,*" *Foreign Policy,* Spring 1972.
Goar, J.C., "Bloody Times in Blanco County," *Frontier Times,* Aug. 1929.
Goodwin, Richard N., "Dismantling the Presidency: Advise, Consent & Restrain," *Rolling Stone,* Mar. 14, 1974.
Graebner, Norman A., "The Cold War Revisited" (a review) *Virginia Quarterly Review,* Spring 1978.
Graham, John, "The Universal Military Obligation," *The Fund for the Republic,* June 1958.

Halberstam, David, "Notes from the Bottom of the Mountain," *Harper's*, June 1968; "Lyndon," *Esquire*, Aug. 1972; "How It All Began," *Progressive*, April 1973.
Hall, Joseph S., ed. "Horace M. Hall's Letters from Gillespie Co., Texas, 1871–1873," *Southwestern Historical Quarterly*, Jan. 1959.
Harriman, W. Averell, "From Stalin to Kosygin: The Myths and the Realities," *Look*, Oct. 3, 1967.
Harris, Joseph P., "The Senatorial Rejection of Leland Olds: A Case Study," *The American Political Science Review*, Sept. 1951.
Harris, Richard, "Justice," *New Yorker*, Nov. 8, 15, 22, 1969
Harrison, Selig S., "Lyndon Johnson's World," *New Republic*, June 13, 1960.
Healy, Paul F., "The Frantic Gentleman from Texas," *Saturday Evening Post*, May 19, 1951.
Heilbroner, Robert, "Counterrevolutionary America," *Commentary*, April 1967.
Holden, W.S., "Law and Lawlessness on the Texas Frontier," *Southwestern Historical Quarterly*, vol. 44, pp. 188–203.
Howe, Quincy, "The New Age of the Journalist Historian," *Saturday Review*, May 20, 1967.
Huie, William Bradford, "Murder in Texas," *Cavalier Magazine*, Aug. 1961.
Humphrey, Hubert, "Tax Loop Holes," *Public Affairs Institute*, foreword Paul Douglas, 1952 (a pamphlet).
Hurt III, Harry, "The Most Powerful Texans," *Texas Monthly*, April 1976.
Janeway, Eliot, "Johnson of the 'Watchdog Committee'," *NYT Magazine*, June 17, 1951.
Janeway, Michael C., "Lyndon Johnson's Other Wars," *Atlantic Monthly*, Sept. 1967; Interviewer, "Bill Moyers talks about LBJ, Power, Poverty, War, and the Young," *Atlantic Monthly*, July 1968.
Janos, Leo, "The Last Days of the President, LBJ in Retirement," *Atlantic Monthly*, July 1973.
Jenkins, Peter, "H.H.H.: 'What this country needs is a nice man as President of the United States," *NYT Magazine*, May 28, 1972
Johnson, Lyndon B., "A Helping Hand for Youth," *Texas Municipalities*, Nov., 1935; "My Political Philosophy," *Texas Quarterly*, Winter 1958.
Johnson, Mrs. Lyndon B., "Help Your Husband Guard His Heart," *This Week*, Feb. 1956 (as told to J. H. Pollack); "The Story of the LBJ Ranch" (an account Mrs. Johnson gave her husband for his fifty-seventh birthday) *AAS*, Aug. 28, 1965.
Kautsky, John H., "Myth, Self-fulfilling Prophecy, and Symbolic Reassurance in the East-West Conflict," *The Journal of Conflict Resolution*, Mar. 1965, reprinted in *Current*, July 1965.
Kearns, Doris, "The Art of Biography: The Power and Pathos of LBJ," *New Republic*, Mar. 3, 1979.
Kemp, L.W., "A Blanco County Tragedy," *Frontier Times*, June, 1934.
Kempton, Murray, "The Bloody Ground of Texas Politics," *New Republic*, Feb. 1, 1964.
Kiker, Douglas, "Russell of Georgia, The Old Guard at Its Shrewdest," *Harper's*, Sept. 1966; "Robert Kennedy and the *What If* Game," *Atlantic Monthly*, Oct. 1966.
King, Larry L., "Lyndon Slept Here," *Los Angeles Times WEST* (magazine), Jan. 7, 1968; "LBJ through Watergate-colored glasses," *New Times*, Aug. 23, 1974.
Knebel, Fletcher, "Lyndon Johnson: Trained for Power," *Look*, Dec. 31, 1963.
Kornitzer, Bela, "President Johnson Talks About His Mother & His Father," *Parade*, Jan. 5, 1964.
Larner, Jeremy, "Nobody Knows . . . Reflections on the McCarthy Campaign," *Harper's*, April and May 1969.
Lasch, Robert, "How We Got Where We Are," *Progressive*, July 1971.
Lindberg, Anne Morrow, "As I See Our First Lady," *Look*, May 17, 1964.
Link, Arthur S., "The Case for Woodrow Wilson," *Harper's*, April 1967.
Link, J.B., ed., "George W. Baines, Sr.," *Texas Historical and Biographical Magazine*, 1891.
Lisagor, Peter, "Lyndon Johnson Discusses His Failure with American Youth," *True*, Mar. 1969.
Martin, Roscoe C., "The People's Party in Texas, a Study in Third Party Politics," *The University of Texas Bulletin No. 3308*, Feb. 22, 1933.
McCarry, Charles, "Mourning Becomes Senator Fulbright," *Esquire*, June 1970.
McGovern, George, "Why Don't You Speak Out, Senator?'" *New Republic*, Mar. 18, 1967.
Meryman, Richard (interviewer), "Hubert Humphrey Takes His Self-Portrait," *Life*, Sept. 27, 1968.
Meyerson, Harvey, "Choppers and the New Kind of War," *Look*, Apr. 30, 1968.
Montgomery, Robert H., "Texas—A Colony of Manhattan," *Summer Texan*, June 20, 1937.
Morgenthau, Hans J., "Globalism, Johnson's Moral Crusade," *New Republic*, July 3, 1965; "Truth and Power, the Intellectuals and the Johnson Administration," *New Republic*, Nov. 26, 1966.
Morris, Willie; Northcott, Kaye; and Cartwright, Gary, "Billy Lee Brammer, 1929–1979," *Texas Observer*, Mar. 3, 1979.
Moynihan, Daniel P., "The Democrats, Kennedy & the Murder of Dr. King," *Commentary*, May 1968.
Nation, Carol, "A Rendezvous with Destiny," *Texas Highways*, Mar. 1964.
Osborne, John, "Concern About LBJ," *New Republic*, July 24, 1965.
Pachter, Henry, "Revisionist Historians & the Cold War," *Dissent*, Nov.-Dec. 1968.
Rodell, Fred, "The Complexities of Mr. Justice Fortas," *NYT Magazine*, July 28, 1968.
Rostow, Eugene V., "L.B.J. Reconsidered," *Esquire*, April 1971.

Rothchild, John, "The Screwing of the Average Man," *Washington Monthly,* Oct. 1971.
Schendel, Gordon, "Something is Rotten in the State of Texas," *Collier's,* June 9, 1951.
Schlesinger, Jr., Arthur, "On The Writing of Contemporary History," *Atlantic Monthly,* Mar. 1967.
Schreiber, Flora Rheta, "Lady Bird: She's LBJ's Political Partner, Too," *Family Weekly,* Jan. 17, 1965; "First Year of Marriage," *Woman's Day,* Dec. 1967.
Seib, Charles B., and Otten, Alan L., "Abe, Help—L.B.J.," *Esquire,* June 1965.
Severeid, Eric, "The Final Troubled Hours of Adlai Stevenson," *Look,* Nov. 30, 1965.
Shannon, William V., "Lyndon Johnson" (a biographical series) *New York Post,* May 28-June 2, 1956; "Lyndon Johnson: Conservative," *Progressive,* Jan. 1960.
Sherrill, Robert, "The Democratic Rebels in Congress," *Nation,* Oct. 10, 1966; " 'The Last of the Great Populists' Takes on the Foundations, the Banks, the Federal Reserve, the Treasury," *NYT Magazine,* Mar. 16, 1969.
Shearer, Lloyd, "Can LBJ find happiness in Johnson City?" *Parade,* July 7, 1968.
Sidey, Hugh, "The Presidency," Sidey's column in *Life,* under various dates, some specified here by subtitles: "Departure of a 'Deputy President,' " Mar. 6, 1964; "Two Years in Office, Measure of the Man," Dec. 3, 1965; "L.B.J. Populist versus L.B.J. Entrepreneur," Sept. 9, 1966; "Time of Imperative Privacy as Crises Pile Up," Aug. 16, 1967; "Beyond Politics, the reality of faith," Aug. 11, 1967; "Big Shoes for the U.S. to Fill," Dec. 8, 1967; "The Private Preserve of the President," July 5, 1968; "Deep Grow the Roots of the Alamo," May 31, 1969.
Smith, Hedrick, "How the President Keeps Informed," *NYT Magazine,* Aug. 30, 1964.
Smith, Ralph, "The Farmer's Alliance in Texas, 1875–1900," *Southwestern Historical Quarterly,* pp. 346–69.
Steele, John L., "A Kingmaker or a Dark Horse?" *Life,* June 25, 1956.
Stegner, Wallace, "History, Myth, and the Western Writer," *American West,* May 1967.
Stevenson, Adlai, "America's Broken Mainspring," *Progressive,* March, 1959; "The Most Important Fact in the World Today," *Progressive,* July 1959.
Symington, Stuart, "Congress' Right to Know," *NYT Magazine,* Aug. 9, 1970.
Velie, Lester, "Do You Know Your State's Secret Boss?" *Reader's Digest,* Feb. 1953.
Viereck, Peter, "The New Conservatism," *New Republic,* Sept. 24, 1962.
Waugh, Gene Barnwell, "The Boyhood Days of Our President," *SAEN,* April 25, 1965, reprinted from the *Texas Public Employee,* Mar. 1964.
Wells, Samuel F., Jr., "The Lessons of the [Korean] War," *Wilson Quarterly,* Summer 1978.
Welsh, David, "Building Lyndon Johnson," *Ramparts,* Dec. 1967.
Wheeler, Keith, and Lambert, William, "The Man Who Is the President," two parts, *Life,* Aug. 14, 21, 1964.
White, William S., "The Two Texans Who Will Run Congress," *NYT Magazine,* Dec. 30, 1956; "Who *Is* Lyndon Johnson," *Harper's,* March 1958.
Wicker, Tom, "Requiem for the Great Society," *Saturday Evening Post,* Jan. 25, 1969.
Williams, T. Harry, "Huey, Lyndon, and Southern Radicalism," *The Journal of American History,* Sept. 1973.
Wills, Garry, "Singing 'Mammy' to Doris," *New York Review,* June 24, 1976.
Wiltz, John E., "The Korean War and American Society," *Wilson Quarterly,* Summer 1978.
Young, Joanne B., "The LBJ White House," *American Home,* Mar. 1964.

Newspapers Cited

Abilene (Tx.) *Reporter-News*
Alice (Tx.) *Daily Echo*
Austin American
Austin American-Statesman
Austin Statesman
Austin Tribune
Baltimore Sun
Blanco County (Tx.) *Record*
Blanco (Tx.) *News*
Brenham (Tx.) *Banner-Press*
Campus Chat (student, NTSU, Denton, Tx.)
Charlotte (N.C.) *News*
Chicago Sun-Times
Chicago Tribune
College Star (student, STSTC, San Marcos, Tx.)
Corpus Christi Caller
Corpus Christi Caller-Times
Corpus Christi Times
Cuero (Tx.) *Record*
Daily Texan (student, UT Austin, Austin, Tx.)
Dallas Morning News
Dallas Times-Herald
Dayton (Oh.) *Daily News*
Denton (Tx.) *Record-Chronicle*
Denver Post
Des Moines Register
El Paso Herald-Post
El Paso Times
Fort Worth Press
Fort Worth Star-Telegram
Fredericksburg (Tx.) *Standard*
Galveston News
Hays County (Tx.) *Citizen*
Hays County (Tx.) *Times*
Houston Chronicle
Houston Post
Houston Press
Interscholastic Leaguer (Tx.)

Johnson City (Tx.) *Record-Courier*
Madison (Wis.) *Capital Times*
Memphis Commercial-Appeal
Milwaukee Journal
National Observer
New York Daily Mirror
New York Daily News
New York Herald-Tribune
New York Journal-American
New York Post
New York Times
Onion Creek (Tx.) *Free Press*
Paris (Tx.) *News*
RFD News (Ohio)
San Antonio Express
San Antonio Express-News
San Antonio Light
San Antonio News
San Marcos (Tx.) *Record*
Shreveport Journal
Southern Mercury
State Gazette (Tx.)
St. Louis Post-Dispatch
Summer Texan (student, UT-Austin, Austin, Tx.)
Uvalde (Tx.) *Leader News*
Wall Street Journal
Washington Daily News
Washington Evening Star
Washington Post
Washington Post and Times-Herald

Interviews by the Author

(In the case of telephone interviews, the city listed is where the interviewee was)

Acheson, Dean, Washington, D.C., May 1959.
Acreman, Harry, Houston, Oct. 23, 1967.
Adams, Harry, Alice, Tx., May 22, 1970.
Adams, Mark, Austin, Sept. 21, 1967, Jan. 26, 1968.
Allen, Robert S., Washington, D.C., April 3, 1968.
Allred, Dave, Wichita Falls, Tx., Oct. 30, 1967.
Allred, Raymond, Odessa, Tx., Mar. 11, 1968.
Anderson, David, Austin, Oct. 6, 1967.
Archer, Roy, Austin, Feb. 12, 1968.
Babcock, John, Austin, Aug. 7, 1967.
Ball, Ellana, Houston, Oct. 16, 1967.
Banks, Jimmy, Jan. 26, 1968.
Barclay, John, Austin, Feb. 9, 1968.
Baren, Harry, El Cajon, Ca., July 11, 1978.
Barr, Willard, Fort Worth, Oct. 24, 1967.
Barron, John, Washington, D.C., July 15, 1967, May 26, 1968.
Barton, Bob, San Marcos, Dec. 30, 1966; Buda, Tx., Nov. 21, 1979, Nov. 21, 1981.
Bean, Woodrow, El Paso, Oct. 31, 1968.
Beard, Pat, Waco, Tx., April 4, 1970.
Beto, George, Huntsville, Tx., Jan. 24, 1968.
Birdwell, Sherman, Austin, Feb. 13, 1968.
Black, Hugo, Washington, D.C., Mar. 25, 1968.
Blair, John, Washington, D.C., May 20–24, 1969.
Bloom, Mrs. Ida, Giddings, Tx., Oct. 11, 1967.
Botsford, Mrs. H.C., Corpus Christi, May 19, 1970.
Braly, Mac, Washington, D.C., Mar. 27, 1968.
Brammer, Bill, Washington, D.C., May, 1959; Austin, Sept. 21, 1968.
Brammer, Sydney, Austin, Mar. 17, 1979.
Bravo, M.B., Zapata, Tx., Nov. 20, 1969.
Brewton, A.R., Houston, Oct. 18, 1967.
Brick, John, Washington, D.C., April 9, 1968.
Broide, Mace, Washington, D.C., Mar. 26, 1968.
Brooks, Jack, Washington, D.C., April 10, 1968.
Brown, Wales, Washington, D.C., May 20–24, 1969.
Buck, Raymond, Fort Worth, Oct. 26, 1967.
Buoncristiani, Margaret, Austin, Dec. 11, 1977.
Burnett, Gay, Austin, Oct. 18, 1966.
Burris, Sam, Alice, Tx., May 22, 1970.
Byers, Bo, Austin, Feb. 28, 1964, Aug. 29, 1977.
Caldwell, Charles (Chuck), Austin, Mar. 8, 1968, Nov. 21, 1970.
Calvert, Robert, Austin, Feb. 9, 1968.
Carlton, Sarge, Washington, D.C., Sept. 20, 1977.
Carter, Jack, Fort Worth, Oct. 24, 1967.
Carter, Margaret, Fort Worth, Oct. 24, 1967.
Cater, Douglass, Washington, D.C., Dec. 14, 1967.

Chemery, Frank, Washington, D.C., April 4, 1968.
Christian, George, Washington, D.C., Dec. 13, 15, 1967.
Clark, Ed, San Antonio, summer, 1968; Salado, Tx., Dec. 5, 1969; Austin, Dec. 18, 1981.
Clark, Joseph, Washington, D.C., May 1959.
Cochran, Bob, Washington, D.C., Feb. 7, 1967.
Cochran, Clay, Washington, D.C., April 4, 1968.
Cofer, John, Austin, Jan. 8, 1968, Aug. 27, 1969.
Coffin, Tristram, Washington, D.C., Oct. 30, 1978.
Collier, Everett, Houston, Oct. 13, 1967.
Connally, John, Austin, early August, 1968.
Conner, B.E., Austin, Feb. 1, 1968.
Corson, W.R., Washington, D.C., Mar. 26, 1968.
Crider, Ben, Austin, Jan. 30, 1968.
Crider, Otto, Cloverdale, Ca., July 22, 1969.
Crider, Tom, Houston, Oct. 15, 1967.
Crozier, Harry Benge, Austin, Jan. 29, 1969.
Dauplaise, Marie, Houston, Oct. 12, 1967.
Davidson, T. Whitfield, Dallas, Oct. 26, 1967.
Davis, Ethel, San Marcos, Tx., May 27, 1971.
Davis, Will, Austin, Jan. 29, 1968.
Dealey, Mrs. Roy, Houston, Oct. 13, 1967.
Deakin, James, Washington, D.C., April 2, 1968.
Dean, Homer, Alice, Tx., May 23, 1970.
Dickson, Fagan, Austin, Nov. 30, 1967, Aug. 19–20, 1969.
Dixie, Chris, Houston, July 7, 1967.
Dodgen, Howard, Austin, Feb. 6, 1968.
Donald, Tom, Alice, Tx., May 23, 1970.
Dorman, Mike, Washington, D.C., Mar. 31, 1968.
Dougherty, Dudley, Beeville, Tx., May 2, 1967, April 2, 1970.
Douglas, Paul, Washington, D.C., May, 1959, April 11, 1969.
Dudman, Richard, Austin, Nov. 21, 1966.
Durr, Virginia and Clifford, Austin, spring, 1975.
Eckhardt, Celia, Washington, D.C., April 2, 1979.
Eckhardt, Nadine Brammer, Washington, D.C., Mar. 31, 1968; Houston, June 1, 1979.
Eckhardt, Robert C., Washington, D.C., Feb. 6, 1967; Austin, Oct. 1967; Washington, D.C., Jan. 18, 1971.
Edwards, Clyda, Washington, D.C., Mar. 25, 1968; as Mrs. Clyda Gugenberger, San Jose, Ca., Dec. 2, 1981.
Edwards, Don, Washington, D.C., Mar. 25, 1968, Dec. 2, 1981.
Ellinger, Don, Austin, Dec. 3, 1967.
Elliott, O.H., Austin, Sept. 15, 1967.
Ellis, Mary Beth, San Diego, Tx., summer 1981.
Evans, Rowland, Austin, Oct. 6, 1966.
Evans, Roy, Austin, Aug. 16, 1967.
Fannin, Oliver, Jr., Fort Worth, Oct. 24, 1967.
Farr, Dick, Washington, D.C., April 1, 1968.
Fath, Creekmore, Aug. 24, 28, 1967, Feb. 1, 1968, Aug. 29, 1974.
Faulk, John Henry, Austin, early Dec. 1966, Aug. 15, 1967, Jan. 28, 1968.
Ferrell, Bob, Bloomington, Ind., Jan. 22, 1982.
Findlay, Marion, Austin, Feb. 7, 1968.
Finney, John, Washington, D.C., Mar. 2, 1971.
Fleming, Richard S., Austin, Nov. 14, 1967; Nov. 19, Dec. 20, 1972.
Francis, Charles I, Houston, Oct. 17, 1967.
Frankel, Max, Austin, Dec. 7, 1966.
Frantz, Joe, Austin, Oct. 14, 1968, Feb. 20, 1970, Dec. 11, 1977.
Friedman, Saul, Austin, April 18, 1968.
Fritts, Jim, Austin, Sept. 13, 1967.
Fuermann, George, Houston, Oct. 12, 1967.
Fulbright, William, Washington, D.C., Mar. 27, 1968.
Galbraith, John Kenneth, Austin, May 6, 1970.
Gibbons, Harold, Houston, Oct. 18, 1967.
Gliddon, Reverdy, Austin, 1967.
Glynn, Dr. James D., Austin, Jan. 30, 1968.
Gold, Harold, Washington, D.C., April 2, 1968.
Gonzalez, Henry B., Washington, D.C., May 26, 1969, and Austin, a series of interviews, 1980–81.
Goulden, Joe, Washington, D.C., Mar. 25, 1968.
Graham, Callan, Austin, Sept. 13, 1967.
Greene, H.M., Fall River Mills, Ca., July 21, 1969.

Grinspoon, Lester, Boston, Mar. 1, 1971.
Gugenberger, Mrs. Clyda, see Edwards, Clyda.
Haley, J. Evetts, Canyon, Tx., Oct. 30, 1967.
Hall, Walter, League City, Tx., June 15, Oct. 13, 17–18, 1967; Galveston, Tx., May 13, 1970; at Hall's Ranch, July 1, 1978, April 27, 1980.
Harbin, Estelle, San Antonio, May 25, 1971.
Harris, Fred, San Antonio, Dec. 12, 1975.
Harrison, Gilbert, Washington, D.C., Feb. 6, 1967.
Harrison, Joe, Washington, D.C., Mar. 27, 1968.
Hazelrigg, Hal, Houston, Oct. 14, 1967.
Herring, Charles, Austin, Mar. 13, 1968.
Hodges, Harmon, Austin, Feb. 9, 1968.
Hoffard, Allen, Washington, D.C., Mar. 3, 1968.
Holley, Lamar, Dallas, Oct. 20, 1967.
Hopkins, Welly, Washington, D.C., Mar. 29, 1968.
Hughes, Charles, Sherman, Tx., Oct. 26, 1967.
Humphrey, Hubert, Washington, D.C., May, 1959.
Hyde, Rosel, Washington, D.C., Mar. 29, 1968.
Ivins, Molly, Austin, Jan. 6, 1972.
Jackson, Robert, Corpus Christi, April 14, 1970.
Janeway, Michael, Boston, Mar. 1, 1971.
Jenkins, Walter, Austin, Dec. 11, 1977.
Johnson, Mrs. Elizabeth, Cotulla, Tx., May 25, 1971.
Johnson, Lyndon B., at the LBJ Ranch, Dec. 1955; Washington, D.C., May 1959 (two interviews); Washington, D.C., Dec. 13, 14–15, 16, 1967, and Mar. 23, 1968. (In addition, Carl Degen, chief of the division of audiovisual arts of the National Park Service, interviewed Lyndon and Claudia Johnson Sept. 1972 at the LBJ Ranch, and I listened to the tape recordings of this held by the National Park Service at Harper's Ferry, W. Va.—for short designated "Harper's Ferry tapes.")
Johnson, Mrs. Lyndon B., at the LBJ Ranch, Jan. 18, 1975 (recorded by the Johnson Library).
Johnson, Sam Houston, Washington, D.C., May, 1959, and Austin, Aug. 14, 1972, Feb. 8, 1973, June 6, 1975.
Johnson, Tom, Dallas, Sept. 21, 1973.
Jones, George F., Washington, D.C., Mar. 25, 1968.
Jones, Luther, Corpus Christi, April 15, 1970.
Kantor, Seth, Washington, D.C., Mar. 25, 1968.
Keach, Mr. and Mrs. Carroll, Robstown, Tx., May 21, 1970.
Kellam, J.C., Austin, Dec. 9, 1959.
Kennard, Don, Austin, Jan. 12, 19, 1967, Jan. 14, 1971; Fort Worth, Oct. 24, 1967.
Kennedy, Robert F., Washington, D.C., Feb. 1967.
Kennedy, Roderick, Austin, Feb. 12, 1968.
King, Larry L., Austin, Oct. 9, 1967.
Kingsbery, E.G., Austin, Jan. 30, 1968.
Kingsbery, John, Austin, Jan. 29, 1968.
Kinney, C.S., Austin, Feb. 7, 1968.
Kittrell, Mrs. William H., Dallas, Oct. 20, 1967.
Kleberg, Mrs. Richard, Corpus Christi, May 19, 1970.
Knight, James, Austin, Feb. 4, 1971; San Antonio, Sept. 21, 1975.
Koeniger, John Fritz, Austin, Feb. 10, 1968.
Korioth, Tony, Austin, Aug. 1, 1968.
Korth, Fred, Washington, D.C., April 11, 1968.
Kotlow, Milton, Washington, D.C., Mar. 27, 1968.
Laudermilk, Jack, Washington, D.C., Mar. 29, 1968.
Lawrence, Foe A., Austin, Feb. 9, 1968.
Leavitt, William, Washington, D.C., Mar. 25, 1968.
Lee, Mrs. Jean, Austin, Nov. 10, 1966.
Lee, Ray, Austin, Jan. 31, 1968.
Lemberger, Dr. Ernst, Washington, D.C., Mar. 25, 1968.
Leo, Leo J., Lay Joya, Tx., Nov. 20, 1969.
Lichten, Bob, Dallas, Oct. 24, 1967.
Lloyd, Ed, Alice, Tx., May 22, 1970.
Lloyd, O.B., Washington, D.C., April 12, 1968.
Long, Bob, Austin, Jan. 29, 1968.
Long, Stuart, Austin, Jan. 30, 1968.
Love, Dan, Austin, Feb. 1, 1968.
Low, Sam D.W., Houston, Oct. 12, 1967.
Lowry, Ray, Austin, Feb. 12, 1968.
Maloney, Jim, Houston, Oct. 12, 1967.

Mankiewicz, Frank, Washington, D.C., Mar. 3, 1971.
Manning, Robert, Boston, Mar. 7, 1971.
Marcus, Stanley, Dallas, Oct. 6, 1973.
Martens, Clarence, Alice, Tx., May 23, 1970.
Martin, Winston, San Antonio, early May 1973.
Mashman, Jim, Fort Worth, Oct. 24, 1967.
Maverick, Maury, Jr., Austin and San Antonio, Oct. 6, Nov. 24, 1966, May 25, 1975, Mar. 18, 1977, April 1979.
Mayor, Jim, Houston, Oct. 12, 1967.
McCrocklin, James, San Marcos, Tx., April 24, 1967.
McCrory, James, San Antonio, Nov. 1966, April 2, 1970.
McLean, Kenneth, Washington, D.C., April 11, 1974.
McNeel, Jess, San Antonio, Oct. 7, 1975.
McNees, Donald, Dallas, Oct. 20, 1967.
McPherson, Harry, Washington, D.C., Dec. 14, 1967.
Miller, Joseph, Washington, D.C., Mar. 25, 1968.
Mollenhoff, Clark, Washington, D.C., Mar. 27, 1968, Mar. 1971.
Montague, Joe, Fort Worth, Oct. 26, 1967.
Montgomery, Gladys, Austin, Feb. 12, 1968.
Montgomery, Robert, Austin, Feb. 12, 1968.
Moody, Mrs. Dan, Austin, Feb. 6, 1968.
Mooney, Booth, Washington, D.C., April 1, 1968.
Moorhead, Dean, Austin, Feb. 7, 8, 1968.
Morgan, Edward P., Washington, D.C., Mar. 25, 1968.
Morgan, Everett, Austin, Dec. 2, 1967 and 1973.
Morgan, Guiton, Austin, Feb. 14, 1968.
Moriss, Jim, Austin, Feb. 14, 1968.
Morrow, Wright, Houston, Oct. 13, 17, 1967.
Moyers, Bill, Garden City, N.Y., Dec. 20, 1967, April 11, 1968.
Newfield, Jack, New York City, Feb. 1967.
Nolle, Alfred H., San Marcos, Tx., May 27, 1971.
Novak, Robert, Austin, Dec. 27, 1967.
Parker, Byron, Houston, Oct. 13, 1967.
Parr, M. H., San Antonio, Dec. 15, 1981.
Parr, Thelma, Corpus Christi, May 19, 1970.
Parten, J.R., Houston, Nov. 18, 1967, Sept. 6, 1968, and Jan. 23, 1971; Madisonville, Tx., Feb. 25, 1969.
Patman, Elmer, Austin, Jan. 25, Feb. 9, 14, April 17, 1968.
Patman, Wright, Washington, D.C., April 5, 1968.
Payne, Harvey, Austin, Feb. 12, 1968.
Perry, Dell, Washington, D.C., Mar. 28, 1968.
Pipes, Richard, Austin, Aug. 6, 1968.
Pool, William, Austin, Feb. 1, 1968.
Porter, J. H. (Jack), Houston, May 13, 1970.
Potter, Cliff, Houston, Oct. 18, 1967.
Powers, Dave, Waltham, Mass., May 24, 1977.
Price, C. W. "Dinky," Alice, Tx., May 22, 1970.
Procter, Les, Austin, Feb. 6, 1968.
Proxmire, William, Washington, D.C., May, 1959.
Pryor, Cactus, Austin, Jan. 29, Feb. 6, 1968.
Quill, Dan, San Antonio, Dec. 16, 1981.
Ragovin, Mitchell, Washington, D.C., Mar. 28, 1968.
Randolph, Mrs. R. D., Houston, Feb. 1, Oct. 14, 1967.
Ransom, Harry, Austin, Feb. 6, 1968.
Rapoport, Bernard, Charlottesville, Va., April 10, 1977, Waco, Tx., Dec. 14, 1981.
Rauh, Joe, Washington, D.C., May 1959, Mar. 29, 1968.
Redford, Cecil, Corpus Christi, May 19, 1970.
Redford, Emmette, Austin, Jan. 23, 1968.
Reilly, Wallace, Dallas, Oct. 20, 1967.
Rice, Downey, Washington, D.C., Mar. 28, April 1968.
Rice, F.R. (Friendly), Austin, Nov. 14, 1967.
Roberts, Henry, San Antonio, Dec. 9, 1977.
Rolnick, Harry, Dallas, Oct. 26, 1967.
Rosenblatt, Maurice, Washington, D.C., May 1959.
Roundtree, Payne, Austin, Sept. 15, 1967.
Rowe, James, Corpus Christi, Jan. 21, April 14, 1970.
Roy, Miss Jessie, Austin, Sept. 14, 15, 1967.
Ryon, Don, Jr., Fort Worth, Oct. 24, 1967.

Sain, Hubert T., Alice, Tx., May 23, 1970.
Salas, Luis, Alice, Tx., Jan. 24, 25, May 22, 1970, Aug. 14, 1975.
Sanderford, Ghent, Austin, Feb. 8, 1968.
Sanders, Barefoot, Austin, Feb. 13, 1970.
Schlesinger, Arthur, Jr., New York City, Feb. 1967.
Schmidt, Fred, Austin, Dec. 28, 1966; San Antonio, spring 1978.
Schnabel, Charles, Austin, Sept. 3, 1974.
Schnitzer, Paul, Washington, D.C., April 3, 1968.
Schreiber, Harry, Galveston, May 13, 1970.
Scofield, Frank, Austin, Sept. 15, 1967.
Scofield, Frank, Jr., Austin, Mar. 7, 1968.
Semple, Robert, Bloomsbury, Md., May 17, 1972.
Seymour, Jim, Austin, Jan. 19, 1975.
Sheehan, Neil, Austin, Dec. 31, 1968, April 22, 1970.
Shelton, Polk, Austin, Nov. 14, 1967.
Shuffler, Henderson, Austin, Sept. 14, 1967.
Shuman, Howard, Washington, D.C., May 1959.
Siemiller, Roy, Washington, D.C., Mar. 25, 1968.
Silber, John, San Antonio, April 15, 1978.
Skaggs, Jack, Harlingen, Tx., Nov. 20, 1969.
Slagle, R.C., Jr., Sherman, Tx., Oct. 30, 1967.
Small, C.C., Austin, Sept. 15, 1967.
Small, Joe, Austin, Sept. 16, 1967.
Smith, Brad, Austin, Nov. 14, 1967.
Smith, Mrs. Margaret, Mission, Tx., Nov. 20, 1969.
Sorenson, Theodore, Washington, D.C., May 1959, April 11, 1968.
Spampinato, Michael, Houston, May 13, 22, 1970.
Spelce, Neil, Austin, Jan. 20, 1968.
Stevenson, Coke, at his ranch near Junction, Tx., April 15, 1968.
Taylor, Barney, Austin, May 30, 1970.
Thompson, Mrs. Marie, San Diego, Tx., summer 1981.
Travis, Edmunds, Austin, Nov. 14, 1967.
Truitt, James, San Miguel de Allende, Mexico, Aug. 4, 13, 1974.
Turner, W. Earl, Austin, Jan. 26, 1968.
Tyler, Lyon, Washington, D.C., April 1, 1968.
Vale, A.J., Rio Grande City, Tx., Nov. 20, 1969.
Vance, Dorothy, Austin, Mar. 3, 1979.
Vessels, Jay, Austin, Sept. 14, 1967.
Waldron, Martin, Dallas, Nov. 1, 1967.
Walker, James Stanley, Austin, Mar. 7, 1968.
Waugh, Gene, Austin, Feb. 7, 1968.
Weatherred, Preston, Dallas, Oct. 20, 1967.
Webb, Mrs. Terrell Maverick, Austin, Jan. 26, 1968.
Weeg, William J., Feb. 15, 1968.
Wells, L.N.D., Dallas, Oct. 23, 1967.
West, Wesley, Houston, Oct. 12, 1967.
Wheeler, Bob, Austin, Oct. 6, 1966.
Wild, Claude C., Austin, Jan. 29, 30, 1968.
Wilson, Will, Austin, Jan. 24, 25, 1968.
Wright, Douglas, Austin, Sept. 21, 1967.
Yarborough, Ralph W., Austin, Dec. 30, 1966, summer 1968.
Yarmolinsky, Adam, Warrenton, Va., Feb. 22, 1971.
Yellott, Mrs. Oscar, Beaumont, May 13, 1970.
Young, Harold, Odessa, Tx., Oct. 29, 30, 1968.
Zimmerman, Julian, Austin, Aug. 19–20, 1969.

(And others who are not listed here for various reasons)

Oral History Interviews

(Consulted at the Johnson Library, Austin, Texas)

I.W. Abel
Gardner C. Ackley
Edie Adams
George Aiken
Lonnelle Aikman
Mrs. Dorothy Palmie Alford
Ivan Allen
Robert S. Allen
J. Lindsay Almond, Jr.
Stewart Alsop

Clinton P. Anderson
Lucille G. Anderson
Robert B. Anderson
David W. Angevine
Harry Ashmore
Wayne Aspinall
Toinette Bachelder
Charles Fitz Baird
Donald M. Baker
John Austin Baker
Robert M. Ball
Ben Barnes
Malcolm Bardwell
Joseph M. Barr
Joseph W. Barr
Charles L. Bartlett
Mrs. E. L. (Bob) Bartlett
Birch Bayh
Joseph A. Beirne
Frederick C. Belen
Ivan L. Bennett, Jr.
Robert Bennett
Sen. and Mrs. Lloyd Bentsen, Jr.
Maurice M. Bernbaum
Howard Bertsch
W. Sherman Birdwell
Eugene Black
William M. Blackburn
Roger M. Blough
James H. Blundell
Charles K. Boatner
Hale Boggs
Charles E. Bohlen
Chester Bowles
Alan S. Boyd
Percy Brigham
Edmund G. Brown
H.S. Hank Brown
Lester Brown
Oliver N. Bruck
C. Farris Bryant
Raymond E. Buck
Gordon Bunshaft
George G. Burkley
Omar Burleson
John M. Cabot
Clifton C. Carter
Hodding Carter
Margaret Carter
Douglass Cater
Anthony J. Celebrezze
Emanuel Celler
George E. Christian
Frank Church
Ramsey Clark
Tom C. Clark
Edward P. Cliff
Clark Clifford
Wilbur J. Cohen
Chester L. Cooper
Ben Crider
John H. Crooker, Sr.
James O. Cross
Jesse Curry
Lloyd N. Cutler
Price Daniel, Sr.
Jonathan Daniels
George R. Davis
W. True Davis
Willard Deason
Frederick Deike
Marjorie Delafield
Frank Denius
Charles Diggs
C. Douglas Dillon
Everett McKinley Dirksen
Helen Gahagan Douglas
Paul H. Douglas
Ralph Dungan
Clifford and Virginia Durr
James O. Eastland
India Edwards
Milton S. Eisenhower
James A. Elkins, Jr.
Allen J. Ellender
Courtney A. Evans
James Farmer
Thomas K. Finletter
Congressman O.C. Fisher
Thomas W. Fletcher
Mr. and Mrs. Sam Fore, Jr.
Abe Fortas
Henry Fowler
Sanford E. Fox
Orville Freeman
Gordon Fulcher
Betty Furness
James Gaither
Dr. Hector Garcia
E.D. Germany
Sam Gideon
Donald Gilpatric
Arthur L. and Elizabeth W. Goldschmidt
Andrew J. Goodpaster
Elmer Graham
Katherine Graham
H.M. Greene
Ernest Gruening
James C. Hagerty
Walter G. Hall
Charles A. Halleck
Robert Hardesty
W. Averell Harriman
Patricia Roberts Harris
George B. Hartzog
Mrs. Jessie Hatcher
Carl Hayden
Brooks Hays
Wayne L. Hays
Richard Helms
Aaron E. Henry
Charles Herring
Lewis B. Hershey
Theodore Hesburgh
Bourke B. Hickenlooper
Lister Hill
Roger Hilsman
Luther H. Hodges, Sr.
Anna Rosenberg Hoffman
Jerry Holleman
Welly Z. Hopkins
Walter C. Hornaday
Harold Howe
Gov. and Mrs. Richard J. Hughes

Sarah T. Hughes
Don Hummel
Hubert H. Humphrey
Frank E. Ikard
Robert M. Jackson
Jake Jacobsen
Mrs. Dorothy H. Jacobson
Lyndon B. Johnson (by Hoover Library; Robert McKay; Elspeth Rostow)
Luther E. Jones, Jr.
Marvin Jones
Carroll Keach
Claude Kellam
Leon Keyserling
Raymond H. Lapin
Gene Latimer
Oscar Laurel
Philip R. Lee
Ray Lee
Gould Lincoln
Otto Lindig
Stuart M. Long
J.C. Looney
Katie Louchheim
John J. McCloy
Gale McGee
George S. McGovern
Harry McPherson
Lester Maddox
Stanley Marcus
Leonard Marks
Ernest May
George Meany
Robert Menzies
Emma Guffy Miller
Clarence Mitchell
Mike A.S. Monroney
Robert H. Montgomery
Booth Mooney
Charles S. Murphy
Dorothy J. Nichols
Paul H. Nitze
Frank "Posh" Oltorf
J.R. Parten
Wright Patman
Drew Pearson
Harry Provence
Richard S. "Cactus" Pryor
Daniel J. Quill
A. Philip Randolph
Mary Rather
George Reedy
Chalmers Roberts
A. Willis Robertson
Laurance Rockefeller
Eugene Rostow
Stanley Ruttenberg
Mrs. Josefa Baines Saunders
Harry Schreiber
Allan Shivers
Gerald W. Siegel
C.R. Smith
John Sparkman
Mr. and Mrs. Max Starcke
John C. Stennis
William H. Stewart
Jule M. Sugarman
William H. Sullivan
O.B. Summy
Herman Talmadge
Antonio J. Taylor
Hobart Taylor, Jr.
Hobart Taylor, Sr.
Willie Day Taylor
R.E. Thomason
Homer Thornberry
Alexander Trowbridge
Stewart Udall
Jack Valenti
Carl Vinson
Fred M. Vinson, Jr.
James E. Webb
Edwin L. Weisl, Jr.
Edwin L. Weisl, Sr.
Robert M. White
William S. and June White
Walter Wilcox
Claude C. Wild, Sr.
Roy Wilkins
G. Mennen Williams
Logan Wilson
Mrs. Alvin J. Wirtz
Whitney M. Young, Jr.

Oral History Interviews

(Consulted at the Kennedy Library, Waltham, Mass.)

Elie Abel
Robert Amory
William Attwood
John A. Baker
Charles Baldwin
Ross Barnett
Jack Bell
Hale Boggs
Richard Bolling
Simeon S. Booker
Juan Bosch
Chester Bowles
Henry Brandon
Dave Burke
George C. Burkley
Cesar Chavez
Lucius D. Clay
Charles U. Daly
George H. Decker
Richardson Dilworth
William O. Douglas
Fred Dutton
Philip J. Farley
Ed Folliard
Elizabeth Gatov
Roswell Gilpatric

Albert Gore
Charles Halleck
Raymond Hare
Seymour E. Harris
Andrew J. Houvouras
George Kennan
Robert F. Kennedy
Roger Kent
Michael J. Kirwan
William E. Knox
Foy D. Kohler
Joseph Kraft
Arthur Krock
David L. Lawrence
William Lawrence
Anthony Lewis
Gould Lincoln
Peter Lisagor
John W. McCormack
David McDonald
Burke Marshall
Charles Murphy
Robert Nathan
Gaylord A. Nelson
Maurine Neuberger
Robert Notti
Jacqueline Kennedy Onassis
Bradley Patterson
William Proxmire
Joseph Rauh
James J. Reynolds
Charles Roberts
Norbert A. Schlei
Robert C. Seamans
Hugh Sidey
John B. Swainson
Stanley Tretick
Wernher von Braun
Donald M. Wilson
Harris Wofford
Leonard Woodcock

Documents

Carpenter, Elizabeth, and Johnson, Mrs. Lyndon B. "The Story of the LBJ Ranch and Home," privately printed.
Democratic National Conventions:
Official Report of the Proceedings of the Democratic National Convention Held at Chicago, Ill., July 15–18, 1940.
Official Report of the Proceedings of the Democratic National Convention, Chicago, Ill., July 19–21, 1944.
Democracy at Work, The Official Report of the Democratic National Convention, Philadelphia, Pa., July 12–14, 1948.
Official Report of the Proceedings of the Democratic National Convention, Chicago, Ill, July 21–26, 1952, Democratic National Committee.
Jeffersonian Democrats: "Jeffersonian Democrats of Texas, A Declaration. . . . Unanimously Adopted at the Organization Meeting at Dallas, August 1, 1936," and "To Democrats: Report of the National Jeffersonian Democrats on the Detroit Conference," Aug. 7–8, 1936.
Johnson, Lyndon B.: Newsletters; Political Handbills; Speeches.
Johnson Library: "A National Tribute to Lady Bird Johnson on the Occasion of her 65th Birthday," Dec. 11, 1977.
Texas, State of, Attorney General: *Attorney General's Opinion C-748,* Aug. 31, 1966.

COURTS
Court of Civil Appeals, Third Supreme Judicial District, *No. 9984, Texas Federation of Labor vs. Brown & Root,* Feb. 6, 1952.
Court of Civil Appeals, Fourth Supreme Judicial District (San Antonio), *No. 12081, Mrs. Frank J. Martin, Appellant, vs. Mrs. Lela B. Martin, Appellee* (opinion by W.O. Murray, Chief Justice).

LEGISLATURE
House Journal, 1893.
Members of the Legislature of the State of Texas from 1846 to 1939, 1939.
Record of Proceedings of the High Court of Impeachment on the Trial of Hon. James E. Ferguson, Governor, Before the Senate of the State of Texas, Aug. 1–Sept. 29, 1917, Texas Legislature.

SECRETARY OF STATE
Biennial Report of the Secretary of State, 1892.
Corporate charter files.
Texas State Federation of Labor: *Proceedings,* 1947, 1948, 1950, 1952.
United States, CONGRESS: *Senate / Committee on Armed Services, Nomination of Mon C. Wallgren to be Chairman of the National Security Resources Board, Feb. 17–25, 1949.*

GENERAL SERVICES ADMINISTRATION
The Public Papers of the Presidents, Lyndon B. Johnson. Nov. 1963–Jan. 1969, Office of the Federal Register, National Archives and Records Service, General Services Administration;

Government Printing Office, Washington, D.C. Two volumes are printed for each period 1963–1964, 1965, 1966, 1967, and 1968–69.

NATIONAL LABOR RELATIONS BOARD

Decisions and Orders, Brown & Root, Inc., and UAW-CIO, Case No. 39–CA–322, 1955.

NATIONAL SECURITY TRAINING COMMISSION

Twentieth Century Minutemen, A Report to the President on a Reserve Forces Training Program, Dec. 1, 1953, Government Printing Office, Washington, D.C.

COURTS

Court of Appeals, Eighth Circuit (St. Louis), *No. 14680, NLRB v. Brown & Root, et al.*, Jan. 4, 1963.

District Court, Fort Worth, *No. 1640 Civil, Coke R. Stevenson vs. Tom L. Tyson, Vann M. Kennedy, and Lyndon B. Johnson* (a file which includes transcripts of hearings on the 1948 U.S. Senate election contest).

Letters, Memoranda, and Telegrams Except in the Johnson Library

Adams, H. L., to RD, May 28, 1970.
Allred, Dave, to RD, Dec. 7, 1967.
Allred, Mrs. Dave, to RD, Mar. 9, 1968.
Allred, James V. to LJ, Mar. 8, 1949.
Amrine, Michael, to RD, Jan. 31, 1968.
Anderson, Martin, to RD, Nov. 25, 1967, Feb. 12, 1968.
Anderson, Samuel E., to RD, Mar. 12, 1968, Dec. 25, 1975.
Baker, Roy D., to RD, Sept. 15, 1974.
Black, Hugo L., to RD, Sept. 1, 1967, April 18, 1968.
Bloodgood, Grant, to RD, July 15, 1959.
Booth, Brown, to Sam Rayburn, April 11, 1959, *RL*.
Boykin, Frank, to H. L. Hunt, June 14, 1960.
Brammer, Bill, to RD and Jean Dugger, 1956 to mid-1960s.
Brammer, Nadine, to RD and Jean Dugger, 1956.
Christian, George, to RD, Mar. 25, 1968.
Clark, Joseph S., to Joseph Alsop, Mar. 21, 1960, KL.
Cochran, Clay, to RD, Oct. 10, 1967.
Coffin, Tristram, to RD, Dec. 2, 1966, Jan. 26, 1968.
Corcoran, Tom, May 24, 1941 (memo on a call from him), FDRL.
Cousins, W. R., Sr., to John Tower, Feb. 21, 1964.
Cowart, George, to RD, Mar. 1, 1968.
Curley, Frederick N., to RD, June 19, 1959.
Detlefsen, Mrs. Harold (Eileen) to RD, Sept. 1974.
Dickson, Fagan, to LJ, April 8, 1954, Feb. 2, 1957, Jan. 8, 1964; to John F. Kennedy, April 18, 1963.
Doherty, John F., to RD, Sept. 4, Dec. 24, 1974.
Downs, R.B., to RD, Oct. 20, 1967.
Drewry, Pat, to Franklin Roosevelt, Oct. 2, 1940, FDRL.
Dungan, Ralph, to John F. Kennedy (memo), Oct. 3, 1962, KL.
Durr, Virginia, to RD, Mar. 3, 19, 1973.
Eastman, James N., Jr., to RD, Aug. 23, 1978.
Ellinger, W. Don, to RD, Feb. 13, 1968.
Emanuel, Victor, to RD, Jan. 14, 1968.
Faulk, John Henry, to RD, Aug. 29, 1974.
Fay, Albert, to Peter O'Donnell, Feb. 29, 1960.
Galbraith, John Kenneth, to John F. Kennedy, May 15, Aug. 15, 1961, Mar. 2, 1962, KL.
George, Larry, to RD, June 1, 1959.
Gibbons, Harold, to RD, Aug. 31, Oct. 11, Oct. 24, 1967.
Golze, Alfred R., to RD, June 29, 1959.
Graham, Katherine, to James Truitt, Sept. 2, 1964.
Graham, Philip L., to John F. Kennedy, Oct. 5, 1962, *KL*.
Griswold, Erwin N., to Fagan Dickson, April 26, 1963.
Hall, Walter, to RD, Aug. 29, Sept. 5, Oct. 7, 1974.
Hawkes, George L., to RD, May 29, Oct. 4, 1967.
Heiman, Grover C., to RD, Mar. 15, 1968.
Hymoff, Edward, to RD, Dec. 1, 1975.
Johnson, Lyndon, to Austin Catholic Centennial Committee, April 14, 1939, as in *CR 1939*, vol. 84, p. A1749; Austin Trades Council, May 12, 1941; Matthew Connelly, Nov. 8, 1945, TL; Fagan Dickson,

April 12, May 19, 1954, Feb. 13, 1957, Oct. 7, 1958, April 9, 1959; RD, June 1, 1959; Luther E. Jones, Jr., Dec. 6, 1931, Feb. 13, 26, April 18, 1932; John F. Kennedy, Jan. 12, Aug. 3, 1956, April 28, 1961, Jan. 9 (or 7), Nov. 2, 1962, Jan. 15, April 22, July 31, 1963, all KL; Alfred H. Nolle, April 10, 1957; Sam Rayburn, Oct. 22, Nov. 14, 1940, Jan. 6, 1946, all RL; Franklin Roosevelt, July 29, 1939, Oct. 1, Nov. 14, 1940, May 24, 1941 (tgm.), Dec. 8, 1941, all FDRL; Harry Truman, Dec. 15, 1945, Aug. 2, 1947, June 28, 1950, all TL.

Johnson, Zeake W., Jr., to RD, Jan. 26, 1968.

Jones, Luther E., Jr., to Eric Goldman, April 6, 1965 (marked "not mailed").

Kennedy, John F., to LJ, April 20, Sept. 30, 1961, April 17, 1963, Feb. 21, 1963, KL.

King, Ray T., to RD, Sept. 15, 1967.

Kirbow, Charles B., to RD, Sept. 8, 1967.

Kleberg, Richard M., to G. F. Newheuser, Oct. 26, 1933.

Kuyper, Adrian, to RD, Oct. 18, Nov. 22, 1967.

Mansfield, Paul J., to RD, Aug. 20, 1974.

Mares, William, to RD, Sept. 25, 1974.

Maverick, Maury, Sr., to Sam Rayburn, Oct. 5, 1940, RL; Franklin Roosevelt, Oct. 8, 1940, FDRL.

McCarthy, David J., to RD, Nov. 3, 1977.

McClary, James D., to RD, Jan. 26, 1968.

McClennahan, Mrs. E. L., to RD, Sept. 9, 1974.

McCoy, Harold D, to RD, June 9, 1959.

Mullen, Bob, to RD, Dec. 3, 1966, and undated memo, RL.

Munden, H. Ed, to Dr. William Prendergast, Feb. 28, 1964.

Nixon, Richard, to LJ, Sept. 27, 1954.

Petty, William B., to RD, Oct. 3, 18, 1967.

Rayburn, Sam, to R.H. Cochran, Feb. 10, 1948; Clara Driscoll, Feb. 10, 1944; C. C. Miller, Sept. 19, 1956; J. W. Potter, Oct. 22, 1956, all RL.

Randall, Marian T., to RD, Sept. 20, 1974.

Roosevelt, Franklin, to LJ, Aug. 2, 1939, Nov. 25, 1940, and May 26, June 3, 27, 1941 (three tgms.); Mac (Marvin McIntyre, presumably) (memo), Oct. 4, 1940; W. Lee O'Daniel, June 27, 1941 (tgm.), all above FDRL; Sam Rayburn, Jan. 6, 1943, RL.

Rowe, James, to Franklin Roosevelt, June 3, 1941 (memo), FDRL.

Rowe, James, (of Corpus Christi, Texas,) to RD, Aug. 27, 1974.

Russell, D. R., to RD, Aug. 24, 1974.

Saholsky, B. A., to RD, July 27, 1959.

Sawyer, Roland, to RD, Mar. 14, 1967.

Schieffer, Bob, to RD, Mar. 31, 1975.

Schlesinger, Arthur, Jr., to John F. Kennedy, Aug. 26, 30, 1960, KL.

Schmidt, Fred, to RD, June 17, 1979.

Shalowitz, Aaron L., to RD, Oct. 8, 1967.

Shelton, Edgar, to RD, May 15, 1951.

Sherrill, Robert, to RD, April, 1979.

Sherrod, Robert, to RD, Dec. 10, 1974, Oct. 11, 1977.

Shuford, Gene, to RD, April 23, 1979.

Small, Stephen J., to RD, Oct. 23, 1974.

Smith, Tad R., to Joe Harrison, Sept. 8, 26, 1964.

Stanley, Albert A., to RD, Oct. 16, 1967.

Stevenson, Adlai, E., to LJ, Aug. 30, 1952.

Stewart, Jack L., to RD, Aug. 25, 1974.

Sumner, Jane, to Tad Smith, Sept. 9, 1964.

Tarrance, Lance, to Joe Harrison, Oct. 3, 1964, and Peter O'Donnell, Joe Harrison, and John Tower, Sept. 24, 1964 (memo).

Tower, John, to W. R. Cousins, Sr., Feb. 28, 1964.

Truman, Harry, to LJ, Dec. 19, 1945, Aug. 6, 1947, June 30, 1950, all TL; Sam Rayburn, Aug. 15, 1950, and undated (c. 1956 or 1957), RL.

Twyman, Harvey, to RD, Sept. 15, 1974.

Wardlaw, Frank, to RD, Mar. 23, 1970.

Watson, Edwin M., to Edward J. Flynn, Sept. 19, 1940 (tgm.), FDRL.

Willis, Doyle, to RD, undated (c. 1974).

Wirtz, A. J., to James Rowe, June 3, 1941 (tgm.), FDRL.

Young, Warren E., to RD, July 20, 1959.

Youngblood, Grant, to RD, July 15, 1959.

Letters, Memoranda, and Telegrams in the Johnson Library

Birdwell, Sherman, to LJ, April 12, 1946.
Bolton, Paul, to Walter Jenkins, Feb. 3, 1947.
Brown, George, to LaBJ, Mar. 20, June 13, 1942; LJ, April 16, May 2, 13, 19, 27, June 12, 28, 1939, Oct. 27, 1939, Mar. 5, Oct. 19, 1940 (tgm.) Oct. 5, 1942 (tgm.), Oct. 24, 1956, Feb. 25, 1957, Jan. 8, 1958; Roy Miller, May 1, 1939 (copy to LJ).
Brown, Herman, to J. E. Van Hoose, Oct. 11, 1939 (copy to LJ); LJ, Jan. 7, 1958.
Clark, Ed, to LJ, Oct. 8, 20, 27, 1943, Mar. 29, June 17, 1944.
Connally, John, to LJ, Jan. 7, 9, 1942.
Cook, Don, to LJ, July 30, 1948.
Foley, E.H., Jr., to Roy Fry, July 15, 1937; C. McDonough, Oct. 10, 1935.
Francis, Charles I, to Tom Connally, June 28, 1949; LJ, April 13, June 28, Oct. 13, 1949.
Gideon, W. S., to Frank W. Kuehl, May 6, 1940.
Hamilton, Claude E., Jr., to Powell, Rauhut & Gideon, July 1, 1940.
Hopkins, Welly, to Roy Miller, Nov. 25, 1931.
Jenkins, Walter, to Herman Brown, Sept. 10, 1954; Tom Carson, Dec. 9, 1952; George Frey, Dec. 9, 1952; LJ, Oct. 24, Nov. 15, 18, 1949 (memos); Bill Kennedy, Dec. 9, 1952; W.F. Matheny, June 22, July 21, 1948; Glynn Stegall, Nov. 9, 1948; Bob Tatum, Dec. 9, 1952.
Jester, Beal, to LaBJ, April 6, 1942.
Johnson, Lyndon B., to Sherman Birdwell, April 16, 1946; George Brown, April 28, May 5, 16, June 13, Aug. 11, 1939 (tgm.), Feb. 27, Oct. 21, Nov. 5, 1941, Sept. 25, Oct. 8, 1942, Dec. 17, 1948, Jan. 14, Dec. 15, 1955, Jan. 3, 1957, Jan. 15, Nov. 3, 1958; Mrs. George Brown, Mar. 19, 1951, Jan. 17, 1958; the George Browns, Sept. 28, 1953, Jan. 11, 1954, Aug. 31, 1956, Aug. 28, 1957; Herman Brown, Aug. 11, 1939 (tgm.), Oct. 10, 1944 (tgm.), Aug. 29, 1956, Aug. 23, 1958; the Herman Browns, Sept. 28, 1953; Ed Clark, Oct. 30, 1943; John Connally, Aug. 27, 1942; Hugh Roy Cullen, Aug. 15, 1950; Willard Deason, undated (c. Feb. 1948); E.M. DeGuerin, July 5, 1944; Jesse Kellam, Oct. 19, 1946; Everett Looney, June 26, 1943; E.F. Matheny, May 5, 1948 (tgm); Sam Rayburn, May 13, 1939; Sid Richardson, Sept. 18, Nov. 24, 1941, Jan. 3, Nov. 28 (with enclosures), 1949; Alvin Wirtz, Feb. 21 (tgm.), Dec. 22, 1938.
Johnson, Mrs. Lyndon B., to George Brown, June 17, July 3, 1942.
Kellam, Jesse, to LJ, July 14, 1942; to the Lyndon Johnsons, May 20, July 7, 1947.
Latimer, Gene, to Mrs. George Brown, Nov. 9, 1938.
Marsh, Charles, to Herman Brown, July 28, 1934; Gordon Fulcher, April 26, 1941; LJ, April 16, May 21, 1940, Jan. 8 (memo), Oct. 13, 31, Nov. 5 (memo), 1941; Charles Marsh (himself), Mar. 4, 1942; Henry Wallace, Nov. 20, 1941 (memo).
Matheny, W. F., to Walter Jenkins, June 22, 1948; Waldemar A. Von Schoeler, July 24, 1948.
McDonough, C., to LJ, July 6, 1937, April 1, 1938 (tgm.).
Powell, Rauhut and Gideon, to Claude E. Hamilton, Aug. 20, 1940.
Richardson, Sid, to Charles Marsh, Dec. 5, 1941.
Wirtz, A. J., to Carl F. Farbach, Oct. 13, 1937; LJ, May 7 (memo), Aug. 12, 13, 17, 21 (tgm.), 1937, Feb. 23, 23 (tgm.), Mar. 12, June 4, 7, 15 (tgm.), 1938, April 29, Aug. 1, 12, Oct. 7, 1939, May 20, June 24, 1940, Feb. 27, 1943, Feb. 6, 1948, and tgm., Wirtz to LJ, undated; C. McDonough, Nov. 1, 1935 (memo).

Miscellaneous

American Broadcasting Company, "Edward P. Morgan and the News," ABC radio, July 13, 1966.
Benson, James, and Anthony Sisto, comp., "The College Star: The Student Editorials of Lyndon Baines Johnson," 1968.
Boulding, K. E. et al., "The U.S. and Revolution," an Occasional Paper on the Free Society, Center for the Study of Democratic Institutions, 1961.
Brown & Root, Inc., "Brownbilt," "Marine," and "Brownbuilder," Brown & Root publications.
Butterfield, Jack C., "Clara Driscoll Rescued the Alamo," privately published for the Daughters of the Republic of Texas, Dallas, 1961.
Columbia Broadcasting System, "Face the Nation," Oct. 11, 1959, Dec. 31, 1967; four programs taken from 13 hours of interviewing of LJ by Walter Cronkite in the autumn of 1969, "LBJ, 'Why I Chose Not to Run," Dec. 27, 1969; "LBJ: The Decision to Halt the Bombing," Feb. 6, 1970; "LBJ: Tragedy and Transition," May 2, 1970; "LBJ: Lyndon Johnson Talks Politics," Jan. 27, 1972.
Johnson, Rebekah Baines, "The Mother's Book," a looseleaf scrapbook Johnson's mother gave him in 1954 and he later showed to reporters, including the author.
"The Journey of Lyndon Johnson," a film of the Johnson Library.
National Broadcasting Company, "The Hill Country: Lyndon Johnson's Texas," May 9, 1966.
National Educational Television, "The President from Texas," in the series, "At Issue," Nov. 28, 1963.

Periodic publications other than newspapers and magazines: *National Labor Relations Manual;* Newsletters of LJ, National Republican Congressional Committee, Wright Patman, University of Texas System; *Newsletter of the Democratic Left; Pedagog,* student annual, Southwest Texas State Teachers College, 1927–29; *Texas Almanac; Texian Annual; Texas Review.*

Political materials: campaign documents; speech texts; press releases; "Jeffersonian Democrats of Texas," Aug. 1, 1936; "To the Democrats: Report of the National Jeffersonian Democrats to the Detroit Conference," Aug. 7–8, 1936; *Johnson Journal,* Aug. 1948; *Texas Argus,* 1964.

Reference Works, among others: *The Handbook of Texas; Encyclopaedia Britannica; Texas Almanac;* various U.S. almanacs.

Rowe, James, unpublished manuscript on George Parr.

Index